THE WILEY GUIDE TO FINANCE FACULTY

Compiled by

James R. Hasselback

College of Business
Florida State University
Tallahassee, Florida

WILEY

JOHN WILEY & SONS, INC.
New York   Chichester   Brisbane   Toronto   Singapore

©1993 by **John Wiley & Sons, Inc.**

605 Third Avenue

New York, NY 10158

All rights reserved.

10 9 8 7 6 5 4 3 2 1

ISBN: 0-471-59345--1

Printed in the United States of America

Dear Professor:

We at John Wiley & Sons, Inc. are delighted to offer this **Guide to Finance Faculty** as a service to the academic Finance community. As a committed supporter of the students in this community, Wiley publishes some of the highest-quality Finance textbooks available. And as an equally committed supporter of practitioners and academics in this community, Wiley also publishes a wide array of reference titles in Finance.

All of these titles are described in detail in the "Guide to Wiley Finance Offerings" beginning on page vii. As you browse through this catalog at your leisure, keep a record of books in which you are particularly interested; then, use the order form at the back of the **Guide to Finance Faculty** to request examination copies of those texts. Or, place your order by calling our toll-free number: (800) 248-5334.

Again, we are hopeful that this desk reference will prove to be a valuable resource for you and that you will view it as tangible evidence of Wiley's commitment to you and your students.

Sincerely,

Carolyn Henderson
Marketing Manager
Finance

Whitney Blake
Executive Editor
Finance

Please send all corrections/additions for the **Wiley Guide to Finance Faculty** to:

James R. Hasselback
College of Business
R-53A
Florida State University
Tallahassee, FL   32306-1042

904-644-7884 (ph)
904-644-5265 (fax)

TABLE OF CONTENTS

Guide to Wiley Finance Offerings vii

Introduction to the Directory xxiii

List of Institutions Included xv

Finance Faculty Alphabetical by School 1

Finance Faculty Alphabetical by Individual 147

NEW

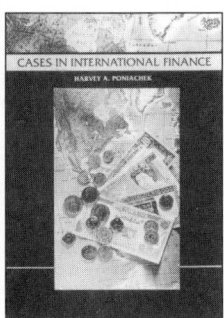

CASES IN INTERNATIONAL FINANCE

Harvey A. Poniachek, New York University, Stern School of Business
53678-4, 336 pp., paper, 1993

This latest title in the **Wiley Series in Finance** addresses the need students and practitioners alike have to learn about and benefit from the opportunities available in an ever-increasingly competitive international marketplace. With the globalization of financial markets and the growing trend toward integration of the markets for goods and services, it is vital for corporate management to keep pace with global financial issues. The author addresses not only these issues but also the need for corporations to penetrate the international marketplace.

The use of case studies facilitates the student's introduction to issues, information, and business situations that are normally beyond the scope of international finance textbooks. This method also provides students with a unique opportunity to learn the theory of international corporate financial management, while at the same time learning how to apply their own analytical and decision-making skills. What's more, because it is accompanied by a comprehensive **Instructor's Resource Guide**, **Cases In International Finance** is amazingly easy to use in the classroom.

TABLE OF CONTENTS

FINANCIAL MARKETS AND FINANCIAL TRANSACTIONS

Case 1. **Atlantic Financial Services, Ltd.** Currency Rate Projections.
Case 2. **Société Montage.** Hedging International Transactions with Traditional Forward Exchange Transactions and Currency Options, and the Cost-Benefit of Alternative Hedging Strategies.
Case 3. **Fidelity Trust Company.** Forward Rate Agreement and Eurodollar Futures Designed to Hedge Interest Rate Risk on a Future Loan Commitment.
Case 4. **Madesco, Inc.** Hedging Export Receipts Through Forward Contracts and Currency Options.
Case 5. **Chase Options, Inc.** Hedging Foreign Currency Exposure Through Currency Options.
Case 6. **Metro Corporation, Inc.** Investing Internationally with an Asset Swap.

CURRENCY EXPOSURE, PRICE EXPOSURE, AND HEDGING

Case 7. **The American Electric Engine Corporation.** Foreign Currency Exposure Management and Eurocurrency Funding.
Case 8. **The International Chemical Corporation, Inc.** Positioning of Global Activities, Currency Exposure, and Funding.
Case 9. **The Manhattan Trading Corporation, Inc.** Hedging Through the Futures Commodity Market.
Case 10. **ABC Airlines.** Managing Strategic Risks.

CORPORATE FUNDING AND CAPITAL STRUCTURE

Case 11. **Intel Overseas Corporation.** Notes Funding, Cost, and the Capital Structure of the Parent and the Subsidiary.
Case 12. **Hydro-Québec.** The Evolution of the International Financial Policy of Canada's Major Public Utility Corporation.
Case 13. **Guinness Peat Aviation.** Going Public, International Funding, and Currency Exposure.
Case 14. **Genentech, Inc. and Royal Gist-brocades, nv.** Capital Structure and the Cost of Capital in Biotechnology Corporations Across Countries.

INTERNATIONAL CASH AND WORKING CAPITAL MANAGEMENT

Case 15. **World Tours, Inc.** Cash Management Swaps.
Case 16. **The Computerized Numerical Control (CNC) Corporation, Inc.** Projecting the Yen/Dollar Exchange Rate, Hedging Divide Remittances from Japan, and Positioning of Funds in the MNC.

INTERNATIONAL PORTFOLIO INVESTMENT

Case 17. **Templeton Growth Fund, Inc.** International Portfolio Investment Management.

INTERNATIONAL CAPITAL BUDGETING: DIRECT FOREIGN INVESTMENT

Case 18. **IBM and Thailand.** Factors Considered in a Decision-Making Process of Investing Abroad.
Case 19. **The Dallas Energy Corporation, Inc.** The Feasibility, Funding, Currency Hedging, and Debt Conversion Option of Direct Foreign Investment in Southern Europe.

Continued on next page

Case 20. **The FMC Corporation.** Investment Bankers Assess the Feasibility of Foreign Direct Investment, Risk, and Funding Methods.
Case 21. **Ford Motor Company.** Direct Foreign Investment in Mexico.
Case 22. **The Anglo-French War for the Irish Distillers Group.** An International Acquisition of an Industrial Company in the European Community.
Case 23. **The Ginza Motor Corporation, Ltd., Tokyo.** Japanese Investment in the U.S. Motor Vehicle Parts Industry.
INTERNATIONAL CORPORATE TAXATION
Case 24. **Harvey Pharmaceutical Corporation, Inc.** International Intercompany Transfer Pricing Determination.
Case 25. **The Teleport Project in St. Petersburg and Moscow.** A Telecommunications Joint Venture in Russia.
Case 26. **Irving Oil Versus the Queen.** A Case Study in Transfer Pricing.
Case 27. **Mobil Corporation.** International Taxation and the Implications of Foreign Tax Credit.
ENVIRONMENTAL ISSUES AND ANALYSIS
Case 28. **The EC-1992 Program.** The Implications for U.S. Multinational Corporations.
Case 29. **The Chip War.** United States-Japan Trade Conflict in Semiconductors.
Case 30. **Country Risk Assessment.** Assessing Qualitatively Country Risk and Default.
Case 31. **The World Commercial Aircraft Industry.** Booming into the 1990s.

NEW

PERSONAL FINANCE

Fifth Edition
Robert Rosefsky
54978-9, 704 pp., cloth, 1993

This comprehensive and practical guide gives students a unique opportunity to learn about the various aspects of personal money management and consumer economics, while gaining invaluable insight into the impact of global economic trends. Using a friendly, hands-on approach, the author covers a wide range of topics — from the role of the economy in everyday life to advice on investment, financial planning, insurance, and much more. The author's clear and concise writing style enables students at all levels to grasp the principles of money management and master the basic skills necessary to cope with the real-life challenges of personal finance.

The Fifth Edition has been completely revised to reflect recent economic trends and world events. Additionally, enhanced pedagogical aids make this edition the most accessible, engaging, and practical ever. These new learning devices include:

• **Ups and Downs: The Practical Economics of Everyday Life.** Each chapter contains a section devoted to microeconomic trends and gives students an awareness of how and why these affect personal finances and planning.

• **Expanded End-of-Chapter Reviews.** An important new feature of this edition, these sections include practical applications such as *What If...* and *Number Cruncher* sections which test students on the real-life financial situations covered in each chapter. Also included are *Consumer Alert, Personal Action Checklist,* and *Strategies for Success* sections which give students the advantage of being prepared when faced with potential opportunities and/or problems in the future.

• **Comprehensive and Up-to-Date Coverage of Practical Issues.** Tips on shopping wisely, avoiding frauds and swindles, buying a car, obtaining life and health insurance, and filing tax returns are just some of the many helpful topics contained in this edition.

The following newly prepared teaching and learning aids are also available:

• **Instructor's Manual**
This supplement plays an important role in helping and guiding instructors through the preparation of the course material. For example, *Lecture Hot Spots* provide an invaluable teaching aid to instructors who wish to update their own presentations. *On the Other Hand...* sections are designed specifically to promote and stimulate class discussion. Also contained are reviews of end-of-chapter material and a comprehensive test bank.

• **IBM Microtest**
This full-featured, easy-to-use, fully-supported test creation program enables instructors to choose test questions from the **Instructor's Manual**, print the tests out for use in the classroom, and save the tests for later use or modification.

• **Study Guide**
Includes learning objectives, *What's It To You?* sections, word plays, group exercises, exercises in which students analyze current trends, real-world discussion questions, and sample test questions.

• **Telecourse Study System**
Includes both the **Viewer's Guide** to accompany the Personal Finance Telecourse (a step-by-step guide through each television program which features reproductions/clarifications of the video's graphics and highlights of critical video segments) *and* the **Study Guide** described above — all for just a few dollars more than the price of the **Study Guide** alone.

TABLE OF CONTENTS
BASIC CONCERNS
1. The Economy: How it Works and What It Means to You.
2. Work and Income.
GETTING WHAT YOU NEED
3. Creating a Workable Plan: Goal Setting and Budgeting.
4. The Smart Shopper.
5. Frauds and Swindles and How To Avoid Them.
6. Transportation: Buying, Financing, and Insuring Your Cars.
7. Leisure and Recreation.
A ROOF OVER YOUR HEAD
8. Buying a Home.
9. Financing a Home.
10. Housing Costs and Regulations.
11. Renting.
12. Selling Your Home.
WHERE THE MONEY IS
13. Financial Institutions.
14. Credit and Borrowing.
MAKING YOUR MONEY GROW
15. Making Your Money Grow: An Overview.
16. Making Your Money Grow: The Money Market.
17. Making Your Money Grow: The Stock Market.
18. Making Your Money Grow: Real Estate and Other Opportunities.
PROTECTING WHAT YOU WORK FOR
19. Life, Health, and Income Insurance.
20. Financial Planning For Later Years.
21. Estate Planning.
22. Income Taxes.
Appendix ... How To Solve Consumer Problems.
Glossary.

NEW

NON-LINEAR DYNAMICS, CHAOS AND ECONOMETRICS

M. Hashem Pesaran, University of Cambridge, UK
Simon M. Potter, University of California, Los Angeles
208 pp., cloth, 1993

This unique new book, which includes contributions from many of the most influential thinkers in this important and rapidly developing field, examines and assesses the latest techniques in non-linear dynamics. It will be of special interest to advanced students and academics in econometrics and also financial econometricians seeking insight into the very latest thinking in this field.

The text is unique in its detailing of the important advances made during the last two decades in the mathematical and statistical analysis of dynamic systems. In an area of vital importance, this book fulfills a real need for statisticians and researchers in the field and facilitates understanding of complex theoretical material.

TABLE OF CONTENTS

1. "Nonlinear Dynamics and Econometrics: An Introduction," by Pesaran & Potter.
2. "Complex Economic Dynamics: Obvious in History, Generic in Theory, Elusive in Data," by R.H. Day.
3. "Using the Correlation Exponent to Decide if an Economic Series Is Chaotic," by Liu, Granger & Heller.
4. "Lyapunov Exponents as a Nonparametric Diagnostic for Stability Analysis," by Dechert & Gencay.
5. "The Liklihood Ratio Text Under Non-Standard Conditions: Testing the Markov Trend Model of GNP," by B.E. Hansen.
6. "Merger Waves and the Structure of Merger and Acquisition Time Series," by R. Town.
7. "Nonlinear Dynamics in a Structural Model of Employment," by S.M. Burgess.
8. "Modelling Nonlinearities in Business Cycles Using Smooth Transition Autoregressive Models," by Terasvirta & Anderson.
9. "Forecast Improvements Using a Volatility Index," by B. LeBaron.
10. "Multivariate Nearest Neighbour Forecasts of EMS Exchange Rates," by B. Mizrach.
11. "Nonlinear Time Series Analysis of Stock Volatilities," by Cao & Tsay.
12. "The Comparative Power of the TRTEST Against Simple Threshold Models," by P. Rothman.
13. Conference Programme: Econometric Inference Using Simulation Techniques. June 5-6, 1992.
14. Conference Announcement: Calibration Techniques in Time Series Econometrics. July, 1993.

NEW

TRADER VIC II: PRINCIPLES OF PROFESSIONAL SPECULATION

Victor Sperandeo with T. Sullivan Brown, Rand Management Corporation
53577-X, 400 pp., cloth, 1993

In this sequel to his bestselling **Trader Vic: Methods of a Wall Street Master**, Victor Sperandeo expounds his highly individual investment philosophy. The man described by Barron's as "The Ultimate Wall Street Pro" elaborates on the techniques that are fundamental to his powerful and successful investment approach.

A few of the text's many outstanding features:

• Fresh insights into traditional investment techniques, including Dow Theory, technical analysis, the use of historical data in risk assessment, and economic forecasting.
• Victor Sperandeo's proven and comprehensive trading approach combines ideas from technical and fundamental analysis, statistics and probability, economics, politics, and psychology.
• Illustration of significant investment techniques with the use of over 100 charts from the stock, futures, and options markets.

TABLE OF CONTENTS

1. The Fundamental Principles of a Sound Investment Philosophy. 2. The Economic Principles of Market Forecasting. 3. Money, Credit, and The Business Cycle.
4. Applications of Fundamental Economic Analysis.
5. Key Economic Indicators.
6. GNP Growth Versus Stock Market Volatility.
7. Dow Theory: A Proven Method of Economic Forecasting. 8. Dow Theory's Record as a Trading Tool. 9. The Technical Basis of Risk/Reward Analysis. 10. The Technical Principles of Market Analysis Applied.
11. The Technical Principles of Stock Selection Applied. 12. Options: The Key to Triple-Digit Returns. 13. Understanding the Institutional Psychology. 14. A Professional Trader's Character and Personality Traits.

CASES IN FINANCIAL MANAGEMENT

Joseph M. Sulock, University of North Carolina - Asheville
John S. Dunkelberg, Wake Forest University
52904-4, 416 pp., paper, 1992

This original and in-depth casebook provides students with firsthand experience in a variety of financial management areas. All fifty cases are authentic and have been carefully selected to reflect the wide-ranging diversity of the subject matter, from elementary principles of finance to more complex issues such as business ethics and international finance. All cases are accompanied by inventive and creative questions to guide student analysis.

The cases are based on interviews with more than thirty corporate executives. Students are encouraged to participate actively in the problem-solving process, and the final section contains a number of comprehensive, unstructured cases for students to work through and further hone their problem-solving skills.

The text is supplemented by the following teaching and learning aids:

• Instructor's Resource Guide
• Spreadsheet Templates (available on 5.25" and 3.5" disks)
• Spreadsheet Instructor's Guide

TABLE OF CONTENTS
FINANCE FUNDAMENTALS
1. Financial Planning, Part 1 (*Time Value of Money*).
2. Financial Planning, Part II (*Time Value of Money*).
3. Professor Kinney (*Risk and Return*). 4. American Brands (*Valuation*). 5. Jefferson Hardware (*Accounting Fundamentals*). 6. U.S. Business Products (*Economic Fundamentals*).
FINANCIAL ANALYSIS AND PLANNING
7. Tiny Tim Toys (*Ratio Analysis*). 8. Regina (*Ratio Analysis*). 9. Gravely (*Ratio Analysis*). 10. Hickory Soups, Part I (*Financial Forecasting*). 11. Friends (*Breakeven Analysis*).
12. Dr. Soft (*Breakeven Analysis*).
WORKING CAPITAL MANAGEMENT
13. Berlin's (*Working Capital Policy*). 14. Lyle's Enterprises (*Inventory*).
15. Chemco (*Accounts Receivable*). 16. Lyle's Enterprises (*Cash Budget*). 17. Mountain View Lodge (*Cash Budget*).
CAPITAL BUDGETING
18. Knight International (*Capital Budgeting*). 19. Solar Energy (*Capital Budgeting*).
20. Anderson Clayton Co. (*Equipment Replacement*).
21. Valley Forge Plastics (*Make or Buy*). 22. La Casa (*Return on Equity*). 23. Surgisound (*Capital Budgeting*).
24. Midland-Michigan (*Capital Budgeting*).
25. Morrison Products (*Risk Classes*).
26. Quomaca Major (*Probability Distributions*).
CAPITAL STRUCTURE/COST OF CAPITAL
27. Pelco (*Cost of Capital*). 28. Salem Foods (*Cost of Capital*). 29. Conroy (*Cost of Capital*).
30. Kenwood (*Debt/Equity Choice*).
31. Bowmon Mowers (*Debt/Equity Choice*).
32. Hickory Soups, Part II (*Miller & Modigliani*).
VALUATION
33. Landmark (*Valuation*). 34. B&G Pies (*Valuation*).
35. Ozark Bottling (*Valuation*).
36. Benjamin's (*Valuation*).
INTERNATIONAL FINANCE
37. GM-Europe (*International Finance*).
38. Powercell (*Capital Budgeting*).
MISCELLANEOUS TOPICS
39. Boe of Colombia (*Business Ethics*).
40. Gunther Paving (*Financial Lease*). 41. Bennet Construction (*Financial Lease*). 42. AT&T (*Dividend Policy*). 43. Stinson (*Dividend Policy*).
COMPREHENSIVE CASES
44. Holcombe Scientific. 45. Blockbuster Video.
46. New England Graphics. 47. Medalist Golf Equipment. 48. Burdette's. 49. Shuckers.
50. Martin Enterprises.

FUNDAMENTALS OF RISK AND INSURANCE
Sixth Edition

Emmett J. Vaughan,
University of Iowa
54552-X, 800 pp., cloth, 1992

This text continues to be one of the most comprehensive and flexible presentations of risk and insurance ever published. While reflecting important new changes in the insurance sector, the new Sixth Edition retains its well-organized and structured presentation. The author favors a tried and tested functional approach; for example, each chapter features an *Important Concepts to Remember* section which has proven to be a better teaching tool than the chapter summary.

This comprehensive text is divided into three sections:

• The first section presents a complete overview of the insurance industry and includes detailed coverage of the concept of risk, the nature of the insurance device, and the principles of risk management.

• The second section deals with the fields of life and health insurance. The social security system, workers' compensation, and other social insurance programs are discussed to enable the student to integrate these into the overall concept of income protection planning.

• The final section details the risks associated with the ownership of property and legal liability. For greater ease, separate chapters are devoted to individual or family coverage and coverage designed specifically for corporate purposes.

The text is supplemented by the following teaching and learning aids:

• **Instructor's Resource Guide**
• **Transparency Masters**
• **Study Guide Manual**

TABLE OF CONTENTS
1. The Conceptual Framework.
2. The Insurance Device.
3. Risk Management.
4. The Fields of Insurance.
5. The Private Insurance Industry.
6. Functions of Insurers.
7. Financial Aspects of Insurer Operations.
8. The Government as an Insurer.
9. Regulation of Insurance.
10. The Legal Framework.
11. Introduction to Life Insurance.
12. Actuarial Basis of Life Insurance.
13. Life Insurance Contract - Part I.
14. Life Insurance Contract - Part II.
15. Special Policy Forms.
16. Health Insurance - Disability Income.
17. Health Insurance - Medical Expenses.
18. Old-Age and Retirement Insurance.
19. Other Compulsory Compensation Programs.
20. Programming Life Insurance.
21. Buying Life Insurance.
22. Business Uses of Life and Health.
23. Homeowners - Part I.
24. Homeowners - Part II.
25. Other Personal Forms of Insurance.
26. Negligence and Legal Liability.
27. Personal Liability Insurance.
28. The Auto and Its Environment.
29. The Personal Auto Policy.
30. Commercial Property Coverage.
31. Commercial Liability Coverage.
32. Surety Bonds and Credit Insurance.
33. Insurance and the Future.

THE BASICS OF INVESTING
Fifth Edition
Benton E. Gup, The University of Alabama
54853-7, 496 pp., cloth, 1992

This concise and understandable text offers an ideal blend of accessibility, the latest developments and terminology in the field, and reference material. The book is organized into five logical parts, all written in the clear and straightforward style for which Benton Gup is known, so technical equations can be understood by students who do not have a mathematical orientation.

The Fifth Edition deals with topical issues such as insider trading and investment fraud and features coverage of global markets, investment in tangible assets, and, in view of the increased incidence of Leveraged Buyouts and corporate restructurings, a significantly revised chapter on financial statement analysis and valuation.

The text is supplemented by an **Instructor's Resource Guide/Test Bank**.

TABLE OF CONTENTS
INVESTING IN SECURITIES AND OTHER ASSETS
1. An Overview of Investment Alternatives. 2. Equity Markets. 3. Debt Securities. 4. Risks and Returns.
THE SECURITIES BUSINESS
5. How the Securities Business Works. 6. Services of Stock Brokerage Firms. 7. The New York Stock Exchange. 8. Averages and Indexes.
ANALYZING SECURITIES
9. Sources of Information. 10. Analyzing the Economy. 11. Analyzing Industries. 12. Analyzing Companies. 13. Financial Statement Analysis and Valuation. 14. Technical Analysis, Formula Plans, and Investment Strategies.
INVESTMENT ADMINISTRATION
15. Making Investment Decisions. 16. Taxes and Tax Shelters. 17. Real Estate Investments. 18. Antiques, Gems, and Other Investments.
SPECIAL SITUATIONS
19. Stock and Index Options. 20. Convertible Securities, Warrants, and Rights. 21. Commodities.
Appendices.
Glossary.

THE PORTABLE MBA IN FINANCE AND ACCOUNTING
John Leslie Livingstone, CPA
53226-6, 524 pp., cloth, 1992

John Leslie Livingstone examines the concepts of finance and accounting and their practical applications in running and managing a business. This functional approach to the subject matter gives students valuable insights into the mechanisms that help to generate a successful business approach.

Some of the outstanding features of **The Portable MBA in Finance and Accounting** include:

• Coverage of what leading business schools teach about finance and accounting: contributors from schools like Harvard, the University of Washington, Babson College, Indiana State University, George Washington University, and Georgia Institute of Technology.
• Detailed analysis of financial statement costs, budgeting, business plans, and capital budgeting to ensure that students gain a thorough understanding of these fundamental concepts.

TABLE OF CONTENTS
UNDERSTANDING THE NUMBERS
1. Understanding and Analyzing Financial Statements. 2. Cost-Profit-Volume Analysis. 3. Activity-Based Costing. 4. Using the Computer in Finance and Accounting. 5. Budgetary Control Analysis: Techniques for Measuring Productivity.
PLANNING AND FORECASTING
6. Choosing a Business Form: To Incorporate or Not to Incorporate. 7. The Business Plan: A Step-By-Step Guide. 8. Forecasts and Budgets. 9. Managing Long-Term Investments: Financial Structure, Cost of Capital, and Capital Budgeting. 10. Taxes and Business Decisions. 11. The Impact of Globalization on Management and Financial Reporting.
MAKING KEY STRATEGIC DECISIONS
12. Going Public. 13. Mergers and Acquisitions: Strategies for Growth. 14. Corporate Governance: The Board of Directors. 15. Bankruptcy.
Chapter Notes.
About the Authors.
Index.

THE STOCK MARKET
Sixth Edition
Richard J. Teweles
Edward S. Bradley
Ted M. Teweles
54019-6, 576 pp., cloth, 1992

With sales of over 120,000 copies in its five editions, this bestseller is the most extensively used practical guide to the stock market. The prestigious authors are widely recognized in professional and academic circles as experts in the field; their combined years of experience enhance the practical qualities of the text, giving students the opportunity to gain a thorough working knowledge of the stock market and the many factors which influence it.

The Sixth Edition has now been completely revised and updated to reflect today's stock market and features coverage of such current topics as electronic trading, the globalization of the securities business, regulatory changes, and program trading.

TABLE OF CONTENTS
FUNDAMENTAL INFORMATION
1. Securities Markets and Securities Owners.
2. Corporate Securities.
3. U.S. Government and Municipal Securities.
4. Reading the Financial Page.
WORK OF THE STOCK EXCHANGES
5. The New York Stock Exchange: Its Functions and History. 6. The New York Stock Exchange: Its Organization and Membership. 7. Stock and Bond Lists, Tickers, and Quotations. 8. Trading Procedures. 9. The NASDAQ Market. 10. The American Stock Exchange and Other U.S. Securities Exchanges. 11. Foreign Stock Markets.
WORK OF THE SECURITIES HOUSES
12. The Customer and the Broker. 13. Margin Trading. 14. Investment Banking.
15. Securities Delivery, Transfer, and Clearing.
REGULATIONS
16. Manipulation in the Old Market. 17. Regulation, Self-Regulation, and Compliance.
INVESTING PRACTICES AND SPECIAL INSTRUMENTS
18. Stock Price Averages and Indexes. 19. Investing and Trading in Common Stocks. 20. Investment Companies. 21. Fundamentals of Stock Prices.
22. Technical Analysis of Stock Prices. 23. Securities Options. 24. Convertible Securities, Warrants, and Rights. 25. Sources of Information and Security Rating.
Glossary.
Index.

LEO MELAMED ON THE MARKETS: TWENTY YEARS OF FINANCIAL HISTORY AS SEEN BY THE MAN WHO REVOLUTIONIZED THE MARKETS
Leo Melamed
57524-0, 265 pp., cloth, 1992

One of the most influential financial figures of the 1980s, Leo Melamed played a pivotal role in the creation of the financial futures markets. In this book, Melamed takes a retrospective look at the last twenty years of financial history and looks ahead into the 1990s. He describes the impact of the futures markets on the financial sector in the 1980s and goes on to discuss such topics as:

• How he helped create the financial futures markets, and how those markets changed the financial world in the 1980s.
• The role and importance of futures markets in the world economy.
• The debate over futures markets in the wake of the 1987 crash.
• The future of electronic global markets in the 1990s.

This is a compelling treatment of one of the most interesting phenomena to occur in the world of finance in recent years. The book contains a foreword by the Nobel prize-winning economist, Milton Friedman.

TABLE OF CONTENTS
THE SOUL OF THE TRADER
Be A Lover, Not a Fighter. The Art of Futures Trading. A Technical Approach to Trading.
The Psychology of a Successful Trader. On Tips and Tipping. Market Liquidity and the Technique of Spreading. Our American Free Markets.

THE BIRTH OF A MARKET — FINANCIAL FUTURES
A Futures Market in Currencies. Chicago's Future in Futures. The "Sleazy" Speculator. The Birth of LIFFE. The Future of Futures. Financial Futures and the Banks. Homecoming.
FUTURES — THEIR ROLE AND POTENTIAL
The Futures of Chicago. The Food-Price Crisis. The Birth of the CFTC. Pioneerism Needs No Economic Justification. The Fed Study on Futures and Options. The Coveted Scapegoat. Fixed Exchange Rate Foolishness. The Debate over Index Participation Contracts.
THE 1987 CRASH
A Call to Arms. Embracing Reality. Who Killed Cock Robin? Chicken Little Revisited. Excerpts from Testimony Relating to the 1987 Stock Market Crash. Quintessential Lessons. The Jaws of Victory.
GLOBALIZATION AND THE NEW WORLD ORDER
Responding to Globalization: A CME Perspective. The Third Milestone. GLOBEX and World Markets. The Impossible Dream: Free Markets in Moscow. Free Market Victory. Financial Markets in the Coming Decade. The New World Order. Markets of the Pacific Rim. Tomorrow's Technological Tidal Wave. Protectionism — The Scourge of Markets.

INVESTMENTS: ANALYSIS AND MANAGEMENT
Third Edition
Charles P. Jones, North Carolina State University
52839-0, 736 pp., cloth, 1991

This text presents balanced coverage of investment topics in a well-organized and structured format and is particularly recommended for undergraduate students. Some of the outstanding features which make this text one of the best available for the course are its excellent pedagogy, clear presentation, and unique topic coverage. These features, together with the superior package of supplements, set this text far apart from the competition.

New and exciting features of this edition include a chapter on international investment and the introduction of new software, the *Investment Calculator*. This is an invaluable course component designed to perform eleven different key calculations from data entered by students to facilitate investment analysis and is packaged with every copy of **Investments** at no extra cost.

The text is supplemented by the following teaching and learning aids:

• **Instructor's Manual**
• **Study Guide**
• **Testbank**
• **Microtest**
• **Transparency Masters**

(Fourth Edition to be published in October, 1993.)

TABLE OF CONTENTS
BACKGROUND
1. A Background for Understanding Investments.
2. Types of Securities. 3. Securities Markets. 4. Sources of Investment Information. 5. Return and Risk Concepts.
FIXED INCOME SECURITIES: ANALYSIS AND EVALUATION
6. The Basics of Bonds. 7. Bond Valuation.
COMMON STOCKS: ANALYSIS AND VALUATION
8. Common Stocks. 9. Common Stock Valuation and Analysis.
COMMON STOCKS: THE FUNDAMENTAL APPROACH
10. Market Analysis. 11. Industry Analysis. 12. Company Analysis.
COMMON STOCKS: OTHER APPROACHES
13. Technical Analysis. 14. Efficient Markets.
ADDITIONAL INVESTMENT OPPORTUNITIES
15. Options. 16. Warrants and Convertible Securities.
17. Futures Markets.
18. Investment Companies.
PORTFOLIO MANAGEMENT
19. Portfolio Theory. 20. International Investing and Extended Diversification.
21. Capital Market Theory. 22. Measuring Portfolio Performance.

MODERN PORTFOLIO THEORY AND INVESTMENT ANALYSIS

Fourth Edition
Edwin J. Elton, New York University
Martin J. Gruber, New York University
53248-7, 736 pp., cloth, 1991

This renowned text on portfolio theory and investment analysis features extensive use of empirical examples and evidence, making the subject matter relevant and easy to understand. This focused, structured text manages to present a rigorous treatment of portfolio theory and investment analysis without becoming overly abstract.

The text is supplemented by an **Instructor's Manual**.

TABLE OF CONTENTS
1. Introduction.
PORTFOLIO ANALYSIS
Section One: Mean Variance Portfolio Theory.
2. The Characteristics of the Opportunity Set Under Risk. 3. Delineating Efficient Portfolios. 4. Techniques for Calculating the Efficient Frontier.
Section Two: Simplifying the Portfolio Selection Process.
5. The Correlation Structure of Security Returns: The Single Index Model.
6. The Correlation Structure of Security Returns: Multi-Index Models and Grouping Technique.
7. Simple Techniques for Determining the Efficient Frontier.
Section Three: Selecting the Optimum Portfolio.
8. Utility Analysis. 9. Other Portfolio Selection Models.
Section Four: Widening the Selection Universe.
10. International Diversification.
MODELS OF EQUILIBRIUM IN THE CAPITAL MARKETS
11. The Standard Capital Asset Pricing Model.
12. Nonstandard Forms of Capital Asset Pricing Models. 13. Empirical Tests of Equilibrium Models.
14. The Arbitrage Pricing Model of APT — A New Approach to Explaining Asset Prices.
SECURITY ANALYSIS AND PORTFOLIO THEORY
15. Efficient Markets. 16. The Valuation Process.
17. Earnings Estimation.
18. Interest Rate Theory and the Pricing of Bonds.
19. The Management of Bond Portfolios. 20. Option Pricing Theory. 21. The Valuation and Uses of Financial Futures.
EVALUATING THE INVESTMENT PROCESS
22. Evaluation of Portfolio Performance.
23. Evaluation of Security Analysis. 24. Portfolio Management Revisited.

WORKING CAPITAL MANAGEMENT

John J. Hampton,
The College of Insurance, New York
Cecilia Wagner, Seton Hall University
60260-4, 527 pp., paper, 1989

This comprehensive textbook provides balanced coverage of the basic concepts of working capital management together with practical techniques for measuring the liquidity of a company and analyzing sources of financing. The authors' practical approach ensures the accessibility of the text and includes such features as case studies, spreadsheet models, and detailed end-of-chapter analysis material.

The inclusion of spreadsheet models — the package contains a student disk with Lotus 1-2-3 spreadsheets for use with the cases — enables instructors to integrate computerized decision-making into the course.

The text is supplemented by the following teaching and learning aids:

- **Instructor's Manual**
- **Student Disk**
- **Instructor Disk**

TABLE OF CONTENTS
FRAMEWORK
1. Working Capital Management.
THE BANKING SYSTEM
2. Understanding the Flow of Money. 3. Managing Disbursements and Collections.
4. Commercial Bank Packages for Cash Management.
CASH MANAGEMENT
5. Cash Forecasting. 6. Cash Forecasting: Advanced Techniques. 7. Investing Excess Cash: A Risk Return Framework. 8. International Cash Management. 9. Cash Flow Analysis.
ANALYZING WORKING CAPITAL
10. Working Capital Adequacy. 11. Economics of Short Term Financing.
12. Sources of Near Term Financing.
CREDITING COLLECTIONS
13. Analyzing Credit Capacity of Customers.
14. Developing Credit Policies.
15. Collection Policies and Government Regulations.
CONSUMER AND BUSINESS LENDING
16. Consumer Loans. 17. Small Business Loans.
18. Credit Scoring Systems.
INVENTORY
19. Inventory Management. 20. Inventory Planning.
Appendix.

BANK MANAGEMENT: TEXT AND CASES
Third Edition
George H. Hempel, Southern Methodist University
Alan B. Coleman
Donald G. Simonson, University of New Mexico
62178-1, 816 pp., cloth, 1989

This comprehensive guide to funds and financial management in commercial banking covers a wide range of issues, including such topics as:

- The changing financial environment for banking.
- Basic measures of risk and return.
- Bank investment and funding instruments.
- Interest rate and yield curve analysis.
- Measuring and meeting liquidity needs.
- Investment and capital planning.
- Risk management.

The text is supplemented by an **Instructor's Manual**.

TABLE OF CONTENTS
INTRODUCTION TO BANK MANAGEMENT
1. The Changing Nature of Bank Management.
2. Understanding a Bank's Financial Statement.
3. A Model for Measuring Bank Returns and Risks.
4. Evaluation of a Bank's Performance. *Cases.*
BASIC ASSET, LIABILITY, AND CAPITAL DECISIONS
5. Measuring and Providing Reserves and Liquidity.
6. Managing the Security Portfolio.
7. Trends in Acquisition and Cost of Bank Funds.
8. Financing the Bank's Capital Needs.
Cases.
MANAGING THE LOAN PORTFOLIO
9. Organizing the Bank's Lending Effort. 10. Lending Principles and the Business Borrower. 11. Commercial Lending. 12. Consumer Lending. 13. Special Markets for Bank Loans. *Cases.*
INTEGRATIVE BANK FINANCIAL DECISIONS
14. Interest Margin, Interest Sensitivity, Duration, and Hedging. 15. Innovations in Products and Pricing.
16. International Banking. 17. Long-Range Planning for Future Performance. *Cases.*
Appendix: Bank President Micro Simulation

COMMERCIAL BANK MANAGEMENT

Benton E. Gup, The University of Alabama
Donald R. Fraser, Texas A&M University
James W. Kolari, Texas A&M University
84676-7, 496 pp., cloth, 1988

This text includes twenty chapters with end-of-chapter exercises and problems covering a wide range of topics — from the basic principles of commercial bank management such as assets, liabilities, and equity to those which require a more detailed analysis such as international banking, off-balance sheet products and services, and management issues.

The authors also highlight the practical aspects of commercial bank management and the inclusion of carefully developed end-of-chapter analysis material gives students many opportunities to acquire a realistic working knowledge of the problems and issues which can arise in the commercial banking sector.

The text is supplemented by an **Instructor's Manual**.

TABLE OF CONTENTS
INTRODUCTION
1. Overview of Banking System. 2. Fundamentals of Investments.
ASSETS
3. Evaluating Bank Performance. 4. Liquidity Management. 5. Investment Management. 6. Principles of Commercial Lending. 7. Process of Commercial Lending. 8. Process of Commercial Lending (Continued). 9. Real Estate Lending. 10. Consumer Lending.
LIABILITIES AND EQUITY
11. Managing Bank Liabilities. 12. Bank Capital Management.
ASSET/LIABILITY MANAGEMENT
13. An Overview of Asset/Liability Management. 14. Techniques of Asset/Liability Management: Dollar Gap and Duration Gap. 15. Techniques of Asset/Liability Management: Future Options and Swaps.
INTERNATIONAL BANKING
16. International Banking. 17. International Finance and Lending.
OFF BALANCE SHEET PRODUCTS AND SERVICES
18. Off Balance Sheet Activities. 19. The Payments System. 20. Bank Management Issues.

REAL ESTATE
Third Edition

Larry E. Wofford, C&L Systems Corporation
Terrence M. Clauretie, University of Nevada
54848-0, 672 pp., cloth, 1992

This text is organized around the components of the real estate profession, facilitating students' understanding of the differences and relationships between the various components. The authors cover not only the standard topics but also some less traditional topics such as real estate counseling and markets, so instructors can tailor the subject matter to suit individual course requirements.

All the principles are fully supported and illustrated by independent examples and an on-going example (Blackacre Farm) that is incorporated into many chapters, providing a consistent theme and frame of reference. Thus, students are encouraged to learn both the conceptual principles and their application in real-life situations. The revised Third Edition not only reflects changes in tax legislation, but also includes expanded chapters on taxation and the basic principles of income property investment.

The text is supplemented by an **Instructor's Resource Guide, Newsletter,** and **State-Specific Updates**.

TABLE OF CONTENTS
DEVELOPING A PERSPECTIVE
1. Real Estate in the Overall Scheme of Things.
2. Real Estate Business Environment.
REAL ESTATE FUNDAMENTALS
3. Real Estate: Physical Characteristics and Description.
4. Legal Fundamentals: Interests in Real Property.
5. Legal Fundamentals: Conveying and Protecting Title to Real Property.
6. Legal Fundamentals: Contracts. 7. The Urban Area: Real Estate Economics and Location.
8. The Urban Area: Planning and Land Use Controls.
9. Real Estate Markets.
10. Taxation: Real Property. 11. Taxation: Basic

REAL ESTATE INVESTMENT STRATEGY, ANALYSIS, AND DECISIONS
Second Edition

Stephen A. Pyhrr, Davis & Associates, Inc.
James R. Cooper, Georgia State University
Stephen Kapplin, University of South Florida
Larry Wofford, C&L Systems Corporation
87953-3, 962 pp., cloth, 1989

The practical text features an emphasis on decision-making tools and return and risk concepts. The integration of other topics — such as marketing and negotiation — not normally included in competing textbooks, but equally important to a thorough understanding of the subject, complement the practical and comprehensive nature of the text.

TABLE OF CONTENTS
REAL ESTATE INVESTMENT: THE STATE OF THE ART
1. The Nature and Scope of Real Estate Investment.
2. Overview of the Investment Decision Process.
3. Decision-Making Approaches to Real Estate Investment.
SYSTEMATIC INVESTMENT ANALYSIS
4. Investment Strategy. 5. Selecting the Ownership Entity. Concepts of Federal Income Taxation.
12. Fundamental Financial Concepts and Applications.
REAL ESTATE DECISION AREAS
13. Real Estate Lending: Legal Considerations. 14. Real Estate Lending: Sources of Funds, Interest Rates, Loan Types. 15. Real Estate Lending: Decision Making.
16. Equity Investment: Basic Concepts of Income.
17. Equity Investment: Making the Investment Decision.
REAL ESTATE DECISION SUPPORT AREAS
18. Marketing: Overview - The Brokerage Business and the Real Estate Transaction.
19. Marketing: Public Regulations of the Brokerage Business.
20. Property Management. 21. Real Estate Appraisal: Basic Concepts and the Appraisal Process.
22. Real Estate Appraisal: Applying Appraisal Concepts.
23. Real Estate Counseling.

6. Preliminary Financial Feasibility Analysis.
7. Discounted-Cash-Flow and Ratio Analysis. 8. Risk Analysis and Risk Management: Single Projects.
9. Financing and Refinancing Decisions. 10. Tax Planning and Detailed Financial Analysis.
ANALYZING REAL ESTATE MARKETS UNDER CHANGING CONDITIONS
11. Urban Analysis. 12. Market Analysis.
13. Marketability Analysis.
14. Inflation, Deflation, and Real Estate Cycles.
Appendix to Part III: Sources of Market Data for Real Estate Investors.
NEGOTIATIONS, MANAGEMENT, AND TERMINATION DECISIONS
15. The Art of Real Estate Negotiations. 16. Property and Asset Management.
17. Termination of the Investment.
PORTFOLIO STRATEGY AND INVESTMENT OUTLOOK
18. Institutional Real Estate Portfolios. 19. Developing a Personal Portfolio with Real Estate. 20. The Real Estate Investment Outlook.
PROPERTY SELECTION
21. Property Types and Selection. 22. Apartments.
23. Shopping Centers. 24. Office Buildings.

HOW TO REQUEST EXAMINATION COPIES

You can request a complimentary copy of any text described in this catalog in one of three ways:

1. Complete, clip, and mail the attached reply coupon to:
   John Wiley & Sons, Inc., attn: C. Henderson, Dept. 3-4210 HB,
   605 Third Avenue, New York, NY 10158
2. Contact your local Wiley representative.
3. FAX us at (212) 850-6118, to the attention of Carolyn Henderson..

Please send me an examination copy of: _____
_____
_____

Your Name _____
School _____ Dept _____
Street _____
City _____ State _____ Zip _____
Telephone _____ Office Hours _____
Course Title and Number _____
Total Annual Course Enrollment: Fall _____ Spring _____ Summer _____
Current Text/Author _____
Probability of a text change is: ❏ Definite ❏ Possible ❏ Unlikely
Most important adoption criteria _____
_____ Decision Date _____

John Wiley & Sons, Inc., attn: C. Henderson
605 Third Avenue
WILEY New York, New York 10158   3-4210 HB

Please send me an examination copy of: _____
_____
_____

Your Name _____
School _____ Dept _____
Street _____
City _____ State _____ Zip _____
Telephone _____ Office Hours _____
Course Title and Number _____
Total Annual Course Enrollment: Fall _____ Spring _____ Summer _____
Current Text/Author _____
Probability of a text change is: ❏ Definite ❏ Possible ❏ Unlikely
Most important adoption criteria _____
_____ Decision Date _____

John Wiley & Sons, Inc., attn: C. Henderson
605 Third Avenue
WILEY New York, New York 10158   3-4210 HB

JOHN WILEY & SONS, INC.
DIRECTORY OF FINANCE FACULTY
Compiled by
James R. Hasselback
College of Business   R-53A
Florida State University
Tallahassee, Florida 32306-1042
904-644-7884 Phone/Recorder
904-644-5265 Fax

This is the first FINANCE FACULTY DIRECTORY published by John Wiley & Sons, Inc. The Directory includes a listing of the Dean, Department Chairperson, and full-time Finance Faculty from over 800 schools. It is compiled for information provided by the respective schools. Typically at least three requests went to any school not responding. Only that information received by February 20, 1992, is included in the Directory. Some missing information was filled in from other sources.

The Directory covers the academic year 1991-92. United States schools are followed by Canadian and then other foreign schools in the school listing.

At the right side of the first line of each school are the degrees offered by the department. The years in the right side of the second line are the AACSB Bachelors and Masters accreditation dates. The school's bitnode is on the line following the area code.

The columns are as follows:
Name   Rank School-Phone Bitnet Teaching Research Degree Start
    $ next to a Dean or Chairman indicates "Acting"

For the Chairman, the title and rank are:
C   Chairman   D   Director   H   Head
Pr   Professor   Ac   Associate   As   Assistant

The degree column represents the highest earned degree or "all but dissertation," date received, and school.

The start column is for the year of beginning full-time employment at that school.

The teaching and research columns are as follows:

1 Corporate Finance	A. Agency Theory
	B. Bankruptcy & Finl Distress
	C. Capital Budgeting
	D. Capital Structure
	E. Cost of Capital
	F. Financial Analysis
	G. Mergers, Acq & Restructuring
	H. Strategic & Long-Term Fin Pl
	I. Working Capital Management
2 Investments	J. Asset Pricing Models
	K. Fixed Income Securities
	L. Futures & Options
	M. Portfolio Management
	N. Risk Measurement & Behavior
	O. Valuation Models
3 Financial Institutions & Markets	P. Commercial Banking
	Q. Investment Banking
	R. Issues in Monetary & Econ Pl
	S. Mutual Funds & Other Instit
	T. Security Markets Structure
4 International Finance	U. Intl Corporate Finance
	V. Intl Financial Markets
	W. Intl Investments
	X. Personal Financial Planning
	Y. Financial Education
	Z. Methodological Issues
6 Real Estate	&. Real Estate
7 Insurance	#. Insurance

Any mistakes in the Directory are my responsibility. However, some of the misinformation belongs to schools not providing complete information.

Any corrections, additional information, and new schools should be sent directly to me. If your schools is not included, did you send me a listing?

James R. Hasselback

JAMES R. HASSELBACK

James R. Hasselback is a Professor of Taxation at Florida State University and has previously taught at Eastern Michigan University, the University of Florida, and Texas A&M University. A member of the American Accounting Association and the American Taxation Association, he has published over 120 papers in professional and academic journals, including THE ACCOUNTING REVIEW, THE TAX ADVISER, FINANCIAL MANAGMENT, JOURNAL OF REAL ESTATE TAXATION, and the AMERICAN BUSINESS LAW JOURNAL.

He has presented papers at numerous national and regional professional meetings, and served as chairman at tax sessions of professional conferences. He is co-author on a two-volume introductory taxation textbook published by Commerce Clearning House, serving as technical editor on the second volume. In addition to compiling the DIRECTORY OF FINANCE FACULTY, he has compiled an Accounting Faculty Directory published by Prentice Hall for the past eighteen years. The ACCOUNTING FACULTY DIRECTORY may be the most cited reference in the Accounting field. Jim Hasselback also compiles a Directory of Management Faculty and a Directory of Marketing Faculty. He has begun work on a Directory of Engineering Faculty and a Directory of Computer Science Faculty.

ALABAMA
University of Alabama
U of Alabama at Birmingham
U of Alabama in Huntsville
Alabama A&M University
Alabama State University
Athens State College
Auburn University
Auburn U at Montgomery
Birmingham–Southern College
Jacksonville State Univ
Livingston University
University of Montevallo
University of North Alabama
Samford University
University of South Alabama
Troy State University
Tuskegee University
ALASKA
Univ of Alaska, Anchorage
Univ of Alaska – Fairbanks
ARIZONA
American Grad Sch Intl Mgt
University of Arizona
Arizona State University
Arizona St U – West Campus
Northern Arizona University
ARKANSAS
Arkansas College
University of Arkansas
U of Arkansas at Little Rock
U of Arkansas at Monticello
U of Arkansas at Pine Bluff
Arkansas State University
Arkansas Tech University
Univ of Central Arkansas
Fayetteville State Univ
Harding University
Henderson State University
Southern Arkansas Univ
CALIFORNIA
Azusa Pacific University
U of California–Berkeley
Univ of California–Davis
Univ of Calif–Irvine
Univ of Calif, Los Angeles
Univ of Calif, Riverside
U of Calif, Santa Barbara
Calif Polytechnic State U
Calif State Poly U–Pomona
Calif State U., Bakersfield
Calif State Univ, Chico
Calif St U–Dominguez Hills
Calif State Univ–Fresno
Calif State Univ, Fullerton
Calif State Univ, Hayward
Calif State Univ – Humboldt
Calif State Univ, Long Beach
Calif State U–Los Angeles
Calif State Univ, Northridge
Calif State Univ–Sacramento
Calif St U–San Bernardino
Calif State U – San Marcos
Calif State U, Stanislaus
Chapman College
Claremont McKenna College
Golden Gate University
John F. Kennedy University
LaSierra University
University of LaVerne
Loyola Marymount Univ
Naval Postgraduate School
University of the Pacific
Pacific Union College
Pepperdine Univ–Los Angeles
Pepperdine Univ–Malibu
Saint Mary's College
University of San Diego
San Diego State University
University of San Francisco
San Francisco State Univ
San Jose State University
Santa Clara University
Sonoma State University
Univ of Southern California
Stanford University
United States Intl Univ
Woodbury University
COLORADO
Univ of Colorado at Boulder
U of Colorado at Co Springs
Univ of Colorado at Denver
Colorado State University
University of Denver
Fort Lewis College
Mesa State College
Metropolitan State College
Univ of Northern Colorado
Univ of Southern Colorado
U.S. Air Force Academy
Western State College of CO

CONNECTICUT
University of Bridgeport
Central Connecticut St Univ
University of Connecticut
Eastern Conn State Univ
Fairfield Universy
University of Hartford
University of New Haven
Post College
Quinnipiac College
Southern Connecticut St Un
Western Conn State Univ
Yale University
DELAWARE
University of Delaware
Delaware State College
Wesley College
FLORIDA
Barry University
Bethune-Cookman College
Univ of Central Florida
Embry-Riddle Aeronautical U
University of Florida
Florida A&M University
Florida Atlantic Univ
Florida International Univ
Florida Southern University
Florida State University
Jacksonville University
University of Miami
University of North Florida
Rollins College
St. Thomas University–FL
University of South Florida
Stetson University
University of Tampa
University of West Florida
GEORGIA
Albany State College
Augusta College
Berry College
Clark Atlanta University
Clayton State College
Columbus College
Emory University
Fort Valley State College
Georgia College
University of Georgia
Georgia Institute Tech
Georgia Southern University
Georgia Southwestern College
Georgia State University
Kennesaw College
Mercer University–Atlanta
Mercer University–Macon
Morehouse College
Morris Brown College
Oglethorpe University
Piedmont College
Savannah State College
Valdosta State College
West Georgia College
HAWAII
Brigham Young Univ–Hawaii
Chaminade University
University of Hawaii at Hilo
Univ of Hawaii at Manoa
Hawaii Pacific College
IDAHO
Boise State University
University of Idaho
Idaho State University
ILLINOIS
Augustana College
Aurora University
University of Chicago
Chicago State University
DePaul University
Eastern Illinois Univ
Elmhurst College
Governors State University
University of Illinois
Univ of Illinois at Chicago
Illinois Benedictine College
Illinois Institute of Tech
Illinois State University
Illinois Wesleyan University
Loyola University of Chicago
Millikin University
Northeastern Illinois Univ
Northern Illinois Univ
Northwestern University
Quincy College
Roosevelt University
Saint Xavier College
Sangamon State University
Southern Illinois Univ
So Illinois, Edwardsville
Western Illinois University

INDIANA
Ball State University
Butler University
DePauw University
University of Evansville
Goshen College
Indiana University
Indiana Univ – Purdue Univ
Indiana Univ at Kokomo
Indiana Univ at South Bend
Indiana Univ Northwest
Indiana Univ Southeast
Indiana State University
University of Indianapolis
Marian College
University of Notre Dame
Purdue University
Saint Marys College
Univ of Southern Indiana
Tri State University
Valparaiso University
IOWA
Buena Vista College
Drake University
University of Iowa
Iowa State University
Loras College
Luther College
University of Northern Iowa
St. Ambrose University
Wartburg College
KANSAS
Emporia State University
Fort Hays State University
University of Kansas
Kansas State University
MidAmerica Nazarene College
Pittsburg State University
Washburn Univ of Topeka
Wichita State University
KENTUCKY
Bellarmine College
Brescia College
Cumberland College
Eastern Kentucky University
University of Kentucky
Kentucky State University
University of Louisville
Morehead State University
Murray State University
Northern Kentucky Univ
Transylvania University
Western Kentucky University
LOUISIANA
Dillard University
Grambling State University
Louisiana State University
Louisiana St in Shreveport
Louisiana Tech University
Loyola Univ–New Orleans
Mc Neese State University
University of New Orleans
Nicholls State University
Northeast Louisiana Univ
Northwestern State U of La
Southeastern Louisiana Univ
Southern University
U of Southwestern Louisiana
Tulane University
MAINE
Univ of Maine
Univ of Southern Maine
MARYLAND
University of Baltimore
Frostburg State University
Loyola College in Maryland
University of Maryland
Morgan State University
Salisbury State University
Towson State University
MASSACHUSETTS
American International Coll
Assumption College
Babson College
Bentley College
Boston College
Boston University
Clark University
Fitchburg State College
Harvard University
College of the Holy Cross
University of Massachusetts
U Massachusetts at Dartmouth
U Massachusetts at Boston
U Massachusetts at Lowell
Massachusetts Inst of Tech
Merrimack College
Nichols College
North Adams State College
Northeastern University
Salem State College

Simmons College
Stonehill College
Suffolk University
Western New England College
Westfield State College
Worcester State College
MICHIGAN
Adrian College
Albion College
Alma College
Andrews University
Calvin College
Central Michigan University
University of Detroit
Eastern Michigan University
Ferris State University
GMI Engineering & Mgt Inst
Grand Valley State Univ
Hillsdale College
Hope College
Lake Superior State Univ
Lawrence Technological Univ
University of Michigan
Univ of Michigan–Dearborn
Univ of Michigan–Flint
Michigan State University
Michigan Technological Univ
Northern Michigan Univ
Northwood Institute
Oakland University
Olivet College
Saginaw Valley State Univ
Wayne State University
Western Michigan University
MINNESOTA
Bemidji State University
Concordia College
Gustavus Adolphus College
Mankato State University
University of Minnesota
U of Minnesota – Duluth
Moorhead State University
St. Cloud State University
University of St. Thomas–MN
Southwest State University
Winona State University
MISSISSIPPI
Belhaven College
Delta State University
Jackson State University
Millsaps College
Mississippi College
University of Mississippi
Mississippi State Univ
Mississippi Valley St Univ
U of Southern Mississippi
MISSOURI
Central Missouri State Univ
Drury College
Fontbonne College
Lincoln University
U of Missouri at Columbia
U Missouri--Kansas City
U Missouri--St. Louis
Missouri Southern St Col
Missouri Western St College
Northeast Missouri State U
Northwest Missouri St Univ
Rockhurst College
Saint Louis University
Southeast Missouri St Univ
Southwest Baptist Univ
Southwest Missouri St Univ
Washington University
Webster University
William Jewell College
MONTANA
Eastern Montana College
University of Montana
Montana State University
NEBRASKA
Bellevue College
Creighton University
Kearney State College
University of Nebraska
Univ of Nebraska at Omaha
Wayne State College
NEVADA
Univ of Nevada, Las Vegas
University of Nevada, Reno
NEW HAMPSHIRE
Dartmouth College
Keene State College
New Hampshire College
University of New Hampshire
Plymouth State College

NEW JERSEY
  Centenary College
  Fairleigh Dickinson–Madison
  Fairleigh Dickinson–Rutherf
  Fairleigh Dickinson–Teaneck
  Glassboro State College
  Jersey City State College
  Monmouth College
  Montclair State College
  Ramapo College of New Jersey
  Rider College
  Rutgers University–Camden
  Rutgers Univ–Newark Undergrd
  Rutgers University–Newark
  Rutgers Univ–New Brunswick
  Saint Peter's College
  Seton Hall University
  Trenton State College
  Upsala College
NEW MEXICO
  Eastern New Mexico Univ
  University of New Mexico
  New Mexico Highlands Univ
  New Mexico State Univ
NEW YORK
  Adelphi University
  Alfred University
  Canisius College
  CUNY–Baruch College
  CUNY–Brooklyn College
  CUNY–H Lehman College
  CUNY–Hunter College
  CUNY–Queens College
  CUNY–Col of Staten Island
  Clarkson University
  Columbia University
  Cornell University
  Fordham University
  Hofstra University
  The College of Insurance
  Iona College
  Ithaca College
  LeMoyne College
  Long Isl U, Brooklyn Campus
  Long Island U–C.W. Post
  Long Isl Univ–Southhampton
  Manhattan College
  Marist College
  New York University
  New York University–Grad
  New York Inst of Tech
  Niagara University
  Pace University
  Pace University–Pleasantvil
  Pace University–Westchester
  Rensselaer Poly Institute
  University of Rochester
  Rochester Inst of Technology
  Russell Sage College
  Saint Bonaventure Univ
  St. Francis College
  St. John Fisher College
  St. John's University
  College of Saint Rose
  Siena College
  Skidmore College
  SUNY College at Fredonia
  SUNY College at Geneseo
  SUNY College at Oswego
  SUNY College at Old Westbury
  SUNY College at Stony Brook
  SUNY at Albany
  SUNY at Binghamton
  SUNY at Buffalo
  SUNY at New Paltz
  SUNY at Plattsburgh
  Syracuse University
  Union College
  Utica College
  Wagner College
  Yeshiva University
NORTH CAROLINA
  Appalachian State Univ
  Barton College
  Campbell University
  Catawba College
  Duke University
  East Carolina University
  Elon College
  Greensboro College
  Guilford College
  Lees–McRae College
  Mars Hill College
  Meredith College
  North Carolina at Ashville
  University of North Carolina
  North Carolina at Charlotte
  North Carolina at Greensboro
  North Carolina at Wilmington
  North Carolina A&T State Un
  North Carolina Central Univ

  North Carolina State Univ
  Pfeiffer College
  Wake Forest University
  Wake Forest University–Grad
  Western Carolina University
  Winston–Salem State Univ
NORTH DAKOTA
  Dickinson State University
  Jamestown College
  University of Mary
  Minot State University
  University of North Dakota
  North Dakota State Univ
OHIO
  Air Force Institute of Tech
  University of Akron
  Ashland University
  Baldwin–Wallace College
  Bowling Green State Univ
  Bradley University
  Capital University
  Case Western Reserve Univ
  Cedarville College
  Central State Univ–Ohio
  University of Cincinnati
  Cleveland State University
  University of Dayton
  Franklin University
  Heidelberg College
  John Carroll University
  Kent State University
  Marietta College
  Miami University
  Ohio University
  Ohio Northern University
  Ohio State University
  Ohio Wesleyan University
  Otterbein College
  University of Rio Grande
  University of Toledo
  Wittenberg University
  Wright State University
  Xavier University
  Youngstown State University
OKLAHOMA
  Cameron University
  Univ of Central Oklahoma
  East Central University
  Northeastern State Univ
  University of Oklahoma
  Oklahoma Christian College
  Oklahoma City University
  Oklahoma State University
  Oral Roberts University
  Southeastern Oklahoma State
  Southwestern Oklahoma St Un
  University of Tulsa
OREGON
  Lewis & Clark College
  Linfield College
  University of Oregon
  Oregon State University
  University of Portland
  Portland State University
  Southern Oregon St College
  Willamette University
PENNSYLVANIA
  Albright College
  Beaver College
  Bloomsburg University
  Bucknell University
  Calif Univ of Pennsylvania
  Carnegie Mellon University
  Cheyney University
  Clarion University
  Drexel University
  Duquesne University
  Elizabethtown College
  Franklin and Marshall Coll
  Gannon University
  Geneva College
  Gettysburg College
  Immaculata College
  Indiana U of Pennsylvania
  LaSalle University
  Lehigh University
  Lock Haven University
  Lycoming College
  Marywood College
  Millersville State Univ
  Mulhenberg College
  University of Pennsylvania
  Penn State University
  Penn State Univ–Erie
  Penn State Univ–Harrisburg
  University of Pittsburgh
  U of Pittsburgh at Johnstown
  Robert Morris College
  Saint Francis College
  Saint Joseph's University
  University of Scranton

  Shippensburg University
  Slippery Rock University
  Susquehanna University
  Temple University
  Villanova University
  West Chester University
  Widener University
  York College of Pennsylvania
RHODE ISLAND
  Bryant College
  Providence College
  University of Rhode Island
SOUTH CAROLINA
  Benedict College
  College of Charleston
  The Citadel
  Clemson University
  Francis Marion College
  Furman University
  Lander College
  Univ So Carolina at Aiken
  South Carolina–Coastal Carol
  Univ of South Carolina
  U South Carolina at Spartanb
  South Carolina St College
  Winthrop College
  Wofford College
SOUTH DAKOTA
  Augustana College SD
  Northern State University
  University of South Dakota
TENNESSEE
  Austin Peay State University
  Belmont College
  Carson–Newman College
  Christian Brothers College
  David Lipscomb University
  East Tennessee State Univ
  Fisk University
  Freed Hardeman University
  Memphis State University
  Middle Tennessee State Univ
  Rhodes College
  Southern Col of 7th Day Adv
  University of Tennessee
  Tennessee at Chattanooga
  Univ of Tennessee at Martin
  Tennessee State University
  Tennessee Technological Un
  Vanderbilt University
TEXAS
  Abilene Christian Univ
  Angelo State University
  Baylor University
  Corpus Christi State Univ
  University of Dallas
  East Texas State Univ
  Hardin–Simmons University
  University of Houston
  Univ of Houston–Clear Lake
  Univ of Houston–Downtown
  Houston Baptist University
  Lamar University
  Laredo State University
  Univ of Mary Hardin–Baylor
  Midwestern State University
  University of North Texas
  Prairie View A&M University
  Rice University
  St. Edward's University
  St. Mary's University
  University of St. Thomas–TX
  Sam Houston State Univ
  Southern Methodist Univ
  Southwest Texas State Univ
  Southwestern University
  Stephen F. Austin St Univ
  Tarleton State University
  U of Texas at Arlington
  Univ of Texas at Austin
  Univ of Texas at Dallas
  Univ of Texas at El Paso
  Univ of Texas–Pan American
  U of Texas of Permian Basin
  Un of Texas at San Antonio
  Univ of Texas at Tyler
  Texas A&I University
  Texas A&M University
  Texas Christian University
  Texas Southern University
  Texas Tech University
  Texas Wesleyan University
  Texas Woman's University
  Trinity University
  West Texas State Univ
UTAH
  Brigham Young University
  University of Utah
  Utah State University
  Weber State College

VERMONT
  Lyndon State College
  Norwich University
  University of Vermont
VIRGINIA
  Christopher Newport College
  Emory and Henry College
  George Mason University
  Hampton University
  James Madison University
  Liberty University
  Longwood College
  Lynchburg College
  Mary Baldwin College
  Mary Washington College
  Marymount University
  Norfolk State University
  Old Dominion University
  Radford University
  Regent University
  University of Richmond
  Roanoke College
  Shenandoah College
  University of Virginia
  University of Virginia–Grad
  Virginia Commonwealth Univ
  Virginia Poly Inst & St Un
  Virginia State University
  Virginia Union University
  Washington and Lee Univ
  College of William & Mary
WASHINGTON
  Central Washington Univ
  Eastern Washington Univ
  Gonzaga University
  Pacific Lutheran University
  University of Puget Sound
  Saint Martin's College
  Seattle University
  Seattle Pacific University
  University of Washington
  Washington State University
  Western Washington Univ
WASHINGTON DC
  The American University
  Catholic University
  Univ of District of Columbia
  George Washington Univ
  Georgetown University
  Howard University
  Southeastern University
WEST VIRGINIA
  Alderson–Broaddus College
  Marshall University
  Shepherd College
  West Virginia University
WISCONSIN
  Carroll College
  Marquette University
  St. Norbert College
  U of Wisconsin–Eau Claire
  Univ of Wisconsin–Green Bay
  U of Wisconsin–La Crosse
  Univ of Wisconsin–Madison
  Univ of Wisconsin–Milwaukee
  Univ of Wisconsin–Oshkosh
  Univ of Wisconsin–Parkside
  U of Wisconsin–Platteville
  U of Wisconsin–River Falls
  U of Wisconsin–Stevens Point
  Univ of Wisconsin–Superior
  U of Wisconsin–Whitewater
WYOMING
  University of Wyoming

1991-92 FINANCE FACULTY DIRECTORY
ALPHABETICAL BY SCHOOL

NAME	RANK	PHONE	BITNET	TCH	RESR	DEGREE			START
Abilene Christian Univ									BA,BBA
Dept of Management Sciences									
College of Business Adm									
Abilene, Texas 79699-0001									
Area Code (915) Fax 674-2564									
Griggs, Jack	Dean	674-2245		13	P	PHD	71	Texas	1991
Reinsch Jr., N. L.	C-Pr	674-2053	REINSCH		Mgt	PHD	73	Kansas	1984
Gunter, Rick	Inst	674-2429		12		MBA	87	W Tx St	1990
Adelphi University									BBA,MBA,MS
Dept of Banking Econ & Fin									
School of Business Adm									
Garden City, NY 11530									
Area Code (516) Fax 294-6128									
Waters, Winston	Dean$	877-4690			Law	JD	61	Seton Hl	1988
Chorun, Joseph	Assoc					PHD	65	Columbia	
Felheim, Robert	Assoc					PHD	74	NYU	
Patchias, James C.	Assoc					MPHL	84	NYU	
Swensen, R. Bruce	Assoc					DSW	82	Columbia	
Emami, Aristotle	Asst					PHD	81	Wash St	
Heinowitz, Harvey J.	Asst					MBA	75	Adelphi	
Laudor, Charles R.	Asst					PHD	70	Columbia	
Nowicki, Lawrence W.	Asst					PHD	84	Paris	
Adrian College									BBA
Finance Faculty									
Dept of Atg & Bus Adm									
Adrian, Michigan 49221-2575									
Area Code (517) Fax									
Bachman, William	C-Pr	265-5161			Mgt	ABD	73	Kentucky	1981
Stevenson, Ben	Prof	265-4298		12	HP	PHD		Ohio St	1980
Air Force Institute of Tech									
Finance Faculty									
School of Systems & Log									
Wright-Patter OH 45433-6583									
Area Code (513) Fax									
Did Not Respond									
University of Akron									BS,MBA,MS
Department of Finance									1966,1976
College of Business Adm									
Akron, Ohio 44325-4803									
Area Code (216) Fax 972-6588									
AKRONVM									
Petersen, Russell J.	Dean	972-7442			Atg	PHD	71	U Wash	1989
Wentz, Arthur G.	C-Ac	972-6329				PHD	69	Ohio St	1982
Durst, David R.	Prof	972-6332				DBA	72	Geo St	1968
Inman, James E.	Prof	972-7043				JD	71	Akron	1966
Litka, Michael P.	Prof	972-6884				JD	58	Iowa	1971
Shedlarz, Robert J.	Prof	972-7303				JD	72	Notre Dm	1972
Williams, John D.	Prof	972-6886				DBA	71	Kent St	1969
Jose, Manuel L.	Assoc	972-6883				PHD	83	Va Tech	1990
Kahl, Douglas R.	Assoc	972-6755				PHD	81	Iowa	1989
Lahey, Karen E.	Assoc	972-5436				PHD	85	Fla St	
Winick, Bernard S.	Assoc	972-6108				JD	64	Akron	1979
Anderson, Allen S.	Asst	972-6331				PHD	78	Arkansas	1984
Canda, Francis E.	Asst	972-6885				MBA	86	Kent St	1990
Ramcharran, Harridutt	Asst	972-6882				PHD	78	SUNY-Bin	1986
Redle, David A.	Asst	972-6085				JD	80	Akron	1981
Billow, Patricia M.	Inst	972-7390				JD	81	Akron	1984
Walker, Angela	Inst	972-5361							

University of Alabama
Dept Econ, Fnce & Legal Stde
College Comm & Bus Adm
Tuscaloosa, AL 35487-0224
Area Code (205) Fax 348-2951
UA1VM

BS,MA,PHD
1929,1963

Name	Rank	Phone	Code		Field	Degree	Age	School	Year
Mason, J. Barry	Dean	348-7443	BMASON		Mktg	PHD	67	Alabama	1967
Russell Professsor of Business Administration									
Helms, Billy P.	H-Pr	348-7842	BHELMS	1		PHD	73	Tenn	1973
Gup, Benton E.	Prof	348-7842	BGUP	3		PHD	66	Cinn	1983
Robert Hunt Cochrane/Alabama Bankers Chair									
Jean, William H.	Prof	348-7842	WJEAN	2		PHD	64	Purdue	1973
Rudolph, Patricia M.	Prof	348-8966	PRUDOLPH	3		PHD		N Carol	1976
Schlesinger, Harris	Prof	348-7859	HSCHLESI	1		PHD		Illinois	1987
Frank Park Samford Chair of Insurance									
Wu, H. K.	Prof	348-7842		3		PHD	63	Penn	1972
Zumpano, Leonard V.	Prof	348-7842	LZUMPANO	3		PHD	76	Penn St	1975
Chair of Real Estate									
Downs, Thomas W.	Assoc	348-4590	TDOWNS	2		PHD		Purdue	1989
McLeod, Robert W.	Assoc	348-8993	RMCLEOD	3		PHD		Texas	1978
Brooks, Robert E.	Asst	348-8987	RBROOKS	2		PHD		Florida	1989
Carroll, Carolyn	Asst	348-9791	CCARROLL	2		PHD		Illinois	1984
Ligon, James	Asst	348-7842	JLIGON	3		PHD		Penn	1991
Page, Frank H.	Asst	348-7842		1		PHD		Illinois	1991

U of Alabama at Birmingham
Department of Finance
School of Business
Birmingham, AL 35294-4460
Area Code (205) Fax 975-6234

BS,MAC,MBA
1973,1977

Name	Rank	Phone		Code	Field	Degree	Age	School	Year
Newport, M. Gene	Dean	934-8810			Mgt	PHD	63	Illinois	1971
Hill, Kendall Pat	C-Ac	934-8860	13		SM	PHD	81	Okla St	1982
Burns, Richard M.	Assoc	934-8860	1		CI	PHD	86	Georgia	1987
Fetherston, Thomas A.	Asst	934-8860	43		VS	PHD	85	Rutgers	1987
Walker, Joe	Asst	934-8860	12		CI	PHD	79	Tx A&M	1987

U of Alabama in Huntsville
Dept of Economics & Finance
College of Adm Science
Huntsville, AL 35899
Area Code (205) Fax 895-6328

BS,MAS

Name	Rank	Phone	Field	Degree	Age	School	Year
Billings, C. David	Dean	895-6735	Econ	PHD	69	Missouri	1981
Forbes, Shawn M.	Prof	895-6762		PHD	85	Georgia	1988
on leave to Georgia Southern, 1991-92							
Evans, Dorla A.	Assoc	895-6764		PHD	85	Arkansas	1991

Alabama A&M University
Economics & Finance Dept
School of Business
Normal, Alabama 35762
Area Code (205) Fax 851-5839
Did Not Respond--Taken from Catalog; Department Phone 851-5294

BS,BA,MBA

Name	Rank	Phone	Degree	Age	School
Williams II, Ira	Dean	851-5485			
Chang, Peter T.	Prof	Ext 228	PHD		Okla St
Esensoy, Yilmaz	Prof	Ext 227	PHD	69	Ohio St
Kim, Yang H.	Prof	Ext 226	PHD		Utah
Patnaik, Promode K.	Prof	Ext 232	PHD		Alabama
Rao, Yedla K.	Prof	Ext 222	PHD	64	Maryland
Salib, Anis B.	Prof	Ext 229	PHD		Vanderb
Alexander, James	Assoc	851-5685	ABD		Texas
Rahimian, Eric N.	Assoc	Ext 225	PHD		Indiana
Elike, Uchenna I.	Asst	Ext 224	PHD		Alabama
Karumanchi, V. R.	Asst	Ext 221	MS		Alab A&M
Yousif, Salah A.	Asst	Ext 230	MA		Howard
Briggs, Charles		851-5389			

Alabama State University
Dept of Accounting & Finance
College of Business Adm
Montgomery, AL 36101-0271
Area Code (205) Fax 265-9144

Name	Rank	Phone	Field	Degree	Age	School	Year
Vaughn Jr., Percy J.	Dean	293-4123	Mktg	DBA		Tx Tech	1974
Crawford, Jean G.	C-Ac	293-4133	Atg	PHD	87	Alabama	1989
Amdafo, Sampson	Asst	240-6809	F	ABD		Denver	1990
Huang, Gow-Cheng	Asst	240-6920	F	PHD	91	Alabama	1989

Univ of Alaska, Anchorage   BBA,MBA
Department of Business Adm
School of Business
Anchorage, AK 99508
Area Code (907) Fax 786-1914
  Blachman, William L.   Dean   786-1758   Econ   PHD   63 Wiscon   1988
  Essayyad, Musa   Assoc   786-1791   PHD   85 Alabama   1985
    William H. Seward Professor of International Finance
  Srivastava, Suresh C.   Asst   786-1761   PHD   88 Maryland   1987

Univ of Alaska – Fairbanks   BBA
Dept of Business Adm   1988,1988
School of Management
Fairbanks, AK 99775-1070
Area Code (907) Fax 474-5219
ALASKA
  Lehman, John   Dean$ 474-7461   Mis   PHD   82 Michigan   1987
  Taylor, John N.   H-Pr   474-6534
  Rice, Michael L.   Prof   474-7461   PHD   75 N Carol
    Interim Vice Chancellor for Administration
  Lindahl, Mary R.   Assoc   474-6656   PHD   75 Illinois   1986
  Pace, Kelley R.   Assoc   474-6657   PHD   85 Georgia   1986
  Kumar, Hari   Asst

Albany State College
Department of Business Adm
School of Business Adm
Albany, Georgia 31705
Area Code (912) Fax 430-5119
  Burgess, Walter J.   Dean   430-4772   Mgt   PHD   72 Geo St
  Kooti, Ghanbar   Assoc   430-4772   PHD   80 Mich St
  Vu, Liem   Asst   430-4772

Albion College   BA
Finance Faculty
Dept of Economics & Mgt
Albion, Michigan 49224-1899
Area Code (517) Fax 629-0509
ALBION
  Steinhauer, Larry E.   C-Pr   629-0423 LSTEIN Econ   PHD   74 Chicago   1968
  Hooks, Jon A.   Asst   PHD   89 Mich St   1989

Albright College
Finance Faculty
Business Box 15234
Reading, Penn 19612-5234
Area Code (215) Fax
  Reilly, Terence J.   C-Pr   921-2381   Atg   MS   67 Northeas   1975
  Martin, David A.   Assoc   921-2381   DA   80 Lehigh   1983

Alderson-Broaddus College
Finance Faculty
Dept of Bus Adm & Econ
Philippi, WV 26416
Area Code (304) Fax
Did Not Respond

Alfred University   1987
Finance Faculty
College of Bus & Adm
Alfred, New York 14802
Area Code (607) Fax 871-2114
CERAMICS
  Kulonda, Dennis   Dean   871-2124 BUSDEAN   PHD   N Car St   1991
  Hannum, John E.   Asst   871-2124   PHD   N Carol   1987

Alma College   BA
Finance Faculty
Business Adm Dept
Alma, Michigan 48801
Area Code (517) Fax 463-7277
  Gazmararian, George   C-Pr   463-7184   MBA   Detroit   1966
    Charels A. Dana Professor of Business Administration

The American University BS,MSA,MST,MBA
Dept Finance & Real Estate
Kogod College of Bus Ad
Washington, DC 20016-8044
Area Code (202) Fax 885-1946
AUVM2

Tuggle, Francis D. (Doug)	Dean	885-1986		Mgt	PHD	71	Car Mel	1990
Baker, H. Kent	C-Pr	885-1949	1	TVH	DBA	72	Maryland	1975
Edelman, Richard B.	Prof	885-1948	1	TM	DBA	75	Maryland	1983
Cao, Andrew D.	Assoc	885-1955	1	UX	DBA	76	Geo Wash	1976
Chinloy, Peter	Assoc	885-1951	6	&	PHD	74	Harvard	1991
Realtor Chair and Homer Hoyt Faculty Fellow								
Kokus, Jr., John	Assoc	885-1952	6	&	PHD	71	American	1969
Kumar, Parmeswar C.	Assoc	885-1947	21	CMR	PHD	75	Penn St	1980
Losey, Robert L.	Assoc	885-1941	3	LP	PHD	77	Kentucky	1982
Benjamin, John D.	Asst	885-1892	1	&	PHD	88	LSU	1990
Megbolugbe, Isaac F.	Asst	885-1994	6	&	PHD	83	Penn	1991
Musumeci, James J.	Asst	885-1995	1	ZP	PHD	87	Texas	1991
Phillips, Aaron L.	Asst	885-1980			DBA	86	So Illin	1989
Riddick, Leigh A.	Asst	885-1944	12	MNW	PHD	88	Wiscon	1989

American Grad Sch Intl Mgt MIM
Department of Finance
Business
Glendale, AZ 85306-3399
Area Code (602) Fax 439-5432

Mathis, F. John	C-Pr	978-7151	PHD	66	Iowa	
Foster, Robert D.	Prof	978-7788	PHD	68	Oregon	
Heathcotte, Bryan	Prof	978-7296	DBA	70	Indiana	
Carrada-Bravo, Francisco	Assoc	978-7170	PHD	80	Colorado	1971
Keat, Paul G.	Assoc	978-7298	PHD	59	Chicago	
Tuzzolino, Frank A.	Assoc	978-7155	PHD	87	Ariz St	
Vor der Landwehr, Dale	Assoc	978-7162	PHD	74	Wayne St	
Kuhlmann, Arkadi	Inst	978-7825				

American International Coll BS
Finance Faculty
School of Business Adm
Springfield, MA 01109-3189
Area Code (413) Fax 737-2803

Smolowitz, Ira E.	Dean	737-7000	PHD	84	RPI	1988
Stanio, Raymond F.	Asst	737-7000	MBA	64	Hartford	1983

Andrews University BS,MBA
Dept of Atg, Econ & Finance
School of Business
Berrien Spr, MI 49104-0020
Area Code (616) Fax 473-4425

Saliba, Slimen J.	Dean	471-3102		Mktg	PHD	85	Northwes	1980
Russell, Malcolm B. M.	C	471-3104		Econ	PHD	77	J Hopkin	1979
Chikaonda, Matthew A.	Prof	471-3118	12	MNOZ	PHD	90	Mass	1991

Angelo State University BBA,MBA
Finance Faculty
Dept of Atg, Econ & Fin
San Angelo, TX 76909
Area Code (915) Fax 942-2038

Hegglund, Robert K.	Dean	942-2337		Mgt	PHD	72	Arkansas	1972
Dane, Andrew J.	H-Pr	942-2046		Econ	PHD	75	Oklahoma	1973
Bankston, Thomas A.	Prof	942-2076	12	EL	PHD	75	Florida	1974
Harlow, Forrest W.	Prof	942-2076	1	E	PHD	76	N Texas	1983
McGaughy, Cheryl A.	Inst	942-2076	12	M	MBA	76	Miss	1984
McKinney, William	Inst	942-2076	6	&	MA	77	Txs A&M	1984

Appalachian State Univ BS,MS
Dept Finance, Insur & Real E 1976,1981
Walker College of Bus
Boone, N Carolin 28608
Area Code (704) Fax 262-2094

Peacock, Ken	Dean$			Atg	PHD	79	LSU	1983
Davis, Harry M.	C-Pr	262-4030	34	PV	PHD		Georgia	1977
Bowden, Elbert V.	Prof		34	PV	PHD		Duke	1977
Jones Jr., Ray G.	Prof	262-4030	2	MK	DBA		Miss St	1973
Johnson, Linda L.	Assoc	262-4030			PHD		Georgia	1981
Wood, David D.	Assoc	262-6234	12	NA	DBA		La Tech	1985

Fletcher, J. Stuart	Asst	262-4030		34	PV	PHD		Fla St 1988
Followill, Richard A.	Asst			2	LJ	PHD		Alabama 1985
Goff, Delbert C.	Asst			12	EM	PHD	91	Fla St 1991
Keasler, Terrill R.	Asst			1	DE	PHD		Alabama 1987

University of Arizona BA,MBA,MAC,PHD
Dept Finance & Real Estate 1948,1966
College of Bus & Pub Ad
Tucson, Arizona 85721
Area Code (602) Fax 621-7483
ARIZRVAX

Smith, Kenneth R.	Dean	621-2165	Econ	PHD	68	Northwes	1980
Dyl, Edward A.	H-Pr	621-7554		PHD	73	Stanford	1987
Bierwag, Gerald O.	Prof	621-7488		PHD	62	Northwes	1981
Carleton, Willard T.	Prof	621-1520		PHD	62	Wiscon	1984
Atkins, Allen B.	Asst	621-5406		PHD	88	Texas	1988
Brenner, Robin J.	Asst	621-1701		PHD	89	Cornell	1989
Bronfman, Corinne M.	Asst	621-7490		PHD	88	New York	1988
on leave							
Harlow III, W. Van	Asst			PHD	86	Texas	1986
on leave							
Kwan, Simon	Asst	621-5569		PHD	90	N Carol	1990
Sternberg, Joel R.	Asst	621-3378		PHD	86	Stanford	1990
Harjes, Richard H.	Inst	621-7489		ABD			

Arizona State University BS,MBA,PHD
Department of Finance 1962,1964
College of Business
Tempe, Arizona 85287-3906
Area Code (602) Fax 965-8539
ASUACAD

Penley, Larry E.	Dean	965-5516	Mgt	PHD	76	Georgia	1985
Smith, Richard L.	C-Pr	965-3131	13 AGQ	PHD		UCLA	1981
Joehnk, Michael D.	Prof	965-7281	12 DKMO	PHD		Arizona	1982
Poe, Jerry B.	Prof	965-6212	1 FH	DBA	63	Harvard	1974
Sushka, Marie E.	Prof	965-6581	13 BGPQ	PHD		Geotown	1984
Cesta, John R.	Assoc	965-2969	JM	PHD	74	Fla St	1975
Hoffmeister, J. Ronald	Assoc	965-4389	13 GT	PHD		Illinois	1983
Martin, Linda J.	Assoc	965-6819		DBA		La Tech	1980
on leave 1991-92							
Wilt Jr., Glenn A.	Assoc	965-6355	12 FMX	PHD	63	Michigan	1963
Amel, Eric	Asst	965-4603	12 DQT	PHD		Wash U	1988
Bessembinder, Hendrik	Asst	965-4603	24 LNUV	PHD		U Wash	1989
Booth, James R.	Asst	965-5698	13 AGPQ	PHD		Alabama	1980
Chan, Kalok	Asst	965-6878	24 JLVW	PHD		Ohio St	1990
Chang, Saeyoung	Asst	965-6855	12 AG	PHD		Ohio St	1988
Gallinger, George W.	Asst	965-4221	12 FHI	PHD		Purdue	1977
Hertzel, Michael G.	Asst	965-6869	1 ADGV	PHD		Oregon	1987

Arizona State Univ West BS,MBA
Department of Finance
Business Prog Box 37100
Phoenix, Arizona 85069-7100
Area Code (602) Fax 543-6221
ASUACAD

Greenhut, John G.	Assoc	543-6212	ICJGG	21	MGPU	PHD	1989
McWilliams, Victoria B.	Asst	543-6223	ICVBM	1	GZD	PHD	1990

Arkansas College
Finance Faculty
Business Program
Batesville, AK 72501
Area Code (501) Fax
No Finance Faculty

Adams, Clarence	C-Pr			Mgt	PHD	N Carol 1989

University of Arkansas BS,MS,PHD
Department of Finance 1931,1963
College of Business Adm
Fayetteville, AR 72701
Area Code (501) Fax 575-7687
Bitnet: Adm #UAFSYSA; Academic #UAFSYSB

Smith, Stanley D.	Dean	575-5949	Fnce	PHD	79	Ariz St	1985
Hearth, Douglas P.	H-Ac	575-2044		PHD		Iowa	1989

Dominick, John A.   Prof   575-2204   PHD   Alabama   1970
  Arkansas Bankers Assoc Chair in Banking & J.W. Bellamey Chair of Bank & Fin
Hardin, William F.   Prof   575-6143   PHD   66 N Carol   1968
Kennedy, Robert E.   Prof   575-6149   PHD   Texas   1957
Lynch, Gene C.   Prof   575-6147   PHD   Texas   1973
Millar, James A.   Prof   575-4908   PHD   71 Oklahoma   1970
Liu, Pu   Assoc 575-6095   PHD   Indiana   1984
Perry, Larry G.   Assoc 575-6154   DBA   La Tech   1982
Benefield, Michael E.   Asst   575-6094   MBA   Ark St   1988
Rimbey, James N.   Asst   575-5259   DBA   Kentucky   1988

U of Arkansas at Little Rock   BS
Department of Finance   1976,1982
College of Business
Little Rock, AR 72204
Area Code (501) Fax 569-8915
UALR
  Culpepper, Robert C.   Dean   569-3351 RCCULPEP   Atg   PHD   69 Arkansas   1975
  Dorfman, Mark S.   Prof   569-3354   PHD   Illinois
  Glubok, Allan   Prof   569-3354   2   DBA   Wash U
  Terry, Andy   Asst   569-3354

U of Arkansas at Monticello
Department of Finance
Dept of Business Adm
Monticello, AR 71655
Area Code (501) Fax
  Barringer, David F.   H $ 460-1141   MBA   91
  McGregor, Michael   Inst   460-1041   MBA   87

U of Arkansas at Pine Bluff   BS
Finance Faculty
School of Bus & Mgt
Pine Bluff, AR 71601
Area Code (501) Fax 534-1012
  Fluker, John E.   Dean$ 541-6827   Quan   PHD   Houston   1989
  Cudjoe, Kwamena A.   Assoc 541-6830   PHD   Penn St   1987

Arkansas State University   BS,MBA
Dept of Bus Adm & Econ   1979,1985
College of Business
State Univ, AR 72467-0239
Area Code (501) Fax 972-3868
  Talbert, Lonnie E.   Dean   972-3035   Econ   PHD   74 N Car St   1966
  Crawford, Jerry L.   C-Pr   972-3416   Econ   PHD   69 Arkansas   1966
  Moody, George E.   Prof   226-2641   DBA   Indiana
  Taylor, Richard W.   Prof   972-3416   PHD   76 LSU   1984
  Williams, William M.   Assoc 972-3416   PHD   78 Miss St   1978
  Washam, James O.   Inst   972-3416   ABD   Miss   1989

Arkansas Tech University   BS
Finance Faculty
School of Business
Russellville, AR 72801-2222
Area Code (501) Fax 968-0677
  Cole, Raymond E.   Dean   968-0490   Econ   PHD   76 Arkansas   1970
  Smith, Richard   Asst   968-0493   23   PV   PHD   74 Texas   1991

Ashland University   BS
Department of Finance
School of Bus Adm, Econ
Ashland, Ohio 44805
Area Code (419) Fax 289-5333
  Rafeld, Frederick J.   Dean   289-5733   PHD   68 Ohio St   1970
  Shockney, Thomas D.   C-Pr   289-5231   Mgt   PHD   71 Ohio St   1964
  Piper, Beverly   Assoc 289-5230   MS   78 Toledo   1979
  Stuck, Charles   Asst   289-5223   MBA   85 Xavier   1985
  Lathovich, Sharon

Assumption College BA,MBA
Finance Faculty
Department of Economics
Worcester, Mass 01615-0005
Area Code (508) Fax 756-1780
Did Not Respond--Taken from College Catalog; Phone 752-5615
McCarthy, James	C			Econ	PHD	63 Yale	
Aiello, John P.	Lect				MBA	88 Bryant	1988
Mayer, John M.	Lect				MBA	80 Babson	1982

Athens State College
Finance Faculty
Division of Business
Athens, Alabama 35611
Area Code (205) Fax 233-8164
Haynes, James F.	H	233-8116	37	P#	PHD	Vanderbi	1981
Bartlett, Jerry	Prof	233-8201	7	&	JD	Cumberla	1965
Garino, James	Assoc	233-8295	12	FN	MA	Indiana	1968
Edmondson, Rey	Inst	233-8211	1	F	MBA	Alabama	1975

Auburn University BS,MS,MBA,PHD
Department of Finance 1976,1980
College of Business
Auburn, Alabama 36849-5245
Area Code (205) Fax 844-4016
AUDUCVAX
Bellenger, Danny N.	Dean	844-4030		Mktg	PHD	72 Alabama	1989
Jahera, John S.	C-Ac	844-5344	1	ADG	PHD	Georgia	1980
Barth, James R.	Prof	844-2469	3	PS	PHD	Ohio St	1989
Lowder Eminet Scholar Professor							
Edmonds, Charles P.	Prof	844-3003	1	O	PHD	72 Arkansas	1973
Hand, John H.	Prof	844-3004	3	PS	PHD	65 MIT	1974
Lloyd, William P.	Prof	844-6511	1	ADE	DBA	73 Indiana	1979
Associate Dean							
McCord, Sammy O.	Assoc	844-2909	4	UV	PHD	71 Arkansas	1973
Page, Daniel E.	Assoc	844-3008	2	ADE	PHD	Georgia	1984
Tole, Thomas M.	Assoc	844-3011	2	HC	DBA	74 Oklahoma	1974
Crutchley, Claire E.	Asst	844-3002	1	A	PHD	Va Tech	1989
Hudson, Carl D.	Asst	844-3005	3	PT	PHD	Ariz St	1988
Jensen, R. H. Marlin	Asst	844-3006	1	EH	PHD	Tx A&M	1988
Pugh, William N.	Asst	844-3009	24	DG	PHD	Fla St	1986

Auburn U at Montgomery BSBA,MBA
Dept of Accounting & Finance 1988,1988
School of Business
Montgomery, AL 36117-3596
Area Code (205) Fax 244-3762
Budden, Michael C.	Dean	244-3478		Mktg	PHD	82 Arkansas	1988
Rogow, Robert B.	H-Pr	244-3490		Atg	PHD	76 Arkansas	1986
Johnson, Raymond M.	Assoc	244-3490	34	PRUK	PHD	Okla St	1970
Heier, Jan R.	Asst	244-3490	12	FPX	DBA	86 Miss St	1986
Lange, David	Asst	244-3490	12	KXY	DBA	89 Kentucky	1990
Wilbourn, Macon	Asst	244-3490	12	NS	DBA	Miss St	1982

Augusta College BBA,MBA
Department of Finance
School of Business Adm
Augusta, Georgia 30910
Area Code (404) Fax 737-1773
Brannen, Dalton E.	Dean$	737-1418		Mgt	PHD	76 Miss	1990
Dowling, William A.	C	737-1560	13		DBA	84 Tenn	1990
Kuniansky, Harry R.	Prof	733-4465	13	HIM	DBA	70 Geo St	1980
Sherrouse, M. Teresa	Assoc	737-1560	14	IMV	ABD	Georgia	1975
Ziobrowski, Brigitte J.	Assoc	737-1560	13	HRU	ABD	Kent St	1991

Augustana College IL BA
Finance Faculty
Dept of Business Adm
Rock Island, IL 61201-2296
Area Code (309) Fax 794-7431
Selbyg, Arne	Dean	794-7311			PHD	75 Chicago	1988
Lonergan, Janis	C-Ac	794-7472			PHD	78 So Ill	1976
Hammermeister, John F.	Inst	794-7399			MBA	Oregon	

Augustana College SD BA,MASS
Finance Faculty
Dept of Bus Adm & Econ
Sioux Falls, SD 57197
Area Code (605) Fax 336-5477
  English, Richard D. C-Ac 336-5312   Atg MBA 68 Wash U 1974
  Danford, Gregory Assoc 336-5321 14 JVW PHD 87 Wash St 1990

Aurora University BA
Atg, Econ & Finance Division
Sch Bus & Prof Studies
Aurora, Illinois 60506-4892
Area Code (708) Fax
  Popper, Edward T. Dean 344-5529   DBA 78 Harvard 1991
  Gash, Dennis N. C-As   MS 78 Northwes 1989
  Voris, Frank K. Lect   MBA 81 No Illin 1985

Austin Peay State University
Dept of Accounting & Finance
College of Business
Clarksville, TN 37044
Area Code (615) Fax
  Reagan, Carmen Dean$ 648-7674 Mktg DBA 83 Miss St 1988
  Fortner, Wesley O. C-Pr 648-7557 Atg PHD 67 Alabama 1983
  Phillips, Michael Assoc 648-7556   ABD 1991
  Richards, Charles Asst 648-7556   1991

Azusa Pacific University
Finance Faculty
School of Bus & Mgt
Azusa, Calif 91702-7000
Area Code (818) Fax 969-7180
  Grant, Donald Dean$ 969-3434   EDD So Calif 1991
  Conover, Roger Asst   MA Sn Diego 1991

Babson College BS,MBA
Division of Finance 1980,1981
School of Management
Babson Park, MA 02157-0901
Area Code (617) Fax 239-5230
BABSON
  Cohen, A. Dean 239-4316   Mgt DBA 67 Harvard
  Kimball, Ralph C. C-Ac 2394404 32 PQ PHD Berkeley
  Edmunds, John C. Assoc 14 UVW DBA Harvard
  Perry, James E. Assoc 1 P PHD Oklahoma
  Thomas, Annie Assoc 23 PHD Yale
  Yener, Demir Assoc 239-5577 41 MT PHD Gazi
  Alt, Christopher Asst 1 DC PHD MIT
  Ballantine Jr., John W. Asst 239-4630 13 P PHD New York
  Minahan, John R. VAsst 2 AS PHD MIT
  Santini, Donald Asst 1 SI PHD Boston U
  Stoller, Linda Lect 6 & JD Boston U

Baldwin-Wallace College BA
Finance Faculty
Div of Business Adm
Berea, Ohio 44017
Area Code (216) Fax 826-2329
  Ehresman, Ronald L. C-Pr 826-2392   Case Wes
  Donahue, Thomas Prof 826-2392 12 CXFL DBA S Calif
  Peck, Earl M. Prof 826-2392 14 UW PHD 74 Colorado
  Sears, Paul Assoc 826-2392 12 HPUX PHD Case Wes
  DeVille, Susan Asst 826-2392 13 FQ PHD Case Wes

Ball State University BS,MS
Department of Finance 1978,1984
College of Business
Muncie, Indiana 47306-0345
Area Code (317) Fax 285-8024
BSUVAX1
  Palomba, Neil A. Dean 285-8192 Econ PHD 66 Minn 1984
  Fitzgerald, John F. C-Pr 285-5200 23 PX PHD 71 Wiscon 1984
  Black, Joseph B. Emer 285-1152 13 AK BBA 65 Illinois 1973

Faulhaber, Bert C. on leave	Prof			34	VV	PHD	56	Insbruck	1978
Hoban Jr., James P.	Prof	285-1814		23	NH	PHD	76	Utah	1976
Mantripragada, Krishna G.	Prof	285-3727		23	PT	PHD	71	Minn	1979
Wells, Grant J.	Prof	285-5219		23	KP	PHD	73	Wiscon	1966
Williams, Numan A.	Prof	285-5220		23	XY	PHD	73	Wiscon	1973
Banerjee, Harpogal	Asst	285-5215		13	PT	PHD	89	Illinois	1989
Baur, Michael N.	Asst	285-5214		12	AD	PHD	91	Texas	1990
Benkato, Omar M.	Asst	285-5210		12	FL	PHD		Cinn	1989
Rathinasamy, Rathina S.	Asst	285-1660		24	GD	PHD	87	Tennesse	1988
Sundaran, Srinivasan	Asst	285-5217		12	DL	PHD	90	Cinn	1991
Sweeney, Larry E.	Asst	285-1152		12	GD	PHD	85	W Virg	1988
Creviston, D. Carlene	Inst	285-5205		23	XY	MA	62	Ball St	1973

University of Baltimore
Dept of Economics & Finance
Merrick Sch of Business
Baltimore, MD 21201-5779
Area Code (410) Fax 752-2821
Bitnet: UBE.UB.UMD.EDU
BS,MST
1983,1989

Costello, Daniel E.	Dean	625-3255			Comm	PHD	68	Mich St	1990
Register, Charles A.	C-Ac	625-3303			Econ	PHD		Okla St	
Chambers, Donald R.	Assoc	625-3309				PHD		N Carol	
Ford, Deborah A.	Assoc	625-3311				PHD		Penn	
Morse, Joel N.	Assoc	625-3301				PHD		Mass	
Cebenoyan, A. Sinan	Asst	625-3020				PHD		NYU	
Cooperman, Elizabeth S.	Asst	625-3421				PHD		Georgia	
Fung, Hung-Gay	Asst	625-3303				PHD		Geo St	
Isberg, Steven C.	Asst	625-3026				PHD		SUNY-Bin	
Nawalkha, Sanjay	Asst	625-3306				PHD		Mass	
Thies, Clifford F.	Asst	625-3312				PHD		Boston C	

Barry University
Finance Faculty
Andreas School of Bus
Miami Shores, FL 33161-6695
Area Code (305) Fax 892-6412
BARRYU
BS,MBA,MPA

Elgart, Lloyd D.	Dean	899-3500			Mgt	DBA		Nova	1979
Broihahn, Michael	Assoc	899-3506		12	MOX	MBA		Wiscon	1988
Daghestani, Eddie	Assoc	899-3509				PHD		Colorado	1988
Duchatelet, Martine	Assoc	899-3510	DUCHAELE	12	EOT	PHD		Stanford	1989
Rocourt, George F.	Adj	899-3521		13	EFKR	ABD	75	JHopkins	1991

Barton College
Finance Faculty
Dept of Business Prog
Wilson, NC 27893
Area Code (919) Fax 237-4957

Davis, Mark	Dean	399-6343				PHD		1978
Kaplan, Ralph	C-As	399-6417				PHD	Maryland	1989
Cummings, Michael	Asst	399-6419				MBA	E Carol	1983
Edmondson, Robert	Asst	399-6429				MBA	Wake For	1991
Mitchell, Kay	Asst	399-6428				MBA	Campbell	1986
Petway, C. Briggs	Asst	399-6425				MA	N Car St	1989

Baylor University
Department of Finance
Hankamer Sch Business
Waco, Texas 76798-8002
Area Code (817) Fax 755-2421
BBA,MBA,MT
1950,1969

Scott, Richard C.	Dean	755-1211			Mgt	DBA	68	Indiana	1968
Maness, Terry S.	C-Pr	755-2263	1	FI	DBA		Indiana	1972
Carr P. Collins Professor of Finance								
Cook, Alan	Prof		4	U	PHD		Arkansas	1969
Cretien, Paul D.	Prof	755-1667	23	L	PHD		Texas	1985
Ghee, William K.	Prof		1		PHD		Penn	1981
Rose, John T.	Prof	755-2263	3	P	PHD		Wash U	1984
Lacy Chair in Banking								
Cunningham, Donald F.	Assoc		1		PHD		Ohio St	1984
Potts, J. Franklin	Assoc		1		PHD		LSU	1968
Potts, Tom L.	Assoc	755-2263	15	X	PHD		Illinois	1971
Reichenstein, William	Assoc		2	JLM	PHD		Ntr Dame	1990
Powers Chair of Investment Management								
Tipton, James McCall	Assoc		23		PHD		Florida	1980
Director of the Center for Securities Research and Education								
Rich, Steven Paul	Asst		12		PHD		Indiana	1982
Seward, J. Allen	Asst		1	G	PHD		Penn	1976
Busby, James E.	Lect	755-2263	1		MBA		Baylor	1985

Beaver College — BS,BA
Finance Faculty
Dept of Bus Adm & Econ
Glenside, PA 19038-3295
Area Code (215) Fax 572-0240

Name	Rank	Phone			Field	Degree	Yr	School	Yr
Biggs, William D.	C-Pr	572-2937		H		PHD	74	Penn St	1980
Halpin, Annette A.	Asst	572-2900	1	X		ABD		Drexel	1983

Belhaven College — BS
Finance Faculty
Div of Business Adm
Jackson, Miss 39202
Area Code (601) Fax
Did Not Respond

| Park, James W. | C-Pr | 968-5965 | | | Atg | PHD | 77 | | |

Bellarmine College
Dept of Bus Adm & Econ
Ruble Sch- 2001 Newburg
Louisville, KY 40205-0671
Area Code (502) Fax

| Feltner, Richard L. | Dean | 452-8240 | | | | PHD | 65 | N Car St | 1986 |
| Sharef, G. A. | Prof | 452-8240 | | | | PHD | | Alabama | |

Bellevue College — BS,BA,BTS
Finance Faculty
Faculty of Business
Bellevue, Neb 68005
Area Code (402) Fax

| Polson, Houston H. | C-As | 291-8100 | 12 | BF | | JD | 89 | Creighto | 1985 |

Belmont College — BS,MBA
Finance Faculty
Massey School of Bus
Nashville, Tenn 37212-3757
Area Code (615) 385-6455

Cotham III, James C.	Dean$	385-6482			Mgt	DBA	67	Indiana	1986
Edwards, Charles	VProf	385-6480				PHD		N Carol	
Winn Jr., Edward L.	Prof	385-6463							
Associate Dean									

Bemidji State University
Finance Faculty
Dept of Business Adm
Bemidji, MN 56601
Area Code (218) Fax

Norris, Gerald	Dean					PHD			
Kyryluk, Robert	C-Ac	755-2758			Mgt	MBA		Mankato	1978
Gendreau, Richard J.	Prof	755-2755				MBS		St Cloud	1969
Fauchald, Thomas	Assoc	755-3717				MS		N Color	1982

Benedict College — BS
Finance Faculty
Business
Columbia, SC 29204
Area Code (803) Fax

Scott, Robert L.	C-Pr				Mgt	EDD		S Carol	
Mahdi, Syed	H-Pr	253-5190			Econ	PHD		Mass	
Nadig, Narayanaswamy	Asst	253-5192				MBA		Atlanta	

Bentley College — BS,MBA,MS 1989,1989
Department of Finance
College of Business
Waltham, Mass 02254-4705
Area Code (617) Fax 891-2819
BENTLEY

Schlorff, H. Lee	Dean	891-2113			Atg	PHD	73	Missouri	1978
Hachey, George	C-Ac	891-2514	GHACHEY	3	KPQV	PHD	85	New Hamp	1983
Nelson, David T.	Prof	891-2511	DNELSON	13	FHP	PHD	74	Wiscon	1983
Sullivan, Timothy	Prof	891-2737		1	DFH	PHD	71	Michigan	1980
Feldman, Stanley	Assoc	891-2384		1	DFH	PHD	76	New York	1988
Rosenthal, Leonard	Assoc	891-2516		2	GWVB	PHD	77	CUNY	1983
Balogh, Colin	Asst	891-2772	CBALOGH		ReEs	PHD	91	Georgia	1989

```
                                                                                                                  11

    Datta, Sudip             Asst    891-2513 SDATTA      12 ABGK   PHD    89 SUNY      1989
    Fletcher, Donna          Asst    891-2982 DFLETCHE    12 UVW    PHD    91 LeHigh    1991
    Gupta, Atul              Asst    891-2512 AGUPTA      12 AGPU   PHD    85 Texas
    Gupta, Keshav            Asst    891-2099 KGUPTA      12 DGJL   PHD    84 Pitt      1987
    Keating, William         Asst    891-2722 WKEATING    13 AJPT   PHD    91 Arizona   1990
    Kim, Sangphill           Asst    891-2088 SKIM        12 DJMV   PHD    84 Ohio      1988
    Leabman, Jerry           Asst    891-2771             12 FMX    MST    84 Bentley   1987
    Martel, Robert           Asst    891-2729             2  LMNX   MS     66 MIT       1989
    Milton, David            Asst    891-2734             13 CMSX   MBA    85 Bentley   1983
    Sultan, Jahangir         Asst    891-2518 JSULTAN     14 JMVW   PHD    86 Arizona   1989
    Young, Colin M.          Asst    891-2679 CYOUNG      13 HOTV   PHD    82 London    1986

Berry College                                                                             BS,MBA
Finance Faculty
Dept of Business & Econ
Rome, Georgia  30149
Area Code (404)  Fax
    Brown, William J.        H-Pr    236-1713             13 AGP    PHD

Bethune-Cookman College
Finance Faculty
Division of Business
Daytona Beach FL  32015
Area Code (904)  Fax
Phone 255-1401; No Finance Faculty
    Long, Aubrey E.          C-Ac    Ext 355                        PHD       Ohio St   1988

Birmingham-Southern College                                                               BS
Finance Faculty
Business Department
Birmingham, AL  35254
Area Code (205)  Fax 226-4627
    Gunter, Marjorie         C-Pr    226-4818                Atg    MBA    71 Samford    1978
    Cleveland, Paul          Asst    226-4817             12 CEMN   PHD    85 Tx A&M    1990

Bloomsburg University                                                                     BS,MBA
Dept of Finance & Bus Law
College of Business
Bloomsburg, PA  17815
Area Code (717)  Fax 389-3892
    Matteson, Carol          Dean    389-4019
    Heskel, David G.         C-Ac    389-4394                                              1976
    Dill, Bernard            Prof    389-4393             12 FMXY   DBA    71 Geo Wash  1968
    Guttha, Raj              Assoc   389-4761                                              1988
    Siergiej, Lalana         Assoc   389-4816             13 JTVW   ABD       Kent St   1989

Boise State University                                                         BBA,BS,BA,MBA
Dept of Marketing & Finance                                                         1979,1985
College of Business
Boise, Idaho  83725
Area Code (208)  Fax 385-3637
IDBSU
    Dudley, Orie             Dean    385-1125                Mgt    BS        Stanford   1991
    Lincoln, Douglas J.      C-Pr    385-3848                Mktg   PHD       Va Tech    1980
    Frankle, Alan W.         Prof    385-3462                       PHD       Arizona    1984
    Stitzel, Thomas E.       Prof    385-3150                       PHD       Oregon     1975
    Barney, Dwayne           Assoc   385-3429                       PHD       Tx A&M     1986
    Maher, Matt              Asst    385-4046                       PHD       Illinois   1989
    Schooley, Diane K.       Asst    385-4047                       DBA       Colorado   1989
    White, Harry L.          Asst    385-3546                       PHD       Tx A&M     1988

Boston College                                                                 BS,MSF,MBA,PHD
Department of Finance                                                                1956,1975
W.E. Carroll Sch of Mgt
Chestnut Hl, MA  02167-3808
Area Code (617)  Fax 552-2097
BCVMS
    Neuhauser, John J.       Dean    552-3925 NEUHAUJO       Sys    PHD    68 Rens Pol   1969
    Tehranian, Hassan        C-Pr    552-3944             12 FM     PHD       Alabama
    Greaney Jr., Walter T.   Prof    552-3986 GREANEY     3         PHD    60 Harvard
    Maung, Mya               Prof    552-3709 MAUNG       34 PV     PHD    61 Catholic   1966
    Taggart, Robert A.       Prof    552-4113 TAGGARTR    1         PHD       MIT
    Aragon, George A.        Assoc   552-3957 ARAGON      12        DBA    75 Harvard    1975
    Benveniste, Larry        Assoc   552-3974 BENVENIL    2         PHD       Berkeley
```

12

Marcus, Alan	Assoc	552-2767	MARCUSAL	21	LO	PHD		MIT	
Preston, John G.	Assoc	552-3987	PRESTON	12		DBA	65	Harvard	1969
Travlos, Nickolaos G.	Assoc	552-8519	TRAVLOS	1	F	PHD		NYU	
Hevert, Kathleen T.	Asst	552-3992	HEVERT	12	F	PHD		N Carol	
Holderness, Clifford	Asst	552-2768	HOLDERNE	1		JD		Stanford	
McClaughlin, Robyn M.	Asst	552-3240	MCLAUGH		DF	PHD		MIT	
Mech, Timothy	Asst	552-3976	MECH	12		PHD		Rochest	
Mehran, Hamid	Asst	552-8656	MEHRAN	13	D	PHD		N Carol	
Singh, Manoj	Asst	552-3980	SINGHMA	21	L	PHD		Purdue	
Strock, Elizabeth A.	Asst	552-3994	STROCK	12	F	PHD		Mass	
Wilhelm, William J.	Asst	552-3990	WILHELMW	2	L	PHD		LSU	

Boston University
Dept of Finance & Economics
School of Management
Boston, Mass 02215
Area Code (617) Fax 353-6667
BUACCA

BS,MBA,PHD
1921,1965

Lataif, Louis E.	Dean	353-2668		Mgt	MBA		Harvard	1991
Aber, Jack W.	C-Ac	353-4404			DBA	72	Harvard	1972
Bodie, Zvi	Prof	353-4160			PHD		MIT	
Cox, Edwin B.	Prof	353-4808			PHD		Penn	
Ahmed, Hassan M.	Assoc	353-5713			PHD		Stanford	
Kulatilaka, Nalin	Assoc	353-2514			PHD		MIT	
Michel, Allen J.	Assoc	353-4167			PHD		Cornell	
Salinger, Michael	Assoc	353-4608			PHD		MIT	
Samuelson, William F.	Assoc	353-3631			PHD		Harvard	
Shaked, Israel M.	Assoc	353-2665			DBA		Harvard	
Smith, Donald J.	Assoc	353-2037			PHD		Berkeley	
Ball, Sheryl	Asst	353-4614			PHD		Northwes	
Daskin, Alan J.	Asst	353-2353			PHD		MIT	
Feinstein, Steven P.	Asst	353-2514			PHD		Yale	
Fremault, Anne	Asst	353-5713			PHD		Penn	
Gandal, Neil S.	Asst	353-4615			PHD		Berkeley	
Jackson III, William E.	Asst	353-2514			PHD		Chicago	
Kahn, Shulamit B.	Asst	353-4299			PHD		MIT	
Lane, Sarah J.	Asst	353-4285			PHD		Stanford	
Perotti, Enrico C.	Asst	353-5715			PHD		MIT	
Schary, Martha A.	Asst	353-2317			PHD		MIT	
Trigeorgis, Lenos	Asst	353-2514			PHD		Harvard	
Clarke, Gerald L.	Inst	353-2364			BS		MIT	
Hamid, Shaikh A.	Inst	353-5716					Dhaka	
Speros, Jonathan	Inst	353-4158			ABD		Boston C	
Weil, David	Lect				PHD		Harvard	

Bowling Green State Univ
Department of Finance
College of Business
Bowling Gr, Ohio 43403-0264
Area Code (419) Fax 372-2875
BGSUOPIE

BS,MAC,MBA
1954,1966

Williams, Fred E.	Dean	372-2747			MgtS	PHD	70	Purdue	1990
Mueller, Paul A.	C-Ac	372-2520		12		DBA	77	Kentucky	1976
Skomp, Stephen E.	Prof	372-2594	SSKOMP	1	FG	DBA		Oklahoma	1986
Pachraraj, Raj A.	Assoc	372-8291		1	ACFO	PHD		Ohio St	1976
Bae, Sung C.	Asst	372-2520	SBAE	12	GHOQ	PHD		Florida	1987
Dyer, Michael A.	Asst	372-2668		13	PRS	ABD		Illinois	1991
Johnson, Shane A.	Asst	372-6058	SJOHNSO	3	ABDP	PHD		LSU	1991
Klein, Daniel P.	Asst	372-2520	DKLEIN	12	AFLQ	PHD		Kansas	1989
Laatsch, Francis E.	Asst	372-2520	FLAATSC	2	L	PHD		Oklahoma	1988

Bradley University
Department of Finance
College of Business Adm
Peoria, Illinois 61625
Area Code (309) Fax 677-3374

BS,BA
1978,1983

Sullenberger, A. Gale	Dean	677-2255			Mis	PHD	71	Oklahoma	1986
Bhandari, Shyam B.	Prof	677-2269		12	CFKU	PHD	77	Iowa	1976
Horvath, Philip A.	Prof	677-2313		12	NOK	DBA	75	Kent St	1977
Rubash, Arlyn R.	Assoc	677-2258		24	LQUW	PHD	75	Penn St	1974
Webster, Allen L.	Assoc	677-2312		12	AGR	PHD	79	Fla St	1990
Showers, Vince E.	Asst	677-2291			YFV	PHD	88	Ohio St	1987
Webster, Patricia C.	Asst	677-3581		1	ABG	PHD	90	Kentucky	1990
Rubash, Marjorie A.	Inst	677-2295		1		MBA		Bradley	1988

13

Brescia College — BS
Finance Faculty
Division of Business
Owensboro, KY 42301
Area Code (502) Fax
Did Not Respond
  Treesh, Mark A.   C-As 686-4311   Atg MS 81 Purdue 1989

University of Bridgeport — BS,MBA 1970,1982
Dept of Finance & Banking
Col of Bus & Public Mgt
Bridgeport, Conn 06601-2449
Area Code (203) Fax 576-4941

Name	Title	Phone	Field	Deg	Yr	School	Yr
Blackshaw, Lance	Dean	576-4111	Eng	PHD		N Carol	
Moriya, Frank E.	D-Pr	576-4384	Mktg	DBA	67	Geo Wash	1967
Katsimbris, George	Prof	576-4383		PHD		Conn	
Harvey Hubbell Professor of Economics & Finance							
Goon, Robert		576-4372					
Noulas, Athansios		576-4360					
Teall, John		576-4370					

Brigham Young University — BS,MBA 1963,1971
Finance Group
Marriott School of Mgt
Provo, Utah 84602
Area Code (801) Fax 378-5984
BYUVAX

Name	Title	Phone		Field	Deg	Yr	School	Yr
Skousen, K. Fred	Dean	378-4122		Atg	PHD	68	Illinois	1970
KPMG Peat Marwick Professor								
Hill, Ned C.	C-Pr	378-2407	12	DIMO	PHD	76	Cornell	1987
Call, Ivan T.	Prof	378-4993	13	IPXY	PHD	69	Indiana	1963
Daines, Robert H.	Prof	378-2447		FGH	DBA	66	Indiana	1959
Heaton, Hal B.	Prof	378-2132	31	OTLJ	PHD	83	Stanford	1982
Smith, Milton E.	Prof	378-6823	31	XYP	PHD	81	Utah	1966
Associate Director								
Stone, Bernell K.	Prof	378-2295	12	DIJM	PHD	68	MIT	1986
Cox, Charles M.	Assoc	378-2120	1	BCDH	PHD	78	U Wash	1965
Lambert, William J.	Assoc	378-4232	12	FMN	DBA	69	Indiana	1962
Pinegar, Michael J.	Assoc	378-3088	14	DOVG	PHD	82	Utah	1987
Wilson, Brent	Assoc	378-4867	14	UGDE	DBA	79	Harvard	1982
McQueen, Grant R.	Asst	378-3017	1	JMS	PHD	89	U Wash	1989
Thorley, Steven	Asst	378-6065	12	ANTZ	PHD	91	U Wash	1991

Brigham Young Univ-Hawaii — BS
Finance Faculty
Business Division
Laie, Hawaii 96762-1294
Area Code (808) Fax 293-3322

Name	Title	Phone		Field	Deg	Yr	School	Yr
Neal, William G.	C-Pr	293-3580		Sys	EDD	77	Va Tech	1984
Keliiliki, Dale K.	Asst	293-3590	7	V	MS	71	Brig Yg	1972
McKenzie, Roger I.	Asst	293-3595	38	BILY	MBA	67	Harvard	1982

Bryant College — BS,MBA,MST
Department of Finance
College of Business
Smithfield, RI 02917-1284
Area Code (401) Fax 232-6319

Name	Title	Phone	Field	Deg	Yr	School	Yr
Patterson, Michael B.	Dean	232-6060	B	DBA	75	Geo Wash	1986
Rubens, Jack H.	C-Ac	232-6435	MP	DBA	84	Kent St	1991
Lewis, Chantee	Prof	232-6155		DBA		Geo Wash	
Li, H. C.	Prof	232-6079		PHD	71	Mass	
Gudikunst, Arthur C.	Assoc	232-6387		PHD	74	Renssel	1990
McCarthy, Joseph	Assoc	232-6446	KLMN	DBA	83	Colorado	1989
Ketcham, David C.	Asst	232-6456		PHD	88	Penn St	1991
Louton, David	Asst	232-6343		PHD	91	Mich St	1991
Yobaccio, Elizabeth J.	Asst	232-6460		DBA	91	Boston U	1991

Bucknell University — BS,MS
Finance Faculty
Dept of Management
Lewisburg, Penn 17837
Area Code (717) Fax 524-3760

Name	Title	Phone	Deg	Yr	School	Yr
Sweeney, Timothy	C-Pr	524-3386	PHD	72	Penn St	1980
Kester, George W.	Assoc	524-3745	DBA	83	Virginia	1983
McGoun, Elton G.	Asst	524-3732	PHD	87	Indiana	1987

Buena Vista College BS
Finance Faculty
School of Business
Storm Lake, Iowa 50588
Area Code (712) Fax 749-2037
    Kerby, Joe Kent   Dean   749-2411   Mktg   PHD 66 Columbia 1989
    Russell, Paul W.   Prof   749-2422   EDD   N Carol   1967
    Hardt II, Henry W.   Assoc 749-2414   MBA   Arkansas 1983
    Binder, Mike   Asst   749-2423   MBA   Drake   1975

Butler University   BS, MBA
Department of Finance
College of Business
Indianapolis, IN 46208
Area Code (317) Fax 283-9930
    Engledow, Jack L.   Dean   283-9221   Mktg   DBA 71 Indiana
    Rieber, William J.   C   283-9846   14 OV   PHD 79 Pitt
    Uchida, Mark   Assoc 283-9460   12   PHD 76 Illinois
    Templeton, William K.   Asst   283-9419   12 BPY   PHD 90 Kent St

Calif Univ of Pennsylvania   BS
Finance Faculty
Business & Econ Dept
California, PA 15419-1394
Area Code (412) Fax
    Hart, Richard   Dean   PHD   Minn   1978
    Chawdhry, Arshad   C-Pr   938-4371   13 P   PHD   Illinois 1976
    Rossell, Fred   Asst   938-5993   12   MBA   Calif-PA 1990

U of California-Berkeley   BS,MBA,PHD
Faculty of Finance   1916,1963
Haas School of Business
Berkeley, Calif 94720
Area Code (415) Fax 643-8460
UCBCMSA
Real Estate Taken from College Catalog
    Hasler, William A.   Dean   642-1425   MBA 67 Harvard   1991
    --Finance Faculty
    Modest, David M.   C-Ac   642-4593   PHD 81 MIT   1986
    Garman, Mark B.   Prof   642-7526   PHD 69 Car Mel   1969
    Hakanson, Nils H.   Prof   642-1686   PHD 66 UCLA   1969
      Sylvan C. Coleman Professor of Finance and Accounting
    Jaffee, Dwight M.   Prof   642-1273   PHD 68 MIT   1991
    Leland, Hayne E.   Prof   642-8694   PHD 68 Harvard   1974
      Arno A. Rayner Professor of Finance and Management
    Pyle, David H.   Prof   642-4417   PHD 68 MIT   1968
      Willis H. Booth Professor of Banking and Finance
    Rubinstein, Mark E.   Prof   642-3580   PHD 71 UCLA   1972
    Kyle, Albert S.   Assoc 642-0951   PHD 81 Chicago   1987
    Marsh, Terry A.   Assoc 642-1651   PHD 81 Chicago   1986
    Wilcox, James A.   Assoc 642-3535   PHD 80 Northwes 1978
    Gennotte, Gerard   Asst   642-6590   PHD 85 MIT   1985
    He, Hua   Asst   642-6452   PHD 90 MIT   1989
    Stanton, Richard H.   Asst   642-7382   PHD 91 Stanford 1991
    --Real Estate Faculty
    Edelstein, Robert H.   Prof   6 &   PHD   Harvard
      Chair in Real Estate Development
    Rosen, Kenneth T.   Prof   6 &   PHD   MIT
      California Real Estate Chair
    Smith, Wallace F.   Prof   6 &   PHD   U Wash
    Wallace, Nancy E.   Asst   6 &   PHD   Michigan

Univ of California-Davis   MMGT,PHD
Finance Faculty
Graduate School of Mgt
Davis, Calif 95616-8609
Area Code (916) Fax 752-2924
    Smiley, Robert H.   Dean   752-7366   MgtS   PHD 73 Stanford 1989
    Clark, Peter K.   Prof   752-7606   PHD   Harvard
    Griffin, Paul A.   Prof   PHD   Ohio St
    Castanias II, Richard P. Assoc 752-8064   PHD   Car Mel
    Algert, Peter   Asst   ABD   Berkeley
    Barber, Brad M.   Asst   PHD 91 Chicago

14

Univ of Calif-Irvine MBA,PHD
Finance Faculty 1987
Graduate School of Mgt
Irvine, Calif 92717
Area Code (714) Fax 856-8469
UCI

Aigner, Dennis J.	Dean	856-6855	DJAIGNER		Econ	PHD	63 Berkeley	1988
McKenzie, Richard B.	C-Pr	856-8156	RBMCKEN		Econ	PHD	72 Va Tech	1991
Chen, Nai-Fu	Prof	856-8156	NCHEN	12	JLMO	PHD	75 Berkeley	1989
on leave Fall 1991								
Haugen, Robert	Prof	856-8391	RAHAUGEN	12	ABDL	PHD	68 Illinois	1989
Stoughton, Neal M.	Assoc	856-4944	NMSTOUGH	12	ADLM	PHD	83 Stanford	1986
Talmor, Eli	Assoc	856-6639	ETALMOR	12	ABD	PHD	81 N Carol	1989
Connolly, Robert A.	Asst	856-6639	RACONNOL	43	NY	PHD	82 Maryland	1985
on leave to Univ of North Carolina								
Cuny, Charles	Asst	856-8467	CJCUNY	12	JL	PHD	89 Stanford	1989

Univ of Calif, Los Angeles MBA,PHD
Finance Faculty 1939
Graduate School of Mgt
Los Angeles, CA 90024-1481
Area Code (213) Fax 206-2002
UCLAMVS

LaForce Jr., J. Clayburn	Dean	825-7982			Econ	PHD	62 UCLA	1978
Cornell, Bradford	H-Pr	825-2922		2	J	PHD	75 Stanford	1979
Brennan, Michael J.	Prof	825-5387		3	R	PHD	70 MIT	1986
Goldyne and Irwin Hearsh Professor of Money and Banking								
Eiteman, David K.	Prof	825-2508		4	U	PHD	59 Northwes	1959
Hofflander, Alfred E.	Prof	825-2445		4	U	PHD	64 Penn	1966
Roll, Richard W.	Prof	825-6118				PHD	69 Chicago	1976
Allstate Professor of Insurance and Finance								
Schwartz, Eduardo S.	Prof	825-2873		12	J	PHD	75 Brit Col	1986
California Professor of Real Estate and Land Economics								
Titman, Sheridan D.	Prof	825-2218		16	&	PHD	81 Car Mel	1980
Weston, J. Fred	Prof	825-2200				PHD	48 Chicago	1949
Warren C. Cordner Professor of Money and Financial Markets								
Andersen, Theodore A.	Assoc	825-2764				PHD	49 Wiscon	1956
Geske, Robert L.	Assoc	825-3670		2	J	PHD	77 Berkeley	1977
Grinblatt, Mark S.	Assoc	825-1098		2	M	PHD	82 Yale	1981
Hirshleifer, David A.	Assoc	825-2508		2	L	PHD	85 Chicago	1984
Torous, Walter N.	Assoc	825-4059		2	K	PHD	81 Penn	1988
Chowdhry, Bhagwan	Asst	825-5883		4	U	PHD	89 Chicago	1988
Jegadeesh, Narasinhan	Asst	825-5355		2		PHD	87 Columbia	1987
Welch, Ivo I.	Asst	825-2633		1		PHD	91 Chicago	1990
Cockrum, William M.	Adj	825-2985		3	S	MBA	61 Harvard	1984
May, Marvin M.	Adj	825-1142		1	E	PHD	69 UCLA	1972
Weil, Leonard	Adj	825-1922		3	P	BA	43 UCLA	1987

Univ of Calif, Riverside
Finance Faculty
Graduate School of Mgt
Riverside, Calif 92521-0203
Area Code (714) Fax 787-3970

Balow, Irving	Dean$	787-4238		Educ	PHD	Minn	1959
Auerbach, Robert D.	Prof	787-6329			PHD	Chicago	1983
Khoury, Sarkis J.	Prof	787-6329			PHD	Penn	1984
Park, Jinsop	Asst	787-6329			PHD	Berkeley	1987

U of Calif, Santa Barbara BA
Finance Faculty
Department of Economics
Santa Barbara CA 93106
Area Code (805) Fax 961-8830

Deacon, Robert	C-Pr$	893-3569		Econ	PHD	72 U Wash	1972
Krouse, Clem	Prof	893-3804					
LeRoy, Stephen	Prof						
Mehra, Rajnish	Prof	893-3238					
Morgan, Doug	Prof	893-2653					
Sonstelie, Jon							
Stuart, Charlie	Prof	893-4791					

Calif Polytechnic State U
Business Adm Department
School of Business
S Luis Obispo CA 93407
Area Code (805) Fax 756-1473
CALPOLY

BS,MBA
1981,1987

Name	Rank	Phone		Field	Deg	Yr	School	Yr
Boyes, William	Dean	756-2704		Econ	PHD	74	Claremont	1991
Rogers, John C.	C-Pr				PHD	79	Va Tech	1986
Lindvall, John R.	Prof	756-2381		12 MZ	DBA	73	Illinois	1973
Perlick, Walter W.	Prof	756-2657		13 CHPY	PHD	73	Penn St	1979
Riener, Kenneth	Prof	756-2822		12 KDE	PHD	76	Purdue	1983
Soenen, L. A.	Prof	756-2822		14 UVW	DBA	77	Harvard	1989
Dobson, John	Assoc	756-1606		1 AN	PHD	88	S Carol	1990
Weatherford, Alan M.	Assoc	756-2822	DDAAAAK	12 LHMN	PHD	86	Tx-Dalla	1986

Calif State Poly U-Pomona
Finance, Real Est & Law Dept
College of Business Adm
Pomona, Calif 91768-4083
Area Code (714) Fax 869-2350

BS,MS,MBA

Name	Rank	Phone	Field	Deg	Yr	School	Yr
Eaves, Ronald W.	Dean	869-2400		PHD	76	UCLA	1968
Kashefinejad, Djavad	C-Pr	869-2396	12 FL	PHD	81	Claremont	1980
Carney, Michael	Prof	869-2409	1 O	PHD	81	UCLA	1981
Jin, Hyung Ki	Prof	869-2399	12 FW	DBA	71	S Calif	1977
McKee Jr., Gilbert James	Prof	869-3229	13 FR	PHD	72	Claremont	1969
Parry, David L.	Prof	869-2394	1 O	PHD	76	S Calif	1980
Sibbald, Peter G.	Prof	869-2403	2 XM	PHD	77	Claremont	1977
Sohrabian, Ahmad	Assoc	869-3795	4 V	PHD	84	Ca-SanBr	1986
Muhtaseb, Majed R.	Asst	869-4287	12 AO	PHD	87	Tenn	1988
Sarmas, Paul	Asst	869-4435	13 FV	PHD		Claremont	1991
Ghazanfari, Farrokh		869-4436	13 PS	DBA	85	Miss St	1990
Kholdy-Sabety, Shady		869-3797	14 GW	PHD	84	Ca-SanBr	1990

Calif State U., Bakersfield
Department of Finance
Sch of Bus & Public Adm
Bakersfield, CA 93311-1099
Area Code (805) Fax 664-3194
CALSTATE

BS,MBA
1975,1982

Name	Rank	Phone	Field	Deg	Yr	School	Yr
Wood, Glenn	C	664-2320	#	PHD			1970
Fletcher, Robert G.	Prof	664-2328	U&	PHD	71	UCLA	1974
Shakorri, Ken	Prof	664-2311	PT	PHD			1986
Weber, Carlene	Asst	664-2157	M	PHD			1989

Calif State Univ, Chico
Dept of Finance & Marketing
College of Business
Chico, Calif 95929-0051
Area Code (916) Fax 898-6824

BS,MBA,MS
1972,1976

Name	Rank	Phone	Field	Deg	Yr	School	Yr
Rethans, Arno J.	Dean	898-6271	Mktg	PHD	79	Oregon	1987
Chen, Chang-Yi	Prof	898-6244		PHD	85	Oregon	1984
Gill, Edward	VProf			PHD	68	Oregon	1991
Hsu, H. Christine	Prof	895-6387		PHD		Penn St	
Moosa, Suleman A.	Prof	898-5920		PHD	72	Penn	1980
Olsen, Robert A.	Prof	895-5666		PHD	74	Oregon	1975
Ponarul, Richard R.	Prof	343-2760		PHD		Chicago	
Prestopino, Chris J. on leave	Prof			PHD	74	Penn	1972
Scott, Robert on leave	Prof			PHD	61	Harvard	1987
Troughton, George H.	Prof	898-6430		PHD	61	Mass	1987
Khaki, Mohammed	Lect	898-5376		ABD		Oregon	1988

Calif St U-Dominguez Hills
Dept of Finance & Quant Mths
School of Management
Carson, Calif 90747
Area Code (213) Fax 516-3664
Phone: 516-3557

BS,MBA

Name	Rank	Phone	Field	Deg	Yr	School	Yr
Neumann, Yoram	Dean	516-3548	OrgB	PHD	76	Cornell	1990
Yavas, Burhan F.	C-As	516-3557		PHD	83	S Calif	1983
Blyn, Martin R.	Prof	516-3557		PHD	66	NYU	1969
Dheeriya, Prakash L.	Prof	516-3557					
Lopilato, Carol	Prof	516-3557		PHD	80	S Calif	1975
Milgrim, Herbert	Prof	516-3557		PHD	68	NYY	1972
Nashif, Mazin K.	Prof	515-3557		PHD	72	Nebraska	1973
Ulivi, Ricardo M.	Prof	516-3557		PHD	81	Arkansas	1985
Vasseer, Potkin	Prof	516-3557					
Yoshida, Kosaku	Prof	516-3557		PHD	75	NYU	1975

Calif State Univ-Fresno   BS,MBA,MS,MSA
Dept of Finance & Bus Law   1959,1977
School of Bus & Adm Sci
Fresno, Calif 93740-0006
Area Code (209) Fax 278-4911
  Penbera, Joseph J.   Dean   278-2482   Mgt   PHD   70 America   1985
  Lange, Paul M.   C-Pr   278-4992   JD   65 Minn   1968
  Chen, Kuang C.   Prof   278-4964   PHD   Ohio St   1988
  Doyel, Tom   Prof   278-4962   PHD   71 UCLA   1970
  Jassim, Amir A.   Prof   278-2546   PHD   Georgia   1985
  Martin, Gerald D.   Prof   278-4967   PHD   Ariz St   1980
  Shahrokhi, Manuchehr   Prof   278-2107   PHD   Ohio St   1986
  Smith, Charles R.   Prof   278-4954   PHD   Penn St   1980
  Tseng, Kuo-Cheng   Prof   278-4981   PHD   Penn St   1984
  Waters, Alan Rufus   Prof   278-2349   PHD   Rice   1986
  Wilson, Joseph W.   Prof   278-2344   PHD   Arkansas   1982
  Yazdipour, Rassoul   Assoc   278-4987   PHD   Ohio St   1987
  Laiss, Barry   278-4976

Calif State Univ, Fullerton   BS,MBA,MS,MST
Department of Finance   1965,1972
School of Bus Adm & Ec
Fullerton, Calif 92634-9480
Area Code (714) Fax 449-7101
CALSTATE
  Smith, Ephraim P.   Dean   773-2592   Atg   PHD   68 Illinois   1990
  Emery, John T.   C-Pr   773-2217   PHD   Wash   1985
  Bueso, Alberto T.   Prof   779-3754   PHD   75 Texas   1974
  Crane, Donald B.   Prof   773-3956   DBA   S Calif   1976
  Fredman, Albert J.   Prof   773-3963   PHD   UCLA   1975
  Lai, Tsong-Yue   Prof   773-2218   PHD   Yale   1991
  Mlynaryk, Peter M.   Prof   773-3954   DBA   72 S Calif   1967
  O'Connor, Dennis J.   Prof   773-2233   PHD   67 SocResea   1971
  Plattueu, Robert   Prof   448-7126   PHD   Michigan   1991
  Stolz, Richard W.   Prof   773-2907   PHD   Mich St   1987
  Tonietti, Marco E.   Prof   773-3822   PHD   72 St Louis   1970
  Chan, Su Han   Assoc   773-3679   PHD   Texas   1988
  Chang, Carolyn C. WU   Assoc   773-3953   PHD   So Cal   1990
  Erickson, John R.   Assoc   773-3957   PHD   CA-Davis   1979
  Lee, Daniel   Assoc   773-3647   PHD   Berkeley   1990
  Stickels, Perry James   Assoc   773-3955   PHD   Claremon   1977
  Walgren, Blaine   Assoc   773-3716   PHD   U Wash   1990
  Wang, Ko   Assoc   773-3074   PHD   Texas   1988

Calif State Univ, Hayward   BS,MBA,MTA
Dept Management & Finance   1973,1981
Sch of Business & Econ
Hayward, Calif 94542-3069
Area Code (510) Fax 727-2039
  Tontz, Jay L.   Dean   881-3291   Econ   PHD   66 N Carol   1969
  Basu, Sam N.   Prof   881-3556   PHD   75 Houston   1988
  Johnson, Craig   Prof   881-3139   1   AI   PHD   68 UCLA   1980
  Wort, Donald H.   Prof   881-4276   PHD   73 Mich St   1984
  Zock, Richard   Prof   881-3307   31   PS   DBA   71 Colorado   1984
  Behzah, Hadi   Assoc   881-3825   3   PRS   PHD   89 Indiana   1989
  Major, John B.   Assoc   881-3294   6   PHD   73 Illinois   1988
  Pan, Fung-Shine L.   Assoc   881-3556   62   JO   PHD   86 Berkeley   1990
  Pradhan, Surendra   Assoc   881-3611   4   UVW   PHD   85 Tx-Dalla   1985

Calif State Univ - Humboldt   BS,MBA
Dept of Business Adm
College of Prof Studies
Arcata, Calif 95521-4957
Area Code (707) Fax 826-5555
CALSTATE
  Lowery, Bette A.   Dean   826-3961   EDD   Montana   1983
  Aziz, Abdul   Prof   826-3336   PHD   84 Texas   1986
  Mortazavi, Saeed   Prof   826-3846   PHD   83 Texas   1984

Calif State Univ, Long Beach   BS
Dept of Fnce, Real Es & Law   1971,1977
Sch of Business Adm 092
Long Beach, CA 90840-1004
Area Code (213) Fax 985-7586
  Deans, Robert H.   Dean   985-2466   4   Econ   PHD   66 Pitt
  Runyon, Richard   C-Pr   985-5668   2   DBA   70 S Calif   1968

Beecher, Earl	Prof	985-4568	1		PHD	65	UCLA	1961
Dilbeck, Harold R.	Emer	730-1661		1991				
Harlow, Charles	Prof	985-7526	12		DBA	68	S Calif	1968
McCulloch, Wendell	Prof	985-4565	4		J			1974
Sachdeva, Darshan	Prof	985-5671	12		PHD			1977
Trippi, Robert	Prof	985-5072	12		PHD			1989
Bilici, Hamdi	Assoc	985-1560	1		DBA			1988
Le, S. V.	Assoc	985-1608	12		PHD			1986
Morris, Gene P.	Assoc	985-4563	1		MA			1967
Rhee, Thomas A.	Assoc	986-1501	2		PHD			1988
Yang, Tyler	Asst		1					1991
Seegers, Weldon	Lect	985-7996	2		MBA			

Calif State U-Los Angeles BS,MBA,MS
Department of Finance & Law 1960,1964
School of Bus & Econ
Los Angeles, CA 90032-8125
Area Code (213) Fax 343-2813

Inacker, Charles J.	Dean	343-2800	B Ed	EDD	73	Temple	1973
Chang, Jack S. K.	Prof	343-2873		PHD	83	Houston	1985
Engler, George N.	Prof	343-2875		PHD	69	UCLA	1975
Fang, Hsing	Prof	343-2846		PHD	86	Ariz St	
Kim, Taewon	Prof	343-2921		PHD	86	Georgia	1987
Lai, Sung-Chung	Prof	343-2875		PHD	88	S Calif	1987
Loo, Ching-Hsing	Prof	343-2874		PHD	84	Ohio St	1985
Schnitzel, Paul E.	Prof	343-2870		PHD	71	NYU	1974

Calif State Univ, Northridge BS,MBA,MS
Dept Fnce, Real Est & Insu 1977,1982
Sch of Bus Adm & Econ
Northridge, CA 91330
Area Code (818) Fax 885-4903

Hosek, William R.	Dean	885-2455			PHD	67	CA-S Br	1988
Jennings, William	C $	885-2459	12	ANST	PHD	81	UCLA	1977
Berger, Jay	Prof	885-2459	32	OH	PHD	67	UCLA	1965
Buchalter, Sol	Prof	885-2459	13	P	MBA	50	New York	1963
Buchwald, Joseph	Prof	885-2459	12	Q	PHD	65	UCLA	1961
Dunn, Michael	Prof	885-2459	12	E	PHD	71	UCLA	1968
Launie, Joseph	Prof	885-2459	13	RF	PHD	68	UCLA	1965
Phillips, Michael	Prof	885-2459	12	GR	PHD	82	CS-Domin	1985
Taitt, Arthur	Prof	885-2459	1	X	DBA	59	Indiana	1965
Bleich, Donald	Assoc	885-2459	32	JH	PHD	85	UCLA	1985
Cary, David	Assoc	885-2459	1	CE	PHD	83	UCLA	1978
Chen, Chao	Assoc	885-2459	23	LB	PHD	88	Maryland	1988
Mudaliar, Vishwa	Assoc	885-2459	14	WV	PHD	85	So Carol	1982
Williams, James	Assoc	885-2459	12	MO	PHD	64		1982
Jeng, Jau-lian	Asst	885-2459	13	FLJ	PHD	91	CS-Domin	1991

Calif State Univ-Sacramento BS,MBA,MS
Finance Area 1963,1970
School of Bus & Pub Adm
Sacramento, CA 95819-6088
Area Code (916) Fax 278-5437
CSUS.EDU

Moorehead, Josef D.	Dean	278-6578			REst	PHD	71	S Calif	1974
--Dept of Management									
Blake Jr., Herbert	C	278-6459	HBLAKE		Mgt	PHD	85	Santa Cl	1979
Ahmadi, Hamid	Prof	278-6374		21	JMNO	PHD	83	Claremon	1983
Cheshier, Pataricia	Prof	278-7386		71	X#	PHD	82	Nebraska	1984
Heflin, Thomas L.	Prof	278-6407		71	X#	PHD	72	Oregon	1984
Kaufman, Richard F.	Prof	278-7198		12	BKN	PHD	77	Tx-Arlin	1979
Kuhle, James L.	Prof	278-7058		21	JNS&	PHD	85	Texas	1984
Pletcher, Dale D.	Prof	278-6849		13	BFGI	DBA	74	Kent St	1975
Schaffer, Burton F.	Prof	278-7228		21	NY	DBA	76	S Calif	1975
Sharp, Peter A.	Prof	278-6958		41	LV	PHD	84	Claremon	1982
Stockdale, John M.	Prof	278-7228		1	X	PHD	70	Iowa	1969
Walther, Carl H.	Prof	278-7073		1	JMW	PHD	83	Mich St	1984
Chung, M. C. (Marcus)	Assoc	278-6272		31	JOP	PHD	91	Mich St	1989
Pope, Ralph A.	Assoc	278-6921		1	CJNS	DBA	84	Miss St	1989
--Dept of Org Beh & Environ									
Sparks, P. Michael	C	278-6463			Mgt	PHD	74	S Calif	1976
Fountain, J. R.	Prof	278-6705		6	&	PHD	77	UCLA	1976
Koehler, Cortus T.	Prof	278-6023		6	&	PHD	72	Claremon	1973
Stanley, Craig E.	Prof	278-6482		6	&	PHD	74	Claremon	1981
West, Bill W.	Prof	278-6153		6	&	JD	72	Berkeley	1970
Alvayay, Jaime R.	Assoc	278-6510		6	&	PHD		Georgia	1991

Calif St U-San Bernardino BA,BS,MBA
Dept of Accounting & Finance
Sch of Bus & Public Adm
S Bernardino, CA 92407-2397
Area Code (714) Fax

Porter, David O.	Dean	880-5700		Mgt	PHD	70 Syracuse	1986
Lewis, Eldon C.	C-Pr	880-5704		Atg	PHD	67 Missouri	1987
Khan, Rauf A.	Prof	880-5713	12		DBA	73 Colorado	1976
Thygerson, Kenneth	Prof	880-5775	13		PHD	73 Northwes	1990
Vaziri, Mohammad T.	Prof	880-5718	14		PHD	79 Oklahoma	1986
Andrusco, Gene L.	Assoc	880-5705	13		PHD	84 Claremon	1977
Beer, Francisca	Assoc	880-5709	14		PHD	90	1990
Kim, Dongman	Assoc	880-5783	12		PHD	90 Ariz St	1990
Nelson, Edward A.	Assoc	880-5719	13		PHD	68 UCLA	1987
Schalow, David L.	Assoc	880-5789	12		PHD	84 Arkansas	1991

Calif State U - San Marcos BS
Finance Faculty
800 W. Los Vallecitos
San Marcos, CA 92069-1477
Area Code (619) Fax

Hinton, Bernard L.	Dean$	752-4242	Mgt	PHD	66 Stanford	
Kwan, Edmond	Prof	752-4225		PHD	72 Cornell	1990
Kang, Eun	Asst	752-4223		PHD	91 Penn	1991

Calif State U, Stanislaus BS,MBA
Department of Finance
School of Business Adm
Turlock, Calif 95380
Area Code (209) Fax 667-3333

Geisler, Jerry L.	Dean	667-3287		Mgt	PHD	75 Missouri	1989
Vellenga, Daniel R.	C-Pr	667-3671	12	CFMO	PHD	74 Mich St	1986
Cherukuri, U. Rao	Prof	667-3278	1	CEFY	PHD	72 N Carol	1970
VandenDool, Peter	Prof	667-3278	1	CEFY	PHD	66 Oregon	1970

Calvin College BS,BA
Dept of Economics & Business
Division of Social Sci
Grand Rapids, MI 49546
Area Code (616) Fax 957-8551

Roberts, Frank C.	Dean	957-6203		PHD	73 Vanderbi	1965
Roels, Shirley J.	C-Ac	957-6479	Mgt	ABD	Mich St	1979
Kuipers, Kenneth J.	Prof	957-6188		MA	Mich St	
Cook, David	Asst	957-7025		MBA	Grand V	

Cameron University BS
Dept of Accounting & Finance
School of Business
Lawton, Oklahoma 73505-6377
Area Code (405) Fax

McClung, Jacquetta J.	Dean	581-2267	3	Fnce	PHD	85 Oklahoma	1990
Sheets, Bob	C-Ac	581-2848		Atg	PHD	87 Oklahoma	1980
Bhattacharya, T. K.	Asst	581-2847	12		ABD	Oklahoma	1990

Campbell University
Department of Finance
Lundy-Fetterman Sch Bus
Buies Creek, NC 27506
Area Code (919) Fax
Phone 893-4111

Fowell Jr., Thomas Harold	Dean	Ext 7000		MA	Duke	1963
Zinkhan, Christian	C $	Ext 7000		DBA	Miss St	1987

Canisius College BS,MBA
Dept of Economics & Finance 1977,1982
Wehle School of Bus
Buffalo, NY 14208-1098
Area Code (716) Fax 888-2525
CANISIUS

Shick, Richard A.	Dean	888-2160	1	GH	PHD	73 SUNY-Buf	1978
Palumbo, George M.	Prof	888-2667	3	OR	PHD	77 Syracuse	1978
Wall, Richard A.	Prof	888-2666	13	PT	PHD	84 SUNY-Buf	1981
Bosshardt, Donald I.	Assoc	888-2676	12	DG	PHD	78 Wiscon	1987
Falkowski, Daniel C.	Assoc	888-2668	4	UV	PHD	72 New York	1975

Pfaff, Philip	Assoc	888-2675	12	H	PHD	73	Mich St	1979
Reiber, Ronald R.	Assoc	888-2665	12	JM	PHD	74	Arizona	1971
Zaporowski, Mark P.	Assoc	888-2679	3	RV	PHD	85	SUNY-Alb	1984
Beaves, Robert G.	Asst	888-2694	12	LM	PHD	78	Iowa	1989
Eisenhauer, Joseph G.	Asst	888-2688	2	N	PHD	91	SUNY-Buf	1989

Capital University
Dept of Bus Adm & Econ
College of Arts & Sci
Columbus, Ohio 43209
Area Code (614) Fax

McGary, Daina	Dean	236-6204		PHD		Unior Gr	1979
Schwab, Richard	C-Pr	236-6132		JD		Ohio St	1956
George H. Mour Professor of Business Administration & Economics							
Mittler, Dale L.	Assoc	236-6598		MBA		Capital	1978

Carnegie Mellon University BS,MS,PHD
Finance Faculty 1982,1957
Grad School of Ind Adm
Pittsburgh, PA 15213-3890
Area Code (412) Fax 268-6837
ANDREW

Sullivan, Robert S.	Dean	268-2265	OMgt	PHD	76	Penn St	1991
Spatt, Chester S.	Prof			PHD	79	Penn	1979
Srivastava, Sanjay	Prof			PHD	82	MIT	1982
Green, Richard C.	Assoc	268-2302		PHD		Wiscon	1982
Bhattacharyya, Sugato	Asst			PHD	90	Harvard	1988
Ketterer, Juan	Asst			PHD	88	Minn	1988
Kumar, Praveen	Asst			PHD	81	Stanford	1985
Zin, Stanley E.	Asst			PHD	87	Toronto	1988

Carroll College BS
Finance Faculty
College of Business
Waukesha, Wiscon 53186
Area Code (414) Fax
APRA # CARROLL1.CC.EDU

Olsen, Gary L.	C-Ac	547-1211	GOLSEN	Atg	PHD		Marquett	1975
Debrecht, Dennis M.	Asst	547-1211			PHD		Iowa St	1984
Kunz, Jeffrey T.	Asst	547-1211			MS		Wiscon	1981

Carson-Newman College BS
Finance Faculty
Division of Bus & Econ
Jefferson Cy, TN 37760
Area Code (615) Fax 471-3317

Driver, Phyllis N.	C-Ac	471-3317		Atg	ABD		Tenn	1978
Clark, Donald W.	Assoc	471-3417	1		MBA		Memph St	1981

Case Western Reserve Univ BS,MBA,MA,PHD
Dept of Banking & Finance 1979,1958
Weatherhead Sch of Mgt
Cleveland, Ohio 44106-7235
Area Code (216) Fax 368-4776
CWRU

Cowen, Scott S.	Dean	368-2046		Atg	DBA	75	Geo Wash	1976
Bowers, David A.	C-Pr	368-2165			PHD	63	So Meth	
Mayne, Lucille S.	Prof	368-2151			PHD	66	Northwes	
Morrissey, Thomas F.	Prof	368-2079			PHD	70	Syracuse	
Ritchken, Peter	Prof	386-3849			PHD		Case Wes	
Silvers, J. B.	Prof	368-2143			PHD		Stanford	
Elizabeth M. & William C. Treuhaft Professor of Management								
Borokhovich, Kenneth A.	Asst	292-2830			PHD		Ohio St	
Kauer, Robert T.	Asst	368-2938			PHD		Case Wes	
Wilson, Arthur J.	Asst	386-2040	23	LP	PHD	90	Chicago	

Catawba College BA
Finance Faculty
Ketner School of Bus
Salisbury, NC 28144-2488
Area Code (704) Fax 637-4304

Terrell, Junius H.	Dean	637-4320	Atg	PHD	66	Texas	1990
Ralph W. Ketner Chair in Business Administration							
Carter, J. Alvin	Assoc	637-4406		MA		Geo St	

Catholic University BA,MA,PHD
Finance Faculty
Dept of Econ & Business
Washington D.C. 20064
Area Code (202) Fax
 Piedra, Alberto M. C Econ PHD
 Koutmos, Gregory Asst 319-5236 CDEJ
 Nuven, Diep Asst 319-5236 FHKL
 Saidi, Reza Asst 329-5236 JBAF
 Uppal, Jamshed Asst 319-5236 BFGI

Cedarville College BA
Finance Faculty
Business Adm Department
Cedarville, Ohio 45314-0601
Area Code (513) Fax 766-2760
 Walker, Ronald J. C-Pr 766-2211 1 DSci DBA 86 Kent St 1978
 Cassidy, John Assoc 766-2211 14 DBA 80 Fla St 1991
 Hazen, Marinos Assoc 766-2211 12 ABD Cleve St 1983

Centenary College
Finance Faculty
Business
Hackettstown, NJ 07840-9989
Area Code (901) Fax
 Quade, Robert C-Ac   Mktg MBA Iowa 1986
 Lewthwaite, Barbara Jayne Asst 45 MBA St Johns 1987

Univ of Central Arkansas BBA,MBA
Department of Finance 1984,1990
College of Business Adm
Conway, Arkansas 72032
Area Code (501) Fax 327-9938
 Johnson, W. Clint Dean 450-3106 Econ PHD 75 Txs Tech 1975
 Lamberson, Morris A. Prof 450-5340   PHD 72 Arkansas
 McNew, Ben B. Prof 450-5332 3 P PHD Texas
  Carmichael Professor of Economics
 Packer, James Assoc 450-5334   DBA LSU

Central Connecticut St Univ BS
Department of Finance
School of Business
New Britain, CT 06050
Area Code (203) Fax 827-7200
 Short, Larry E. Dean 827-7285 Mgt DBA 71 Colorado
 Rosenberg, Seymour L. C-Ac 827-7317 14 CUV PHD   1981
 Lawson, Larry L. Assoc 827-7317 32 PSR PHD   1989
 Cutler, Mary M. Asst 827-7249 14 CUV PHD   1987
 Sfiridis, James M. Asst 827-7249 12 CJM PHD   1990

Univ of Central Florida BA,PHD
Department of Finance 1975,1979
College of Business Adm
Orlando, Florida 32816-4000
Area Code (407) Fax 823-5741
UCF1VM
 Huseman, Richard C. Dean 823-2182 Com PHD 65 Illinois 1990
 Clayton, Ronnie J. C-Ac 823-5567   PHD Georgia 1988
 Klock, David R. Prof 823-5903   PHD Illinois 1981
 Reiff, Wallace W. Prof 823-5567   DBA 62 Indiana 1970
 Scott Jr., David F. Prof 823-2632   PHD Florida 1982
  Chairholder/Della Philips-Martha D. Schenck Chair: American Private Enterpris
 Atkinson, Stanley M. Assoc 823-5567   DBA Miss St 1981
 Cheney, John M. Assoc 823-5567   DBA Tenn 1977
 Graham, Sharon S. Assoc 823-5567   PHD Penn St 1984
 Modani, Naval K. Assoc 823-5567   PHD So Carol 1983
 Weaver, William C. Assoc 823-5567   PHD Geo St 1985
 Neustel, Arthur D. VAsst 632-0098   PHD Va Tech 1984
 Park, Hoon Asst 823-5567   PHD Geo St 1988
 Spudeck, Raymond E. Asst 823-5567   DBA Tx Tech 1987

Central Michigan University — BS 1983 1989
Department of Finance
College of Business Adm
Mt. Pleasant, MI 48859
Area Code (517) Fax 774-3450

Name	Rank	Phone		Field	Deg		School	Year
Plachta, Leonard E.	Dean	774-3337		Atg	PHD	64	Mich St	1972
Sussman, M. Richard	C-Pr	774-3362	12	FJMO	PHD	61	Michigan	1978
Billingham, Carol J.	Prof	774-3478	21	KOMP	PHD	54	New York	1967
Stout, R. Gene	Prof	774-3322	13	BEFH	PHD	72	Iowa St	1981
Cox, Raymond A. K.	Assoc	774-4714	13	GHIP	PHD	86	Mich St	1989
Prasad, Rose M.	Assoc	774-3411	31	PSTU	PHD	87	Cinn	1985
Schneid, Daniel L.	Assoc	774-3722	12	BGHX	PHD	74	Ohio St	1978
Vetter, Daniel E.	Assoc	774-7969	12	DFHI	PHD	83	Nebraska	1988
Felton, James M.	Asst	774-3269	31	FMNO	PHD	90	Arkansas	1989
Mitchell, John B.	Asst	774-3651	41	FVUW	DBA	78	Kent St	1975

Central Missouri State Univ — BSBA,MBA
Dept of Economics & Finance
College of Bus & Econ
Warrensburg, MO 64093-5071
Area Code (816) Fax 747-7813

Name	Rank	Phone	Field	Deg		School	Year
Shaffer, Paul	Dean	429-4560	Mgt	PHD	74	Oklahoma	1986
Engelmann, Paul	C $	543-4788	Econ	PHD	76	Oklahoma	1972

Univ of Central Oklahoma — BS,MBA
Department of Finance
College of Business Adm
Edmond, Oklahoma 73034-0115
Area Code (405) Fax 341-4964

Name	Rank	Phone	Field	Deg		School	Year
Wert, Frank S.	Dean	341-2980	Econ	PHD	72	Colo St	1972
Elliott, Mary L.	C-Pr	341-2980		EDD	70	Oklahoma	1968
Fleming, Donald E.	Prof	341-2980		DBA	74	Tx Tech	1976
McKown, Ellen	Assoc	341-2980		PHD	79	Oklahoma	1980
Ice, Randall D.	Asst	341-2980		MBA	82	Michigan	1984
Johnson, Arnell	Asst	341-2980		ABD		Oklahoma	1980
Black, Stephen	Inst	341-2980		ABD		Okla St	1990
Epplin, Maryellen P.	Inst	341-2980		ABD		Okla St	1991

Central State Univ-Ohio — BS
Finance Faculty
College of Business
Wilberforce, OH 45384
Area Code (513) Fax 376-6652

Name	Rank	Phone		Field	Deg	School	Year
Showell Jr., Charles H.	Dean	376-6441		BAdm	PHD	Ohio St	1988
Braxton, Keylon	Asst	376-6492	13	EFPV	MBA	Wiscon	1987

Central Washington Univ
Finance Faculty
School of Bus & Econ
Ellensburg, WA 98926
Area Code (509) Fax 963-3042
* Faculty located in Seattle

Name		Rank	Phone	Field	Deg		School	Year
Cleveland, Gerald L.		Dean	963-1955	Atg	PHD	65	U Wash	1987
Fairburn, Wayne A.		Prof	963-2032		PHD	75	Mich St	1972
Johnson, Eldon C.	*	Prof			MS		Colo St	1977
Jacobs, Stanley	*	Assoc			DBA		Kent St	1983
Smith, Patrick		Assoc	963-3082					
Lasik, John		Asst			MBA		Miss St	1985
Bagamery, Bruce	*							

Chaminade University — BBA
Finance Faculty
School of Business
Honolulu, Hawaii 96816-1578
Area Code (808) Fax 735-4734
Did Not Respond

Name	Rank	Phone	Field	Deg	School	Year
Murray, Peter	Dean	735-4744		MBA	Penn	1966

Chapman University — BS,BA,MBA,MHRM
Finance Faculty
School of Bus & Econ
Orange, Calif 92666-1032
Area Code (714) Fax 532-6081
VAXLIB

Name	Rank	Phone		Field	Deg		School	Year
McDowell, Richard L.	Dean	997-6684	MCDOWELL	Adm	PHD	74	Tufts	1991
Sarmas, Paul	Asst	997-6822			PHD		Claremon	1985

23

College of Charleston BS,BA
Department of Finance 1988
Sch of Bus Adm & Econ
Charleston, SC 29424-0001
Area Code (803) Fax 792-5627
  Rudd, Howard F.   Dean   792-5627   PHD 73 Tx Tech   1984
  Livingston, Thomas   Assoc 792-5627   PHD 77 S Carol   1977
  Woodside III, B. Perry Assoc 792-5627   PHD 74 S Carol   1987

Cheyney University
Finance Faculty
Business Adm Department
Cheyney, Penn 19319
Area Code (215) Fax
  Williams, Edward   C   Mgt   PHD   Drexel   1972
  Chowdhury, Monayem   Prof   399-2202

University of Chicago MS,PHD
Finance Faculty 1916
Graduate School of Bus
Chicago, IL 60637-1561
Area Code (312) Fax 702-0458
ARPANET Node GSBACD.UCHICAGO.EDU
  Gould, John P.   Dean   702-7121   Econ   PHD 66 Chicago   1965
    Distinguished Service Professor of Economics
  Aliber, Robert Z.   Prof   702-7401   PHD 62 Yale   1965
    Director, Center for Studies in International Finance
  Constantinides, George M. Prof 702-7258 12 JKLO   DBA 74 Indiana   1978
    Leon Carroll Marshall Professor of Finance
  Diamond, Douglas W.   Prof   702-7283 FAC_DOUG 3 ABP PHD 80 Yale   1979
  Fama, Eugene F.   Prof   702-7282   PHD 64 Chicago   1963
    Theodore O. Yntema Distinguished Service Professor of Finance
  French, Kenneth R.   Prof   702-7138   12 JKLN   PHD 83 Rochest   1983
    Leo Melamed Professor of Finance
  Hamada, Robert S.   Prof   702-1680   13 BDEH   PHD 69 MIT   1966
    Edward Eagle Brown Professor of Finance
  Harris, Milton   Prof   702-2549 MILT 1 ABDG PHD 74 Chicago   1987
    Chicago Board of Trade Professor of Finance and Business Economics
  Leftwich, Richard W.   Prof   702-7266   PHD 80 Rochest   1979
  Lorie, James H.   Prof   702-7276   PHD 47 Chicago   1947
    Eli B. and Harriet B. Williams Professor of Business Administration
  Miller, Merton H.   Prof   702-7201   PHD 52 JohnsHop 1961
    Robert R. McCormick Distinguished Service Professor of Finance
  Vishny, Robert W.   Prof   702-2522   13   PHD 85 MIT   1985
  Ferson, Wayne E.   Assoc 702-7039   24 JNKW   PHD 82 Stanford 1983
  Sanders, Anthony B.   VAsoc 702-9026   23 KNR   PHD 79 Georgia   1991
    visiting from Ohio State Univ
  Seyhun, H. Nejat   VAsoc   PHD 84 Rochest   1991
    visiting from Univ of Michigan
  Kaplan, Steven Neil   Asst   702-4513   1 GU   PHD 88 Harvard   1988
  Mitchell, Mark L.   Asst   702-7290   1 DG   PHD 87 Clemson   1990
  Nelson, Daniel B.   Asst   702-3231 FAC_DBN 2 JN PHD 88 MIT   1988
  Petersen, Mitchell A.   Asst   702-0925 FAC_MAP 13 CDT PHD 90 MIT   1990
  Rajan, Raghuram   Asst   702-9299   13 BDPQ PHD 91 MIT   1991

Chicago State University BS
Dept of Accounting & Finance
College of Bus & Adm
Chicago, IL 60628-1598
Area Code (312) Fax
  Bristow, Clinton   Dean   995-3976   Mgt   PHD   Northwes 1981
  Vaughn, Thomas E.   C-Ac   995-3503   Law   JD   78 Kansas   1982
  Choi, Chang K.   Prof   995-3955   DBA   UCLA
  Hunt, Atha   Assoc 995-3978   JD   DePaul   1975
  Dale, Walter R.   Asst   995-3802   LLM 83 J Marsha 1989
  Osaghae, Vincent   Inst   995-3940   MBA 86 Gov St   1989

Christian Brothers Univ BS
Department of Finance
School of Business
Memphis, Tenn 38104-5581
Area Code (901) Fax
Did Not Respond
  House, Ray S.   Dean   722-0316   Mktg   PHD 66 Miss   1985
  Brittingham, Robert   H-Pr   PHD   St Louis
  Schultz, Jeffrey A.   Prof   PHD   Case Ins

24

Christopher Newport College BS
Dept of Economics & Finance
School of Bus & Econ
Newport News, VA 23606-2988
Area Code (804) Fax

Pendergrass, Wesley L.	Dean$	594-7184		Law	JD	78 Tenn	1982
Park, Sang O.	C-Pr	594-7265		Econ	PHD		1982
Rowell, Dexter	Assoc	594-7148			PHD	Penn	1981
Winder, Robert	Assoc	594-7420			PHD	Rutgers	1991
Rahim, Naizur	Asst	594-7727			MBA	Hampton	1988

University of Cincinnati BA,MBA,MAT,PHD
Department of Finance 1919,1966
College of Business Adm
Cincinnati, Ohio 45221-0195
Area Code (513) Fax 556-4891

Schnee, Jerome E.	Dean	556-7002		Mgt	PHD	70 Penn	1988
Barngrover, Charles L.	Prof	556-7076	1	HX	PHD	66 Cinn	1960
Henderson Jr., Glenn V.	Prof	556-7079	1	CEZ	DBA	74 Fla St	1987
Johnson, Timothy E.	Prof	556-7074	2	JK	PHD	71 Illinois	1970
Kim, Yong H.	Prof	556-7084	14	IU	PHD	81 Penn St	1978
CBA Faculty Fellow							
Melnyk, Z. Lew	Prof	556-7080	1	GH	PHD	61 Mich St	1964
Miller, Norman G.	Prof	556-7088	6	&	PHD	77 Ohio St	1980
Walker, Michael C.	Prof	556-7078	13	CDP	PHD	71 Houston	1985
Lin, Cheyeh	Assoc	556-7075	12	JT	DBA	69 Indiana	1967
Swanson, Jr. Paul J.	Assoc	556-7085	2	MO	PHD	62 Illinois	1967
Wyatt, Steve B.	Assoc	556-7083	12	LOT	PHD	80 Tx-Dalla	1987
Adams, Paul D.	Asst	556-7072	1	FZ&	PHD	82 Ohio St	1987
Brunarski, Kelly R.	Asst	556-7041	13	AGP	ABD	Ohio St	1991
Geltner, David M.	Asst	556-7071	6	&	PHD	89 MIT	1989
Kluger, Brian D.	Asst	556-7073	13	DI&	PHD	83 Tulane	1987
Riddiough, Timothy R.	Asst	556-7045	6	&	PHD	91 Wiscon	1991
Venkatesh, P. C.	Asst	556-7064	12	T	PHD	83 Florida	1991

The Citadel BBA,MBA
Finance Faculty
Dept of Business Adm
Charleston, SC 29409-0215
Area Code (803) Fax 792-7084

Bebensee, Mark A.	H-Ac	792-5056		PHD	77 Duke	1977
Spivey, Christopher B.	Prof	792-5158		PHD	N Texas	
Wittschen Jr., J. Harvey	Prof	792-5152		PHD	Alabama	
Stewart, Brent A.		792-6954				

CUNY-Baruch College BS,MBA,PHD
Dept of Economics & Finance 1933,1981
Sch of Bus & Public Adm
New York, NY 10010
Area Code (212) Fax 447-3364
CUNYVM

Connelly, Francis J.	Dean	447-3280		Mgt	DBA	72 Indiana	1972
Ross, Howard N.	C-Pr	447-3140		Econ	PHD	Columbia	
Francis, Jack Clark	Prof	447-3147	12		PHD	69 U Wash	
Markowitz, Harry	Prof	447-3151	2	M	PHD	Chicago	
Speiser Distinguished Professor							
O'Neill, June	Prof	387-1150			PHD	Columbia	
Rentzler, Joel	Prof	447-3135	2	L	PHD	NYU	
Vora, Ashok	Prof	447-3169	2	L	PHD	Northwes	
Allen, Linda	Assoc	447-3156	3	PQ	PHD	NYU	
Ballabon, Maurice	Assoc	447-3149			PHD	McGill	
Harpaz, Giora	Assoc	447-3155	12		PHD	Indiana	
Hessel, Chris	Assoc	447-3173	12		PHD	NYU	
Joyce, Theodore	Assoc	447-3603			PHD	CUNY	
Katz, Steven	Assoc	447-3149	12		PHD	NYU	
Martell, Terry	Assoc	447-3395	2	L	PHD	Penn St	
Tandon, Kishore	Assoc	447-345	4		PHD	80 Pitt	
Weiss, Jeffrey	Assoc	447-3155			PHD	Wiscon	
Wolf, Avner	Assoc	447-3143	2	L	PHD	Columbia	
Hsin, Chin-Wen	Asst	447-3148	2	L	PHD	Illinois	
Huckins, Larry	Asst	447-3156			PHD	Chicago	
Webb, Gwendolyn P.	Asst		12		PHD	NYU	

CUNY-Brooklyn College   BS,MA
Finance Faculty
Department of Economics
Brooklyn, NY 11210
Area Code (718) Fax 951-6885

Name	Rank	Phone			Degree		School	Year
Sardy, Hyman	C-Pr	780-5317			PHD			1957
Bell, Robert	Prof	780-5686			PHD			1986
Friedman, Hersey H.	Prof	780-5119			PHD			1986
Mobilia, Pam	Asst	780-5569			PHD			1991

CUNY-H Lehman College
Department of Finance
College of Business
Bronx, New York 10468-1589
Area Code (212) Fax
Did Not Respond

Fisch, Oscar	Dean							1987

CUNY-Hunter College   BS
Department of Economics
Div of Social Science
New York, NY 10021
Area Code (212) Fax

Friedlander, Judith	Dean				PHD			
Honig, Marjorie	C				PHD			
Shull, Bernard	Prof	772-5437			PHD		Wiscon	
Smith, Ronald	Prof	772-5431			DBA		LSU	
Golbe, Devra	Assoc	772-5408			PHD		Brown	
Seeley, Eric	Asst	772-5544			PHD		New York	

CUNY-Queens College   BA
Finance Faculty
Business
Flushing, NY 11367-0904
Area Code (718) Fax
Did Not Respond

CUNY-Col of Staten Island   AAS,BS
Finance Faculty
Department of Business
Staten Isl, NY 10301
Area Code (718) Fax
Did Not Respond

Affron, Mirella	Dean	390-7553			PHD		Yale	1969

Claremont McKenna College   BA,MBA
Finance Faculty
Department of Economics
Claremont, Calif 91711-6400
Area Code (714) Fax 621-8249
Phone 621-8000

Name	Rank	Phone			Degree	Yr	School	Year
Fucaloro, Anthony	Dean$	621-8117			PHD	69	Arizona	1974
Burdekin, Richard	Asst	Ext 4221	3	PR	PHD	85	Houston	1989
Burnett, Nancy	Asst	Ext 2884	12	DEJO	PHD	88	UCLA	1988
Prag, Jules	Asst	Ext 3899	3	PR	PHD	88	Rochester	1986

Clarion University   BS,MBA
Department of Finance
College of Business
Clarion, Penn 16214
Area Code (814) Fax 226-2039

Name	Rank	Phone			Degree	Yr	School	Year
Grunenwald, Joseph P.	Dean	226-2600			DBA	81	Kent St	1978
Eicher, Jeffrey	C-Ac				JD		Pitt	1983
Ewedemi, Soga O.	Prof	226-2644			PHD		Penn	1988
Stuhldreher, Thomas J.	Prof				DBA		Kent St	1985
Vanlandingham, Marguerite H.		Prof	226-2056		PHD		Florida	1981
Bish, Gerald C.	Asst				JD		Suffolk	1976
Henry, William L.	Asst				JD		West Vir	1974
Hall, Anita J.	Inst				MS		Penn St	1977
Belloit, Jerry					PHD		Florida	1990

25

26

Clark University
Finance Faculty 1986,1986
Grad School of Mgt
Worcester, Mass 01610-1477
Area Code (508) Fax 793-8890

Name	Rank	Phone		Field	Deg	Yr	School	Yr
Ullrich, Robert A.	Dean	793-7670		Beh	DBA	68	Wash U	1988
Tamarkin, Maurry J.	Assoc	793-7657	12	MD	PHD	79	Wash U	
Golec, Joseph H.	Asst	793-7652	2	N	PHD	86	Wash U	

Clark Atlanta University
Department of Finance 1974
School of Business Adm
Atlanta, Georgia 30314-4391
Area Code (404) Fax 880-8458

Name	Rank	Phone		Field	Deg	Yr	School	Yr
Irons, Edward D.	Dean	880-8454		Fnce	DBA	60	Harvard	1990
Williams, Alex O.	C-Pr	880-8475			PHD		Penn	
Robert Woodruff Professor								
Welch, Oliver	Prof	880-8453			PHD		Geo St	1991
Alli, Kasim L.	Asst	880-8740			PHD		Geo St	
Carter, Juanita	Asst	880-8785			MS		Illinois	
Edmond, Steve	Asst				MBA		Tx South	
Ingram, Marcus	Asst	880-8476			PHD		Geo St	1991
Mohammad, Latiff	Lect	880-8459			MBA		Atlanta	

Clarkson University BS,MS,MBA
Dept of Economics & Finance 1977,1982
School of Management
Potsdam, NY 13699-9999
Area Code (315) Fax 268-3810
CLVM

Name	Rank	Phone			Field	Deg	Yr	School	Yr
Sheldon, George	Dean$	268-2300			Atg	PHD	71	Mass	1981
Morse, Wayne J.	C-Pr	268-3998	MORSEW		Atg	PHD	71	Mich St	1983
Theodossiou, Panayiotis T.	Asst	268-6425		24	N	PHD	87	CUNY	1989
Davis, Eleanor	Inst	268-3870		14		MBA	85	Plymouth	1989

Clayton State College BS
Finance Faculty
School of Business
Morrow, Georgia 30260
Area Code (404) Fax 961-3700
Did Not Respond

Name	Rank	Phone		Field	Deg	Yr	School	Yr
Oglesby, Norman	Dean	961-3410		Mgt	PHD	77	Georgia	1991

Clemson University BS,MA,PHD
Department of Finance 1977,1983
Coll of Commerce & Ind
Clemson, S Carol 29634-1305
Area Code (803) Fax 656-2015
CLEMSON

Name	Rank	Phone		Field	Deg	Yr	School	Yr
Amacher, Ryan C.	Dean	656-3177	1	Econ	PHD	71	Virginia	1981
Mabry, R. H.	H-Pr	656-2249	13	Econ	PHD	75	N Carol	1981
Marr Jr., M. Wayne	Prof	656-7096	23	AGQS	PHD	83	Tx Tech	1980
Barnhart, S. W.	Assoc	656-4486	23	LR	PHD	84	Texas	1988
Harris Jr., J. M.	Assoc	656-2610	14	DLUV	PHD	80	S Carol	1986
Klein, Richard H.	Assoc	656-3746	1	Y	PHD	69	Texas	1978
McElreath Jr., R. B.	Assoc	656-3743	12	FH	PHD	76	Geo St	1987
Mulherin III, J. H.	Assoc	656-1023	13	AGST	PHD	84	Calif	1988
Spivey, M. F.	Assoc	656-3744	31	GOPQ	PHD	87	Tenn	1987
Alexander Jr., John C.	Asst	656-0547	21	GJMN	PHD	91	Fla St	1990
Kim, Y. C.	Asst	656-2249	14	BDGU	PHD	87	Ohio St	1991
Springer, T. M.	Asst	656-3954	6	&	PHD	86	Georgia	1988
Sridharan, U. V.	Asst	656-0421	12	ADGH	PHD	90	Iowa	1989
Waller, N. G.	Asst	656-4878	6	&	PHD	86	Texas	1988
Rouse, J. R.	VInst	656-2848	1	BCGL	MPA		Clemson	

Cleveland State University BA,MBA,MAC,DBA
Department of Finance 1974,1978
Nance Col of Bus Adm
Cleveland, Ohio 44115
Area Code (216) Fax 687-9354
CSUOHIO

Name	Rank	Phone		Field	Deg	Yr	School	Yr
Muczyk, Jan P.	Dean$	687-3786		Mgt	DBA		Maryland	1973
Domonkos, John A.	C-Ac$	687-4736	12	KMR	PHD	72	Case Wes	1969
Kamath, Ravindra R.	Prof	687-3727	12	CMOS	PHD	76	Cinn	1976
Reichert, Alan K.	Prof	687-6958	3	PZ	PHD	75	Ohio St	1989

Webb, James R.	Prof	687-4732				PHD	79	Illinois	1989
Bond, Michael T.	Assoc	687-3728				PHD	85	Case Wes	1986
Rini, Charles T.	Assoc	687-4737			F	DBA	71	Kent St	1975
Sharma, Jandhyala L.	Assoc	687-3687				PHD	75	Arkansas	1979
Liang, Youguo	Asst	687-4722	R0111	12	KLMP	PHD	91	Kentucky	1991
Mougoue, Mbodja	Asst	687-4708		24	JMOW	PHD	89	N Orlean	1989
Myer, Francis C. Neil	Asst	687-3809	R0543	12	JMSE	PHD	89	St Louis	1989
Whyte, Ann Marie	Asst	687-5053		34	PV	PHD	91	Fl Atlan	1991

Univ of Colorado at Boulder
Department of Finance
College of Bus & Adm
Boulder, Colo 80309-0419
Area Code (303) Fax 492-5962
CUBLDR
Bitnode address is CUBLDR.COLORADO.EDU

BS,MBA,MS,PHD
1938,1967

Nelson, J. Russell	Dean	492-1809		Mgt	PHD	62	UCLA	1989
Darnell, Jerome C.	H-Pr	492-8793			DBA	65	Indiana	1965
Rush, David F.	H-Pr	492-8215			DBA	71	Indiana	1968
Bhagat, Sanjai	Prof	492-7821			PHD	82	U Wash	1989

First Bank Business Affiliated Scholar

Lymberopoulos, P. John	Prof	492-7541		PHD	65	Texas	1964

Associate Dean for Student Services

Melicher, Ronald W.	Prof	492-3182		DBA	68	Wash U	1969

William H. Baughn Distinguished Scholar

Richey, Clyde	Prof	492-7905		PHD	69	Indiana	1969
Palmer, Michael	Assoc	492-7125		PHD	67	Wash	1967
Winn, Daryl	Assoc	492-6186		PHD	73	Michigan	1971
Cook, Douglas O.	Asst	492-8400		PHD	87	Texas	1987
Jefferis Jr., Richard H.	Asst	492-5665		PHD	85	Stanford	1990
Krueger, Mark K.	Asst	492-3224		PHD	89	Illinois	1988
Ravichandran, R.	Asst	492-4013		PHD	86	Iowa	1988
Wobbekind, Richard	Asst	492-1147		PHD	84	Colorado	1985
Correll, Mark	Inst	492-0440		PHD	86	Wiscon	1988

U of Colorado at Co Springs
Accounting & Finance Dept
College of Bus & Adm
Colorado Spr, CO 80933-7150
Area Code (719) Fax 593-3362
COLOSPGS

BS,BA,MBA
1965,1967

Rothe, James T.	Dean	593-3113	JTROTHE		Mgt	PHD		Wiscon	1986
Wilcox, Kirkland A.	C-Ac	593-3413	KAWILCOX		Atg	PHD	72	Texas	1972
Belden, Susan A.	Asst	593-3349	SABELDEN	34	QK	PHD		Utah	1987
Reddy, Venkat	Asst	593-3666	VKREDDY	12	D	ABD		Penn St	1991
Zwirlein, Thomas J.	Asst	593-3241	TJZWIRLE	12	DG	PHD		Oregon	1984

Univ of Colorado at Denver
Department of Finance
College of Bus & Adm
Denver, Colorado 80204-5300
Area Code (303) Fax 628-1299
CUDNVR
Did Not Respond--Taken from College Catalog

1986,1986

Kochenberger, Gary	Dean$	628-1205		Mgt	PHD	69	Colorado	1988
Arak, Marcelle	Prof	628-1289			PHD		Berkeley	
Morris, James R.	Prof				PHD		Mich St	
Stevens, Donald L.	Prof				PHD	71	Mich St	1982
Taylor, Dean G.	Prof	628-1288			PHD		Chicago	
Bosch, Jean-Claude	Assoc	628-1230			PHD		U Wash	
Cook, Richard	Asst	628-1264						
Foster, Richard W.	Asst	628-1286						
Radosevich, Barbara	Inst				EDS		West St	

Colorado State University
Dept Finance & Real Estate
College of Business
Fort Collins, CO 80523
Area Code (303) Fax 491-0596
Internet VINES.COLOSTATE.EDU

BS,MBA,MS
1970,1976

Pegnetter, Richard	Dean	491-6471		IndR	PHD	71	Cornell	1986
Zumwalt, J. Kenton	C-Pr	491-6681			PHD		Missouri	
Gallagher, Timothy J.	Prof	491-5637			PHD		Illinois	
Ellis, John W.	Assoc	491-5670			PHD		Mich St	
Hoeven, James A.	Assoc	491-5547			PHD		Colo St	
Johnson, Richard D.	Assoc	491-5564			PHD		Oregon	
Olienyic, John P.	Assoc	491-5673			PHD		Colo St	
Bajtelsmit, Vickie	Asst	491-0610						
Prill, Ed	Asst	491-7273			PHD		Illinois	
Worzala, Elaine	Asst	491-6337						

Columbia University MBA,PHD
Department of Finance 1916
Graduate School of Bus
New York, NY 10027
Area Code (212)   Fax 864-4857

Name	Rank	Phone			Field	Deg	Yr	School	Year
Feldberg, Meyer	Dean	854-6083			Mgt	PHD	69	Capetown	1989
Edwards, Franklin R.	C-Pr	854-4202	32			PHD	64	Harvard	1966
Adler, Michael	Prof	854-4682	4	V		PHD	63	Harvard	1968
Arzac, Enrique	Prof	854-4401	1	DGO		PHD	68	Columbia	1971
Donaldson, John B.	Prof	854-4436	12	J		PHD	76	Car Mel	1977
Greenwald, Bruce	Prof	854-3491	3	P		PHD	78	MIT	1991
Huberman, Gur	Prof	854-4100	1	J		PHD	80	Yale	1989
Lehmann, Bruce N.	Prof	854-2475	2			PHD	83	Chicago	1981
Selden, Larry	Prof	854-4353	2			PHD	76	Penn	1976
Sundaresan, Suresh	Prof	854-4423	2	O		PHD	80	Car Mel	1980
Detemple, Jerome	Assoc	854-8694	12	JLNO		PHD	83	Penn	1984
Glosten, Larry R.	Assoc	854-2476	3			PHD	80	Northwes	1989
Hite, Gailen L.	Assoc	854-4224	1			PHD	75	U Wash	1987
Jorion, Philippe	Assoc	854-4240	4	V		PHD	83	Chicago	1984
Chemmanur, Thomas J.	Asst	854-4109	1	ACGO		PHD	90	NYU	1990
Fulghieri, Paolo	Asst	854-4107	1	ADHQ		PHD	87	Penn	1987
Goetzmann, William	Asst	854-5685	2	O		PHD	90	Yale	1990
Hamao, Yasushi	Asst	854-5631	2	O		PHD	87	Yale	1990
Spiegel, Matthew	Asst	854-8888	12	GNT		PHD	87	Princet	1986
Subrahmanyam, A.	Asst	854-7335	3	LNT		PHD	90	UCLA	1990
Sun, Tong-sheng	Asst	854-3461	1	JKLO		PHD	87	Stanford	1990
Freeman, James		854-4412	3	Q		MBA	69	Wharton	1990

Columbus College BBA
Dept of Accounting & Finance
Turner School of Bus
Columbus, GA 31992-2399
Area Code (404)   Fax 568-2284

Name	Rank	Phone			Field	Deg	Yr	School	Year
Klein, Ronald D.	Dean$	568-2044			Mgt	PHD	80	Geo St	1974
Kundey, Gary E.	C $	568-2150	12			PHD	75	Florida	1974
Arthur, William J.	Prof	568-2150	14			DBA	69	Virginia	1985
Henderson, Malcolm R.	Prof	568-2150	12			PHD	65	Alabama	1970
Bohannon, John L.	Assoc	568-2150	1			MBA	68	Georgia	1970
Cook, Cline G.	Assoc	568-2150	1			PHD	87	Geo St	1985

Concordia College BA
Finance Faculty
Dept of Econ & Bus Adm
Moorhead, MN 56562
Area Code (218)   Fax 299-3947

Name	Rank	Phone			Field	Deg	Yr	School	Year
Harrison, Cliff	C-Pr	299-3476			Mgt	EDD		Fairl Di	1986
Spilde, Roger						ABD			

University of Connecticut BS,MBA,PHD
Department of Finance 1958,1971
School of Business Adm
Storrs, Conn 06269-2041
Area Code (203)   Fax 486-0349
UCONNVM

Name	Rank	Phone			Field	Deg	Yr	School	Year
Veiga, John	Dean$	486-2317			Mgt	DBA	71	Kent St	1972
Johnson, Keith B.	H-Pr	486-3040	31	PF		DBA	63	Wash U	1963
Clapp, John M.	Prof	486-3227	2	JNZ		PHD	74	Columbia	1981
Emerzian, A. D. Joseph	Prof	486-4324				PHD	55	New York	1948
Johnson, Harry M.	Prof	486-5631	3	XS		PHD	62	Penn	1962
Mandell, Lewis	Prof	486-4690	23	PX		PHD	70	Texas	1980
Messner, Stephen D.	Prof	486-3227	23	LNPV		DBA	66	Indiana	1966
Norgaard, Richard L.	Prof	486-4413	12	CL		PHD	62	Minn	1969
Sirmans Jr., Clemon F.	Prof	486-3227	12	AO		PHD	76	Georgia	1991
Dolde, Walter	Assoc	322-1673	14	LNUV		PHD	73	Yale	1990
Fields, Joseph A.	Assoc	486-2774	23	NSX		PHD	86	Penn St	1984
Giaccotto, Carmelo	Assoc	488-3040	21	LOCF		PHD	78	Kentucky	1981
Hegde, Shantaram P.	Assoc	486-5135	21	LTDQ		PHD	80	Mass	1990
Nunn Jr., Kenneth P.	Assoc	486-3360	14	FMSU		PHD	79	Mass	1979
O'Brien, Thomas J.	Assoc	486-3041	42	OKU		PHD	80	Florida	1986
Beliveau, Barbara C.	Asst	486-4485	14	AJNZ		PHD	80	Yale	1978
Biolsi, Robert	Asst	322-1673	21	LF		PHD	89	CUNY	1990
Ghosh, Chinmoy	Asst	486-4431	12	DGW		PHD	86	Penn St	1986
Klein, Linda S.	Asst	486-2765	12	TK		PHD	87	Fla St	1988
Knight, John R.	Asst	486-3227	21	MO		PHD	90	LSU	1990
Brennan, James E.	Lect	486-5433	32	XSN		MBA	57	Penn	1983
Kramer, Jeffrey A.	Lect	486-4121				PHD	89	Conn	1981
Stadtmueller, Katherine	Lect	486-3227	2			JD	86	Boston C	1991

28

Cornell University MBA,PHD
Finance Faculty 1950
Johnson Grad Sch of Mgt
Ithaca, New York 14853-4201
Area Code (607) Fax 254-4590
  Merten, Alan G.   Dean 255-6418   Sys PHD 70 Wiscon 1989
    The Anne & Elmer Lindseth Dean
  Bierman, Harold   Prof   HAL 1 CDE PHD 55 Michigan 1956
    Nicholas H. Noyes Professor of Business Administration
  Hass, Jerome E.   Prof 255-3901 JERRY 1 CDE PHD 69 Car Mel 1967
  Jarrow, Robert A.   Prof   JARROW 2 KLJO PHD 79 MIT 1979
    Ronald P. and Susan E. Lynch Professor of Investment Management
  O'Hara, Maureen   Prof   OHARA 3 PT PHD 79 Northwes 1979
  Smidt, Seymour   Prof 255-2384 SSMIDT 1 TC PHD 54 Chicago 1956
    Nicholas H. Noyes Proessor of Economics and Finance
  Bailey, Warren B.   Asst   BAILEY 4 VW PHD 86 UCLA 1990
  Carr, Peter P.   Asst 255-6255 PETER 2 L PHD 88 UCLA 1988
  Jacquier, Eric   Asst   JACQUIER 1 LJ PHD 91 Chicago 1990
  Michaely, Roni   Asst   RONI 1 DEG PHD 90 NYU 1990
  Wiggins, James B.   Asst   JIM 2 LN PHD 86 MIT 1986

Corpus Christi State Univ MPACC,MBA
Department of Finance
College of Business Adm
Corp Christi, TX 78412
Area Code (512) Fax 994-2725
CCSUVM1
  Abdelsamad, Moustafa H.   Dean 994-2655   Fnce DBA 70 Geo Wash 1991
  Whitmire, Ray E.   Prof 994-2490   PHD   Texas
  Desreumaux, James O.   Assoc 994-2483   DBA   Miss St
  Shum, Connie   Asst 994-2489   DBA   La Tech
  Sells Jr., Traylor D.   Lect 994-2704   BBA   Southwes

Creighton University BSBA
Dept of Economics & Finance 1949,1981
College of Business Adm
Omaha, Nebraska 68178-0130
Area Code (402) Fax 280-1874
  Banville, Guy R.   Dean 280-2852   Mktg PHD 69 Alabama 1982
  Allen, Robert F.   C-Pr   PHD 69 Mich St 1987
  Salvatore, Valentino   Prof   3   PHD 54 Nebraska 1954
  Gasper, Juli-Ann   Assoc   13 QS PHD 84 Nebraska 1982
  Phillips, Joseph M.   Assoc   3 PR PHD 82 Notre Dm 1982
  Schweig, Barry B.   Assoc   1 NX PHD 77 Penn 1981
  Sherman, Jerome F.   Assoc   12 F PHD 73 Miss 1976
  Johnson, Robert R.   Asst   12 AM PHD 88 Nebraska 1984

Cumberland College BS
Finance Faculty
Business Adm Department
Williamsburg, KY 40769-7056
Area Code (606) Fax
  Hubbard, Harold F.   C-Pr 549-2200   Atg MBA 60 Kentucky 1960
  Gadd, Susan G.   Asst Ext 4350 13 FX MS 89 Kentucky 1990

University of Dallas
Finance Faculty
Graduate School of Mgmt
Irving, Texas 75062-4799
Area Code (214) Fax 721-5254
  Gellerman, Saul W.   Dean 721-5008   PHD 56 Penn
  Higgins, David   Assoc 721-5304   PHD 79 Texas

Dartmouth College MBA
Finance Faculty 1916
Amos Tuck Sch of Bus Ad
Hanover, NH 03755-1798
Area Code (603) Fax 646-1308
  Fox, Edward A.   Dean 646-2460   MBA 60 NYU 1990
  Blayden, Colin   Prof 646-3160   PHD 66 Harvard 1983
  Logue, Dennis   Prof 646-2801   PHD 71 Cornell 1974
    Associate Dean
  Rojalski, Richard   Prof 646-2512   PHD 74 Michigan 1976
  Williamson, J. Peter   Prof 646-2842   DBA 61 Harvard 1961
  Hansen, Robert   Assoc 646-2079   PHD 84 UCLA 1983

Name	Rank	Phone		Field	Degree	Yr	School	Yr
Maloney, Kevin	Assoc	646-2691			PHD	83	U Wash	1983
Baker, Jonathan	Asst	646-2843			PHD	86	Stanford	1986
Seward, James	Asst	646-3423			PHD	87	Wiscon	1987
Shyam-Sunder, Lakshmi	Asst	646-3937			PHD	89	MIT	1987
Sundaram, Anant	Asst	646-3415			PHD	87	Yale	1986
Willner, Ram	Asst	646-2667			DBA	86	Harvard	1987

David Lipscomb University BS,BA
Finance Faculty
Dept of Business Adm
Nashville, Tenn 37204-3951
Area Code (615) Fax 269-1796
Did Not Respond--Taken from College Catalog

Name	Rank	Phone		Field	Degree		School	Yr
Fulks, L. Gerald	H-Pr	269-2232		Mgt	DA		Mid Tenn	1978
Swang, Axel W.	C-Pr				PHD		Alabama	
Boulware, George	Prof				PHD		S Carol	
Dugger, Patty I.	Prof				EDS		Peabody	
Ingram, William c.	Prof				PHD		W Virgin	
Carmody, Seth F.	Assoc				PHD		Missouri	
Eubanks, Dorothy G.	Assoc				MA		Peabody	
Frasier, Charales E.	Assoc				MA		Alabama	
Crawford, John E.	Asst				PHD		Alabama	
Steger, Randy A.	Asst				DBA		Kentucky	
Jackson, Robert L.	Inst				MA		Cen Mich	
Moore, Perry G.	Inst				MA		Alabama	
Parham, W. Jackson	Inst				MBA		Virginia	
Wright, Gene	Inst				MBA		Vanderb	

University of Dayton BS,MBA
Dept of Economics & Finance
School of Business Adm
Dayton, Ohio 45469-2240
Area Code (513) Fax 229-4000
DAYTON 1983,1988

Name	Rank	Phone		Field	Degree	Yr	School	Yr
Gould, Sam	Dean	229-3731		Mgt	PHD	75	Mich St	1985
Chen, Carl R.	C-Pr	229-2418	12	JMNS	PHD	77	Georgia	1977
Winger, Bernard J.	Prof	229-2410	12	FMX	ABD		Cinn	1966
Stick, Henry H.	Assoc	229-2409	12	G	PHD	57	Ohio St	1975
Chong, Beng S.	Asst	229-2419	13	P	PHD	90	Wash U	1990
Kao, Glenda Wenchi	Asst	229-2404	14	FLNV	PHD	84	Illinois	1991
Mohan, Nancy K.	Asst	229-2458	1	GU	PHD	86	Cinn	1987
Sauer, David A.	Asst	229-2757	12	DE	ABD		Michigan	1991

University of Delaware BS,MBA
Department of Finance
College of Bus & Econ
Newark, Delaware 19716
Area Code (302) Fax 831-6750
UDELVM 1966,1982

Name	Rank	Phone		Field	Degree	Yr	School	Yr
Biederman, Kenneth R.	Dean	831-2551		Econ	PHD		Purdue	
Schweitzer, Robert	C-Pr	831-1015	3	P	PHD		Duke	
Puglisi, Donald	Prof	831-1779	23	KP	DBA	72	Indiana	1971
Bonner, Gordon R.	Assoc	831-1761	1	F	PHD	65	Syracuse	
D'Souza, Rudolph E.	Assoc	831-1766	12	KM	PHD		So Carol	
Fields, M. Andrew	Assoc	831-1762	1	G	PHD		Va Tech	
Lee, Insup	Assoc	831-1920	12	JM	PHD		Houston	
Ngassam, Christopher	Asst	831-1788	24	V	PHD		Tx-Arlin	
Todd, Janet	Asst		13	D	ABD		Mich St	1991
Varma, Raj	Asst	831-1786	1	D	PHD		Penn St	

Delaware State College BS
Finance Faculty
Dept of Econ & Bus Adm
Dover, Delaware 19901-4932
Area Code (302) Fax

Name	Rank	Phone	Field	Degree	School
Awadzi, Winston	C-Ac	739-3521	Mktg	PHD	LSU
Bieker, Richard	Prof	739-3526		PHD	Kentucky
Ikein, Augustine	Assoc	739-5188		PHD	Atlanta
Wendelburg, George	Inst	739-5247		MBA	Temple

Delta State University BBA,MBA
Division of Econ & Finance
School of Business
Cleveland, Miss 38733
Area Code (601) Fax 846-4185

Name	Rank	Phone		Field	Degree	Yr	School	Yr
Moore, Roy N.	Dean	846-4200		Mgt	PHD	71	Alabama	
Hinton, Walter Val	Prof	846-4197	12		PHD	82	Arkansas	1989
Moore, B. C.	Assoc	846-4209	23		ABD		Miss	1986
Eduardo, Marcelo	Asst	846-4198	13		MBA	86	Delta St	1986

University of Denver
Department of Finance
College of Business
Denver, Colorado 80208-0233
Area Code (303) Fax 871-2156
DUCAIR

BS,MBA,MA,MAT
1923,1966

Hutton, Bruce	Dean	871-2273			PHD	77	Florida	1976
Clouse, Maclyn L.	C-Ac	871-3320	13	DGHP	PHD		U Wash	1977
Giles, Leon G.	Prof	871-4228	1	CDGH	PHD	71	Illinois	1970
Rizzuto, Tonald J.	Prof	871-2010	1	CDEG	PHD		New York	1975
Cook, Tom	Assoc	871-2012	12	CDEH	PHD		U Wash	1983
D'Antonio, Lou	Assoc	871-2011	23	PKL	DBA		Colorado	1980
Howard, Charles Thomas	Assoc	871-4402	24	JLMV	PHD		U Wash	1978
Abrahamson, Allen	Asst	871-2131	23	JKLM	PHD		Arizona	1990
Basu, Somnath	Asst	871-2004	24	JLNV	PHD		Arizona	1989
Johnsen, Thomajean	Asst	871-2282	12	ABJO	PHD		Colorado	1988
Speltz, John	Asst	871-2132	14	ABGU	PHD	90	Fla St	1990

DePaul University
Department of Finance
College of Commerce
Chicago, IL 60604-2287
Area Code (312) Fax 362-6566

BS,MA,MBA,MS
1957,1963

Patten, Ronald J.	Dean	362-6781	Atg	PHD	63	Alabama	1989
Hirt, Geoffrey A.	C	362-5119		PHD		Illinois	
Howe, Keith M.	Prof	362-5126		PHD		Nebraska	
Dr. William M. Scholl Professor of Finance							
Berry, Thomas D.	Assoc	362-8360		PHD		Missouri	
Junkus, Joan C.	Assoc	362-6177		PHD		Illinois	
Benet, Bruce A.	Asst	362-6907		PHD		N Carol	
Broome, Carroll D.	Asst	362-8472		PHD		Geo St	
Luft, Carl F.	Asst	362-8428		PHD		Geo St	

DePauw University
Finance Faculty
Dept of Econ & Business
Greencastle, IN 46135
Area Code (317) Fax 658-4177
Did Not Respond

Lemon, Gary Dale	C-Ac			PHD	82	Kansas	1976

University of Detroit Mercy
Finance Program POBox 19900
College of Business Adm
Detroit, Mich 48219-3599
Area Code (313) Fax 993-1052

BS,MBA
1949,1963

Ulferts, Gregory W.	Dean	993-1204		DBA	75	La Tech	1983
Kim, Suk H.	D-Pr	993-3325		PHD	75	St Louis	1977
Crick, T.	Assoc	993-1225		PHD	81	Iowa	1981
Severn, A.	Assoc	993-1161		PHD	69	Penn	1988
Shinkel, B.	Assoc	993-1232		PHD	76	Purdue	1989
Rowland, M.	Asst	993-1200		MA	84	Wayne St	1990
Swinnerton, G.	Asst	993-1172		PHD	88	Kent St	1989

Dickinson State University
Finance Faculty
School of Bus & Adm
Dickinson, ND 58601
Area Code (701) Fax 227-2006

BS,BA

Goetz, William G.	Dean	227-2333	Atg	MA	67	N Dakota	1967
Binde, Boyd L.	Asst	227-2319		MCAA	84	N Dakota	1984
Ford, Kent	Asst	227-2140					

Dillard University
Finance Faculty
College of Business
New Orleans, LA 70122
Area Code (504) Fax

Chase III, Edgar L.	C-Pr	286-4697	Fine	JD	Loyola
Fugar, Chris	Assoc	286-4699		PHD	

Univ of District of Columbia BPA,BBA,MBA,MPA
Department of Finance
Col of Bus & Public Mgt
Washington, DC 20008
Area Code (202) Fax 727-1907
Did Not Respond
  Daljit, Singh   Dean   727-2224   PMgt   PHD   Claremon   1970

Drake University BS,MBA
Department of Finance 1949,1973
Col of Bus & Pub Adm
Des Moines, Iowa 50311-4505
Area Code (515) Fax 271-2001
DRAKE
  Weinbrenner, Hugh   Dean   271-2871   Mgt   PHD   73 Colorado   1979
  Grube, R. Corwin   Prof   271-3811   12 GMQT   PHD   74 Mich St   1988
  Lawrence, David B.   Prof   271-2912   3   Pr   PHD   79 Iowa St   1979
  Ketcher, David N.   Asst   271-3138 DK1631R 12 FNOS   PHD   91 Missouri   1990
  Rozycki, John   Asst   271-2886 JR2921R 13 CDLU   PHD   91 Penn St   1990

Drexel University BS,MBA,MTA,PHD
Department of Finance 1967,1978
College of Bus & Adm
Philadelphia, PA 19104
Area Code (215) Fax 895-2891
DUVM
  Dascher, Paul E.   Dean   895-2110   Atg   PHD   69 Penn St   1973
  Hindelang, T. J.   H-Pr   895-1741   14 CU   DBA   73 Indiana   1973
  Chiang, Thomas C.   Prof   895-1745   41 VG   PHD   Penn St   1981
  Gombola, Michael J.   Assoc 895-1743   32 TO   PHD   So Carol   1985
  Grebis, Thomas J.   Asst   26 T&   MBA   Drexel   1958
    Assistant Department Head
  Oh, Kap-Soo   Asst   12 DF   PHD   Penn   1988
  Szewczyk, Sam   Asst   3   T   PHD   Penn St   1987
  Thomas, Martin   Asst   23 T   PHD   90 Penn St   1989
  Tsetsekos, George   Asst   4   V   PHD   Tenn   1988
  Boyer, Edward   Inst   1   GC   PHD   Temple   1987
  Hykes, Richard   Inst   16 F&   MBA   New York   1988
  Thomas, Sam   Inst

Drury College
Finance Faculty
Breech Sch of Bus Adm
Springfield, MO 65802
Area Code (417) Fax
  Strube, W. Curtis   D-Pr   865-8731   PHD   72 Arkansas
    Burlington Northern Chair in Business Administration
  Nowak, Paul   Assoc   PHD   79 Fla St

Duke University MBA,PHD
Finance Faculty 1979
Fuqua School of Bus
Durham, N Carol 27706
Area Code (919) Fax 684-2818
DUKEFSB
  Keller, Thomas F.   Dean   684-2495   Atg   PHD   60 Michigan   1959
    R. J. Reynolds Professor of Business Administration
  Whaley, Robert E.   C-Pr   660-7781   PHD   Toronto
  Breeden, Douglas T.   Prof   660-7762   PHD   Stanford
  Cohen, J. Kalman   Prof   660-7816   PHD   Car Mel
  Forsyth, John D.   Prof   660-7783   PHD   Illinois
  Foster, Douglas F.   Assoc 660-7786   PHD   Cornell
  Harvey, Campbell R.   Assoc 660-7768   PHD   86 Chicago
  Hsieh, David A.   Assoc 660-7779   PHD   MIT
  Kyle, Alfred   Assoc 660-7797
  Viswanathan, S.   Assoc 660-7784   PHD   Northwes
  Delgado, Francisco   Asst   660-7756   PHD   Penn
  Foster, F. Douglas   Asst   684-2859   PHD   Cornell
  Hemler, Michael L.   Asst   660-7766   PHD   88 Chicago
  Kishimoto, Naoki   Asst   660-7765   PHD   NYU
  Muthuswamy, Jayram   Asst   660-7767   PHD   90 Chicago
  Smith, Thomas M.   Asst   660-7778   PHD   Stanford

Duquesne University
Department of Finance
School of Bus & Adm
Pittsburgh, Penn 15282-0104
Area Code (412) Fax 642-9106

BS,MBA
1961,1963

Murrin, Thomas	Dean				DMS	Duquesne	1991
Presutti Jr., William D.	C-Ac	434-6269		Mktg	PHD	Car Mel	
Ahkam, Sharif Nurul	Assoc	434-6256			DBA	Kent St	
McCue, Thomas E.	Assoc	434-5643			PHD	N Carol	
Bhaskar, Vashishta	Asst	434-6273			ABD	Penn St	
Carlson, William	Asst	434-6270			PHD	Car Mel	
Sukhwani, Manobarlal	Asst	434-5152			ABD	Pitt	

East Carolina University
Department of Finance
School of Business
Greenville, NC 27858-4353
Area Code (919) Fax 757-6618
ECUVM1

BS,MBA
1967,1976

Uhr, Ernest B.	Dean	757-6966			Mktg	PHD	69	Renssel	1983
Sprecher, C. Ronald	C-Pr	757-6670	FISPRECH	12	KMNT	PHD	69	Illinois	1989
Hunt, Jerry G.	Prof	757-6560		24	FLNV	PHD	68	Colorado	1975
Stansell, Stanley R.	Prof	757-6636	FISTANSE	23	FOPV	PHD	71	Georgia	1988
Buck, James F.	Assoc	757-6625		12	JLMN	DBA	78	Fla St	1979
Eakins, Stanley G.	Assoc	757-6359	FIEAKINS	13	AGS	PHD	90	Ariz St	1990
Banning, Peter D.	Asst	757-6365	FIBANNIN	13	ABGP	MS	71	UCLA	1989
Schadler, Frederick P.	Asst	757-6987	FIFFSCHA	12	ADFQ	PHD	87	S Carol	1988
Sewell, Susan P.	Asst	757-6628	FISEWELL	14	JSUW	PHD	90	Tx-Dalla	1990

East Central University
Department of Finance
School of Business
Ada, Oklahoma 74820-6899
Area Code (405) Fax
Phone 332-8000

BS

Kaufman, Jerry M.	Dean	Ext 649		Atg	PHD	74	Okla St	1990
Reed, Morris	Asst	Ext 527			MBA	70	Hawaii	1975
Smith, Weldon	Asst	Ext 531			MBA	72	Oklahoma	1980

East Tennessee State Univ
Dept of Economics & Finance
College of Business
Johnson City, TN 37614-0002
Area Code (615) Fax 929-5274
ETSU

BS,MBA
1987,1987

Spritzer, Allan D.	Dean	929-5489	I64SPRIT		Mgt	PHD	71	Cornell	1981
Bartell Jr., H. Robert	Prof	929-4402				PHD	63	Columbia	1989
Chair of Banking and Director Center of Excellence in Banking									
Granger, George L.	Prof					PHD	71	Penn	1961
Garrison, Sharon H.	Assoc					PHD	83	Tx-Arlin	1986
Mason, W. Joe	Assoc	929-5368				PHD	87	S Carol	1984
Acting Assistant Director Center for Banking									
Waheed, Amjad	Asst					PHD	91	So Ill	1991

East Texas State Univ
Dept of Economics & Finance
College of Business
Commerce, Texas 75429
Area Code (214) Fax 886-5650

BBA
1975,1982

Pressley, Trezzie A.	Dean	886-5189		Mgt	PHD	66	Arkansas	1965
Hakala, Donald R.	H-Pr	886-5673			PHD		Indiana	
Kersey, Bruce L.	Prof	886-5678			PHD	70	LSU	1970
Avard, Stephen L.	Assoc	886-5680			PHD		N Texas	

Eastern Conn State Univ
Dept of Econ & Mgt Sciences
School of Prof Studies
Willimantic, CT 06226-2295
Area Code (203) Fax 456-2331

Comer, Kelvie C.	Dean	456-5293			EDD	Temple
St. Onge, John	C-Ac	456-5321		Mgt		
Krishnamurti, Chandrasekhar	Asst	456-5366				
on leave of absence 1992-93 to India						

34

Eastern Illinois Univ
Dept Atg, Data Proc & Fnce
Lumpkin College of Bus
Charleston, IL 61920-3099
Area Code (217) Fax 581-6247

BS,MBA

Ivarie, Theordore W.	Dean	581-3526		BusE	EDD	68	Ariz St	1979
Clark, Frank L.	C-Pr	581-3023	12	FIXY	PHD	75	Arkansas	1990
Dudley, Dean A.	Prof	581-5957	3	PSD	PHD	65	U Wash	1985
Gover, Timothy D.	Prof	581-6004	3	F	MS	61	Illinois	1963
Hogan, Stephen	Assoc	581-6930	2	GMHY	PHD	77	Oklahoma	1990
Walker, C. Lankford	Assoc	581-6009	3	PBH	PHD	80	Georgia	1987
Born, Waldo L.	Asst	581-6201	61	&CFO	PHD	84	Texas	1988
Jordan-Wagner, James	Asst	581-6931	4	NUVW	PHD	89	N Texas	1990
Michelson, Stuart	Asst	581-6940	12	CALO	PHD	91	Kansas	1991

Eastern Kentucky University
Dept of Finance & Bus Sys
College of Business
Richmond, KY 40475-3111
Area Code (606) Fax 622-2359

BA,MBA

Falk, Charles F.	Dean	622-1409	Ed	EDD	75	N Illin	1986
Brewer, Virgil L.	C-Pr			DBA		Tx Tech	1980
Alford, James D.	Assoc	622-4978		MBA	59	Kentucky	1969
Bickum, Gilbert W.	VAsst	623-4454		PHD		Florida	1987
Robinson, Richard M.	Asst	622-1590		PHD		Oregon	1985
Thompson, J. C.	Asst	622-6156		DBA	90	Kentucky	1991

Eastern Michigan University
Department of Finance
College of Business
Ypsilanti, Mich 48197
Area Code (313) Fax 487-7099

BBA,MSA
1973,1982

Tubbs, Stewart L.	Dean	487-4140	OrgB	PHD	69	Kansas	1986
Garg, Ramesh	Prof	487-0249		DBA	74	Kent St	1978
Diallo, Alahassane	Assoc	487-1022		PHD	85	Ohio St	1985
Hutchins, Ron	Assoc	487-0054		PHD	77	Missouri	1977
Weeks, Wayne	Assoc	487-0054		DBA	78	Kent St	1978
Kiss, Robert	Asst	487-1481		PHD	90	Kent St	1990
Moeller, Susan	Asst	487-0249		PHD	85	Mich St	1990
Rahman, Mahmud	Asst	487-1481		PHD	91	Texas	1991
Valenti, Dennis	Lect	487-3132		MBA	84	Mich St	1989

Eastern Montana College
Department of Finance
School of Business
Billings, MT 59101-0298
Area Code (406) Fax 657-2289

BSBA

Corbeau, Andre B.	Dean	657-2295	Mgt	PHD	63	Tulane	1983
Harris, R. Scott	C-Pr	657-1653	Econ	PHD	85	Calif	1988
Farsio, Farzad	Asst	657-2033		PHD	89	Claremont	1987

Eastern New Mexico Univ
Department of Finance
College of Business
Portales, NM 88130
Area Code (505) Fax 562-4331

BS,BBA,MBA

Davis, Dale N.	Dean	562-2345		Mgt	DBA	80	Geo St	1982
Brewer, Betty L.	Assoc	562-2332	1	W	PHD	76	Nebraska	1987
Brunsen, William H.	Assoc	562-2744	3	XP	PHD	76	Nebraska	1987
Elston, Frank A.	Asst	562-2365	1	PQ	PHD	79	Virginia	1988

Eastern Washington Univ
Department of Finance
College of Business Adm
Cheney, Wash 99004-2490
Area Code (509) Fax 359-6649

BA,MBA
1975,1981

Evans, Fred J.	Dean	359-2455		BusP	PHD	75	U Wash	1988
Bown, Charles C.	Prof	359-6644	12	FNO	PHD	66	U Wash	1969
Hunter, Hugh O.	Prof	359-2806	23	JPQ	DBA	76	S Carol	1980
Eagle, David M.	Asst	359-6630	14	AUV	PHD	86	Minn	1989

Elizabethtown College — BS
Finance Faculty
Department of Business
Elizabethtown PA 17022-2298
Area Code (717) Fax 367-7567
Phone 367-1151
  Stone, Richard G.   C-Ac Ext 269   Mgt PHD 88 Temple   1987
  Trostle, Randolph L. Assoc Ext 284   12 FM   PHD 72 Lehigh   1970

Elmhurst College
Finance Faculty
Center for Bus & Econ
Elmhurst, IL 60126-3296
Area Code (708) Fax
  Bohnert, John E.   Dean 617-3123   PHD   S Illin   1967
  Heiney, Joseph N.   Dir   617-3123   Econ PHD   Chicago   1977
  Hogenboom, Marion Asst   MM   Northwes   1984

Elon College — BS,BA,MBA
Finance Faculty
Love School of Business
Elon College, NC 27244-2010
Area Code (919) Fax 584-2575
  Tiemann, Thomas K. Dean 584-2558   Econ PHD 74 Vanderb   1984
  Synn, Wonhi J.   Asst 584-2181   PHD 89 SUNY-Buf   1989

Embry-Riddle Aeronautical U
Finance Faculty
Aviation Bus Adm
Daytona Bch, FL 32114
Area Code (904) Fax 226-6459
  Fleming, Kenneth   C-Pr   226-6694   Econ PHD   CA-S Dgo 1988
  Chadbourne, Bruce D. Prof   226-6730   7 EFX   PHD 69 Iowa   1988
  Block, Linda J.   Assoc 226-6653   12 DFI   PHD 78 Purdue   1988
  Maulden, Hoyt P.   Assoc 226-6702   12 EFX   MSBA 68 Geo Wash 1985
  Vasigh, Bijan   Asst   226-6732   12 EFS   PHD 84 SUNY   1990

Emory University — BBA,MBA 1949,1963
Finance Area
School of Business Adm
Atlanta, Georgia 30322
Area Code (404) Fax 727-6313
EMUBUS
  Frank, Ronald E.   Dean 727-6377   Mktg PHD 60 Chicago   1989
  Asa Griggs Candler Professor of Marketing
  Rosenfeld, James D. C-Ac   PHD 81 NYU   1983
  Benston, George J.   Prof   727-7831   PHD 63 Chicago   1987
  John H. Harland Professor of Finance, Accounting, and Economics
  Andrews, John J.   Assoc   PHD 65 Ohio St   1970
  Hunter, William C.   Assoc   PHD 79 Northwes   1980
  Mian, Shezad   Asst   PHD 87 Rochest   1989
  Mishra, Banikanta   Asst   727-6302   PHD 85 NYU   1988
  Rosensweig, Jeffrey A. Asst   PHD 85 MIT   1988
  Thornton, Billy   Asst   PHD 89 Harvard   1989
  Valerio, Nicholas   Asst   PHD 91 Penn   1990
  Zacharias, John   Asst   PHD 91 Penn   1990

Emory and Henry College
Finance Faculty
Dept of Econ & Business
Emory, Virginia 24327
Area Code (703) Fax 944-4338
Did Not Respond
  Cumbo, James   C   994-4121   Mgt   PHD 81 Va Tech   1975

Emporia State University — BS
Dept of Mgt, Mktg, Fin & Eco
School of Business
Emporia, Kansas 66801-5087
Area Code (316) Fax 341-5997
  Hashmi, Sajjad A.   Dean 341-5274   PHD 66 Penn   1983
  Titus, Varkey K.   C-Pr   341-5347   PHD   Wash St   1979
  Greenlee, Robert   Assoc 341-5420   67   EDS 64 Kan St   1967
  Pettengill, Glenn   Assoc 341-5389   23   PHD 76 Arkansas   1989
  Kelm, Kathryn   Asst   23   ABD   Missouri   1992
  Sundaram, Sridhar   Asst   341-5377   12   DBA 90 Illinois   1989

University of Evansville BS
Finance Faculty
School of Business Adm
Evansville, IN 47722
Area Code (812) Fax 479-2320

Name	Rank	Phone			Field	Deg		School	Year
Reeder, David B.	Dean$	479-2851			Atg	DBA	80	Kentucky	1968
De, Soumendra N.	Asst	479-2863		14	DGV	DBA	88	So Illin	1988
Khan, Walayet	Asst	479-2869		32	FJTV	PHD	90	Arkansas	1989

Fairfield Universiy BS
Finance Faculty
School of Business
Fairfield, Conn 06430-7524
Area Code (203) Fax 254-4105
FAIR1
Phone 254-4000

Name	Rank	Phone	Code		Field	Deg		School	Year
Martin, R. Keith	Dean	Ext 4070	RKMARTIN		Atg	PHD	73	U Wash	1979
Conine Jr., Thomas E.	C-Pr	Ext 2818	CONINE	12	JOED	PHD	79	New York	1980
Boisjoly, Russell P.	Prof	Ext 2622		12	BG	DBA	78	Indiana	1989
Associate Dean									
Madden, Gerald P.	Assoc	Ext 2834	GPMADDEN	2	MND	PHD	76	Penn St	1985
Bhalla, Bharat B.	Asst	Ext 2838	BBBHALLA	41	UV	PHD	66	Cornell	1987
Eldridge, Robert M.	Asst	Ext 2832		14	LNVI	DBA	87	Geo Wash	1988
Hlawitschka, Walter F.	Asst	Ext 2826	WFHLAWIT	21	JNW	PHD	89	Virginia	1988
Tucker, Michael T.	Asst	Ext 2833	TUCKER	1	NJPK	DBA	88	Boston	1988

Fairleigh Dickinson Univ BS,MA,MBA
Department of Finance
Silberman Col of Bus Ad
Madison, NJ 07940
Area Code (201) Fax 593-8804

Name	Rank	Phone			Field	Deg		School	Year
Dickey, Ron	Prof	593-8830		6	&	PHD			
Rust, A.	Prof	593-8893		1		PHD			
Malitz, Ileen	Assoc	539-8830		1	ADHK	PHD		Maryland	1990
Kierhan, Joseph	Asst	593-8830		13	XY	PHD			
Norton, Edgar A.	Asst	593-8838		12	DFMN	PHD	84	Illinois	1988
Woods, John C.	Asst	593-8898		1	CDEF	PHD	89	New York	1990

Fairleigh Dickinson Univ BS,MBA
Finance Faculty
Business
Rutherford, NJ 07070
Area Code (201) Fax 460-5498
Did Not Respond

Fairleigh Dickinson Univ
Dept of Economics & Finance
College of Business Adm
Teaneck, NJ 07666
Area Code (201) Fax 692-0185
Did Not Respond

Name	Rank	Phone				Deg		School	Year
Lerman, Paul	Dean	692-2134				PHD	74	New York	

Fayetteville State Univ
Dept of Economics & Finance
Sch of Business & Econ
Fayetteville, NC 28301-4298
Area Code (919) Fax

Name	Rank	Phone			Field	Deg	School
Tavakoli, Assad	Dean$				Mgt	PHD	Aston
Nijhawan, Inder P.	C-Pr	486-1618			Econ	PHD	N Carol
Walker, Moses S.	Prof	486-1165				PHD	Iowa St
McClean, Larry E.	Assoc	486-1488				PHD	Syracuse
Roayaei, Jean	Assoc	486-1592				PHD	Fla St
Iledare, Wumi	Asst	486-1984				PHD	W Virg

Ferris State University BS,MACC
Department of Finance
School of Business
Big Rapids, Mich 49307
Area Code (616) Fax 592-2990

Name	Rank	Phone			Field	Deg		School	Year
Hansen, Richard C.	Dean	592-2422			Mgt	PHD	71	Wiscon	1983
Boras, William	H-Pr$	592-2427				PHD		Mich St	1975
Shin, Kilman	Prof	592-2465				PHD		Conn	1989
Giller, Marshall	Assoc	592-2474				PHD			1978
Lunden, John H.	Assoc	592-2474				MBA		Michigan	1988
Fairbanks, John G.	Asst	592-2471				MBA		Cen Mich	1980
Nazar, Vivian	Asst	592-2478				MBA		London	1988

36

Fisk University
Finance Faculty
Div of Business Adm
Nashville, TN 37208-3051
Area Code (615) Fax
  Smith, Solomon S.   Dean$ 329-8573   PHD   So Illin
  Hiremath, B. N.   Prof   329-8698

Fitchburg State College
Finance Faculty
Dept of Business Adm
Fitchburg, MA 01420-2697
Area Code (508) Fax 343-8603
Phone 345-2151
  Cox, Howard B.   C-Pr   Ext 3378   PHD   Ohio St   1988
  McAloon, Joseph   Asst   Ext 3378   16 BCF& MBA   S Dakota   1984

University of Florida   BSA,MBA,MAC,PHD
Dept Finance, Insur & Rl Est   1929,1963
College of Business Adm
Gainesville, FL 32611-2017
Area Code (904) Fax 392-6250
UFFSC
  Kraft, John   Dean   392-2397   Econ   PHD   71 Pitt   1990
  Crum, Roy Lee   C-Pr   392-0153   PHD   74 Texas   1974
  McCollough, W. Andrew   Prof   392-8436   PHD   71 Florida   1969
    Associate Dean
  Brigham, Eugene F.   Prof   392-0142   PHD   62 Berkeley 1971
    Graduate Research Professor
  Flannery, Mark J.   Prof   392-3184   PHD   Yale   1989
    Barnett Bank Eminent Scholar
  Heggestad, Arnold A.   Prof   392-2610   PHD   73 Mich St   1974
    William H. Dial Professor; Director, Financial Institutions Center
  James, Christopher   Prof   392-3486   PHD   78 Michigan 1989
    SunBank/William H. Dial Eminent Scholar
  Levy, Haim   Prof   392-0340   PHD   Jerusale   1981
    Walter J. Matherly Professor; Graduate Research Professor
  Livingston, Miles B.   Prof   392-4316   PHD   New York   1982
    on leave to College of William & Mary, 1991-92
  Nye, David J.   Prof   392-6649   7 #   PHD   73 Penn   1971
    Director Florida Insurance Research Center
  Smith, Halbert C.   Prof   392-0157   6 &   DBA   62 Illinois   1971
    Director, Real Estate Research Center
  Ling, David C.   Assoc 392-9307   6 &   PHD   Ohio St   1989
  Radcliffe, Robert C.   Assoc 392-0138   PHD   71 Ohio St   1971
  Archer, Wayne R.   Asst   392-1330   6 &   PHD   74 Indiana   1971
  Brown, David T.   Asst   392-5844   PHD   Wash U   1986
  Desai, Anand S.   Asst   392-5843   PHD   Michigan   1987
  Houston, Joel F.   Asst   392-7546   PHD   Penn   1987
  Mooradian, Robert M.   Asst   392-5808   PHD   Penn   1988
  Nimalendran, Mahendrarajah VAsst 392-9526   PHD   Michigan   1990
  Ryngaert, Michael D.   Asst   392-9765   PHD   88 Chicago   1987
  Smith, Marc T.   Asst   392-3781   6 &   PHD   Ohio St   1986
  Venkataraman, Subramanyan VAsst 392-7357   PHD   Wiscon   1988

Florida A&M University   BS,MBA
Finance Faculty
Sch of Bus & Industry
Tallahassee, FL 32307
Area Code (904) Fax 599-3533
  Mobley, Sybil C.   Dean   599-3565   Atg   PHD   64 Illinois   1963
  Atkinson, Robert   C-Ac   599-3170   Mktg   PHD   76 Carnegie 1982
  Frieder, Larry A.   Prof   599-3787   PHD   Arizona
  Cole, John A.   Asst   561-2341   PHD   Michigan
  Reuben, Lucy J.   Asst   561-2338   PHD   Michigan
  King, Jules   561-2339   PHD   Stanford

Florida Atlantic Univ   BS,MBA,MACC,PHD
Finance, Insur, Rl Est Dept   1977,1977
College of Business
Boca Raton, FL 33431-0991
Area Code (407) Fax 367-3978
FAUVAX
Office Phone 367-2607
  Hille, Stanley J.   Dean   367-3630   PHD   66 Minn   1988
  McCarty, Daniel E.   C-Pr   367-3995   PHD   73 Geo St   1981

Madura, Jeff	Prof	367-3677			DBA	83	Fla St	1987
McDaniel, Wm R.	Prof	367-3193			PHD	75	Geo St	1975
Caks, John	Assoc	367-3997			PHD	84	Penn	1989
Jessell, Kenneth A.	Assoc	367-3196			PHD	85	Fla St	1983
Associate Dean								
Laird, Thomas	Assoc	367-3677			PHD	77	Miami	1974
McNulty, James	Assoc	367-2708			PHD	75	N Carol	1989
Akhigbe, Aigbe	Asst	367-2702			PHD	90	Houston	1991
Bartunek, Kenneth	Asst	367-3923			PHD	91	Louisian	1991
Brown, Craig	Asst	367-3923			ABD		Georgia	1991
Dare, William	Asst	367-3923			ABD		Tx Tech	1991
Dickinson, Amy	Asst	367-3669			PHD	89	Fla St	1989
Wiant, Kenneth	Asst	367-3493			PHD	91	S Carol	1990
Zarruk, Emilio	Asst	367-2710			PHD	85	LSU	1990

Florida International Univ
Dept of Finance, DM 368
College of Business Adm
Miami, Florida 33199
Area Code (305) Fax 348-3278
SERVAX
                                                          BBA,MA,MST
                                                          1983,1986

Wyman, Harold E.	Dean	348-2754		Atg	PHD	67	Stanford	1990
Prakash, Arun J.	C-Pr	348-2680			PHD	81	Oregon	
Bear, Robert	Prof	355-5285			PHD	70	Iowa	
Beaton, William R.	Prof	348-3282			PHD	58	Ohio St	
Bierwag, Gerald O.	Prof	348-2680			PHD	62	Northwes	
Ryder Systems Professor of Finance								
Parhizgari, Ali M.	Prof	348-3326			PHD	76	Maryland	
Roussakis, Emmanuel N.	Prof	348-3328			PHD	68	Louvain	
Simmons, George B.	Prof	940-5870			PHD	61	Indiana	
Distinguished Service Professor								
Zdanowicz, John S.	Prof	348-2771			PHD	71	Mich St	
Director, Center for Banking and Finance								
Daigler, Robert T.	Assoc	348-3325			PHD	76	Oklahoma	
Dandapani, Krishnan	Assoc	348-3323			PHD		Penn St	
Pak, Simon	Assoc	348-2774			PHD	80	Berkeley	
Welch, William	Assoc	348-2772			PHD	74	Michigan	
Chang, Chung-Hao	Asst	348-2845			PHD	88	Northwes	
Hamid, Shahid	Asst	348-2680			PHD	88	Maryland	
Sullivan, Michael	Asst	348-3274			ABD	88	Yale	
Keys, James D.	Inst	348-3268			MBA	87	Fla Intl	

Florida Southern University
Finance Faculty
Dept of Business Adm
Lakeland, Fl 33801-5698
Area Code (813) Fax 680-4126

O'Leary, Harold	Assoc	680-4289	23		DBA			1978
Wiley, C. Jeffery	Asst	680-4276	23		MBA			1978

Florida State University
Department of Finance
College of Business
Tallahassee, FL 32306-1042
Area Code (904) Fax 644-4225
FSUAVM
                                                            BS,MBA,PHD
                                                           1962,1964

Stith, Melvin T.	Dean	644-3090			Mktg	PHD	77	Syracuse	1985
--Department of Finance	FAX =	644-4225							
Nast, Donald A.	C-Ac	644-4220		12	FNO	PHD	75	Penn St	1974
Ang, James S.	Prof	644-8208		1	DGQU	PHD	72	Purdue	1980
William O. Cullom Professor									
Braswell, Ronald C.	Prof	644-7896		12	KMSX	DBA	73	Fla St	1976
Brown, Stewart L.	Prof	644-9657		23	LNPF	PHD	74	Florida	1974
Celec, Stephen E.	Prof	644-3090		1	CDEJ	PHD	76	N Carol	1977
Coats, Pamela K.	Prof	644-8203	PCOATS	1	BFHZ	PHD	78	Nebraska	1978
Humphrey, David B.	Prof	644-7899		34	PW	PHD	69	Berkeley	1991
The Fannie Wilson Smith Eminent Scholar Chair in Banking									
Nosari, E. Joe	Prof	644-3090		3	P	PHD	72	Kentucky	1970
Associate Dean									
Osteryoung, Jerome S.	Prof	644-7898				PHD	71	Geo St	1974
Peterson, David R.	Prof	644-8200	DPETERS	12	JLNO	PHD	81	N Carol	1981
Peterson, Pamela P.	Prof	644-7895	PPETERS	1	DGZB	PHD	81	N Carol	1981
Turner, Robert F.	Prof	644-7897		23	KPX	PHD	69	Kentucky	1970
Benesh, Gary A.	Assoc	644-8209		12	DMN	PHD	81	Va Tech	1981
Christiansen, William A.	Assoc	644-8202				PHD	83	Utah	1983
Clark, Jeffrey A.	Assoc	644-8211	JCLARK	13	GPRZ	PHD	80	Illinois	1983

Edgeworth, Hubert C.   Assoc   644-8205   PHD 57 Alabama   1957
  Teaching Spring Semesters Only
Scott, Elton   Assoc   644-7894   24 JLNV   DBA 74 Fla St   1975
Broughton, John B.   Asst   644-7876 JBROUGH   2 JLMO   PHD 89 Va Tech   1989
Mikaya, Ivy Locke   Asst   644-7871 ILOCKE   12 FK   ABD   Florida   1990
Perfect, Steven B.   Asst   644-7868 SPERFEC   12 FLN   PHD 91 Texas   1990
Woodbury, Denise   Asst   644-9847   ABD   Utah   1989
--Dept Risk Mgt/Insur & RL E   FAX =   644-4077
Marshall, Robert A.   C-Pr   644-4070   7   #   PHD 68 Penn   1976
  Kathryn Magee Kip Professor of Life Insurance
Corbett, Richard B.   Prof   644-8219   7   #   PHD 74 Geo St   1980
  Independent Life & Accident Insurance Company Professor
Diskin, Barry A.   Prof   644-8212   6   &   PHD 82 Geo St   1980
Lewis, John R.   Prof   644-6554   6   &   PHD 69 Wiscon   1969
Lilly III, Claude C.   Prof   644-6550   7   #   PHD 73 Geo St   1978
Maroney, Patrick F.   Prof   644-8217   7   #   JD   75 Florida   1981
Solomon, E. Ray   Prof   644-7885   7   #   PHD 62 Wiscon   1962
  Midyette Eminent Scholar Chair in Insurance
Boggs II, Glenn H.   Assoc   644-8220   6   &   JD   75 Fla St   1981
Sirmans, G. Stacy   Assoc   644-8214   6   &   PHD 80 Georgia   1988
Sutton-Bell, Nancy S.   Assoc   644-8213   7   #   PHD 85 Georgia   1983
Young, E. Neil   Assoc   644-8222   7   #   JD   65 Miss   1972
Butler, Ann M.   Asst   644-4039   7   #   ABD   Penn   1990
Eastman, Kevin L.   Asst   644-8218   7   #   ABD   Penn   1989
Gatzlaff, Dean H.   Asst   644-5710   6   &   PHD 90 Florida   1990

Fontbonne College
Finance Faculty
Dept of Business & Adm
St. Louis, MO 63105
Area Code (314) Fax
Did Not Respond
  Friedman, William M.   C-Pr   862-3456   PHD   St Louis 1976

Fordham University   BS,MBA
Department of Finance   1939,1982
School of Business Adm
New York, NY 10023
Area Code (212) Fax 765-5573
FORDHULC
Did Not Respond--Taken from College Catalog
  Taylor, Arthur R.   Dean   841-5521   MA   Brown   1985
  Malley, Susan L.   Assoc   889-8985   PHD 80 NYU
  Chatterjee, Sris   Asst   932-4195   PHD   Columbia 1989
  Fishcer, Klaus P.   Asst   841-5487
  Leistikow, Dean A.   Asst   841-5497   PHD   Brown   1987
  Shao, Lawrence P.   Asst   841-5497   PHD   Tenn   1989

Fort Hays State University   BBA,MBA
Dept of Economics & Finance
College of Business
Hays, Kansas 67601-4099
Area Code (913) Fax 628-5398
  McCullick, Jack   Dean   628-5339   Econ   PHD 70 Kan St   1966
  Rickman, Bill D.   C-Pr   628-5805   Econ   PHD 82 Okla St   1972
  Gilson, Preston   Asst   628-4107   MA   82 Sangamon 1988
  Johansen, Thomas C.   Asst   628-5867   PHD 90 Okla St   1989

Fort Lewis College   BA
Department of Finance   1974
School of Business Adm
Durango, Colo 81301-3999
Area Code (303) Fax 247-7310
FLC
  Cave Jr., John E.   Dean   247-7294   Mgt   PHD 67 Minn   1990
  Burn, Karen Sue   C $ 247-7557   PHD
  Fluck, Roland F.   Prof   247-7265   DBA 84 Colorado 1984
  Goff, J. Larry   Prof   247-7406   JD   72 Oklahoma 1985
  Memon, Iqbal A.   Asst   247-7210   DBA 84 Miss St   1988

Fort Valley State College   BBA
Dept of Business Adm & Econ
Sch of Arts & Sciences
Fort Valley, GA 31030
Area Code (912) Fax 825-6394
No full-time Finance faculty
  Jolley Jr., Samuel D.   Dean   825-6454   Math   EDD 74 Indiana   1967
  Wilson, Richard   H $ 825-6715   Econ   PHD 82 Missouri 1991

Francis Marion College   BBA,MBA,BA,BS
Dept of Bus Adm & Economics
School of Business
Florence, SC 29501-0056
Area Code (803) Fax 661-1165

Kinard, Jerry L.	Dean	661-1420		Mgt	DBA	71 Miss St	1989
Palmetto Professor of Business							
McFadyen, James	Prof	661-1433	12		PHD	73 Kentucky	1989
Stanton, Thomas	Prof	661-1210	23		DBA	74 Geo Wash	1983
President of Francis Marion College							
Riley, Neil	Assoc	661-1415	12		PHD	86 Miss	1991

Franklin University   BS
Finance Program
College of Business
Columbus, Ohio 43215-5399
Area Code (614) Fax 221-7723

Proulx, Gena	Dean	341-6211		Cpt	PHD	SUNY-Buf	
Whitney, Howard R.	D-Pr	224-6237	23	FKPR	PHD	71 Oregon	1979
Clark, Susan B.	Prof	224-6237	12	FNTX	MBA	84 Ohio St	1987

Franklin and Marshall Coll   AB
Finance Faculty
Dept of Busines Adm
Lancaster, Penn 17604-3003
Area Code (717) Fax 291-4329
FANDM

Glazer, Alan S.	C-Ac	291-4069		Atg	PHD	78 Penn	1975
Leeds, Eva M.	Asst	291-3895	12	IRT	PHD		1987

Freed Hardeman University
Finance Faculty
Department of Business
Henderson, TN 38340-2399
Area Code (901) Fax

Wilson, Dwayne	Dean	989-6091	12	FIM	PHD	91 Miss	1975
Edmonds, Jim	Asst	989-6096	37	PX	JD	80 Tenn	1983
Assistant to the Dean							

Frostburg State University   BS,BA
Dept of Business Adm
School of Business
Frostburg, MD 21532-1099
Area Code (301) Fax 689-4737

Wilkinson, Steven P.	D-Pr	689-4089			PHD	77 S Illin	1987
Sharma, Anil F.	C-As	689-4297		Mktg	DBA	89 US Intl	1987
Park, John C.	Prof	689-4363	12		PHD	Nebraska	1970
Shin, Hung-Sik	Asst	689-7269	34		PHD	Pitt	1991
Handley, Mark	Inst	689-4259	13		MBA	Ball St	1988
Madan, Rippy	Inst	689-4258	13		MBA	Marshall	1990

Furman University   BA
Finance Faculty
Dept of Econ & Bus Adm
Greenville, SC 29613
Area Code (803) Fax

Stanford, Richard A.	C-Pr	294-3322		Econ	PHD	71 Georgia	1968
Brown, Bruce	Prof	294-3319		PQR	PHD	84 S Carol	1984
Cunningham, Dixon C.	Prof	294-3312		PST	DBA	70 Virginia	1983

Gannon University   BS,MBA
Dept of Economics & Finance
Dahlkemper Sch Bus Adm
Erie, Penn 16541
Area Code (814) Fax

Licata, Betty Jo	Dean	871-7582		PHD	Renssela
Bennett, Charles A.	C-Ac	871-7585		MA	Fordham 1975
Aburachis, Abe	Assoc	871-7584		PHD	73 Pitt
Jay, Nancy	Asst	871-7568			
Wallace, Robert	Asst	871-7565		DBA	Kent St
MBA Director					

40

GMI Engineering & Mgt Inst BS,MS
Finance Faculty
Management Department
Flint, Michigan 48504-4898
Area Code (313) Fax 762-9807
Did Not Respond--Taken from College Catalog
  Kangas, J. Eugene   Dean   762-7966   Mktg PHD 65 Cinn   1990
  Bornholtz, Evan F.   Prof   762-7967   MBA 66 Iowa   1966
  McCarthy, Neil T.   Assoc 762-7970   PHD 77 Renssela 1973

Geneva College BSBA
Finance Faculty
Dept of Econ & Bus Adm
Beaver Falls, PA 15010-3599
Area Code (412) Fax 847-6687
  Mitchell, John M.   C-Ac$ 847-6612   Atg   MBA 62 Pitt   1962
  Lee, Stewart M.   Prof   847-6616   PHD 56 Pitt   1949
  Raver, Daniel H.   Asst   847-6618 12 CDJK   MBA 85 Pitt   1980

George Mason University BS,MBA,MS
Department of Finance 1989,1989
School of Business Adm
Fairfax, Virg 22030-4444
Area Code (703) Fax 764-4692
GMUVAX
  dekluyver, Cornelis A. Dean   993-1807   PHD 74 Case Wes 1991
  Crockett Jr., John H. C-Ac   993-1851   PHD 75 N Carol   1985
  Ferri, Michael G.   Prof   323-2756   PHD 75 N Carol   1987
  Hanweck, Gerald A.   Prof   993-1855   PHD   Wash U   1986
  Crawford, Peggy Joyce Assoc   PHD 79 Purdue   1982
  Hysom, John Leland   Assoc 993-1863   PHD 73 American 1977
  Johnston, Robert Dail Assoc 993-1852   PHD 74 Alabama   1976
  Hogan, Arthur M. B.   Asst   993-1895   PHD 88 Texas   1988
  Sugrue, Timothy F.   Asst   993-1853   PHD 85 Mass   1997
  Yau, Jot K.   Asst   993-1862   PHD 88 Mass   1988
  Erickson, Mary K.   Lect   993-1854   MBA 85 G Mason   1985

George Washington Univ BACCT,MAC,DBA
Department of Finance 1977,1982
Sch of Bus & Public Mgt
Washington, DC 20052
Area Code (202) Fax 994-5014
GWUVM
  Burdetsky, Ben   Dean   994-6380   Mgt   PHD 68 American 1962
  Barnhill, Theodore M. C-Pr   994-6053   PHD 74 Michigan
  Amling, Frederick   Prof   676-6670   PHD 57 Penn
  Handorf, William C.   Prof   994-1414   PHD
  Seale, William E.   Prof   994-3669   PHD 75 Kentucky
  Cohen, Neil   Assoc 994-7276   DBA 75 Virginia
  Klock, Mark S.   Assoc 994-8342   JD   88 Maryland
  Peyser, Paul   Assoc 994-8205   PHD 79 Wiscon
  Sachlis, J. Minor   Assoc 994-6068   DBA 75 Maryland
  Jabbour, George   Asst   994-3879   PHD
  Jenkins, Sarah B.   Asst   994-5911   PHD

Georgetown University BSBA,MBA,MS
Department of Finance 1983,1988
School of Business Adm
Washington, DC 20057
Area Code (202) Fax 687-4031
  Parker, Robert S.   Dean   687-3877   Fnce PHD 69 Wharton   1986
  Droms, William G.   Prof   687-3820   23 MNOS   DBA 75 Geo Wash 1973
  Sweeney, Richard J.   Prof   687-3742   43 VRNJ   PHD 72 Princeto 1989
    Sullivan/Dean Chair in International Business
  Walker, David A.   Prof   687-4582   1 PR   PHD 68 Iowa St   1973
  Brewer, Thomas L.   Assoc 687-3798   4 W   PHD 82 Michigan 1985
  Rivoli, Pietra   Assoc 687-3775   1 V   PHD 84 Florida   1983
  Aggarwal, Reena   Asst   687-3784   12 BEVM   PHD 85 Maryland 1986
  Angel, James G.   Asst   687-3765 ANGELJ 2T MDV PHD 91 Berkeley 1991
  Eberhart, Allan C.   Asst   687-4584   1 ABN   PHD 89 S Carol   1989
  Wilson, Berry K.   Asst   687-3822   1 BPJ   PHD 88 NYU   1988

41

University of Georgia BA,MBA,MA,PHD
Department of Finance 1926,1964
Terry College of Bus
Athens, Georgia 30602
Area Code (404)   Fax 542-3743
UGA

Name	Title	Phone		Field	Degree	Yr	School	Yr
Niemi Jr., Albert W.	Dean	542-8100		Econ	PHD	69	Conn	1968
--Department of Finance								
Verbrugge, James A.	H-Pr	542-3657	3	FHPQ	PHD	68	Kentucky	1968
Hiles Professor of Finance								
Beranek, William	Prof	542-3645	1	EIR	PHD	53	UCLA	1977
C&S Mills Bee Lane Professor								
Fortson, James C.	Prof	542-1186	1	CN	PHD	69	Georgia	1969
Hilliard, Jimmy E.	Prof	542-3646	24	LMNV	PHD	72	Tenn	1972
C. Herman & Mary Virginia Terry Chair of Finance								
Legler, John B.	Prof	542-3634	1	CDE	PHD	67	Purdue	1971
Sinkey Jr., Joseph F.	Prof	542-3649	3	P	PHD	71	Boston C	1976
Georgia Banking Association Professor of Finance								
Blackwell, David W.	Assoc	542-3637	13	GPQ	PHD	86	Tenn	1985
Poulsen, Annette B.	Assoc	542-3654	14	BGTV	PHD	83	Ohio St	1987
Scott, Louis O.	Assoc	542-3650	2	JLN	PHD	82	Virginia	1989
Gregory, Deborah W.	Asst	542-3644	4	UVW	PHD	87	Florida	1988
Jones, Steven L.	Asst	542-3639	2	JMNO	PHD	88	Purdue	1988
Megginson, William L.	Asst	542-3648	14	DGHV	PHD	86	Fla St	1986
Netter, Jeffry M.	Asst	542-3638	13	ABGT	PHD	88	Ohio St	1989
--Dept of Insurance Legal St								
Gustavson, Sandra G.	H-Pr	542-4290			PHD		Illinois	
Floyd, Charles F.	Prof	542-3801	6	&	PHD		N Carol	
Kau, James B.	Prof	542-9110	6	&	PHD		Wash	
C. Herman & Mary Virginia Terry Distinguished Chairholder in Business Adm								
Leverett Jr., E. J.	Prof	542-3780			DBA		Indiana	
Nourse, Hugh O.	Prof	542-3809	6	&	PHD		Chicago	
Shenkel, William M.	Prof	542-2379	6	&	PHD		Wash	
Trieschmann, James S.	Prof	542-3550			DBA		Indiana	
Dudley L. Moore, Jr. Chairholder								
Browne, Mark J.	Asst	542-3799						
Cox, Larry A.	Asst	542-5160			PHD		S Carol	
Hoyt, Robert	Asst	542-3808						

Georgia College BBA,MBA
Dept of Economics & Finance
School of Business
Milledgeville GA 31061
Area Code (912)   Fax 453-5249

Name	Title	Phone		Field	Degree	Yr	School	Yr
Jones, Jo Ann	Dean	453-5497			PHD	77	La Tech	1976
Wolfenbarger, J. Larry	C-Pr	453-4210	3	J	PHD		Tenn	1987
Samprone Jr., Joseph C.	Assoc	453-4210	2		PHD		Cal-SanB	1983
Farr, William Kendrick	Asst	453-4210			PHD		Georgia	1985
Lord, Richard A.	Asst	453-4210	12	CDEF	PHD		Tx-Arlin	1988
Soundararajan, L.	Asst	453-4210	12	CDEF	ABD		Georgia	1988

Georgia Institute Tech BS,MS,PHD
Department of Finance 1969,1969
College of Management
Atlanta, Georgia 30332-0520
Area Code (404)   Fax 894-6030

Name	Title	Phone		Field	Degree	Yr	School	Yr
Parsons, Charles K.	Dean$	894-4921		Mgt	PHD	80	Illinois	1979
Nachman, David C.	H-Pr	894-4906	1	BDOT	PHD	73	Northwes	1973
Smith, Stephen D.	Prof	894-5110	13		PHD	80	Florida	1986
Mills Bee Lane Professor of Banking and Finance; on leave to Geo St Spring 92								
Jayaraman, Narayanan	Asst		1		PHD	86	Pitt	1986
on leave								
Shrikhande, Milind	Asst		24		PHD	91	Penn	1991

Georgia Southern University BBA
Dept of Finance & Economics 1977,1982
School of Business
Statesboro, GA 30460-8151
Area Code (912)   Fax 681-0292

Name	Title	Phone		Field	Degree	Yr	School	Yr
Gooding, Carl W.	Dean	681-5106		Mgt	PHD	76	Georgia	1986
Whitaker, William M.	H-Pr	681-5161	1	SOC	PHD	68	Kentucky	1989
Carnes Jr., Lon Melson	Prof	681-5437	1	I	DBA	72	Geo St	1967
Hodges Jr., J. Frank	Prof	681-5576	3	SA	PHD	73	Georgia	1980
Forbes, Shawn M.	Assoc	681-5161	3	P	PHD	85	Georgia	1991
Budack, John J.	Asst	681-5577	3	SD	MBA	70	Drake	1974
Hatem, John J.	Asst	681-0086	2	MTV	PHD	90	LSU	1990
Stewart, Lewis M.	Asst	681-5985	1	R	MBA	60	Tx Tech	1970
White, John B.	Asst	681-0591	1	CGR	PHD	85	Virginia	1989
Jones, Wesley W.	Inst	681-5161	1	F	MBA	89	Geo So	1990

Georgia Southwestern College
Finance Faculty
Division of Bus Adm
Americus, GA 31709
Area Code (912) Fax
No other Finance Faculty
  Henry, John   Prof   928-1340   Fine   PHD   Alabama

Georgia State University   BA,MP,MB,MT,PHD
Finance, Real Estate & Insur   1960,1963
College of Bus Adm
Atlanta, Georgia 30303-3083
Area Code (404) Fax 651-2804
GSUVM1
  Hogan, John D.   Dean   651-2604   Econ   PHD   52 Syracuse   1991
  --Department of Finance
  Andrews, Victor L.   C-Pr   651-2699   PHD   58 MIT   1968
    Mills Bee Lane Chair of Banking and Finance
  Cochran, John S.   Prof   658-2628   PHD   61 Harvard   1967
  Eisemann, Peter C.   Prof   651-2633   PHD   74 Michigan   1974
  Ewert, David C.   Prof   651-2646   PHD   68 Stanford   1969
  Gay, Gerald D.   Prof   651-2628   PHD   Florida
  Henry, William Ray   Prof   PHD   57 N Carol   1970
  Mehta, Dileep R.   Prof   658-2632   DBA   65 Harvard   1973
  Morin, Roger-Andre   Prof   651-2628   PHD   Penn
  Smith, Stephen D.   Prof   651-2628   PHD   80 Florida   1992
  White, Daniel L.   Prof   PHD   Northwes
  Woods, Donald H.   Prof   651-2631   DBA   65 Harvard   1970
  Owers, James   Assoc   651-2619   PHD   1991
  Swift, Ernest W.   Assoc   651-2833   PHD   Oklahoma
  Thompson II, Donald J.   Assoc   651-2691   DBA   Harvard
  Timme, Stephen G.   Assoc   PHD   Geo St
  Kale, Jayant R.   Asst   651-2798   PHD   Texas
  Noe, Thomas H.   Asst   231-9264   PHD   Texas
  Ramamurtie, Sailesh   Asst   651-2710   PHD   Minn   1990
  Rebello, Michael   Asst   651-2781   PHD   Texas   1990
  --Department of Real Estate
  Brown, Robert K.   C-Pr   6 &   PHD   Pitt
  Cooper, James R.   Prof   6 &   JD   Penn
  Carn, Neil G.   Assoc   6 &   PHD   Geo St
  Vernor, James D.   Assoc   6 &   PHD   Wiscon
  Black, Roy T.   Asst   6 &   PHD   Georgia
  --Dept of Risk Mgt & Insur
  Kellison, Stephen G.   C-Pr   7 #   MS   Nebraska
  Batten, Robert W.   Prof   7 #   MA   Duke
  Black Jr., Kenneth   Prof   7 #   PHD   Penn
    Regents' Prof of Risk Mgt & Ins & Holder of the C.V. Starr Chair of Intl Ins
  Gaunt, Larry D.   Prof   7 #   PHD   Geo St
  Palmer, Bruce Allen   Prof   7 #   PHD   Penn
  Skipper, Harold D.   Prof   7 #   PHD   Penn
  Chollet, Deborah J.   Assoc   7 #   PHD   Syracuse
  Feldhaus, William R.   Assoc   7 #   PHD   Geo St
  Brown, John E.   Asst   7 #   PHD   N Car St
  Dean, Stephen F.   Inst   7 #   MI   Geor St
  Gaunt, Deborah S.   Inst   7 #   MI   Geor St

Gettysburg College   BA
Finance Faculty
Dept of Management
Gettysburg, PA 17325-1486
Area Code (717) Fax 337-6251
  Redding, Rodney J.   C-Pr   337-6654   Atg   PHD   79 Penn St   1989
  Pitts, Robert   Prof   337-6651   PHD   Harvard

Glassboro State College   BS,MBA
Dept of Accounting & Finance
School of Business Adm
Glassboro, NJ 08028-1748
Area Code (609) Fax 863-6553
GLASSBOR
  Fleming, Robert S.   Dean$ 863-6025   EDD   Temple   1990
  Welsh, Carol N.   C-As   863-6343   Atg   MBA   Drexel   1983
  Pritchard, Robert E.   Prof   863-6027   16 CX&   EDD   Penn   1971
  Meric, Gulser   Assoc   863-6409   3 DFPV   PHD   Lehigh   1987

Golden Gate University
Department of Finance
Graduate School of Tax
San Francisco CA 94105-2968
Area Code (415) Fax 495-2671
Did Not Respond; 632 exchange has 213 area code; 648 exchg has 916 area code
  Hawkey, R. Stevenson   Dean 442-7252
  Bohn, Robert F.   C   442-7221

Gonzaga University   BBA,MBA
Dept of Atg, Econ, & Finance   1991,1991
School of Business Adm
Spokane, Wash 99258-0001
Area Code (509) Fax
GONZAGA
  Barnes, Clarence H.   Dean 328-4220   Econ PHD 73 Tenn   1973
  Wiseman, Alexander C. C-Ac 328-4220   Econ PHD 67 Wash   1981
  Carrica, Jean L.   Prof 328-4220   PHD 87 Nebraska 1984
  Shrader, Mark J.   Asst 328-4220   PHD 88 Tx Tech   1988

Goshen College   BA
Dept of Atg, Bus, & Econ
Business
Goshen, Indiana 46526
Area Code (219) Fax 535-7660
  Eby, John   Dean 535-7503   Mgt   PHD   Cornell   1989
  Good, Delmar   C-Pr 535-7452   Mgt   PHD   Illinois 1967
  Ankney, Carolyn   Asst 535-7453   12   MBA   Ball St   1990

Governors State University
Department of Finance
College Bus & Pub Adm
Univ Park, IL 60466-0975
Area Code (312) Fax 534-0054
UIUCVMD
Did Not Respond; 534-5000
  Finkley, Richard H.   Dean$ Ext 2269   Law   LLM 84 DePaul   1979

Grambling State University   BS,MBA
Dept of Accounting & Finance
College of Business
Grambling, LA 71245
Area Code (318) Fax 274-2191
  Dhanani, Karim   Dean   274-2275   Atg   DBA 86 La Tech   1977
  Wilkie Jr., Macil C.   H-Pr   274-3110   Atg   PHD 68 LSU   1985
  Hopusch, Edgar   Assoc 274-2776   1   DBA 70 Colorado 1983

Grand Valley State Univ   MBA,MST
Department of Finance
Seidman Sch Bus & Adm
Allendale, Mich 49401
Area Code (616) Fax 895-3286
  Pitman Glenn   Dean   895-2163   Mktg PHD 77 Penn St 1990
  Dimkoff, Gregg   C-Pr   895-2157   1   G   PHD 78 Mich St 1975
  Bornhofen, John O.   Prof   895-2153   31   R   PHD 67 Illinois 1973
  Griggs, Frank   Assoc 895-2151 GRIGGSF 21   BGLO PHD 90 Ariz St 1990
  Planisek, Sandra   Assoc 895-2151   14   UV   PHD 80 Kent St 1985
  Sprow, James   Asst   895-2149   12   NWM ABD 87 Wash St 1991

Greensboro College   BA,BS
Finance Faculty
Div of Bus Adm & Econ
Greesnboro, NC 27401-1875
Area Code (919) Fax
  Jones Jr., Thomas O. C-Pr   272-7102   DBA 72 Geo Wash 1986
    Fred L. Proctor Sr. Professor
  Branan, N. Carson   Assoc 271-2234   MS   N Car St

Guilford College   BS,BAS
Department of Management
College of Business
Greensboro, NC 27410
Area Code (919) Fax
  Bobko, Peter B.   C-Ac 316-2243   DBA 83 Indiana   1984
  Turner, Betty   Asst 316-2111

45

Gustavus Adolphus College
Finance Faculty
Econ & Management Dept
Saint Peter, MN 56082-9989
Area Code (507) Fax
  Bungum, John   C-Ac 933-7406   13   &   PHD 77 Nebraska   1979
  McRostie, Clair M.   Prof   933-7407   PHD 64 Wiscon   1957

Hampton University   BS
Dept of Accounting & Finance
School of Business
Hampton, Virg 23668
Area Code (804) Fax 727-5048
  Carter, Alphonse H.   Dean 727-5361   Mgt   PHD   Cinn   1988
  Adeyiga, Janet A.   C-Ac 727-5765   Atg   PHD 80 Missouri   1991
  Pyatt, Edward J.   Prof   727-5762   PHD 85 Temple   1984
  Ekpoudom, Edidiong O.   Assoc 727-5360   PHD   Nebraska
  Ananaba, Agu J.   Asst   727-5763   MS   Nrflk St   1987
  Parson, Wayman   Asst   JD   N Car Ce 1988
  Askew, Robert C.   Inst   MSM

Hardin-Simmons University   BBA,BS,MA,MBA
Dept of Atg Fin & Economics
School of Business
Abilene, Texas 79698
Area Code (915) Fax 670-1572
  Presley, Ronald W.,   Dean 670-1356   Econ   PHD 75 Oklahoma 1988
  Curtis, William   H-As 670-1364   ABD 76 Texas   1976
  King, Barry   C-Pr 670-1508   Atg   PHD
  Eberle, Jeanette   Asst   670-1297   PHD 91 Columbia 1990

Harding University   BBA,MS
Finance Faculty
Sch of Business Box 774
Searcy, Arkansas 72143-5590
Area Code (501) Fax
Did Not Respond
  Oliver, George H.   Dean   Mktg   MSA 85 Cen Mich

University of Hartford   BS,MBA,MS
Dept of Insurance & Finance
Barney Sch Bus & P Adm
W Hartford, CT 06117-0395
Area Code (203) Fax 243-4198
HARTFORD
  Lievano, R. J.   Dean   768-4243   PHD   Houston
  Lashgari, Malek   C-Ac   243-4511   PHD   NYU
  Cohn, Richard A.   Prof   243-4809   MBA   Stanford
  Ivry, David A.   Prof   243-4521   7   #   MBA   Wharton
  Kouatly, Youssef I.   Prof   342-4821   7   #   PHD   Penn
  Costello, Ann   Assoc 243-4503   7   #   PHD   Penn
  Brennwald, Heinz H.   Asst   768-4682   PHD   Zurich
  Shalagan, Susan   Asst   768-4690   PHD   Pace
  Wahab, Mahmoud   Asst   768-5119

Harvard University   MBA,DBA,PHD
Department of Finance   1916
Grad School of Bus Adm
Boston, Mass 02163
Area Code (617) Fax 495-6001
HARVBUS1
  McArthur, John H.   Dean   495-6550   Fnce   DBA   Harvard   1959
  Fruhan, William E.   C-Pr   495-6350   DBA 70 Harvard
  Baldwin, Carliss Y.   Prof   495-6673
  Crane, Dwight B.   Prof   495-6679   PHD 65 Car Mel   1969
    Senior Associate Dean
  Donaldson, Gordon   Prof   495-6274   DCS 56 Harvard
  Fenster, Steven R.   VProf 495-6672
  Froot, Ken   VProf 495-6677
  Hayes, III, Samuel L.   Prof   495-6240
  Kester, W. Carl   Prof   495-6351
  Light, Jay O.   Prof   495-6358
    Senior Associate Dean
  Mason, Scott P.   Prof   495-6674
  Merton, Robert C.   Prof   495-6678   PHD 70 MIT

Name	Title	Phone		Field	Degree	Yr	School	Yr
Piper, Thomas R.	Prof	495-6370						
Senior Associate Dean								
Reiling, Henry B.	Prof	495-6531			JD	65	Columbia	
Ruback, Richard	Prof	495-6422						
Sahlman, William A.	Prof	495-6593						
Senior Associate Dean								
Luehrman, Timothy	Assoc	495-6682						
Edleson, Michael	Asst	495-6675						
Gilson, Stuart C.	Asst	495-6243						
Lerner, Joshua	Asst	495-6065						
Meulbroek, Lisa	Asst	495-6992						
Sirri, Erik R.	Asst	495-6856						
Tufano, Peter	Asst	495-6855						
Moore, Ronald W.	Adj	495-6670						

University of Hawaii at Hilo
Div of Bus Adm & Econ
Coll of Arts & Sciences
Hilo, Hawaii 96720-4091
Area Code (808) Fax 933-3685
UHCCVM
BBA

Name	Title	Phone		Field	Degree	Yr	School	Yr
Fullerton, Charles M.	Dean	933-3300			PHD	66	NMIM&T	1966
Stack, Robert T.	H	933-3432			PHD	78	Mich St	1984
Wilson, William E.	Asst	933-3469	12 FLW		PHD	90	Indiana	1989

Univ of Hawaii at Manoa
Dept Financial Econ & Inst
College of Business Adm
Honolulu, Hawaii 96822
Area Code (808) Fax 956-9887
UHCCVM
BBA,MBA
1967,1972

Name	Title	Phone	Code	Field	Degree	Yr	School	Yr
Bess, H. David	Dean	956-8377	CBAODBE	Tran	PHD	67	UCLA	
Dawson, Steven	C-Pr	956-7119	CBAFSDA		PHD	71	Michigan	1971
Freitas, Lewis P.	Prof	956-8736	CBAFLFR		PHD	66	Columbia	1966
Taussig, Russell A.	Prof	956-8752	CBAFRTA		PHD	62	Berkeley	1970
Chua, Lena	Asst	956-8738	CBAFLCH		PHD	91	Ariz St	1991
Constand, R. L.	Asst	956-7679	CBAFRCO		PHD	89	Fla St	1988
Mais, Eric L.	Asst	956-7493	CBAFERA		PHD	88	S Carol	1988
Robbins, Ed	Asst	956-7592	CABFERO		PHD	87	Stanford	1988

Hawaii Pacific University
Finance Faculty
Business
Honolulu, Hawaii 96813
Area Code (808) Fax 544-0243
BA,MBA,MS,MA

Name	Title	Phone		Field	Degree	Yr	School	Yr
Ward, Richard T.	Dean	544-0213		Mgt	EDD	86	S Calif	1986
Hines, D. Spencer	Assoc	544-1115			MBA	82	Pepperdi	1989
Karbens, John	Assoc	544-1156			EDD		Hawaii	
Wee, Warren	Assoc	544-0280			PHD	82	U Wash	1988
Kam, Thomas	Asst	544-1119			MBA		Hawaii	
Kearns, Daniel	Asst	544-1107			MBA		Chaminad	
Curammeng, Mary	Inst	544-1119			MACC		Hawaii	
Sakata, Jenny	Inst	544-1119			MACC		Hawaii	

Heidelberg College
Finance Faculty
Dept of Bus Adm & Econ
Tiffin, Ohio 44883
Area Code (419) Fax 448-2124

Name	Title	Phone		Field	Degree	Yr	School	Yr
Wickham, William T.	C-Pr	448-2280		Mgt	PHD	56	Case Wes	1977
Kirklin, W. Wayne	Assoc	488-2280						

Henderson State University
Dept of Adm Sciences
School of Business
Arkadelphia, AR 71923
Area Code (501) Fax 246-3199

Name	Title	Phone		Field	Degree	Yr	School	Yr
Fisher, Robert C.	Dean	246-5511			PHD	75	Arkansas	1986
Edwards, Robert G.	Prof	246-5511			PHD	68	Arkansas	1969

47

Hillsdale, College
Finance Faculty
Dept of Econ, Bus & Atg
Hillsdale, Mich 49242
Area Code (517) Fax 437-3923
phone 437-7341

VanEaton, Charles	C-Pr	Ext 2412		Econ	PHD	Tulane	1978
Morris, Howard	Asst	Ext 2423			MBA	88 Penn	1991
Parham, Jack	Asst	Ext 2421			MBA	Virginia	1991

Hofstra University BS,MBA,MTA
Banking & Finance Department 1968,1982
School of Business
Hempstead, NY 11550
Area Code (516) Fax 564-4296

Haynes, Ulric	Dean	463-5015						
Papaioannou, George J.	C-Ac	463-5699		13	DGQT	PHD	79 Penn St	1982
Groppelli, Angelico	Prof	463-5083	FINAGG	12	SMOT	PHD	70 NYU	1977
Bishnoi, Rahul	Assoc	463-5697	FINRKB	14	EGHU	PHD	84 Mass	1986
Lyn, Esmeralda	Assoc	463-5700	FINEOL	12	ADGU	PHD	82 CUNY Bar	1982
Nikbakht, Ehsan	Assoc	463-5676		12		PHD	82 Geo Wash	1982
Ahmad, Syed	Asst	463-5348	FINSMA	12	UVWJ	PHD	86 Purdue	1987
Alaganar, V. T.	Asst	463-5701	FINVTA	12	AJMN	PHD	89 Wisc Mil	1989
Huckins, Nancy	Asst	463-5334		1	ADL	MPHI	91 CUNY	1991
Kim, Yu K.	Asst	463-5702	FINYKK	12	ACDZ	PHD	91 Rutgers	1990
Krull, Steven	Asst	463-5329	FINSBK	23	KLMO	PHD	90 CUNY Bar	1986
Rai, Anoop	Asst	463-5356	FINAZR	14	KUVW	PHD	87 Indiana	1988
Ramakrishnan, Kumoli	Asst	463-5141	FINKZR	14	JOPU	PHD	85 Texas	1985
Sankaran, Jayanthi	Asst	463-5784	FINJZS	12	LKOT	ABD	91 Syracuse	1991
Viswanathan, K. G.	Asst	463-5355	FINKGV	14	PV	PHD	91 Tenn	1989
Zychowicz, Edward	Asst	463-5354	FINEJZ	13	ADHS	PHD	89 SUNY Bin	1989
Bales, Gioia	Inst	463-5328		23	KPQT	MBA	86 Hofstra	1990
Witzenburg, James	Inst	463-5328		26		MBA	83 Hofstra	1987

College of the Holy Cross BS
Finance Faculty
Dept of Economics
Worcester, Mass 01610
Area Code (508) Fax 793-2677
Offers No Business Curriculum

Hope College BA,BS
Finance Faculty
Econ & Business Adm
Holland, Mich 49423-3698
Area Code (616) Fax 394-7922
no Finance Faculty available

Heisler, James B.	C-Pr	394-7915		Econ	PHD	75 Nebraska	1981

University of Houston BBA,MBA,MAC,PHD
Department of Finance 1964,1967
College of Business Adm
Houston, Texas 77204-6282
Area Code (713) Fax 749-6800
UHUPVM1

Ivancevich, John M.	Dean	749-2911	MANA6HZ		OrgB	DBA	68 Maryland	1974
Kretlow, William J.	C-Ac	749-1126		12	I	PHD	67 Purdue	1971
Horvitz, Paul M.	Prof			3	QP	PHD	58 MIT	1977
Judge James A. Elkins Professor of Banking and Finance								
Pettit, R. Richardson	Prof			2	N	PHD	69 UCLA	1977
Duncan Professor of Finance								
Hochman, Shalom J.	Assoc	749-1126		12	J	PHD	80 Toronto	1980
Owens, Emiel W.	Assoc			3	R	PHD	56 Ohio St	1971
Rabinovitch, Ramon	Assoc			2	L	PHD	74 New York	1980
Singer, Ronald F.	Assoc	749-6812		12	LO	PHD	75 Mich St	1982
Brinkmann, Emile J.	Asst			31	TQ	PHD	90 Purdue	1991
Easterwood, John C.	Asst			31	T	PHD	85 Texas	1984
Fry, Clifford	Asst			3	R	PHD	72 Tx A&M	1975
He, Jia	Asst					PHD	89 Penn	1991
Kadapakkam, Palani-Rasan	Asst	749-6822		13	D	PHD	85 Michigan	1985
Peevey, Robert M.	Asst			2	J	PHD	91 Tx A&M	1991
Seth, Sarabjeet	Asst	749-6813		1	DG	PHD	57 Michigan	1985
Sisneros, Phillip M.	Asst			12	ACD	PHD	89 Tx Tech	1991
Woodruff, Catherine	Asst			21	H	PHD	84 Texas	1989

48

Univ of Houston-Clear Lake
Department of Finance
Sch of Bus & Public Adm
Houston, Texas 77058-1098
Area Code (713) Fax
UHCL

BA,BS,BA,MS,MBA
1981,1986

Staples, William A.	Dean	283-3100	Mktg	PHD	68	Houston	1979
Weed, Norman L.	C-Pr	283-3208		PHD	68	Tulane	1974
Cloninger, Dale O.	Prof	283-3210		DBA	73	Fla St	1974
Marks, Barry R.	Prof	283-3214		PHD		Purdue	
Hodgin, Robert F.	Assoc	283-3211		DA		No Illin	
Marchesini, Roberto	Assoc	283-3215		PHD		Texas	
Bendeck, Yvette M.	Asst	283-3212		PHD		Ariz St	
McCormack, Joseph Patrick	Asst	283-3217		PHD		Tx A&M	
Perdue, Daniel Grady	Asst	283-3213		PHD		Alabama	

Univ of Houston-Downtown
Finance, Atg & CIS Dept
College of Business
Houston, Texas 77002
Area Code (713) Fax 221-8064

BS

Bizzell, Bobby G.	Dean	221-8179	Mgt	PHD	71	Texas	1989
Leavins, John R.	C-Ac	221-8017	Atg	PHD	87	Houston	1978
Pelaez, Rolando F.	Assoc	221-8577	KPN	PHD		Houston	1986
Penkar, Samuel H.	Assoc			PHD	84	Miss St	1984

Houston Baptist University
Department of Finance
College of Bus & Econ
Houston, Texas 77074-3298
Area Code (713) Fax 995-3408

BS,BA,MA,MBA

Garrison, R. Bruce	Dean	995-3325			PHD	75	N Colo	1983
Driver, Robert E.	C-Ac	995-3286	12	DGLM	PHD	73	Texas	1988
Prince-Chavanne Professor in Christian Business Ethics								
Rush, Robert	Prof		13	CEPQ	PHD		Texas	
Flower, George M.	Asst		12	FHNO	MBA	83	Wiscon	19

Howard University
Dept of Finance & Insurance
School of Business
Washington, DC 20059
Area Code (202) Fax 797-6393

BA
1976,1980

Johnson, Lawrence	Dean$	806-1505		Mktg	PHD	70	Stanford	
Fanara, Philip	C-Pr	806-1593	12	DHMW	PHD	80	Indiana	1985
Ramakomud, Sriprinya	C-Ac	806-1585	14	CFIU	PHD	63	Indiana	1977
Barbee, William	Assoc	806-1594	23	KLTN	PHD	74	Catholic	1975
Lee, Youngho	Assoc	806-1591	24	LVWH	PHD	81	Geo Wash	1986
Cassidy, Steven	Asst	806-1592	1	NDXY	PHD	88	Fla St	1989
Iwarere, Jide	Asst	806-1634	1	JM	PHD	87	Georgia	1986
Ziorklui, Sam	Asst	806-1592	34	RVWF	PHD	86	Howard	1984
Assar, Hamid	Lect	806-1598	13	GP	ABD		Southern	1989
Brent, William H.	Lect	806-1593	1	ABD	ABD		Nova	1990
Gordon-McNeil, Elizabeth	Lect	806-1593	1	UV	MPA	88	Howard	1988

University of Idaho
Department of Business
College of Bus & Econ
Moscow, Idaho 83843
Area Code (208) Fax 885-8939
IDUI1

BS

Dangerfield, Byron	Dean	885-6478		Mgt	PHD	85	U Wash	1981
Byers, C. Randall	C-Ac	885-7341		Mgt	PHD	73	Minn	1972
Geiger, Joseph J.	Prof	885-7154	12	FHMO	EDD	77	Colorado	1988
Narayanaswamy, C. R.	Assoc	885-6854	12	DHJM	PHD	84	Temple	1990
Johnson, Mark S.	Asst	885-6788	12	ADKL	PHD	87	Wash St	1987
Reyes, Mario G.	Asst	885-7146 CBEINVES	13	LSWZ	PHD	87	Arkansas	1985

Idaho State University
Department of Finance
College of Business
Pocatello, Idaho 83209-0009
Area Code (208) Fax 236-4367

BA,MBA
1975,1980

Fannin, William R.	Dean	236-3585	Mgt	PHD	80	Tx A&M	1988
Longmore, Dean R.	C-Pr$			PHD	80	Missouri	1979
Wells, Gary R.	Prof	236-2259		PHD	71	Utah	1972
Hackert, Ann M.	Asst	236-2506		PHD	87	Iowa Sta	1984
Millington, Kent	Asst			MBA		Brig Yg	

University of Illinois
Department of Finance
College Comm & Bus Adm
Champaign, IL 61820
Area Code (217) Fax 244-3118
UIUCVMD

BS,MS,MBA,PHD
1924,1963

Thomas, Howard	Dean$	333-2747	PHD	70	Edinburg	1982
Boyle, Phelim P.	Prof	333-1505	PHD	70	Dublin	1991
Bryan, William R.	Prof	333-2332	PHD	61	Wiscon	1966
Bull, Ivan O.	Prof	333-7953	PHD	87	Illinois	1987
Colwell, Peter F.	Prof	333-1185	PHD	73	Wayne St	1973
Finnerty, Joseph E.	Prof	333-2815	PHD	74	Michigan	1984
Gentry, James A.	Prof	333-7995	PHD	66	Indiana	1966
Lakonishof, Josef	Prof	333-7185	PHD	76	Cornell	1987
Linke, Charles M.	Prof	333-7100	PHD	66	Indiana	1966
Cannaday, Roger E.	Assoc	333-2278	PHD	80	S Carol	1979
D'Arcy, Stephen P.	Assoc	333-0772	PHD	82	Illinois	1981
Lynge, Morgan J.	Assoc	333-7099	PHD	75	Michigan	1974
Park, Hun Y.	Assoc	333-0659	PHD	82	Ohio St	1982
Pennacchi, George G.	Assoc	244-0952	PHD	84	MIT	1990
Ritter, Jay R.	Assoc	333-4522	PHD	81	Chicago	1989
Whitford, David T.	Assoc	333-4638	PHD	80	Georgia	1977
Chan, Louis K. C.	Asst	333-6391	PHD	84	Rochest	1988
Dokko, Yoon	Asst	333-7675	PHD	84	Penn	1984
Flesaker, Bjorn	Asst	244-0490	PHD	90	Berkeley	1990
France, Virginia Grace	Asst	333-0704	PHD	86	Chicago	1988
Quigg, Laura J.	Asst	333-9127	PHD	91	Berkeley	1990
Sarkar, Asani	Asst	333-9128	PHD	89	Penn	1989
MacPhee, William A.	Adj	244-8143	MBA	72	Vanderb	1990
Rushing, Philip J.	Adj	333-4506	PHD	71	Illinois	1975
Sinow, David M.	Adj	333-4506	PHD	82	Illinois	1986

Univ of Illinois at Chicago
Dept of Finance M/C 168
College of Bus Adm 240
Chicago, IL 60680-2451
Area Code (312) Fax 996-0773
UICVM

1971,1981

				DecS				
Abrams, Robert	Dean$	996-2671	2		PHD			
Pliska, Staney R.	Prof		3	R	PHD		Case Wes	
Gregory, Owen K.	Assoc		18	DZN	PHD		Chicago	
Binder, John	Asst		2	K	PHD		Penn	1984
Dermody, Jaime Cuevas	Asst	996-2782	2	J	PHD		Northwes	
Feldman, David	Asst		4	VW	ABD			
Kendall, Coleman S.	Asst		2	L				
Monroe, Margaret	Asst		2	JKL				
Morton, Andrew	Asst		2	L	PHD		Columbia	
Shelan, Catherine	Asst		2	K				
Sung, Jaeyoung	Asst							

Illinois Benedictine College
Department of Finance
College of Business
Lisle, Illinois 60532
Area Code (312) Fax
Did Not Respond

Eber, John	Dean	960-1500

Illinois Institute of Tech
Finance Faculty
Stuart School Business
Chicago, IL 60616
Area Code (312) Fax 567-9360
IITVAX

BBA,MBA,PHD

Hassan, M. Zia	Dean	567-5120		Atg	PHD	65	IIT	1960
Shang, Paul	Asst	567-5104	24	JKLW	PHD	90	Northwes	1989

Illinois State University
Dept of Finance & Law
College of Business
Normal, Illinois 61761-6901
Area Code (309) Fax 438-5510

BS,MS
1981,1986

Jefferson, Robert W.	Dean	438-2251		Mktg	PHD	69	Iowa	1989
McGuire, Charles Robert	C-Pr			BLaw	JD		Ill Urb	
Mills, Dixie L.	Prof	438-8388			PHD	80	Cinn	1980
Naidu, G. N.	Prof	438-2735			PHD	76	Iowa	1976

Scott, William	Prof	438-2827	13	DQS	PHD	71	Houston	1984
Chang, S. J.	Assoc	438-2826	12	DJLW	PHD	86	Iowa	1989
Hagias, James	Assoc	438-2467			PHD	75	Cinn	1986
Kang, Han Bin	Assoc	438-2683			PHD	84	Illinois	1985
Gilberg, Erika	Asst	438-5188	13	DGIA	PHD	86	S Ill	1989
Howe, Thomas S.	Asst	438-5269			PHD	86	Tx Tech	1985
Lockett, Michael	Asst	438-2448			PHD	87	Tx Tech	1985

Illinois Wesleyan University BA,BS
Finance Faculty
Dept of Business Adm
Bloomington, IL 61702-2900
Area Code (309) Fax 556-3411
Did Not Respond
  Gardner, Mona J. Dean 556-3171 23 PHD Cinn 1988
    Adlai H. Rust Professor of Finance/Insurance

Immaculata College
Finance Faculty
Business
Immaculata, Penn 19345-0901
Area Code (215) Fax
Did Not Respond 647-4400

Indiana University BS,MBA,PHD
Department of Finance 1921,1963
School of Business
Bloomington, IN 47405
Area Code (812) Fax 855-8679
IUGOLD
274- phone # have (317) area code & INDYVAX bitnet node

Wentworth, Jack R.	Dean	855-8489		Mktg	DBA	59	Indiana	
Klemkosky, Robert	C-Pr	335-7972			PHD	71	Mich St	
Fred T. Greene Professor of Finance								
Boquist, John A.	Prof	855-8568			PHD	73	Purdue	1973
Hettenhouse, George W.	Prof	855-8924			PHD	70	Purdue	1969
Associate Dean for Research & Operations								
Jennings, Robert H.	Prof	855-8568			PHD	59	Indiana	1967
Simkowitz, Michael A.	Prof	855-8568			PHD	70	NYU	
Thakor, Anjan	Prof	855-8568			PHD	79	Northwes	
Tuttle, Donald L.	Prof	855-8568			PHD	65	N Carol	1970
Bagnoli, Mark	Assoc	855-8568						
Fisher, Jeffrey D.	Assoc	855-7794						
Resnick, Bruce	Assoc	855-8568						
Sartoris, William L.	Assoc	855-8568			PHD	70	Purdue	
Bliss, Robert	Asst	855-8568						
Holden, Craig	Asst	855-8568						
Kamma, Sreenivas	Asst	855-8568			PHD	87	SUNY-Buf	
Lentz, George H.	Asst	274-4121	6	&	MBA	82	Indiana	
Nanisetty, Prasad	Asst	855-3407			PHD	86	Michigan	
Shiekh, Amir	Asst	855-8568			PHD	87	Calif	
Smart, Scott	Asst	855-8568						
Webb, R. Brian	Asst	855-8568						
Brown, David P.	Asst	855-8568			PHD	84	Stanford	

Indiana Univ - Purdue Univ BS
Department of Finance 1987,1987
School of Bus & Mgt Sci
Fort Wayne, IN 46805-1499
Area Code (219) Fax 481-6880
Did Not Respond

Dunlap, James W.	Dean$	481-6461		Fnce	PHD	63	Arkansas	1991
Karna, Adi S.	Prof	481-6495			PHD	68	Ohio St	1984
Crowley, Frederick D.	Asst	481-6464			PHD	84	NYU	1982

Indiana Univ at Kokomo BS
Finance Faculty
Div of Business & Econ
Kokomo, Indiana 46904-9003
Area Code (317) Fax
  Von der Embse, Thomas J. C-Pr 455-9446   Mgt PHD 68 Ohio St 1990

Indiana Univ at South Bend
Finance Faculty
Div of Business & Econ
South Bend, IN 46634
Area Code (219) Fax 237-4599   BS,MBA
                                                                                                               1989,1989
  Joray, Paul A.   Dean   237-4227   Mgt   PHD
  Swanda Jr., John R.   D-Pr   237-4294   Mgt   PHD   68 Illinois   1968
  Mehran, Jamshid   Assoc   237-4216   12   MVO   PHD   83 Arkansas   1986
  Blodgett, Linda L.   Asst   237-4329   14   UVW   PHD   87 Michigan   1987
  Kohli, Raj K.   Asst   237-4144   13   GN   DBA   90 Miss St   1990
  Phelps, Katherine L.   Asst   237-4729   12   R   PHD   88 S Carol   1987

Indiana Univ Northwest
Finance Faculty
Div of Business & Econ
Gary, Indiana 46408
Area Code (219) Fax 980-6579   BS,MBA
                                                                                                               1986,1986
  Vasquez, Marilyn   Dean   980-6633   Law   JD   88 Valparis   1979
  Arshanapalli, Bala G.   Assoc   980-6919   12   PHD   88 N Ill   1991
  Nelson, William B.   Assoc   980-6908   12   CF   PHD   74 Rice   1979

Indiana Univ Southeast
Finance Faculty
Div of Business & Econ
New Albany, IN 47150
Area Code (812) Fax 941-2672   BA,MBA
                                                                                                               1989
  Greckel, Fay E.   Dean$ 941-2363   Econ   PHD   69 Indiana   1967
  Wong, Alan   Assoc   941-2362   23   PV   PHD   85 N Texas   1985

Indiana U of Pennsylvania   BS,MBA,MS
Dept Finance & Legal Studies
College of Business
Indiana, Penn 15705-1087
Area Code (412) Fax 357-5743
  Camp, Robert C.   Dean   357-2520   Econ   PHD   75 Miss   1988
  Ray, Terry T.   C   357-5744
  Boldin, Robert J.   Prof   357-2465
  Duhala, Karen   Assoc   357-5767   12   CDGJ   PHD   87 Penn St   1990
  Walia, Tirlochan S.   Assoc   357-5771
  McCaffrey, Michael A.   Asst   357-5761
  Welker, James E.   Asst   357-7952

Indiana State University   BS
Dept Management & Finance   1980,1983
School of Business
Terre Haute, IN 47809
Area Code (812) Fax 237-7675
INDST
  Ross, Herbert L.   Dean   237-2000   Mktg   PHD   68 Illinois   1967
  Chait, Herschel N.   C-Ac$ 237-2103   Mgt   PHD   Indiana   1981
  Kim, David J.   Prof   237-2117   PHD   Wiscon   1975
  Ferreira, Eurico J.   Assoc   237-2095
  Query, Tim   Assoc   237-2109
  Zietlow, John   Assoc   237-2091   PHD   Memphis   1989
  Warfel, William   237-2122   7   #
  Zaher, Tarek   237-2093

University of Indianapolis   BS,BA,MBA
Finance Faculty
School of Business
Indianapolis, IN 46227-3697
Area Code (317) Fax 788-3275
  Livesay, Robin R.   Dean   788-3370   Mgt   PHD   Ohio St   1978
  Conrad, James   Prof   788-3378   PHD   Purdue   1978
  Foost, James D.   Assoc   788-3378   PHD   S Carol   1982

The College of Insurance   BBA,BS,MBA
Insurance Faculty
101 Murray Street
New York, NY 10007
Area Code (212) Fax
  Hampton, John J.   Prof   17   #   DBA   Geo Wash
  Thrower, Ellen   Prof   7   #   PHD   Geo St
    President of the College

Bilik, Laurie J.	Assoc		7		MA	NYU	
Holliday, Richard	Assoc		7		MA	Insuranc	
Hourigan, Frank E.	Assoc		7	#	EDM	Columbia	
Mintz, Seymour D.	Assoc		12		JD	Toura Lw	
Nelson, Jack M.	Assoc		17	#	PHD	Penn	
Ramanujam, Srinivasa	Assoc		7	#	PHD	Brown	
LaMonica, Judith A.	Asst		7	#	MS	Brooklyn	
Luckstone Jr., Harold C.	Asst		7	#	MA	NYU	
Mead, Ken	Asst		7		MA	Rutgers	
Santoro, Lawrence	Asst		7	#	MA	CUNY	

Iona College
Department of Finance
Hagan School of Bus
New Rochelle, NY 10801-1890
Area Code (914) Fax
Did Not Respond

BBA

O'Donnell, Charles F.	Dean	633-2256		Econ	PHD			1961
Ford, Joseph William	C-Ac				PHD	66	Fordham	1984
Hammerbacher, Irene M.	Prof				PHD	69	NYU	1969
Karcic, Berislav	Prof	633-2263			PHD	66	Columbia	1959
McGrath, Francis J.	Prof				PHD	69	Fordham	1979
Perez, Robert	Assoc				PHD	66	NYU	1982
Pescatrice, Donn	Assoc				PHD	75	Purdue	1983
Crosby, Suzanne M.	Asst				PHD	89	No Ill	1988
Ottaviani, Alberto	Asst				MBA	83	Iona	1982
Shetty, Anand	Asst				PHD	87	Pitt	1988

University of Iowa
Department of Finance
College of Business Adm
Iowa City, Iowa 52242
Area Code (319) Fax 335-1956
UIAMVS

BBA,MA,PHD
1923,1963

Daly, George	Dean	335-0866		Econ	PHD	67	Northwes	1983
Schweser, G. Carl	C-Ac	335-0930			PHD	76	Georgia	1976
Phillips, Susan M.	Prof				PHD	73	LSU	1974
Reinganum, Marc R.	Prof				PHD	79	Chicago	1987
Soldofsky, Robert M.	Emer	335-0945		1991	PHD	54	Wash U	1954
Murray Professor								
Stevenson, Richard A.	Prof	335-0944			PHD	65	Mich St	1967
Vaughan, Emmett J.	Prof				PHD	63	Nebraska	1963
J. E. Partington Professor								
Sa-Aadu, Jarjisu	Assoc				PHD	80	Wiscon	1981
Suchanek, Gerry	Assoc				PHD	77	Northwes	1989
Weller, Paul	Assoc				PHD	81	Essex	1990
Beaglehole, David	Asst				PHD	91	Chicago	1991
Bhattacharya, Utpal	Asst				PHD	90	Columbia	1990
Evans, Jocelyn	Asst				PHD	91	So Carol	1991
Martin, Kenneth J.	Asst	335-0895			PHD	87	Purdue	1987
Oh, Gyutaeg	Asst				PHD	91	Yale	1991
Parameswakan, Sunil	Asst				PHD	91	Duke	1991
Peck, Sarah	Asst				PHD	91	Rochest	1990
Sant, Rajiv	Asst	335-0943			PHD	87	Pitt	1985

Iowa State University
Department of Finance
College of Business Adm
Ames, Iowa 50011-2065
Area Code (515) Fax 294-6060
ISUMVS

BBA,BS,MS,MBA

Shrock, David	Dean	294-6060			Tran	DBA	74	Indiana	1989
Ralston, August	Prof	294-9355				PHD	73	Penn	1982
Stover, Roger	Prof	294-8114		3	P	DBA	75	Virginia	1979
Koppenhaver, Gary D.	Assoc	294-8119	K1.GDK	32	LP	PHD	80	Iowa	1988
Power, Mark L.	Assoc	294-5651				PHD	81	Iowa	1983
Van Auken, Howard E.	Assoc	294-2478	S1.VAN	24	UV	PHD	80	Oklahoma	1980
Carter, Richard B.	Asst	294-9438	K1.RBC	12	ADMQ	PHD	87	Utah	1986
Cowan, Arnold M.	Asst	294-9439	K1.ARC	12	GQUZ	PHD	88	Iowa	1988
Dark, Frederick H.	Asst	294-5922	K1.FHD	1	AGQT	PHD	87	Utah	1988
Singh, Ajai K.	Asst	294-8104	K1.AKS	12	ADQT	PHD	88	Iowa	1987

53

Ithaca College
Department of Finance
School of Business
Ithaca, New York 14850
Area Code (607)   Fax 274-1137
ITHACA
BS

Name	Rank	Phone			Field	Deg	Yr	School	Yr
Long, David K.	Dean	274-3341			Beh	PHD	74	Kent	1973
Zaman, M. Raquib	C-Pr	274-3692		24	QV	PHD	70	Cornell	1974
Bramhandkar, Alka J.	Assoc	274-3065		16	UV	PHD	89	SUNY-Bin	1984
Cheng, Joseph M.	Assoc	274-3067		13		PHD	86	SUNY-Bin	1983
Mulugetta, Abraham	Assoc	274-3950		14	FV	PHD	86	Wiscon	1984
Movassaghi, Hormoz	Asst	274-3956		14	VW	ADB	91	Wiscon	1988
Raad, Elias A.	Asst	274-1318		13	D	PHD	89	Alabama	1989
Ryan, Jr., Robert J.	Asst	274-1551		12	D	PHD	89	Syracuse	1990

Jackson State University
Dept of Econ Fin & Gen Bus
School of Business
Jackson, Miss 39217
Area Code (601)   Fax 968-2358
BS,BBA,MBA

Name	Rank				Field	Deg	Yr	School	Yr
Swinton, David H.	Dean				Econ	PHD	75	Harvard	1987
Hurley, John F.	C-Ac				Econ	PHD		Illinois	1972
Goree, Janace Harvey	Assoc					JD		Illinois	1974
Agahro, Steve B.	Asst					MBA		Jacks St	1984
Denard, Deborah	Asst					TD		Tx So	1988
Petrovich, James	Asst					MBA		W Fla	1984

Jacksonville University
Finance Faculty
College of Business
Jacksonville, FL 32211
Area Code (904)   Fax 744-0101
Phone 744-3950
BS,BA

Name	Rank	Phone			Field	Deg	Yr	School	Yr
Livingston, Felix R.	Dean	744-3950			Econ	PHD	75	Kan St	1989
Broske, Mary S.	Assoc	Ext 4441				PHD	82	Florida	1990
Director MBA Program									
Bush, Robert G.	Asst	Ext 4448				MBA	81	Florida	1981

Jacksonville State Univ
Department of Finance
College Comm & Bus Adm
Jacksonville, AL 36265
Area Code (205)   Fax 782-5312
BS,MBA

Name	Rank	Phone			Field	Deg	Yr	School	Yr
O'Brien, Patrick	Dean	782-5773			Econ	PHD	77	Okla St	1991
Brown, Thomas L.	Prof					PHD		Miss	1974
Fielding, William T.	Prof					PHD		S Carol	1968
Jones, Gail Graham	Prof					JD		Alabama	1973
Trivoli, George W.	Prof					PHD	70	Virginia	1990
Scroggins Jr., William A.	Assoc					DBA		Miss St	1979
Bennett, Doris	Asst					PHD		Alabama	1986
Padgham, Gene L.	Inst					MBA		Jack St	1981
Rhea, Joy L.	Inst	547-0825				MBA		Samford	1984

James Madison University
Dept of Finance & Bus Law
College of Business
Harrisonburg, VA 22807
Area Code (703)   Fax 568-6619
JMUVAX1
BBA,MBA
1982,1985

Name	Rank	Phone	Email		Field	Deg	Yr	School	Yr
Holmes, Robert E.	Dean	568-6341			Mgt	PHD	71	Arkansas	1983
Albert, Joseph D.	H	568-6478	JALBERT	12	LN	PHD	78	Georgia	1985
Damanpour, Faramarz	Prof	568-3079	FDAMANPO	34	PV	PHD	77	Texas	1980
Francfort, Alfred J.	Prof	568-6009	AFRANCFO	12	FH	PHD	72	Pitt	1983
Hobson, Hugh	Prof	568-3076	HOBSON	1	RE	PHD	76	Georgia	1983
Weaver, Carl G.K.	Prof	568-6840	WEAVER	13	EHP	PHD	75	Fla St	1980
Berry, Michael A.	Assoc	568-3019		12	JLO	PHD	82	Ariz St	1990
Marshall, S. Brooks	Assoc	568-3075	SMARSHAL	12	LN	PHD	85	Virginia	1985
Maxwell, Philip H.	Assoc	568-6006	MAXWELL	12	F	PHD	74	Fla St	1974
Frazier, Jennifer	Asst	568-3018	JFRAZIER	1	CE		90	Jms Madi	1991
Ruscher, Charles	Asst	568-3077	CRUSHER	13	PT		89	Jms Madi	1990

54

Jamestown College
Finance Faculty
Bus Adm Dept Box 6009
Jamestown, ND 58401-3401
Area Code (701) Fax 253-2318
Phone 252-3467

Name	Rank	Phone				Degree	Age	School	Year
Klaudt, William J.	C-Ac	Ext 2552				MED	64	Black Hl	1967
Heck, Tom	Assoc	Ext 2573				MS	75	N Dakota	1977

Jersey City State College
Finance Faculty
Dept of Business Adm
Jersey City, NJ 07305-1597
Area Code (201) Fax

Antrosiglio, Victor	D-As	200-3353		Atg	MBA	71	Wharton	1980
Egan, John	C-Ac	200-3353			PHD		NYU	
Ettinger, Marilyn	Asst	200-3353			MBA		NYU	
O'Neil, Barbara	Asst	200-3353			MBA			

John Carroll University   BS,MBA
Dept of Economics & Finance   1988,1988
School of Business
Cleveland, Ohio 44118
Area Code (216) Fax 397-4256
JCUVAX
Department Phone 397-4508

Navratil, Frank J.	Dean	397-4391	NAVRATIL	3	Econ	PHD	74	Notre Dm	1973
Cima, Lawrence R.	C-Ac	397-4534	LRCIMA		Econ	PHD	82	W Virg	1971
Aggarwal, Raj	Prof	397-4584	AGGARWAL	14	COUV	DBA	75	Kent St	1987
Edward J. and Louise E. Mellen Chair Professor									
Coyne, Thomas J.	Prof					PHD		WstrnRes	1981
Schirm, David C.	Assoc	397-4468	SCHIRM	13	PRVW	PHD	83	Penn St	1984
Moore, Scott	Asst	397-4531	MOORE	13	AFPR	PHD	89	Kentucky	1986

John F. Kennedy University   MSBA,MBA,MACDV
Finance Faculty
School of Management
Walnut Creek, CA 94596
Area Code (510) Fax 295-0604
Did Not Respond

Proehl, Rebecca A.	Dean	295-0600		Mgt	PHD		Wright I	1986
Garrett, Suzanne	C	295-0643		Mgt	MBA		JFKenned	1988

University of Kansas   BS,MS,PHD
Finance Faculty   1925,1970
School of Business
Lawrence, Kansas 66045-2003
Area Code (913) Fax 864-5328
UKANVM

Bauman, L. Joseph	Dean	864-7575			MEng	BS	61	Kansas	1990
Beedles, William L.	Prof	864-7530		1	GEN	PHD		Texas	1978
Gaumnitz, Jack E.	Prof	864-7539		23	MNPT	PHD	67	Stanford	1967
Hirschey, Mark	Prof	864-7563		12	AOM	PHD	77	Wiscon	1988
Joy, O. Maurice	Prof	864-7541		1	CFO	PHD	69	N Carol	1969
Joyce C. Hall Distinguished Professor of Business									
Pinches, George E.	Prof	864-7533		1	CDGH	PHD	68	Mich St	1977
Koch, Paul D.	Assoc	864-7503		24	LRTV	PHD		Mich St	1988

Kansas State University   BS,MAC
Department of Finance   1973,1980
College of Business Adm
Manhattan, KS 66506
Area Code (913) Fax 532-7024

Donnelly, David P.	Dean$	532-7190			Atg	PHD	83	Illinois	1981
Fatemi, Ali M.	H-Pr	532-6892	FATEMI	14	DGUV	PHD	79	Okla St	1980
Robert F. Hagans Professor									
Hollinger, Robert D.	Prof	532-7190	HOLINGER	12	AEM	PHD	64	Ks St	1966
Associate Dean									
Richards, Verlyn D.	Prof	532-6892				PHD	66	Illinois	1965
LWOP for current academic year									
Dukas, Stephen P.	Asst	532-6892	SPDUKAS	12	CEJK	PHD	90	Fla St	1990
Ekman, Peter D.	Asst	532-6892	PDEK	24	JLTW	PHD	89	Purdue	1989
Park, Jinwoo	Asst	532-6892	JWP	13	LNTW	PHD	90	Iowa	1990
Tavokkol, Amir	Asst	532-6892	ZAR9KOV8	14	UV	PHD	79	Ks St	1988

Keene State College — BS
Finance Faculty
Dept of Management
Keene, New Hamp 03431-4183
Area Code (603) Fax

Name	Rank	Phone	Field	Degree	Yr	School	Year
Pruchansky, Neal R.	C-Ac	358-2624	Mgt	PHD		Mass	1983
Charkey, Barbara	Asst	358-2621		MS	85	Mass	1986
Hawes, Elizabeth	Asst	358-2618		MBA	84	Mass	1986
Martin, Roger E.	Asst	358-2614		ABD		Vanderb	1985

Kennesaw College — BBA, MBA
Dept of Economics & Finance
School of Business Adm
Marietta, GA 30061-0444
Area Code (404) Fax 423-6539
USCH.USC

Name	Rank	Phone	Field	Degree	Yr	School	Year
Mescon, Timothy S.	Dean	423-6342		PHD	79	Georgia	1990
Curley, Michael D.	C-Pr			PHD	74	Kentucky	1984
Henssler, Gene W.	Prof			PHD	71	Michigan	1986
Miller, Thomas	Prof			DBA	74	Indiana	1989
Anderson, Thomas C.	Assoc	423-6111		PHD	72	Berkeley	1985
Kochman, Ladd M.	Assoc			DBA	80	Kentucky	1988
Park, Jong H.	Assoc	423-6091		PHD	74	Okla St	1988
Ingram, Virginia C.	Asst	423-6379		MA	79	Cen Fla	1986
Pennington, James W.	Asst			ABD		Harvard	1990

Kent State University — BS, MBA, MS, PHD 1964, 1965
Department of Finance
College of Business Adm
Kent, Ohio 44242-0001
Area Code (216) Fax 672-2448
KENTVM

Name	Rank	Phone		Field	Degree	Yr	School	Year
Upton, Charles W.	Dean	672-2772		Econ	PHD	69	Car Mel	1989
Boyd, James W.	C-Ac	672-2426	62	K&	PHD	83	Arkansas	1984
Baker, James C.	Prof	672-2426	34	PV	DBA	66	Indiana	1976
Curcio, Richard J.	Prof	672-2426	1	FV	PHD	73	Penn St	1971
Hexter, J. Lawrence	Prof	672-2426	1	AH	PHD	66	Wiscon	1974
Lee, Wayne Y.	Prof	672-2426	1	H	PHD	73	UCLA	1991
Firestone Chair of Corporate Finance								
Severiens, Jacobus T.	Prof	672-2426	13	PV	PHD	72	Iowa	1983
Twark, Allan J.	Prof	672-2426	2	O	PHD	59	Illinois	1966
Schroath, Frederick W.	Asst	672-2426	47	V#	PHD	87	S Carol	1985

University of Kentucky — BS, MS, PHD 1926, 1963
Department of Finance
College of Bus & Econ
Lexington, KY 40506-0034
Area Code (606) Fax 257-8938
UKCC.UKY

Name	Rank	Phone	Field	Degree	Yr	School	Year
Furst, Richard W.	Dean	257-8939	Fnce	DBA	68	Wash	1981
Chew, I. Keong	C-Ac$	257-5703		PHD	77	S Carol	
Carpenter, Michael D.	Prof	257-1934		PHD	76	Ariz St	
Hackbart, Merl M.	Prof	257-3592		PHD	68	Kans St	
Haywood, Charles F.	Prof	257-7668		PHD	55	Calif	
Mullineaux, Donald J.	C-Pr	257-2890		PHD	71	Boston C	
Du Pont Chair in Banking and Finance							
Johnson, Keith H.	Assoc	257-3865		PHD	70	Illinois	
Officer, Dennis T.	Assoc	257-2882		PHD		Arkansas	1979
McIntosh, Willard	Asst	257-2968		PHD	87	N Tx St	

Kentucky State University — BA
Finance Faculty
School of Business
Frankfort, KY 40601
Area Code (502) Fax

Name	Rank	Phone	Field	Degree	Yr	School	Year
Lee, Dae Sung	Dean	227-6708	Econ	PHD	69	Mass	1969

Lake Superior State Univ — BS
Finance Faculty
Business Administration
Sault S Marie MI 49783-1699
Area Code (906) Fax 635-2193

Name	Rank	Phone	Field	Degree	Yr	School	Year
Harger, Bruce	H-Ac	635-2421	Econ	ABD		Mich St	1967
Gaertner, Robert	Assoc	635-2177		MBA		Notre Dm	1965

Lamar University BBA
Dept of Economics & Finance 1980,1986
College of Business
Beaumont, Texas 77710
Area Code (409) Fax 880-8088
  Sethna, Beheruz N.   Dean   880-8603   Mktg   PHD   76   Columbia   1989
  Hawkins, Charles F.   C-Pr   Econ   PHD   LSU   1966
    Regents' Professor of Economics
  Brost, Melvin   Prof   880-8632   12   JM   PHD   N Tx St   1978
  Cherry, Richard   Prof   880-8631   23   NPO   PHD   Texas   1966
  Moss, Jimmy D.   Assoc   880-8633   12   FJM   PHD   Miss St   1986

Lander College BS
Finance Faculty
School of Business Adm
Greenwood, SC 29649
Area Code (803) Fax 229-8890
  Molander, J. Dale   Dean   229-8232   Mktg   PHD   66   U Wash   1989
  Gray, Otha L.   Prof   229-8302   2   Y   PHD   61   Alabama   1985
  Ziobrowski, Alan   Asst   229-8392   1   F   PHD   90   Kent St   1991

Laredo State University BBA,MBA
Finance Faculty
Grad Sch Intl Trade/BA
Laredo, Texas 78040-9960
Area Code (512) Fax 726-3405
Did Not Respond
  Fatemi, Khosron   Dean   722-8001   Mgt   PHD   S Calif   1982

LaSalle University BS,MBA
Department of Finance
School of Business
Philadelphia, PA 19141
Area Code (215) Fax 951-1892
  Kane, Joseph A.   Dean   951-1040   Econ   PHD   Temple   1961
  Barenbaum, Lester   C-Pr   951-1649   PHD   Rutgers1   196
  Buch, Joshua   Assoc   951-1030   PHD   Penn   1971
  Kelly, James M.   Assoc   951-1044   PHD   Geo St   1978
  Rhoda, Kenneth L.   Assoc   951-1033   PHD   SUNY-Buf   1981
  Schubert, Walter   Assoc   951-1034   PHD   Rutgers   1980
  Toyne, Michael   Asst   951-1481
  Trinidad, Jose   Asst   951-1103   MBA   Rutgers   1988
  Ambrose, Janet   Inst   951-1332
  McNichol, Kathleen   Inst   951-1824

LaSierra University BA,BBA,MBA
Finance Faculty
School of Bus & Mgt
Riverside, CA 92515-8247
Area Code (714) Fax 785-2901
  Yacoub, Ignatius I.   Dean   785-2064   Mgt   PHD   76   Claremon   1984
  McClymont, Trevor L.   Assoc   785-2314   1   CDEF   DBA   88   Int Gr S   1991
  Ford Jr., Robert M.   Asst   785-2316   12   CELM   MBA   86   LomaLind   1986

University of LaVerne
Finance Faculty
School of Bus & Econ
LaVerne, CA 91750
Area Code (714) Fax
Did Not Respond
  Han, H'tein   H   593-3337   PHD   Claremon   1972

Lawrence Technological Univ BSBA,BSIM,MBA
Department of Finance
School of Management
Southfield, Mich 48075-1058
Area Code (313) Fax EXT 3005
LTUVAX
Did Not Respond
  Koch, Douglass V.   Dean   356-0200   PHD   80

Lees-McRae College BS
Finance Faculty
Business
Banner Elk, NC 28604
Area Code (704) Fax 898-4310
  Fuller, Floyd   C   898-8796

Lehigh University BS,MBA,PHD
Department of Finance 1938,1963
College of Bus & Econ
Bethlehem, Penn 18015
Area Code (215) Fax 758-4499
LEHIGH

Barsness, Richard W.	Dean	758-3402	RWBO		Mgt	PHD	63 Minn	1978
Beidleman, Carl R.	C-Pr	758-3435	CRB2	24	EKPV	PHD	68 Penn	1967
DuBois Professor								
Buell, Stephen G.	Assoc	758-3436	SGB2	12	KBEY	PHD	77 Lehigh	1973
Greenleaf, James A.	Assoc	758-3437	JAG2	12	KLMW	PHD	73 New York	1970
Thode, Stephen F.	Assoc	758-4557	SFTO	1	GHIO	DBA	80 Indiana	1982
Kish, Richard J.	Asst	758-4205	URJKISH	12	EGKY	PHD	88 Florida	1988
Schranz, Mary S.	Asst	758-4533	MSOP	23	AGPT	PHD	88 Wash U	1990
Swindle, C. Sloan	Asst	758-4950	CSS4	23	AGPR	PHD	91 Florida	1991
Vasconcellos, Geraldo M.	Asst	758-5347	GMVO	34	UVGP	PHD	86 Illinois	1988

LeMoyne College BS
Finance Faculty
Dept of Business Adm
Syracuse, NY 13214-1399
Area Code (315) Fax 445-4540
LEMOYNE

Carlson, John W.	Dean	445-4310					
Elmer, Wally	C-Pr	445-4433		Mktg	PHD	80 Syracuse	1979
Consler, John E.	Assoc	445-4428	2	JKLM	DBA	78 Colorado	1984
Foote, William	Assoc	445-4682	1	CJ	PHD	84 Fordham	1988
Kim, Chongyoul	Asst	445-4391	3	RU	PHD	82 Rutgers	1986

Lewis & Clark College BS,BA
Finance Faculty
Dept of Bus & Adm Stds
Portland, Oregon 97219
Area Code (503) Fax 768-7379
Did Not Respond–information taken from college catalog
  Schleef, Harold   C-Pr   Fine   PHD   77 Chicago

Liberty University BS,HRM,MBA
Dept of Finance & Accounting
School of Bus & Gov
Lynchburg, Virg 24506-8001
Area Code (804) Fax
Did Not Respond--Taken from College Catalog

Forbus, H. Frank	Dean	582-2480	Mgt	ABD	Nova	1979
Mather, Geoffrey R.	C-Ac	Ext 2465	Atg	MBA	Michigan	1985
Mateer, Robert N.	Assoc	582-2338		MBA	Tulane	1984

Lincoln University
Finance Faculty
Dept of Business & Econ
Jefferson Cty MO 65101
Area Code (314) Fax 681-6074
No Finance Faculty
  Hirst, Richard   Dean   681-5488   PHD   1991

Linfield College
Finance Faculty
Dept of Economics & Bus
McMinnville, OR 97128-6894
Area Code (503) Fax 472-3198

Emery, Richard F.	C-As			Tax	MBA	71 ENMU	1986
Chambers, Scott	Asst		12		PHD	88 Cal-Davi	1990

58

Livingston University — BS
Finance Faculty
College of Bus & Comm
Livingston, AL 35470
Area Code (205) Fax

Name	Title	Phone		Field	Degree		School	Year
Skelly, Gerald U.	Dean	652-9661		Mktg	DBA	78	Fla St	1990
Said, Hassan A.	Asst	652-9661			MBA		Cl Insur	1988

Lock Haven University — BS
Finance Faculty
Dept Cpt Sc, Mgt & Atg
Lock Haven, Penn 17745
Area Code (717) Fax 893-2600

Pacl, Lawrence	C-Ac	893-2328		Atg	ABD		Miss	1987

Long Isl U, Brooklyn Campus — BS,MBA,MS
Department of Finance
Sch Bus, Adm & Info Sci
Brooklyn, NY 11201-5372
Area Code (718) Fax 852-3447

Petrello, George J.	Dean	403-1070			PHD	69	NYU	
Gadgil, Shashi	C-Pr	403-1070		Mktg	PHD		New York	
Markovich, Michael	Prof	403-1070			PHD		Paris	
Paulas, John	Assoc	403-1070			MBA		Columbia	
McMeen, Albert R.	Asst	403-1070			MBA	66	Columbia	

Long Island U.-C.W. Post — BS,MS,MST
Department of Finance
School of Business
Brookville, NY 11548-0570
Area Code (516) Fax 299-2297
Did Not Respond--Taken from College Catalog

Silver, Donald P.	Ac-Dn	299-2364		Atg	MBA	61	Columbia	1984
Ewald, Peter K.	Prof				PHD		NYU	
Levine, Jules M.	Prof				DBA		Indiana	
Avestruz, Fred S.	Assoc				PHD		Philipin	
Farhi, Victor	Assoc				PHD		NYU	
Anderson, Charles	Asst				PHD		SchSoRes	
Hiris, Lorene	Asst				MBA		Lg Isl	
Lupo, Theresa	Inst				MBA		Lg Isl	
Strickland, William A.	Inst				MBA		Lg Isl	

Long Isl Univ-Southampton
Finance Faculty
Sch of Bus & Public Adm
Southampton, NY 11968
Area Code (516) Fax
Did Not Respond

Granitz, Elizabeth	D-As				MA		UCLA	

Longwood College — BS
Finance Faculty
School of Bus & Econ
Farmville, Virg 23901
Area Code (804) Fax 395-2203
Vernet/Internet Address LWCVM1.LWC.EDU;

Farmer, Berkwood	D-Pr	395-2045		Econ	PHD	70	N Car St	1991
Brastow, Ray	C $							
Lavely, Joseph A.	Prof	395-2376	13	BDGT	PHD	70	Iowa	1989
McWee, Wayne	Assoc	395-2367	1	FXYZ	EDD		N Colo	1984
Bacon, Frank	Asst	395-2131	12	ABDE	PHD	90	Va Comm	1990

Loras College — BA
Finance Faculty
Dept Accounting & Bus
Dubuque, Iowa 52004-0178
Area Code (319) Fax 588-7964

Cosgrove, Margaret Mary	C-Ac	588-7765		Atg	MBA	80	Iowa	1987
Upstrom, John P.	Assoc	588-7202	12	CJLM	MBA	82	Ill St	1984
Bernardi, Joseph C.	Asst	588-7267	23	KHSR	MBA	82	Ill St	1986

Louisiana State University BA,MS,PHD
Department of Finance 1931,1963
College of Business Adm
Baton Rouge, LA 70803-6308
Area Code (504) Fax
LSUVM

Name	Rank	Phone	Email		Field	Deg	Age	School	Year
Henry, James B.	Dean	338-3211		1	Fnce	PHD	70	Syracuse	1984
Booth, G. Geoffrey	C-Pr	388-6291	FIBOOT	24	NPVW	PHD	71	Michigan	1986
Union National Life Insurance Co. Endowed Professorship in Insurance									
Crary, David T.	Prof	388-6354		1		PHD	66	Ohio St	1972
Frankfurter, George M.	Prof	388-6369	FIFRAN	12	DGMO	PHD	71	SUNY-Buf	1987
Lloyd F. Collette Endowed Chair of Insurance and Financial Markets									
Slovin, Myron B.	Prof	388-6260	FISLOV	3	PQR	PHD	72	Princeto	1987
Premier Bank/Chuck McCoy Distinguished Professorship in Financial Institution									
Staats, William F.	Prof	388-6285	FISTAA	3	PR	PHD	65	Texas	1971
Louisiana Bankers' Association Chair of Banking									
Glascock, John L.	Assoc	388-6256	FIGLAS	12	CGLN	PHD	84	N Texas	1988
Howe, John S.	Assoc	388-6254	FIHOWE	24	GJTV	PHD	81	Purdue	1988
Lane, William R.	Assoc	388-6367	FILANE	1	AGP	PHD	76	N Carol	1977
Sanger, Gary C.	Assoc	388-6353	FIGSAN	12	JNTZ	PHD	80	Purdue	1985
Boehmer, Ekkehart	Asst	388-6239	FIBOEH	13	GQZA	PHD	91	Georgia	1991
Hughes, William	Asst	388-6255	FIHUGH	2	JNO	PHD	90	Georgia	1990
Leung, Wai-Kin	Asst	388-6320	FILEUN	1	LOV	PHD	86	Texas	1986
Lin, Ji-Chai	Asst	388-6252	FILIN	12	DGJN	PHD	88	Iowa	1988
Mustafa, Chowdhury	Asst	388-6334	FIMUST	24	JLNW	PHD	88	CS-Diego	1988

Louisiana St in Shreveport BS
Dept of Economics & Finance
College of Business
Shreveport, LA 71115-2399
Area Code (318) Fax 797-5156

Name	Rank	Phone			Field	Deg	Age	School	Year
Clark, Lawrence S.	Dean	797-5383			Law	LLM	78	DePaul	1981
Bible, Douglas	Prof	797-5026		6	&	PHD	77	Ohio St	1985
Real Estate Professorship									
Harju, Melvin	Prof	797-5241		34	CNPV	PHD	72	Florida	1977
Hsieh, Chen-Ho		797-5145		14	A&	PHD	90	LSU	1989
Vines, Tim		797-5016		23	PKLN	ABD		Tenn	1989

Louisiana Tech University BS,MBA,MPA,DBA
Dept of Economics & Finance 1955,1979
College of Adm & Bus
Ruston, LA 71272-0046
Area Code (318) Fax

Name	Rank	Phone			Field	Deg	Age	School	Year
Owens, Bob R.	Dean	257-4526			Mgt	PHD	65	Arkansas	1965
Sale III, Tom S.	H-Pr	257-4149		2	O	PHD		LSU	1965
Anderson, Dwight C.	Prof	257-3359		1	CEFI	PHD	74	Alabama	1979
Cross, Mark L.	Assoc	257-3593		12	AJOS	PHD		Missouri	1987
Dickens, Ross N.	Asst	257-3871		3	PQ	DBA		Tenn	1991
Nance, Deana Renee	Asst	257-4464		1	ABDE	PHD		N Texas	1989
Shelor, Roger M.	Asst	257-3593		1	DE	DBA		Kentucky	1989

University of Louisville BS,MBA
Dept of Economics & Finance 1982,1987
School of Business
Louisville, KY 40292
Area Code (502) Fax 588-7557
ULKYVM

Name	Rank	Phone	Email		Field	Deg	Age	School	Year
Taylor, Robert L.	Dean	588-6443	RLTAYL01		Mgt	DBA	72	Indiana	1984
McCabe, James R.	C-Ac	588-7832	JRMCCA01	13	R	PHD	74	Missouri	1973
Brandi, Jay T.	Assoc	588-7832	JTBRAN01	12	BFX	PHD	85	Arizona	1982
Johnson, Hazel J.	Assoc	588-7832	HJJOHN01	13	CNPV	PHD	87	Florida	1990
Monath, Donald R.	Assoc	588-7832	DRMONA01	12	FJO	PHD	69	Florida	1969
Ray, Russ	Assoc	588-7832	JRRAY01	14	VWLO	PHD	78	Michigan	1983
Siegel, Fred W.	Assoc	588-7832	FWSIEG01	1	CIEN	PHD	74	Illinois	1977
Preece, Dianna C.	Asst	588-7832	DCPREE01	13	AD	PHD	90	Kentucky	1989

Loyola College in Maryland BBA,MBA,MSF
Department of Finance 1988,1988
School of Bus & Mgt
Baltimore, MD 21210-2699
Area Code (410) Fax 323-2768
LOYVAX

Name	Rank	Phone			Field	Deg	School	Year
Anton SJ,, Ronald J.	Dean	617-2301			Mgt	PHD	Northwes	1989
Reinhart, Walter J.	C-Ac	617-2818		21	MH	PHD	N Carol	1984
Fletcher, Harold D.	Prof	617-2570		1	H	PHD	Illinois	1981
Martinelli, Patrick A.	Prof	617-2382		1	GH	PHD	Ohio St	

Eddy, Albert R.	Assoc	617-2594	1	HI	PHD		SUNY Buf	1984
Holman Jr., Walter R.	Assoc	617-2841	1	GH	PHD		Syracuse	1982
Merriken III, Harry E.	Assoc	617-2617	3	PQ	PHD		Maryland	1980
Allotey, Traci	Asst	617-5192	7		MA			1992
Cotner, John S.	Asst	617-2473	12	CL	PHD		St Louis	1989
Fairchild, Lisa M.	Asst	617-2681	12	FK	BBA			1991
Hitselberger, Thomas E.	V-As	617-2616	4		MA		Geo Wash	1986
Swanson, H. Gene	Asst	617-2524	2	N	PHD			1991

Loyola University of Chicago BBA,MBA
Department of Finance 1955,1980
School of Business Adm
Chicago, IL 60611
Area Code (312) Fax 915-6619
LUCCPUA

Meyer, Donald G.	Dean	915-6113		Mktg	PHD	65	Northwes	1961
Tarhan, Vefa	C-Pr	915-7073	14	GPRV	PHD		CA-SanBr	1978
Kaufman, George G.	Prof	915-7075	3	PRT	PHD		Iowa	1981
John Smith Professor								
Lash, Nicholas A.	Prof	915-7074	3	PR	PHD		Wayne St	1980
Urrutia, Jorge L.	Assoc	915-7072	24	LVW#	PHD		Texas	1985
Hoque, Monzurul	Asst	915-7067	12	FIL	PHD		Illinois	1988
Lee, Suk H.	Asst	915-7071	14	DEUV	PHD		So Calif	1988
Mishra, Chandra	Asst	915-7069	13	AGP	PHD		Houston	1990
Sung, Hyun Mo	Asst	915-7065	12	GLZ	PHD		Illinois	1990

Loyola Univ-New Orleans BBA
Department of Finance 1950,1974
College of Business Adm
New Orleans, LA 70118
Area Code (504) Fax 865-3496

New, J. Randolph	Dean	865-3547		Mgt	PHD	78	Ariz St	1989
Hood, Jerry M.	Prof	482-1682	13	P	PHD	71	Tx Tech	1989
Sibley, Albin M.	Prof	865-3839	14	CUW	PHD	72	S Carol	1979
Christner, Ronald	Assoc	835-7168	26	&X	PHD	71	Minn	1974
Wood, J. Stuart	Assoc	866-7200	12	CD	PHD	78	NYU	1984

Loyola Marymount Univ BS,MBA
Dept Finance & Cpt Info Sys 1981,1987
College of Business Adm
Los Angeles, CA 90045
Area Code (310) Fax 338-5187

Wholihan, John T.	Dean	338-7504		Mgt	PHD	73	American	1984
Katz, Rachelle	C-Pr	338-4526	13		PHD	80	Stanford	1976
Byrne, Martin	Prof	338-1524	14		PHD	59	UCLA	1968
Higgins, Charles J.	Assoc	338-8734	12		PHD	85	Claremon	1982
Manning, Christopher A.	Assoc	338-3113	16		PHD	83	UCLA	1986
Tai, Lawrence	Assoc			14	PHD	83	Geo St	1990

Luther College BA
Finance Faculty
Dept of Econ & Business
Decorah, Iowa 52101-1045
Area Code (319) Fax 387-1657

Kaschins, Edward A.	H-Pr	387-1130	Econ	PHD	73	Iowa	1961
Berg, Warren	Prof	387-1279		PHD	60	Iowa	1948
Evensen, Donald	Prof	387-1189		MBA	48	Northwes	1950
Lund, Mark	Prof	387-1275		PHD	75	Iowa St	1969
Nelson, John	Prof	387-1568		MBA	65	Iowa	1958
Ryksund, Conrod	Prof	387-1274		PHD	70	Chicago	1954
Heltne, Mari	Assoc	387-1338		PHD	88	Arizona	1968
Leake, Richard	Assoc	387-1812		ABD	75	Ohio	
Rudolf, Uwe	Assoc	387-1295		MBA	78	S Calif	1968
Christianson, Charles	Asst	387-1187		MBA	75	S Dakota	1974
Gomersall, Nicholas	Asst	387-1133		PHD	90	Cornell	1967
Moorcroft, Christian	Asst	387-1035		MBA	85	Wi-LaCro	1966
Nelson, Ramona	Asst	387-1569		MBT	85	Minn	1975
Schweizer, Timothy	Asst	387-1131		PHD	88	Arkansas	1980

Lycoming College BA
Finance Faculty
Dept of Business Adm
Williamsport, PA 17701
Area Code (717) Fax

Weaver, H. Bruce	C-Pr	321-4186	Fine	JD	

Lynchburg College
Department of Finance
School of Business
Lynchburg, VA 24501-3199
Area Code (804) Fax
  Savoian, Roy T.   Dean   522-8256   Econ   PHD   75   S Calif   1984
  Abouzeid, Kamal M.   Prof   522-8257   PHD   Texas   1978

Lyndon State College   BS,BA,MS
Finance Faculty
College of Business
Lyndonville, VT 05851
Area Code (802) Fax 626-9770
  Myers, Rex   Dean   626-9371   Hst   PHD   72   Montana   1991
  Mitchell, Linda M.   C-As   626-9371   Mktg   MBA   Columbia   1989
  Siegel, Rachel   Asst   626-9371   MPPM   Yale   1990

University of Maine   BS,MBA
Finance Faculty   1974,1982
College of Business Adm
Orono, Maine 04469-0158
Area Code (207) Fax 581-1930
  Devino, W. Stanley   Dean   581-1968   Econ   PHD   59   Mich St   1960
  Ford, John   Prof   581-1990   PHD   77   Harvard   1981
  Strong, Robert   Assoc   581-1986   PHD   83   Penn St   1983
  McConnell, Dennis   Asst   581-1988   PHD   82   Maryland

Manhattan College   BS,MBA
Department of Finance
School of Business
Riverdale, NY 10471
Area Code (212) Fax 884-0255
MANVAX
Did Not Respond
  Suarez, James   Dean   920-0440   PHD   72   Columbia   1984
  Akcay, Osman   920-0469
  Elias, Carlos   920-0462

Mankato State University   BS,MBA
Dept Finance, Insur & Rl Est
College of Business
Mankato, Minn 56001-8400
Area Code (507) Fax 389-5497
  Abouelenein, Gaber A.   Dean   389-5420   PHD   69   Illinois   1968
  Okleshen, Henry N.   C-Pr   389-1319   PHD   Arkansas   1980
  Huntley, Kennes C.   Prof   PHD   Iowa   1967
  Lee, Chan H.   Prof   389-2076   PHD   No Illin   1982
  Moosally, Joseph G.   Prof   PHD   Iowa   1969
  Severns, Roger   Prof   PHD   Nebraska   1987
  Swanson, Richard N.   Prof   EDD   Florida   1968
  Thiewes, Harold   Prof   PHD   Iowa   1984
  Wilcox, Steve   Assoc   PHD   Nebraska   1991
  Jernberg, Mary Jean   Inst   MBA   Mankato   1990

Marian College
Accounting & Finance Dept
Business
Indianapolis, IN 46222-1997
Area Code (317) Fax 929-0263
  Akin, Timothy R.   C-Pr   929-0221   Atg   MBA   73   Xavier   1975
  Huston, Kevin   Asst   929-0221   JD   Duke   1989

Marietta College   BA
Department of Finance
College of Business
Marietta, Ohio 45750-3031
Area Code (614) Fax 374-4763
No Finance Faculty
  Osborne, Edward H.   C-Pr   374-4632   Atg   MBA   65   Indiana   1971

Marist College — BS,MBA,MPA
Finance Faculty
Division of Mgt Studies
Poughkeepsie, NY 12601-1387
Area Code (914) Fax 575-3225

Name	Rank	Phone		Field	Deg	Yr	School	Yr
Kelly, John C.	Dean	575-3225			PHD		Boston C	1962
Kapoor, Ashok K.	Asst	575-3000	12 FR		ABD			1988
Kobos, Chester	Asst	575-3000	12 J		PHD		Fordham	1982

Marquette University — BS,MBA
Department of Finance — 1928,1963
Straz College of Bus Ad
Milwaukee, WI 53233
Area Code (414) Fax 288-1660
MUCSD

Name	Rank	Phone	Field	Deg	Yr	School	Yr
Bausch, Thomas A.	Dean	288-7141	Econ	DBA	69	Indiana	1978
Stoffels, John D.	C $	288-6200		PHD	69	Mich St	1980
Seifert, James A.	Assoc	288-1456		PHD		Wiscon	1976
Kutner, George W.	Asst	288-1448		PHD		Northwes	1985
McBain, Michael L.	Asst	288-1455		PHD		Mass	1985
Porte, David	Asst	288-1461		PHD		W Ontar	1988
Torregrosa, Paul	Asst	288-1464		PHD		Va Tech	1988
Weaver, Daniel	Asst	288-1462		PHD		Rutgers	1990

Mars Hill College
Finance Faculty
Div of Bus Adm & Econ
Mars Hill, NC 28754
Area Code (704) Fax

Name	Rank	Phone		Field	Deg	Yr	School	Yr
Grose, Jack N.	C-Pr	689-1179		Mgt	DBA	74	Miss St	1964
Narron, Charlie C.	Prof	689-1129	12		MA	58	E Carol	1958

Marshall University — BBA,BS,MBA,MS
Dept of Finance & Bus Law
College of Business
Huntington, WV 25755-2320
Area Code (304) Fax 696-6565

Name	Rank	Phone	Field	Deg	Yr	School	Yr
Alexander, Robert P.	Dean	696-2314	Mgt	PHD	69	Ohio U	1969
Singh, Dayal	C-Pr	696-2667		DBA	65	Indiana	
Holdren, Don P.	Prof	696-2668		PHD	79	Nebraska	
Brozik, Dallas	Assoc	696-2663		PHD	84	S Carol	

University of Mary — BA,BS
Finance Faculty
Division of Business
Bismarck, ND 58501-9652
Area Code (701) Fax
Phone 255-7500

Name	Rank	Phone	Field	Deg	Yr	School	Yr
Mielke, Carol A.	C-Ac	Ext 391	Atg	MS	79	N Dakota	1981
Brown, Larry	Asst	Ext 434		MBA	82	Temple	1982

Mary Baldwin College — BA
Finance Faculty
Business Administration
Staunton, Virg 24401
Area Code (703) Fax

Name	Rank	Phone		Field	Deg	Yr	School	Yr
Ewing, Janet S.	H-Ac	887-7059	12 ISY		ABD		Va Comm	1977
Douglas, Patricia C.	Asst	887-7274	12 CFJO		MS	90	Virginia	1990

Univ of Mary Hardin-Baylor — BBA
Finance Faculty
School of Business
Belton, Texas 76513-2599
Area Code (817) Fax 939-4535

Name	Rank	Phone		Field	Deg	Yr	School	Yr
Walther, George H.	Dean$	939-4644		Mgt	PHD	73	Texas	1985
Fabritius, Michael M.	Prof	939-4655	12	FPY	PHD	87	Texas	1987
Horton, Howard	Asst	939-4647	3	X	MBA	80	SW Tx St	1981

Mary Washington College — BS
Finance Faculty
Dept of Business Adm
FredericksburgVA 22401-5358
Area Code (703) Fax 899-4373

Name	Rank	Phone	Field	Deg	Yr	School	Yr
Evans, Gano S.	C-Pr	899-4099		PHD	69	U Wash	
Scull, Robert W.	Assoc	899-4603		PHD		Mass	1987

University of Maryland BS,MBA,PHD
Department of Finance 1940,1964
College of Bus & Mgt
College Park, MD 20742
Area Code (301) Fax 314-9157
UMDD

Lamone, Rudolph P.	Dean	405-2308		Mgt	PHD	66 N Carol	1966
Kolodny, Richard	C-Pr	405-2257			PHD	72 New York	
Bradford, William	Prof	405-2306			PHD	72 Ohio St	
Chen, Son-Nan	Prof	405-2244			PHD	75 Georgia	
Haslem, John A.	Prof	454-2236			PHD	67 N Carol	
Senbet, Lemma W.	Prof	405-2242			PHD	75 SUNY Buf	
William Mayer Professor of Finance							
Chang, Eric C.	Assoc	405-2246			PHD	82 Purdue	
Eun, Cheol S.	Assoc	405-2261			PHD	81 New York	
on leave to Pennsylvania							
Madan, Dilip	Asst	405-2127			PHD	75 Maryland	
Pichler, Pegaret	Asst	405-2219			PHD	90 Stanford	
Unal, Haluk	Asst	405-2256			PHD	85 Ohio St	

Marymount University BBA,MBA
Dept of Business & Economics
School of Business Adm
Arlington, VA 22207-4299
Area Code (703) Fax 284-1653

Sigethy, Robert	Dean	284-1652		Mgt	PHD	American	1983
Hassanein, Saad	Prof	284-1652	1	F	PHD	Catholic	1988
Kaitz, Edward M.	Prof	284-1652	1	DE	PHD	Harvard	
Miller, Charles W.	Assoc	284-1652	2	M	MBA	Geo Wash	

Marywood College BS,MBA,MS/MIS
Department of Finance
Bus & Mgr Science Prog
Scranton, Penn 18509-1598
Area Code (717) Fax 348-1817

Adams, David C.	C			Mgt	PHD	Syracuse	
Dagher, Samir P.	Prof	348-6274	24		PHD	74 Ohio St	1989

University of Massachusetts BBA,MBA,PHD
Dept of Gen Bus & Finance 1958,1963
School of Management
Amherst, Mass 01003
Area Code (413) Fax 545-3858
UMASS

O'Brien, Thomas	Dean	545-5581			PHD	69 Cornell	1987
Moore, Craig L.	C-Pr	545-5633			PHD	72 Syrcuse	
Barges, Alexander	Prof	545-5623	1	EG	PHD	62 Northwes	
Branch, Ben S.	Prof	545-5690	21	MB	PHD	70 Michigan	1975
Owers, James E.	Prof	545-5637	1	GB	PHD	82 Ohio St	
Schneeweis, Thomas	Prof	545-5641	24	LMB	PHD	77 Iowa	
Lacey, Nelson J.	Assoc	545-5630	37	P	PHD	85 Penn St	
Milonas, Nikos	Assoc	545-5632	2	LK	PHD	84 Baruch	
Kazemi, Hossein B.	Asst	545-5629	2	JKO	PHD	85 Michigan	
Sinha, Sidharth	Asst	545-5642	1	DE	PHD	87 Berkeley	
Verma, Avinash Kumar	Asst	545-5643	23	JPR	PHD	88 Berkeley	

U Massachusetts at Boston BS,MBA
Department of Finance
College of Management
Boston, Mass 02125-3393
Area Code (617) Fax 265-7173

Shimshak, Daniel	Dean$	287-7700		MgtS	PHD	76 CUNY	1978
Chugh, Lal C.	C-Ac	287-7671	13	DEPV	PHD	70 Harvard	1985
Franko, Lawrence	Prof	287-7676	4	UW	DBA	69 Harvard	1986
Bandopadhyaya, Arindam	Asst	287-7854	14	UV	PHD	91 Indiana	1991
Ehsani, Hassan B.	Asst	287-7685	12	LN	PHD	87 Houston	1991
Jaggia, Priscilla	Asst	287-7687	1	DG	PHD	90 Indiana	1990
Kim, Chan-Wung	Asst	287-7672	12	LO	PHD	91 Iowa	1991
Thosar, Satish B.	Asst	287-7686	12	CGO	PHD	89 Indiana	1989

U Massachusetts-Dartmouth SB,MBA
Dept of Accounting & Finance
College of Bus & Indus
No Dartmouth, MA 02747
Area Code (508) Fax 999-8776

Jackson, Raymond	C-Pr	999-8422	12	CM	PHD	67 Boston U	1973
Gart, Alan	Prof	999-8445	13	FP	PHD	67 Penn	1989
Maskooki, Kooros	Assoc	999-8759	14	HN	PHD	77 Nebraska	1981

U of Massachusetts at Lowell　　　　　　　　　　　　　　　　　　　　　　　BS,MBA
Dept Management & Finance　　　　　　　　　　　　　　　　　　　　　　　1987,1987
College of Management
Lowell, Mass 01854
Area Code (508) Fax 934-3011
Phone 934-2801

Kahalas, Harvey	Dean	Ext 2845		Mgt	PHD	71	Mass	
Freedman, Stuart	C-Pr	Ext 2776		Mgt	PHD	77	Cornell	
Downey, Gerald	Prof	Ext 2805	32	J	PHD	71	Boston C	
Pullara, Santo J.	Prof	Ext 2808	31	H	PHD	62	Syracuse	
Puri, Yash	Prof	Ext 2807	41	UV	DBA	77	Indiana	
Carlson, Severin C.	Assoc	Ext 2832	1	G	DBA	79	Indiana	
Koundinya, Raina	Assoc	Ext 2806	41	PQ	PHD	77	NYU	
Awerbuch, Shimon	Asst	Ext 2804	1	H	PHD	75	RPI	
Echevarria, David	Asst	Ext 2803	21	L	PHD	88	Mass	

Massachusetts Inst of Tech　　　　　　　　　　　　　　　　　　　　　　　　MS,PHD
Finance Faculty　　　　　　　　　　　　　　　　　　　　　　　　　　　　　　1957,1963
Sloan School of Mgt
Cambridge, Mass 02139
Area Code (617) Fax 258-6855
Did Not Respond--1991 Listing; Faculty Phone 253-2659

Thurow, Lester C.	Dean	253-2932		Econ	PHD		Harvard	1964
Beja, Avraham	VProf				PHD			
Cox, John Carrington	Prof				PHD			
Normura Professor of Finance								
Fabozzi, Frank J.	VProf	253-3439			PHD			
Huang, Chi-fu	Prof				PHD			
Myers, Stewart Clay	Prof	253-6696			PHD	67	Stanford	1966
Gordon Y. Billard Professor of Finance								
Pindyck, Robert Stephen	Prof				PHD	71	MIT	1971
Mitsubishi Bank Professor of Finance								
Asquith, Paul	Assoc				PHD			
Lo, Andrew W.	Assoc				PHD			
Mello, Antonio S.	VAsst				PHD			
Parsons, John Emery	Asst				PHD			
Scharfstein, David	Asst				PHD			
Vila, Jean-Luc	Asst				PHD	85	Paris	

McNeese State University　　　　　　　　　　　　　　　　　　　　　　　　　　　BS
Dept of Economics & Finance　　　　　　　　　　　　　　　　　　　　　　　1989,1989
College of Business
Lake Charles, LA 70609-1415
Area Code (318) Fax 475-5010

Mondy, R. Wayne	Dean	475-5514			DBA	74	La Tech	1986
Caples, Stephen	Assoc	475-5553	1		PHD		UTA	
Patin Jr., Roy P.	Assoc	475-5560	1	LS	DBA	80	Miss St	1980
Mishra, Banamber	Asst	475-5559	1		PHD		Alabama	

Memphis State University　　　　　　　　　　　　　　　　　　　　　BBA,MBA,MS,PHD
Dept Finance, Insur & Real E　　　　　　　　　　　　　　　　　　　　　　1970,1971
Fogelman Col Bus & Econ
Memphis, Tenn 38152
Area Code (901) Fax 678-4282
MEMSTVX1

Baskin, Otis W.	Dean	678-2432		Mgt	PHD	75	Texas	1991
Pertl, Mars	C-Ac	678-2436	7	#	PHD	74	Iowa	1982
Bond, M. E.	Prof	678-4203			PHD	67	Iowa	1979
Greer, Gaylon E.	Prof	678-4643			PHD	74	Colorado	1986
Fogelman Professor of Real Estate								
McInish, Thomas H.	Prof	678-4662			PHD	78	Pitt	1982
Wunderlich Chair of Excellence in Finance								
Pyun, C. S.	Prof	678-4645			PHD	66	Georgia	1970
Tankersley, Irvin Lee	Prof	678-4635			JD	73	Tulane	1973
Wood, Robert A.	Prof	678-2676			PHD	78	Pitt	1990
Distinguished Professor of Finance								
Boyd, Donald A.	Assoc	678-2787			PHD	72	Miss	1957
Chu, Chen-Chin	Assoc	678-4643			PHD	84	Illinois	1984
Chung, Kee-Ho	Assoc	678-4642			PHD	86	Cinn	1988
Ferris, Stephen P.	Assoc	678-4936			PHD	84	Pitt	1991
visiting from Virginia Tech								
Phillips, William	Assoc	678-4637			CLU	78	Memphis	1965
Sruggs Jr., Leslie S.	Assoc	678-3567			PHD	74	Vanderbt	1969
Kolbe, Phillip T.	Asst	678-4090	6	&	PHD	88	Arizona	1989
Means Jr., Dwight B.	Asst	678-4103			PHD	84	Pitt	1989
Moore, Larry	Asst	678-4624			JD	76	Wash U	1967
Puelz, Robert	Asst	678-3657	7	#	PHD	90	Georgia	1990
Schwartz, Leonard	Asst	678-2454			JD	79	Wayne St	1986
Theerathorn, Pochara	Asst	678-2657			PHD	83	Northwes	1989
Patton, Charles H.	Adj				JD	75	Memph St	1986

Mercer University-Atlanta   BBA,MBA,MSHCA
Finance Faculty
Stetson Sch of Bus & Ec
Atlanta, Georgia 30341
Area Code (404) Fax 986-3337
 Beigeleisen, Alan   Dean   986-3162   PHD   Geo St   1982
 Schlenker, Austin   D-Ac   986-3169   PHD   Cal-Coas   1984
 Ghannadian, Frank   Asst   986-3233   PHD   Geo St   1988
 Miller, John R.   Asst   986-3166   MBA   Geo St   1975

Mercer University-Macon   BBA,MBA
Finance Faculty
Stetson Sch Bus & Econ
Macon, Georgia 31207-0001
Area Code (912) Fax 752-2635
 Joiner, W. Carl   Dean   752-2832   Mgt   PHD 78 Alabama   1974
 Hood, William   Asst   MBA 84 N Carol   1984
 Luckie Jr., William Vernon Asst   MBA 68 Miss   1976

Meredith College   BS,MBA
Finance Faculty
Dept of Business & Econ
Raleigh, N Carol 27607-5298
Area Code (919) Fax 829-2828
 Spanton, Donald L.   H-Pr   829-8470   Mgt   PHD   American   1983
 Johnson, James R.   Assoc   829-8487   12 CM   PHD   Duke   1979
 Wakeman, Douglas J.   Assoc   829-8482   12 GN   PHD   N Carol   1984
 Spencer, Theresa   Asst   829-8483   3 PJ   PHD   N Car St   1985

Merrimack College   BS,BA
Dept of Accounting & Finance
Division Business Adm
North Andover MA 01845
Area Code (617) Fax 831-5013
 Lonardo, Vincent J.   Dean   837-5000   Atg   MBA 50 Boston U   1969
 Lee, Philip H.   Assoc   837-5000   MBA 57 Syracuse
 Andrews, Frank E.   Asst   837-5000   MBA   Babson C
 Quinn, Frances A.   Asst   837-5000   MS   Bentley

Mesa State College   BBA
Finance Faculty
School of Business
Grand Junctio CO 81502
Area Code (303) Fax 248-1903
 Mazzeno, Lauarence W.   Dean$ 248-1213
 Ralser, Tom   Asst   248-1731   12 FM

Metropolitan St Col Denver   BS
Department of Finance
School of Business
Denver, Colorado 80217
Area Code (303) Fax 556-4429
 Sullivan, Claire F.   Dean   556-3245   Mktg   PHD 73 N Texas   1989
 Boswell, Jerry   Prof   556-3006   12 DEMY   DBA 69 Indiana   1986
 DyReyes, Felix   Prof   556-3007   34 RV   PHD 74 Iowa St   1977
 Foster, Phillip   Assoc   556-3126   6 &   PHD 68 Oregon   1976
 Griffin, C. Ramon   Assoc   556-3747   65 X&   PHD 79 Geo St   1986
 Huggins, Kenneth M.   Assoc   556-8312   12 DFMS   PHD 73 Tx Tech   1988
 Choi, Ducksang   Asst   556-4687   12 DETV   DBA 91 Miss St   1990

University of Miami   BBA,MBA,PHD
Department of Finance   1957,1963
School of Business Adm
Coral Gables, FL 33124-6552
Area Code (305) Fax 284-4800
UMIAMIVM
 Fedor, Kenneth J.   Dean   284-4643   Mgt   PHD 66 Tenn   1990
 Chiang, Raymond   C-Pr   284-4397   1 LVT&   PHD 79 Penn   1985
 Goldberg, Lawrence G   Prof   284-4362 C70CLP9F 31 PAVQ PHD 72 Chicago   1981
 Heuson, William G.   Prof   284-4362   34 V   PHD 54 St Louis   1948
 Kolb, Robert W.   Prof   284-4362   2 LMKV   PHD 74 N Carol   1983
 Barrett, W. Brian   Assoc   284-4362 WBARRETT 12 KML   PHD 83 Ga Tech   1983
 Bruce, Thor W.   Assoc   284-4362   12 EJMO   PHD 71 Wash U   1968
 Heuson, Andrea J.   Assoc   284-4362 GR4GHC9F 61 SKPT   PHD 82 Illinois   1982

Landsea, William F.	Assoc	284-4362		61	&F	PHD	66 Illinois	1965
Ledford, Manfred H.	Assoc	284-4362		13	#	PHD	73 Kentucky	1973
Sawyer, James A.	Assoc	284-4362		12	O	PHD	64 Illinois	1964
Gosnell, Thomas F.	Asst	284-4362	TGOSNELL	12	BT&V	PHD	87 Va Tech	1987
Rodriguez, Ricardo J. bitnode @UMIAMI	Asst	284-4362	RJRFAC9F	12	CIKO	PHD	86 Texas	1985

Miami University BS,MBA,MACC
Department of Finance 1932,1963
School of Business Adm
Oxford, Ohio 45056
Area Code (513) Fax 529-6992
MIAMIU

Robeson, James F.	Dean	529-3631	Mktg	PHD	67 Penn St	1985
Conn, Robert L.	C-Pr	529-1560		PHD	73 Houston	1989
Leonard, David C.	Prof	529-1562		PHD	76 Illinois	
Olson, Bruce H.	Prof	529-1566		DBA	61 Indiana	
Serraino, William J.	Prof	529-1567		PHD	62 Ohio St	
Adelman, Saul W.	Assoc	529-1578		PHD	80 Georgia	
Gorman, Raymond F.	Assoc	529-1569		DBA	82 Indiana	
Kehr, James B.	Assoc	529-1571		PHD	74 Ohio St	
Lewis, Barbara J.	Assoc	529-1573		PHD	83 Cinn	
Filbeck, Greg	Asst	529-1575		PHD	86 Kentucky	
Marshall, David	Asst	529-1577		PHD	88 Illinois	
Shull, David M.	Asst	529-1565		PHD	88 Indiana	
Wyatt, Jeffrey G.	Asst	529-1563		PHD	89 S Carol	
Rudd, E. Ann	Inst	529-1564		ABD		

University of Michigan BBA,MAC,MBA,PHD
Department of Finance 1919,1963
School of Business Adm
Ann Arbor, Mich 48109-1234
Area Code (313) Fax 763-5688

White, B. Joseph	Dean	764-1361	Econ	PHD	75 Michigan	1987
Bradley, Michael	C-Pr			PHD	79 Chicago	1981
Everett E. Berg Professor of Business Administration						
Capozza, Dennis R.	Prof			PHD	72 JohnsHop	1989
Kim, E. Han	Prof	764-2282		PHD	75 SUNY-Buf	1980
Fred M. Taylor Professor of Business Administration						
Kon, Stanley J.	Prof			PHD	76 SUNY-Buf	1982
Varian, Hal R.	Prof			PHD	73 Berkeley	1977
Reuben Kempf Professor of Economics						
Brophy, David J.	Assoc			PHD	65 Ohio St	1966
Reilly, Raymond R.	Assoc	763-1008		PHD	70 Penn St	1970
Amin, Kaushik	Asst			PHD	89 Cornell	1989
Berkovitch, Elazar	Asst			PHD	86 Northwes	1986
Bodurtha Jr., James N.	Asst			PHD	83 New York	1987
Israel, Ronen	Asst			PHD	89 Northwes	1987
Kaul, Gautam	Asst			PHD	85 Chicago	1985
Kazarian, Dickran	Asst			PHD	91 Chicago	1991
Khanna, Naveen	Asst	763-2170		PHD	86 Northwes	1985
Kodres, Laura E.	Asst			PHD	88 Northwes	1989
Narayanan, M. P.	Asst			PHD	83 Northwes	1986
Ng, Victor K.	Asst			PHD	89 Calif	1989
Seyhun, H. Nejat on leave to Univ of Chicago	Asst			PHD	84 Rochest	1984
Shen, Qi	Asst			PHD	91 Penn	1991
Slezak, Steve L.	Asst			PHD	89 Calif	1989
Weiss, Kathleen A.	Asst	764-2305		PHD	88 Florida	1988

Univ of Michigan-Dearborn BA,BS,MBA
Department of Finance
School of Management
Dearborn, Mich 48128-1491
Area Code (313) Fax 593-5436

Krachenberg, A.Richard	Dean$	593-5248		Mgt	PHD	63 Michigan	1962
Chou, Yu-Min	Prof	593-5373	24		PHD	59 Illinois	1966
Fricke, Cedric	Prof	593-5086	13		PHD	59 Michigan	1960
Murray, Barbara	Assoc	593-5538	23		PHD	67 Wayne St	1978
Yohannes, Arefaine	Assoc	593-5286	13		PHD	76 Northwes	1985

Univ of Michigan-Flint BBA,MBA
Finance Faculty 1982,1986
School of Management
Flint, Michigan 48502-2186
Area Code (313) Fax 762-3687
UMICHUB
  Fortner, Richard W.   Dean   762-3164   Atg   DBA 64 Indiana   1980
  McGowan Jr., Carl B.   VAsoc 762-3160   14 NUVY PHD 80 Mich St   1991
  Kretovich, Duncan J.   Asst   762-3295   12 DIOU PHD 85 Mich St   1988
  Mensah, Samuel   Lect   762-3318   12 DLOV ABD   Toronto   1991

Michigan State University BA,MBA,PHD
Dept of Finance & Insurance 1953,1963
Grad School of Bus Adm
East Lansing, MI 48824-1303
Area Code (517) Fax 336-1111
MSU
  Lewis, Richard J.   Dean   355-8378   Mktg DBA 64 Mich St   1961
  Simonds, Richard R.   C-Pr   337-7721   PHD   Michigan 1974
  Brick, John R.   Prof   353-1705   PHD   Wiscon
  Cox, Samuel H.   Prof   PHD   LSU
    A.J. Pasant Chair in Life Insurance and Financeial Services
  Grunewald, Alan E.   Prof   353-1705   PHD 55 Wiscon
  O'Donnell, John L.   Prof   353-1745   DBA 54 Indiana
  Gilster, John E.   Assoc 353-1705
  Ahn, Chang   Asst   PHD   Wiscon
  Bange, Mary   Asst   PHD   Wiscon
  Butler, Kirt C.   Asst   PHD   Mich St
  Domian, Dale Louis   Asst   353-1705
  Kremer, Ann S.   Asst   353-1705   MBA   U Wash
  Mazzeo, Michael A.   Asst   PHD   Indiana

Michigan Technological Univ BS,MS
Department of Finance
School of Bus & Eng Adm
Houghton, Mich 49931-1295
Area Code (906) Fax 487-2944
MTUS5
  McCoy, Walter D.   Dean   487-2181 WMCCOY   Mgt PHD 80 Texas   1989
  Sen, Swapen   Asst   487-2668 SSEN   2 U   ABD   Nebraska 1991

MidAmerica Nazarene College BA
Finance Faculty
Div of Business Adm
Olathe, Kansas 66061-1776
Area Code (913) Fax 791-3290
Phone 782-3750
  McGee, Corlis   C   Ext   170   DA   87 M Tenn
  Wehmeyer, Willadee   Assoc Ext 179   3 P

Middle Tennessee State Univ BS,MBA,MS
Dept of Economics & Finance 1977,1983
School of Business
Murfreesboro, TN 37132
Area Code (615) Fax 898-5538
  Haskew, Barbara S.   Dean   898-2764   Econ PHD 69 Tenn   1988
  Lee, John T.   C-Pr   898-2528   3 PI   PHD 77 Georgia   1984
  Ford, William F.   Prof   898-2889   3 P   PHD 66 Michigan   1991
    Weatherford Chair of Finance
  Graddy, Duane B.   Prof   898-2525   3 P   PHD 74 Lehigh   1972
  Homafair, Ghassem   Prof   898-2384   42   PHD 82 Alabama   1982
  Kittrell, Fred J.   Prof   898-2364   1   PHD 70 Miss   1971
  Strickland, Thomas H.   Assoc 885-8196   1   PHD 79 Oklahoma   1988
  Feller, James F.   Asst   898-2365   2   PHD 79 Florida   1984
  Sarver, F. Lee   Asst   898-5919   1   PHD 87 Tenn   1991

Midwestern State University BBA
Department of Finance
Div of Business Adm
Wichita Falls TX 76308-2099
Area Code (817) Fax
Phone 692-6611
  McCullough, Charles   Dean   Ext 4360   Mktg PHD   Tx Tech   1985
  Fukasawa, Yoshikazu   Prof   Ext 4247   PHD   Kans St   1978
  Hadley, Garland R.   Prof   Ext 4247   PHD 74 Missouri   1983
  Krienke, Albert B.   Prof   Ext 4247   PHD   Txs A&M   1965
  Welch, Robert G.   Prof   Ext 4247   PHD   OregonSt   1966
  Van Geem, Henry   Assoc Ext 4247   DBA   Tx Tech   1964
  Harmel Jr., Robert   Asst   Ext 4247

67

Millersville Univ of PA
Finance Faculty
Dept of Business Adm
Millersville, PA 17551
Area Code (717) Fax
  Frazer, J. Douglas   C-Ac 872-3566   Atg   PHD 87 Temple 1987
  Leinberger, Gary   Assoc 872-3752   PHD 83 Okla St 1986
  Guo, Enyang   Asst 872-3857   PHD 91 Va Tech 1982

Millikin University   BS
Department of Finance
Tabor School Bus & Eng
Decatur, IL 62522
Area Code (217) Fax 424-3993
  Mannweiler, R. A.   Dean 424-6284
  Byler, Ezra U.   Prof 424-6203   12 ACJO DBA   1988

Millsaps College   BBA,MBA
Finance Faculty   1990,1990
Else School of Mgt
Jackson, Miss 39210-0001
Area Code (601) Fax 974-1260
  Whitt, Jerry D.   Dean 974-1250   Mgt PHD 73 Arkansas 1980
  Neely, Walter P.   Prof 974-1263   GMPW PHD 74 Georgia 1980
  Brister, William M.   Asst 974-1271   BKPW PHD 90 Arkansas 1989

University of Minnesota   BS,MBA,MBT,PHD
Department of Finance   1920,1963
Carlson School of Mgt
Minneapolis, MN 55455-0413
Area Code (612) Fax 624-2873
UMNSOM
  Kidwell, David S.   Dean 625-0027   Fnce PHD 75 Oregon 1991
  Kareken, John   C-Pr 624-3861   PHD
    Minnesota Chair in Banking and Finance
  Alexander, Gordon J.   Prof 624-8598   PHD 75 Michigan 1975
    IDS Professor in Finance
  Dothan, Michael   Prof 624-7594   PHD
  LeRoy, Stephen   Prof 624-5051
    Carlson Professor of Finance
  Natell, Timothy   Prof 624-3558
    Gelco Professor of Finance
  Whitman, Andrew   Prof 625-2553
  Gahlon, James   Assoc 624-5869
  Hess, Patrick   Assoc 625-5256   PHD
  Jagannathan, Ravi   Assoc 624-4863
  Rosko, Peter   Assoc 624-0312
  Stutzer, Michael   Assoc 624-1018
  Chang, Chung   Asst 624-8305   PHD
  Harris, Ellie   Asst 624-6582   PHD
  Lee, Bong-Soo   Asst 624-5763   PHD

U of Minnesota - Duluth   BBA,BAC,MBA,MS
Dept of Finance & MIS
School of Bus & Econ
Duluth, Minn 55812-2496
Area Code (218) Fax 726-6338
UMDDUL
  Vose, David A.   Dean 726-7281   AgEc PHD 66 Wiscon 1966
  Merrier, Patricia   C-Pr 726-7388
  Kim, Hyung K.   Prof 726-8760   13   PHD 67 U Wash
    retiring May 1992
  Wong, Shee Q.   Assoc 726-8506   12   PHD 83 Wi-Milwa
  Vaidya, Ramesh   Asst 726-7539   1   PHD 81 Cornell

Minot State University
Finance Faculty
Business Administration
Minot, ND 58701-5002
Area Code (701) Fax 857-3111
  Robinson, Earl J.   Dean 857-3110   Mgt PHD 77 Georgia 1991
  Witwer, Keith L.   C-As 857-3313   MBA Michigan 1982
  Schlapman, Richard   Prof 857-3314   EDD N Dakota 1964
  Davison, Carl W.   Inst 857-3571   MBA S Illin 1989

Mississippi College BS
Finance Faculty
School of Business Adm
Clinton, MS 39058
Area Code (601) Fax 925-3804

Lee, Gerald D.	Dean	925-3220		Econ	PHD	73 Miss	
Davidge, William	Prof	925-3816			PHD	75	1988

University of Mississippi BA,MA,PHD
Dept of Economics & Finance 1944,1972
School of Business Adm
University, Miss 38677
Area Code (601) Fax 232-7010
UMSVM

Boxx, William Randy	Dean$	232-5820		Mgt	PHD	71 Arkansas	1971
Womer, Norman Keith	C-Pr				PHD	Penn St	
McKenzie, Richard Bunn	Prof				PHD	72 Va Tech	
Hearin-Hess Professor of Economics and Finance; on leave to Cal-Irvine							
Malone, Rodney Phil	Assoc	232-5464			PHD	74 Florida	1973
Blenman, Lloyd Patrick	Asst				PHD	Ohio St	
Boose, Mary Ann	Asst	232-7291			PHD	Wash U	
Graham, Alexander Steven	Asst	232-7076			PHD	Queen's	
Hatfield, Gay B.	Asst	342-3066			DBA	La Tech	
Hawley, Delvin D.	Asst	232-5128			MBA	Mich St	
Jung, Minje	Asst				PHD	89 Fla St	
McIntyre Jr., James Edgar	Asst				PHD	Georgia	
Rayborn, William	Asst				DBA	Memphis	
Walker, Milan Mark	Asst	232-7721			PHD	Mich St	

Mississippi State Univ BPA,MPA,DBA
Dept of Finance & Economics 1960,1964
College of Bus & Indus
Miss St, Miss 39762-6135
Area Code (601) Fax 325-2410
MSSTATE

Leyden, Dennis R.	Dean	325-2580			Econ	PHD	76 Virginia	
Kohers, Theodore	Prof	323-2998		13 GHTU		PHD	71 Oregon	1971
Liano, Kartono	Prof	324-3176	KL1	32 JLTZ		PHD	89 Alabama	1989
Gilmer, R. H.	Assoc	324-3232		12 DJN		PHD	82 Illinoia	1988
White, Larry R.	Assoc	324-2312		13 FMOP		PHD	85 Georgia	1984
Duett Jr., Edwin H.	Asst	323-2679		13 PTDG		PHD	87 Georgia	1987
Kelly, Gary Wayne	Asst	324-3542	GWK	13 BCET		PHD	88 Alabama	1984
Merikas, Andreas G.	Asst	323-3458		14 HKLU		PHD	88 Oklahoma	1987

Mississippi Valley St Univ
Finance Faculty
Business Adm Department
Itta Bena, Miss 38941
Area Code (601) Fax

Williams, Cliff F.	C-Pr			BEd	EDD	Houston	1960
Rajanikanth, Nareseeyappa	Inst	Ext 6573			MS	Miss St	1987

U of Missouri at Columbia BAC,MS,MACC,PHD
Department of Finance 1926,1964
College Bus & Pub Adm
Columbia, MO 65211
Area Code (314) Fax 882-0365
UMCVUMB

Walker, Bruce J.	Dean	882-6688			Mktg	PHD	71 Colorado	
Stowe, John D.	C-Pr	882-2465	FINSTOWE	1	FIS	PHD	74 Houston	1980
Pettway, Richard H.	Prof	882-3800	FIN0177	13	PVW	PHD	65 Texas	
Missouri Bankers Chair								
West, David A.	Prof	882-6373		&		PHD	61 Arkansas	
Jordan, Bradford	Assoc	882-7302		1		PHD	Florida	
Brooks, Ray	Asst	881-1931	FINRMB	1		ABD	Wash U	1991
Corrado, Charles J.	Asst	882-5390		2		PHD	Arizona	1990
Hall, Jr., John R.	Asst	882-1930	FINJRH	1		ABD	Indiana	1991
Jordan, Susan D.	Asst	882-6681		23	MKJ	PHD	Georgia	
Lee, Yul	Asst	882-7852		1		PHD	Texas	
Patel, Ajay	Asst	882-3667	FINPATEL	4	UVW	PHD	Georgia	

U Missouri--Kansas City BS,MS
Department of Finance 1969,1971
Bloch School of Bus
Kansas City, MO 64110-2499
Area Code (816) Fax 235-2312
  Eddy, William B.   Dean   235-2204   OrgB   PHD   65   Mich St   1965
  Hays, Fred H.   Prof   276-2314   DBA   Kent St   1971
  Schrock, Robert D.   Prof   276-2319   PHD   70   Kansas   1965
  Belt, Brian L.   Assoc   276-2322   PHD   N Texas   1977
  Smith, Chris   Asst   PHD   Indiana   1989

U Missouri--St. Louis BS,MBA,MAC
Department of Finance 1970,1973
School of Business Adm
St. Louis, MO 63121-4499
Area Code (314) Fax 553-6420
UMSLVMA
  Nauss, Robert M.   Dean   553-5886   PHD   74   UCLA
  Kummer, Donald R.   H-Ac   553-6270   23   PM   PHD   75   Oregon
  Arshadi, Nasser   Assoc   553-6272   13   AGP   PHD   82   Nebraska   1982
  Driemeier, Donald H.   Assoc   553-5886   DBA   69   Wash U   1965
  Lawrence, Edward C.   Assoc   553-6148   13   BP   PHD   82   Penn St   1982
  Alderson, Michael J.   Asst   845-3656   1   DE   PHD   84   Illinois
  Eyssell, Thomas H.   Asst   553-6273   1   AG   PHD   Tx A&M
  Hancock, D'Anne Gorum   Asst   553-6149   2   LM   PHD   N Orlean

Missouri Southern St Col BSBA
Finance Faculty
School of Business
Joplin, Missouri 64801-1595
Area Code (417) Fax 625-3121
  Gray, James M.   Dean   625-9601   MBA   69   Arkansas   1969
  LaNear, Richard E.   Assoc   625-9530   PHD   Miss   1987

Missouri Western St College BSBA
Finance Faculty
Dept of Business & Econ
Saint Joseph, MO 64507-2294
Area Code (816) Fax
  Perkins, Charles A.   C-Ac   271-4338   X   PHD   Geo Wash   1991

Monmouth College BS
Dept of Economics & Finance
School of Business Adm
W Long Branch NJ 07764
Area Code (201) Fax 571-3523
  Dempsey, William A.   Dean   571-3423   Mktg   DBA   73   Maryland   1989
  Feist, William R.   C-Ac   571-3641   F   PHD   87   Temple   1966
  Weber, Richard E.   Prof   PHD   Rutgers   1979
  Kim, Sang-Hoon   Assoc   PHD   Wiscon   1987
  Mahajan, Y. Lal   Assoc   PHD   No Ill   1979

University of Montana BS,MBA,MACCT
Department of Finance 1949,1982
School of Business Adm
Missoula, MT 59812-1216
Area Code (406) Fax 243-2086
  Gianchetta, Larry D.   Dean   243-4831   Mgt   PHD   75   Txs A&M   1969
  Goode, Rudyard B.   Prof   243-6716   1   F   PHD   53   Virginia   1974
  Weber, David W.   Prof   243-4962   43   L   DBA   73   Colorado   1974
  Denker, Claudia   Asst   243-5872   13   AC   DBA   90   La Tech   1990
  Manuel, Timothy A.   Asst   243-2511   13   HP   PHD   88   S Carol   1991

Montana State University BS
Department of Business 1981
College of Business
Bozeman, Montana 59717-0306
Area Code (406) Fax 994-6206
  Lee, James B.   Dean$ 994-4423   PHD   74   Arizona
  Taylor, Shannon   H $ PHD   76   Colorado
  Drenk, Dean   Assoc   994-6190   3   PHD   74   Michigan
  Lin, James W. H.   Asst   994-2062   2   NSJ   PHD   87   Arizona
  Owen, Mike   994-2057   1   MS   63   MIT

Montclair State College
Dept of Fin & Quant Methods
School of Business
U Montclair, NJ 07043
Area Code (201) Fax
Did Not Respond
Rossetti, Albert D.	Dean			EDD		Rutgers	
Blumberg, Harvey	C			PHD		NYU	
Chen, Chuan Yu				PHD		NYU	
Oppenheim, Alan J.				PHD		NYU	
Sohn, Ira				PHD		NYU	

University of Montevallo   BBA
Finance Faculty   1987
College of Business
Montevallo, AL 35115-6540
Area Code (205) Fax 665-6003
| Word, William R. | Dean | 665-6540 | | Econ | PHD | 70 | Tenn | 1979 |
| Blevins, Dallas R. | Assoc | | | | DBA | 76 | Fla St | 1983 |

Moorhead State University   BS,MBA
Department of Finance
Bus, Ind & Applied Prog
Moorhead, Minn 56560
Area Code (218) Fax
Nelson, David C.	Dean	236-2076		AgEc	PHD	64	Nebraska	1974
Kalra, Rajiv	Assoc	236-4655	2	M	PHD	89	Cinn	1989
Chan, Johnny	Asst		14	N	PHD	90	Alabama	1990
Clapp, Benjamin	Asst		36		MBA	76	America	1990
Noehl, James	Asst		6		MBA	69	Minn	1972
Weber, Marsha	Asst		3		MBA	88	Moorhead	1989
Williams, Sandra	Inst		1		MBA	85	Moorhead	1988

Morehead State University   BBA,MBA
Department of Finance
Sch of Business & Econ
Morehead, KY 40351-1689
Area Code (606) Fax 783-2678
MOREKYVM
Did Not Respond
Davis, Bernard	Dean	783-2174	Mgt	PHD	67	Kentucky	1978
Osborne, John W.	C-As			MBA		E Kentuc	1977
Conyers, Alex D.	Assoc			MBA		Kentucky	1958
Peavler, Rosemary C.	Asst	783-2777		DBA		Kentucky	1983

Morehouse College   BA
Finance Faculty
Dept of Econ & Bus Adm
Atlanta, Georgia 30314
Area Code (404) Fax 681-2650
Sheftall Jr., Willis B	C	681-2800	Econ	PHD		Geo St	1986
Charles E. Merrill Professor of Economics							
Williams, John E.	Prof			PHD		Geo St	1976
Mills B. Lane Professor of Banking and Finance							
Abghori, M. Hossein	Assoc			PHD		Georgia	1988
Sillah, Marion	Assoc		F&	PHD		S Carol	1987

Morgan State University   BS
Dept of Accounting & Finance
School of Bus & Mgt
Baltimore, MD 21239
Area Code (410) Fax
Thomas, Otis A.	Dean	319-3160	QMth	PHD	71	American	1972
McNamara, James B.	C-Pr	319-3445	Atg	PHD	78	Arkansas	1989
Nwanna, Gladson	Assoc						
Tang, Alex	Asst	319-3517		PHD		Houston	
Isimbabi, Michael		319-3254		PHD			

Morris Brown College   BS
Finance Faculty
Dept of Econ & Bus Adm
Atlanta, GA 30314
Area Code (404) Fax 688-5985
Did Not Respond
| Heyliger, Wilton | C | 220-0233 | | PHD | 81 | Indiana | |

Mulhenberg College
Finance Faculty
Dept of Econ & Business
Allentown, PA 18104
Area Code (215) Fax
Did Not Respond
 Frary, Paul E. H-Pr   PHD Arkansas 1990

Murray State University   BS,MBA
Dept of Economics & Finance   1976,1981
Coll Bus & Public Affrs
Murray, Kentucky 42071-3304
Area Code (502) Fax

Name	Rank	Phone			Field	Deg	Yr	School	Yr
Thompson, John A.	Dean	762-4181			Atg	PHD	74	Arkansas	1967
Mathis, Gilbert L.	C-Pr				Econ	PHD	66	Ohio St	1966
Devine, John W.	Prof					PHD	62	Indiana	1963
Guin, Larry D.	Assoc	762-4323				DBA		Miss St	1978
Maxwell, Charles E.	Assoc	762-4188				PHD		Cinn	1988
Cheng, Louis T. W.	Asst	753-1170				DBA		LSU	1989
Driver, Betty A.	VLect					MBA		MurraySt	1983

Naval Postgraduate School   MS
Finance Faculty
Dept of Adm Sciences
Monterey, Calif 93943-5104
Area Code (408) Fax 646-3407
NAVPGS
No Finance Faculty Members
 Whipple, David R. C-Pr 646-2161   Econ PHD 71 Kansas 1971

University of Nebraska   BS,MBA,MS,PHD
Department of Finance   1916,1963
College of Business Adm
Lincoln, NE 68588-0491
Area Code (402) Fax 472-5855
UNLVM

Name	Rank	Phone	Code		Field	Deg	Yr	School	Yr
Schwendiman, Gary	Dean	472-2311			BCom	PHD	71	Brig Yg	1973
Peterson, Manferd	C-Pr	472-2330		13	CPQT	PHD	71	Mich St	1976
McCabe, George M.	Prof	472-3309		13	CDGI	PHD	75	Penn	1981
DeFusco, Richard A.	Assoc	472-6763	BUFI022	24	NSD	PHD	85	Tenn	1985
Karels, Gordon V.	Assoc	472-3860	BUFI027	13	PQ	PHD	79	Purdue	1986
Zorn, Thomas S.	Assoc	472-6049		12		PHD	78	UCLA	1981
De La Torre, Chris	Asst	472-3005	BUFI003	12	CD	PHD	90	Texas	1989
Geddert, John M.	Asst	472-3370	BUFI002	24	LVD	PHD	89	Purdue	1989

Univ of Nebraska at Kearney   BS,BA,MBA
Department of Finance
School of Business
Kearney, NE 68849-0518
Area Code (308) Fax 234-8669

Name	Rank	Phone	Field	Deg	Yr	School	Yr
Hadley, Galen	Dean	234-8342	Acct	PHD	75	Nebraska	1991
Reno, Sam C.	Prof	234-8620	BusE	EDD	72	Nebraska	1967
Borden, Karl	Assoc	234-8515		EDD	75	Mass	1986
Shade, Phil	Assoc	234-8243		DBA		Indiana	1982

Univ of Nebraska at Omaha   BS,MPA
Dept of Finance Bank & Ins   1965,1981
College of Business Adm
Omaha, Nebraska 68182-0048
Area Code (402) Fax 554-3363
UNOMA1

Name	Rank	Phone	Field	Deg	School
Specht, Pam	Dean$	554-2599	Mgt	PHD	Nebraska
Abdullah, Fuad A.	C-Pr	554-2818		PHD	Penn
Benecke, Robert W.	Prof			DBA	Colorado
Hakim, Sam	Asst	554-2818		MA	Cal St
Medeweitz, Jeanette N.	Asst	554-2655		MS	St Louis
Mitenko, Graham R.	Asst	554-2532		DBA	Memphis
Beal, Laura	Inst	554-2818			
Volkman, David A.	Inst	554-2818		BA	Nebraska

72

Univ of Nevada, Las Vegas BS,MS,MBA
Department of Finance
College of Bus & Econ
Las Vegas, NV 89154-6008
Area Code (702) Fax 739-3606
UNSVAX

Name	Rank	Phone		Field	Deg	Yr	School	Yr
Pohl, Norval F.	Dean	739-3362		Atg	PHD	73	Ariz St	1986
Chatfield, Robert E.	C	739-3019			PHD	79	Purdue	1988
Clauretie, Terrence	Prof	739-3223			PHD		Wash St	1988
Newbould, Gerald D.	Prof	739-1381			PHD		Liverpol	1988
Hoyt, Dick	Assoc	739-3493			PHD			
Anderson, Ron	Asst	739-3498			ABD		Arizona	
Choi, Seungmook	Asst	739-4668			PHD	79	Texas	1991
Hardigree, Donald W.	Asst	739-3856			PHD		Georgia	1990
Jameson, Mel	Asst	739-1025			PHD		Berkeley	1989
Poon, Percy S.	Asst	739-3017			PHD		LSU	1989
Sullivan, Michael J.	Asst	739-4669			PHD	89	Fla St	1991

University of Nevada, Reno BS,MBA
Dept Mgt Sci-Finance Faculty 1961,1971
Col Bus Adm Stop 028
Reno, Nevada 89557-0016
Area Code (702) Fax 784-1769
UNGV

Name	Rank	Phone		Field	Deg	Yr	School	Yr
Larwood, Laurie G.	Dean	784-4912		Mgt	PHD	74	Tulane	1990
Austin, M.	Asst	784-4871	12	FJLM	PHD		NYU	1986
Demaskey, Andrea	Asst	784-6811	14	LUWV	PHD	87	Kent St	1986

University of New Hampshire BA,MBA
Dept of Accounting & Finance
Whittemore Sch Bus & Ec
Durham, New Hamp 03824-3593
Area Code (603) Fax 862-4468

Name	Rank	Phone		Field	Deg	Yr	School	Yr
Goodridge, Lyndon E.	Dean	862-1983		Econ	PHD	71	Purdue	1990
Horrigan, James O.	C-Pr	862-3364		Atg	PHD	67	Chicago	1966
Kaen, Fred R.	Prof	862-3354	1	A	PHD	72	Michigan	1973
Wrightsman, Dwayne E.	Prof		13	DR	PHD	64	Mich St	1964
Etebari, Ahmad	Assoc	868-1447	12	FJ	PHD	79	N Texas	1980
Smith, Patricia B.	Asst		12	L	PHD	87	New York	1989

New Hampshire College BS,MBA,MS
Dept of Economics & Finance
USB
Manchester, NH 03104-1394
Area Code (603) Fax 645-9603

Name	Rank	Phone	Field	Deg	Yr	School	Yr
Kaliski, Burt D.	Dean	668-2211	Atg	MBA	61	Denver	1991
Widener, Steven	C-As			PHD		New Hamp	
Johnson, R. Larry	Prof			DBA		Geo Wash	
Hall, Yvonne C.	Assoc			PHD		Col St	
White, Charles	Assoc			PHD		Ohio St	
Hussan, Mahboubal	Asst			MA		New Hamp	

University of New Haven BS,MBA,MS,MST
Department of Finance
School of Business
West Haven, CT 06516-1999
Area Code (203) Fax 933-2036

Name	Rank	Phone	Deg	School	Yr
McLaughlin, Marilou	Dean	932-7115	PHD	Wiscon	1977
Downe, Edward	C	932-7418	PHD	N Sch Re	
Berman, Peter	Prof	932-7466	PHD	J Hopkin	
Parker, Joseph	Prof	932-7349	PHD	Oklahoma	
Finance Coordinator					
Rainish, Robert	Prof	932-7363	PHD	CUNY	
Tedefalk, Rolf	Prof	932-7124	PHD	Minn	
Shapiro, Steven	Asst	932-7356	PHD	Geotown	

University of New Mexico BBA,MBA,MA,EMBA
Department of Finance 1975,1975
R O Anderson Sch of Mgt
Albuquerque, NM 87131
Area Code (505) Fax 277-7108
UNMB

Name	Rank	Phone		Field	Deg	Yr	School	Yr
Walters, Kenneth D.	Dean	277-6471		Mgt	PHD	72	Berkeley	1990
Finkelstein, John M.	C-Ac	299-6522	13	R	PHD	76	Penn	1984
Grant, Dwight	Prof	277-6471	14	UW	PHD	74	Penn	1985

Simonson, Donald G.	Prof	277-8445	3	PR	PHD	72	Michigan	1971
Schatzberg, John D.	Assoc	277-3018	12	OJZ	PHD	84	Michigan	1990
Vora, Gautam	Asst	277-6471	12	LQV$	PHD	82	Indiana	1989
Weeks, David E.	Asst	277-7102	12	DKHO	PHD	87	Texas	1986
Woodard, Nelson	Asst	277-8890	12	JHOW	ABD		Virginia	1988

New Mexico Highlands Univ BA,MBA
Department of Business
School of Prof Studies
Las Vegas, NM 87701-4211
Area Code (505) Fax 454-0026
Did Not Respond

Sanchez, Lorenzo	C-As	454-3522		Atg	MBA	77	North Tx	1991

New Mexico State Univ BA,MA
Dept Finance, Ins & Real Est 1973,1981
College Bus Adm & Econ
Las Cruces, NM 88003-0001
Area Code (505) Fax 646-6155
NMSUVM1

Graham, Curtis C.	Dean	646-2821			PHD	68	Oklahoma	1979
Smith, Barry D.	H	646-3201	7	#	PHD	83	Penn	1986
Hawkins, Clark A.	Prof	646-6027	12	K	PHD	64	Purdue	1985
Goldman, Sam	Assoc	646-5749	36	Jd	JD	65	Northwes	1980
Lee, Boyden	Assoc	646-2727	13	P	PHD	71	Manchest	1980
Maese, Judy	Assoc	646-5195	13	V	PHD	82	Oregon	1980
Fortin, Rich	Asst	646-3099	12	J	PHD	88	Kansas	1988
Mull, Rick	Asst	646-1236	12	D	PHD	90	Georgia	1990

University of New Orleans BS,MBA,MS,PHD
Dept of Economics & Finance 1969,1975
College of Business Adm
New Orleans, LA 70148
Area Code (504) Fax 286-6958
UNO

Davis, J. Ronnie	Dean	286-6954			Econ	PHD	67	Virginia	1989
Whitney, Gerald A.	C-Pr$	286-6903	GAWEFEUN		Econ	PHD	77	Tulane	1979
Miller, Edward M.	Prof	943-3395				PHD		MIT	
Mukherjee, Tarun K.	Prof	286-7146		12	CDGO	DBA		Tx Tech	
Ragas, Wade R.	Prof	286-6739		6	&P	PHD	76	Ohio St	1976
Director Real Estate Market Data Center									
Wilford, Walton T.	Prof	286-6899		34	PRVW	PHD	64	So Meth	1986
Burns, Michele A.	Assoc	286-6898		23	KPTV	PHD	80	Arkansas	1979
Meurer Jr., Emil M.	Assoc					PHD		Nebraska	
Miestchovich Jr., Ivan J.	Assoc	286-6663		6	&	PHD	86	So Miss	1978
Director Center for Economic Development									
Varela, Oscar A.	Assoc	286-6905	OAVEF	14	DNUW	PHD	81	Alabama	1982
Akella, Srinivas R.	Asst	286-6488				PHD		Northwes	1990
Hassan, M. Kabir	Asst		MKHEF	13	ALPU	PHD	90	Nebraska	1990
Wei, Peihwang P.	Asst	286-6602	PPWEF	12	ALT&	PHD		LSU	1989

New York University BS,MBA,MS,PHD
Department of Finance 1916,1916
Stern School of Bus
New York, NY 10006
Area Code (212) Fax 995-4000
NYUVX1

West, Richard R.	Dean	285-6200		Fnce	PHD	64	Chicago
Gruber, Martin J.	C-Pr	285-6146			PHD	66	Columbia
Nomura Professor of Finance							
Altman, Edward I.	Prof	285-6100			PHD	67	UCLA
Chairman of Master of Business Administration Program							
Amihud, Yakov	VProf	285-6159			PHD	75	New York
Bloch, Ernest	Prof	285-6154			PHD	62	Columbia
Charles William Gerstenberg Professor of Finance							
Brenner, Menachem	VProf	285-6125			PHD	74	Cornell
Brown, Stephen J.	Prof	285-6952			PHD	76	Chicago
Elton, Edwin J.	Prof	285-6151			PHD	70	Car Mel
Nomura Professor of Finance							
Figlewski, Stephen	Prof	285-8822			PHD	76	MIT
John, Kose	Prof	285-6154			PHD	78	Florida
Kavesh, Robert A.	Prof	285-6141			PHD	54	Harvard
Marcus Nadler Professor of Finance and Economics							
Lamb, Robert B.	Prof	285-6924			PHD	70	London
Levich, Richard M.	Prof	285-6924			PHD	77	Chicago
Lindsay, Robert	Prof	285-6163			PHD	55	Harvard

Name	Rank	Phone		Degree	Year	School
Maldonado-Bear, Rita	Prof	285-6032		PHD	69	New York
Renwick, Fred B.	Prof	285-6153		PHD	66	New York
Saunders, Anthony	Prof	285-6103		PHD	81	London
Schwartz, Robert A.	Prof	285-6167		PHD	66	Columbia
Silber, William L.	Prof	285-6100		PHD	66	Princeto
Director, L. Glucksman Institute for Research in Securities Markets						
Smith, Roy C.	Prof	285-6177		MBA	66	Harvard
Clinical Professor of Finance and International Business						
Subrahmanyam, Marti G.	Prof	285-6902		PHD	74	MIT
Walter, Ingo	Prof	285-6970		PHD	66	New York
Dean Abraham L. Gitlow Professor of Finance, Chairman of International Bus						
Damodaran, Aswath	Assoc	285-6145		PHD	85	UCLA
Engberg, Holger L.	Assoc	285-8827		PHD	63	Columbia
Hasbrouck, Joel	Assoc	285-6160		PHD	81	Penn
Kallberg, Jarl G.	Assoc	285-6123		PHD	79	Brit Col
Keenan, W. Michael	Assoc	285-6155		PHD	67	Car Mel
Udell, Gregory F.	Assoc	285-6100		PHD	83	Indiana
Acharya, Sankarshan	Asst	285-6160		PHD	86	Northwes
Baldzuzzi, Pierluigi	Asst	285-6154				
Berlin, Mitchell	Asst	285-6178		PHD	86	Penn
Boudoukh, Jacob	Asst	285-8919				
Chang, P. H. Kevin	Asst	285-8920		PHD	88	Mass
Christensen, Bent	Asst	285-6154		MS		
Handa, Puneet	Asst	285-6147		PHD	86	Iowa
Lang, Larry	Asst	285-6026				
Liu, Crocker H.	Asst	285-8497		PHD	88	Texas
Madrigal, Vincent	Asst	285-6123		PHD	89	Princeto
Mei, Jiaping	Asst	285-6026				
Ofek, Eli	Asst	285-6027				
Tuckman, Bruce	Asst	285-6027		PHD	88	MIT
Whitelaw, Robert F.	Asst	285-6154				
Carbone, Dominick	Adj	285-6951		MS	75	Columbia
Copeland, Thomas	Adj	285-6951				
Friedman, Harry M.	Adj	285-8931		PHD	72	Cal-SanB
Gendreau, Brian	Adj	285-6160		MA	76	JohnsHop
Gordon, Robert	Adj	285-6951				
Latimer, Steve	Adj	285-8497				
Levy, Jerome	Adj	285-6160				
Moore, Keith	Adj	285-6160				
Parkinson, Ken	Adj	285-6160		MBA	76	Penn
Pilzer, Paul	Adj	285-8497		LLD	74	SUNY
Regan, Edward	Adj	285-6951		PHD	50	Illinois
Rice, Sherman T.	Adj	285-6160		PMD	74	Harvard
Riehl, Heinz	Adj	285-8927				
Rosenfeld, Gerald	Adj	285-6951				
Sonnenreich, William	Adj	285-6149				
Stovall, Robert H.	Adj	285-6951		MBA	57	New York
Sullivan Jr., Frank L.	Adj	285-8497		MBA	71	Penn
Teall, John	Adj	285-6032				
Zhu, Yu	Adj	285-6160				

New York University-Grad MSM,MPA,DPA,PHD
Department of Finance
738 Tisch 40 W 4th St
New York, NY 10003
Area Code (212) Fax 995-4162

Name	Rank	Phone			Degree	Year	School	
Newman, Howard	Dean	998-7410		Law	JD	70	Temple	1988
Berne, Robert	Prof	998-7438	1		PHD	77	Cornell	1976
Finkler, Steven A.	Prof	998-7463	1		PHD	78	Stanford	1984
Stiefel, Leanna	Assoc	998-7437	1		PHD	72	Wiscon	1976

New York Institute of Tech BS,MS,MBA
Finance Faculty
School of Management
Old Westbury, NY 11568
Area Code (516) Fax

Schwartz, Carol H.	Dean	686-7554	PHD
Weiss, Nitzan	Prof	686-7554	PHD
Drescher, Sol	Assoc	686-7554	PHD
Kutasovic, Paul	Assoc	686-7554	PHD
Stanley, William	Assoc	399-8330	MBA
area code (212)			
Silverstein, Ethel	Asst	686-7554	MBA

76
BA,BS,BBA

Niagara University
Department of Commerce
College of Business
Niagara Univ, NY 14109
Area Code (716) Fax
Phone 285-1212
  Praetzel, Gary D. Dean Ext 237 Econ PHD SUNY-Buf 1981
  Pikas, Bodhans C-Pr Ext 544 Mktg MS Niagara 1968
  Warren, Stanton A. Assoc 285-1212 PHD SUNY-Buf 1981
  Janowsky, Dale Adj Ext 544
  Pikas, Ann Adj Ext 544

Nicholls State University
Dept of Economics & Finance
Col of Business Box2015
Thibodaux, LA 70310
Area Code (504) Fax 448-4922
BS,BA
1983,1989
  Kooros, Syrous K. Dean 448-4172 PHD 1991
  McManis, Bruce H-Pr 448-4188 23 MOP PHD 1978
  Stanley, Thomas O. Assoc 448-4194 3 P
  Guidry, K. Asst 448-4216 6 & PHD 1990
  Lajaunie, John Asst 448-4210 24 LMVW ABD 1991
  Lee, Sang Asst 448-4235 1 PHD 1991

Nichols College
Dept of Accounting & Finance
Div of Business & Econ
Dudley, Mass 01571-5000
Area Code (617) Fax EXT 102
943-1560 Phone for all
BS
  Warren, Ed Dean Ext 201 PHD 79 Brown 1974
  Olive, Frank C-Ac Ext 253 12 Atg MBA 80 Maryland 1982
  Lasher, William Asst Ext 263 12 FH PHD 77 So Metho 1988

Norfolk State University
Dept of Finance & Marketing
School of Business
Norfolk, VA 23504
Area Code (804) Fax 683-8084
BS
  Boyd, Joseph L. Dean 683-8920 Atg PHD 77 S Carol 1983
  Friedman, Marshall Myron C-Pr 683-8915 Mktg PHD Nebraska 1973
  Choudhury, Santosh K. Prof 683-8913 PHD Northwes 1974
  Randolph, William L. Assoc 683-2563 PHD Alabama 1989
  Zemedkun, Wold Assoc 683-2562 MA Columbia 1977

North Adams State College
Finance Faculty
Business Adm/Econ Dept
North Adams, MA 01247
Area Code Fax
  Markou, Peter J. Dean MSBA Suffolk
  Croteau, Barbara A. C-As MBA Providen
  Hajizadeh, Avaz Prof PHD Renssel
  Yanow, Richad Prof MBA Harvard

University of North Alabama
Department of Finance
School of Business
Florence, AL 35632-0001
Area Code (205) Fax 760+4270
BS
  Johnson, Robert S. Dean 760-4261
  Copeland, Joe B. H-Pr 760-4270 Econ PHD 74 Arkansas 1983
  Free, Veronica A. Prof PHD 70 Miss St 1984
  Morris, Barry K. Prof PHD 74 Arkansas 1974
  Gordon, Bruce L. Inst MA 86 Alabama 1986
  Wells, Bill

North Carolina at Ashville
Finance Faculty
Dept of Management
Ashville, NC 28804-3329
Area Code (704) Fax
UNCA
No Finance Faculty
BS
  Lisnerski, Donald O. C-Ac 251-6554 LISNERSK HAdm DPH 74 N Carol 1982

University of North Carolina BS,MBA,MAC,PHD
Dept of Finance, CB #3490 1923,1963
Kenan Flagler Bus Sch
Chapel Hill, NC 27599-3490
Area Code (919) Fax 962-0054
UNC

Name	Rank	Phone	Email		Field	Deg	Yr	School	Yr
Rizzo, Paul J.	Dean	962-3232			Mgt	JD	69	Michigan	1987
Eisenbeis, Robert A.	C-Pr	962-3203	EISEES	3	PS	PHD	71	Wiscon	1982
Wachovia Professor of Banking; Associate Dean of Research									
McEnally, Richard W.	Prof	962-3194	UUURWM	23	KMNQ	PHD	69	N Carol	1973
Meade H. Willis, Sr. Professor of Investment Banking									
Pringle, John J.	Prof	962-3180	UPRING	14	EFUV	PHD	72	Stanford	1973
C. Knox Massey Professor of Business Administration									
Rendleman, Richard J.	Prof	962-3188	RR006088	12	DKLM	PHD	76	N Carol	1983
Smith, James F.	Prof	962-3176	JS007758	14	EHV	PHD	71	So Meth	1988
Gultekin, Mustafa N.	Assoc	962-3153	UMGMXG	24	JMOL	PHD	84	New York	1985
Hartzell, David J.	Assoc	962-3160	HARTZELL	2	K	PHD	85	N Carol	1988
Ravenscraft, David J.	Assoc	962-3187	DR00706	12	AGHW	PHD	80	Northwes	1987
Connolly, Robert A.	Asst	962-0053	CONNOLLY	24	JV	PHD	82	Maryland	1990
Conrad, Jennifer S.	Asst	962-3132	UBILBO	12	JNTZ	PHD	86	Chicago	1985
Snow, Karl N.	Asst	962-3182	KS012078	24	JKLW	PHD	91	Chicago	1990
Wiles, Kenneth W.	Asst	962-3202	KWILES	13	AGPQ	PHD	91	Texas	1990
Zenner, Marc	Asst	962-3210	ZENNER	14	DGQU	PHD	89	Purdue	1989

North Carolina at Charlotte
Dept of Finance & Bus Law
College of Business Adm 1983,1985
Charlotte, NC 28223
Area Code (704) Fax 547-4888

Name	Rank	Phone	Email		Field	Deg	Yr	School	Yr
Neel, Richard E.	Dean	547-2165			Econ	PHD	60	Ohio St	1978
Nunnally Jr., Bennie H.	C $	547-2063		1		DBA		Virginia	1978
Walls, Edward L.	Prof	547-4418		1		DBA	70	Harvard	1971
R. S. Dickson Professor of Finance									
Kennedy, William F.	Assoc	547-4427		3		PHD		Va Tech	1978
Blose, Laurence E.	Asst	547-4415		2		PHD	87	Texas	1990
Khan, A. Qayyum	Asst	547-2007		4		PHD		Geo St	1989
Lamb, Reinhold P.	Asst	547-4125		1		PHD	90	Fla St	1990
Plath, D. Anthony	Asst	547-4413		1		DBA		Kent St	1987

North Carolina at Greensboro
Department of Finance BS,MSA
Bryan Sch of Bus & Econ 1982,1982
Greensboro, NC 27412-5001
Area Code (919) Fax 334-5580
UNCG

Name	Rank	Phone	Email	Field	Deg	Yr	School	Yr
Weeks, James K.	Dean$	334-5338	WEEKSJK	Opm	PHD	74	S Carol	1976
Jud, G. Donald	H-Pr	334-3055	JUDDON		PHD	71	Iowa	1971
Flanigan, George B.	Prof	334-3055			PHD	73	Iowa	1973
Johnson, Joseph E.	Prof	334-3055			DBA	69	Geo St	1969
Balbirer, Sheldon D.	Assoc	334-3096			PHD		N Carol	1974
Wingler, Tony R.	Assoc	334-3092			DBA		Kentucky	1976
Simms, John M.	Asst	334-3055			PHD		N Carol	1985
Winkler, Daniel T.	Asst	334-3094	WINKLER		PHD		S Carol	1986
Oglesby, Nicholas P.	Lect	334-3055			BS		Virginia	1985

North Carolina at Wilmington
Dept of Econ & Finance BS,MBA
Cameron Sch of Bus Adm
Wilmington, NC 28403-3297
Area Code (919) Fax 395-3815
UNCWIL

Name	Rank	Phone	Email		Field	Deg	Yr	School	Yr
Kaylor, Norman R.	Dean	395-3501	KAYLOR		Atg	PHD	71	Miss	1971
Hill, Roger P.	C-Pr	395-3510		1	FHI	PHD	68	Mich St	1970
Copley, Ronald E.	Assoc	395-3510		2	JMLN	PHD	81	S Carol	1982
Bojanic, Sharon Lee	Asst	395-3510		1	CDH	DBA	88	Kentucky	1988
Comeskey, Harry A.	Asst	395-3510		1	DH	DBA	83	Colorado	1984
Harriss, James D.	Asst	395-3510		3	PRQT	DBA	88	Miss St	1986
Sigler, Kevin J.	Asst	395-3510		2	JMLN	PHD	86	Nebraska	1981

North Carolina A&T State Un
Department of Business Adm BS
School Business & Econ 1979
Greensboro, NC 27411
Area Code (919) Fax 334-7093
ATSUVAXI

Name	Rank	Phone	Field	Deg	Yr	School	Yr
Craig, Quiester	Dean	334-7632	Atg	PHD	71	Missouri	1972
Nkange, Japhet N.	C-Pr			PHD		N Carol	
Angell, Robert J.	Prof	334-7656		DBA	74	Fla St	
Howard, Robert	Assoc	334-7656		PHD	78	Ohio St	
Redmon, Alonzo L.	Assoc	334-7656		PHD	87	N Carol	

78

North Carolina Central Univ
Finance Faculty
School of Business
Durham, N Carol 27707
Area Code (919) Fax 560-6413
Fleming, Sundar W.	Dean	560-6458		Mktg	PHD	77	Duke	1987
Pickett, H. R.	Assoc	560-6546	1	FH	DBA	73	Virginia	1982

North Carolina State Univ BA,MSM
Finance Faculty
Div of Econ & Business
Raleigh, N Carol 27695-8109
Area Code (919) Fax 515-5560
NCSUMVS
Clark, R. L.	H-Pr$	515-5560		Mgt	PHD	74	Duke	1975
Holthausen, D.	H-Pr	515-5567			PHD	74	Northwes	1976
Agrawal, Anup	Prof	515-5590			PHD	86	Pittsbur	
Jones, Charles P.	Prof	515-5567			PHD	69	N Carol	
Mitchell, Karlyn	Prof	515-5590			PHD	82	Michigan	
Poindexter, J. C.	Prof	515-5584			PHD		Ohio St	
Wilson, J.	Prof	515-5567			PHD	66	Oklahoma	

University of North Dakota BS,MBA
Department of Finance 1984,1990
Box 8097, Univ Station
Grand Forks, ND 58202
Area Code (701) Fax 777-5099
NDSUVM1
777-2396 Office Phone
Lawrence, W. Fred	Dean	777-2135		Mgt	PHD	80	Geo St	1986
Nelson, Theron R.	C-Ac	777-2396	6	E	PHD		Geo St	1984
Escarraz, Donald R.	Prof	777-2396	1	CDEF	PHD	64	Okla St	1984
Markovich, Denise E.	Assoc	777-2396	13	GP	PHD	79	Manitoba	1986
Lee, Jeong Wan	Asst	777-4149	2	LM	PHD	86	Texas	1986
Potter, Thomas A.	Asst	777-4699	1	FIDE	DBA	86	Colorado	1986

North Dakota State Univ BS,MBA
Department of Finance
College of Business Adm
Fargo, N Dakota 58105-5137
Area Code (701) Fax 237-7050
NDSUVM1
Scheibelhut, John H.	Dean	237-8651		Mktg	PHD	70	Oregon	
Bathal, Chenchu	Asst	237-8128			PHD	90	Texas	1990
Walker, Matthew	Inst	237-8529			ABD		Texas	1990

University of North Florida BS,MBA,MAC
Dept of Accounting & Finance 1976,1981
College of Business Adm
Jacksonville, FL 32216-6699
Area Code (904) Fax 646-2594
Johnson, Edward A.	Dean	646-2590		Mgt	PHD	68	Mich St	1989
Bates, Homer L.	C-Pr	646-2630		Atg	PHD	77	Illinois	1984
Wiggins, C. Donald	Prof	646-2630	12	CFMO	DBA		La Tech	
White, Richard E.	Assoc	646-2630			PHD	73	Missouri	1973
Frohlich, Cheryl J.	Asst	646-2630	23	JKPS	PHD		Illinois	
Kare, Dilip K.	Asst	646-2630	24	LNVW	PHD		Tx Arlin	
Howard, Sue Beck	Inst	646-2630	12	CFXJ	MBA	83	Fla St	

University of North Texas BS,MS,MBA,PHD
Department of Finance 1961,1966
College of Business Adm
Denton, Texas 76203-3677
Area Code (817) Fax 565-4930
UNTVM1
Singleton, J. Clay	Dean	565-3037		Fnce	PHD	79	Missouri	1991
McDonald, James L.	C-Ac	565-3051	13	PCDH	PHD	79	Oklahoma	1976
Chandy, P. R.	Prof	565-3063	12	IJLM	DBA	80	Tx Tech	1981
Roden, Foster	Prof	565-3059	12	ADEO	PHD	70	N Texas	1974
Schutte, David	Prof	565-3060	12	ADLO	PHD	81	Minn	1989
Karafiath, Imre	Assoc	565-3065	34	PZUV	PHD	83	Tx A&M	1984
Kensinger, John W.	Assoc	565-3069	12	ALGO	PHD	83	Ohio St	1991
Chopin, Marc	VAsst	565-3064	13	PRGD	PHD	91	Tx A&M	1991
Cole, C. Steven	Asst	565-3075	13	PTCD	PHD	89	Arkansas	1988
Conover, James A.	Asst	565-3061	14	UVLM	PHD	89	Tx A&M	1989
Impson, C. Michael	Asst	565-3055	12	ADJO	DBA	87	La Tech	1987
MacDonald, Don N.	Asst	565-3072	2	JLNO	PHD	84	Tx A&M	1989
Siddiqi, Mazhar	Asst	565-3052	14	UVAG	ABD		U Wash	1991
Tripathy, Niranjan	Asst	565-3068	12	ADGJ	PHD	87	Tx Tech	1987

Northeast Louisiana Univ BBA,MBA
Dept of Economics & Finance 1972,1977
College of Business Adm
Monroe, LA 71209-0130
Area Code (318) Fax 342-5161

Name	Rank	Phone			Field	Deg	Yr	School	Yr
Bethke, Arthur L.	Dean	342-1100			Mgt	PHD	72	Nebraska	1974
Moser, Ernest R.	H-Ac	342-1150			Econ	PHD	73	Tx A&M	1976
Caldwell, James L.	Prof	342-1167	1	Y		PHD	63	LSU	1975
Ingram, Franklin Jerry	Prof	342-1153	1	XY		PHD	79	S Carol	1986
Cheatham, Leo R.	Assoc	342-1161	13	FIP		PHD	74	Arkansas	1986
Parker, Michael E.	Asst	342-1168	12	ADQ		DBA	91	Miss St	1990
Sharma, Maneesh K.	Asst	342-1166	24	GTV		PHD	91	Alabama	1991

Northeast Missouri State U BS,MA
Finance Faculty
Div of Business & Accty
Kirksville, MO 63501
Area Code (816) Fax EXT 4366
NEMOUS
Phone 785-4346

Name	Rank	Phone			Field	Deg	Yr	School	Yr
Dager, Robert A.	H-Pr	Ext 4346	BU15		Mgt	EDD	74	Ball St	1974
Fellows, Paul	Assoc	Ext 4346	BU38	23	LM	PHD	85	Illinois	1991
Lin, Jason	Assoc	Ext 4349	BU30	13	HI	PHD	85	Wayne St	1986
Mun, Kyung	Asst	Ext 4346	BU54	14	AF	PHD	91	Va Tech	1991

Northeastern University BS,MS
Finance & Insurance Group 1962,1974
College of Business Adm
Boston, Mass 02115
Area Code (617) Fax 437-2056

Name	Rank	Phone			Field	Deg	Yr	School	Yr
Boyd, David P.	Dean	437-3239			Mgt	PHD		Oxford	1978
Welch, Jonathan B.	C-Pr	437-4572				PHD		Conn	
Marple, Wesley W.	Prof	437-4569		13	AGQ	DBA	67	Harvard	1966
Meador, Joseph Wayne	Prof	437-4713				PHD		Penn	
Bolster, Paul J.	Assoc	437-5051	NUHUB	2	ROM	PHD		Va Tech	1985
Joseph G. Riesman Research Professor									
Born, Jeffrey A.	Assoc	437-5054				PHD		N Carol	1988
Margotta, Donald G.	Assoc	437-4739				PHD		N Carol	1983
Pantalone, Coleen C.	Assoc	437-4741		13	PS	PHD		Iowa St	1981
Platt, Harlan D.	Assoc	437-4740			BB	PHD		Michigan	1981
Alford, Alan	Asst	437-4775	ALFORD	4	JUWV	PHD		S Carol	1989
Badrinath, S. G.	Asst	437-4782	NOHUB	12	JMNT	PHD		Purdue	1985
Ball, Jay N.	Asst	437-5030				PHD		Georgia	1988
Faria, Hugo J.	Asst	437-5098	NUHUM	14	ADGR	PHD		S Carol	1988
Felgran, Steven D.	Asst	437-2197		23	PQRN	PHD		Yale	1989
Janjigian, Vahan	Asst	437-2812		12	DGOY	PHD		Va Tech	1990
Joshi, Yash Pal	Asst	437-4778				PHD		Pitt	1989
Sounders, Edward M.	Asst	437-4571				PHD		Geo St	1985
Srinivasan, Venkatesan	Asst	437-3720		1	I	PHD		Cinn	1985
Trahan, Emery A.	Asst	437-4568	EATQ38	13	AGR	PHD		SUNY-Alb	1988
Fletcher, Peggy L.	Lect	437-4738				ABD		Pitt	1985
Gurley, Darryl E. J.	Lect	437-2741	GURLEYD	1	ABY	ABD		Colorado	
Khan, Bibi Zorina	Lect	437-4704	ZORINA	34		PHD		UCLA	1990
Schellhorn, Carolin D.	Lect	437-5965				ABD		Texas	

Northeastern Illinois Univ BS,MBA
Dept Atg, Finance & Bus Law
College Business & Mgt
Chicago, IL 60625-4699
Area Code (312) Fax 794-6288

Name	Rank	Phone			Field	Deg	Yr	School	Yr
Englehardt, Olga E.	Dean	794-5247			OrgB	PHD	44	Columbia	1981
Chen, Chong-Tong	C-Pr	794-2657			Atg	PHD	72	Illinois	1985
Balsara, Nauzer	Assoc	794-2654		13	LN	PHD	86	Columbia	1987
Rao, Narendar	Asst	794-2879		12	BD	PHD	89	Cinn	1990
Rezranian, Rasoul	Asst	794-2649		13	PQR	PHD	89	So Ill	1990

Northeastern State Univ
Department of Finance
Division of Business
Tahlequah, OK 74464-2399
Area Code   Fax

Name	Rank	Phone			Field	Deg	Yr	School	Yr
Williams, Earl R.	Dean	456-5511			Econ	PHD	68	Tenn St	1968
Greubel, Robert T.	Prof	456-5511		2		PHD	72	Arkansas	1965
Vaidyanathan, Ravi	Asst	456-5511		4		DBA	91		1991
Goddard, Jack B.	Inst	456-5511		3		MS	76	N Txs St	1976
Haney, Jack	Inst	586-0750				MBA			1991
Schmidt, Ned	Inst	456-5511				MBA			1991

Northern Arizona University BS,MBA
Department of Finance 1969,1977
College of Business Adm
Flagstaff, AZ 86011-5066
Area Code (602) Fax 523-7331
NAUVM

Name	Rank	Phone		Field	Deg	Yr	School	Year
Walka, Joseph J.	Dean	523-3657		Econ	PHD	69	Harvard	1986
Tallman, Gary D.	Prof	523-7339			DBA		Colorado	1976
Maberly, Edwin D.	Assoc	523-7409			PHD		Tx A&M	1987
Allen, David S.	Asst	523-7378			PHD		Va Tech	1988
Borstadt, Lisa F.	Asst	523-7400			PHD		Utah	1990

Univ of Northern Colorado BS
Department of Finance
College of Business Adm
Greeley, Colo 80639
Area Code (303) Fax 351-2500

Name	Rank	Phone		Field	Deg	Yr	School	Year
Duff Jr., William L.	Dean	351-2764			PHD	69	UCLA	1971
Clinebell, John M.	C-Ac	351-2275	12 JMN	DBA	88	S Illin	1987
Allen, Garth H.	Assoc	353-6918	7 #	JD	72	Iowa	1973
Haskins, James P.	Asst	223-7442	13 PKCF	PHD	91	Colo St	1987
Johnson, David	Asst	330-6023	13 KOP	PHD	89	Tenn	1990
McDonald, James E.	Asst	352-6463	14 GVWA	DBA	88	La Tech	1989

Northern Illinois Univ BS,MS
Department of Finance 1969,1977
College of Business
Dekalb, Illinois 60115-2854
Area Code (815) Fax 753-8515
NIU
800-323-8714

Name	Rank	Phone	Code		Field	Deg	Yr	School	Year
Brown, Richard D.	Dean	753-1755			Bus	PHD	67	Illinois	1971
Miller, Robert E.	C-Ac	753-0250	M40REM1	2	QT	PHD	75	Kansas	1989
Bauman, W. Scott	Prof	753-1354	M40WSB1	2	M	PHD	61	Indiana	1981
Johnson, James M.	Prof	753-1116	M40JMJ1	1	BF	PHD	75	Ohio St	1987
Dowen, Richard J.	Assoc	753-6394	M40RJD1	1	FMT	PHD	83	SUNY Bin	1983
Dran Jr., John J.	Assoc	753-6393	M40JJD1	1	CI	PHD	70	Kent St	1982
Miller, Roger L.	Assoc	753-0398	M40RLM1	1	FI	PHD	65	Illinois	1976
Weiss, Donald E.	Assoc	753-6398	M40DEW1	1	CF	PHD	76	Wiscon	1974
Iskandar, Mai E.	Asst	753-6396	M40MEI1	1	K	PHD	86	Missouri	1991
Jensen, Gerald R.	Asst	753-6399	M40GRJ1	1	BF	PHD	87	Nebraska	1987
Mercer, Jeffrey M.	Asst	753-6362	M40JMM1	12	PT	PHD	91	Tx Tech	1991
Newman, Joseph A.	Asst	753-0322	M40JAN1	3	PA	PHD	89	Tennesse	1989
McNeil, Melanie	Inst	753-6395	M40MJM1	1		MS	89	No Ill	1989
Sparrow, Gregory B.	Inst	753-0685	M40GBS1			MBA	80	No Ill	1980

University of Northern Iowa BA
Department of Finance
College of Business Adm
Cedar Falls, IA 50614-0124
Area Code (319) Fax 273-2922
ISCSVAX
Bitnet name: ISCSVAX.UNI.EDU

Name	Rank	Phone			Field	Deg	Yr	School	Year
Minter, Robert L.	Dean	273-6240			Mgt	PHD	69	Purdue	1991
Thompson, A. Frank	H-Pr	273-2949	THOMPSON		FKNP	PHD	77	Nebraska	1990
Isakson, Hans R.	Prof	273-6096	ISAKSON	3	BGP	PHD	78	Wiscon	1990
Rappaport, Allen	Prof	273-2800		14	HPW	PHD	68	Texas	1982
Mills, Geoffrey T.	Assoc	273-6243		14	FUV	PHD	79	Illinois	1983
Wyatt, Robert W.	Assoc	273-6385		34	PQV	PHD	78	Iowa	1980
Bowlin, Lyle	Asst	273-6312		12	ALM	MA	85	Iowa	1987
Cox, Arthur T.	Asst	273-6986	COX	12	CNM	PHD	91	Iowa	1988
Okoruwa, Ason	Asst	273-2948		13	AOQ	PHD	85	Georgia	1991

Northern Kentucky Univ BS,MBA
Department of Finance
College of Business
Highland Hght KY 41076-1448
Area Code (606) Fax 572-5566

Name	Rank	Phone		Field	Deg	Yr	School	Year
Comte, Thomas E.	Dean	572-5551		Mgt	PHD	78	Missouri	1991
Clayton, Gary E.	Prof	572-6542	12 BFKU	PHD	73	Utah	1980
Ramjee, Anju	Assoc	572-5158	12 BDHG	PHD	87	Cinn	1988
Ramjee, Balasubramani	Assoc	572-5695	12 CDHL	PHD	87	Cinn	1988

Northern Michigan Univ
Dept of Accounting & Finance BS
Walker L. Cisler Sch Bs
Marquette, Mich 49855
Area Code (906) Fax 227-1333
NMUMUS

Gnauck, Brian G.	Dean	227-2947		Econ	PHD	68 Minn	1963
Graci, Samuel P.	H-Ac	227-2603		Atg	PHD	82 Arkansas	1980
Guenther, Harry P.	Prof	227-2603			DBA	59 Indiana	1989
Rayhorn, Charles	Asst	227-1839	FACE		ABD	Colorado	1989
Rayome, David	Asst	227-1802	FADV		MBA	88 Akron	1990

Northern State University
Department of Finance BA,BS
School of Bus & Industr
Aberdeen, SD 57401-7198
Area Code (605) Fax 622-3022

Jasinski, Harry	Dean	622-2400	Mgt	EDD	65 N Colo	1966
Lo, Harry	Asst	622-3001		PHD	86 Geo St	1989

Northwest Missouri St Univ
Dept of Accounting & Finance BS,MBA
Coll Bus, Gov & Cpt Sci
Maryville, MO 64468-6001
Area Code (816) Fax 562-1900

DeYoung, Ron C.	Dean	582-7682	BEd	EDD	71 N Illin	1984
McLaughlin, Patrick	C-Ac	562-1280	Law	JD	Mo-KC	1978
Kelly, Al	Prof	562-1698		PHD	Kentucky	1975
Wilson, Michael J.	Asst	562-1278		MSBA	S Illin	1986

Northwestern University
Dept of Finance Leverone Hl MM,PHD
Kellogg Grad Sch of Mgt 1916
Evanston, IL 60208-2006
Area Code (708) Fax 491-5719
NUACC

Jacobs, Donald P.	Dean	491-3300	13	PRU	PHD	57	Columbia
Gaylord Freeman Distinguished Professor of Banking							
--Department of Finance							
McDonald, Robert L.	C-Pr	491-8344	12	CDL	PHD	82	MIT
Breen, William J.	Prof	491-8335	12	HJMO	PHD	65	Cornell
Greenbaum, Stuart I.	Prof	491-5498	13	PQRU	PHD	64	JHopkins
Norman Strunk Distinguished Professor of Financial Institutions; Assoc Dean							
Hodrick, Robert J.	Prof	491-4113	4	JWZ	PHD	76	Chicago
Tokai Bank Professor of International Finance							
Lerner, Eugene M.	Prof	491-8337	1		PHD	54	Chicago
Mills, Edwin S.	Prof	491-8340	23	CDKM	PHD	56	Birmingh
Alan E. Peterson Distinguished Professor of Finance							
Raviv, Artur	Prof	491-8342	1	ABDQ	PHD	74	Northwes
Roberson, John	AdjPr	491-7843	13		MBA	64	Harvard
Bollerslev, Tim	Assoc	491-8338	24	JNW	PHD	86	CA-S Dgo
Korajczyk, Robert A.	Assoc	491-8336	12	DJMW	PHD	83	Chicago
Andersen, Torben G.	Asst	467-1285	24	BJOZ	PHD	91	Yale
Bagwell, Laurie Simon	Asst	491-2671	1	DEGH	PHD	88	Stanford
on leave							
Bizer, David	Asst	491-3562	13	ABDM	PHD	88	Stanford
on leave							
Boot, Arnoud W. A.	Asst	467-1191	13	ADGP	PHD	87	Indiana
Braun, Phillip A.	Asst	467-1963	23	JKOR	PHD	91	Chicago
DeMarzo, Peter	Asst	491-5941	13	ABDM	PHD	89	Stanford
Fishman, Michael	Asst	491-8332	13	GT	PHD	86	Chicago
Hagerty, Kathleen M.	Asst	491-8345	23	AST	PHD	85	Stanford
Lucas, Deborah	Asst	491-8333	13	DJP	PHD	88	Chicago
Marshall, David	Asst	491-7436	12	JNOR	PHD	88	Car Mel
Rebelo, Sergio	Asst	491-4510	24	JW	PHD	88	Rochest
on leave							
Rietz, Thomas	Asst	491-8339	23	JNRZ	PHD	88	Iowa
Winton, Andrew	Asst	467-1841	13	ADP	PHD	90	Penn
Chaplinsky, Susan	V	467-1281	1	DEGH	PHD	84	Chicago
Ofer, Aharon R.	V	491-2681	12	ADQS	PHD	73	Penn
--Real Estate							
Mills, Edwin	C-Pr	491-8340	6	&	PHD	56	Birmingh
Kendall, Leon	Prof	491-7704	6	&HPS	DBA	56	Indiana
Masotti, Lou	Prof	491-8697	6	&	PHD	64	Northwes

Northwestern State U of LA
Finance Faculty
Division of Business
Natchitoches, LA 71497
Area Code (318) Fax 357-5161   BS

Name	Rank	Phone			Degree		School	Year
Smiley, Barry A.	D-Pr	357-5163			DBA		La Tech	
Elliott, Robert Stephen	Assoc	357-5700			PHD		La Tech	
Kromis, Stephen G.	Assoc	357-5699			PHD		La Tech	
Washington, Dorothy M.	Inst	357-4581			MBA		Michigan	

Northwood Institute
Finance Faculty
College of Business
Midland, Mich 48640-2398
Area Code (517) Fax 832-9590   BBA

Name	Rank	Phone			Degree	Yr	School	Year
Haywood, Dale	Prof	837-4291			PHD	80		1972
Hunkins, Donald	Prof	837-4211			BA	71		1978
Nash, Timothy	Assoc	837-4371			MA	87		1981
Sumi, Barbara	Assoc	837-4250			MS	80		1980
Tofteland, Elmer	Assoc	837-			MBA	78		1981
Schell, Richard	Asst	837-4257			MBA	70		1988

Norwich University
Finance Faculty
Div of Business & Mgt
Northfield, VT 05663
Area Code (802) Fax 485-2580
Did Not Respond

Name	Rank	Phone			Degree	Yr	School	Year
Vanecek, Frank T.	H	485-2212			DBA	82	Kent St	1976

University of Notre Dame
Dept of Finance & Bus Econ
College of Business Adm
Notre Dame, IN 46556
Area Code (219) Fax 239-5255
IRISHMVS   BBA,MBA
                                                                                                   1962,1972

Name	Rank	Phone		Field	Degree	Yr	School	Year
Keane, John G.	Dean	239-7992		Mgt	PHD	65	Pitt	1989
Keating, Barry P.	C-Pr	239-6370		Econ	PHD	74	Notre Dm	
McDonald, Bill D.	Prof	239-5137	12					
Reilly, Frank K.	Prof	239-6393	2		PHD		Chicago	
Tavis, Lee A.	Prof	239-7617	41		DBA		Indiana	
C. R. Smith Professor								
Conway, Paul F.	Assoc	239-6253	1		MSC	51	SUNY-Alb	1956
Halloran, John A.	Assoc	239-5305	13					
Lanser, Howard P.	Assoc	239-6370	1		PHD	72	Purdue	1971
Affleck-Graves, John	Asst	239-6760	12					
Bowers, Helen M.	Asst	239-6762	1					
Fehrs, Don	Asst	239-5540	12		PHD	87	Fla St	
Kremer, Joseph W.	Asst	239-6766	2		PHD		S Carol	
Mendenhall, Richard	Asst	239-6076	12					
Niden, Cathy M.	Asst	239-8434	12		PHD	88	Chicago	
Peterson, James	Asst	239-8301	12					
Scanlon, Kevin P.	Asst	239-6077	2		PHD		Florida	
Spiess, Katherine	Asst	239-6268	1					
Wright, David J.	Asst	239-6499	2		PHD		Illinois	

Oakland University
Dept of Accounting & Finance
School of Bus Adm
Rochester, Mich 48309-4401
Area Code (313) Fax 370-4275
OAKLAND   BS,MBA
                                                                                                   1988,1988

Name	Rank	Phone		Field	Degree	Yr	School	Year
Stevens, George E.	Dean	370-3286		Mgt	DBA		Kent St	1991
Dillon, Gadis J.	C-Pr	370-4289		Atg	PHD	77	Michigan	1987
Horwitz, Ronald M.	Prof	370-2432	1	FH	PHD	64	Mich St	1979
Mittra, Sid	Prof	370-3539	12	XO	PHD	62	Florida	1967
Farragher, Edward J.	Assoc	370-4094	1	CI	PHD	71	Illinois	1987
Kleiman, Robert	Assoc	370-3509	12	GN	PHD	86	Mich St	1985
Murphy, J. Austin	Assoc	370-2125	24	LKOV	PHD	84	Georgia	1984

Oglethorpe University
Finance Faculty
Div of Business & Econ
Atlanta, Georgia 30319-2797
Area Code (404) Fax   BBA

Name	Rank	Phone		Field	Degree	Yr	School	Year
Tucker, Dean	C-Ac	261-1441		Mgt	PHD	79	Mich St	1988
Middleton, Mary	Assoc	261-1441	1	N	PHD	88	Georgia	1988
Straley, William	Assoc	261-1441	12	MO	PHD	79	Auburn	1990

Ohio University BA,MBA
Department of Finance 1950,1969
College of Business Adm
Athens, Ohio 45701-2979
Area Code (614) Fax 593-1388
  Day, William A.   Dean   593-2000   Mgt   DBA   67 Harvard   1965
  Rakes, Ganas K.   C-Pr   593-2056   DBA   Wash U
    O'Bleness Professor of Banking and Finance
  Mikhail, Azmi D.   Prof   593-2054   PHD   62 Ohio St   1967
  Patterson, Harlan R.   Prof   593-8752   PHD   63 Mich St
  Pugh, Dwight A.   Assoc   PHD   69 Ohio U   1969
  Berlin, Bruce S.   Asst   593-2052   PHD   85 Mich St   1984

Ohio Northern University BSBA
Finance Faculty
College of Business Adm
Ada, Ohio 45810
Area Code (419) Fax 772-1932
  Maris, Terry L.   Dean   772-2070   PHD   79 Nebraska
  Cooper, Ken   Prof   772-2235   12 AF   PHD   84 Minn   1986
  Mohan, Santhosh   Asst   772-2075   12 ADLO   PHD   90 Indiana   1991

Ohio State University BS,MBA,MAC,PHD
Department of Finance 1916,1963
College of Business
Columbus, Ohio 43210-1399
Area Code (614) Fax 292-2418
  Alutto, Joseph A.   Dean   292-2666   Mgt   PHD   68 Cornell
  Gibson, Frank F.   C-Pr   JD   52 New York
  Buser, Stephen A.   Prof   PHD   72 Boston C
  Cole, David W.   Prof   292-8441   DBA   65 Indiana
  Hendershott, Patric H.   Prof   6 &   PHD   65 Purdue
    Galbreath Professor of Real Estate
  Jennings, Edward H.   Prof   PHD   Michigan
  Kane, Edward J.   Prof   292-8708   PHD   60 MIT
  Mayers, David   Prof   9 #   PHD   Rochest
    Shepard Professorship in Insurance
  Racster, Ronald L.   Prof   PHD   67 Illinois 1968
    Associate Dean
  Stulz, Rene M.   Prof   292-1970   PHD   MIT
    Riklis Chair of Business and its Environment
  Ballam, Deborah   Assoc   JD   Ohio St
  Blackburn, John   Assoc   JD   Cinn
  Chan, Ka-Kung C.   Assoc   PHD   Chicago
  Harvey, Roger K.   Emer   292-7562   DBA   67 Indiana   1967
  Klayman, Elliot I.   Assoc   LLM   Harvard
  Sanders, Anthony B.   Assoc   23 KNR   PHD   79 Georgia
    on leave to Univ of Chicago
  Smith, Michael L.   Assoc   PHD   Minn
  Walkling, Ralph A.   Assoc   292-1580   PHD   Maryland
  Wood, Justin   VAsoc
    visting from Univ of Australia
  Betker, Brian   Asst   PHD   91 UCLA
  Darr, Frank   Asst   JD   Ohio St
  Forster, Margaret M.   Asst   PHD   Cornell
  Franke, Janice R.   Asst   JD   Ohio St
  George, Thomas J.   Asst   PHD   Michigan
  Karolyi, G. Andrew   Asst   PHD   89 Chicago
  Longstaff, Francis A.   Asst   PHD   87 Chicago
  Persons, John C.   Asst   PHD   91 Chicago
  Schultz, Paul H.   Asst   PHD   88 Chicago
  Whittaker, Maria C.   Asst   JD   Chicago

Ohio Wesleyan University BA
Finance Faculty
Department of Economics
Delaware, Ohio 43015
Area Code (614) Fax 368-3535
OWUCOMCN
  Harvey, Joann P.   C-Ac   368-3541   Atg   MBA   82 Ohio St   1981
  Boos, John D.   Assoc   368-3546   JD   66 Geo Wash   1983

University of Oklahoma BAC,BBA,MAC,PHD
Department of Finance 1926,1963
College of Business Adm
Norman Oklahoma 73019-0450
Area Code (405) Fax 325-7688
UOKMVSA
Lusch, Robert F.	Dean	325-3611			Mktg	PHD	75	Wiscon	1987
Emery, Gary W.	D-Ac	325-5591		1	BCGI	PHD	78	Kansas	1987
Ederington, Louis H.	Assoc	325-5591		23	KLPR	PHD	72	Wash U	1989
Linn, Scott C.	Assoc	325-5591		1	AGJO	PHD	82	Purdue	1989
Stock, Duane R.	Assoc	325-5591	BA1863	23	KLMP	PHD	79	Illinois	1979
Lee, Jae Ha	Asst	325-5591		12	GJLT	PHD	88	Indiana	1989
Nayar, Nandkumar	Asst	325-5591		12	DGLQ	PHD	88	Iowa	1988

Oklahoma Baptist University BBA
Finance Faculty
School of Business
Shawnee, Okla 74801-2590
Area Code (405) Fax 878-2069
Phone 878-2115
Babb, Robert M.	Dean	Ext 2115				EDD	89	Kentucky	1989
Brattin, Max A.	Assoc	Ext 2124		23	RX	MBA	62	LSU	1966
Reeder, Danny B.	Asst			23	BMPQ	PHD	91	Okla St	1991

Oklahoma Christian College
Finance Faculty
Division of Business
Oklahoma City OK 73136-1100
Area Code (405) Fax 425-5149
Skaggs, W. Jack	C $	425-5567				EDD		Okla St	
Rix, James A.	Prof	425-5569		12	CGMD	PHD		Arkansas	1989

Oklahoma City University BS,MBA
Department of Finance
Meinders School of Bus
Oklahoma City,OK 73106
Area Code (405) Fax 521-5098
Brown, Thomas L.	Dean	521-5276				PHD	Okla St	1990
C.R. Anthony Chair of Competitive Enterprise								
Meyer, James E.	C	521-5099		14	BGHU	PHD	N Carol	1987
Fitzgerald, Pat	Prof	521-5168		12		PHD	Texas	1981
Altshuler, Jerry	Assoc	521-5218		13		MA	S Calif	1982
Belford, Ray	Asst	521-5282		12		MBA	Okla Cty	1987
Shao, John	Asst	521-5108		12	AFM	PHD	Va Tech	1991

Oklahoma State University BS,MS,PHD
Department of Finance 1958,1964
College of Business Adm
Stillwater, Okla 74078-0555
Area Code (405) Fax 744-5180
OSUCC
Sandmeyer, Robert L.	Dean	744-5064	MGMTRLS		Econ	PHD	62	Okla St	1962
Jadlow, Janice W.	H-Ac	744-5199		4	V	PHD		Okla St	1984
Simpson, W. Gary	Prof	744-5199		3	P	PHD		Txs A&M	1978
OBA Chair of Commercial Bank Management									
Jackson, James F.	Assoc	744-5104		1	F	PHD	64	Texas	1963
Miller, Ronald K.	Assoc	744-8604		1	CH	PHD		Missouri	1981
Polonchek, John A.	Assoc	744-5114		3	GQ	PHD		Ga Tech	1983
Wingender, John R.	Assoc	744-8603		2	Jn	PHD		Nebraska	1985
Gleason, Anne E.	Asst	744-8663		3	P	PHD	90	Fla St	1989
Krehbiel, Timothy L.	Asst	744-8660		3	L	PHD		Purdue	1989
Terry, Rory	Asst	744-5113		2	AJ	ABD		Utah	1991

Old Dominion University BS
Department of Finance 1974,1980
College of Bus & Pub Ad
Norfolk, Virg 23529-0223
Area Code (804) Fax 683-5155
ODUVM
Wallace, William W.	Dean	683-3521		13		PHD	62		
Doukas, John	C-Pr	683-3501		14	UVW	PHD		NYU	1989
Cho, Dongsae	Assoc	683-3551		7	#				
Choi, Kwang S.	Assoc	683-3507		1		PHD	72	Cinn	1971
Crunkleto, Jon R.	Assoc	683-3540		6	&	PHD		S Carol	1978

Name	Rank	Phone			Deg	Yr	School	Yr
Rubin, Bruce L. on leave	Assoc		12	CDEL	PHD		Case Wes	1981
Seifert, Bruce	Assoc	683-3552	14		PHD		Michigan	1984
Gibson, Robert A.	Asst	683-4232	6	&	MS		Wiscon	1985
Hudgins, Sylvia C.	Asst	683-3510	13	PQST	PHD		Va Tech	1989
Najand, Mohammed	Asst	683-4708	1		PHD		Syracuse	
Noronha, Gregory	Asst	683-3563	1					
Rahman, Hamid	Asst	683-3240	1					
Yung, Kenneth K.	Asst	683-3573	1		PHD		Geo St	

Olivet College
Finance Faculty
Dept of Business & Econ
Olivet, Michigan 49076
Area Code (616) Fax 749-7650

Nanney, Jerry	C-Pr	749-7610			PHD	80	Ocean Pa	1989

Oral Roberts University   BS,MBA
Finance Faculty
School of Business
Tulsa, Oklahoma 74171
Area Code (918) Fax 495-6033

Swearingen, Eugene	Dean	495-7040		Mgt	PHD	55	Stanford	1982
Martin, Rinne	Prof	495-6113	12	MX	PHD	84	Cincinna	1977
Greer, Jack	Asst	495-6669	13		MBA	65	Oklahoma	1990
Bovee, Steve	Inst	495-6119	13		MBA	90	Oral Rob	1991

University of Oregon   BS,BA,MBA,PHD
Department of Finance   1923,1963
College of Business Adm
Eugene, Oregon 97403-1208
Area Code (503) Fax 346-3341
OREGON

Reinmuth, James E.	Dean	346-3300 JER	Quan	PHD	69	Oreg St	
Wier, Peggy	H-Ac			PHD	81	Rochest	1982
Dann, Larry	Prof	LDANN		PHD	80	UCLA	1977
Richard W. Lindholm Professor of Finance and Taxation							
Dasso, Jerome J.	Prof	686-3325		PHD	64	Wiscon	1966
H. T. Miner Professor of Real Estate							
Hopewell, Michael H.	Assoc			PHD	72	U Wash	1969
Mikkelson, Wayne H.	Assoc			PHD	80	Rochest	1984
Partch, M. Megan	Assoc			PHD	81	Wiscon	1981
Racette, George A.	Assoc			PHD	72	U Wash	1974
Campbell, Alyce Rita	Asst			PHD	87	Brit Col	1987
Mullins, Helena M.	Asst			PHD	90	Berkeley	1990

Oregon State University   BS
Dept of Finance & Int Bus   1960,1970
College of Business
Corvallis, OR 97331-2603
Area Code (503) Fax 737-4890

Parker, Donald F.	Dean	737-6025	Mgt	PHD	75	Cornell	1991
Widicus, Wilbur W.	C-Pr	737-2551	Fnce	PHD	64	Columbia	1964
Neilsen, James F.	Prof	737-3326		DBA	72	Colorado	1974
Nielson, Norma L.	Prof	737-3689		PHD	79	Penn	1985
Dickerson, Bodil	Inst	737-6048		MBA	84	Oreg St	1981
Dunsdon, David	Inst	737-6044		MBA	80	Cen Mich	1981

Otterbein College   BA,BS
Finance Faculty
Dept of Bus, Atg & Econ
Westerville, OH 43081
Area Code (614) Fax 898-1200

Brown, Gerald C.	C-Ac	898-1468		Atg	PHD	67	Ohio St	1988
Wallenbrock, Terry	Asst	898-1310	13	F	MBA	82	Michigan	1983

Pace University   BBA,MBA,MS,DPS
Department of Finance
Lubin School of Bus Adm
New York, NY 10038-1502
Area Code (212) Fax 488-1613
Did Not Respond--Taken from College Catalog

Centonze, Arthur	Dean	346-1962	Adm	PHD	83	NYU	1991
Johnson, Clarke C.	Prof	346-1818		PHD		Purdue	1979

Seligman, Barnard	Prof	346-1817					
Sharp, J. Franklin	Prof			PHD		Purdue	1985
Janus, Frank	Assoc			PHD		NYU	1965
Larrain, Maurice	Assoc			PHD		Columbia	1989
Crego, Carl R.	Asst			DBA		Geo Wash	1985

Pace University-Westchester BBA,MBA
Department of Finance
Business
Pleasantville NY 10570-2799
Area Code (914) Fax 773-3541
Did Not Respond
  Centonze, Aurthur   Dean$ 773-3716   Adm   PHD   83 NYU   1972

University of the Pacific BS
Finance Faculty 1983
School of Bus & Pub Adm
Stockton, Calif 95211
Area Code (209) Fax 946-2586
INTERNET MAXVAX.UOP.EDU

Plovnick, Mark S.	Dean	946-2476	MPLOVNIC	Mgt	PHD	75	MIT	1989
Bryan, Donald W.	Assoc	946-2476			PHD	74	Syracuse	1974
Tatsch, Paul A.	Assoc	946-2476			PHD	77	SUNY	
Lee, Unro	Asst	946-2476			PHD	86	Purdue	

Pacific Lutheran University BBA
Department of Finance 1971,1976
School of Business Adm
Tacoma, Wash 98447
Area Code (206) Fax 535-8320
Did Not Respond
  King, Gundar J.   Dean   535-7251   Mgt   PHD   63 Stanford   1960

Pacific Union College BBA,BA,BS
Finance Faculty
Dept of Bus Adm & Econ
Angwin, Calif 94508-9797
Area Code (707) Fax 965-6237

Voth, Richard	Dean	965-6238		Mgt	PHD	73	Ariz St	1968
Hardcastle, Rodney	Asst	965-2832			MBA	89	Gold Gt	1989

University of Pennsylvania BSE,MBA,PHD
Department of Finance 1916,1963
Wharton Sch 2028 SH-DH
Philadelphia, PA 19104-6370
Area Code (215) Fax 898-0401
WHARTON
  Gerrity, Thomas P.   Dean   898-4851   Mgt   PHD   70 MIT   1990
  --Department of Finance
  Kihlstrom, Richard E.   C-Pr   898-4378   PHD   68 Minn   1979
    Ervin Miller-Arthur M. Freedman Professor of Finance
  Abel, Andrew B.   Prof   PHD   78 MIT   1987
  Blume, Marshall E.   Prof   PHD   68 Chicago   1978
    Howard Butcher III Professor of Financial Management
  Dumas, Bernard   Prof   PHD   73 Columbia 1990
    Nippon Life Professor of Finance
  Gibbons, Michael R.   Prof   PHD   80 Chicago   1989
    Drexel Burnham Lambert Professor of Investment Banking
  Grossman, Sanford J.   Prof   PHD   75 Chicago   1989
    Steinberg Trustee Professor of Finance
  Guttentag, Jack M.   Prof   PHD   58 Columbia 1962
    Jacob Safra Professor of International Banking
  Herring, Richard J.   Prof   PHD   73 Princeton 1972
  Inman, Robert   Prof   PHD   71 Harvard   1971
    Senior Fellow, Leonard Davis Institute of Health Economics
  Linneman, Peter D.   Prof   PHD   77 Chicago   1978
    Albert Sussman Professor of Real Estate
  Litzenberger, Robert H. Prof   896-6413   PHD   69 N Carol   1986
    Edward Hopkins, Jr. Professor of Investment Banking
  MacKinlay, A. Craig   Prof   PHD   85 Chicago   1985
  Marston, Richard   Prof   PHD   72 MIT   1972
    James R. F. Guy Professor of Finance & Economics
  Mendelson, Morris   Prof   PHD   50 Cornell   1961
  Ramaswamy, Krishna   Prof   PHD   78 Stanford 1985

Santomero, Anthony M.	Prof		PHD	71 Brown	1972
Richard King Mellow Professor of Finance					
Siegel, Jeremy J.	Prof				
Stambaugh, Robert F.	Prof		PHD	81 Chicago	1979
Ronald O. Perelma Professor of Finance					
Allen, Franklin H.	Assoc	898-3629	PHD	80 Oxford	1980
Calomiris, Charles	VAsoc				
visiting from Northwestern Univ					
Eun, Cheol S.	VAsoc		PHD	81 New York	
visiting from Univ of Maryland					
Ghandhi, Jamshed K. S.	Assoc		PHD	60 Cambridg	1965
Gorton, Gary Bernard	Assoc		PHD	83 Rochest	1990
Gultekin, N. Bulent	Assoc		PHD	76 Penn	1990
Gyourko, Joseph E.	Assoc		PHD	84 Chicago	1984
Jaffe, Jeffrey	Assoc		PHD	72 Chicago	1973
Kandel, Shmuel	VAsoc				
visiting from Tel Aviv Univ					
Keim, Donald B.	Assoc		PHD	83 Chicago	1981
Lewis, Karen K.	Assoc		PHD	85 Chicago	1991
Sarig, Oded	VAsoc				
visiting from Tel Aviv Univ					
Wachter, Susan M.	Assoc		PHD	74 Boston C	1974
Zeldes, Stephen	Assoc		PHD	84 MIT	1982
Bates, David S.	Asst		PHD	88 Princeto	1988
Bohn, Henning	Asst				
Dravid, Ajay R.	Asst		PHD	90 Stanford	1989
Eberly, Janice C.	Asst		PHD	91 MIT	1991
James G. Campbell, Jr. Memorial Term Assistant Professor of Finance					
Glen, Jack	Asst		PHD	87 Northwes	1987
Alumni of Goldman Sachs Term Assistant Professor of Finance					
Leach, J. Christopher	Asst		PHD	88 Cornell	1988
Donaldson, Lufkin & Jenrette Term Assistant Professor of Finance					
Madhavan, Ananth N.	Asst		PHD	88 Cornell	1988
W. P. Carey & Co. Term Assistant Professor of Finance					
Mizrach, Bruce	VAsst				
visiting from Boston College					
Richardson, Matthew P.	Asst		PHD	89 Stanford	1989
Elliott Baim Term Assistant Professor of Finance					
Grundy, Bruce	Lect		PHD	78 Chicago	1990
Donald B. Stott Lecturer in Finance					
Inselbag, Isik	Adj		PHD	73 Columbia	1979
Kaufold, Howard S.	Adj		PHD	81 Princeto	1980
--Insurance & Risk Mgt Dept					
Rosenbloom, Jerry S.	C-Pr				
Frederick H. Ecker Professor					
Cummins, J. David	Prof				
Harry J. Loman Professor of Property & Liability Insurance					
Doherty, Neil A.	Prof				
Lemaire, Jean	Prof				
Joseph Wharton Term Professor of Insurance & Actuarial Science					
Babbel, David F.	Assoc				
Berger, Lawrence A.	Asst		PHD	85 Penn	
Tennyson, Sharon	Asst				
Matthew R. Kornreich Term Assistant Professor					
Bartlett III, Dwight K,	VExec				
Visiting Executive Professor of Insurance					

Penn State University BS,MBA,MS,PHD
Finance Faculty 609 Bus Adm 1957,1963
Smeal College Bus Adm
Univ Park, PA 16802
Area Code (814) Fax 865-3362
PSUVM
Insurance/Real Estate and Acturial Science Taken from College Catalog

Hammond, J. D.	Dean	863-0448	7 #	PHD	61 Penn	1961
--Department of Finance						
Kracaw, William A.	C	863-0486		PHD	69 Penn	1970
Curley, Anthony J.	Prof	865-9201		PHD	79 Penn St	1970
Ezzell, John R.	Prof	863-0486		PHD	Penn St	1980
Miles, James A.	Prof	863-3565		PHD	Iowa	1979
Woolridge, J. Randall	Prof	865-1160		PHD	83 Purdue	
Muscarella, Chris J.	Assoc	865-1481		PHD	Oregon	1989
Brous, Peter	Asst	865-9590		PHD	90 Chicago	1990
Choe, Hyuk	Asst	863-3566		PHD	NYU	1989
Freund, Steven	Asst	885-1483		PHD	Purdue	1986
Kini, Omesh	Asst	865-5191		PHD	McGill	1988
Padmanabhan, Prasad	Asst	865-3763		PHD	Cornell	
Lemke, Graham	Inst	863-3564		ABD		

--Dept Insurance & Real Est
  Lusht, Kenneth M.   C-Pr   PHD   Geo St
--Dept of Acturial Science
  Shapiro, Arnold F.   C-Pr   PHD   Penn

Penn State Univ-Erie   BS,MBA
Finance Faculty
School of Business
Erie, Penn 16563-1400
Area Code (814) Fax 898-6233
PSUVM
  Magenau, John M.   Dir   898-6173   Mgt   PHD   81 SUNY-Buf   1985
  Chan, Stanley W.   Asst   898-6439   12 DW   PHD   86 Houston   1987

Penn State Univ-Harrisburg   BS,MBA
Finance Faculty
School of Business Adm
Middleton, PA 17057
Area Code (717) Fax
PSUVM
  Dhir, Krishna S.   Dir   948-6141 KSD3   DBA   75 Colorado   1991
  Christofi, Andreas C.   Assoc   948-6161   PHD   84 Penn St   1986
  Kulkarni, Mukund S.   Assoc   948-6342
  Arbelaez, Harvey   Asst   PHD   90 Temple   1991
  Musser, William A.   Inst   948-6145   MBA   75 Geo Wash   1978

Pepperdine Univ-Los Angeles   BS,MBA
Department of Finance
School of Bus & Mgt
Culver City, CA 90230
Area Code (213) Fax 568-5727
Non 568- numbers have (818) area code
  Wilburn, James R.   Dean   568-5500   Econ   PHD   71 UCLA   1970
  Kinsman, Michael   Prof   568-5539   PHD   75 Stanford   1975
  Stanley, Darrol   Prof   568-5539   DBA   73 So Calif   1973
  Feiganbaum, Bernard   Assoc   568-5539   Econ   PHD   81 UCLA   1990

Pepperdine Univ-Malibu   BS
Department of Finance
Seaver College
Malibu, Calif 90263
Area Code (213) Fax 456-4758
PEPVAX
  Wilson, John   Dean   456-4281 JWILSON   Rel   PHD   67 Iowa   1983
  Johnson, David   Assoc   456-4380   12 DFIX PHD   89 Cinn   1991

Pfeiffer College   AB,BS,MBA,MCE
Finance Faculty
Div of Business & Econ
Misenheimer, NC 28109
Area Code (704) Fax 463-2046
  Bleau, Barbara Lee   H-Pr   463-1360   PHD   80 Penn St   1986
    Jefferson-Pilot Professor of Management Science
  Spruill, Charles R.   Prof   521-9116   13   PHD   75 So Illin
  Booth III, W. Scott   Assoc   463-1360   2   MA   71 Appal St   1982
  Jozsa Jr., Frank P.   Assoc   463-1360   13   PHD   77 Geo St   1991
  Poplin, Toby L.   Assoc   463-1360   13   MA   68 Appal St   1976

Piedmont College
Finance Faculty
Division of Business
Demorest, GA 30535-0010
Area Code (404) Fax
  Blair, Allen G.   H-Pr   DBA   67 Harvard
  Welch, H. Oliver   Prof   778-2889   DBA   Geo St

Pittsburg State University   BS,MBA
Dept Econ, Finance & Banking
Kelce School Bus & Econ
Pittsburg, KS 66762
Area Code (316) Fax 232-7515
Did Not Respond
  Mendenhall, Terry L.   Dean   235-4598   Mgt   PHD   81 Kans St   1964

```
Fisher, Charles C.        Prof                              PHD       Wash St
Hay, Richard              Prof                              PHD       Kent St
Cortes, Bienviendo        Asst                              PHD       Okla St
Muoghalu, Michael         Asst                              DBA       La Tech
Scribner, Curtis D.       Asst    231-7000

University of Pittsburgh                                              MBA,PHD
Department of Finance                                                 1979,1916
Katz Grad School of Bus
Pittsburgh, Penn  15260
Area Code (412)  Fax 648-1693
PITTVMS
Did Not Respond
  Zoffer, H. J.           Dean    648-1561       Bus       PHD   56  Pitt         1953
  Mandelker, Gershon N.   Prof    648-1713                 PHD       Chicago
  Makhija, Anil K.        Assoc   648-1709
  Shastri, Kuldeep        Assoc   648-1708

U of Pittsburgh at Johnstown
Finance Faculty
Dept of Business Econ
Johnstown, Penn  15904
Area Code (814)  Fax
  Letcher, George E.      Dean    269-2964       Atg       MA    66  St Fran      1981
  Vickroy, Ronald         C-Ac    269-2965       Mgt       MS    80  CMU          1985
  Thompson, Raymond       Assoc   269-2970       MS        DBA   84  Nova         1980
  Byely, Larry            Asst                             DBA   89  Ind St

Plymouth State College                                                BS,MBA
Finance Faculty
Department of Business
Plymouth, NH  03264
Area Code (603)  Fax
Did Not Respond
  Datta, Anindya          C       536-5000       Econ      MA    68  Wash U

University of Portland                                                BBA
Department of Finance                                                 1977,1981
School of Business Adm
Portland, Oregon  97203-5798
Area Code (503)  Fax 283-7399
  Robertson, James W.     Dean    283-7224       Atg       PHD   63  U Wash       1988
  Gritta, Richard D.      Prof    283-7224                 DBA   71  Maryland     1972
  Shank, Todd             Asst    283-7279                 ADB   91  Cen Fla      1991
  Leitch, Gordon          Adj     283-7466                 PHD   87  Tulane       1991

Portland State University                                             BS,BA,MT,MBA
Finance Area                                                          1970,1982
School of Business Adm
Portland, Oregon  97207-0751
Area Code (503)  Fax 725-4882
PSUORVM
  Oh, John S.             Dean$   725-3703          Fnce   PHD   78  Virginia     1979
  Anderson, Leslie P.     Prof    725-4746       34 PURV   PHD   60  Wiscon       1986
  Hsia, Chi-Cheng         Prof    725-3762                 PHD   74  UCLA         1988
  Settle, John W.         Assoc   725-3767 HEJS  12 EFMO   PHD   78  U Wash       1984
  Fuller, Beverly R.      Asst    725-3744                 PHD   87  Va Tech      1987
  Hamilton, Janet G.      Asst    725-3731 HEJH  12 EGHO   PHD   86  Mich St      1986
  Rahman, Shafiqur        Asst    725-4766                 PHD   86  Illinois     1986

Post College
Department of Finance
School of Business Adm
Waterbury, CT  06708
Area Code (203)  Fax
Did Not Respond
  Hartman, Frederic C.    Dean    755-0121                 MBA
```

Prairie View A&M University BBA,MBA
Dept of Economics & Finance
College of Bus Box 957
Prairie View, TX 77446-0951
Area Code (409) Fax 857-4956
Did Not Respond
  Jones, Barbara A. P.   Dean   857-4310   Econ   PHD   73   Geo St   1987
  Soliman, Mostafa   Assoc   PHD   Iowa St   1971
  Thiagarajan, Kuttalam R.   Asst   MA   Annamali
  Song, Kean P.

Providence College BS,MBA
Division of Finance
Dept of Business Adm
Providence, RI 02918-0001
Area Code (401) Fax 865-2057
  Maloney, Paul J.   D-As   865-2658   12 GOX   MBA   McGill U   1980
  Cerwonka, Ronald P.   Prof   865-2657   12 DM   PHD   73   Rhde Isl   1974
  Okere, Vivian O.   Asst   865-2671   12 DKPV   PHD   Rhde Isl   1987
  Tamule, Harold B.   Asst   865-2009   12 ABGH   PHD   Mass   1990
  Zalewski, David A.   Asst   865-2009   34 JNRV   ABD   Clark   1990
  Deely, Thomas J.   Inst   865-2659   13 CIQ   MBA   St Johns   1976
  Gaus, Kenneth   Adj   865-2009   12 FHLN   MBA   Penn   1990

University of Puget Sound BA
Department of Finance
School of Bus & Pub Adm
Tacoma, Wash 98416-0121
Area Code (206) Fax 756-3500
Did Not Respond
  Dickson, John P.   Dean   756-3153   Mktg   PHD   74   Oregon

Purdue University BS,MS,PHD
Department of Finance 1967,1969
Krannert School of Mgt
W Lafayette, IN 47907-1310
Area Code (317) Fax 494-9658
PURCCVM
  Weidenaar, Dennis J.   Dean   494-4366   PHD   69   Purdue   1966
  Johnson, Robert W.   Prof   494-4380   13 BP   PHD   52   Northwes   1964
  Lewellen, Wilbur G.   Prof   494-4493   14 EG   PHD   67   MIT   1964
  McConnell, John J.   Prof   494-5910   12 GK   PHD   74   Purdue   1976
  Smith, Keith V.   Prof   494-7337   12 IM   PHD   66   Purdue   1979
  Sheehan, Dennis P.   Assoc   494-4508   12 AD   PHD   81   Berkeley   1986
  Sullivan, A. Charlene   Assoc   494-4382   13 BP   PHD   78   Purdue   1978
  Phillips, Gordon   Asst   12 DG   PHD   91   Harvard   1991

Quincy College BS
Finance Faculty
Div Bus & Computer Sci
Quincy, Illinois 62301-2699
Area Code (217) Fax
Did Not Respond

Quinnipiac College BS,MBA
Department of Finance
School of Business
Hamden, Conn 06518-0569
Area Code (203) Fax 281-8664
  Strang, Roger   Dean   281-8720   Mgt   DBA   Harvard
  Driscoll, Vincent   C   281-8788   12 FC   PHD   N Sch So
  Clyde, William   Assoc   281-8574   14 VLM   PHD   Edinburg
  Miller, Walter   Assoc   281-8798   23 PH   PHD   NYU

Radford University
Accounting & Finance Dept
College of Bus & Econ
Radford, VA 24142
Area Code (703) Fax 831-5669
VTVM1
  Kroeber, Donald W.   Dean   831-5300   Sys   PHD   76   Georgia
  Little, Philip L.   C-Ac   Atg   DBA   La Tech
  Rose, Clarence C.   Prof   PHD   Va Tech
  Perumpral, Shalini E.   Assoc   831-5233   PHD   Va Tech   1975
  Torabzadeh, Khalil M.   Assoc   831-5382   PHD   Miss St
  Sen, Nilanjan   Asst   PHD   Va Tech
  Woodruff, Criss G.   Asst   ABD   Miss st

Ramapo College - New Jersey							BS
Finance Faculty
School of Adm & Bus
Mahwah, N Jersey 07430-1680
Area Code (201) Fax 529-7508
    Raciti, Sebastian J.   D   529-7377   PHD   68 Fordham   1971
    Essig, James   Asst   PHD   New York
    Sabrin, Murray   Asst   PHD   Rutgers   1985

Regent University
Finance Faculty
College of Adm & Bus
Virginia Bch, VA 23464-9800
Area Code (804) Fax 424-7051
    Mulford, John E.   Dean   424-4354   Econ   PHD   Cornell
    Redmer, Timothy A. O.   Prof   424-4360   PHD   89 Va Comm   1991

Rensselaer Poly Institute							1977,1983
Department of Finance
School of Management
Troy, New York 12180-3590
Area Code (518) Fax 276-8661
RPITSMTS
    Hawkins, Robert G.   Dean   276-6802   Mgt   PHD   NYU
    Paulson, Albert S.   Prof   276-6850   23   PHD   67 Va Tech   1972
    Goldenberg, David H.   Assoc   276-6582   13   PHD   Florida   1986
    Bessler, Wolfgang   Asst   276-2996   12   PHD   Hamburg   1990

University of Rhode Island							BS,MBA,MS
Department of Finance							1969,1973
College of Business
Kingston, R Isl 02881-0801
Area Code (401) Fax 792-4312
URIMVS
    Stern, Sydney V.   Dean   792-2337   Engr   PHD   62 Ga Tech   1990
    Dash Jr., Gordon H.   C-Pr   792-2086   DBA   78 Colorado   1979
    Rhee, S. Ghon   Prof   792-4324   PHD   78 Ohio St   1989
    Chang, Rosita P.   Assoc   792-2086   PHD   82 Pitt   1988
    Oppenheimer, Henry R.   Assoc   792-2086   PHD   79 Purdue   1987
    Lai, Gene C.   Asst   792-2086   PHD   87 Texas   1988
    McNamara, Michael J.   Asst   792-2086   PHD   88 Nebraska   1988
    Yasuhara, Akio   Asst   792-2086   PHD   82 Ohio St   1988
    Hamilton, Karen   792-2086
    Kang, Jun-Koo   792-2086   MS   86 Iowa St   1991
    Palmisciano, William   792-2086

Rhodes College
Finance Faculty
Dept of Econ & Bus Adm
Memphis, Tenn 38112
Area Code (901) Fax
    Planchon, John M.   C-Ac   726-3798   Mktg   PHD   Alabama
    Pittman, Debbie   Inst   726-3738   ABD   Memphis

Rice University							MAC,MBA,PHD
Finance Faculty
Jones Grad Sch of Adm
Houston, Texas 77251
Area Code (713) Fax 285-5251
RICE
    Bailar, Benjamin F.   Dean   527-4838   Adm   MBA   59 Harvard   1987
    Barnea, Amir   Prof   285-5383   PHD   72 Cornell   1989
    Williams, Edward E.   Prof   285-5381   PHD   68 Texas   1978
      Henry Gardiner Symonds Professor
    Taylor, William M.   Assoc   285-5387   PHD   79 Chicago   1988
    Abraham, Abraham   Asst   285-5384   PHD   89 Boston   1989
    Ikenberry, David   Asst   285-5385

University of Richmond   BSBA,MBA
Department of Finance   1965,1981
E. C. Robins Sch of Bus
Richmond, Virg 23173
Area Code (804)   Fax 289-8878
URVAX
  Poole, R. Clifton   Dean   289-8550   13 Fnce   PHD   74 S Carol   1975
  Phillips, Robert Wesley   C-Pr   289-8588   13 DEFS   DBA   69 Indiana   1974
  Earl Jr., John H.   Assoc   289-8589   23 MPS   PHD   Ariz St   1981
  Stevens, Jerry L.   Assoc   289-8597   24 JOUV   PHD   81 Illinois   1986
  Burnett, Amy   Asst   289-8580   12 MO   ABD   Texas   1990
  Lancaster, M. Carol   Asst   289-8955   13 CES   PHD   84 Ariz St   1989

Rider College   BCOMM
Department of Finance
School of Business Adm
Lawrenceville NJ 08648-3099
Area Code (609)   Fax 895-0448
RIDER
  Ruch, Richard S.   Dean   896-5152   Org   PHD   76 Rennesl   1982
  Randall, Maury R.   C-Ac   895-5584   PHD   New York
  Meric, Ilhan   Prof   895-5537   PHD   Lehigh
  Carroll, Anne M.   Asst   PHD   Penn
  Ghosh, Asim   Asst   895-5502   PHD   Kentucky
  Loh, Charmen   Asst   PHD   Arkansas
  Ratner, Mitchell   Asst   PHD   Drexel
  Shih, Feng-Ying L.   Asst   895-5404   MBA   Drexel
  Suk, David   Asst   PHD   Drexel
  Zantout, Zaher   Asst

University of Rio Grande   BS
Finance Faculty
College of Business Mgt
Rio Grande, Ohio 45674
Area Code (614)   Fax 245-9220
Phone: 245-5353
  Palmer, Charles F.   Dean   Ext 268   PHD   76 Va Tech   1988
  Medley, William   Asst   Ext 269   1 R   JD   80 Akron   1987

Roanoke College   BBA,BS,BA
Finance Faculty
Business
Salem, Virginia 24153-3794
Area Code (703)   Fax 375-2426
  Gibson, Gerald W.   Dean   PHD   84 Tenn   1984
  Fleming, Garry A.   Assoc   375-2428   24   PHD   Kentucky   1987
  Lynch, Larry A.   Assoc   375-2413   12 B   PHD   Va Tech   1978

Robert Morris College   BS,MS,MBA
Dept of Economics & Finance
School of Management
Corappolis, Penn 15108-1189
Area Code (412)   Fax 391-3329
  Moricz, Joseph M.   Dean   262-8241   Mgt   DBA   64 Indiana   1969
  Dudley, Bob G.   C   262-8342   Econ   MS   Tx A&M   1971
  Alford, Ray   Prof   262-8476   PHD   Renssel
  DeLosSantos, Adora   Asst   227-6847   PHD   Penn St
  Dennick-Ream, Zane A.   Asst   262-8435   MBA   Iowa
  Letterman, Denise   Asst   262-8434   MBA   Penn St
  Miller, Richard K.   Asst   227-6802
  Swanson, Diane   Asst   227-6889   MA   Missouri

University of Rochester   MBA,PHD
Department of Finance   1964
Simon Grad Sch of BusAd
Rochester, NY 14627
Area Code (716)   Fax 271-8752
  Plosser, Charles I.   Dean$ 275-3316   Econ   PHD   76 Chicago   1978
    Fred H. Gowen Professor of Business Administration
  Jarrell, Gregg A.   Prof   275-3915   PHD   Chicago
    Director of the Simon School's Bradley Policy Research Center
  Long Jr., John B.   Prof   PHD   71 Car Mel   1969
  Pearson, Neil D.   Prof   PHD   MIT
  Schwert, G. William   Prof   275-2470   PHD   Chicago
    Gleason Professor of Finance & Statistics

Shanken, Jay A.   Prof   PHD   Car Mel
Smith Jr., Clifford W.   Prof   275-3217   PHD   N Carol
  Clarey Professor of Finance and Economics
Warner, Jerold B.   Prof   PHD   Chicago
  Chairperson of PHD Program
Watts, Ross L.   Prof   275-4278   PHD   71 Chicago   1971
  Rochester Telephone Corporation Professor
Barclay, Michael J.   Asst   PHD   Stanford
Bodnar, Gordon M.   Asst   ABD   Princeto

Rochester Inst of Technology   BS,MBA
Dept of Accounting & Finance   1988,1988
College of Business
Rochester, NY 14623-0887
Area Code (716) Fax 475-7055
RITVAX
  Rosett, Richard N.   Dean   475-6915 RNRBBU   Econ   PHD   57 Yale   1990
  Woerheide, Walter J.   C-Pr   475-5268 WJWBBU   23 MSX   PHD   77 Wash U   1990
  Helmuth, John   Assoc   475-2718 JAHBBU   13 C   PHD   S Carol   1981
  Mattson, Kyle Logan   Asst   475-5191 KLMBBU   12 M   DBA   88 Kentucky   1989
  Galloway, James   475-2083 JCGBBU   12   PHD   Virginia
  Lessard, Jeffrey P.   475-6136 JPLBBU   12 G   PHD   83 Arkansas   1989
  Robin, Ashok J.   475-5211 AJRBBU   14 J   PHD   79 SUNY-Buf   1989

Rockhurst College   BSBA,MBA
Finance Faculty
School of Mangement
Kansas City, MO 64110-2508
Area Code (816) Fax 926-4666
  Clark, Robert M.   Dean   926-4200   PHD   88 Syracuse   1991
  Lyn, Thomas L.   Prof   926-4200   PHD   70 Missouri   1975
  Fitzpatrick, Brian   Asst   926-4200   PHD   90 St Louis   1990
  Satyanarayan,   926-4200   MA   85 Toledo   1991

Rollins College   MBA
Department of Finance   1985
Crummer Grad Sch of Bus
Winter Park, FL 32789-4499
Area Code (407) Fax 646-1550
ROLLINS
  Certo, Samuel C.   Dean   646-2249 SCERTO   PHD   73 Ohio   1986
  Moses, Edward A.   Prof   646-2610 EMOSES   12 DFJM   PHD   70 Georgia   1989
  Veit, E. Theodore   Prof   646-2538 TVEIT   12 DIMO   PHD   77 Arkansas   1988
  Currie, David M.   Assoc   646-2154 DCURRIE   13 BR   PHD   76 S Carol   1978
  Trifts, Jack W.   Assoc   646-2404 JTRIFTS   12 FGJO   PHD   84 Florida   1989

Roosevelt University   BS,MBA,MS
Department of Finance
Heller College Bus Adm
Chicago, IL 60605-1394
Area Code (312) Fax 341-3659
  Matasar, Ann B.   Dean   341-3820   Mgt   PHD   Columbia   1984
  Swanton, Donald W.   C-Ac   341-3805   12 RS   PHD   74 Northwes   1978
  Williams, Bismarck   Prof   341-3716   12   ABD   Chicago   1964
  Liberman, Joseph   Assoc   341-3779   12 EM   PHD   82 Chicago   1988
  Krabbenhoft, Alan   Asst   341-3835   12 UV   ABD   Wayne St   1991

Russell Sage College
Finance Faculty
Econ & Business Dept
Troy, New York 12180-4115
Area Code (518) Fax 271-4545
  Brandt, Frederick   D-Ac   445-1763   Mgt   PHD   Ariz St   1982
  Nikolaos, Adamou   Asst   445-1763   1   CFO   PHD   1989

Rutgers University-Camden   BA,BS
Finance Faculty
School of Business
Camden, N Jersey 08102
Area Code (609) Fax 757-6231
  Leontiades, Milton   Dean   757-6216   Mgt   PHD   66 American   1974
  LaBarge, Richard A.   Prof
  Yaari, Uzi   Assoc   757-6216   PHD   Chicago
  Gregory-Allen, Russell B.   Asst   757-6216   PHD   N Txs St
  LaBarge, Karin   Asst   757-6218   PHD   Berkeley

94

Rutgers Un-Newark Undergrd BS,MBA
Department of Finance
Div of Mgt Studies
Newark, NJ 07102
Area Code (201) Fax
Did Not Respond

Rutgers Univ-Newark Grad MS,MBA,PHD
Dept of Business Adm 1983,1941
Grad School of Mgt
Newark, N Jersey 07102
Area Code (201) Fax 648-5889
DRACO
  Farris, George F. Dean$ 648-5128 Mgt PHD 66 Michigan 1980
  Crew, Michael A. H-Pr 648-5049 PHD Bradford
  Bicksler, James L. Prof 64853153 PHD 67 NYU
  Brick, Ivan E. Prof 648-5221 PHD Columbia
  Dunning, John VProf 648-5885 PHD Upsala
    State of New Jersey Professor of International Business
  Fisher, Lawrence Prof 648-5981 PHD Chicago
    First Fidelity Bank Reseach Professor
  Marshall, Richard D. Prof 648-5295 LLB 56 Howard 1972
  Mellon, W. Giles Prof 648-5297 PHD Princeto
  Whitcomb, David K. Prof 648-5264 PHD 68 Columbia 1975
  Long, Michael Assoc 648-5471 PHD Purdue
  Ravid, S. Abraham Assoc 648-5540 PHD Cornell
  Chang, LyJune Asst 648-5836 PHD Car Mel
  Kim, Yong O. Asst 648-5272 PHD New York
  Murthy, Shashidhar N. Asst 648-5395 PHD Columbia
  Nadler, Paul S. Asst 648-5685 PHD New York
  Tessitore, Anthony Asst 648-1147 ABD Baruch
  Viswanath, P. V. Asst 648-5899 PHD Chicago

Rutgers Univ-New Brunswick BS
Department of Finance
School of Business
New Brunswick NJ 08903
Area Code (908) Fax 932-5647
  Kraft, Arthur Dean 932-3582 Econ PHD 70 SUNY 1987
  Lee, Cheng-Few C 932-3530 Econ PHD 73 SUNY 1988
  Hardouvelis, Gikas Assoc 932-4188 PHD 84 UC 1989
  Palmon, Oded Assoc 932-4209 PHD 81 Chicago 1988
  Cakici, Nusret Asst 932-5109 PHD 89 CUNY 1988
  Chen, Ren-Raw Asst 932-4236 PHD 90 Illinois 1990
  Kim, Dongcheol Asst 932-4195 PHD 89 Michigan 1989

Saginaw Valley State Univ BBA,MBA
Department of Finance
School of Bus & Mgt
Univ Center, MI 48710
Area Code (517) Fax 790-1314
  Mitchell, James L. Dean 790-4064 Atg DBA 67 Mich St 1977
  Mackie, Wayne Prof 790-4311 24 PHD 86 Mich St 1977
  Wetmore, Jill L. Assoc 790-4326 31 PHD 88 Mich St 1981
  Jurn, Iksu Asst 790-4169 14 PHD 89 Nebraska 1990

St. Ambrose University BA,BS,MBA,MACC
Department of Finance
College of Business
Davenport, Iowa 52803
Area Code (319) Fax 383-8791
  Jensen, James O. C $ 383-8759 Mgt PHD 69 Iowa 1980
  Chohan, Ray V. Prof 383-8738 79 UZ PHD 75 Port St 1978
  Mullins, James E. Prof 383-8714 79 UZ MA 65 Marquett 1969
  Shovlain, Ray Prof 383-8773 19 AZ MBA 80 St Ambro 1982
  Withrow, Linda Prof 383-8708 19 AZ MBA 84 St Ambro 1987

Saint Bonaventure Univ BBA,MBA
Department of Finance
School of Business
S Bonaventure NY 14778
Area Code (716) Fax 375-2005
  Burns, John Dean 375-2200 12 FD PHD 70 Mich St 1991
  Kirk, Eugene C-As 375-2111 34 PV PHD 73 Boston C 1972
  Parikh, Rajeev Assoc 375-2111 12 FIO PHD 82 Buffalo 1982
  Martin, David Asst 375-2111 1 PHD 91 St Louis 1988
  Peterson, Jeffrey Asst 375-2111 21 LM PHD 91 Alabama 1984

St. Cloud State University BS,MBA,MS
Dept Management & Finance 1976,1982
College of Business
Saint Cloud, MN 56301-4498
Area Code (612) Fax 255-3986
MSUS1

Name	Title	Phone		Field	Degree	Yr	School	Year
Kelly, James M.	Dean	255-3213		Mgt	DBA	67	Colorado	1987
Tallant, Dwayne	C-Pr	255-3226		Mgt	PHD	70	Nebraska	1979
Kravel, George R.	Prof	255-3067	6 &		DBA	79	Colorado	1980
Rhee, Yinsong	Prof	255-4989			PHD	85	Minn	1988
Young, Peter C.	Prof	255-4986	7 #		PHD	88	Minn	1987
Legg, Thomas D.	Assoc	654-5149			BA	75	Minn	1989
Mooney, Stephen P.	Assoc	255-3074	6 &		MS	82	So Meth	1986
Thomas, David J. on leave	Assoc	255-2247			PHD	79	Nebraska	1980
Yook, Ken C.	Assoc	255-2241 KYOOK	12 DG		PHD	89	Nebraska	1989
Bohnen, Howard W.	Asst	255-2257			MBA	72	St Cloud	1973

St. Edward's University BBA,MBA
Department of Finance
School of Business Adm
Austin, Texas 78704
Area Code (512) Fax 488-8492

Name	Title	Phone		Field	Degree	Yr	School	Year
Oveisi, Hadi F.	Dean	448-8696		Fnce	PHD	79	Texas	1981
Lambert Jr., Eugene W.	Assoc	448-8673	12		PHD	63	Alabama	1989

St. Francis College BS
Department of Finance
Business
Brooklyn Hght NY 11201
Area Code (718) Fax 522-1274
Did Not Repsond; Phone 522-2300

Name	Title				Degree		School	
O'hare, Emett N.	C	$			MS		NY Ins T	

Saint Francis College BS
Finance Faculty
Dept of Business Adm
Loretto, Penn 15940
Area Code (814) Fax 472-3044
Did Not Respond

Name	Title	Phone		Field	Degree	Yr	School	Year
Maher, Thomas	Dean	472-3004			PHD			
Frye, Randy L.	C-Pr	472-3087		Atg	MBA	80	Ind-PA	1980

St. John Fisher College MBA
Finance Faculty
Grad School of Mgt
Rochester, NY 14618
Area Code (716) Fax 385-8094

Name	Title	Phone	Degree	School
Sen, Asim	Dir	385-8079	PHD	Rutgers
Ilter, Selim S.	C		PHD	Geo St
Sakariya, Sohanraj	Assoc	385-8132	MBA	Cal St
Stendardi, Edward J.	Assoc	385-8093	MBA	SUNY-Alb
Lakehal-Ayat, Merouane	Asst	385-8429	MIM	Denver

St. John's University 1968,1982
Dept of Economics & Finance
College of Business
Jamaica, N York 11439
Area Code (718) Fax 380-3803

Name	Title	Phone	Degree	Yr	School	Year
Mauer, Laurence J.	Dean	990-6477	PHD		Tenn	
Chen, Thomas	C	990-6420	PHD			
Carvounis, Chris	Prof	390-4518	PHD		N Sch Re	
Eng, Maximo	Prof	990-6161	PHD	66	NYU	
Lees, Francis A.	Prof	990-6161	PHD	61	NYU	1960
Ellis, M. E.	Assoc	537-6194	PHD		S Carol	
Flowers, Edward B.	Assoc	990-6161	PHD		Geo St	
Harris, Malcolm C.	Assoc	990-6161	PHD			
Marshall, John F.	Assoc	990-6161	PHD		SUNY-SBr	
Bansal, Vipul	Asst	990-6161	PHD			
Dorigan, Michael	Asst	390-4518	PHD			
Haye, Eric	Asst	990-6161	PHD			
Kim, Chang-soo	Asst	990-6161	PHD			
Lee, Sung	Asst	990-6161	PHD			
Liaw, K. Thomas	Asst	990-6161	PHD			
Moy, Ronald	Asst	390-4518	PHD			
Wong, Matthew	Asst	990-6161	PHD			
Yuyuenyongwatana, Robert P.	Asst	990-6161	PHD			

Saint Joseph's University
Department of Finance
College of Bus & Adm
Philadelphia, PA 19131-1395
Area Code (215) Fax 660-1625
SJUPHIL

Lord, John B.	Dean	660-1645 JLORD		Mktg	PHD	84 Temple	1975
Webster Jr., George H.	C-As				PHD	81 SUNY-Bin	1980
Foster, Paul L.	Prof	660-1669			DBA	69 Virginia	1979
Tezel, Ahmet	Assoc				PHD	73 Berkeley	1985
Coyne, Christopher	Asst				PHD	86 Temple	1978
Rahmlow, Harold F.	Asst				PHD	65 Wash St	1987
Tharthare, Suresh K.	Asst				PHD	87 Temple	1985
Fuhrmann, Thomas							
McManus, Ginette							
Pescow, Michael							

Saint Louis University   BS,MPA,PHD
Department of Finance   1948,1978
School of Bus & Adm
St. Louis, MO 63108
Area Code (314) Fax 658-3874
SLUVCA

Turner, Emery C.	Dean	658-3833		Atg	DBA	66 Wash U	1985
Tyree, Donald A.	C-Pr	658-3858	1		PHD	59 Texas	
Guithues, Henry J.	Prof	658-3847	1		PHD	64 St Louis	
James, Charles A.	Prof		3		PHD	70 St Louis	
Kim, Seung Hee	Prof	658-3898	4		PHD	69 New York	
Seitz, Neil E.	Prof		1		PHD	73 Ohio St	1973
Yeager, Frederick Conrad	Prof		3		PHD	72 W Virgin	
Gillespie, William B.	Assoc		2		PHD	Florida	
Nasseh, Alireza	Assoc		3		PHD	Mich St	
Wright, Thomas V.	Assoc	658-3863	3		PHD	Wash U	
Loughlin, John	Inst		2				
Nichols, Michael	Inst		4				
Singer, Robert	Inst						

Saint Martin's College   BS
Finance Faculty
Business Division
Lacey, Wash 98503
Area Code (206) Fax
  Knutson, Jerry L.   Dean

Saint Mary's College   BS
Finance Faculty
Sch of Econ & Bus Adm
Moraga, Calif 94575
Area Code (415) Fax 631-4000

Walter, C. J.	Dean	631-4604			PHD	66 Iowa	1983
Snyder, D.	Prof	631-4607	12 RV		PHDj	71 Penn St	1990
Thompson, J.	Prof	631-4607	13 PCD		MBA	63 Chicago	1979

Saint Marys College   BBA,BA
Finance Faculty
Dept of Bus Adm & Econ
Notre Dame, IN 46556-5001
Area Code (219) Fax 284-4716

McElroy, Jerome L.	C-Pr	284-4501	4 R		PHD	71 Colorado	1982
Robinson, Michael L.	Asst	284-4511	23 F		MBA	78 Loyola	1984
Vihtelic, Jill Lynn	Asst	284-4507	14 RX		MBA	82 Mich St	1987

St. Mary's University-Tx
Dept of Decision Support
School of Bus & Adm
San Antonio, TX 78284
Area Code (512) Fax 431-2115
STMARYTX

Manuel, David	Dean			Econ	PHD	75 Miss	
Bauer Jr., Richard J.	Assoc	661-3268			PHD	85 Tx Tech	
Dahlquist, Julie D.	Asst				ABD	Tx A&M	
Davis, Maria F.	Asst				MBA	77 Trinity	
Hamilton, Thomas R.	Asst	436-3705			ABD	Tx Tech	

96

St. Norbert College BBA
Finance Faculty
Dept of Business Adm
DePere, Wiscon 54115-2099
Area Code (414) Fax 337-4073
INTERNET SNCAC SNC EDU
  Ritter, Jeffrey D.   D-As 337-3234 RITTER   Atg MBA 74 Miami U 1983
  Bursik, Paul B.   Asst   337-3241 BURSIK 13 ADMN ABD 89 Wash St 1990
  Varamini, M. Hossein Asst   337-3237 VARAMINI 24 CJLV PHD 85 Kans St 1987

Saint Peter's College
Department of Finance
College of Business
Jersey City, NJ 07306
Area Code (201) Fax 435-3662
Did Not Respond

College of Saint Rose BS,MS,MBA
Finance Faculty
School of Business
Albany, New York 12203
Area Code (518) Fax 438-3293
Did Not Respond
  Hughes, Barry J.   C-As 458-5466   Atg MBA   St Rose 1984

College of St Scholastica
Finance Faculty
Management Department
Duluth, Minn 55811
Area Code (218) Fax 723-6290
Did Not Respond
  Jones, Patricia   C   723-6000

St. Thomas University
Finance Faculty
Business
Miami, Florida 33054
Area Code (305) Fax 628-6510
Did Not Respond

University of St. Thomas-MN BA
Department of Finance
Business Adm Mail #6010
St. Paul, Minn 55105-1096
Area Code (612) Fax 647-5897
Did Not Respond
  Beckmann, Heino   Assoc 647-5810   PHD   Penn   1986
  Williams, Melvin D. Assoc 647-5677
  Vang, David O.   Asst   647-5649   PHD   Iowa St 1988

University of St. Thomas-TX BA,BBA,MBA
Finance Faculty
Cameron School of Bus
Houston, Texas 77006-4696
Area Code (713) Fax
  Ho, Yhi-Min   Dean   PHD   Vanderbi
  Wilbratte, Barry F. C-Pr   522-7911   12   PHD   Tulane
  Shirvani, Hassan M. Assoc 522-7911   12   PHD   Harvard 1986

Saint Xavier College BA,MBA
Finance Faculty
Graham School of Mgt
Chicago, IL 60655
Area Code (312) Fax 799-9073
  Rahman, Faisal   Dean   779-8661   Mgt   PHD   St Louis 1989
  Weeks, Benjamin   D-Ac   779-8661   Mgt   PHD   St Louis 1986
  Varjavand, Reza   Assoc 779-8661   PHD   Oklahoma 1986
  Brown, Mary Robbie Asst   779-8661   ABD   Northwes 1988
  Galvan, Mary   Asst   779-8661   PHD   N Ill   1987
  Tainer, Elevina   Asst   779-8661   PHD

Salem State College BS,MBA
Department of Finance
School of Business
Salem, Mass 01970-4589
Area Code (508) Fax
Phone 741-6000
McLanahen, Craig	Dean$	Ext 6630			MBA		
Ryan, Carolyn J.	Assoc	Ext 7274	12	DEFK	PHD	Clark	1990
Spangler, Gordon	Assoc	Ext 7274	13	CF	PHD	Tufts	1984
McGee, Paul	Asst	Ext 6630	12	FI	MS	Boston C	1990

Salisbury State University BS,MBA
Department of Finance
Franklin Perdue Sch Bus
Salisbury, MD 21801-6860
Area Code (301) Fax 543-6068
Bebee, Richard F.	Dean	543-6316		Atg	DBA	71 Colorado	1991
Bello, Zakri Y.	Assoc	543-6327			PHD	83 Va Tech	1987
Khazeh, Khashayar	Assoc	543-6328			PHD	85 Tenn	1985
Tirtiroglu, Dogan	Asst	543-6320			PHD	91	1991

Sam Houston State Univ BBA,MBA,MS
Dept of Gen Bus & Finance
College of Business Adm
Huntsville, TX 77341
Area Code (409) Fax 294-3612
Did Not Respond
Gilmore, James E.	Dean	294-1254	Fnce	EDD	69 Houston	1956
Ashorn Jr., Leroy W.	C-Pr	294-1278		PHD	Arkansas	
Carter, Michael	Asst			MBA	Baylor	

Samford University
Finance Faculty
School of Business
Birmingham, AL 35229
Area Code (205) Fax 870-2464
Did Not Respond
David, Robert T.	Dean	870-2308		MBA	Harvard	1988

University of San Diego BS,MS,MBA,MIB
Finance Faculty 1980,1981
School of Business Adm
San Diego, Calif 92110
Area Code (619) Fax 260-4891
ACUSD
Did Not Respond--Taken from College Catalog
Burns, James M.	Dean	260-4886	Mgt	DBA	68 Harvard	1974
Picconi, Mario J.	Prof			PHD	Rutgers	
Hennigar, Elizabeth S.	Assoc	260-4843		DBA	Indiana	
Rivetti, Daniel A.	Assoc	260-4844		DBA	Kent St	
Zocco, Dennis	Assoc			PHD	Lehigh	
Deshpande, Shreesh D.	Asst	260-4863				

San Diego State University BS,MS,MBA
Department of Finance 1959,1963
College of Business Adm
San Diego, Calif 92182-0096
Area Code (619) Fax 594-1573
INTERNET @SCIENCES.SDSU.EDU
Bailey, Allan R.	Dean	594-5259	ABAILEY		Atg	PHD	69 UCLA	1968
Varaiya, Nikhil P.	C	594-5323	NVARALYA	1	DGHP	PHD	83 U Wash	1988
Gitman, Lawrence J.	Prof	594-6417		1	CIDF	PHD	Cinn	1989
Haddad, Kamal M.	Prof	594-5311		1	CFI	PHD	Nebraska	1981
Hutchins, Robert C.	Prof	594-6844		2	M#	PHD	71 S Calif	1968
Nye, William A.	Prof	594-2661		27	M#	PHD	62 Penn	1962
Reints, William W.	Prof	594-4411		1	CDEF	PHD	66 U Wash	1966
Salehizadeh, Mehdi	Prof	594-4305	MSALEHIZ	4	UVW	PHD		1980
Short, James L.	Prof	594-4894		6	&	PHD	73 UCLA	1973
Sterk, William E.	Prof	594-4788		1	CDLO	PHD	Wiscon	1978
Vandenberg, Pieter A.	Prof	594-3027		1	CDLO	DBA	72 S Calif	1969
Warschauer, Thomas Associate Dean	Prof	594-5259	TWARSCHA	3	MNXS	PHD		1977
Block, Russell L.	Assoc	594-2496				JD	Berkeley	1969
Bost, John L.	Assoc	594-5690				JD	Hastings	1979
Cherin, Tony C.	Assoc	594-5657	TCHERIN	27	KPTX	PHD		1982

Houston, Arthur L.	Assoc	594-2721		17	D&	PHD		U Wash	1986
Omberg, Edward	Assoc	594-6418	EOMBERG	4	LUVW	PHD		UCLA	1989
Sachdeva, Kanwal S.	Assoc	594-2477		1	CDLO	PHD			1976
Wilbur, Robert W.	Assoc	594-4749		16	&	PHD		U Wash	1974
Do, Andrew Q.	Asst	594-5324		6	&	PHD		LSU	1990
Ely, David P.	Asst	594-6842	DELY	3	PRG	PHD		Ohio St	1986
Hanson, Robert C.	Asst	594-7774	RHANSON	1	DGOF	PHD		Utah	1987
Hittle, Linda C.	Asst	594-2830	LHITTLE	1	DEIO	PHD		Colorado	1987
Kim, Tong Suk	Asst	594-2699	TKIM	2	LUVW	PHD		Ohio St	1989
Song, Moon	Asst	594-5334	MSONG	1	DGA	PHD		Ohio St	1988

University of San Francisco
Department of Finance
McLaren Sch of Business
San Francisco CA 94117-1080
Area Code (415) Fax 666-2502
Did Not Respond--Taken from College Catalog
BS
1953,1982

Williams, Gary G.	Dean	666-6384	Mktg	PHD	66	Stanford	1978
Nye, Blaine	Prof	666-6519		PHD	84	Stanford	1988
Doyle, Barry W.	Assoc	666-6129		PHD		Oregon	
Bi, Keqian	Asst	666-6414		PHD	89	Florida	1989
Gardner, William	Asst	666-6696		PHD	59	Indiana	1975

San Francisco State Univ
Department of Finance
School of Business
San Francisco CA 94132
Area Code (415) Fax 338-6237
BS,MBA
1963,1975

Cunningham, Arthur F.	Dean	338-1276		Mktg	JD	53	Brooklyn	1974
Chen, Yea Mow	Prof	338-1038	13	PRT	PHD	84	Ohio St	1984
Hsiao, P.	Prof	338-2975	12	AJMN	PHD	89	S Calif	1989
Jung, A.	Prof	338-7487	12	HJLN	PHD	90	Berkeley	1989
Mansinghka, S.	Prof	338-1032	13	DFGH	PHD	71	UCLA	1975
Messina, J.	Prof	338-6348	13	EFHN	PHD	79	Berkeley	1977
Platt, W. G.	Prof	338-7470	12	BFJN	PHD	73	Wayne	1976
Somanath, V. S.	Prof	338-1508	14	UVW	PHD	81	New York	1988
Sortino, F.	Prof	338-2380	12	KMNO	PHD	81	Oregon	1980
Tzang, Dah Nein	Prof	338-6084	13	LMRT	PHD	86	Illinois	1989
Wade, J.	Prof	338-6085	13	PY	PHD	72	Stanford	1969
Wong, S.	Prof	338-7488	12	LMNO	PHD	65	Berkeley	1967

San Jose State University
Dept of Accounting & Finance
School of Business
San Jose, Calif 95192-0066
Area Code (408) Fax 924-3419
BS
1967,1973

Burak, Marshall J.	Dean	924-3400	Fnce	DBA	68	S Calif	1981
Mori, Joseph E.	C-Pr	924-3460	Atg	PHD	72	Santa Cl	1964
Ashley, William L.	Prof	924-8466		PHD	80	Georg St	1984
Campsey, Billy J.	Prof	924-3400		PHD	79	Tx Arlin	1982
Associate Dean							
Harper, Charles P.	Prof	924-3464		PHD	79	Tx A&M	1984
Rose, Lawrence	Prof	924-3486		PHD	85	Tx A&M	1985
Zaima, Janis K.	Prof	924-3490		PHD	80	U Wash	1986
Black, Joseph H.	Assoc	924-3478		MBA	77	San Jose	1987
Cochran, R. Bruce	Assoc	924-3491					
Elan, Don	Assoc	924-1339					
Solt, Michael E.	Assoc	924-3497					
Sun, Y. Elizabeth	Assoc	725-1021					

Sangamon State University
Department of Finance
School of Bus & Mgt
Springfield, IL 62794-9243
Area Code (217) Fax 786-7188
Did Not Respond
BA,MA

Nosari, John S.	Dean	786-6355	Atg	PHD	84	St Louis	1978
Heshmat, Shahram	Asst	786-6306					

Santa Clara University BS,MBA
Department of Finance 1953,1963
Leavey School Bus & Adm
Santa Clara, CA 95053
Area Code (408)   Fax 554-4571
SCU
  Koch, James L. Dean 554-4523 Mgt PHD 72 UCLA 1990
  Statman, Meir C 554-4147 MSTATMAN Fnce PHD 79 Columbia 1979
  Shefrin, Hersh Prof 554-6893 HSHEFRIN PHD 74 London 1979
  Chow, Edward Asst 554-2777 PHD 90 Indiana 1990
  Hamilton, Sally A. Asst 554-2776 SHAMILTO PHD 87 UCLA 1988
  Jo, Hoje Asst 544-4779 PHD 86 Florida 1990

Savannah State College BBA
Department of Finance
School of Business
Savannah, GA 31404
Area Code (912) Fax
  Honeycutt, Andrew E. Dean 356-2816 Mktg DBA 75 Harvard 1991
  Alemayehu, Tsehai Prof 356-2830 14 UW PHD Kentucky 1985

University of Scranton BS,MBA
Department of Finance
School of Management
Scranton, Penn 18510-4602
Area Code (717)   Fax 941-4201
SCRANTON
  Horton, Joseph J. Dean 941-4208 JH446 Econ PHD 68 So Meth 1986
  Giunta, A. John Prof 941-6179 PHD 56 Syracuse 1960
  Bose, Mrigen Assoc 941-7727 PHD 72 Utah 1968
  Corcione, Frank P. Assoc 941-7720 PHD 75 Lehigh 1978
  Grambo Jr., Ralph W. Assoc 941-7417 PHD 73 Penn 1973
  Hussain, Riaz Assoc 941-7497 PHD 73 J Hopkin 1967
  Kallianiotis, Ioannis Assoc 941-7577 PHD 85 CUNY 1990
  Nguyen, Hong V. Assoc 941-7475 PHD 81 SUNY-Bin 1979
  Ghosh, Satyajit P. Asst 941-6197 PHD 90 SUNY-Buf 1986
  Rajan, Murli Asst 941-6240 MBA 85 Scranton 1989
  Scahill, Edward M. Asst 941-4187 PHD 83 SUNY-Bin 1989
  Trussler, Susan Asst 941-6122 PHD 89 Penn St 1985

Seattle University BA
Dept of Econ & Finance 1965,1980
Albers School of Bus
Seattle, Wash 98122-4460
Area Code (206)   Fax 461-5795
  Viscione, Jerry A. Dean 296-5700 Econ PHD 73 Boston U 1988
  Dibee, Khalil Prof 296-5716 12 FICD PHD 62 Texas 1964
  Hendrickson, Hildegard R. Prof 296-5704 13 PR PHD 66 U Wash 1967
  Erickson, Suzanne M. Asst 296-5736 1 ADG PHD 87 U Wash 1986
  Robertson, J. Fiona Asst 296-5791 12 AJL MA 82 Queens 1987
  Trevino, Ruben C. Asst 296-5745 12 KLMW PHD 80 Alabama 1987

Seattle Pacific University BA,MBA
Finance Faculty
School of Bus & Econ
Seattle, Wash 98119
Area Code (206)   Fax 281-2500
  Knight, Kenneth Dean 281-2992 Mgt PHD 63 Carnegie 1989
  Kierulff, Herbert Prof 281-3523 DBA 66 S Calif 1980
  Hess, Daniel Assoc 281-2192 PHD 82 Arizona 1987

Seton Hall University BS,MBA,MST
Finance Faculty 1978,1984
Stillman Sch Business
South Orange, NJ 07079-2692
Area Code (201)   Fax 761-9217
  Kelly, Fredrick J. Dean 761-9013 PHD 74 Columbia
  Hunter Jr., Richard C $ 761-9237 JD 76 Notre Dm
  Arnold, Henry Prof 761-9255 PHD 82 New Sch
  Harrington, John Prof 761-9231 PHD 77 New York
  Manley, John Prof 761-9103 MBA 81 Baruch
  Pasmantier, Anita Prof 761-9707 PHD 89 Fordham
  Phillips, Philip Prof 761-9505 PHD 62 New York
  Sawyer, Granville Prof 761-9233 PHD 85 Tenn
  Wagner, Cecilia Prof 761-9535 PHD 88 China
  Yoon, Yeomin Prof 761-9229 PHD 75 Penn

Shenandoah College — BBA,MBA
Finance Faculty
Byrd School of Business
Winchester, VA 22601-5195
Area Code (703) Fax 665-4508
Did Not Respond
 Ladd, Richard   Dean$ 665-4526   Econ PHD 67 Conn   1987

Shepherd College — BS
Finance Faculty
Division of Bus Adm
Shepherdstown,WV 25443-1569
Area Code (304) Fax
Did Not Respond
 Rath, G. Norris   C-Pr 876-2511   Mgt   MS   W Virg   1963

Shippensburg University — BS
Dept Fin Adm, Mgt Sci & IS   1981
College of Business
Shippensburg, PA 17257
Area Code (717) Fax 532-1273
 Armstrong, Ruth D.   Dean$ 532-1435   Bis   DED 67 Penn St   1967
 Roth, Herbert J.   C-Pr$ 532-1768   16 CF&   PHD 68 Ohio St   1968
 Hocking, Ralph T.   Prof 532-9565   12 JLMN   DBA 72 Kent St   1972
 Barrow, Janice M.   Assoc 532-1398   13 ABPR   PHD   Houstonn   1988
 Pan, Ming-Shiun   Assoc 532-1683 MSPANO 12 JLNV PHD   Alabama   1989
 Rim, Hong K.   Assoc 532-1172   14 LVW   PHD   Penn St   1986

Siena College — BA,BS,BBA
Department of Finance
Division of Business
Loundonville, NY 12211-1462
Area Code (518) Fax 783-4293
 Kopp, Thomas   H-Ac 783-4272   34 GR   PHD 83 SUNY-Bin   1984
 Trent, Paul A.   Prof 783-4251   67 &   MBA   Long Is   1977
 Richardson, Linda L. Assoc 782-2927   12 DGM   PHD   Arkansas   1991
 Ruggeri, Paul J.   Assoc 783-4254   14 IY   ABD   Renssela   1984
 Dwyer, Jr., Paul F.   Asst 783-2983   16 &   JD   New Eng   1987
 Sheridan, Patrick J. Asst 783-4287   12 M   MBA   Siena C   1979
 Shtzel, Elwood W.   Asst 783-4264   1 F   MBA   New Hamp   1980
 Sparling, Beverly   Asst 783-4275   12 M   ABD   Renssela   1988

Simmons College — BA
Finance Faculty
Dept of Management
Boston, Mass 02115-5898
Area Code (617) Fax 738-2099
 Robinson, John S.   Dean 738-3127   DED 71 Harvard
 Betters-Reed, Bonita L. C-Ac 738-2201   Mgt   PHD 83 Boston C
 Rouse, Michael   Inst 738-2201   MBA 81 Boston U

Skidmore College — BS
Finance Faculty
Department of Business
Saratoga Sprg NY 12866-1632
Area Code (518) Fax 584-3023
Phone 584-5000
 Balevic, Betty V.   C-Ac Ext 2330   Mgt   MS   SUNY-Alb   1969
 Trimble, Donald   Assoc   13   MBA   Harvard   1986
 McCarthy, David   Asst Ext 2757   14 JLW   MBA   Stanford   1991

Slippery Rock University — BS
Dept of Economics & Finance
Business
Slippery Rock PA 16057-1326
Area Code (412) Fax 738-2098
 Mastrianna, Frank V. Dean 738-2008   Econ PHD 68 Cinn   1987
 Mamoozadeh, G. Abbas C   738-2578   PHD   Kent   1981
 Noorbakhsh, Abbas   Assoc 738-2576   PHD   Kansas   1990

Sonoma State University
Finance Faculty
School Business & Econ
Rohnert Park, CA 94928
Area Code (707) Fax 664-4009

BA,MBA

Name	Rank	Phone		Field	Degree		School	Year
Doutt, Jeffrey	Dean	664-2220		Mktg	PHD	79	Berkeley	1973
Anderson, Sherri C.	C $	664-2377		Mgt	MBA	83	Sn Frn S	1980
Allen, Chester L.	Prof	664-3067	1	CF	PHD	73	Tx Tech	1985
Schickele, Sandra	Prof	664-2298	3	PQ	PHD	77	Chicago	1973
Taylor, Keith L.	Prof	664-2220	2	JM	PHD	81	Ariz St	1985

University of South Alabama
Dept of Economics & Finance
Col Bus & Mgt Studies
Mobile, Alabama 36688
Area Code (205) Fax 460-6529

BS,MACC,MBA
1976,1980

Name	Rank	Phone		Field	Degree		School	Year
Moore, Carl C.	Dean	460-6418		Mgt	PHD	71	Alabama	1973
Filer, John E.	Prof		3	PR	PHD		Chicago	1987
Reid, Donald W.	Assoc				PHD		Kentucky	1990
Cromwell, Nancy	Asst		12		PHD		Georgia	1991
McKenna, Frederick W.	Asst	460-7171	13	N	PHD		S Carol	1985
Pereira, Fabio T.	Asst	752-7842	12	VL	PHD		Alabama	1988
Tawarangkoon, W.	Asst				PHD		Mississi	1989
Yoder, James A.	Asst		12	JL	PHD		Florida	1988

Univ So Carolina at Aiken
Finance Faculty
School Bus Adm & Econ
Aiken, S Carol 29801
Area Code (803) Fax 641-3302

BS

Name	Rank	Phone	Field	Degree	School	Year
Hargrove, C. LaFye	H-As	648-6851	Mgt	PHD	Geo Col	1987
Marsh, William H.	Prof	648-6851		PHD	S Carol	

South Carolina-Coastal Carol
Finance Faculty
Wall School of Bus Adm
Conway, S Carol 29526
Area Code (803) Fax 349-2455

BS

Name	Rank	Phone	Field	Degree		School	Year
Baxley, William J.	Dean	349-2641		MBA	62	Alabama	1973
Boyles, Gerald V.	Prof	448-1481		PHD	72	S Carol	
Kendree II, Jack M.	Assoc	349-2641		PHD	89	S Carol	1985
Burney, Robert B.	Asst	349-2641		ABD		S Carol	1991

Univ of South Carolina
Dept Banking,Finance,Insu,RE
College of Bus Adm
Columbia, SC 29208
Area Code (803) Fax 777-6876
BAGAMCOK

BS,MAC,MTX,PHD
1962,1964

Name	Rank	Phone		Field	Degree		School	Year
Kane, James F.	Dean	777-3176		Mktg	DBA	64	Wash U	1967
Roenfeldt, Rodney L.	C-Pr	777-6644	1		DBA	72	Indiana	1974
Brooks, Leroy D.	Prof	777-4906	1		PHD	71	Mich St	
Folks, William R.	Prof	777-3600	4		DBA	70	Harvard	1969
Harrington, Scott E.	Prof	777-4925	7	#	PHD	77	Illinois	
Koch, Timothy W.	Prof	777-6748			PHD	76	Purdue	
Chair of Banking								
Korth, C. M.	Prof	777-3607						
Pritchett, S. Travis	Prof	777-4928	7	#X	DBA	69	Indiana	1973
Wood Jr., Oliver G.	Prof	777-6055	3		PHD	65	Florida	1965
Moore, William T.	Assoc	777-4905	4		PHD	82	Va Tech	
Niehaus, Gregory R.	Assoc	777-7254	7	#	PHD	85	Wash U	
Porter, Robert J.	Assoc	777-6980	1		PHD	65	N Carol	
Rogers, Ronald C.	Assoc	777-5960	6	&	PHD	83	Ohio St	
Sicherman, Neil W.	Assoc	777-7632	12		PHD	86	Florida	
Doerpinglaus, Helen I.	Asst	777-4926	7	#	PHD	89	Penn	
Kwok, Chuck C. Y.	Asst	777-3606	4					
Mann, Steven V.	Asst	777-4929	2		PHD	87	Nebraska	
Ramanlal, Pradipkumer	Asst	777-4928	1		PHD	91	Michigan	

U South Carolina/Spartanburg
Finance Faculty
School of Bus Adm & Eco
Spartanburg, SC 29303
Area Code (803) Fax 599-2598

BSBA

Name	Rank	Phone		Field	Degree		School	Year
Bennett, Jerome V.	Dean	599-2593		Atg	PHD	76	S Carol	1986
Mullis, David L.	Assoc	599-2588	13	FS	DBA	74	Miss St	1986

South Carolina St College
Dept of Bus Administration
School of Business
Orangeburg, SC 29117
Area Code (803)   Fax 536-8066
```
  Wright, Karl S.         Dean  536-7994            AgBs  PHD              1985
  Martinez, Zaida L.      C-As  536-8443
  Baral, Suresh           Asst  536-8982
```

University of South Dakota   BS,MPA,MBA
Department of Finance   1949,1965
School of Business
Vermillion, SD 57069-2390
Area Code (605)   Fax 677-5427
SDNET
```
  Johnson, Jerry W.       Dean  677-5455            Econ  PHD  71 Iowa St    1967
  Oppedahl, Richard A.    Prof  677-5543                  PHD  67 Wash
  Simmons, Joseph T.      Prof  677-5554                  PHD  74 Nebraska   1975
  Turner, Terry L.        Prof  677-5566                  PHD  73 Car Mel
```

University of South Florida   BA,MBA,MACC,PHD
Department of Finance   1969,1980
College of Business Adm
Tampa, Florida 33620-5500
Area Code (813)   Fax 974-3030
CFRVM
```
  Pappas, James L.        Dean  974-4281            Fnce  PHD  68 UCLA       1986
  Kanatas, George         C-Pr                            PHD  78 J Hopkin   1990
  Beenhakker, Arie        Prof  974-2081                  PHD  64 Purdue     1973
  Bolten, Steven E.       Prof  974-2081                  PHD  69 New York   1978
  Kapplin, Steven D.      Prof                            PHD  79 Geo St     1974
  Meyer, Richard L.       Prof  974-2081                  PHD  71 Wiscon     1970
  Power, Fred B.          Prof                            MED  64 Florida    1964
  Schwartz, Arthur L.     Prof  893-9543                  PHD  75 Oregon     1982
  Wieand, Kenneth F.      Prof                            PHD  70 Wash U     1980
  Bulmash, Samuel B.      Assoc 974-2081                  PHD  81 Northwes   1985
  Johnson, Dale A.        Assoc                           DBA  73 Geo St     1970
  Kares, Peter            Assoc 974-2081                  PHD  68 Purdue     1969
  Rivard, Richard J.      Assoc 974-2081                  PHD  78 Tx A&M     1977
  Besley, Scott           Asst  974-2081                  PHD  84 Fla St     1982
  Lee, Hei Wai            Asst                            PHD  89 Illinois   1990
  Modrow, William G.      Asst                            MS   63 Tx A&M     1963
  Quintero, Socorro M.    Asst  974-2081                  PHD  89 Texas      1990
  Sanders, Ralph          Asst                            PHD  88 SUNY       1991
```

Southeast Missouri St Univ   BS,MBA
Dept of Accounting & Finance
College of Business Adm
C Girardeau, MO 63701-4799
Area Code (314)   Fax 651-2909
```
  Schmidt, Richard J.     Dean  651-2112            Atg   PHD  79 Santa Cl   1988
  Russell, Keith A.       C-Ac  651-2118            Atg   PHD  80 Arkansas   1985
  Devaney, Michael T.     Assoc 651-2319       12         PHD  82 Arkansas   1988
  Kunz, David             Assoc 651-2326       14         PHD  88 St Louis   1990
  Uzoau, Ben              Assoc 651-2313       24         PHD  74 Columbia   1986
  Walker, William H.      Assoc 651-2998       14         DBA  82 La Tech    1987
```

Southeastern University   BS,MS,MBA
Dept of Finance Bank & Econ
School of Business
Washington D.C. 20024
Area Code (202)   Fax 488-8093
```
  Agbonyitor, Florence    Dean  488-8162                  EDD
  Safa, Mohammed          H-Pr  488-8162            Econ  PHD     Ruhr
  Colantuoni, Ido E.                                      PHD     NYU
  Dike, Stephen           Adj   488-8162                  PHD
  Fineberg, George                                        MBA     American
  James, Dennison M.                                      MA      Howard
  Kim, Wheegook           Adj                             PHD
  Pilzer, Arthur                                          MBA     American
  Rhoads, Thomas B.                                       MS      Geo Wash
  Stern, Stephen M.                                       MBA     Wharton
  Stubblefield, Ronald                                    MSW     NYU
  Tran, Trong             Adj                             PHD
```

Southeastern Louisiana Univ BS,MBA
Dept of Marketing & Finance 1987,1987
College of Business
Hammond, LA 70402
Area Code (504) Fax 549-5038
  Miller, Joseph H.   Dean   549-2258   Adv   PHD   77 Miss   1971
  Cudd, Robert M.   Prof   549-2146   12 DHM   PHD   Arkansas   1977
  Connell Jr., Frederick L.   Asst   549-2277   14 GU   PHD   88 Fla St   1983
  Duggal, Rakesh   Asst   549-2277   12 GHM   PHD   Arkansas   1989

Southeastern Oklahoma State BS
Dept Bus Adm & Management
School of Business
Durant, Oklahoma 74701
Area Code (405) Fax 924-7313
924-0121 Phone
  Buckles, Richard   Dean   Ext 706   JD   73 S Dakota   1990
  Oliver, Robert   C-Ac   Ext 467   Mgt   PHD   74 Colo St   1984
  Ellis, Barry   Asst   Ext 467   12   MBA   80 E Texas   1982

Southern Col of 7th Day Adv BBA
Finance Faculty
Dept of Bus & Office Ad
Collegedale, TN 37315-0370
Area Code (615) Fax
  Vandevere, Wayne E.   C-Pr   238-2750   Atg   PHD   67 Mich St   1956
  Rolfe, Cecil   Prof   238-2752   PHD   66 Maryland   1964

Southern University BS,MPA
Dept of Economics & Finance
College of Business
Baton Rouge, LA 70813-2064
Area Code (504) Fax 771-2495
  Eisa, Mohamed S.   Dean$ 771-5641   Atg   ABD   LSU
  Hademenos, George   Asst   771-5641   PHD   Houston

Southern Arkansas Univ BBA
Department of Finance
School of Business Adm
Magnolia, AR 71753
Area Code (501) Fax 235-5005
  White, Gayle W.   Dean   235-4300   BEd   EDD   72 Miss   1966
  Rankin, David Foster   C-Pr   235-4310   PHD   Miss   1968
  Boaz, Ralph S.   Prof   235-4303   PHD   Arkansas   1963

Univ of Southern California BS,MBA,PHD
Dept of Finance & Bus Econ 1922,1963
School of Business Adm
Los Angeles, CA 90089-1421
Area Code (213) Fax 740-6650
USCVM
  Borsting, Jack R.   Dean   740-6422   PHD   51 Oregon
  Westerfield, Randolph W.   C-Pr   740-6413   PHD
    Charles B. Thornton Professorship in Finance
  Chan, Yuk-Shee   Prof   740-6538   PHD
  DeAngelo, Harry   Prof   740-6541   PHD   77 UCLA   1991
    Charles E. Cook/Community Bank Chair in Banking Finance & Business Economics
  Shapiro, Alan C.   Prof   454-7318   PHD
    Theodore and Ivadelle Johnson Professor Finance & Business Economics
  Stancill, James   Prof   740-6543   PHD   65 Penn   1964
  Andre, James M.   Asst

Univ of Southern Colorado BSBA
Department of Finance
School of Business
Pueblo, Colorado 81001-4901
Area Code (719) Fax
  Askwig, William J.   Dean   549-2142   Mgt   PHD   69 Tx Tech
  Dhatt, Yoshwonb   Assoc   549-2450   PHD
  Noreiko, Gary   Assoc   549-2200   PHD

105

Southern Connecticut St Un BSBA
Dept of Economics & Finance
School of Business
New Haven, Conn 06515
Area Code (203) Fax 397-4207
```
Leader, Alan H.         Dean   397-4461              Mgt   DBA  63 Indiana
Crakes, Gary            C-Pr   397-4462              Econ  PHD     Conn
Buck, Donald T.         Prof   397-4468                    MA      New Hamp
Hsiao, James C.         Prof   397-4472                    PHD     Conn
Morgan, Alfred D.       Prof   397-4466                    PHD     Harvard
Matsumoto, Keishiro     Assoc  397-4465                    PHD     Minn
Mostaghimi, Mehdi       Assoc  397-4462                    MS      W Mich
```

Southern Illinois Univ BS,MBA,MA,DBA
Department of Finance 1962,1972
College of Bus & Adm
Carbondale, IL 62901-4626
Area Code (618) Fax 453-7961
SIUCVMB
```
Gutteridge, Thomas G.   Dean   453-3328        Mgt   PHD  71 Purdue    1983
Mathur, Iqbal           C-Pr   453-2459     14 CU    PHD  74 Cinn      1977
Davidson III, Wallace N. Prof  453-1429      1 GI    PHD  82 Ohio St   1989
  Rehn Professor of Finance
Elsaid, Hussein H.      Prof   453-1418     13 CU    PHD  68 Illinois  1967
Vaughn, Donald E.       Prof   453-1426     12 M     PHD  61 Texas     1970
Waters, Gola E.         Prof   453-1428              PHD  70 Iowa      1965
Cornett, Marcia M.      Assoc  453-1417     13 GP    PHD  83 Indiana   1990
Rangan, Nanda K.        Assoc  453-1422     13 GP    PHD  86 Tx A&M    1986
Tyler, R. Stanley       Assoc  453-1425              JD   52 Illinois  1970
Rosenstein, Stuart N.   Asst   453-1423     12 GJ    PHD  87 Colorado  1987
Schwarz, Thomas V.      Asst   453-1424     12 JL    PHD  84 Fla St    1988
Szakmary, Andrew C.     Asst   453-1419     14 UV    PHD  91 N Orlean  1991
```

So Illinois, Edwardsville BS,MBA
Dept of Finance & Op Mgt 1975,1980
School of Business
Edwardsville, IL 62026-1104
Area Code (618) Fax 692-3979
SIUEMUS
```
Ault, David E.          Dean   692-3823              Econ  PHD  69 Illinois  1969
So, Jacky C.            C-Ac   692-2980 BGO1               PHD  83 Ohio St   1983
Aucamp, Donald C.       Prof   692-2931                    PHD  71 Wash U    1971
Nyerges, Richard T.     Assoc  692-2939                    PHD  72 Mich St   1980
Bharati, Rakesh C.      Asst   692-2549                    PHD  91 Indiana   1989
Skinner, David L.       Asst   692-2974                    PHD  87 Mich St   1988
```

Univ of Southern Indiana
Finance Faculty
Business
Evansvillle, IN 47712
Area Code (812) Fax 464-1960
```
Fisher, Philip          Dean   464-1718           Mgt    PHD  79 Stanford   1991
Hartl, Robert J.        Assoc  464-1721       13 CIPX    PHD  77 Arkansas   1989
Rhim, Jong C.           Asst   465-1637       12 AEJ     PHD  90 Missouri   1989
```

Univ of Southern Maine BS
Finance Faculty
Sch of Bus, Econ, & Mgt
Portland, Maine 04103-4899
Area Code (207) Fax 780-4662
```
Patton, Robert          Dean   780-4020
Neveu, Raymond P.       Prof   780-4307              PHD  68 Pitt       1982
Sanders, Thomas         Asst   780-4401              PHD  87 Colorado   1988
```

Southern Methodist Univ BBA,MBA
Department of Finance 1925,1979
Cox School of Business
Dallas, Texas 75275-0333
Area Code (214) Fax 692-4099
```
Blake, David H.         Dean   692-3012                    PHD  68 Rutgers   1990
Bowman, Robert G.       Prof   692-3778 J_BOWMAN  12 CDEN  PHD  78 Stanford  1991
Chen, Andrew H.         Prof   692-3179           12 BDLM  PHD  69 Berkeley  1983
  Distinguished Professor of Finance
Frame, Robert J.        Prof   692-2547           12 L     PHD  66 Colorado  1966
Guedes, Jose            Prof   692-4110            1 EHGA  PHD  90 Ohio St   1990
```

Hempel, George H.	Prof	692-2995		31	PFSV	PHD	64	Michigan	1977
Corrigan Professor of Finance									
Peavy III, John W.	Prof	692-3148		12	DMNO	PHD	78	Tx-Arlin	1979
Mary Jo Vaughn Rauscher Chair in Financial Investments									
Thompson, Rex	Prof	692-3052		12	GJZN	PHD	78	Rochest	1988
Caruth Professor of Financial Mangement									
Lam, Chun H.	Assoc	692-2240		13	GKPQ	PHD	77	Duke	1981
Jarrell, Sherry L.	Asst	692-2632		12	AGM	PHD	91	Chicago	1990
Nabar, Prafulla	Asst	692-4157		1	JL	PHD	86	NYU	1987
Opler, Tim	Asst	692-2627		12	BDGJ	PHD	90	UCLA	1991
Sharathchandra, Gopalakrishn		Asst	692-3155		24	JK	PHD 89Berkeley		1988
Vetsuypens, Michael R.	Asst	692-2022		14	BGQ	PHD	83	U Wash	1986

U of Southern Mississippi BSBA,MBA
Department of Finance 1976,1980
College of Business
Hattiesburg, MS 39406-5076
Area Code (601) Fax 266-4630
USMCP6

Black, Tyrone	Dean	266-4659			Econ	PHD	70	Tulane	1978
Daniel, Donnie L.	C-Pr	266-4638	DDANIEL	13	P	PHD	73	Illinois	1977
Dennis, Charles N.	Prof	266-5667		2	KMO	PHD	72	Arkansas	1972
King, Roger	Prof	266-4862		1	P	PHD	69	Tx Tech	1969
Lindley, James T.	Prof	266-4637	LINDLEY	13	PT	PHD	77	Georgia	1990
Taylor, Walt	Assoc	865-4505		2	MN	PHD	73	Penn St	1991
Madaris, Michael	Asst	266-5766	MADARIS	12	GT	PHD	89	Alabama	1989
Sacley, William	Asst	266-4852	SACKLEY	3	P	PHD	90	Nebraska	1990
Cockerham, Mary	Inst	266-5775		1		MBA	83	So Miss	1983
Sirmon, William A.		266-4659							
Associate Dean									

Southern Oregon St College BS,BA,MSBA
Department of Finance
School of Business
Ashland, Oregon 97520-5022
Area Code (503) Fax 482-6429

Carney, Keith T.	Dean	482-6483			Atg	PHD	76	N Colo	1965

Southwest Baptist Univ BS
Finance Faculty
School of Business
Bolivar, MO 65613-2496
Area Code (417) Fax 326-1652

DeBauche, G.	Dean	326-1752			Mgt	EDD		Arkansas	1975

Southwest Missouri St Univ BS,MACC
Finance & Gen Bus Dept
College of Business
Springfield, MO 65804-0094
Area Code (417) Fax 836-6337
SMSVMA

Bottin, Ronald R.	Dean	836-5646			Atg	PHD	74	Missouri	1990
Swales, George S.	H-Ac$	836-5504		12	MNS	PHD	84	Arkansas	1982
Kim, Kee S.	Assoc	836-6345		12	BEV	PHD	78	Texas	1988
Litvan, John K.	Assoc	836-5567		13	BCP	PHD	81	Arkansas	1980
Pettijohn, James B.	Assoc	836-5646		1	FY	PHD	80	Nebraska	1982
Associate Dean									
Squires, Jan R.	Assoc	836-5566		13	FMP	DBA	84	Virginia	1987
Chang, C. Edward	Asst	836-5563		14	PRV	PHD	89	Illinois	1989
Elayan, Fayez A.	Asst	836-5569		14	BGP	PHD	85	LSU	1990
Scott, James R.	Asst	836-5362		13	FY	ABD		Georgia	1988
Young, Philip J.	Asst	836-5580		13	AG	PHD	90	Arkansas	1990

Southwest State University BS
Finance Faculty
Business
Marshall, Minn 56258
Area Code (507) Fax 537-7154

Steel, Carolyn	Dean	537-6218				PHD	73	Chicago	1989
Mitchell, George	C	537-6223			Mgt	ABD			
Abbott, Joann	Asst	537-6194		12	CFJM	MS	91	St Cloud	1987

Southwest Texas State Univ
Dept of Finance & Economics
School of Business
San Marcos, TX 78666-4616
Area Code (512) Fax 245-3089

BBA,MBA

Gowens, Paul R.	Dean	245-2311		Econ	PHD	73	Miss	1980
Morgan, Celia A.	C $	245-2547	3		PHD	71	Houston	1971
Carman, D. Gary	Prof	245-2547	2	XY	PHD	73		1975
Garnett, Robert H.	Assoc	245-2547	13	KZ	PHD	81	Penn	1982
Bae, Gi-Beom	Asst	245-2547	14	PV	ABD		Geo St	1990
Lang, Darla F.	Asst	245-2547	1	AF	ABD		Houston	1991
Schmitz, Paula	Asst	245-2547	12	KM	PHD	91	Texas	1990
Stutzman, James F.	Asst	245-2547	14	EF	PHD	82	Houston	1988

Southwestern University
Finance Faculty
Dept of Econ & Bus Adm
Georgetown, TX 78627-0770
Area Code (512) Fax 863-5788

BA

Giesecke, Leonard F.	C-Pr	863-1574		Econ	PHD	75	Texas	1968
Valentine, Jerome L.	Assoc	863-1592			PHD		N Texas	1988
John Shearn Chair in Business Administration								

U of Southwestern Louisiana
Dept of Econ & Finance
Col of Bus Adm Box44570
Lafayette, LA 70504-4570
Area Code (318) Fax 231-5898
USL.EDU

BS

Duggar, Jan W.	Dean	231-6491		Econ	PHD	67	Fla St	1989
Payne, Bruce C.	C-Pr$	231-6672	12	OJDW	PHD	77	La St	1975
Womack, Douglas	Prof	231-6673	3	PR	PHD	71	Alabama	1971
Boudreaux, Denis O.	Asst	231-6670	12	ODJW	PHD	88	Miss St	1986
Lapoint, James J.	Asst	231-6671	1	MFIY	MS	64	So Miss	1964
Min, Sungky	Asst	231-6098	1	OLHV	PHD	90		1990
Rao, Spuma	Asst	231-6099	2	FGMN	PHD	88	Miss St	1988
Yu, Geungu	Asst	231-6675	2	KLMO	PHD	86	Miss St	1987

Southwestern Oklahoma St Un
Dept of Accounting & Finance
School of Business
Weatherford, OK 73096-3098
Area Code (405) Fax 772-5447

BA,MBA

Reeder, Robert	Dean	774-3282		Mgt	PHD			
Page, Charles	C-Pr	774-3755		Atg	EDD	70	N Carol	1970
May, Ralph	Asst	774-3279			PHD	75	Purdue	1989
Buddy, Nancy	Inst	774-3755			MBA	86	SW Ok St	1986

Stanford University
Finance Faculty
Graduate School of Bus
Stanford, Calif 94305-5015
Area Code (415) Fax 725-7979

MBA,PHD
1926

Spence, A. Michael	Dean			Econ	PHD	72	Harvard	1990
Philip H. Knight Professor of Economics & Management								
McDonald, John G.	Prof	723-4037	14	MOUV	PHD	67	Stanford	1968
The IBJ Professor of Finance and Business School Trust Faculty Fellow 90-91								
Parker, George C.	Prof	723-9117	13	GHPQ	PHD	67	Stanford	
Scholes, Myron S.	Prof				PHD	69	Chicago	1983
Frank E. Buck Professor of Finance								
Singleton, Kenneth J.	Prof				PHD	77	Wiscon	1987
C.O.G. Miller Distinguished Professor of Finance								
Van Horne, James C.	Prof	723-2761			PHD	64	Northwes	1965
A. P. Giannini Professor of Banking and Finance								
Admati, Anat R.	Assoc		12	ADJT	PHD	83	Yale	1982
Duffie, J. Darrell	Assoc				PHD	84	Stanford	1984
Kleidon, Allan W.	Assoc		13	AQTV	PHD	83	Chicago	1982
Pfleiderer, Paul C.	Assoc		12	ADJT	PHD	82	Yale	1981
Hindy, Ayman M.	Asst				PHD	90	MIT	1990
Jacklin, Charles J.	Asst		23	LNPQ	PHD	85	Stanford	1987
Werner, Ingrid M.	Asst				PHD	90	Rochest	1990
Zwiebel, Jeffrey	Asst				ABD	91	MIT	1991

SUNY College at Fredonia — BS
Finance Faculty
Dept of Business Adm
Fredonia, NY 14063-1198
Area Code (716) Fax 673-3397

Name	Rank	Phone		Field	Deg	Yr	School	Year
Hopson, James F.	C-Pr	673-3505		Atg	JD	73	So Meth	1989
Smith, Rodney F.	Prof	673-3504	13		PHD		Mass	
Seyedian, Mojtaba	Assoc	673-3503	23		PHD		SUNY	1984
Pencek, Thomas A.	Asst	673-3492	13		DBA		Miss St	1988

SUNY College at Geneseo — BA,BS
Finance Faculty
Jones Sch of Business
Geneseo, NY 14454-1401
Area Code (716) Fax 245-5467

Name	Rank	Phone		Field	Deg	Yr	School	Year
Moore, Gary	H-Pr	245-5367		Econ	PHD	74	Nebraska	1974
Martin, David	Prof	245-5372	3	R	PHD		Syracuse	1966
Harawa, Rex	Asst	245-5366	12	AF	PHD		SUNY-Bin	1989
Howard, Barbara	Inst	245-4363	14	AJ	MBA		Renssela	1988

SUNY College at Old Westbury — BS,BPS
Finance Faculty
Business Division
Old Westbury, NY 11568-0210
Area Code (516) Fax 876-3209
SNYOLDVA

Name	Rank	Phone		Field	Deg	Yr	School	Year
Yasar, Geyikdazi	Prof	876-3331	24	VW	PHD			1983
Leon, G.	Assoc	876-3331	21	FM	PHD			1990
Mickens, Al	Assoc	876-3309	3	PR	PHD			1978
O'Sullivan, P.	Assoc	876-3392	24	VW	PHD			1975
Tabwiztchi, S.	Assoc	876-3318	12	FMN	PHD			1975
Feiner, J.	Inst	876-3309	3	QRS	ABD			1976
Keefe, M.	Inst	876-3318	12	FMN	ABD			1985

SUNY College at Oswego — BS
Finance Faculty
Business Adm Department
Oswego, New York 13126
Area Code (315) Fax 341-3154

Name	Rank	Phone		Field	Deg	Yr	School	Year
Karns, Lanny	C-Pr	341-2272		MgtS	PHD	78	Syracuse	1976
Ntoko, Alfred Ngome	Asst	341-2526	23	OPRV	PHD	85	SUNY-Bin	1985
Shankar, S. Gowri	Asst	341-2522	12	FDLO	PHD	91	Syracuse	1990

SUNY College at Stony Brook — BS,MS
Finance Faculty
Harriman Sch of Mgt
Stony Brook, NY 11794-3775
Area Code (516) Fax 632-7176
SBCCMAIL
Did Not Respond

Name	Rank	Phone	Field	Deg	Yr	School	Year
Wolf, Gerrit	Dean	632-7175	Mgt	PHD	67	Cornell	1985

SUNY at Albany — BS,MS,PHD 1974,1974
Department of Finance
School of Business
Albany, New York 12222
Area Code (518) Fax 442-3944
ALBNYVM1

Name	Rank	Phone	Field	Deg	Yr	School	Year
Hughs, Richard E.	Dean	442-4910	Mgt	PHD	62	Purdue	1991
Forbes, Ronald W.	Prof	442-4919		PHD	68	SUNY-Buf	1968
Leonard, Paul A.	Prof	442-4922		PHD	80	Oregon	1987
Shawky, Hany A.	Assoc	442-4921		PHD	78	Ohio St	1978
Biswas, Rita	Asst	442-4954		PHD	91	Tx A&M	1990
Brucato, Jr., Peter F.	Asst	442-4962		PHD	87	Duke	1989
Janakiramanan, S.	Asst	442-4963		PHD	85	Minn	1985
MacDonald, John A.	Asst	442-4973		PHD	87	Va Tech	1987
Smith, David	Asst	442-4245		PHD	89	Va Tech	1989

SUNY at Binghamton BA,MBA
Department of Finance 1991,1991
School of Management
Binghamton, NY 13902-6000
Area Code (607) Fax 777-4422
BINGVMA
Other Bitnet BINGSOM, BINGVMB

Name	Rank	Phone	Email		Field	Degree	Yr	School	Yr
Roodman, Gary M.	Dean$	777-2314	GROODM@M		Ops	DBA	69	Indiana	1977
Emery, Douglas R.	Prof	777-2555				PHD	77	Kansas	1989
Grier, Paul C.	Assoc	777-2401				PHD	71	New York	1976
Dhillon, Upinder S.	Asst	777-4381				PHD	86	LSU	1987
Lasser, Dennis J.	Asst	777-4874				PHD	84	Indiana	1988
Ramirez, Gabriel	Lect	321-0436				PHD	88	Geo St	1988

SUNY at Buffalo BS,MBA,PHD
Dept of Finance & Mgr Econ 1930,1972
School of Management
Buffalo, N York 14260
Area Code (716) Fax 636-3823
UBVM

Name	Rank	Phone	Email		Field	Degree	Yr	School	Yr
Foster, Howard G.	Dean$	636-3247	MGTRUH		Org	PHD	69	Cornell	1969
Hagerman, Robert L.	Prof	636-3278		12	FMPZ	PHD	72	Rochest	1982
Jen, Frank C.	Prof	636-3272	MGTFJEN	13	ACNO	PHD	63	Wiscon	1964
Manufacturers & Traders Trust Co. Professor of Banking and Finance									
Rozeff, Michael S.	Prof	636-3281	MGTSPEED	2	JMNO	PHD	74	Rochest	1989
Louis M. Jacobs Professor of Corporate Financial Management									
Trzcinka, Charles	Prof	636-3262	MGTCAT	23	JKST	PHD	80	Purdue	1980
Choi, Dosoung	Assoc	636-3271	MGTDOS	1	ADEG	PHD	80	Penn St	1986
Ogden, Joseph P.	Assoc	636-3270	MGTOGDEN	2	JKLN	PHD	82	Purdue	1988
Perry, Philip	Assoc	636-3264		12	JMXZ	PHD	79	Berkeley	1985
Park, Sangsoo	Asst	636-3266	MGTPARK	1	ACGU	PHD	90	Chicago	1990

SUNY at New Paltz BS
Finance Faculty
Dept of Business Adm
New Paltz, NY 12561
Area Code (914) Fax 257-3009
SNYNEWVM

Name	Rank	Phone	Email		Field	Degree	Yr	School	Yr
Bishko, Donald	D-Ac	257-2929				PHD	69	RPI	1982
Salavitabar, Hadi	Assoc	257-2934	SALAVITH	12	CFIL	PHD	82	SUNY-Bin	1982

SUNY at Plattsburgh BS
Finance Faculty
School of Bus & Econ
Plattsburgh, NY 12901-2697
Area Code (518) Fax 564-7827
SNYPLAVA

Name	Rank	Phone	Email		Field	Degree	Yr	School	Yr
Gandhi, Prem P.	Dean	564-3190	GANDHIPP		Econ	PHD	73	New Scho	1966
Thoren, Raymond	C	564-4208				MBA		St Johns	1970

Stephen F. Austin St Univ BBA,MBA
Dept of Economics & Finance 1976,1982
School of Business
Nacogdoches, TX 75962-3009
Area Code (409) Fax 568-1117

Name	Rank	Phone			Field	Degree	Yr	School	Yr
Ashley, Janelle C.	Dean	568-3101			Mgt	PHD	72	N Texas	1965
Solomon, Lynnette K.	C	568-4301				PHD	70	Arkansas	1979
Lewis, John H.	Prof	568-4301				DBA	75	La Tech	1969
Smith, Weldon L.	Prof	568-4301				PHD	74	Tx A&M	1966
Griffith, Reynolds	Assoc	568-4301				PHD	66	Texas	1989
Stine, J. Bert	Assoc	568-4301				DBA	84	La Tech	1986
Wheat, Charles M.	Assoc	568-4301				PHD	68	Arkansas	1988
Simmons, Mark	Asst	568-4301				PHD	87	Tx A&M	1987

Stetson University BBA,MBA,MACC
Dept of Finance & Quant Mth
Sch of Bus Adm Box 8398
Deland, Florida 32720-3757
Area Code (904) Fax 822-8832
STETSON

Name	Rank	Phone				Degree	Yr	School	Yr
Wright, William W.	Dean	822-7406				PHD		Alabama	1984
Lerro, Anthony J.	C-Pr	822-7440				PHD		Alabama	1988
Bear, F. Thomas	Assoc	822-7440				PHD		Georgia	1982
Boyd, G. Michael	Assoc					PHD		Fla St	1980
Mallett, James E.	Assoc	734-4121				PHD		Wayne St	1984
Director of the Roland and Sarah George Institute									
Belcher, Larry	Asst					PHD		Indiana	
Foo, Jennifer	Asst					PHD		Northeas	

Stonehill College
Finance Faculty
Business Adm Department
North Easton, MA 02357-1150
Area Code (508) Fax 238-9253

BA,BS

Burke, William A.	C	230-1378			MBA		NYU	1982
Vaughn Jr., Edward S.		230-1222	13		JD		Suffolk	1981
Whitbread, Joseph E.		230-1219	12		PHD		Syracuse	1989

Suffolk University
Department of Finance
School of Management
Boston, Mass 02108-2770
Area Code (617) Fax 573-8704

BA,MBA,MSF
1989,1989

Brennan, John F.	Dean	573-8300		Mgt	MBA	58	Harvard	1991
Khaksari, Shahriar	C-Ac	573-8641			PHD		St Louis	
O'Hara, H. Thomas	Assoc				PHD			
Prezas, Alexandros P.	Assoc	573-8319			PHD		Northwes	
Anderson, Michael H.	Asst	573-8672			PHD		Indiana	
Bubnys, Edward L.	Asst	573-8449			PHD		Illinois	
Han, Ki C.	Asst	573-8561			PHD		Mich St	
Shawcross, Roger K.	Asst				MS		Rhode Is	

Susquehanna University
Department of Finance
Weis School of Business
Selinsgrove, PA 17870-1001
Area Code (717) Fax 372-4310

Bellas, Carl J.	Dean	372-4455		Mgt	PHD	69	Oregon	1983
Remaley, William	Prof	372-4235			PHD	71	New York	1973
Sauter, Frederick	Asst	372-4462			MBA	67	Columbia	1967

Syracuse University
Department of Finance
School of Management
Syracuse, NY 13244-2130
Area Code (315) Fax 443-5389
SUVM

BS,MBA,MS,PHD
1920,1963

Burman, George	Dean	443-3751				PHD	73	Chicago	1991
Fredrikson, E. Bruce	Prof	443-3398	U1772	12	FHKO	PHD	63	Columbia	1966
Kim, Moon K.	Prof	443-3478	MKK	2	FJ	PHD	74	Illinois	1975
Young, Allan	Prof	443-3476		13	QT	PHD	67	Columbia	1971
Finucane, Thomas J.	Assoc	443-3486	FINUCANE	12	KLO	PHD	86	Cornell	1985
Koveos, Peter	Assoc	443-3427	PETER	14	UV	PHD	77	Penn St	1982
Wu, Chunchi	Assoc	443-3399	SANDY	12	JM	PHD	82	Illinois	1982
Cho, Sung-il	Asst	443-3502	SCHO	12	BMOQ	PHD	89	Michigan	1987
Diz, Fernando	Asst	443-3499	FDIZ	12	KLO	PHD	89	Cornell	1989
Jagtiani, Julapa	Asst	44303422		34	PV	PHD	89	NYU	1990
Polakoff, Michael	Asst	443-3576	POLAKOFF	23	LO	PHD	87	SUNY Bin	1988
Van Inwegen, Greg	Asst	443-3331	GBVANINW	14	UVW	PHD	91	Penn	1991

University of Tampa
Department of Finance
College of Business
Tampa, Florida 33606-1490
Area Code (813) Fax 251-0016

AB,MBA

Vaughn, Ronald L.	Dean	253-6221		Mtkg	PHD	75	Georgia	1984
Jankowski, Joel R.	C-Ac	253-3439	13		ABD		Columbia	1986
Adams, Michael K.	Asst	253-3687	12		PHD	86	Arkansas	1990
Stocker, John	Asst	253-3336	14		ABD		Kent St	1991

Tarleton State University
Dept of Accounting & Finance
College of Business Adm
Stephenville, TX 76402
Area Code (817) Fax

BBA,MBA

DeHay, Jerry M.	Dean	968-9350		Mktg	PHD	78	N Texas	1985
Collier, Boyd D.	C-Ac	968-9910		Atg	PHD	70	Texas	1983
Brocato, Joe M.	Assoc	968-9909			PHD	81	Tenn	1989
Smith, Patricia	Inst	968-9916			MBA	84	Tarleton	1984

Temple University BBA,MBA,MS,PHD
Finance Faculty 1934,1973
School of Bus & Mgt
Philadelphia, PA 19122
Area Code (215) Fax 787-5698
TEMPLEVM
  Dunkelberg, William C.   Dean   787-7605   Econ   PHD   69   Michigan   1987
  Friedman, Joseph   C-Pr   787-8142   3   RD   PHD   Berkeley
  Choi, J. Jay   Prof   787-5084   V515BE   14   VDW   PHD   New York
  Fischer, Gerald C.   Prof   787-8453   3   PQR   PHD   60   Columbia   1967
  Gupta, Manak C.   Prof   787-1697   1   ADG   PHD   67   UCLA
  Phillips, Herbert E.   Prof   787-8141   2   MJ   PHD   68   U Wash   1973
  Ritchie Jr., John C.   Prof   787-8140   12   FKN   PHD   63   Penn
  Kopecky, Kenneth J.   Assoc   787-5827   13   PR   PHD   Brown
  Scott, Jonathan A.   Assoc   787-7605   13   PQR   PHD   80   Purdue
  Tucker, Alan L.   Assoc   787-5887   12   LV   PHD   86   Fla St
  Becker, Kent   Asst   787-8139   12   LM   PHD   Illinois
  Chopra, Navin   Asst   787-1918   12   MO   PHD   Michigan
  Howard, Lorraine M.   Asst   787-8850   3   P   ABD   Penn
  Mehdian, Seyed M.   Asst   787-6827   13   PR   PHD   So Illin
  Puri, Tribhuvan   Asst   787-6066   14   UW   PHD   Tennesse
  Zissu, Anne-Marie   Asst   787-8108   13   GPS   PHD   CUNY

University of Tennessee BS,MBA,MA,PHD
Department of Finance 1941,1971
College of Business Adm
Knoxville, Tenn 37996-0540
Area Code (615) Fax 974-3100
UTKVM1
  Neel, C. Warren   Dean   974-5061   Mgt   PHD   69   Alabama   1969
  Black, H. A.   H-Pr   974-3216   PHD   Ohio St
  Boehm, T. P.   Prof   PHD   71   Wash U
  Philippatos, G. C.   Prof   974-1713   PHD   New York
    Distinguished Chaired Professor of Banking and Finance
  Shrieves, Ronald E.   Prof   974-3216   PHD   72   UCLA   1972
  Wansley, James W.   Prof   974-3216   PHD   S Carol
  Auxier, A. L.   Assoc   PHD   Iowa
  Wachowicz Jr., John M.   Assoc   974-3216   PHD   Illinois
  Collins, M. Cary   Asst   531-3446   PHD   Georgia
  Daves, Phillip R.   Asst   974-1727   PHD   N Carol
  DeGennaro, R. P.   Asst   PHD   Ohio St
  Ehrhardt, Michael C.   Asst   974-3216   PHD   Ga Tech
  Gunthorpe, D.   Asst   PHD   Florida
  Stern, M.   Asst   PHD   Virginia

Tennessee at Chattanooga BS,MBA
Dept of Accounting & Finance 1982,1988
School of Business Adm
Chattanooga, TN 37403-2598
Area Code (615) Fax 755-5255
UTCVM
  Fletcher, Linda Pickthorne   Dean   755-4333   Econ   PHD   64   Penn   1991
  Fulmer Jr., John G.   H-Pr   755-4101   1   BP   PHD   70   Alabama   1977
    Vieth Professor
  Bertin, William J.   Prof   755-4419   WBERTIN   1   GKY   DBA   80   Kent St   1984
  Zivney, Terry L.   Prof   755-4127   TZIVNEY   12   KLMN   PHD   84   Geo St   1988
    Harris Chair of Excellence
  Finch, J. Howard   Asst   755-4047   23   AT   ABD   Alabama   1991
  Wyatt, James C.   Asst   755-5250   13   QR   MBA   90   Tenn-Cha   1991

Univ of Tennessee at Martin
Dept of Economics & Finance
School of Business Adm
Martin, Tenn 38238-5015
Area Code (901) Fax
UTKVM1
Did Not Respond--Taken from College Catalog
  Young, Gary F.   Dean   587-7225   PHD   77   La Tech
  Fletcher, John L.   Prof   PHD   Miss
  Gullett, Nell S.   Asst   MBA   Tenn

Tennessee State University BS,MBA
Dept of Economics & Finance
School of Business
Nashville, Tenn 37203-3401
Area Code (615) Fax 320-3114

Curry, Tilden J.	Dean	251-1505		Plan	PHD	78 Fla St	1976
Hartmann, Bruce	H-Pr	351-1505		Econ	PHD		
Hasty, John M.	Prof	251-1505			PHD	73 Geo St	1973
Holbrook, S. Thomas	Prof	251-1505			PHD	74 Georgia	1971
Weis, Charles	Prof	251-1505			PHD	Ariz St	

Tennessee Technological Un BS
Dept of Econ & Finance 1978,1981
College of Business Adm
Cookeville, Tenn 38505
Area Code (615) Fax 372-6112
TNTECH

Bell, Robert R.	Dean	372-3372	RRB6250	Mgt	PHD	70 Florida	1976
Williams, Norman C.	C-Ac	372-3745			PHD	72 Arkansas	1972
Martin, Deryl W.	Asst	372-3871			PHD	88 Tx A&M	1988
Pashley, Mary M.	Asst	372-3855			PHD	86 Tennesse	1986
Wang, Louie K.	Asst	372-3879			PHD	88 Northwes	1988

U of Texas at Arlington BBA,MBA,MS,PHD
Dept Finance & Real Estate 1969,1973
College of Business Adm
Arlington, Texas 76019-0449
Area Code (817) Fax 794-5793

Mullendore, Walter E.	Dean	273-2881		Econ	PHD	68 Iowa St	1968
Lockwood, Larry J.	C-As	273-3705	B167LJL		PHD	82 Purdue	1982
Apilado, Vincent P.	Prof	273-3840	B868TING		PHD	70 Michigan	1980
Panton, Don Bradley	Prof	273-3833			PHD	72 Arizona	1989
Swanson, Peggy E.	Prof	273-3841	B153PES		PHD	78 So Meth	1978
Diltz, J. David	Assoc	273-3837	BO76DAVE		PHD	80 Illinois	1987
Swidler, Steven	Asst	273-3838	B908RESE		PHD	81 Brown	1988
Hensler, Douglas A.	Asst	273-3842	D191DAH		PHD	89 U Wash	1991

Univ of Texas at Austin BBA,MBA,MPA,PHD
Department of Finance 1916,1963
College of Business Adm
Austin, Texas 78712-1179
Area Code (512) Fax 471-3937

Witt, Robert E.	Dean	471-5921		Mktg	PHD	68 Penn	1968
Centennial Chair in Business Education Leadership							
Tinic, Seha M.	C-Pr	471-4368	23	JNQT	PHD	70 Cornell	1985
James A. Elkins Centennial Chair in Finance							
Crum, Lawrence Lee	Prof	471-4368	3	P	PHD	61 Texas	1969
Texas Commerce Bancshares, Inc., Centennial Professor in Commercial Banking							
Doenges, R. Conrad	Prof	471-4368	1	CE	DBA	65 Colorado	1964
Arthur Andersen & Co. Alumni Centennial Professor in Finance							
Hackett Jr., Charles Wilson	Prof	471-4368	2	X	DBA	55 U Wash	1966
The Capitol City Savings Regents Fellow							
Martin, John D.	Prof	471-4368	1	GH	DBA	73 Tx Tech	1980
The Margaret & Eugene McDermott Centennial Professor in Banking & Finance							
Mettlen, Robert D.	Prof	471-4368	3	PR	DBA	69 Indiana	1966
Lamar Savings Centennial Professor in Finance							
Rao, Ramesh K. S.	Prof	471-4368	1	AD	DBA	78 Indiana	1978
Senchack Jr., Andrew J.	Prof	471-4368	2	LM	PHD	73 UCLA	1973
First Republican Corp. Professorship in Business Administration							
Spellman, Lewis J.	Prof	471-4368	3	P	PHD	71 Stanford	1971
Walker, Ernest Winfield	Prof	471-4368	1	FI	DBA	53 Indiana	1954
Lawrence D. Gale Chair Emeritus in Small Business and Entrepreneurship							
Wolf, Harold Arthur	Prof	471-4368	3	R	PHD	58 Michigan	1968
Young, Leslie	Prof	471-4368	4	R	PHD	71 Oxford	1983
V. F. Neuhaus Centennial Professor in Finance							
Brown, Keith C.	Assoc	471-4368	2	GLMN	PHD	81 Purdue	1984
Ehud, I. Ronn	Assoc	471-4368	12	JKLO	PHD	83 Stanford	1988
Hadaway, Beverly L.	Assoc	471-4368	3	PR	PHD	80 Alabama	1980
MacMinn, Richard D.	Assoc	471-4368	1	F	PHD	78 Illinois	1981
Starks, Laura T.	Assoc	471-4368	12	ANS	PHD	81 Texas	1987
Kothare, Meeta	Asst	471-4368	12	AQ	PHD	91 Rocheste	1991
Laux, Paul A.	Asst	471-4368	2	LT	PHD	88 Vanderbi	1989
Ng, Lilian K.	Asst	471-4368	12	JLZ	PHD	89 Penn	1989
Zapatero, Fernando	Asst	471-4368	1	JOS	PHD	91 Columbia	1991
Williams, Michael E.	SLect	471-4368	14		PHD	80	1988
Duvic, Robert C.	Lect	471-4368	14		PHD	90 Texas	1989
Nolen Jr., James A.	Lect	471-4368	1		MBA	76 Texas	1980
White, Susan	Lect	471-4368	1		PHD	90 Texas	1989
Young, Suzanne Lee	Lect	471-4368	3		MA	76 Canterbu	1983

Univ of Texas at Dallas
Finance Faculty
School of Mgt & Adm
Richardson, TX 75083-0688
Area Code (214) Fax 690-2799

Kroncke, Charles O.	Dean	690-2705	1	Fnce	PHD	68	Minn	1988
Bass, Frank M.	C-Pr	690-2744		Mktg	PHD	54	Illinois	1982
Merville, Larry J.	Prof	690-2711	2	L	PHD	71	Texas	1973
Osborne, Dale K.	Prof	690-2025			PHD	63	Kentucky	1984
Day, Ted E.	Assoc	690-2743	3	D	PHD	81	Stanford	1990
Emanuel, David C.	Assoc	690-2806	1	O	PHD	81	Stanford	1991
Choi, Yoon K.	Asst	690=2678	1	A	PHD	90	Michigan	1990

Univ of Texas at El Paso   BA,BBA,MBA
Dept of Economics & Finance   1989,1989
College of Business Adm
El Paso, Texas 79968-0543
Area Code (915) Fax 747-5147

Hoy, Frank	Dean	747-5241		Mgt	PHD	79	Tx A&M	1991
Herbst, Anthony F.	Prof	747-5245	1		PHD		Purdue	1987
Schauer, David	Assoc	747-5245	3	PR	PHD		Notre Dm	
Sprinkle, Richard	Assoc	747-5245	4	UV	PHD			
Tollen, Robert D.	Assoc	747-5245	12	CDJM	PHD		Texas	1972
Johnson, Stephen A.	Asst	747-5245	12	CDEJ	PHD		Alabama	1987
Smith, Charles	Asst	747-5245	1c	DE	ABD		Tx Tech	1991

Univ of Texas-Pan American   BBA,MBA
Dept Mktg, Finance & Gen Bus   1979,1985
School of Business Adm
Edinburg, Texas 78539-2999
Area Code (512) Fax 381-2354

Brewerton, Francis J.	Dean	381-3311		Mgt	DBA	68	LSU	1981
Dalrymple, Brent B.	Prof	381-3368			PHD	70	LSU	1989
Assefa, Zewdineh	Assoc	381-3316			PHD	80	Illinois	1983

U of Texas of Permian Basin   BBA,MBA
Finance Faculty
Division of Bus Adm
Odessa, Texas 79762-8301
Area Code (915) Fax 367-2115
UTPB
Did Not Respond

Gaulden, Corbett	Dean	367-2187 C_GAULDI	Mktg	PHD	80	LSU	
Watts, William A.	Prof			PHD	66	Iowa	
Buchanan, William K.	Inst			MBA	85	Txs-PeBa	
Fletcher, Kenneth	Inst			ABD		Tx Tech	

Un of Texas at San Antonio   BBA,MPA
Div of Economics & Finance   1980,1980
College of Business
San Antonio, TX 78285-0633
Area Code (512) Fax 691-4308
UTSAVM1

Gaertner, James F.	Dean	691-4313		Atg	PHD	77	Tx A&M	1983
Flory-Truett, Lila	D-Pr	691-4315	14	CU	PHD	72	Iowa	1975
Truett, Dale	Prof	691-5313	14	CU	PHD	67	Texas	1973
Ayers, Ronald	Assoc	691-5302	3	GPR	PHD	78	Tulane	1979
Betty, Winfield	Assoc	691-5314	13	CFHP	PHD	69	N Texas	1981
Fairchild, Keith WM	Assoc	691-5307	14	CGHU	PHD	86	Texas	1981
Misra, Lalatendu	Assoc	691-5349	12	LVGO	PHD	85	Texas	1982
Weiher, Kenneth E.	Assoc	691-5315	3	R	PHD	75	Indiana	1975
Prasad, Devendra	Asst	691-5303	14	CEOU	PHD	90	Oklahoma	1988
Timmons, Douglas J.	Asst	691-5306	2	XO	PHD	86	Florida	1986

Univ of Texas at Tyler   BBA,MBA
Econ, Finance & Gen Bus
School of Business Adm
Tyler, Texas 75701-6699
Area Code (903) Fax 566-7365

Partain, Robert T.	Dean	566-7360	12	Fnce	PHD	67	Texas	1986
Odom, Oris L.	C-Pr$	566-7365	12	FMXY	DBA	79	Oklahoma	1983
Fischer, Donald E.	Prof	566-7365	12	MSDX	DBA	65	Wash	1990

Texas A&I University
Dept of Economics & Finance
College of Business Adm
Kingsville, TX 78363
Area Code (512) Fax 595-2143

BBA,MBA

Name	Rank	Phone		Field	Degree		School	Year
Bigbee, Dalton	Dean$	595-3081	17	F#JL	DBA		Tx Tech	
Matthews, Warren	C-Ac	595-2504	46	UV	PHD		Tx A&M	1972
Kirby, Robert O.	Prof	595-3801			DBA	74	Tx Tech	1974
Nash, Robert	Prof	595-2355	1	FCE	PHD		Tx A&M	1971
Rossman, Joseph	Assoc	595-2506	3	Pr	PHD		Iowa St	1970
Nemec, Richard	Asst	595-2507	12	CDEJ	ABD		Kentucky	1990

Texas A&M University
Department of Finance
College of Business Adm
Coll Station, TX 77843-4218
Area Code (409) Fax 845-3884

BS,MS,PHD
1972,1972

Name	Rank	Phone		Field	Degree		School	Year
Cocanougher, A. Benton	Dean	845-4711		Mktg	PHD	69	Texas	1987
Trennepohl, Gary L.	C-Pr	845-3514	12	LM	PHD	76	Tx Tech	1986
Cooper, S. Kerry	Prof	845-3514	34	U	PHD	71	Texas	1975
Lamar Professor								
Etter, Wayne E.	Prof	845-3514	3		PHD	68	Texas	1969
Fraser, Donald R.	Prof	845-3514	3	P	PHD	69	Arizona	1972
Groth, John C.	Prof	845-3514	12	ST	PHD	76	Purdue	1975
Rose, Peter S.	Prof	845-3514	3	PV	PHD	69	Arizona	1969
Uselton, Gene C.	Prof	845-3514	12	N	PHD	70	Texas	1979
Dubofsky, David A.	Assoc	845-3514	12	LT	PHD	82	U Wash	1981
Haney, Richard L.	Assoc	845-4830	3		PHD	74	Indiana	1978
Kolari, James W.	Assoc	845-4803	3	P	PHD	80	Ariz St	1980
Lummer, Scott L.	Assoc	845-3514	1	AB	PHD	83	Purdue	1983
Mahajan, Arvind	Assoc	845-3514	14	UV	PHD	80	Geo St	1980
Alderson, Michael J.	Asst	845-3514	12	DH	PHD	84	Illinois	1985
on leave to Univ of Missouri-St Louis								
Ellis, David M.	Asst	845-3514	12	JO	PHD	91	N Carol	1990
Kannan, Srinivasan	Asst	845-3514	1	NO	PHD	86	Illinois	1986
Lee, Scott	Asst	845-3514	12	G	PHD	90	Oregon	1990
Walker, Lawrence C.	SLect	845-3514	1	UV	PHD	72	Tx A&M	1984
Reed, Debra	Lect	845-3514	1	O	PHD	82	Purdue	1982

Texas Christian University
Dept of Fin & Decision Scien
MJ Neeley School of Bus
Fort Worth, TX 76129
Area Code (817) Fax 921-7227
TCUAMUS

BS,MBA
1963,1966

Name	Rank	Phone	Office		Field	Degree		School	Year
Downey, H. Kirk	Dean	921-7526	IBO41BU		OrgB	PHD	74	Penn St	1983
French, Dan W.	C-Ac	921-7514	RB231BU	12	LMO	PHD	79	La Tech	1984
Barry, Christopher B.	Prof	921-7550	RB531BU	12	MNQ	DBA	73	Indiana	1988
Block, Stanley B.	Prof	921-7561	RB131BU	12	GMT	PHD	67	LSU	1967
Brauer, Greggory	Prof	921-7420	SBO86R	1	NST	PHD	80	Wash	1990
Stanley, Marjorie T.	Prof	921-7559	RB151BU	24	SVW	PHD	53	Indiana	1965
Boatler, Robert W.	Assoc	921-7549	RB591BU	34	RVW	PHD	73	Cornell	1977
Lipscomb, Joseph B.	Assoc	921-7546	RB451BU	1	CFO	PHD	78	Houston	1977

Texas Southern University
Department of Finance
Jones School of Bus
Houston, Texas 77004
Area Code (713) Fax 527-7701
Did Not Respond--Taken from College Catalog

Name	Rank	Phone		Field	Degree		School	Year
Hyman, Ladelle M.	Dean	527-7700		Atg	PHD	75	N Texas	1981
Grace, Steven H.	V-Ac				PHD		Houston	
Cobb, Kenneth	Asst				MBA		N Ill	
Ducy, Mary E.	Asst				MSA		Geo Wash	

Texas Tech University
Department of Finance
College of Business Adm
Lubbock, Texas 79409-4320
Area Code (806) Fax 742-2099
TTACS

BA,MS,PHD
1958,1981

Name	Rank	Phone	Office		Field	Degree		School	Year
Stem, Carl H.	Dean	742-3186			Econ	PHD	69	Harvard	1970
Hein, Scott E.	C-Pr	742-3433	ODHENTTA	32	KLR	PHD	79	Purdue	1983
Bowlin, Oswald D.	Prof	742-3338		12	DCEF	PHD	59	Illinois	1965
Dukes, William P.	Prof	742-3419		21	ONM	PHD	68	Cornell	1968

Peterson, Richard L.	Prof	742-3365		32	PTLM	PHD	66	Michigan	1982
Briscoe Professor of Bank Management									
Sears, R. Stephen	Prof	742-3377		12	LMNO	PHD	80	N Carol	1988
Goebel, Paul	Assoc	742-3339		2	J	PHD	80	Georgia	1980
Ma, Christopher K.	Assoc	742-3298	ODMARTTA	12	BGKL	PHD	83	Illinois	1988
MacDonald, S. Scott	Assoc	742-1536	ODSSMTTA	32	KLP	PHD	83	Tx A&M	1984
Rao, Ramesh	Assoc	742-3901	ODRAOTTA	1	ABDG	PHD	85	Tx Tech	1987
Ritchey, Robert	Assoc	742-3956		12	JLOF	PHD	81	Arizona	1982
Wade, Charles	Assoc	742-3350		12	CDEF	PHD	66	Oklahoma	1965

Texas Wesleyan University BBA
Finance Faculty
School of Business
Fort Worth, TX 76105-1536
Area Code (817) Fax 531-4814

Norwood, Frank G.	Dean	531-4840	Mgt	PHD	68	Oklahoma	1960
Klaasen, Thomas A.	Prof	531-4842		PHD	69	Mich St	1989
McLain, Louis	Asst	531-4849		MBA	76	So Meth	1978

Texas Woman's University BBA,BS,BA,MBA
Dept of Business & Economics
College of Arts & Scien
Denton, Texas 76204
Area Code (817) Fax 898-3726
TWU
Did Not Respond

Bulls, Derrell W.	C-Pr	898-2102	Mgt	PHD	71	Tx Tech	1977

University of Toledo BBA,MBA
Department of Finance 1955,1963
College of Business Adm
Toledo, Ohio 43606-3390
Area Code (419) Fax 537-7744

Uselding, Paul J.	Dean	537-2558		PHD	70	Northwes	1991
Bowyer, Linda	C-Ac$	537-2194					
Conway, Larry	Prof	537-2437		PHD		Illinois	1975
Smolen, Gerald E.	Prof	537-2389		PHD		Tenn	1986
Ahern, Michael J.	Assoc	537-2889		EDD	74	Tenn	1974
Lindsley, David A.	Assoc	537-4611		PHD		Michigan	1972
Sherman, Michael D.	Assoc	537-4194		PHD		Purdue	1980
Weinraub, Herbert J.	Assoc	537-2440		PHD	72	Mich St	1970
Kuhlman, Bruce R.	Asst	537-2091		PHD		Florida	1988
Meyer, Thomas O.	Asst	537-4273		ABD		Ohio St	1989
Moore, Gary	Asst	537-2610					
Visscher, Sue L.	Asst	537-2541		PHD		Indiana	1987
Wolfe, Glenn A.	Asst	537-2196					

Towson State University BS,BA
Department of Finance
School of Bus & Econ
Towson, Maryland 21204-7097
Area Code (301) Fax 830-3225
TOWSONVX

Barone, Sam	Dean	830-3342	Mgt	PHD	62	Illinois	1985
Haight, G. Timothy	C-Pr	830-2465		DBA	80	Geo Wash	1989
Holt, Arthur L.	Prof	830-3229		PHD	67		1975
Avery, Albert E.	Assoc	830-3185		PHD	78	Purdue	1987
Grimshaw, Alan E.	Assoc	830-2111		DBA	79	Maryland	1987
Vennos, Spyros	Assoc	830-3232		DSC	68		
Kaywan, Sayeed	Asst	830-4080		PHD		American	1982
Rhee, Moon-Whoan	Inst	830-4075		PHD	91	Maryland	1987

Transylvania University
Finance Faculty
300 North Broadway
Lexington, KY 40508
Area Code (606) Fax
Did Not Respond

Lynch, Lawrence K.	C-Pr	233-8104	Econ	PHD	66	Kentucky	1979
Baldwin Jr., William T.	D-Ac			PHD	75	Kentucky	

115

Trenton State College BS
Department of Finance
School of Business
Trenton, NJ 08650-4700
Area Code (609) Fax 530-7686
  Hantjis, Anthony W.   Dean 771-3027   EDD 69 Temple   1965
  Mayo, Herbert   Prof 771-3014   PHD 69 Rutgers   1982
  Thomas, Patrick   Prof 771-2608   PHD 74 Kentucky 1980
  Chung, Ronald   Asst 771-3044   ABD   Drexel   1991

Tri State University BSBA,BS
Finance Faculty
Business
Angola, Indiana 46703-0307
Area Code (219) Fax 665-4292
  Sheffield, Leonard E. Dean   665-4176   Mktg   PHD 75 Mich St   1966
  Walter, William J.   Assoc 665-4179   MBA 61 Northwes 1972

Trinity University BS,BA
Finance Faculty
Business & Adm Studies
San Antonio, TX 78284
Area Code (512) Fax 736-8134
  Walz, Daniel T.   Dean 736-7238 31 VPRT PHD 81 Wash U   1982
  Cooley, Philip L.   Prof 736-7281   1 CGIN PHD 73 Ohio St 1985
    Dick & Peggy Prassel Distinguished Professor of Business Administration
  Hubbard, Carl M.   Assoc 736-7283 12 FORI PHD 75 Tx Tech 1975

Troy State University BS
Dept Atg, Finance & Bus Law
Sorrell College of Bus
Troy, Alabama 36082
Area Code (205) Fax 670-3592
  Lovik, Lawrence W.   Dean 566-8112   Econ PHD 81 Geo St   1985
  Ratcliffe, Thomas A. C-Pr 566-8112   Atg   PHD 78 Alabama 1986
  Curtis, Wayne C.   Prof 566-8112   PHD 71 Miss St 1989
  Bibbins, W. Jerome   Asst 566-8112   PHD 80 Arkansas 1990
  Stewart, Robert E.   Asst 566-8112   MBA 65 Mississi 1967

Tulane University BSM,MBA,PHD
Finance Group 1981,1916
Freeman Sch of Business
New Orleans, LA 70118-5669
Area Code (504) Fax 865-6751
TCSVM
  McFarland, James W. Dean   865-5407   MSci PHD 71 Txs A&M 1988
  Goodman, Seymour S. Prof   865-5470   PHD 59 J Hopkin 1959
  Murphy, James T.   Prof   865-5469   PHD 62 Iowa
  Spindt, Paul   Prof   865-5413
  Trapani, John M.   Prof   865-5667
  Schachter, Barry   Assoc 865-5624
  Boebel, Richard   Asst   865-5486
  Bohannon, John   Asst   865-5479

University of Tulsa BS,MBA,MTX,MAC
Department of Finance 1949,1972
College of Business Adm
Tulsa, Oklahoma 74104-3189
Area Code (918) Fax 631-2124
TULSA
  Monroe, Robert J.   Dean   631-2213   Fnce DBA 70 Indiana   1981
  Bey, Roger P.   C-Pr   631-2946 12 CDGM PHD 74 Penn St   1983
  Burgess, Richard C.   Prof   631-3067 12 JMNO DBA 74 Kentucky 1980
  Collins, J. Markham   Prof   631-2783 14 UVJ   PHD 80 Oklahoma 1979
  Johnson, Larry J.   Assoc 631-2956 12 LMV   DBA 80 Indiana   1984
  Larsen Jr., Glen   Asst   631-2077 23 OJNT DBA 89 Indiana   1990
  Waller, Edward R.   Asst   631-2955 13 TPB   PHD 88 Ariz St   1986

Tuskegee University
Department of Finance
School of Business
Tuskegee, AL 36088
Area Code (205) Fax 727-8451
  Newhouse, Benjamin   Dean 727-8286   Atg   PHD 82 Michigan 1984
  Cheng, William I.   Asst 727-6307   PHD 90 SUNY-Bin 1990

117

Union College BA,BS,PHD
Finance Faculty
Institute of Adm & Mgt
Schenectady, NY 12308-2311
Area Code (518) Fax 370-6789
Did Not Respond
  Lambrinos, James   C-Ac 370-6253   Mgt PHD 79 Rutgers 1979

U.S. Air Force Academy BS
Finance Faculty
Dept of Management
Colorado Spr, CO 80840
Area Code (719) Fax 472-3135
Phone (719)472-4130
  Yoos, Charles J.   H-Pr 472-4130   DBA Colorado
  Woody, James R.   Prof 472-4130   DBA Virginia
  Gay, R. Keith   Asst 472-4130   MBA UCLA
  Vilbert, Michael J.   Asst 472-2328   ABD Wharton
  Hong, Derek M.   Inst 472-4130   MBA Stanford

United States Intl Univ
Department of Finance
School of Bus & Mgt
San Diego, CA 92131
Area Code (619) Fax 693-8562
  Stavenga, Mink   Dean$ 693-4695
  Khalil, Mohammed   Prof 693-4601   4
  Brouthers, Keith   Adj

Upsala College
Finance Faculty
Business
East Orange, NJ 07019-1186
Area Code (201) Fax 266-7000
  Funk, Warren H.   Dean   Reli PHD   Columbia 1976
  Bozzo, Cheryl Zega   Asst 266-7289   1989

University of Utah BA,BS,MHRM,PHD
Department of Finance 1936,1963
College of Business
Salt Lake CY, UT 84112
Area Code (801) Fax 581-7214
UTAHBUS
Did Not Respond--Taken from College Catalog
  Seybolt, John W.   Dean 581-7347   Mgt PHD 75 Cornell 1974
  Brinkley, James A.   C   MBA 69 Texas
  Boardman, Calvin M.   Prof 581-5577   MBA 69 Texas 1976
  Gahir, Fikry S.   Prof   PHD 66 Wiscon 1970
  Huntsman, Blaine   Prof   PHD 68 Penn 1969
  Johnson, Ramon E.   Prof 581-7785   PHD 66 Wiscon 1965
  Jorgensen, Jerry L.   Prof   PHD 65 Penn 1965
  Kalay, Avner   Prof   PHD 79 Rochest 1987
  Lease, Ronald C.   Prof 581-7463   PHD 73 Purdue 1973
  Manaster, Steven   Prof   PHD 77 Chicago 1983
  Pratt, Richard T.   Prof   MBA 62 Utah 1966
  Stewart Jr., Samuel S.   Prof   PHD 70 Stanford 1973
  Coles, Jeffrey L.   Assoc 581-6794   BA 79 Pomona 1983
  Glenn, David W.   Assoc   PHD 74 Stanford 1975
  Schallheim, James S.   Assoc 581-4434   PHD 80 Purdue 1980
  Loewenstein, Uri   Asst   MBA 81 NYU 1984
  Zender, Jaime E.   Asst   PHD 88 Yale 1988

Utah State University BS,BA
Dept of Business Adm 1972,1981
College of Business
Logan, Utah 84322-3510
Area Code (801) Fax 750-1091
  Stephens, David B.   Dean 750-2272   Mgt PHD 75 Texas 1987
  Malko, J. Robert   Prof 750-2363   12 FJO PHD 72 Purdue 1987
  Randle, Paul A.   Prof 750-2370   1 EFJX PHD 70 Illinois 1970
  Swensen, Philip R.   Prof 750-2377   12 FLNO DBA 72 Indiana 1975
  Stephens, Alan A.   Assoc 750-2367   1 CDEX PHD 80 Utah 1984
  Dahl, Drew C.   Asst 750-1911   13 GPQU PHD 85 Tenn 1988

Utica College BS
Finance Faculty
Division of Business
Utica, New York 13502-4892
Area Code (315) Fax 792-3292
  Jones, Edward J.   Assoc   792-3242   12 GIPX   MBA   1976
  Dunn, Bradford   Asst   792-3236   1 CDEI   MS   1984

Valdosta State College BBA
Dept of Accounting & Finance 1990
School of Business
Valdosta, GA 31698
Area Code (912) Fax 245-6498
  Stanley, Kenneth L.   Dean   333-5991   Fnce   PHD   78 Purdue   1984
  Seat, Donald L.   C-Pr   333-5967   Atg   DBA   80 Kentucky   1985
  DeThomas, Arthur R.   Prof   333-5967   DBA   Miss St   1977
  Ray, Marvin E.   Prof   333-5967   PHD   74 Arkansas   1974
  Scott, David   Prof   333-5967   PHD   73 Arkansas   1975

Valparaiso University BS
Finance Area
College of Business
Valparaiso, IN 46383
Area Code (219) Fax 464-5381
VALPO
  Miller, John A.   Dean   464-5040 CBA.JAM   Mktg   DBA   Indiana   1986
  Becker, Michael W.   Asst   464-5044 CBA.MWB   1 DC   ABD   Ill-Chic   1987
  Holder, Mark E.   Asst   464-5407 CBA.MH   12 AD   ABD   Kent St   1990
  Pace, Dan   Asst   464-5158 CBA.RDP   13 PG   PHD   91 Fla St   1991

Vanderbilt University MBA,PHD
Finance Faculty 1979
Owen Grad School of Mgt
Nashville, Tenn 37203
Area Code (615) Fax 343-7177
VUCTRVAX
  Geisel, Martin S.   Dean   322-2316   Mgt   PHD   70 Chicago   1987
  Masulis, Ronald   Prof   322-3687   13 BDQV   PHD   78 Chicago   1990
  Stoll, Hans R.   Prof   322-3674   23 JLT   PHD   66 Chicago   1980
    Walker Professor of Finance
  Weingartner, Martin   Prof   322-3668   16 CIBN   PHD   62 Carnegie   1977
  Ball, Clifford A.   Assoc   322-2909   23 JLOT   PHD   80 New Mex   1990
  Huang, Roger   Assoc   322-3723   24 JKVW   PHD   80 Penn   1988
  Christie, William G.   Asst   343-7802   12 CDMN   PHD   89 Chicago   19-8
  Lewis, Craig M.   Asst   322-2626   12 DGLO   PHD   82 Wiscon   1986
  Sternberg, Theodore   Asst   343-6904   2 B&#   PHD   89 Berkeley   1989

University of Vermont BS,MBA
Finance Faculty 1986,1986
School of Business Adm
Burlington, VT 05405-0158
Area Code (802) Fax 656-8279
UVMVM
  Brandenburg, Richard G. Dean   656-3177   Mgt   PHD   64 Cornell   1987
  Gatti, James F.   Assoc   656-8298   23 PEH   PHD   72 Cornell   1972

Villanova University BS,MAT
Department of Finance 1985,1985
Coll of Commerce & Fin
Villanova, Penn 19085-1678
Area Code (215) Fax 645-7864
VUVAXCOM
  Clay, Alvin A.   Dean   645-4340   Atg   MBA   57 Drexel   1955
  LeClair, Robert T.   C   645-4396   23 MLPX   PHD   72 Northwes   1986
  Clarke, James J.   Assoc   645-4373   3 PJ   PHD   72 Notre Dm   1972
  Dellva, Wilfred L.   Assoc   645-7797   12 FMDS   PHD   80 Oklahoma   1987
  Heck, Jean Louis   Assoc   645-4325   12 NXY   PHD   83 S Carol   1983
  Lamm-Tennant, Joan   Assoc   645-7798   12 MSAB   PHD   83 Texas   1989
  Nawrocki, David N.   Assoc   645-4323   32 MNT   PHD   76 Penn St   1981
  Cochran, Steven J.   Asst   645-4322   12 JNO   PHD   88 Cinn   1987
  Holland, Michael M.   Asst   645-4322   12 BDHN   DBA   75 S Calif   1982
  Olson, Gerard   Asst   645-4377   13 GHSO   PHD   88 Drexel   1988

University of Virginia　　　　　　　　　　　　　　　　　　　　　　　　　　　　　　　　　　　　　BS,MS
Department of Finance　　　　　　　　　　　　　　　　　　　　　　　　　　　　　　　　　　　1925,1981
McIntire School Comm
Charlottesvil VA 22903-2493
Area Code (804) Fax 924-7074
　Shenkir, William G.　　　　　　　　Dean　924-3176　　　　　　Atg　　PHD　64 Texas　　　　1977
　　William Stamps Farrish Professor of Free Enterprise
　Atchison, Michael D.　　　　　　　C-As　924-7093　　　　　　　　　　PHD　　 Mich St
　De Mong, Richard F.　　　　　　　Prof　924-3227　　　　　　　　　　DBA　　 Colorado
　Kemp, Robert S.　　　　　　　　　Assoc　924-3482　　　　　　　　　DBA　81 Fla St
　Overstreet, George A.　　　　　　Assoc　924-7063　　　　　　　　　PHD　　 Alabama
　Pettit Jr., L. C.　　　　　　　　　Assoc　973-4221　　　　　　　　　DBA　　 Virginia
　Webb, Robert I.　　　　　　　　　Assoc　924-7570　　　　　　　　　PHD　　 Chicago
　Marston, Felicia C.　　　　　　　Asst　924-1417　　　　　　　　　　PHD　　 N Carol
　White, Mark A.　　　　　　　　　Asst　924-7365　　　　　　　　　　PHD　　 Mich St

University of Virginia-Grad
Department of Finance　　　　　　　　　　　　　　　　　　　　　　　　　　　　　　　　　　　　 1971
Darden Grad Sch Bus Adm
Charlottesvil VA 22906-6550
Area Code (804) Fax 924-4859
　Rosenblum, John W.　　　　　　　Dean　924-7481 AHUV　　Mgt　　DBA　72 Harvard　　　1979
　　Charles C. Abbott Professor of Business Administration
　Harrington, Diana R.　　　　　　　C-Pr　924-4836　　　24 WOGE DBA　　 Virginia
　Dunstan, James C.　　　　　　　　Prof　924-4807　　　14 WCEF　DBA　73 Virginia　　　1973
　Eaker, Mark R.　　　　　　　　　Prof　924-4811　　　　　　　　　　PHD　　 Stanford
　　Business and Political Economy Chair
　Harris, Robert S.　　　　　　　　Prof　924-4823　　　 1 EGNC　PHD　　 Princeto
　　C. Stewart Sheppard Professor of Business Administration
　Meiburg, Charles O.　　　　　　　Prof　924-4816　　　31 PFHI　 PHD　60 Virginia
　　J. Harvie Wilkinson Jr., Professor of Business Administration
　Sihler, William W.　　　　　　　　Prof　924-7489　　　13 BDPT　DBA　65 Harvard　　 1967
　　Ronald Edward Trzcinski Professor of Business Administration
　Bruner, Robert F.　　　　　　　　Assoc　924-4802　　　13 DGHQ DBA　　 Harvard
　　on leave to INSEAD
　Conroy, Robert M.　　　　　　　　Assoc　924-4829　　　24 LOV　 DBA　　 Indiana
　Eades, Kenneth M.　　　　　　　 Assoc　924-4825　　　12 EJO　 PHD　　 Purdue
　Bonnier, Karl-Adam　　　　　　　Lect　924-3208　　　 14 ADG　 PHD　　 Virginia

Virginia Commonwealth Univ　　　　　　　　　　　　　　　　　　　　　　　　　　　BS,MA,MBA,PHD
Department of Finance　　　　　　　　　　　　　　　　　　　　　　　　　　　　　　　　　　　1975,1981
School of Business
Richmond, VA 23284-4000
Area Code (804) Fax 367-8884
　Trumble, Robert R.　　　　　　　Dean　367-1595　　　　　　Mgt　　PHD　71 Minn　　　　1988
　Murphy, Neil B.　　　　　　　　　Prof　367-1611　　　 3　　　　　　PHD　86 Illinois　　 1988
　Shin, Tai S.　　　　　　　　　　　Prof　367-1734　　　14　　　　　　PHD　69 Illinois　　 1978
　Berry, Sam G.　　　　　　　　　　Assoc　　　　　　　　 1　　　　　　DBA　76 Fla St　　　1971
　Hubbard, Elbert W.　　　　　　　Assoc　367-1486　　　 1　　　　　　PHD　73 Cinn　　　　1981
　Myers, Phyllis S.　　　　　　　　Assoc　367-1486　　　　　　　　　　PHD　84 S Carol　　1982
　Upton, David E.　　　　　　　　　Assoc　367-1734 VCMUVS 2　　　　PHD　76 N Carol　　1987
　Daniels, Kenneth N.　　　　　　　Asst　367-1486　　　 13　　　　　　PHD　91 Conn　　　1990
　Solandro, Daniel　　　　　　　　Asst　367-1734　　　 12　　　　　　PHD　90 Pitt　　　　 1989

Virginia Poly Inst & St Un　　　　　　　　　　　　　　　　　　　　　　　　　　　　　　　　BS,MS,PHD
Dept Finance, Insur & Bus Lw　　　　　　　　　　　　　　　　　　　　　　　　　　　　　　　1966,1971
College of Business
Blacksburg, VA 24061-0221
Area Code (703) Fax 231-7826
VTVM1
　Sorensen, Richard E.　　　　　　Dean　961-6601　　　　　　Mgt　　PHD　73 NYU　　　　1982
　Thompson, G. Rodney　　　　　　H-Pr　231-6523
　Chance, Don M.　　　　　　　　　Prof　231-5061　　　　　　　　　　PHD　80 LSU　　　　1980
　Hansen, Robert S.　　　　　　　　Prof　231-6576　　　　　　　　　　PHD　78 Florida　　1979
　Johnson, Dana J.　　　　　　　　Prof　231-5550　　　　　　　　　　PHD　76 Kent St　　1976
　Keown, Arthur J.　　　　　　　　Prof　231-8647　　　　　　　　　　DBA　74 Indiana　　1974
　Mackay, Robert J.　　　　　　　　Prof　678-6036　　　　　　　　　　PHD　72 N Carol　　1972
　Morgan, George Emir　　　　　　Prof　231-7380　　　　　　　　　　PHD　77 N Carol
　Pinkerton, John M.　　　　　　　Prof　231-5002　　　　　　　　　　PHD　79 Florida　　1977
　Billingsley, Randall S.　　　　　　Assoc　231-7374　　　　　　　　　PHD　81 Txs A&M　1981
　Bonomo, Vittorio A.　　　　　　　Assoc　961-5031　　　　　　　　　PHD　69 Brown　　　1968
　Ferris, Stephen P.　　　　　　　Assoc　　　　　　　　　　　　　　　PHD　84 Pitt　　　　 1983
　　on leave to Memphis State
　Jordan, James　　　　　　　　　Assoc　678-6067　　　　　　　　　PHD　80 N Carol
　Patterson, Douglas M.　　　　　　Assoc　231-5737　　　　　　　　　PHD　78 Wiscon　　1980
　Shome, Dilip K.　　　　　　　　　Assoc　231-5403　　　　　　　　　PHD　83 Florida　　1982
　Denis, David J.　　　　　　　　　Asst　231-4377　　　　　　　　　　PHD　88 Michigan　1989

Denis, Diane K.   Asst   231-4315   MBA   81 Cranfiel   1989
Kumar, Raman   Asst   231-5700   PHD   85 Pitt   1984
Mahle, Stephen   VAsst   231-7750   PHD   84 Ohio St   1986
Shin, Young-Seock   Asst   231-4316   PHD   89 Penn   1989

Virginia State University   BS
Dept of Economics & Finance
School of Business
Petersburg, VA 23803
Area Code (804) Fax 524-6512
  Liverpool, Patrick   Dean   524-5166   Mgt   DBA   85 Kent St   1990
  Bawuah, Kwadwo   C-Ac   524-5363   PHD   Va Tech   1984
  Ogum, George   Asst   524-5498   DBA   Memphis   1990
  White, Garland M.   Asst   524-5373   MC   Richmond   1958

Virginia Union University   BS
Department of Finance
S. Lewis Sch of Bus Adm
Richmond, VA 23220
Area Code (804) Fax
  Altimus, Cyrus A.   Dean   257-5710   BAdm   PHD   71 Penn St   1987
  Odutola, Adelaja   Inst   259-5697   MS   Va State   1983

Wagner College
Department of Finance
Business
Staten Island,NY 10301
Area Code (718) Fax
Did Not Respond
  D'Allesandio, G.   C-Ac   MBA   83 Wagner

Wake Forest University   BS
Finance Faculty   1985
Sch Bus & Accountancy
Winston-Salem NC 27109
Area Code (919) Fax 759-5830
  Taylor, Thomas C.   Dean   759-5304   Atg   PHD   70 LSU   1971
  Dunkelberg, John   Assoc   759-5778   12 IO   PHD   S Carol   1983
  Goho, Thomas S.   Assoc   761-5737   13 XY   PHD   N Carol   1977

Wake Forest University-Grad   MBA
Finance Faculty   1985
Babcock Grad Sch of Mgt
Winston-Salem NC 27109
Area Code (919) Fax 759-5830
  McKinnon, John B.   Dean   759-5418   Fnce   MBA   61 Harvard   1989
  Moyer, R. Charles   Prof   759-5413   14 EADO   PHD   Pitt   1988
    Integon Chair in Finance
  Harris, Frederick   Assoc   759-5112   12 DCAL   PHD   Virginia   1990
  Lamy, Robert E.   Assoc   759-5039   31 PQAD   PHD   LSU   1990
  Claggett, E. Tylor   Asst   761-0707   12 DP   PHD   79 Houston   1988
  Ferner, Jack D.   Lect   759-5575   1 CFGH   MBA   55 Harvard   1971

Wartburg College
Finance Faculty
Dept of Bus Adm & Econ
Waverly, Iowa 50677-1003
Area Code (319) Fax 352-8514
Did Not Respond
  Shipman, William A.   C-Pr   352-8315   Econ   PHD   77 Pitt   1972

Washburn Univ of Topeka   BBA
Department of Finance
School of Business
Topeka, Kansas 66621
Area Code (913) Fax
  McKibbin, Lawrence E.   Dean   231-1010   Mgt   PHD   67 Stanford   1991
  Baker, W. Gary   Prof   PHD   75 Nebraska   1975
  Eck, James Robert   Prof   245-6307   PHD   79 Illinois   1979
  Hines, Mary Alice   Prof   267-4672   PHD   67 Ohio St   1982
    C. W. King Chair of Real Estate and Finance
  Hull, Robert M.   Asst   PHD   90 Kansas   1990

University of Washington
Dept of Finance & Bus Econ
School of Business Adm
Seattle, Wash 98195
Area Code (206) Fax 685-9392
UWACDC

BA,MBA,MPA,PHD
1921,1963

Name	Rank	Phone		Field	Deg	Yr	School	Yr
Leventhal, Robert S.	Dean	543-4752			MBA	56	Harvard	1989
Schall, Lawrence D.	C-Pr	543-4773	1 OG		PHD	69	Chicago	1968
Alberts, William W.	Prof	543-6579	1 CGH		PHD	61	Chicago	1967
Frost, Peter A.	Prof	543-4111	23 MNQ		PHD	66	UCLA	1969
Haley, Charles W.	Prof	543-7697	13		PHD	68	Stanford	1966
Higgins, Robert C.	Prof	543-4379	4		PHD	69	Stanford	1967
Roley, V. Vance	Prof	685-7476	23		PHD	77	Harvard	1983
Siegel, Andrew F.	Prof	543-4476	12 KLO		PHD	77	Stanford	1983
Siegel, Daniel R.	Prof	543-9131	1 ADL		PHD	83	Stanford	1990
Karpoff, Jonathan M.	Assoc	685-4954	1 ADG		PHD	82	UCLA	1983
Malatesta, Paul H.	Assoc	685-1987	12		PHD	69	Rocheste	1980
Rice, Edward M.	Assoc	543-4480	1		PHD	78	UCLA	1979
Bonser-Neal, Catherine A.	Asst	543-8737	4 V		MA	83	Chicago	1987
Kamara, Avraham	Asst	543-0652	2 LT		PHD	86	Columbia	1984
Neal, Robert S.	Asst	685-1089	12 MT		PHD	87	Chicago	1987
Wheatley, Simon	Asst	543-4435	24 JSWR		PHD	86	Rocheste	1984

Washington University
Finance Faculty
Olin School of Business
St. Louis, MO 63130-4899
Area Code (314) Fax 935-6359
WUOLIN

BS,MBA,PHD
1921,1963

Name	Rank	Phone	Login		Field	Deg	Yr	School	Yr
Virgil Jr., Robert L.	Dean	935-6344			Atg	DBA	67	Wash U	1964
Dybvig, Philip H.	Prof	935-4569	DYBVIG	23 DJOP		PHD	79	Yale	1988

Boatmen's Bancshares Professor of Banking and Finance

Back, Kerry E.	Assoc	935-7321	BACK	2 JKLO		PHD	83	Kentucky	1989
Lamoureux, Christopher G.	Assoc	935-6329	LAMOUREU	23 LNOT		PHD	85	Syracuse	1989
Little, James T.	Assoc	935-6393	LITTLEJ	14 FHUV		PHD	77	Minn	1971
Zhou, Guofu	Assoc	935-6384	ZHOU	12 JLMN		PHD	90	Duke	1990
Campbell, Cynthia J.	Asst	935-6394	CAMPBELL	13 DGTV		PHD	86	Michigan	1987
Jender, Jaime	VAsst	935-4527	ZENDER	12 ABDN		PHD	88	Yale	1991
Maheswaran, Srinivasan	Asst	935-5924	MAHESWAR	23 JLOT		ABD	91	Minn	1991
Steeley, James M.	VAsst	935-5883	STEELEY	12 JKLT		PHD	90	Warwick	1990

Washington and Lee Univ
Finance Faculty
Sch Comm, Econ, & Pol
Lexington, Virg 24450
Area Code (703) Fax 463-8945
Did Not Respond; Phone 463-8600

BS
1927

Peppers, Larry C.	Dean	463-8602			Econ	PHD		Vanderbi	1986
Goldsten, Joseph	Prof	463-8619							

Washington State University
Department of Finance
Coll of Business & Econ
Pullman, Wash 99164-4746
Area Code (509) Fax 335-4275
WSUVM1

BA,MAC,PHD
1960,1965

Markin, Rom J.	Dean	335-3596			Mktg	DBA	61	Indiana	1961
Goolsby, William C.	C-Pr	335-8727		6 &		PHD	74	Wiscon	1989
Field, Irv	Prof	335-2322				PHD	66	Oregon	1966
Kerr, Halbert	Prof	335-4469		24 UVW		PHD	76	U Wash	
Petry, Glenn	Prof	335-5609				DBA	73	Colorado	1973
Kling, John	Assoc	335-2160				PHD	83	Purdue	1988
Byrd, John	Asst	335-2347	BYRD	1 ADG		PHD	88	Oregon	1987
Han, Li-Ming	Asst	335-0118	HAN			PHD	87	Texas	1988
Cooney, John W.	Inst	335-7658	COONEY	13 DG		ABD		Utah	1990

Wayne State College
Finance Faculty
Division of Business
Wayne, Nebraska 68787
Area Code (402) Fax

BS,BA

Benson, Vaughn L.	H-Ac	375-7245			Atg	PHD	85	Nebraska	1974
Halsey, Ken	Prof	375-7250		12 FML		PHD	73	N Colora	1987
Conway, Gerald	Asst	375-7252		13 DIN		MSE	73	Chadron	1975
Nelson, Jeryl	Inst	375-7251		13 DFP		MBA	87	S Dakota	1986

Wayne State University BS,BA,MBA
Dept of Finance & Bus Econ 1976,1982
School of Business Adm
Detroit, Mich 48202
Area Code (313) Fax

Volz, William H.	Dean	577-4500		Law	MBA	78	Harvard	1978
Hamilton, James L.	C-Pr	577-4520		Econ	PHD	69	Duke	1974
Price, Kelly	Assoc	577-4542	23	JK	PHD	76	Michigan	1982
Shulman, Joel M.	Assoc	577-4537	12	BI	PHD	84	Mich St	1988
Voorheis, Frank L.	Assoc	577-4498	1	L	PHD	66	Mich St	1969
Ajayi, Richard	Asst	577-4496	14	V	PHD	89	Temple	1989
Bayless, Mark E.	Asst	577-4539	13	AD	PHD	79	Wash U	1988
Cooper, Rick	Asst	577-5951	2	J	PHD	90	Vanderbi	1990
Haddad, Mahmoud M.	Asst	577-4538	24	LW	PHD	84	Alabama	1984
Monroe, Margaret	Asst	577-4520	2	L	PHD	81	Florida	1991

Weber State College BS,MPACC
Department of Finance
School of Bus & Econ
Ogden, Utah 84408-3803
Area Code (801) Fax 626-7930

Vaughan, Mike	Dean	626-6064		Econ	PHD	80	Nebraska	1981
Cooley, Clyde J.	Prof				PHD	77	Utah	1978
Nelson, Mark J.	Prof				PHD	69	Oregon	1973
Lutz, Robert A.	Asst				BA	86	Utah	1991

Webster University
Department of Finance
College of Business
St. Louis, MO 63119-3194
Area Code (314) Fax

George, Neil J.	Dean	968-6915			PHD		Case Wes	
Afshar, Tahmoures A.	Assoc	968-7551			PHD	84	Case Wes	1975
Spillane Jr., Edward Joseph	Assoc	968-7008			PHD	73	St Louis	1986

Wesley College BA,BS
Finance Faculty
Division of Business
Dover, Delaware 19901-9912
Area Code (302) Fax 736-2301
No full-time Finance faculty

Murchison, Richard L.	H-As	736-2451		Mgt	MAS	66	Delaware	1988

West Chester University BS,MBA
Deparatment of Econ & Agt
Sch of Bus & Public Afr
West Chester, PA 19383
Area Code (215) Fax

Fiorentino, Christopher R.	Dean$	436-2236			PHD	89	Temple	1985
DeMoss, Phil	C-Pr	436-2134		Econ	PHD		Kans St	1972
Mohan, Daniel	Assoc	436-2217			PHD		Rutgers	1980

University of West Florida BS,MBA
Dept of Finance & Economics
College of Business
Pensacola, FL 32514-5752
Area Code (904) Fax 474-3131

Dimsdale, Parks B.	Dean	474-2348		Econ	PHD	69	Florida	1978
Elebash, Clarence C.	C-Pr	474-2727			DBA	75	Fla St	1976
Committe, Thomas Carrol	Prof				PHD	66	Alabama	1967
Richey, Thomas Craig	Assoc				ABD	61	Northwes	1968
Wade, Charles M.	Assoc				PHD	77	Miss	1980
Apap, Antonio	Asst				DBA	82	US Intl	1990
Callaway, Mary M.	Asst				LLM	81	Emory	1977

West Georgia College BBA,MBA,MPA
Dept of Accounting & Finance 1984,1990
School of Business
Carrollton, GA 30118
Area Code (404) Fax 836-6720

Hovey Jr., David H.	Dean	836-6467		Mgt	PHD	78	LSU	1984
Volkan, Ara G.	C-Pr	836-6469		F	PHD	79	Alabama	1989
Arsan, Noyan	Prof	836-6469	34	CPUV	PHD	73	Syracuse	1984
Burton, James H.	Prof	836-6469	1	EOQ	PHD	78	Geo St	1990
Poindexter, Eugene O.	Prof	836-6469	12	GIKM	PHD	70	Syracuse	1977

West Texas State Univ BS,MPA
Dept of Atg, Econ & Finance
Sch of Business Box 187
Canyon, Texas 79016-0187
Area Code (806) Fax 656-2071

Dittrich, John E.	Dean	656-2530	Mgt	PHD	73	U Wash	1988
Duman, Barry L.	H-Pr	656-2519		PHD		S Calif	1969
Miller, Jerry D.	Prof	656-2514		PHD		LSU	1970
Gene Edwards Professor of Finance							
Owens, James K.	Prof	656-2516		DBA		Harvard	1978
Walker, Ella J.	Inst	656-2515		MBA		W Txs St	1980

West Virginia University BS,MPA
Department of Finance 1954,1963
Coll of Business & Econ
Morgantown, WV 26506-6025
Area Code (304) Fax 293-7061
WVNVM

Logar, Cyril M.	Dean	293-7800			Mktg	DBA	75	Kent St	1976
Riley, William B.	C-Pr	293-7885	U00CA	12	CFLM	PHD	76	Arkansas	1978
Brewer, Howard L.	Prof	293-7887		1	CFGH	PHD	77	Iowa	1985
Scherr, Frederick C.	Prof	293-7891		12	BCDI	PHD	79	Pitt	1977
Wright, Fred E.	Emer	293-7893				MA	50	W Virg	1951
Rose, Terry L.	Assoc	293-7890				PHD	78	Illinois	1984
Speaker, Paul J.	Assoc	293-7892	U1CC7	12	DP	PHD	81	Purdue	1981
Abbott, Ashok	Asst	293-7888	U3EB7	13	AGPU	PHD	87	Va Tech	1987
Chow, Kewn Victor	Asst	293-7888	U55C9	12	JMNO	PHD	89	Alabama	1989
Denning, Karen Craft	Asst	293-7889	U40F2	12	JMNO	PHD	86	Pitt	1987

Western Carolina University BSBA,MBA
Dept of Economics & Finance 1983,1984
School of Business
Cullowhee, NC 28723-9034
Area Code (704) Fax 227-7414
WCUVAX1

McCreary, John Franklynn	Dean	227-7401	Mgt	EDD	68	Tenn	1977
Boyd, William L.	H-Pr$	227-7401		PHD	78	Tx A&M	1990
Spencer, Austin Harvey	Prof	227-7401		PHD	72	Indiana	1980
Hays, Patrick Allen	Assoc	227-7401		PHD	77	N Carol	1985
Pourian, Heydar	Assoc	227-7403		PHD	80	Wis-Milw	1984
on leave							
Allen, Grace C.	Asst	227-7403		PHD	91	S Carol	1990

Western Conn State Univ
Department of Finance
Ancell School of Bus
Danbury, Conn 06810
Area Code (203) Fax
Did Not Respond

Blaylock, Bruce K.	Dean	797-4316	Mgt	PHD		Geo St	1989
Bondi, Robert J.	C-Ac	797-4277		PHD		New York	
Deastlov, Frank	Assoc	797-4089					
Bliss, W. Michael	Asst			MBA		Harvard	
Morton, Allen D.	Asst	797-2787				Penn	

Western Illinois University BB,MAC
Dept of Mktg Finance & Trans 1978,1983
College of Business
Macomb, Illinois 61455
Area Code (309) Fax 298-2142
ECNCDC

Smith, E. Ray	Dean	298-2442	Atg	PHD		Ohio St	1987
Finlay, Jim	C-Ac	298-1198		MBA		La Tech	1984
Ebeid, Fred J.	Prof	298-1303		PHD		Illinois	1970
Sims Jr., Edwin C.	Prof	298-1198		PHD		Columbia	1972
Chishty, Muhammod	Asst	298-1198					
Kenney, Peppi	Asst	298-1198					
Panici, Joseph	Asst	298-1198					
Tripp, James D.	Asst	298-1198		MBA		Drury	1990
Voss, Richard	Asst	298-1198					

Western Kentucky University BS
Dept of Finance & MIS 1982
College of Business
Bowling Green KY 42101
Area Code (502) Fax
WKYUVM
  Brown, J. Michael   Dean   745-3893   Econ   PHD   71 Kentucky   1988
  Bretz, Robert   H-Ac   745-5283   F   DBA   75 Miss St   1983
  Keck, Peggy   Prof   745-3290   2 XY   EDD   Oklahoma   1968
  Redman, Arnold L.   Assoc   745-2926   12 CD   PHD   79 Illinois   1985
  Wolfe, Edward R.   Assoc   745-6193   13 P   PHD   76 Kentucky   1984
  Chhachhi, Indudeep S.   Asst   745-2928 RFCHHCHH 12 AGMU   DBA   90 So Illin   1990
  Manakyan, Herman   Asst   745-2919 RFMANMAN 12 DGMN   PHD   88 Alabama   1984
  Thapa, Samanta B.   Asst   745-6399 RFTHAPA   14 UVWD   PHD   88 Geo St   1988

Western Michigan University BBA,MS,MBA
Dept of Finance & Comm Law 1970,1981
Haworth College of Bus
Kalamazoo, Mich 49008-3811
Area Code (616) Fax 387-5710
GW.WMICH
  Jones, Darrell G.   Dean   387-7042   BSci   PHD   66 Mich St   1962
  McCarty, William F.   C $ 387-5722   JD   66 Michigan
  Balik, Robert   Prof   387-5674   PHD   84 Iowa
  Burnie, David A.   Prof   387-5764   PHD   84 Syracuse
  Edwards, Adrian   Prof   387-5534   PHD   67 Ohio St
  Issa, Ahmad D.   Prof   387-5532   PHD   67 Illinois
  Jones, Robert   Prof   387-5751   PHD   78 Notre Dm
  KrishnaSwamy, C. R.   Prof   387-5761   PHD   83 Tenn   1977
  Mangla, Inayat U.   Prof   387-5639   PHD   78 Mich St

Western New England College BS,MBA,MS,AC
Dept of Accounting & Finance
School of Business
Springfield, MA 01119-2684
Area Code (413) Fax 782-3111
  Kowalski Jr., Stanley   Dean   782-1224   Econ   PHD   76 Mass   1973
  Bronson, Claire S.   C-Ac   782-1600   23 PYG   PHD   82 Connecti   1983
  Hulbert, William   Assoc   782-3111   1 EI   MA   Syracuse   1972
  Bosworth, William   Asst   782-3111   14 RV   PHD   85 Conn   1988

Western State College of CO BS
Finance Faculty
Dept of Bus & Acctg
Gunnison, CO 81231
Area Code (303) Fax 943-2212
  Blair, Ken   C-Pr   943-2870   Mktg   PHD   76 Ariz St   1986
  Liesz, Thomas   Assoc   943-3055   12   PHD   89 Idaho   1990

Western Washington Univ BA,MBA
Dept Finance, Mktg & Dec Sci 1990,1990
College of Bus & Econ
Bellingham, Wash 98225-5996
Area Code (206) Fax 647-4844
WWU.EDU
Internet numbers rather than Bitnet
  Murphy, Dennis R.   Dean   676-3896   Econ   PHD   74 Indiana   1979
  Benson, Earl D.   C-Pr   676-3375   12 KN   PHD   78 Oregon   1980
  Fewings, David E.   Assoc   647-4815   1 FIO   PHD   75 Toronto   1985
  Rystrom, David S.   Assoc   647-4820   12 LN   PHD   82 Oregon   1983
  Hall, Pamela L.   Asst   676-3906   12 BFG   PHD   91 La Tech   1990

Westfield State College BS
Finance Faculty
Dept of Econ & Bus Mgt
Westfield, Mass 01086
Area Code (413) Fax 562-3613
RCN
Phone 568-3311
  Pellegrino, Kathleen B.   C-Ac   Ext 329   Atg   MBA   76 W N Eng   1978
  Daniel, Cornelia M.   Asst   Ext 696   PHD   Mass   1990
  Healy, Gerald   Asst   Ext 693   CLU   Amer Col 1981
  Jakacky, Gary   Asst   Ext 592

Wichita State University
Dept of Fnce RI Es & Dec Sci
Barton School of Bus
Wichita, Kansas 67208-1595
Area Code (316) Fax 689-3770
TWSUVM

BBA,MPA,MBA,MS
1968,1974

Name	Rank	Phone	Code	Area	Field	Deg	Yr	School	Year
Richards, R. Malcolm	Dean	689-3200		12	Fnce	PHD	74	Michigan	1991
Levi, Donald R.	C-Pr	389-3219		23		PHD	74	Wash St	1980
Nielsen, Carl C.	Assoc	668-3219		23	PQ	PHD	66	Nebraska	1968
Christensen, Donald G.	Asst	689-3219	TWSUVM	12	ADKL	PHD	88	S Carol	1988
Gupta, Manoj	Asst	689-3219	MGUPTA	12	JLMV	PHD	90	Illinois	1990
Lecompte, Richard L.B.	Asst	689-3219	LECOMPTE	13	BGKP	PHD	87	Texas	1989
Nohr, Timothy W.	Inst	689-3219		12		MBA	86	Wichita	1986

Widener University
Department of Finance
School of Management
Chester, Penn 19013-9987
Area Code (215) Fax 876-6598

BS,MS

Name	Rank	Phone			Field	Deg	Yr	School	Year
DiAngelo Jr., Joseph A.	Dean	499-4301			Mgt	EDD	87	Temple	1980
Ozatalay, Savas	H					PHD			
Salam, Ahmad	Prof	499-4315				PHD			
Mansur, Iqbal	Assoc	499-4321		23	MRV	PHD	84	Cinn	1985
Marshall, Paul	Asst	499-1174				PHD			

Willamette University
Finance Faculty
Atkinson Grad Sch Mgt
Salem, Oregon 97301
Area Code (503) Fax 370-3011

MM

Name	Rank	Phone			Field	Deg	Yr	School	Year
Weight, G.Dale	Dean	370-6440			Fnce	PHD	68	Oregon	1990
Archer, Stephen H.	C-Pr	370-6440				PHD	58	Minn	1974
Guy F. Atkinson Professor of Economics and Finance									
Choate, George Marc	Prof	370-6440				PHD	70	Wash	1974

College of William & Mary
Department of Finance
School of Business Adm
Williamsburg, VA 23187
Area Code (804) Fax 221-2937
Phone 221-4100

BBA,MBA,EMBA
1972,1974

Name	Rank	Phone			Field	Deg	Yr	School	Year
Page, Alfred N.	Dean	221-2890			Fnce	PHD	64	Chicago	1990
T. C. Clarke Professor									
Bryce, Herrington J.	Prof	221-2856				PHD		Syracuse	1986
Haltiner, James R.	Prof	221-2904				DBA		Virginia	1976
O'Connell, William E.	Prof	221-2880				DBA	67	Indiana	
Chessie Professor of Business Administration									
Boschen, John F.	Assoc	221-2886				PHD		Brown	1988
Pulley, Lawrence B.	Assoc	221-2869				PHD		Virginia	1985
Strong, John S.	Assoc	221-2864				PHD		Harvard	1985
Williams, Stuart L.	Assoc	221-2873				PHD		Syracuse	1972

William Jewell College
Finance Faculty
Business Department
Liberty, MO 64068-9988
Area Code (816) Fax 781-3164
Phone 781-7700

AB,BS

Name	Rank	Phone			Field	Deg	Yr	School	Year
Helsing, J. Eric	C-Pr	Ext 5698				JD		Rutgers	1988
A. Major & Dorothy Hull Chair of Communication in Business & Leadership									
Miller, Otis	Prof	Ext 5703		13		PHD		Missouri	1978
Harris, Kimberly H.	Asst	Ext 5704		12		JD	78	Kansas	1986

Winona State University
Dept of Economics & Finance
College of Business
Winona, Minn 55987
Area Code (507) Fax 457-5697

BS

Name	Rank	Phone			Field	Deg	Yr	School	Year
Langston, Rosemary	Dean$	457-5014			Nurs	PHD		Minn	1978
Kauffman, Daniel E.	C-Pr					PHD		Nebraska	1983
Murray, Michael J.	Prof					PHD		Notre Dm	1986
Kesler, David W.	Assoc					MBA		Kansas	1984
Wrolstad, Mark A.	Assoc				Fnce	DBA	83	Colorado	1989
Rahnama, Masha	Asst					PHD		Iowa St	1990

Winston-Salem State Univ   BS
Finance Faculty
Division of Bus & Econ
Winston-Salem NC 27110
Area Code (919) Fax
Bailey Sr., Willie H.	Dir	750-2330			Mgt	PHD	74	Illinois	1986
Blackmon, Elsie C.	Asst							

Winthrop College   BS
Dept of Accounting & Finance   1979,1983
School of Business Adm
Rock Hill, SC 29733
Area Code (803) Fax 328-3960
Padgett, Jerry H.	Dean	323-2185			Econ	PHD	68	Purdue	1970
Bond, James G.	C-Pr	323-2186			Atg	PHD	77	S Carol	1979
Duncan, Frederick H.	Assoc	323-2186		34	UV	PHD		S Carol	
Bhardwaj, Ravinder K.	Asst	323-2186		23	MW	MBA		S Carol	
Furneis, Bill	Asst	323-2186		24	RST	PHD	90	Toronto	1988
LeYouvnenu, David	Asst	323-2186		23	TX	DBA	88	La Tech	1988

U of Wisconsin-Eau Claire   BBA
Department of Finance
School of Business
Eau Claire, WI 54701-4004
Area Code (715) Fax 836-2380
Wenner, James F.	Dean	836-5509				Mgt	PHD	65	Iowa	1971
Vanderheiden, Paul A.	Assoc	836-5228		1	CEIY	PHD	80	Florida	1983
Baradwaj, Babu G.	Asst	836-5199	BARADWBG	34	DGPU	PHD	91	Tx A&M	1991
Chen, Su-Jane	Asst	836-2710	CHENS	12	JMPS	PHD	88	Missouri	1991

Univ of Wisconsin-Green Bay   BS,BA,MS
Finance Faculty
Business Administration
Green Bay, WI 54311-7001
Area Code (414) Fax 465-2660
Bauer, Robert	Dean	465-2336						
Alesch, Dan	C-Pr	465-2553			PHD	70	UCLA	1977
Ghanty, A. Sam	Asst	465-2044	24	JLUV	PHD	82	Wiscon	1984
Nagy, Robert	Asst	465-2386	23	MPQ	PHD	80	Miss	1988
Berk, Laurey	Lect	465-2313	12	H	MBA	82	WI-Oshko	1982

U of Wisconsin-La Crosse   BS,MBA
Department of Finance   1982,1987
College of Business
La Crosse, WI 54601
Area Code (608) Fax 785-6700
UWLAX
Fuller, Rex	Dean	785-8090			Econ	PHD	82	CS-Chico	1981
Aiuppa, Thomas	C-Pr	785-8790	AIUPPA	1	AJ	PHD	81	Georgia	1981
Carney, Robert J.	Assoc	785-8117		1	XFO	PHD	87	Iowa	1987
Krueger, Thomas	Assoc	785-6652	KRUEGER	12	YJM	PHD	88	Kentucky	1989
Callaway, Richard	Asst	785-6654		34	UOP	PHD	86	Indiana	1991
Graham, Lise	Asst	785-6653	GRAHAM	12	PF	ABD		Miss St	1991
Morrison, Dianne	Inst	785-6655		1		MBA	87	Wis-LaCr	1990

Univ of Wisconsin-Madison   BBA,MBA,MS,PHD
Department of Finance   1916,1963
School of Business
Madison, Wiscon 53706
Area Code (608) Fax 263-0477
WISCMACC
Policano, Andrew J.	Dean	262-1555	23	Econ	PHD	75	Brown	1991
Johannes, James M.	C-Pr	263-4502	3	PRD	PHD	78	Wiscon	1984
First Wisconsin Professor of Banking								
Krainer, Robert	Prof	263-1253	31	DBR	PHD	64	Michigan	1964
Thompson, Howard E.	Prof	262-1991	1	EG	PHD	64	Wiscon	1963
Chen, Zhiwu	Asst	262-1942	21	JLMN	PHD	90	Yale	1990
DeBondt, Werner	Asst	262-8601	24	JMN	PHD	85	Cornell	1984
Fedenia, Mark	Asst	263-4502	21	JMNO	PHD	88	Wiscon	1986
Mauer, David C.	Asst	262-7867	12	DKNO	PHD	86	Purdue	1986
Ready, Mark	Asst	262-5226	1	ABCT	PHD	90	Cornell	1990
Sherman, Ann	Asst	262-1466	12	Q	PHD	87	Minn	1987
Triantis, Alex	Asst	263-7431	21	LV	PHD	88	Stanford	1989
Knez, Peter	Lect	263-2138	2	JKLM	ABD		Penn	1991

Univ of Wisconsin-Milwaukee   BBA,MS,MAT
Finance Faculty   1970,1971
School of Business Adm
Milwaukee, WI 53201
Area Code (414) Fax 229-6957

Name	Rank	Phone			Field	Deg	Yr	School	Yr
Schenker, Eric	Dean	229-4235				PHD	57	Florida	1959
Hsu, Der-Ann	Prof	229-3828	2	J		PHD	73	Wiscon	1977
Warga, Arthur	Prof	229-4883	1	F		PHD	77	Michigan	1991
Marcus, Richard	Assoc	229-4130	14	FV		PHD	83	Chicago	1985
Ambrose, Brent	Asst	229-4235	3	ST		PHD	89	Georgia	1989
Ancel, Esther	Asst	229-5612	1	F		PHD	85	Texas	1986
Griffiths, Mark	Asst	229-4369	1	F		PHD	90	W Ontari	1988
Klagstad, Harold L.	Asst	229-5686	12	FB		PHD	90	Purdue	1988
Lepley, William H.	Asst	229-4368	23	Q		PHD	87	Wiscon	1986
Mehra, Anita	Asst	229-3840	14	FV		PHD		Temple	1991
Solberg, Donald	Asst	229-4235	2	J		PHD	87	Nebraska	1987
Winters, Drew	Asst	229-6530	1	F		PHD	87	Georgia	1991
Stroyny, Alvin	Lect	229-4092	2	N		MBA	75	Wiscon	1990

Univ of Wisconsin-Oshkosh   BBA,MS,MBA
Dept of Finance & Bus Law   1970,1978
College of Business Adm
Oshkosh, Wiscon 54901-8677
Area Code (414) Fax 424-0010

Name	Rank	Phone			Field	Deg	Yr	School	Yr
Milam, Robert L.	Dean	424-1424			Econ	PHD	68	N Car St	1984
Drzycimski, Eugene	Prof	424-3044				PHD	66	Mich St	1970
Lang, Larry R.	Prof	424-1090				PHD	73	Mich St	1972
Niendorf, Robert M.	Prof	424-2091				PHD	69	Wiscon	1969
Ward, David J.	Prof	424-3032							
Griepentrog, Gary L.	Assoc	424-1329							
Huffman, Stephen P.	Asst	424-3044				PHD	90	Fla St	
Schellenger, Michael H.	Asst	262-6241				DBA		Arkansas	

Univ of Wisconsin-Parkside   BS,MBA
Dept of Accounting & Finance
School of Business
Kenosha, Wiscon 53141-2000
Area Code (414) Fax

Name	Rank	Phone			Field	Deg	Yr	School	Yr
Anderson, Beverlee B.	Dean	595-2243			Mktg	PHD	72	Ohio St	1988
Singer, Ronald M.	C-Ac	595-2348			Atg	PHD	89	Wiscon	1973
Dougherty, Kevin	Asst	595-2449	12	DNTV		PHD	91	Arizona	1990
Seltzer, David F.	Asst	595-2433	12	LQSY		PHD	89	Arizona	1989

U of Wisconsin-Platteville
Department of Finance
Coll Bus, Ind, & Comm
Platteville, WI 53818-3099
Area Code (608) Fax

Name	Rank	Phone			Field	Deg	Yr	School	Yr
Al Yasiri, Kahtan A.	Dean	342-1547			Econ	PHD	65	Iowa St	1965
Gross, Thomas	Asst	342-1459	12			MBA		Madison	1991
Oxenford, Jerry	Asst	342-1459	13			MBA		Iowa	1982

U of Wisconsin-River Falls   BA,BS
Dept of Business Adm
College of Arts & Sci
River Falls, WI 54022-5001
Area Code (715) Fax

Name	Rank	Phone			Field	Deg	Yr	School	Yr
Prochnow, Neal	Dean	425-3366			Phys	PHD		Duke	1964
Corcoran, Charles	Assoc	425-3849	13			PHD		Minn	1988
Rahgozar, Reza	Assoc	425-3335	12			PHD		Claremon	1987

U of Wisconsin-Stevens Point   BA,BS
Division of Business & Econ
Col of Letters & Sci
Stevens Point WI 54481-3897
Area Code (715) Fax 346-4277

Name	Rank	Phone			Field	Deg	Yr	School	Yr
Judy, Richard B.	H-Pr	346-2728			Mgt	PHD	84	Indiana	1985
Love, William	Assoc	346-3871	12			PHD		Arkansas	1982
Conway, Steve	Asst	346-3906	12			MBA		Wiscon	1989

Univ of Wisconsin-Superior   BS
Finance Faculty
Business & Economics
Superior, Wiscon 54880-2898
Area Code (715) Fax

Name	Rank	Phone			Field	Deg	Yr	School	Yr
Abrahamsson, Bernhard	Dean	394-8209			Econ	PHD		Wiscon	1989
Quinn, Patrick	H-Pr	394-8434	13	FHP		EDD		No Illin	1971

U of Wisconsin-Whitewater
Dept of Finance & Bus Law
College of Bus & Econ
Whitewater, WI 53190-1790
Area Code (414) Fax 472-4863

BBA,MS,MBA
1974,1980

Name	Rank	Phone		Field	Deg	Yr	School	Yr
Domitrz, Joseph S.	Dean	472-1343		Econ	PHD	71	So Illin	1976
Sorensen, Donald E.	C-Ac$	472-1316	1	F	PHD		Wiscon	1976
Batra, Harish C.	Prof	472-1945	1	C	PHD	71	Illinois	1971
Associate Dean								
Thatcher, Janet S.	Prof	472-5462	1	D	PHD		Wiscon	1986
Howat, John D.	Assoc	472-5458	2	L	PHD		Illinois	1976
Moini, Abdol H.	Assoc	472-5460	3	V	PHD		Alabama	1985
Thatcher, John	Assoc	472-5446	1	E	PHD		Madison	1991
Crabb, Ronald R.	Asst	472-1290	3	X	PHD		Madison	1986
Olson, Howard G.	Asst	472-5448	3	S	PHD		Madison	1977
Barrett, Peter J.	Lect	472-1880	1	C	ABD		Wis-Milw	1985
Rich, James D.	Lect	472-5447	1		MBA		Wis-Whit	1988
Sullivan, John	Lect	472-4912	3	X	MBA		Wis-Whit	1984

Wittenberg University
Finance Faculty
Dept of Business Adm
Springfield, OH 45501
Area Code (513) Fax 327-6340
Did Not Respond

BA

Maurer, Wayne O.	C-Ac	327-7903		Atg	MBA	74	Wright	1974

Wofford College
Finance Faculty
Dept of Econ & Atg
Spartanburg, SC 29303-3663
Area Code (803) Fax 582-1816

BA,BS

Stephenson, Matthew A.	C-Pr	597-4570		Econ	PHD	65	Tulane	1970
Proctor, James E.	Assoc	585-4821	12	CFMV	PHD	76	Clemson	1981

Woodbury University
Finance Faculty
Accounting & Bus Dept
Burbank, Calif 91510-7846
Area Code (818) Fax 504-9320

Myers, Jon W.	C-Ac	767-0888		Atg	MBA		Berkeley	
Chan, Anthony K.	Asst	767-0888			ABD		Claremon	

Worcester State College
Finance Faculty
Dept of Bus Adm & Econ
Worcester, MA 01602
Area Code (617) Fax
Did Not Respond

Juralewicz, Richard S.	C-Pr	793-8091		Mgt	PHD	66	Rennsela	1973

Wright State University
Dept of Finance/Ins/Real Est
Coll of Business & Adm
Dayton, Ohio 45435
Area Code (513) Fax 873-3545

BS,MBA
1974,1979

Goulet, Waldemar M.	Dean	873-3242		Fnce	PHD	73	Mich St	1975
Kaufman, Daniel J.	C-Ac	873-3175			PHD	86	Ohio St	1985
Bacon, Peter W.	Prof	873-3488			DBA	67	Indiana	1969
Gressis, Nicolas	Prof	873-2765			PHD	75	Penn St	1979
Ahmad, Khurshi	Assoc	873-3185	7	#	PHD	70	Penn	1970
Ainina, M. Fall	Assoc	873-3175			PHD	86	Ariz St	1986
Sweeney, Robert	Assoc	873-2221			PHD	85	S Carol	1989
Williams, Richard E.	Assoc	873-2260			PHD	72	Mich St	1965
Larsen, James E.	Asst	873-2870	6	&	PHD	87	Nebraska	1987

University of Wyoming
Dept of Economicd & Finance
College of Business
Laramie, Wyoming 82071-3985
Area Code (307) Fax 766-5090
UWYO

BS,MBA,MS,PHD
1956,1982

Forster, Bruce A.	Dean$	766-4194						
Crocker, Thomas	C			Econ				

Spahr, Ronald W.	Prof	766-4244	12		PHD			1974
Sterbenz, Frederic	Assoc	766-2201	1		PHD			1981
Gronwoller, Paul L.	Asst	766-5438	27		PHD			1985
Magiera, Frank T.	Asst	268-2413	12		PHD			1987
Pilotte, Eugene A.	Asst	766-5430	14		PHD			1988
Pilotte, Sheree	Asst	766-3848	12		PHD			1989
Sunderman, Mark A.	Asst	766-4199	16		PHD			1985
White, Mark V.	Inst	766-3834	1		ABD			1991

Xavier University BS
Department of Finance
College of Business
Cincinnati, Ohio 45207-1096
Area Code (513) Fax 745-1954
XAVIER

Geeding, Daniel W.	Dean	745-3528			Mgt	PHD	72 Cinn	1969
Johnson, R. Stafford	C-Pr	745-3108	RSJPROJ3	24	LMVW	PHD	76 Kentucky	1980
Rothwell, John	Prof	745-3103		13	FPR	MBA	Xavier	1963
Retiring January 1992								
Glasgo, Philip W.	Assoc	745-3595	GLASGO	13	FOPY	PHD	80 Ohio St	1984
Jankowske, Wayne C.	Assoc	745-3868		1	EGHO	PHD	75 Kentucky	1978
Gerdsen, Julie B.	Asst	745-3377		16	BGX	PHD	81 Cinn	1988
Pawlukiewicz, James E.	Asst	745-3066	JEP	12	CGN	PHD	91 Kentucky	1989

Yale University MPPM,PHD
135 Prospect St, FnceFaculty
Sch Organization & Mgt
New Haven, Conn 06511-3729
Area Code (203) Fax 432-6316

Levine, Michael E.	Dean	432-5964				LLB	Yale	1987
Ingersoll, Jon	Prof	432-6019				PHD	MIT	1982
Romano, Roberta	Prof	432-4965		1		JD	Yale	1984
Ross, Stephen	Prof	432-6016		2	M	PHD	Harvard	1977
Schwartz, Alan	Prof	432-4030		1		LLB	Yale	1987
Shubik, Martin	Prof	432-6054		3		PHD	Princet	1963
Heston, Steven	Asst	432-6030				PHD	Car Mel	1989
Rouwenhorst, G.	Asst	432-6046		4	U	PHD	Rochest	1990
Lindsey, Richard	Lect	432-6036				PHD	91 Berkeley	1991
Ibbotson, Roger	Prac	432-6021				PHD	Chicago	1984

Yeshiva University BS
Finance Faculty
Sy Syms School of Bus
New York, N York 10033-3299
Area Code (212) Fax 960-0055

Schiff, Michael	Dean	960-0845		Atg	PHD	47 NYU	1987
Krausz, Joshua	Prof	960-0845			PHD	79 Renssela	1987
Levine, Philip	Assoc	960-0845			PHD	74 Columbia	1989

York College of Pennsylvania
Finance Faculty
Dept of Business Adm
York, Penn 17403-3426
Area Code (717) Fax
Phone 846-7788

Breircheck, Glenn F.	C	Ext 425		Mgt	PHD	Conn	1975
Leinheiser, Frederick D.	Asst	846-7788			MBA	Shippens	1980
Sherman, Hugh D.	Asst	Ext 497			ABD	Temple	

Youngstown State University BS,MBA
Accounting & Finance Dept
Williamson Sch Bus Adm
Youngstown, Ohio 44555-0001
Area Code (216) Fax 742-1998
YSUB
Did Not Respond--Taken from College Catalog

Cicarelli, James	Dean	742-3062		Econ	PHD	68 Conn	1988
Tackett, James A.	C-Ac	742-3083		Atg	PHD	83 Ohio St	1984
Hankins, Kenneth P.	Prof				PHD	79 Arkansas	
Magner, Richard M.	Prof				MSED	57 Westmins	
Nunthirapakorn, Thakol	Prof				PHD	84 Arkansas	
Petrych, William	Prof				MA	57 Ohio St	
Pullman, Howard W.	Prof				PHD	73 Columbia	
Ross, Ray L.	Prof	742-1876			PHD	73 Illinois	1978
Vopel, Ronald P.	Prof	742-1872			PHD	75 Pitt	

Zetts, Jerome E.	Prof					MBA	67	Wayne St	
Claypool, Gregory A.	Assoc					PHD	88	Kent St	
Gonzalez, Jose A.	Assoc					PHD	81	Kent St	
Grim, John L.	Assoc					PHD	66	Kent St	
Heal, Inez G.	Assoc					MBA	76	Youngstn	
Parsegian, Elsa	Assoc					PHD	85	Pitt	
Borgia, Daniel J.	Asst					MBA	86	Gannon	
Chen, Haiyang	Asst					MA	87	Kent St	
Savage, Helen	Asst					MS	83	Akron	

CANADIAN SCHOOLS

Athabasca University   BCOM,BA,BGS,BN
Department of Finance
Administrative Studies
AthabascaCanada   T0G 2R0
Area Code (403) Fax 675-4222

Murgatroyd, Stephen	Dean	675-6196			Mgt	PHD	87	Open	1986
Crocker, Kevin	Asst	675-6191				MBA	82	Windsor	1986

Acadia University
Department of Finance
Manning Sch of Bus Adm
Wolfville Canada B0P 1X0
Area Code (902) Fax 542-4111
Phone 542-2201

Churchill, John	Asst	Ext 591	CHURCHIL	12	BHIX	PHD			1982
Feltmate, Ian	Lect	Ext 529	FELTMATE	1	F	ABD	90	W Ontar	1919
MacDougall, Shelley	Lect	Ext 514	MACDOUGA	1	CH	ABD		Bradford	1987

University of Alberta   BCOM,MBA,PHD
Dept of Finance & Mgt Sci   1968,1973
Faculty of Business
EdmontonCanada AB T6G 2R6
Area Code (403) Fax 492-3325
UALTAMTS

Malouin, Jean-Louis	Dean	492-3901			Atg	PHD	70	UCLA	1990
Mumey, Glen	C-Pr	492-2457		1	EH	PHD	65	Wash	1970
Barone-Adesi, Giovanni	Prof	492-4716		2	L	PHD	82	Chicago	1981
Hoskins, Colin	Prof	492-3948		1	C	PHD	67	Manchest	1966
Korkie, Robert	Prof	492-5693		2	M	PHD	73	Wash	1973
Mirus, Rolf	Prof	492-2921		4	VW	PHD	73	Minn	1971
Morck, Randall	Prof	492-5683		1	GUR	PHD	86	Harvard	1986
Beveridge, Steve	Assoc	492-3052		2	M	PHD	75	Chicago	1973
Laughton, David	Asst	492-2452		1	CHJ	PHD	87	MIT	1987
Zhang, Chu	Asst	492-3928		23	KM	ABD		Chicago	1991

Bishop's University   BBA,BABUS
Department of Finance
Business Administration
Lennoxvil Canada J1M 1Z7
Area Code (819) Fax 822-9661

Barlow, Stephen	Dean	822-9600	
Scott, Julia	Assoc	822-9600	
Bequet, Sylvie	Asst	822-9600	

Univ of British Columbia   BCO,MBA,MSC,PHD
Department of Finance
Faculty Comm & Bus Adm
VancouverCanada V6T 1Y8
Area Code (604) Fax 224-8489
Did Not Respond

Goldberg, Michael A.	Dean	822-8555				PHD	68	Berkeley	1968
Eckbo, Espen	C								
Jones, Lawrence D.	Prof	224-8326		6	&				

Brock University   BBA,BACTG,BBE
Department of Finance
Faculty of Business
St Catharines,ON L2S 3A1
Area Code (416) Fax 984-4188
Phone 688-5550

Richardson, A. William	Dean	Ext 3921	AFRICHAR		Atg	PHD	66	McMaster	1989
Mann, Harvey	C-Pr	Ext 3136				PHD	72	New York	1987

131

Name	Rank	Phone	Email			Degree	Yr	School	Year
Hanrahan, J. Robert	Prof	Ext 3917		1	T	MBA	60	Harvard	1975
Rege, Udayan	Prof	Ext 3919		1	FX	PHD	74	W Ontar	1984
Barnes, Thomas H.	Assoc	Ext 3797		12	FKMN	PHD	81	Kentucky	1986
Welch, Robert L.	Assoc	Ext 3920		12	DLO	PHD	89	SUNY-Buf	1978
Butko, James	Asst	Ext 3913		3	QX	ABD		Queens	1983

University of Calgary BCOM,MBA,PHD
Department of Finance 1985,1985
Faculty of Management
Calgary, Canada T2N 1N4
Area Code (403) Fax 282-0095
UNCAMULT

Name	Rank	Phone	Email			Degree	Yr	School	Year
Maher, P. Michael	Dean	220-5689	14011		Mgt	PHD	70	Northwes	1981
Sick, Gordon A.	C-Ac	220-7165	GASICK	12	CELN	PHD	81	Brit Col	1988
Chua, Jess	Prof	220-6331	JCHUA	2	DKOM	PHD	76	Michigan	1979
Mokkelbost, Per	Prof	220-7155		34	PQUV	PHD	73	Minn	1975
Woodward, Richard S.	Prof	220-7156	RSWOODWA	14	DORU	PHD	81	Exeter	1982
Chang, Philip C.	Assoc	220-7157	PCCHANG	1	GV	PHD		Illinois	1985
MacMillan, L. W.	Assoc	220-6168		12	LO	PHD	86	Arizona	1987
Robinson, Michael J.	Assoc	220-3342	MROBINSO	12	GJMT	PHD	89	W Ontari	1990
Nathan, Alli	Asst	220-5159	ANATHAN	34	PQVW	PHD	90	Queens	1989
Shivdasani, Anil	Asst	220-7971	SHIVDASA	1	ABDG	PHD	91	Ohio St	1991
Wood, Larry	Inst	220-7167		25	KXYZ	MBA	82	Calgary	1983

Carleton University BCOM,MMS
Department of Finance
School of Business
Ottawa, Ontario K1S 5B6
Area Code (613) Fax 788-2532
CARLTON
Phone 788-2600

Name	Rank	Phone	Email		
Riding, Allan L.	Prof	Ext 2394	ALRIDING	12	ABNS
Jog, Vijay Mukund	Assoc	Ext 2377	VIJAYJOG	12	AGQS
Lawson, William	Assoc	Ext 2391	BILLLAWS	12	ADQT
Srivastava, Ashwani K.	Asst	Ext 2514		12	ADQT

Concordia University BCOM,MBA,D
Department of Finance
Faculty Commerce & Adm
Montreal, Quebec H3G 1M8
Area Code (514) Fax 848-8645
Did Not Respond

Name	Rank	Phone			Degree	Yr	School	Year
Ross, C. A.	Dean$	848-2703						
Jalilvand, Abolhassan	C-Ac	848-2790			PHD	82	W Ontar	1985
Brodt, Abraham I.	Assoc	848-2786						
Patterson, C. S.	Assoc	848-2961						
Shanker, Latha	Assoc	848-2791						

Dalhousie University MBA
Department of Finance
School of Business Adm
Halifax, Canada B3H 1Z5
Area Code (902) Fax 494-1107
Did Not Respond

Ecole des Hautes Etudes Com BAA,MSC,MBA,PHD
Department of Finance
School of Business
Montreal, Canada H3A 2T5
Area Code (514) Fax 340-5635
Did Not Respond

Name	Rank	Phone				Degree		School	
Leroux, Francois	Dean				Econ	DSCE		Grenoble	
Bourgeois, Jacques	Prof	340-6594							
Lavallee, Mario	Prof	340-6602							
Frenois, Jean-Pierre	Assoc	340-6593							
To, Minh Chau	Assoc	340-6599							

Lakehead University BADMIN,HBCOM
Department of Finance
School of Business Adm
Thunder Bay, Ont P7B 5E1
Area Code (807) Fax 343-8023

Name	Rank	Phone			Degree	School	Year
Hartviksen, K. R.	D-Ac	343-8410	12	ABXY	MBA	York	1979
Dadgostar, B.	Assoc	343-8698	42	WK	PHD		1983
Hensel, A. C.	Assoc	343-8533	12	CEF	MBA	Case Wes	1970

Laurentian University
School of Commerce & Admin
Professional Schools
Sudbury, Canada P3E 2C6
Area Code (705) Fax 673-6518

BCOMM,MBA

Name	Rank	Phone	Email					School	Year
Zinger, J. T.	Assoc	673-6540		13	BP	MBA	78	Western	
Assogbavi, T.	Asst	673-6540		12	MQ	PHD		Laval	
Nagarajan, K. V.	Asst	673-6540		13	FJR	PHD	87	Buffalo	
Zhang, H.	Asst	673-6540	HZHANG	12	TV	PHD	87	Concordi	

Universite Laval
Dept of Finance & Insurance
Faculty of Business Adm
Sainte-Foy, Queb G1K 7P4
Area Code (418) Fax 656-2624
LAVALVM1

BCOM,MBA,PHD

Name	Rank	Phone	Email					School	Year
Lussier, Jacques	Dean	656-2216	LUSSIER			DCY	83	Grenoble	
Khoury, Nabil	C-Pr	656-2920		12	LMS	PHD	68	Indiana	
Cosset, Jean-Claude	Prof	656-3380	COSSETJC	41	UVW	PHD		Columbia	
Gagnon, Jean-Marie	Prof	656-5535		12	CMGS	PHD	70	Chicago	1961
Roy, Jean	Prof	656-5472							
Saint-Pierre, Jacques	Prof	656-2499	STPIERJ	1	GH	PHD	70	Louvain	
Gendron, Michel	Assoc	656-7380	GENDRONM	7	N	PHD		Brit Col	1985
Thibeault, Andre	Assoc	656-5456				PHD	84	West Ont	
Fischer, Klaus P.	Asst	656-3679	FISCHERK	34	ADTV	PHD	85	Tx A&M	1990
Lai, Van Son	Asst	656-3943	LAIV		FP	PHD	85	Georgia	1989
Bernie, Gilles									

University of Lethbridge
Department of Finance
Faculty of Management
Lethbridge Alber T1K 3M4
Area Code (403) Fax 329-2038
HG.ULETH

BMGT

Name	Rank	Phone	Email					School	Year
Lemer, George	Dean	329-2633	LEMER	31	PRAG	PHD		McGill	1981
Alam, Shamsul	Assoc	329-2126	ALAM	12	LJ	PHD			1986
Gardner, Eldon J.	Assoc	329-2726		13	P#	PHD			1982
Pratt, Brian	Asst	329-2478	PRATT	24	CLN	PHD			1990

University of Manitoba
Department of Finance
Dept of Business Adm
WinnipegManitoba R3T 2N2
Area Code (204) Fax 275-0181
UOFMCC
Faculty Bitnet MAN23432

BCOM,MBA,MACC

Name	Rank	Phone	Email					School	Year
Mackness, William	Dean	474-9711			Econ	MA	66	W Ontar	1988
Gould, Lawrence I.	H-Pr	474-9362		12	DENO	PHD	75	Toronto	1985
McCallum, John S.	Prof	474-9984		13	PQRT	PHD	73	Toronto	1973
Abeysekera, Sarath P.	Asst	474-8427	ABEYSEK	14	JUVW	PHD	85	Tx A&M	1985
Mittoo, Usha R.	Asst	474-8969	UMITTOO	12	JVWO	PHD	88	Brit Col	1988
Mossman, Charles	Asst	474-9985	MOSSMAN	12	JOCM	ABD		W Ontari	1990
Pratt, Hugh	Asst	474-8954	PRATT	1		PHD	91	Florida	1991
Stangeland, David	Asst	474-6743		1	ACDG	ABD		Alberta	1991
Swartz, L. Mick	Asst	474-8967	SWARTZ	12		ABD		Iowa	1991
Turtle, Harry J.	Asst	474-6391	HTURTLE	23	JMVZ	PHD	91	Alberta	1990
Cooney, Peter W.	Lect	474-6389		1		MBA	79	Manitoba	1978
Harvey, Mahlon O.	Lect	474-8444		1		MBA	70	Wash St	1973

Mc Gill University
Department of Finance
Faculty of Management
Montreal, Canada H3A 1G5
Area Code (514) Fax 398-3876
MCGILL
Bitnet MUSICA.MCGILL.CA or MUSICB.MCGILL.CA

BCOM,MBA,PHD

Name	Rank	Phone	Email					School	Year
Crowston, Wallace	Dean	398-4001	INGR@B			PHD		Car Mel	1987
Duan, Jin-Chuan	Asst	398-4053		12	KLPW	PHD		Wiscon	1986
Hung, Mao-Wei	Asst	398-3614		12	JKLO	PHD		Northwes	1990
Mazumdar, Sumon	Asst	398-4062		13	LPRT	PHD		So Meth	1990
Moreau, Art	Asst	398-4025		2	JLPT	PHD		Iowa	1986
Najarajan, S.	Asst	398-4047		12	ADFT	PHD		Northwes	1988
Sealey, Calvin W.	Asst	398-4054		13	JLPR	PHD		Georgia	1980
Tang, Nai-Pan	Asst	398-4061		12	KLOW	PHD		Northwes	1991

133

Mc Master University   BCOM,HONBCO,MBA
Department of Finance
Faculty of Business
Hamilton, Canada L8S 4M4
Area Code (416) Fax 527-0100
MCMASTER
Phone 525-9140

Name	Rank	Phone				Degree	Yr	School	Year
Truscott, William G.	Dean	Ext 4431		Orp	DBA		73	Indiana	1969
Chan, M. W. Luke	Prof	525-9140			PHD			McMaster	
Associate Dean									
Kwan, Clarence C. Y.	Prof				PHD			Ottawa	
Krinsky, Itzhak	Assoc	525-9140			PHD			McMaster	
Mountain, Dean C.	Assoc				PHD			W Ontari	
Chamberlain, Trevor W.	Asst	525-9140			PHD			Toronto	
Cheung, C. S. Sherman	Asst	525-9140			PHD			Illinois	
Deaves, Richard W.	Asst				PHD			Toronto	
Lee, Yongho	Asst				PHD			Northwes	
Rotenberg, Wendy D.	Asst	525-9140			PHD			Toronto	
Casey, Matthias M.	Lect				MBA			McMaster	

Memorial U of Newfoundland   BCOM,MBA
Department of Finance
Faculty of Business Adm
St.John's Canada A1B 3X5
Area Code (709) Fax 737-7680

Name	Rank	Phone				Degree	Yr	School	Year
Roskin, Rick	Dean	737-8851			OrgB	PHD	77	Bradford	1968
Faseruk, Alexander J.	Assoc	737-8005	12	MNOZ		PHD	90	Mass	1988
Palasvirta, Asmo P.	Assoc	737-7996	41	VNW		PHD	85	Utah	1991
Chikaonda, Mathias	Asst	737-4007	12	MNOZ		PHD	90	Mass	1988
on leave to Andrews Univ									
Krishnan, Ramesh	Asst	737-8854	12	JD		PHD	88	Northwes	1991

Mount Allison University
Department of Finance
Commerce Department
SackvilleCANADA E0A 3C0
Area Code (506) Fax 364-2216

Name	Rank	Phone				Degree	Yr	School	Year
Hudson, Richard	C-Ac	364-2329		Atg		PHD	84	Ottawa	1985
Patridge, Dan C.	Prof	364-2331							
Fred C. Manning Professor									

Mount Saint Vincent Univ   BBA
Department of Finance
Dept of Business Adm
Nova Scotia CDN B3M 2J6
Area Code (902) Fax 445-3960
MSVU
Did Not Respond

University of New Brunswick   BBA,MBA
Department of Finance
Faculty of Adm Box 4400
Fredericton, NB E3B 5A3
Area Code (506) Fax 453-3561
UNB.CA

Name	Rank	Phone	Code			Degree	Yr	School	Year
Storey, Ronald G.	Dean	453-4869	BUS07			PHD	74	Mich St	1989
Mitra, Devashis	Prof	453-4869				PHD	91	Mass	1991
Rashid, Muhammad	Prof	453-4869				PHD		Queen's	1985
Srinivasan, Gopalan	Prof	453-4869				PHD		IMM-Indi	1987
Otuteye, Eben	Asst	453-4869				PHD	90	Queen's	1987

University of Ottawa   BA,MBA
Dept of Finance & Mgt Sci
Faculty of Adm CANADA
Ottawa, Ontario K1N 6N5
Area Code (613) Fax 564-5074

Name	Rank	Phone	Code			Degree	Yr	School	Year
Zussman, David	Dean					PHD			
Henin, Claude G. J.	C-Pr	564-6545		12	FLMO	PHD			1971
Calvet, A. Louis	Prof	564-6583	CALVET	24	GJND	PHD	80	MIT	1979
Gandhi, Dev	Prof	564-5788		14	NUW&	PHD	76	Wharton	1982
Perrakis, Stylianos	Prof	564-7028		12	DLMN	PHD	70	Berkeley	1970
Adjaoud, Fodil	Assoc	564-6849		12	OAFU	PHD			1981
Kahl, Alfred L.	Assoc	564-7004		14	FIMU	PHD			1974
Rentz, William F.	Assoc	564-7025		12	CLMY	PHD	71	Rochest	1975
Ryan, Peter J.	Assoc	564-5049	PRRHG	12	DLO	PHD			1971
Guo, Chen	Asst	564-5047		2	JKLO	PHD			1990
Masson, Jean L.	Asst	564-5996	MASSON	23	TNE	PHD	89	Rochest	1991
Sauve, Lucie	Asst	564-5048		12	JATO	PHD			1987

Queen's University   BCOM,MBA,PHD
Finance Faculty
School of Business
Kingston Ontario K7L 3N6
Area Code (613) Fax 545-2013
QUCDN

Name	Rank	Phone	Email	Yrs	Fields	Deg	Yr	School	Year
Anderson, D.	Dean	545-2305				PHD	75	Queen's	1988
Morgan, I. G.	Prof	545-2366	MORGANIG	2	JL	PHD		Chicago	1978
Neave, E. H.	Prof	545-2348		32	PL	PHD		Berkeley	1991
Turnbull, S. M.	Prof	545-6348		2	L	PHD		Brit Col	1990
Cannon, W. T.	Assoc	545-2355		13	EGPQ	PHD		Harvard	1974
Davis, Alfred	Assoc	545-2353		1	DE	PHD		Penn St	1983
Johnson, Lewis D.	Assoc	545-2358	JOHNSOND	2	GKM	PHD		Toronto	1981
Gagnon, Louis	Asst	545-6707	GAGNONL	2	GLM	PHD		Toronto	1989

University of Regina
Department of Finance
Faculty of Adm
Regina, CANADA S4S OA2
Area Code (306) Fax 585-4805

Name	Rank	Phone	Email	Yrs	Fields	Deg	Yr	School	Year
Turtle, John P.	Dean	585-4731	585-4162	13	AHPS	PHD	74	Wash	1981
Carlson, J.									
Jalan, Pradeep									
Skingle, J.									

St. Francis Xavier Univ   BBA
Department of Finance
Dept of Bus Adm CANADA
Antigonish, NS B2G 1CO
Area Code (902) Fax 867-5153

Name	Rank	Phone				Deg	Yr	School	Year
Spencer, Ian	C-Ac	867-2252				MBA	73	W Ontar	1973
Sears, John T.	Prof	867-2252							
Ross, Donald G.	Asst	867-2305							
Hynes, Tim	Lect	867-2470							

Saint Mary's University   BCOM,MBA
Department of Finance
Faculty of Commerce
Halifax N Scotia B3H 3C3
Area Code (902) Fax 420-5561
HUSKY1

Connelly, Dennis E.	C-Ac	420-5730
Dodds, Colin J.	Prof	420-5406
Boabang, Francis	Asst	420-5735
Dorp, Kieter	Asst	420-5568
Moh'd, Mahmound	Asst	420-5732

Univ of Saskatchewan   BCOM,MSC
Department of Finance
College of Commerce
SaskatoonCanada S7N 0W0
Area Code (306) Fax 966-8709
SASK

Name	Rank	Phone	Email	Yrs	Fields	Deg	Yr	School	Year
Brennan, W. John	Dean	966-4786	BRENNAN		Atg	PHD	72	Michigan	1967
Lee, Moon H.	H $	966-8430	LEE	24	JLDW	PHD	74	Chicago	1970
Chaudhury, Mohammed M.	Assoc	966-8420	CHAUDHUR	12	NTZL	PHD	86	Sim Fras	1982
Cyr, Don	Assoc	966-8424	CYR	24	CJLV	ABD		Alberta	1990
Elfakhani, Said	Assoc	966-8427	YOUNES	12	DMGL	PHD			1988
Tannous, George F.	Assoc	966-6695	TANNOUS	23	PVHL	PHD	88	Rhd Isl	1984

Simon Fraser University   BA,MBA,D
Department of Finance
Faculty of Business Adm
Burnaby, Canada V5A 1S6
Area Code (604) Fax 291-4920
SFU
Did Not Respond; Faculty Office Phone 291-3708

Name	Rank	Phone			Field	Deg		School	Year
Shapiro, Stanley	Dean	291-4183			Mktg	PHD		Penn	1980
Herzog, John P.	Prof	291-4150							

135

University of Toronto   BCOM,MBA,PHD
Department of Finance
Faculty of Management
Toronto, CANADA M5S 1V4
Area Code (416) Fax 978-5433
```
  Wolff, Roger N.        Dean
  Aivazian, Varsuj       Prof    978-2375              12  ABDM   PHD     Ohio St     1981
  Booth, Laurence D.     Prof    978-6311              14  DEOU   PHD     Indiana     1987
  Gordon, Myron J.       Prof    978-3427              13  ADEN   PHD     Harvard     1970
  Halpern, Paul          Prof    978-2825              12  BEG    PHD     Chicago     1971
  Hull, John C.          Prof    978-8615              12  LFOP   PHD     Cranefld    1988
  Kalyman, Ansil         Prof    978-3425              13  DEPR   PHD     Yale        1975
  Winter, Ralph          Prof    978-6345              13  ABD    PHD     Berkeley    1979
  Berkowitz, Michael     Assoc   978-4178              12  ABDM   PHD     SUNY Buf    1973
  Brean, Donald          Assoc   978-3754              14  EUVW   PHD     Toronto     1978
  Rumsey, John           Assoc   978-4915              12  LTN    PHD     York        1991
  White, Alan            Assoc   978-3689              12  KLM    PHD     Toronto     1988
  Puffer, Marlene        Asst    978-3101              24  JNVM   ABD     Rochest     1990
```

University of Victoria
Department of Finance
Business
Victoria, Canada V8W 2Y2
Area Code (604) Fax
Did Not Respond

University of Waterloo   BA,MACC,PHD
Finance Faculty
Faculty of Ats
Waterloo Ontario N2L 3G1
Area Code (519) Fax 888-7562
WATDCS
Phone 885-1211 Ext 6536
```
  Waterhouse, John       D-Pr   888-4827  JWATER                PHD   72  U Wash     1973
  Shen, Fred             Asst   Ext 6993  FSHEN     12  JMOL    PHD   89  Brit Col   1990
  Vetzal, Ken            Asst   Ext 6518  KVETZAL   12  JKLM    ABD       Toronto    1990
  Zhang, G.              Asst   Ext 6513             1  ABCG    ABD       Brit Col   1991
```

Univ of Western Ontario   BA,MBA,PHD
Finance-Economics Area Group
School of Business Adm
London, Ontario N6A 3K7
Area Code (519) Fax 661-3485
bitnode NOVELL.BUSINESS.UWO.CA
```
  Ryans, Adrian B.        Dean   661-3278              Mktg   PHD   73  Stanford   1973
  Wynant, Larry           C      661-3221  LWYNANT   13  PH    DBA       Harvard    1976
  Hatch, James E.         Prof   661-3251  JHATCH    12  PN    PHD       Michigan   1972
  Lecraw, Donald J.       Prof   661-3206  DLECRAW   34  RV    DBA       Harvard    1975
  Shaw, David C.          Prof   661-3261  DSHAW      1  CH    PHD       Penn       1968
  Bishop, Paul M.         Assoc  661-3229  PBISHOP   14  UV    DBA       Harvard    1970
  Humphrey, John A.       Assoc  661-3290             12  FGH   DBA       Harvard    1968
  White, Robert W.        Assoc  661-3293  RWWHITE   13  TB    PHD       MIT        1980
  Wirick, Ronald G.       Assoc  661-3273  RWIRICK   23  KMSR  PHD       W Ontar    1979
  Foerster, Steve R.      Asst   661-3726  SFOERSTE  12  JN    PHD       Penn       1987
  Kairys Jr., Joseph Peter Asst  661-3305  JKAIRYS   13  JM    PHD   90  Chicago    1990
```

Wilfrid Laurier University   MBA,BBA,AD,DMS
Department of Finance
School of Bus & Econ
Waterloo Ontario N2L 3C5
Area Code (519) Fax 884-0201
MACHI.W
phone 884-1970
```
  Murray, J. Alex         Dean    884-1970
  Amoako-Adu, Ben         C-Ac    Ext 2327              12  DOGM   PHD     Toronto    1987
  Schnabel, Jacques A.    Prof    Ext 2529              14  ADUV   PHD     NS Wales   1986
  Warrack, Brian D.       Assoc   Ext 2566              12  LM     PHD     Alberta    1975
  Ackert, Lucy            Asst                          12  CLMQ   PHD     Emory      1991
  Athanassakos, George    Asst    Ext 2561              13  ADJS   PHD     York       1988
  Smith, Brian F.         Asst    Ext 2953              13  DGP    PHD     Western    1987
  Wajstaub, Sandra        Lect    Ext 2670              12  CDO    MBA     Manitoba   1990
```

136

University of Windsor BCOM,MBA
Department of Finance
Faculty of Business Adm
Windsor, Ontario N9B 3P4
Area Code (519) Fax 973-7073
Phone 253-4232

West, Eric	Dean	253-3097		Sys	PHD	70	Iowa St	1983
Bart, J.	Prof	253-4232						
Rosenbaum, E.	Prof	253-4232						
Henrie, G.	Assoc	253-4232						
Musson, H. S.	Assoc	253-4232						
Gunay, Erdal	Asst	253-4232						
Seck, D.	Asst	253-4232						
Ursel, Nancy D.	Asst	253-4232						

York University BBA,MBA,MPA,PHD
Finance Area
Faculty of Adm Studies
No York, Ontario M3J 1P3
Area Code (416) Fax 736-5687
Bitnode ORION.YORKU.CA

Name	Rank	Phone	ID		Field	Deg		School	Year
Horvath, Dezso J.	Dean	736-5070			Mgt	PHD		Umea	
Fowler, David J.	C-Ac	736-5073	AS000057	12		PHD		Toronto	1983
Friedland, Seymour	Prof	736-5073	AS000141			PHD		Harvard	
on sabbatical									
Brewer, Dawson E.	Assoc	736-5073	AS000044			PHD		Northwes	
on sabbitical									
Prisman, Eliezer	Assoc	736-5073	AS000177	2	JKMO	DSC		ITIsrael	1989
Robinson, Christopher M.	Assoc	736-5072	AS000037	1	DFXZ	PHD		Toronto	1983
Chee, Kew-Chul	Asst	736-5073	AS000101	13	CHPU	PHD		NYU	1999
Hebner, Kevin	Asst	736-5072	AS000107			PHD		Queen's	
on leave until August 1992									
Maynes, Elizabeth M.	Asst	736-5072	AS000102	1	EJZO	PHD		Queen's	1986
Verma, Savita	Asst	736-5072	AS000115	14	AGHU	PHD		Brit Col	1989

OTHER FOREIGN SCHOOLS

University of Adelaide BCO,MBA,MEC,PHD
Department of Finance
Dept of Commerce
Adelaide, S Aust 5001
Area Code 61- Fax 224-0464

Name	Rank	Phone			Field	Deg		Year
Evans, Michael D.	Lect	228-4756		12	CEGO	MBA		1989
Rosser, Bruce A.	Lect	228-5534		12	ADGL	MEC		1989

University of Auckland BCOM,MCOM,PHD
Department of Finance
Business
Auckland N ZEALAND
Area Code 64-09 Fax 33429
bitnode ACC.AUKUNI.AC.NZ

Name	Rank	Phone	Cert		Field	Deg		School	Year
Ansley, Craig F.	Prof	737-955	CFA	2	KMNO	PHD	77	Michigan	1988
Cliffe, Cheryl	SLect	737-999	C.CLIFFE	1	F	MCOM			1987
Alastair, Marsden	Lect	737-999		12	CDE	MCOM	84		1991
Austin, Lloyd M.	Lect	737-999		12	CFO	MCOM			1989
Kerr, Helen J.	Lect	737-999		2	KMR	BCOM			1990

Australian National Univ
Department of Finance
Department of Commerce
Camberra Act2601 AUSTRALIA
Area Code (062) Fax 2495005
Did Not Respond

University of Bath
Finance Faculty
School of Management
Claverton Down BA27AY
Area Code 0225 Fax 826473

Name	Rank	Phone			Field	Deg		Year
Beaumont, J. R.	H				Mgt	BA		
Tompkins, C.	Prof	826682		1	H			
Birts, A. N.	Lect	826826		41	UVI	MBA		1989

Bond University BCOM,MBA,PHD
Department of Finance
School of Business
Gold Coast, Qld AUSTRALIA
Area Code (075) Fax 95-1160
BU.OZ.AU

Goldsworthy, Ashley W.	Dean	952202	A_GOLDSW			DIP		Queensld	1991
Carmichael, Jeffrey	Prof	952220		34	PRLN	PHD	79	Princeto	1989
Sinha, Tapen	Assoc	952263		12	FXY	PHD	86	Minn	1989

Bournemouth Polytechnic BA
Department of Finance
Dept of Finance & Law
Dorset ENGLAND BH12 5BB
Area Code 0202 Fax 513293
School: 0202 524111

Hardwick, Phil	Prof	524111	4	SWZ	PHD		1974
Beckett, Tony	SLect	524111	3	HR	BA		1990
Bollen, David	SLect	524111	37	P	BA		1989
Gibbs, Paul	SLect	524111	3	H	BA		1991
Khan, Bahadur	SLect	524111	34	RV	MA		1974
Langmead, John	SLect	524111	34	RV	MSC		1974
Williams, Griff	SLect	524111		EFV	MBA		1991
Navare, Jyoti	PLect	524111	7	#			1991
Willcocks, Geoff	PLect	524111	27	JM#	MBA		1987

University of Bristol BSC,MSC,PHD
Department of Finance
Department of Economics
Bristol BS81HY
Area Code 0272 Fax 251696
Did Not List Any Finance Faculty

University of Canterbury BCO,MCO,MBA,PHD
Dept of Accounting & Finance
Faculty of Commerce
Christchurch1 NZ NewZealand
Area Code (03) Fax 642-727
Bitnet: %canterbury.ac.nz@relay.cs.net

Robb, Alan J.	H $	Ext 6618	12	Z	MCOM	76	Canterbu	1979
Blanchard, Carl	Asst	Ext 6622	12	ABFM	BCOM	91	Canterbu	1991
Lord, Beverly R.	Asst	Ext 6622		CJXY	BCOM	91	Canterbu	1991
Alexander, Peter	Lect	Ext 6628	12	BFZ	BA	83	Waikato	1990
Birchall, Brian	Lect	Ext 6626	13	FDMT	MBA	83	Cape Twn	1991
Hasseldine, D. John	Lect	Ext 6636	23	UVW	MCOM	87	Canterbu	1988
Purchas, Graeme	Lect	Ext 6615	1	ABFH	BCOM	65	Victoria	1989

Chinese Univ of Hong Kong
Department of Finance
Faculty of Business Adm
Shatin, NT HONG KONG
Area Code (852) Fax 6035114
Did Not Respond

Ip, Yiukeung	Prof	06952831

City of London Polytechnic
Department of Finance
Faculty of Business
London EC2M 6SQ
Area Code 071 Fax 256-8845
Did Not Respond; Phone 071-283-1030

Alexander, B.	Dean	Ext 330		Atg	BCOM

City Polytechnic - Hong Kong BA,MBA,MPHL,PHD
Department of Finance
Faculty of Business
Kowloon HONG KONG
Area Code (852) Fax 788-7220
CPHKVX

Levy, F. K.	Dean	788-8450	FKLEVY		Econ	PHD	64	Carn Mel	1991
Cheng, Y. C.	Dir	788 7788	YCCHENG		Engi	PHD	67	Brit Col	1989
Ho, Y. K.	Head	778-8800	RYKHO	3	JLMV	PHD	79	Wiscon	1990
Lui, Y. H.	SLect	788-8814	YHLUI	13	FMV	MA	85	Lancast	1989
Mole, David	SLect	788-8813		4	RV	PHD	87	Toronto	1989
Ho, Y. W.	SLect	788-8380		23	PV	MSC	82	Manchest	1989
Fang, Jimmy	Lect	788-7280		2	KLMT	PHD	90	CUNY	1991
Wong, K. A.	Visit	788-7895		1	DJMV	PHD	75	Liverpool	1991

137

Coventry Polytechnic
Department of Finance
Dept of Bus & Mgt St
Coventry England CV1 5FB
Area Code 0203   Fax 838646
Did Not Respond

Deakin University
Dept of Accounting & Finance
Faculty of Commerce
Geelong Vic 3217 AUSTRALIA
Area Code (052) Fax 41 1542
 Wolnizer, Peter W. Dean 471-275   T PHD 86 Sydney 1989
 Gibson, Robert W. Prof 471-278   CDE PHD 76 Cinn 1977
  Associate Dean
 Dimovski, Bill Lect 471-560 1 HX MBA 82 Geo St 1985
 Kerry, Mike STut   1   BCOM Melbourn 1988
 Norrie, Gweneth STut 471-568 12   BCOM 83 Deakin 1983
 Williams, Sarah STut 471-567 12   BCOM 83 Deakin 1983

Deakin Univ at Warnambool
Dept of Accounting & Finance
Faculty of Commerce
Warrnambool 3280 Australia
Area Code (055) Fax 618320
 Wolnizer, Peter W. Dean 471-275   T PHD 86 Sydney 1989
 Anderson, R. A. Andrew SLect   12 FM MS   Monash 1991

University of Dundee   BACC,MACC,PHD
Dept of Accountancy & Fnce
Business
Dundee, Scotland DD1 4HN
Area Code 0382 Fax 24419
(0382) 23181
 MacDonald, Ronald Prof Ext 4478 34 JLRV PHD   Manchest 1989
 Fraser, Pat Lect Ext 4693 34 RST PHD 90 City 1987
 Lonie, A. Alasdair Lect Ext 4199 13 BCHN MA 62 Glasgow 1982
 Power, David M. Lect Ext 4854 12 BJNS MSC 87 1987

University of East Anglia
Department of Finance
School of Info Systems
Norwich, England NR4 7TJ
Area Code 0603 Fax 507720
 Jones, C. A. H 56161 1 GZ PHD Hull 1985
 Berry, R. H. Prof 56161 1 FPL PHD Warwick 1987
 Baldwin, T. J. Asst 56161 1 P MSC London 1986
 McLintock, A. J. Asst 56161 1 O BCOM Edinburg 1980
 Pitts, C. G. C. Asst 56161 12 LG PHD Oxon 1964
 Russell, P. O. Asst 56161 4 MA Manchest 1981

Polytechnic of East London
Department of Finance
Business
Dagenham, Essex RM8 2AS
Area Code (01) Fax 590-7799
Did Not Respond; School Phone: 081-590-7722

University of Essex   BA,MA,MBA
Finance Faculty
Dept Actg & Fin Mgt
Colchester, Eng CO4 3SQ
Area Code 0206 Fax 873598
UK.AC
Did Not Respond; bitnet AFM@UK.AC.ESSEX

Flinders U of S Australia   BCOM,MCOM,MA,PH
Div of Accounting & Finance
Sch of Soc Sciences
GPO Box2100Ade AUST 5001
Area Code 61-08 Fax 201-2566
 McMahon, Richard G. P. Assoc 201-2840 1 F MBA 80 Adelaide 1978
 Forsaith, David M. Lect 201-2344 12 FMR MSC 75 London 1990

Hall, Katherine H.	Lect	201-2729	23	GTUW	LLB		Adelaide	1990
Mangos, Nicholas C.	Lect	201-2361	12	AF	MBA	85	Adelaide	1990
Mathews, Clive M. H.	Lect	201-2728	12	AF	MBS	89	Massey	1990
Pacceca, Tania	Tutor	201-2006	12	FC	BEC	91	Flinders	1991
Stanger, Anthony M. J.	Tutor	201-2764	67	STR	BCOM	84	Tasmania	1989

Glasgow University BACC,MACC,PHD
Department of Finance
Glasgow Business School
Glasgow Scotland G12 8LE
Area Code 44-41 Fax 330-4442
Area Code (011-44) 041-339-8855

Keane, Simon M.	Prof	Ext 5573	12	CEN	PHD	76	Glasgow	1969
Holland, John B.	SLect	Ext 4136	34	UVPQ	PHD	78	CNAA	1979
McKernan, John F.	Lect	Ext 6029	16	AFJM	MBA			1990

Griffith University BA,BCOM,MA,PHD
Finance Faculty
Div of Commerce & Adm
Nathan, Brisbane AUST 4111
Area Code 61- Fax 875-7550
Did Not Respond

University of Guam BS,MBA
Finance Faculty
College of Bus & Pub Ad
Mangilao, Guam 96923
Area Code (671) Fax 734-5362

Keck, John	Dean$	734-9225		Atg	PHD	Geo St	1989

Hebrew Univ of Jerusalem BA,MBA,PHD
Department of Finance
School of Business Adm
Mount Scopus ISR 91905
Area Code 9722 Fax
Did Not Respond

Ben-Horin, Moshe	Dir	883-235	

Hitotsubashi University BA,MA,DBA
Department of Finance
Faculty of Commerce
Kunitachi, Tokyo 186
Area Code 0425 Fax 74-8992
Phone (0425) 72-1101

Shibakawa, Rinya	H-Pr	Ext 559	1	D	DE	80	Hitotsub	1990
Hanawa, Toshiya	Prof	Ext 465	3		DBA	80	Hitotsub	1969
Kamae, Hiroshi	Prof	Ext 503	2	K	DBA		Hitotsub	1984
Miura, Ryozo	Prof	Ext 593	2	L	PHD	76	UCB	1989
Shimizu, Yoshinori	Prof	Ext 554	3		DBA		Hitotsub	1977
Ogawa, Eiji	Assoc	Ext 484	4		DBA		Hitotsub	1988
Misumi, Takashi	Asst	Ext 452	13	R	DBA		Hitotsub	1990

University of Hong Kong BBA,MBA,PHD
Finance Faculty
Dept of Mgt Studies
Hong Kong HONG KONG
Area Code (852) Fax 858-5614
HKUCC

Redding, S. G.	Dean	859-2266	HRNMSGR		Mgt	PHD		1982
Donleavy, G. D.	Asst	859-1014	GDON	12	HFN			
Tso, P. S.	Asst	859-1007		42	WJ	PHD		1979
Wong, D. W. S.	Asst	859-1006		1	FE	MBA		1976

Humberside Polytechnic BA,MHIL,MBA,PHD
Humberside Business School
ENGLAND
Cottingham, Hull HU6 7RT
Area Code 0482 Fax 440279
Did Not Respond

Adams, Jack	Dean	440-3215	

Intl Inst for Mgt Develop
Finance Faculty
Ch Bellerive 23 Box 915
Lausanne, Switze CH-1001
Area Code 41 21 Fax 26 67 25
  Rada, Juan F.   Dir   618-0111   Mgt PHD   London
  Ellert, James C.   34 VP   PHD   Chicago
  Schar, Kurt   1 H   DBA   Harvard
  Strebel, Paul   4 UV   PHD   Princeto

INSEAD 77305   MBA,PHD
Department of Finance
Business
Fontainbleau FRANCE
Area Code (331) Fax 60724242
FREIBA51
Phone (33)1 60 72 40 00
  Vermaelen, Theo   C-Pr   72 4263   VERMAELE   12 ABDG PHD   80 Chicago   1987
  Langohr, Herwig   Prof   72 4263
  Remmers, H. Lee   Prof   72 4247   REMMERS   14 HUV   PHD   67 Manchest   1962
  Vaillet, Claude   Prof   72 4214   12 EJOW PHD   76 Northwes   1978
  Bruner, Robert F.   Assoc 924-4802   13 DGHQ DBA   Harvard
    visiting from University of Virginia
  Dermine, Jean   Assoc 72 4247   DERMINE   13 PSYV PHD   82 Louvain   1982
  Hietala, Pekka   Assoc 72-4227   HIETALA   14 JUVW PHD   87 Stanford   1987
  Hillion, Pierre   Assoc 72-4214   HILLION   12 DJLO PHD   88 UCLA   1987
  Nielsen, Lars T.   Assoc 72-4227   NIELSON   12 JLM   PHD   85 Harvard   1989
  Dierkens, Nathalie   Asst   72-4227   DIERKENS   14 DFGU PHD   86 MIT   1987

Korea University
Finance Faculty
School of Business Adm
Seoul, Korea 136-701
Area Code   Fax
  Kim, Hie-Jip   Prof   920-1159   12 FMT   PHD   1969
  Lee, Chung   Prof   920-1160   12 AJMO PHD   1968
  Lee, Phill Sang   Prof   920-1164   13 PRTU PHD   1982
  Nam, Sang-Koo   Prof   920-1177   12 DEJL PHD   1983
  Yun, Yong-Sup   Prof   920-1170   13 AKPT PHD   1984
  Jang, Hasung   Asst   920-1180   12 DFQT PHD   1990

Lancaster University   BA,BSC,MBA,PHD
Finance Faculty
Management School
Lancaster, UK LA1 4YX
Area Code 0524 Fax 381454
Area Code (0524) - school phone 65201
  Stapleton, R. C.   Prof   PHD   Sheffiel
  Mace, J. R.   SLect   MS   London
  O'Hanlon, J.   SLect   MA   Lancaste
  Ho, T. S.   Lect   PHD   Lancaste
  Poon,   Lect   PHD   Lancaste
  Taylor, S.   Read   PHD   Lancaste

University of Leeds   BA,BSC,MBA,PHD
Finance Faculty
Sch of Bus & Econ Studi
Leeds, England LS2 9JT
Area Code 44532 Fax 334465
Area Code (0532) school phone # 334466; bitnode UK.AC.LEEDS.CMS1
  Moizer, Peter   C-Pr   334499   ECO6PM   23 MNST MA   83   1989
  Keasey, Kevin   Prof   332618   24 ABD   PHD   81   1990
  Coutts, Andrew   Lect   332630   1 G   MA   1989
  Dempsey, Michael   Lect   334471   14 CDEJ PHD   1990
  Short, Helen   Lect   1 ABD   BA   Kent St   1990

University of Limburg
Finance Group
Faculty Econ & Bus Adm
Maastricht, Neth 6200 MD
Area Code 31-43 Fax 270999
  Wolff, Christian   C-Pr   888 838   MBA   84 Chicago   1988
  Goslings, Jan Willem   Prof   888 861   PHD   74 Amsterda   1989
  Herst, Arthur   Prof   888 817   PHD   81 Rotterd   1989
  Vermaelen, Theo   Prof   888 861   MBA   76 Chicago   1989

Koedijk, Kees	Assoc	888 235			PHD	89	Rotterd	1991
Schotman, Peter	Assoc	888 862			PHD	89	Rotterd	1991
Benink, Harald	Asst	888 104						1989
Corhay, Albert	Asst	888 859			MBA	80	Liege	1989
Selender, Arthur	Asst	888 242			MBA	85	Chicago	1989
Tourani Rad, Alireza	Asst	888 116			MBA	84	Leuven	1988
Zou, Liang	Asst	888 194			MBA	86	Leuven	1990
Bauer, Rob		888 859						1990
Kleeven, Herman		888 859						1991

Liverpool Polytechnic BA
Dept of Accounting & Finance
Business Faculty
Liverpool L3 5UZ
Area Code 44-51 Fax 707-0423
Did Not Respond; School Phone: 051-207-3581

London Business School MBA MSC,PHL,PHD
Department of Finance
Grad Sch of Bus Studies
London, England NW1 4SA
Area Code 447-1 Fax 724-7875
Did Not Respond; Phone number: 262-5050

London School of Economics BSC,MSC,D
Dept of Accounting & Finance
Business
London, England WC2A 2AE
Area Code 44-71 Fax 955-7420

Selby, Michael	Read	405-7686	2	L	PHD	83	London	1987
Webb, David	Prof	405-7686	13	BDRA	PHD	75	London	1991
Board, John	SLect	405-7686	12	JLMD	PHD	85	Newcastl	1986
Tonks, Ian	SLect	405-7686	12	GT	PHD	83	Warwick	1991
Bertero, Elisabetta	Lect	405-7686	14	TVI	PHD	87	London	1991
Connor, Gregory	Lect	405-7686	12	JO	PHD	82	Yale	1991
Doran, Paul	Lect	405-7686	12	LI	PHD	85	Glasgow	1990

Loughborough U of Technology BSC
Finance Faculty
Business School
Loughborough, LE LE11 3JR
Area Code 0509 Fax 210232
Area Code 0509 phone extension: 3141

Sizer, John	D-Pr			Atg	DLIT	Loughbor
Morison, Ian C.	Prof		3	Q	MA	Oxford
Midland Group Professor of Banking and Finance						
Howcroft, J. Barry	SLect		43	VQ	MSC	Wales
Belk, Penelope A.	Lect			X	MA	Lancast
Boocock, Grahame	Lect		2	N	MA	Manchest
Fish, Gerald	Lect				BA	Wales
Hamilton, Robert	Lect				MPHL	Glasgow
McEvoy, Chris P.	Lect				MSC	Bradford

Macquarie University BEC,MEC,PHD
Department of Finance
Sch of Econ & Fin Stds
New South Wales 2109 AUST
Area Code (02) Fax 805-8586
Did Not Respond; School Phone 805-7111

University of Manchester
Department of Finance
Centre for Emp Research
Mancheseter ENGL M13 9PL
Area Code (061) Fax 275-4023
Did Not Respond

University of Manchester BA,MBA,MBS,PHD
Department of Finance
Manchester Bus School
Manchester, Eng M15 6PB
Area Code (061) Fax 273-7732
Did Not Respond; School Bitnet:mbs.uk.ac

Payne, Roy L.	Dean	275-6426	PAYNERL	Mgt	PHD	London	1987

U Manchester Inst Sci & Tech BSC,MSC,MBA,PHD
Department of Finance
School of Management
Manchester UK M60 1QD
Area Code (061) Fax 200-3505
School phone: 061 200 3500
  Ezzamel, Mahmoud   Prof   200-3455   PHD   Sohampto   1990
  Sweeting, Robert C.   SLect   200-3459   PHD   Keele   1979
  Bloomfield, Brian P.   Lect   200-3427   PHD   1987
  Ciancanelli, Penelope L. Lect   200-3457   PHD   New York   1988
  Edwards, Pamela   Lect   200-3454   Manchest   1990
  Robson, Keith   Lect   200-3451   PHD   Manchest   1988
  Watson, Robert   Lect   200-3452   BA   Hull   1988

Massey University BBS,MBS,PHD
Department of Finance
Faculty of Bus Studies
Palmerston N, NZ 30974
Area Code (063) Fax 505617
MASSEY
Phone 356-9099
  Parry, Jennifer R.   Head$ Ext 8116   12 BCF   MBS   1988
  Wilson, Bruce R.   Assoc Ext 8638   12 IO   MECO 74 New Eng   1970
  Black, Carolyn G.   SLect Ext 8408   12 RX   MBA   1990
  Malone, Chris B.   Lect   Ext 8045   24 LNV   MBS   1986
  Ridge, Jenny   SLect Ext 8607   23 XPN   MBS   1980
  Young, Martin R.   SLect Ext 8019   23 MOR   MA   1990

University of Melbourne
Department of Finance
Business
Parkville 3052 Australia
Area Code 03613 Fax 344-6681
  Rose, John   H
  Brownell, Peter   H-Pr   344-5351   Atg   PHD   70 Calif   1991
    Arthur Andersen Professor
  Davis, Kevin T.   Prof   344-5098   12 LPEV MEC   72 ANU   1985
  Nicol, Robert   Prof   344-5314   14 EC   PHD   72 UCLA   1974
  Officer, Robert   Prof   349-8103   12 FOSU PHD   1986
  Hathaway, Neville   Assoc 349-8148   23 EKLO PHD   1984
  Lee, David   Lect   344-7668   12 CM   BEC   77 ANU   1990
  Martini, Christine   Lect   344-5308   23 KL   MSC   Melbourn   1991
  Singh, Ranjit   Lect   344-7482   14 JFW   MEC   90 Monash   1991
  Moloney, Damian   STut   344-7662   12 PZL   MCOM 91 Melbourn   1990
  Woods, Ivan   Read   349-8129   23 FKLO PHD   1978

Murdoch University BCOM,MBA,MP,PHD
Department of Commerce
Sch of Econ, Comm & Law
Murdoch 6150 W AUSTRALI
Area Code (09)   Fax 310 5004
  Rees, David J.   SLect 360-6040   14 RU   PHD   1991

Napier Polytechnic BA
Department of Finance
Business
Edinburgh Scotla EH11 4BN
Area Code (031) Fax 458-5089
Did Not Respond; School Phone: 444 2266/3356

National Chengchi Univ
Department of Finance
Grad Sch of Accountancy
Taipei, Taiwan 11623 ROC
Area Code 886-2 Fax 939-3091
  Cheng, Ting-Wong   Dean   939-3091   Atg   PHD   74 Missouri   1979
  Lin, Joung-yol   C   938-7121   12 CJMU PHD   85 Iowa   1979
  Richards, K.   SLect

143

National Taiwan University BBA,MBA,PHD
Department of Finance
College of Management
Taipei, TAIWAN 10020 ROC
Area Code 886-2 Fax 351-0907
TWNMOE10

Name	Rank	Phone		Fields	Deg	Yr	School	Yr
Hsu, Paul Shih-Chun	Dean	362-2249		Mgt	PHD	74	Michigan	1987
Ho, Hsien-Chan	C $	396-1382		24 UWMJ	PHD	85	Texas	1986
Kuo, Cheng-Kun	Prof	396-1394		42 UL	PHD	86	Texas	1989
Lee, Tsun-Siou	Prof	396-1382		23 JLM	PHD	88	Berkeley	1988
Lin, Yu-Isung	Prof	396-1382		12 MJ	PHD	76	Minnesot	1978
Chiu, Shean-Bi	Assoc	396-1382		32 SGM	PHD	89	Washingt	1989
Lin, Yun	Assoc	396-1382		23 LM	PHD	87	Illinois	1987
Wang, Tay-Chang	Assoc	351-8967		12 JNO	PHD	88	Penn	1988
Yang, Chau-Chen	Assoc	396-1382		13 MSBF	PHD	89	Illinois	1989

University of New England BFA
Dept of Atg & Financial Mgt
Economic Studies
Armidale 2351 AUSTRALIA
Area Code (067) Fax 711778

Name	Rank	Phone		Fields	Deg			Yr
Hutchinson, P.	H-Pr	732365		1 F	PHD			1979
Gilroy, N.	Lect	733159		2 M	MBA			1991
Gregory, W.	Lect	6-501153		2 L	MEC			1990

Univ of New South Wales BCOM,MCOM,PHD
School of Banking & Finance
Faculty of Comm & Econ
Sydney N S Wales AUSTRALIA
Area Code (02) Fax 313-6347
Phone 697-3580

Name	Rank	Phone		Fields	Deg	School	Yr
Sharpe, Ian G.	Head	697-3508		31 PD	PHD	Stanford	1985
Bowden, Roger G.	Prof	697-3534	88B1006	12 EJLM	PHD	Manchest	1988
Skully, Michael T.	Assoc	697-3276		31 PTD	MBA	Utah	1973
Chan, Keith	Asst	697-3246		12 JV	MCOM	NS Wales	1986
Degabriele, M. Rosalle	Asst	697-3246		3 P	MCOM	NS Wales	1989
Gross, M. A. Ernestine	Asst	697-3277	S8600065	1 AGZ	PHD	Sydney	1986
Harris Snr., Malcolm C.	Asst	697-3545		12 U	PHD	Conn	1991
Harris, Thomas C.	Asst	697-3552		2 JV	PHD	UCLA	1991
Lange, Helen P.	Asst	697-2428		32 DP	MCOM	NS Wales	1989
Mackenzie, David L.	Asst	697-3279		1 D	MCOM	NS Wales	1988
Moshirian, Farlborz	Asst	697-2439		41 V	PHD	Monash	1990
Noti, Gabriel	Asst	697-3278		12 JL	PHD	NS Wales	1972
Pham, Toan M.	Asst	697-3279	74B1823	12 BDK	MCOM	NS Wales	1974
Shanmugam, Bala	Asst	697-3533		3 PV	PHD	Wollong	1988
Sim, Ah Boon	Asst	697-3277	89B0078	42 ZW	PHD	Concordi	1989
Woo, Li-Anne	Asst	697-3502	LEWOO	1 DO	BCOM	NS Wales	1986

University of Newcastle
Finance Faculty
Department of Commerce
New South Wales Australia
Area Code (049) Fax
No Finance Faculty

Univ College of North Wales BA,MA,PHD
Department of Finance
Department of Economics
Bangor, Gwynedd LL57 2DG
Area Code 248 Fax 370451
Did Not Respond

Norwegian School Econ & Bus
Department of Finance
NORWAY
Bergen-Sandviken N-5035
Area Code (05) Fax
Phone +475 959324 or +475 959322; Telefax +475 258383

Name	Rank	Phone				Deg	School
Aase, Knut K.	Prof	Ext 249				PHD	Berkeley
Ekern, Steinar	Prof	Ext 279				PHD	Stanford
Hansen, Terje	Prof	Ext 294				PHD	Yale
Johnsen, Thore	Prof	Ext 291				PHD	Carnegie
Jornsten, Kurt	Prof	Ext 552				DREK	Linkopin
Lensberg, Terje	Prof	Ext 206				DOEC	
Schilbred, Cornelius M.	Prof	Ext 268				DOEC	

Berrefjord, Ole   Asst   Ext 546
Bjerksund, Petter   Asst   Ext 548   DOEC
Boye, Knut   Asst   Ext 288
Gjerde, Oystein   Asst   Ext 271   DOEC
Gjerum, Per Ivar   Asst   Ext 285
Stensland, Gunnar   Asst   Ext 273
Svenden, Bjorn   Asst   Ext 292

University of Otago   BCO,MCO,MBA,PHD
Department of Finance
Commerce Division
Dunedin POBox56 N ZEALAND
Area Code (03)   Fax 479-8450
Phone 479-8039

Name	Rank	Ext			Code	Deg	Yr	School	Year
Boyle, Glenn W.	C-Pr	Ext 8039		23	JLRW	PHD	87	Texas	1991
Bartholdy, Jan	SLect	Ext 8072		23	ADPT	PHD	88	Queen's	1989
Brown, Kate M.	SLect	Ext-8068		1	FHYZ	PHD	89	E Conn	1988
Jeong, Jinho	SLect	Ext 8114		12	ADOT	PHD	91	Georgia	1991
Papasyriopoulos, Nicholas	SLect	Ext 8113		14	AUVW	PHD	90	Wiscon	1990

University of Puerto Rico   BBA,MBA
Finance Department
Faculty of Business Adm
San Juan, PR 00931
Area Code (809) Fax
Phone 764-0000

Cabarrouy, Evaldo A.   Assoc   Ext 4042   R_CABARR   34   RV   PHD   81 Texas   1985

University of Queensland   BCO,MFM,MIS,PHD
Finance Faculty
Department of Commerce
Queensland AUST 4067
Area Code (07)   Fax 365-6788

Name	Rank	Phone		Code	Deg	School	Year
Finn, Frank J.	Dean	365-7111	23		PHD	81 Queensld	1969
Bellamy, David	Lect	365-6652	12	FJK	MBA	Queensld	

University of Salford
Department of Finance
Dept of Bus & Mgt Sds
Salford, England M5 4WT
Area Code (061) Fax 745-5999
Did Not Respond; School Phone: 736 5066

University of Stirling   BS,MS,MBA,D
Department of Finance
Business Faculty
Stirling, Scot FK9 4LA
Area Code (011) Fax 786-6300
Phone for all 44-786-3171

Name	Rank	Ext		Code	Deg	School	Year
Ward, Charles W.R.	H-Pr	Ext 7281	12	JMV	PHD	80 Reading	1985
Copeland, Laurence	Prof	Ext 7283	34	JLRV	PHD	85 Manchest	1991
Limmack, Robin J.	Assoc	Ext 7287	12	GJT	MBA	75 Liverpoo	1978
Campbell, Kevin	Asst	Ext 7289	34	LU	PHD	90 Glasgow	1986
Goodacre, Alan	Asst	Ext 7291	12	FN	PHD	82 Exeter	1981
Grant, Clare	Asst	Ext 7292	14	HU	MS	86 Glasgow	1987

University of Strathclyde   BA,BS,MBA,MS,D
Department of Finance
Strathclyde Bus School
Glasgow Scotland G4 OLN
Area Code 44-41 Fax 552-5589
Did Not Respond; School Phone: 552-4400 Ext 3688

University of Sydney   MBA,MPP,MTM
Department of Finance
Faculty of Economics
New South Wales 2006 AUST
Area Code 61-2   Fax 550-8603

Name	Rank	Phone		Code	Deg	School	Year
Walter, Terry S.	Prof	3068	12	AGJO	PHD	WA	1990
Aitken, Michael J.	Assoc	3901	12	AFJN	PHD	NS Wales	1991
Taylor, Stephen L.	Assoc	3066	12		PHD	NS Wales	1985
Lee, Philip J.	Lect	3067	12	AFMO	MCOM	NS Wales	1990

University of Tasmania   BCOM
Department of Finance
Faculty of Business
Sandy Bay Tasman AUSTRAL
Area Code (002) Fax 234520
Area Code (61–002)

Name	Rank	Phone	Email	Fld	Deg	Yr	School	Yr
English, John	SLect	20 2273	JACK.ENG	Fcne	MBA			1989
Thompson, Bradley	Tutor	20 2803	BRAD.THO	Fnce	BCOM			1989

Tel Aviv University   BA,MBA,D
Department of Finance
Faculty of Management
Ramat Aviv Israe 69978
Area Code 972-3 Fax
TAUNIVM
Did Not Respond

Name	Rank	Phone		Fld	Deg	Yr	School	Yr
Ahituv, Niv	Dean	5450–720		Mgt	PHD	79	Tel Aviv	1969
Kandel, Shmuel	Assoc							
on leave to Pennsylvania								
Sarig, Oded	Assoc							
on leave to Pennsylvania								

University of Tsukuba   BS,MS,PHD
Department of Finance
Inst of Socio–Econ Plan
Tsukuba Ibaraki 305 JAPAN
Area Code 0298 Fax 55-3849
Did Not Respond

Victoria University   BCA,MCA,MBA,PHD
Department of Finance
Commerce & Adm Faculty
Wellington NEW ZEALAN
Area Code 64 4 Fax 712 200
Did Not Respond

Mann, Athol W.	Dean	721–000

University College of Wales
Finance Faculty
Perglain
Aberystwyth SY23 3DY
Area Code 0970 Fax 617172

Name	Rank	Phone			Deg	Yr	School	Yr
Macve, Richard H.	H-Lec	622202			MSC	76	London	1979
Butler, D. K.	Lect	623111			BSC	85	Aberys	1988
Frost, Ceri E.	Lect	622203			BSC	84	Aberys	1986
Fuller-Love, Nerys	Lect	623111			MBA	87	Aberys	1989
Gwaliam, D.	Lect							
Holland, Kevin M. P.	Lect	622200			BSC	80	Bangor	1989
Rhys, H.	Lect							1992
Tippett, Mark J.	Lect	623111			MSC	69	Wales	1988
Horton, Joanne	Tutor	622205			BSC	90	Aberys	1991
Rowley, Allan	Tutor	623111			BSC	89	Aberys	1990

Univ of the Virgin Islands   BA
Finance Faculty
Business Adm Division
St. Thomas, VI 00802
Area Code (809) Fax
Did Not Respond

Univ of Western Australia   BCOM,MCOM,PHD
Department of Finance
Faculty of Econ & Comm
Nedlands, W Aust 6009
Area Code (09) Fax 380-1047

Name	Rank	Phone		F	Deg	Yr	School	Yr
Statham, Pamela	Dean	380–2930			PHD	80	Monash	1991
Brown, Philip R.	Prof	380–2899			PHD	68	Chicago	1980
KPMG Peat Marwick Professor of Accounting								
Izan, Hy	Prof	380–2971			PHD	78	Chicago	1981
Allen, Dave	SLect	380–2907		F	MPHL	77	Leic	1987
Clarke, Alex	Lect	380–2902			MCOM	91	W Austra	1983
Dunlop, Ian	Lect	380–2972			PHD	90	Queensla	1988
Johnson, Jaqueline	Lect	380–2444			MCOM	90	W Austra	1985
Woodliff, David	Lect	380–2911			BCOM	82	W Austra	1991
DaSilva Rosa, Raymond	STut	380–3906			BCOM	85	W Austra	1986
How, Janice	STut	380–2914			BCOM	89	W Austra	1989
Mitchell, Jason	STut	380–2798			MACC	89	W Austra	1990
Wood, Sally	Tutor	380–3827			MBA	90	W Austra	1991

University of Wollongong
Department of Accounting
P.O. Box 1144 Australia
Wollongong, NSW AUST 2500
Area Code (042)   Fax 213 097
Steinke, John C.	Dean	213665	J.STEINK		Econ	MA	60	Berkeley	1964
Gaffikin, Michael J. R.	C-Pr	213718	GAFFIKIN	1	FB	PHD		Sydney	1988
Tibbits, Garry E.	Assoc	213731		1	CD	MCOM		Auckland	1977
Frino, Alessandro	Asst	214011		1	AL	MPHI		Camb	1990
Gniewosz, Gerhardt	Asst	213679		4	VW	MCOM			1990

ALPHABETICAL BY INDIVIDUAL

NAME	RANK	SCHOOL	DEGREE			START
Aase, Knut K.	Prof	Norwegian	PHD		Berkeley	
Abbott, Ashok	Asst	W Virginia	PHD	87	Va Tech	1987
Abbott, Joann	Asst	SW State	MS	91	St Cloud	1987
Abdelsamad, Moustafa H.	Dean	Corpus Christi	DBA	70	Geo Wash	1991
Abdullah, Fuad A.	C-Pr	Neb-Omaha	PHD		Penn	
Abel, Andrew B.	Prof	Pennsylvania	PHD	78	MIT	1987
Aber, Jack W.	C-Ac	Boston Univ	DBA	72	Harvard	1972
Abeysekera, Sarath P.	Asst	U Manitoba	PHD	85	Tx A&M	1985
Abghori, M. Hossein	Assoc	Morehouse	PHD		Georgia	1988
Abouzeid, Kamal M.	Prof	Lynchburg	PHD		Texas	1978
Abraham, Abraham	Asst	Rice	PHD	89	Boston	1989
Abrahamson, Allen	Asst	Denver	PHD		Arizona	1990
Aburachis, Abe	Assoc	Gannon	PHD	73	Pitt	
Acharya, Sankarshan	Asst	New York U	PHD	86	Northwes	
Ackert, Lucy	Asst	Wilfrid Laur	PHD		Emory	1991
Adams, David C.	C	Marywood	PHD		Syracuse	
Adams, Michael K.	Asst	Tampa	PHD	86	Arkansas	1990
Adams, Paul D.	Asst	Cincinnati	PHD	82	Ohio St	1987
Adelman, Saul W.	Assoc	Miami U-Ohio	PHD	80	Georgia	
Adjaoud, Fodil	Assoc	Univ Ottawa	PHD			1981
Adler, Michael	Prof	Columbia	PHD	63	Harvard	1968
Admati, Anat R.	Assoc	Stanford	PHD	83	Yale	1982
Affleck-Graves, John	Asst	Notre Dame				
Afshar, Tahmoures A.	Assoc	Webster	PHD	84	Case Wes	1975
Agahro, Steve B.	Asst	Jackson St	MBA		Jacks St	1984
Aggarwal, Raj	Prof	John Carroll	DBA	75	Kent St	1987
Edward J. and Louise E. Mellen Chair Professor						
Aggarwal, Reena	Asst	Georgetown	PHD	85	Maryland	1986
Agrawal, Anup	Prof	N Carol St	PHD	86	Pittsbur	
Ahern, Michael J.	Assoc	Toledo	EDD	74	Tenn	1974
Ahkam, Sharif Nurul	Assoc	Duquesne	DBA		Kent St	
Ahmad, Khurshi	Assoc	Wright State	PHD	70	Penn	1970
Ahmad, Syed	Asst	Hofstra	PHD	86	Purdue	1987
Ahmadi, Hamid	Prof	CS-Sacrament	PHD	83	Claremon	1983
Ahmed, Hassan M.	Assoc	Boston Univ	PHD		Stanford	
Ahn, Chang	Asst	Michigan St	PHD		Wiscon	
Aiello, John P.	Lect	Assumption	MBA	88	Bryant	1988
Ainina, M. Fall	Assoc	Wright State	PHD	86	Ariz St	1986
Aitken, Michael J.	Assoc	Univ Sydney	PHD		NS Wales	1991
Aiuppa, Thomas	C-Pr	Wis-La Cross	PHD	81	Georgia	1981
Aivazian, Varsuj	Prof	Univ Toronto	PHD		Ohio St	1981
Ajayi, Richard	Asst	Wayne State	PHD	89	Temple	1989
Akcay, Osman		Manhattan				
Akella, Srinivas R.	Asst	New Orleans	PHD		Northwes	1990
Akhigbe, Aigbe	Asst	Fla Atlantic	PHD	90	Houston	1991
Alaganar, V. T.	Asst	Hofstra	PHD	89	Wisc Mil	1989
Alam, Shamsul	Assoc	U Lethbridge	PHD			1986
Alastair, Marsden	Lect	U Auckland	MCOM	84		1991
Albert, Joseph D.	H	Jms Madison	PHD	78	Georgia	1985
Alberts, William W.	Prof	U Washington	PHD	61	Chicago	1967
Alderson, Michael J.	Asst	Texas A&M	PHD	84	Illinois	1985
on leave to Univ of Missouri-St Louis						
Alemayehu, Tsehai	Prof	Savannah St	PHD		Kentucky	1985
Alexander Jr., John C.	Asst	Clemson	PHD	91	Fla St	1990
Alexander, Gordon J.	Prof	Minnesota	PHD	75	Michigan	1975
IDS Professor in Finance						
Alexander, James	Assoc	Alabama A&M	ABD		Texas	
Alexander, Peter	Lect	Canterbury	BA	83	Waikato	1990
Alford, Alan	Asst	Northeastern	PHD		S Carol	1989
Alford, James D.	Assoc	E Kentucky	MBA	59	Kentucky	1969
Alford, Ray	Prof	Robt Morris	PHD		Renssel	
Algert, Peter	Asst	Cal-Davis	ABD		Berkeley	
Aliber, Robert Z.	Prof	Chicago	PHD	62	Yale	1965
Allen, Chester L.	Prof	Sonoma State	PHD	73	Tx Tech	1985
Allen, Dave	SLect	W Australia	MPHL	77	Leic	1987
Allen, David S.	Asst	No Arizona	PHD		Va Tech	1988
Allen, Franklin H.	Assoc	Pennsylvania	PHD	80	Oxford	1980
Allen, Garth H.	Assoc	No Colorado	JD	72	Iowa	1973
Allen, Grace C.	Asst	W Carolina	PHD	91	S Carol	1990
Allen, Linda	Assoc	CUNY-Baruch	PHD		NYU	
Allen, Robert F.	C-Pr	Creighton	PHD	69	Mich St	1987
Alli, Kasim L.	Asst	Clark Atlant	PHD		Geo St	
Allotey, Traci	Asst	Loyola-Maryl	MA			1992
Alt, Christopher	Asst	Babson	PHD		MIT	
Altman, Edward I.	Prof	New York U	PHD	67	UCLA	
Altshuler, Jerry	Assoc	Okla City	MA		S Calif	1982
Alvayay, Jaime R.	Assoc	CS-Sacrament	PHD		Georgia	1991

Name	Rank	School	Degree	Yr	From	Year
Ambrose, Brent	Asst	Wis-Milwauke	PHD	89	Georgia	1989
Ambrose, Janet	Inst	LaSalle				
Amdafo, Sampson	Asst	Alabama St	ABD		Denver	1990
Amel, Eric	Asst	Arizona St	PHD		Wash U	1988
Amihud, Yakov	VProf	New York U	PHD	75	New York	
Amin, Kaushik	Asst	Michigan	PHD	89	Cornell	1989
Amling, Frederick	Prof	George Wash	PHD	57	Penn	
Amoako-Adu, Ben	C-Ac	Wilfrid Laur	PHD		Toronto	1987
Ananaba, Agu J.	Asst	Hampton	MS		Nrflk St	1987
Ancel, Esther	Asst	Wis-Milwauke	PHD	85	Texas	1986
Andersen, Theodore A.	Assoc	UCLA	PHD	49	Wiscon	1956
Andersen, Torben G.	Asst	Northwestern	PHD	91	Yale	
Anderson, Allen S.	Asst	Akron	PHD	78	Arkansas	1984
Anderson, Charles	Asst	Lg-Isl-Post	PHD		SchSoRes	
Anderson, Dwight C.	Prof	Louisiana Te	PHD	74	Alabama	1979
Anderson, Leslie P.	Prof	Portland St	PHD	60	Wiscon	1986
Anderson, Michael H.	Asst	Suffolk	PHD		Indiana	
Anderson, R. A. Andrew	SLect	Deakin-Warrn	MS		Monash	1991
Anderson, Ron	Asst	Nev-L Vegas	ABD		Arizona	
Anderson, Sherri C.	C $	Sonoma State	MBA	83	Sn Frn S	1980
Anderson, Thomas C.	Assoc	Kennesaw St	PHD	72	Berkeley	1985
Andre, James M.	Asst	So Calif				
Andrews, Frank E.	Asst	Merrimack	MBA		Babson C	
Andrews, John J.	Assoc	Emory	PHD	65	Ohio St	1970
Andrews, Victor L.	C-Pr	Georgia St	PHD	58	MIT	1968
Mills Bee Lane Chair of Banking and Finance						
Andrusco, Gene L.	Assoc	CS-San Bern	PHD	84	Claremon	1977
Ang, James S.	Prof	Florida St	PHD	72	Purdue	1980
William O. Cullom Professor						
Angel, James G.	Asst	Georgetown	PHD	91	Berkeley	1991
Angell, Robert J.	Prof	N Carol A&T	DBA	74	Fla St	
Ankney, Carolyn	Asst	Goshen	MBA		Ball St	1990
Ansley, Craig F.	Prof	U Auckland	PHD	77	Michigan	1988
Apap, Antonio	Asst	West Florida	DBA	82	US Intl	1990
Apilado, Vincent P.	Prof	Tx-Arlington	PHD	70	Michigan	1980
Aragon, George A.	Assoc	Boston Coll	DBA	75	Harvard	1975
Arak, Marcelle	Prof	Colo-Denver				
Arbelaez, Harvey	Asst	Penn St-Harr	PHD	90	Temple	1991
Archer, Stephen H.	C-Pr	Willamette	PHD	58	Minn	1974
Guy F. Atkinson Professor of Economics and Finance						
Archer, Wayne R.	Asst	Florida	PHD	74	Indiana	1971
Arnold, Henry	Prof	Seton Hall	PHD	82	New Sch	
Arsan, Noyan	Prof	West Georgia	PHD	73	Syracuse	1984
Arshadi, Nasser	Assoc	Mo-St Louis	PHD	82	Nebraska	1982
Arshanapalli, Bala G.	Assoc	Indiana NW	PHD	88	N Ill	1991
Arthur, William J.	Prof	Columbus	DBA	69	Virginia	1985
Arzac, Enrique	Prof	Columbia	PHD	68	Columbia	1971
Ashley, William L.	Prof	San Jose St	PHD	80	Georg St	1984
Ashorn Jr., Leroy W.	C-Pr	Sam Houston	PHD		Arkansas	
Askew, Robert C.	Inst	Hampton	MSM			
Asquith, Paul	Assoc	MIT	PHD			
Assar, Hamid	Lect	Howard	ABD		Southern	1989
Assefa, Zewdineh	Assoc	Tx-Pan Amer	PHD	80	Illinois	1983
Assogbavi, T.	Asst	Laurentian	PHD		Laval	
Atchison, Michael D.	C-As	Virginia	PHD		Mich St	
Athanassakos, George	Asst	Wilfrid Laur	PHD		York	1988
Atkins, Allen B.	Asst	Arizona	PHD	88	Texas	1988
Atkinson, Stanley M.	Assoc	Cen Florida	DBA		Miss St	1981
Aucamp, Donald C.	Prof	S Ill-Edward	PHD	71	Wash U	1971
Auerbach, Robert D.	Prof	Cal-Riversid	PHD		Chicago	1983
Austin, Lloyd M.	Lect	U Auckland	MCOM			1989
Austin, M.	Asst	Nevada-Reno	PHD		NYU	1986
Auxier, A. L.	Assoc	Tennessee	PHD		Iowa	
Avard, Stephen L.	Assoc	East Txs St	PHD		N Texas	
Avery, Albert E.	Assoc	Towson State	PHD	78	Purdue	1987
Avestruz, Fred S.	Assoc	Lg-Isl-Post	PHD		Philipin	
Awerbuch, Shimon	Asst	Mass-Lowell	PHD	75	RPI	
Ayers, Ronald	Assoc	Tx-S Antonio	PHD	78	Tulane	1979
Aziz, Abdul	Prof	CS-Humboldt	PHD	84	Texas	1986
Babbel, David F.	Assoc	Pennsylvania				
Back, Kerry E.	Assoc	Wash Univ	PHD	83	Kentucky	1989
Bacon, Frank	Asst	Longwood	PHD	90	Va Comm	1990
Bacon, Peter W.	Prof	Wright State	DBA	67	Indiana	1969
Badrinath, S. G.	Asst	Northeastern	PHD		Purdue	1985
Bae, Gi-Beom	Asst	SW Texas St	ABD		Geo St	1990
Bae, Sung C.	Asst	Bowling Gr	PHD		Florida	1987
Bagamery, Bruce		Central Wash				
Bagnoli, Mark	Assoc	Indiana				
Bagwell, Laurie Simon	Asst	Northwestern	PHD	88	Stanford	
Bailey, Warren B.	Asst	Cornell	PHD	86	UCLA	1990

Bajtelsmit, Vickie	Asst	Colorado St				
Baker, H. Kent	C-Pr	American U	DBA	72	Maryland	1975
Baker, James C.	Prof	Kent State	DBA	66	Indiana	1976
Baker, Jonathan	Asst	Dartmouth	PHD	86	Stanford	1986
Baker, W. Gary	Prof	Washburn	PHD	75	Nebraska	1975
Balbirer, Sheldon D.	Assoc	N Car-Greens	PHD		N Carol	1974
Baldwin Jr., William T.	D-Ac	Transylvania	PHD	75	Kentucky	
Baldwin, Carliss Y.	Prof	Harvard				
Baldwin, T. J.	Asst	East Anglia	MSC		London	1986
Baldzuzzi, Pierluigi	Asst	New York U				
Bales, Gioia	Inst	Hofstra	MBA	86	Hofstra	1990
Balik, Robert	Prof	W Michigan	PHD	84	Iowa	
Ball, Clifford A.	Assoc	Vanderbilt	PHD	80	New Mex	1990
Ball, Jay N.	Asst	Northeastern	PHD		Georgia	1988
Ball, Sheryl	Asst	Boston Univ	PHD		Northwes	
Ballabon, Maurice	Assoc	CUNY-Baruch	PHD		McGill	
Ballam, Deborah	Assoc	Ohio State	JD		Ohio St	
Ballantine Jr., John W.	Asst	Babson	PHD		New York	
Balogh, Colin	Asst	Bentley	PHD	91	Georgia	1989
Balsara, Nauzer	Assoc	NE Illinois	PHD	86	Columbia	1987
Bandopadhyaya, Arindam	Asst	Mass-Boston	PHD	91	Indiana	1991
Banerjee, Harpogal	Asst	Ball State	PHD	89	Illinois	1989
Bange, Mary	Asst	Michigan St	PHD		Wiscon	
Bankston, Thomas A.	Prof	Angelo State	PHD	75	Florida	1974
Banning, Peter D.	Asst	East Carol	MS	71	UCLA	1989
Bansal, Vipul	Asst	St Johns	PHD			
Baradwaj, Babu G.	Asst	Wis-Eau Clar	PHD	91	Tx A&M	1991
Baral, Suresh	Asst	So Carol St				
Barbee, William	Assoc	Howard	PHD	74	Catholic	1975
Barber, Brad M.	Asst	Cal-Davis	PHD	91	Chicago	
Barclay, Michael J.	Asst	Rochester	PHD		Stanford	
Barenbaum, Lester	C-Pr	LaSalle	PHD		Rutgers1	196
Barges, Alexander	Prof	Massachusett	PHD	62	Northwes	
Barnea, Amir	Prof	Rice	PHD	72	Cornell	1989
Barnes, Thomas H.	Assoc	Brock Univ	PHD	81	Kentucky	1986
Barney, Dwayne	Assoc	Boise State	PHD		Tx A&M	1986
Barngrover, Charles L.	Prof	Cincinnati	PHD	66	Cinn	1960
Barnhart, S. W.	Assoc	Clemson	PHD	84	Texas	1988
Barnhill, Theodore M.	C-Pr	George Wash	PHD	74	Michigan	
Barone-Adesi, Giovanni	Prof	Univ Alberta	PHD	82	Chicago	1981
Barrett, Peter J.	Lect	Wis-Whitewat	ABD		Wis-Milw	1985
Barrett, W. Brian	Assoc	U Miami	PHD	83	Ga Tech	1983
Barrow, Janice M.	Assoc	Shippensburg	PHD		Houstonn	1988
Barry, Christopher B.	Prof	Tx Christian	DBA	73	Indiana	1988
Bart, J.	Prof	Univ Windsor				
Bartell Jr., H. Robert	Prof	East Tenn St	PHD	63	Columbia	1989
Chair of Banking and Director Center of Excellence in Banking						
Barth, James R.	Prof	Auburn	PHD		Ohio St	1989
Lowder Eminet Scholar Professor						
Bartholdy, Jan	SLect	Univ Otago	PHD	88	Queen's	1989
Bartlett III, Dwight K,	VExec	Pennsylvania				
Visiting Executive Professor of Insurance						
Bartlett, Jerry	Prof	Athens	JD		Cumberla	1965
Bartunek, Kenneth	Asst	Fla Atlantic	PHD	91	Louisian	1991
Basu, Sam N.	Prof	CS-Hayward	PHD	75	Houston	1988
Basu, Somnath	Asst	Denver	PHD		Arizona	1989
Bates, David S.	Asst	Pennsylvania	PHD	88	Princeto	1988
Bathal, Chenchu	Asst	N Dakota St	PHD	90	Texas	1990
Batra, Harish C.	Prof	Wis-Whitewat	PHD	71	Illinois	1971
Batten, Robert W.	Prof	Georgia St	MA		Duke	
Bauer Jr., Richard J.	Assoc	St Marys-Txs	PHD	85	Tx Tech	
Bauer, Rob		Limburg				1990
Bauman, W. Scott	Prof	No Illinois	PHD	61	Indiana	1981
Baur, Michael N.	Asst	Ball State	PHD	91	Texas	1990
Bawuah, Kwadwo	C-Ac	Virginia St	PHD		Va Tech	1984
Bayless, Mark E.	Asst	Wayne State	PHD	79	Wash U	1988
Beaglehole, David	Asst	Iowa	PHD	91	Chicago	1991
Beal, Laura	Inst	Neb-Omaha				
Bear, F. Thomas	Assoc	Stetson	PHD		Georgia	1982
Bear, Robert	Prof	Fla Internat	PHD	70	Iowa	
Beaton, William R.	Prof	Fla Internat	PHD	58	Ohio St	
Beaves, Robert G.	Asst	Canisius	PHD	78	Iowa	1989
Becker, Kent	Asst	Temple	PHD		Illinois	
Becker, Michael W.	Asst	Valparaiso	ABD		Ill-Chic	1987
Beckett, Tony	SLect	Bournemouth	BA			1990
Beckmann, Heino	Assoc	St Thomas-MN	PHD		Penn	1986
Beecher, Earl	Prof	CS-Long Bch	PHD	65	UCLA	1961
Beedles, William L.	Prof	Kansas	PHD		Texas	1978
Beenhakker, Arie	Prof	South Fla	PHD	64	Purdue	1973
Beer, Francisca	Assoc	CS-San Bern	PHD	90		1990

Name	Rank	School	Degree	Yr	Grad School	Yr
Behzah, Hadi	Assoc	CS-Hayward	PHD	89	Indiana	1989
Beidleman, Carl R.	C-Pr	Lehigh	PHD	68	Penn	1967
DuBois Professor						
Beja, Avraham	VProf	MIT	PHD			
Belcher, Larry	Asst	Stetson	PHD		Indiana	
Belden, Susan A.	Asst	Colorado Spr	PHD		Utah	1987
Belford, Ray	Asst	Okla City	MBA		Okla Cty	1987
Beliveau, Barbara C.	Asst	Connecticut	PHD	80	Yale	1978
Belk, Penelope A.	Lect	Loughborough	MA		Lancast	
Bell, Robert	Prof	CUNY-Brookly	PHD			1986
Bellamy, David	Lect	Queensland	MBA		Queensld	
Bello, Zakri Y.	Assoc	Salisbury St	PHD	83	Va Tech	1987
Belloit, Jerry		Clarion	PHD		Florida	1990
Belt, Brian L.	Assoc	Mo-Kansas Ct	PHD		N Texas	1977
Bendeck, Yvette M.	Asst	Houston-Cl L	PHD		Ariz St	
Benecke, Robert W.	Prof	Neb-Omaha	DBA		Colorado	
Benefield, Michael E.	Asst	Arkansas	MBA		Ark St	1988
Benesh, Gary A.	Assoc	Florida St	PHD	81	Va Tech	1981
Benet, Bruce A.	Asst	DePaul	PHD		N Carol	
Benink, Harald	Asst	Limburg				1989
Benjamin, John D.	Asst	American U	PHD	88	LSU	1990
Benkato, Omar M.	Asst	Ball State	PHD		Cinn	1989
Bennett, Charles A.	C-Ac	Gannon	MA		Fordham	1975
Bennett, Doris	Asst	Jacksonvl St	PHD		Alabama	1986
Benson, Earl D.	C-Pr	Western Wash	PHD	78	Oregon	1980
Benston, George J.	Prof	Emory	PHD	63	Chicago	1987
John H. Harland Professor of Finance, Accounting, and Economics						
Benveniste, Larry	Assoc	Boston Coll	PHD		Berkeley	
Bequet, Sylvie	Asst	Bishop's Un				
Beranek, William	Prof	Georgia	PHD	53	UCLA	1977
C&S Mills Bee Lane Professor						
Berg, Warren	Prof	Luther	PHD	60	Iowa	1948
Berger, Jay	Prof	CS-Northrdge	PHD	67	UCLA	1965
Berger, Lawrence A.	Asst	Pennsylvania	PHD	85	Penn	
Berk, Laurey	Lect	WI-Green Bay	MBA	82	WI-Oshko	1982
Berkovitch, Elazar	Asst	Michigan	PHD	86	Northwes	1986
Berkowitz, Michael	Assoc	Univ Toronto	PHD		SUNY Buf	1973
Berlin, Bruce S.	Asst	Ohio Univ	PHD	85	Mich St	1984
Berlin, Mitchell	Asst	New York U	PHD	86	Penn	
Berman, Peter	Prof	New Haven	PHD		J Hopkin	
Bernardi, Joseph C.	Asst	Loras	MBA	82	Ill St	1986
Berne, Robert	Prof	New York-Gr	PHD	77	Cornell	1976
Bernie, Gilles		Univ Laval				
Berrefjord, Ole	Asst	Norwegian				
Berry, Michael A.	Assoc	Jms Madison	PHD	82	Ariz St	1990
Berry, R. H.	Prof	East Anglia	PHD		Warwick	1987
Berry, Sam G.	Assoc	Virg Comm	DBA	76	Fla St	1971
Berry, Thomas D.	Assoc	DePaul	PHD		Missouri	
Bertero, Elisabetta	Lect	London Econ	PHD	87	London	1991
Bertin, William J.	Prof	Tenn-Chattan	DBA	80	Kent St	1984
Besley, Scott	Asst	South Fla	DBA	84	Fla St	1982
Bessembinder, Hendrik	Asst	Arizona St	PHD		U Wash	1989
Bessler, Wolfgang	Asst	Rensselaer	PHD		Hamburg	1990
Betker, Brian	Asst	Ohio State	PHD	91	UCLA	
Betty, Winfield	Assoc	Tx-S Antonio	PHD	69	N Texas	1981
Beveridge, Steve	Assoc	Univ Alberta	PHD	75	Chicago	1973
Bey, Roger P.	C-Pr	Tulsa	PHD	74	Penn St	1983
Bhagat, Sanjai	Prof	Colorado	PHD	82	U Wash	1989
First Bank Business Affiliated Scholar						
Bhalla, Bharat B.	Asst	Fairfield	PHD	66	Cornell	1987
Bhandari, Shyam B.	Prof	Bradley	PHD	77	Iowa	1976
Bharati, Rakesh C.	Asst	S Ill-Edward	PHD	91	Indiana	1989
Bhardwaj, Ravinder K.	Asst	Winthrop	MBA		S Carol	
Bhaskar, Vashishta	Asst	Duquesne	ABD		Penn St	
Bhattacharya, T. K.	Asst	Cameron	ABD		Oklahoma	1990
Bhattacharya, Utpal	Asst	Iowa	PHD	90	Columbia	1990
Bhattacharyya, Sugato	Asst	Carnegie Mel	PHD	90	Harvard	1988
Bi, Keqian	Asst	San Francisc	PHD	89	Florida	1989
Bibbins, W. Jerome	Asst	Troy St	PHD	80	Arkansas	1990
Bible, Douglas	Prof	La St-Shreve	PHD	77	Ohio St	1985
Real Estate Professorship						
Bicksler, James L.	Prof	Rutgers-Newk	PHD	67	NYU	
Bickum, Gilbert W.	VAsst	E Kentucky	PHD		Florida	1987
Bieker, Richard	Prof	Delaware St	PHD		Kentucky	
Bierman, Harold	Prof	Cornell	PHD	55	Michigan	1956
Nicholas H. Noyes Professor of Business Administration						
Bierwag, Gerald O.	Prof	Arizona	PHD	62	Northwes	1981
Bierwag, Gerald O.	Prof	Fla Internat	PHD	62	Northwes	
Ryder Systems Professor of Finance						
Bigbee, Dalton	Dean$	Texas A&I	DBA		Tx Tech	

Name	Rank	School	Degree	Yr	From	Yr
Bilici, Hamdi	Assoc	CS-Long Bch	DBA			1988
Bilik, Laurie J.	Assoc	Insurance	MA		NYU	
Billingham, Carol J.	Prof	Cen Michigan	PHD	54	New York	1967
Billingsley, Randall S.	Assoc	Virg Tech	PHD	81	Txs A&M	1981
Billow, Patricia M.	Inst	Akron	JD	81	Akron	1984
Binde, Boyd L.	Asst	Dickinson St	MCAA	84	N Dakota	1984
Binder, John	Asst	Ill-Chicago	PHD		Chicago	
Binder, Mike	Asst	Buena Vista	MBA		Drake	1975
Biolsi, Robert	Asst	Connecticut	PHD	89	CUNY	1990
Birchall, Brian	Lect	Canterbury	MBA	83	Cape Twn	1991
Birts, A. N.	Lect	Univ Bath	MBA			1989
Bish, Gerald C.	Asst	Clarion	JD		Suffolk	1976
Bishnoi, Rahul	Assoc	Hofstra	PHD	84	Mass	1986
Bishop, Paul M.	Assoc	W Ontario	DBA		Harvard	1970
Biswas, Rita	Asst	SUNY-Albany	PHD	91	Tx A&M	1990
Bizer, David	Asst	Northwestern	PHD	88	Stanford	
Bjerksund, Petter	Asst	Norwegian	DOEC			
Black Jr., Kenneth	Prof	Georgia St	PHD		Penn	
Regents' Prof of Risk Mgt & Ins & Holder of the C.V. Starr Chair of Intl Ins						
Black, Carolyn G.	SLect	Massey Univ	MBA			1990
Black, H. A.	H-Pr	Tennessee	PHD		Ohio St	
Black, Joseph B.	Emer	Ball State	BBA	65	Illinois	1973
Black, Joseph H.	Assoc	San Jose St	MBA	77	San Jose	1987
Black, Roy T.	Asst	Georgia St	PHD		Georgia	
Black, Stephen	Inst	Central Okla	ABD		Okla St	1990
Blackburn, John	Assoc	Ohio State	JD		Cinn	
Blackmon, Elsie C.	Asst	Winston-Sal				
Blackwell, David W.	Assoc	Georgia	PHD	86	Tenn	1985
Blair, Allen G.	H-Pr	Piedmont	DBA	67	Harvard	
Blair, Ken	C-Pr	Western St	PHD	76	Ariz St	1986
Blanchard, Carl	Asst	Canterbury	BCOM	91	Canterbu	1991
Blayden, Colin	Prof	Dartmouth	PHD	66	Harvard	1983
Bleich, Donald	Assoc	CS-Northrdge	PHD	85	UCLA	1985
Blenman, Lloyd Patrick	Asst	Mississippi	PHD		Ohio St	
Blevins, Dallas R.	Assoc	Montevallo	DBA	76	Fla St	1983
Bliss, Robert	Asst	Indiana				
Bliss, W. Michael	Asst	Western Conn	MBA		Harvard	
Bloch, Ernest	Prof	New York U	PHD	62	Columbia	
Charles William Gerstenberg Professor of Finance						
Block, Linda J.	Assoc	Embry-Riddle	PHD	78	Purdue	1988
Block, Russell L.	Assoc	San Diego St	JD		Berkeley	1969
Block, Stanley B.	Prof	Tx Christian	PHD	67	LSU	1967
Blodgett, Linda L.	Asst	Ind-So Bend	PHD	87	Michigan	1987
Bloomfield, Brian P.	Lect	Manches Inst	PHD			1987
Blose, Laurence E.	Asst	N Car-Charl	PHD	87	Texas	1990
Blumberg, Harvey	C	Montclair St	PHD		NYU	
Blume, Marshall E.	Prof	Pennsylvania	PHD	68	Chicago	1978
Howard Butcher III Professor of Financial Management						
Blyn, Martin R.	Prof	CS-Dominguez	PHD	66	NYU	1969
Boabang, Francis	Asst	St Marys-Cdn				
Board, John	SLect	London Econ	PHD	85	Newcastl	1986
Boardman, Calvin M.	Prof	Utah	MBA	69	Texas	1976
Boatler, Robert W.	Assoc	Tx Christian	PHD	73	Cornell	1977
Boaz, Ralph S.	Prof	Southern Ark	PHD		Arkansas	1963
Bodie, Zvi	Prof	Boston Univ	PHD		MIT	
Bodnar, Gordon M.	Asst	Rochester	ABD		Princeto	
Bodurtha Jr., James N.	Asst	Michigan	PHD	83	New York	1987
Boebel, Richard	Asst	Tulane				
Boehm, T. P.	Prof	Tennessee	PHD	71	Wash U	
Boehmer, Ekkehart	Asst	Louisiana St	PHD	91	Georgia	1991
Boggs II, Glenn H.	Assoc	Florida St	JD	75	Fla St	1981
Bohannon, John	Asst	Tulane				
Bohannon, John L.	Assoc	Columbus	MBA	68	Georgia	1970
Bohn, Henning	Asst	Pennsylvania				
Bohn, Robert F.	C	Golden Gate				
Bohnen, Howard W.	Asst	St Cloud St	MBA	72	St Cloud	1973
Boisjoly, Russell P.	Prof	Fairfield	DBA	78	Indiana	1989
Bojanic, Sharon Lee	Asst	N Car-Wilmin	DBA	88	Kentucky	1988
Boldin, Robert J.	Prof	Indiana-PA				
Bollen, David	SLect	Bournemouth	BA			1989
Bollerslev, Tim	Assoc	Northwestern	PHD	86	CA-S Dgo	
Bolster, Paul J.	Assoc	Northeastern	PHD		Va Tech	1985
Joseph G. Riesman Research Professor						
Bolten, Steven E.	Prof	South Fla	PHD	69	New York	1978
Bond, M. E.	Prof	Memphis St	PHD	67	Iowa	1979
Bond, Michael T.	Assoc	Cleveland St	PHD	85	Case Wes	1986
Bondi, Robert J.	C-Ac	Western Conn	PHD		New York	
Bonner, Gordon R.	Assoc	Delaware	PHD	65	Syracuse	
Bonnier, Karl-Adam	Lect	Virg-Grad	PHD		Virginia	
Bonomo, Vittorio A.	Assoc	Virg Tech	PHD	69	Brown	1968

Name	Rank	School	Degree	Yr	PhD From	Yr
Bonser-Neal, Catherine A.	Asst	U Washington	MA	83	Chicago	1987
Boocock, Grahame	Lect	Loughborough	MA		Manchest	
Boos, John D.	Assoc	Ohio Wesley	JD	66	Geo Wash	1983
Boose, Mary Ann	Asst	Mississippi	PHD		Wash U	
Boot, Arnoud W. A.	Asst	Northwestern	PHD	87	Indiana	
Booth III, W. Scott	Assoc	Pfeiffer	MA	71	Appal St	1982
Booth, G. Geoffrey	C-Pr	Louisiana St	PHD	71	Michigan	1986
Union National Life Insurance Co. Endowed Professorship in Insurance						
Booth, James R.	Asst	Arizona St	PHD		Alabama	1980
Booth, Laurence D.	Prof	Univ Toronto	PHD		Indiana	1987
Boquist, John A.	Prof	Indiana	PHD	73	Purdue	1973
Boras, William	H-Pr$	Ferris State	PHD		Mich St	1975
Borden, Karl	Assoc	Neb-Kearney	EDD	75	Mass	1986
Borgia, Daniel J.	Asst	Youngstown	MBA	86	Gannon	
Born, Jeffrey A.	Assoc	Northeastern	PHD		N Carol	1988
Born, Waldo L.	Asst	E Illinois	PHD	84	Texas	1988
Bornhofen, John O.	Prof	Grand Valley	PHD	67	Illinois	1973
Bornholtz, Evan F.	Prof	GMI	MBA	66	Iowa	1966
Borokhovich, Kenneth A.	Asst	Case Western	PHD		Ohio St	
Borstadt, Lisa F.	Asst	No Arizona	PHD		Utah	1990
Bosch, Jean-Claude	Assoc	Colo-Denver	PHD		U Wash	
Boschen, John F.	Assoc	Wm & Mary	PHD		Brown	1988
Bose, Mrigen	Assoc	Scranton	PHD	72	Utah	1968
Bosshardt, Donald I.	Assoc	Canisius	PHD	78	Wiscon	1987
Bost, John L.	Assoc	San Diego St	JD		Hastings	1979
Boswell, Jerry	Prof	Metro State	DBA	69	Indiana	1986
Bosworth, William	Asst	W New Eng	PHD	85	Conn	1988
Boudoukh, Jacob	Asst	New York U				
Boudreaux, Denis O.	Asst	SW Louisiana	PHD	88	Miss St	1986
Boulware, George	Prof	David Lipsc	PHD		S Carol	
Bourgeois, Jacques	Prof	HEC-Montreal				
Bovee, Steve	Inst	Oral Roberts	MBA	90	Oral Rob	1991
Bowden, Elbert V.	Prof	Appalach St	PHD		Duke	1977
Bowden, Roger G.	Prof	New So Wales	PHD		Manchest	1988
Bowers, David A.	C-Pr	Case Western	PHD	63	So Meth	
Bowers, Helen M.	Asst	Notre Dame				
Bowlin, Lyle	Asst	No Iowa	MA	85	Iowa	1987
Bowlin, Oswald D.	Prof	Texas Tech	PHD	59	Illinois	1965
Bowman, Robert G.	Prof	So Methodist	PHD	78	Stanford	1991
Bown, Charles C.	Prof	Eastern Wash	PHD	66	U Wash	1969
Bowyer, Linda	C-Ac$	Toledo				
Boyd, Donald A.	Assoc	Memphis St	PHD	72	Miss	1957
Boyd, G. Michael	Assoc	Stetson	PHD		Fla St	1980
Boyd, James W.	C-Ac	Kent State	PHD	83	Arkansas	1984
Boyd, William L.	H-Pr$	W Carolina	PHD	78	Tx A&M	1990
Boye, Knut	Asst	Norwegian				
Boyer, Edward	Inst	Drexel	PHD		Temple	1987
Boyle, Glenn W.	C-Pr	Univ Otago	PHD	87	Texas	1991
Boyle, Phelim P.	Prof	Illinois	PHD	70	Dublin	1991
Boyles, Gerald V.	Prof	SC-Coastal	PHD	72	S Carol	
Bozzo, Cheryl Zega	Asst	Upsala				1989
Bradford, William	Prof	Maryland	PHD	72	Ohio St	
Bradley, Michael	C-Pr	Michigan	PHD	79	Chicago	1981
Everett E. Berg Professor of Business Administration						
Bramhandkar, Alka J.	Assoc	Ithaca	PHD	89	SUNY-Bin	1984
Branan, N. Carson	Assoc	Greensboro	MS		N Car St	
Branch, Ben S.	Prof	Massachusett	PHD	70	Michigan	1975
Brandi, Jay T.	Assoc	Louisville	PHD	85	Arizona	1982
Braswell, Ronald C.	Prof	Florida St	DBA	73	Fla St	1976
Brattin, Max A.	Assoc	Okla Baptist	MBA	62	LSU	1966
Brauer, Greggory	Prof	Tx Christian	PHD	80	Wash	1990
Braun, Phillip A.	Asst	Northwestern	PHD	91	Chicago	
Braxton, Keylon	Asst	Cen St-Ohio	MBA		Wiscon	1987
Brean, Donald	Assoc	Univ Toronto	PHD		Toronto	1978
Breeden, Douglas T.	Prof	Duke	PHD		Stanford	
Breen, William J.	Prof	Northwestern	PHD	65	Cornell	
Brennan, James E.	Lect	Connecticut	MBA	57	Penn	1983
Brennan, Michael J.	Prof	UCLA	PHD	70	MIT	1986
Goldyne and Irwin Hearsh Professor of Money and Banking						
Brenner, Menachem	VProf	New York U	PHD	74	Cornell	
Brenner, Robin J.	Asst	Arizona	PHD	89	Cornell	1989
Brennwald, Heinz H.	Asst	Hartford	PHD		Zurich	
Brent, William H.	Lect	Howard	ABD		Nova	1990
Bretz, Robert	H-Ac	W Kentucky	DBA	75	Miss St	1983
Brewer, Betty L.	Assoc	E New Mexico	PHD	76	Nebraska	1987
Brewer, Dawson E.	Assoc	York Univ	PHD		Northwes	
Brewer, Howard L.	Prof	W Virginia	PHD	77	Iowa	1985
Brewer, Thomas L.	Assoc	Georgetown	PHD	82	Michigan	1985
Brewer, Virgil L.	C-Pr	E Kentucky	DBA		Tx Tech	1980
Brick, Ivan E.	Prof	Rutgers-Newk	PHD		Columbia	

Name	Rank	School	Degree	Yr	From	Yr
Brick, John R.	Prof	Michigan St	PHD		Wiscon	
Briggs, Charles		Alabama A&M				
Brigham, Eugene F.	Prof	Florida	PHD	62	Berkeley	1971
Graduate Research Professor						
Brinkley, James A.	C	Utah	MBA	69	Texas	
Brinkmann, Emile J.	Asst	Houston	PHD	90	Purdue	1991
Brister, William M.	Asst	Millsaps	PHD	90	Arkansas	1989
Brocato, Joe M.	Assoc	Tarleton St	PHD	81	Tenn	1989
Brodt, Abraham I.	Assoc	Concordia U				
Broihahn, Michael	Assoc	Barry	MBA		Wiscon	1988
Bronfman, Corinne M.	Asst	Arizona	PHD	88	New York	1988
Bronson, Claire S.	C-Ac	W New Eng	PHD	82	Connecti	1983
Brooks, Leroy D.	Prof	So Carolina	PHD	71	Mich St	
Brooks, Ray	Asst	Missouri	ABD		Wash U	1991
Brooks, Robert E.	Asst	Alabama	PHD		Florida	1989
Broome, Carroll D.	Asst	DePaul	PHD		Geo St	
Brophy, David J.	Assoc	Michigan	PHD	65	Ohio St	1966
Broske, Mary S.	Assoc	Jacksonvil U	PHD	82	Florida	1990
Brost, Melvin	Prof	Lamar	PHD		N Tx St	1978
Broughton, John B.	Asst	Florida St	PHD	89	Va Tech	1989
Brous, Peter	Asst	Penn State	PHD		Oregon	1989
Brouthers, Keith	Adj	US Intl				
Brown, Bruce	Prof	Furman	PHD	84	S Carol	1984
Brown, Craig	Asst	Fla Atlantic	ABD		Georgia	1991
Brown, David P.	Asst	Indiana	PHD	84	Stanford	
Brown, David T.	Asst	Florida	PHD		Wash U	1986
Brown, John E.	Asst	Georgia St	PHD		N Car St	
Brown, Kate M.	SLect	Univ Otago	PHD	89	E Conn	1988
Brown, Keith C.	Assoc	Texas	PHD	81	Purdue	1984
Brown, Larry	Asst	Mary	MBA	82	Temple	1982
Brown, Mary Robbie	Asst	St Xavier	ABD		Northwes	1988
Brown, Philip R.	Prof	W Australia	PHD	68	Chicago	1980
KPMG Peat Marwick Professor of Accounting						
Brown, Robert K.	C-Pr	Georgia St	PHD		Pitt	
Brown, Stephen J.	Prof	New York U	PHD	76	Chicago	
Brown, Stewart L.	Prof	Florida St	PHD	74	Florida	1974
Brown, Thomas L.	Prof	Jacksonvl St	PHD		Miss	1974
Brown, William J.	H-Pr	Berry	PHD			
Browne, Mark J.	Asst	Georgia				
Brozik, Dallas	Assoc	Marshall	PHD	84	S Carol	
Brucato, Jr., Peter F.	Asst	SUNY-Albany	PHD	87	Duke	1989
Bruce, Thor W.	Assoc	U Miami	PHD	71	Wash U	1968
Brunarski, Kelly R.	Asst	Cincinnati	ABD		Ohio St	1991
Bruner, Robert F.	Assoc	Virg-Grad	DBA		Harvard	
on leave to INSEAD						
Brunsen, William H.	Assoc	E New Mexico	PHD	76	Nebraska	1987
Bryan, Donald W.	Assoc	Pacific	PHD	74	Syracuse	1974
Bryan, William R.	Prof	Illinois	PHD	61	Wiscon	1966
Bryce, Herrington J.	Prof	Wm & Mary	PHD		Syracuse	1986
Bubnys, Edward L.	Asst	Suffolk	PHD		Illinois	
Buch, Joshua	Assoc	LaSalle	PHD		Penn	1971
Buchalter, Sol	Prof	CS-Northrdge	MBA	50	New York	1963
Buchanan, William K.	Inst	Txs-Perm Bas	MBA	85	Txs-PeBa	
Buchwald, Joseph	Prof	CS-Northrdge	PHD	65	UCLA	1961
Buck, Donald T.	Prof	So Conn St	MA		New Hamp	
Buck, James F.	Assoc	East Carol	DBA	78	Fla St	1979
Budack, John J.	Asst	Geo Southern	MBA	70	Drake	1974
Buddy, Nancy	Inst	SW Okla St	MBA	86	SW Ok St	1986
Buell, Stephen G.	Assoc	Lehigh	PHD	77	Lehigh	1973
Bueso, Alberto T.	Prof	CS-Fullerton	PHD	75	Texas	1974
Bull, Ivan O.	Prof	Illinois	PHD	87	Illinois	1987
Bulmash, Samuel B.	Assoc	South Fla	PHD	81	Northwes	1985
Burak, Marshall J.	Dean	San Jose St	DBA	68	S Calif	1981
Burdekin, Richard	Asst	Claremont	PHD	85	Houston	1989
Burgess, Richard C.	Prof	Tulsa	DBA	74	Kentucky	1980
Burn, Karen Sue	C $	Fort Lewis	PHD			
Burnett, Amy	Asst	Richmond	ABD		Texas	1990
Burnett, Nancy	Asst	Claremont	PHD	88	UCLA	1988
Burney, Robert B.	Asst	SC-Coastal	ABD		S Carol	1991
Burnie, David A.	Prof	W Michigan	PHD	84	Syracuse	
Burns, John	Dean	St Bonaventu	PHD	70	Mich St	1991
Burns, Michele A.	Assoc	New Orleans	PHD	80	Arkansas	1979
Burns, Richard M.	Assoc	Alabama-Birm	PHD	86	Georgia	1987
Bursik, Paul B.	Asst	St Norbert	ABD	89	Wash St	1990
Burton, James H.	Prof	West Georgia	PHD	78	Geo St	1990
Busby, James E.	Lect	Baylor	MBA		Baylor	1985
Buser, Stephen A.	Prof	Ohio State	PHD	72	Boston C	
Bush, Robert G.	Asst	Jacksonvil U	MBA	81	Florida	1981
Butko, James	Asst	Brock Univ	ABD		Queens	1983
Butler, Ann M.	Asst	Florida St	ABD		Penn	1990

Butler, D. K.	Lect	Univ Wales	BSC	85	Aberys	1988
Butler, Kirt C.	Asst	Michigan St	PHD		Mich St	
Byely, Larry	Asst	Pitts–Johnst	DBA	89	Ind St	
Byler, Ezra U.	Prof	Millikin	DBA			1988
Byrd, John	Asst	Wash State	PHD	88	Oregon	1987
Byrne, Martin	Prof	Loyola Marym	PHD	59	UCLA	1968
Cabarrouy, Evaldo A.	Assoc	Puerto Rico	PHD	81	Texas	1985
Cakici, Nusret	Asst	Rutgers–N Br	PHD	89	CUNY	1988
Caks, John	Assoc	Fla Atlantic	PHD	84	Penn	1989
Caldwell, James L.	Prof	NE Louisiana	PHD	63	LSU	1975
Call, Ivan T.	Prof	Brigham Yg	PHD	69	Indiana	1963
Callaway, Mary M.	Asst	West Florida	LLM	81	Emory	1977
Callaway, Richard	Asst	Wis–La Cross	PHD	86	Indiana	1991
Calomiris, Charles visiting from Northwestern Univ	VAsoc	Pennsylvania				
Calvet, A. Louis	Prof	Univ Ottawa	PHD	80	MIT	1979
Campbell, Alyce Rita	Asst	Oregon	PHD	87	Brit Col	1987
Campbell, Cynthia J.	Asst	Wash Univ	PHD	86	Michigan	1987
Campbell, Kevin	Asst	Un Stirling	PHD	90	Glasgow	1986
Campsey, Billy J.	Prof	San Jose St	PHD	79	Tx Arlin	1982
Canda, Francis E.	Asst	Akron	MBA	86	Kent St	1990
Cannaday, Roger E.	Assoc	Illinois	PHD	80	S Carol	1979
Cannon, W. T.	Assoc	Queen's Univ	PHD		Harvard	1974
Cao, Andrew D.	Assoc	American U	DBA	76	Geo Wash	1976
Caples, Stephen	Assoc	McNeese St	PHD		UTA	
Capozza, Dennis R.	Prof	Michigan	PHD	72	JohnsHop	1989
Carbone, Dominick	Adj	New York U	MS	75	Columbia	
Carleton, Willard T.	Prof	Arizona	PHD	62	Wiscon	1984
Carlson, J.		Univ Regina				
Carlson, Severin C.	Assoc	Mass–Lowell	DBA	79	Indiana	
Carlson, William	Asst	Duquesne	PHD		Car Mel	
Carman, D. Gary	Prof	SW Texas St	PHD	73		1975
Carmichael, Jeffrey	Prof	Bond Univ	PHD	79	Princeto	1989
Carmody, Seth F.	Assoc	David Lipsc	PHD		Missouri	
Carn, Neil G.	Assoc	Georgia St	PHD		Geo St	
Carnes Jr., Lon Melson	Prof	Geo Southern	DBA	72	Geo St	1967
Carney, Michael	Prof	CS–Pomona	PHD	81	UCLA	1981
Carney, Robert J.	Assoc	Wis–La Cross	PHD	87	Iowa	1987
Carpenter, Michael D.	Prof	Kentucky	PHD	76	Ariz St	
Carr, Peter P.	Asst	Cornell	PHD	88	UCLA	1988
Carrada-Bravo, Francisco	Assoc	Am Grad Intl	PHD	80	Colorado	1971
Carrica, Jean L.	Prof	Gonzaga	PHD	87	Nebraska	1984
Carroll, Anne M.	Asst	Rider	PHD		Penn	
Carroll, Carolyn	Asst	Alabama	PHD		Illinois	1984
Carter, J. Alvin	Assoc	Catawba	MA		Geo St	
Carter, Juanita	Asst	Clark Atlant	MS		Illinois	
Carter, Michael	Asst	Sam Houston	MBA		Baylor	
Carter, Richard B.	Asst	Iowa State	PHD	87	Utah	1986
Carvounis, Chris	Prof	St Johns	PHD		N Sch Re	
Cary, David	Assoc	CS–Northrdge	PHD	83	UCLA	1978
Casey, Matthias M.	Lect	McMaster	MBA		McMaster	
Cassidy, John	Assoc	Cedarville	DBA	80	Fla St	1991
Cassidy, Steven	Asst	Howard	PHD	88	Fla St	1989
Castanias II, Richard P.	Assoc	Cal–Davis	PHD		Car Mel	
Cebenoyan, A. Sinan	Asst	Baltimore	PHD		NYU	
Celec, Stephen E.	Prof	Florida St	PHD	76	N Carol	1977
Certo, Samuel C.	Dean	Rollins	PHD	73	Ohio	1986
Cerwonka, Ronald P.	Prof	Providence	PHD	73	Missouri	1974
Cesta, John R.	Assoc	Arizona St	PHD	74	Fla St	1975
Chadbourne, Bruce D.	Prof	Embry–Riddle	PHD	69	Iowa	1988
Chamberlain, Trevor W.	Asst	McMaster	PHD		Toronto	
Chambers, Donald R.	Assoc	Baltimore	PHD		N Carol	
Chambers, Scott	Asst	Linfield	PHD	88	Cal–Davi	1990
Chan, Anthony K.	Asst	Woodbury	ABD		Claremon	
Chan, Johnny	Asst	Moorhead St	PHD	90	Alabama	1990
Chan, Ka–Kung C.	Assoc	Ohio State	PHD		Chicago	
Chan, Kalok	Asst	Arizona St	PHD		Ohio St	1990
Chan, Keith	Asst	New So Wales	MCOM		NS Wales	1986
Chan, Louis K. C.	Asst	Illinois	PHD	84	Rochest	1988
Chan, M. W. Luke	Prof	McMaster	PHD		McMaster	
Chan, Stanley W.	Asst	Penn St–Erie	PHD	86	Houston	1987
Chan, Su Han	Assoc	CS–Fullerton	PHD		Texas	1988
Chan, Yuk–Shee	Prof	So Calif	PHD			
Chance, Don M.	Prof	Virg Tech	PHD	80	LSU	1980
Chandy, P. R.	Prof	North Texas	DBA	80	Tx Tech	1981
Chang, C. Edward	Asst	SW Missouri	PHD	89	Illinois	1989
Chang, Carolyn C. WU	Assoc	CS–Fullerton	PHD		So Cal	1990
Chang, Chung	Asst	Minnesota	PHD			
Chang, Chung–Hao	Asst	Fla Internat	PHD	88	Northwes	
Chang, Eric C.	Assoc	Maryland	PHD	82	Purdue	

Name	Rank	School	Degree	Yr	Where	Year
Chang, Jack S. K.	Prof	CS-L Angeles	PHD	83	Houston	1985
Chang, LyJune	Asst	Rutgers-Newk	PHD		Car Mel	
Chang, P. H. Kevin	Asst	New York U	PHD	88	Mass	
Chang, Peter T.	Prof	Alabama A&M	PHD		Okla St	
Chang, Philip C.	Assoc	Univ Calgary	PHD		Illinois	1985
Chang, Rosita P.	Assoc	Rhode Island	PHD	82	Pitt	1988
Chang, S. J.	Assoc	Illinois St	PHD	86	Iowa	1989
Chang, Saeyoung	Asst	Arizona St	PHD		Ohio St	1988
Chaplinsky, Susan	V	Northwestern	PHD	84	Chicago	
Charkey, Barbara	Asst	Keene State	MS	85	Mass	1986
Chase III, Edgar L.	C-Pr	Dillard	JD		Loyola	
Chatfield, Robert E.	C	Nev-L Vegas	PHD	79	Purdue	1988
Chatterjee, Sris	Asst	Fordham	PHD		Columbia	1989
Chaudhury, Mohammed M.	Assoc	Saskatchewan	PHD	86	Sim Fras	1982
Cheatham, Leo R.	Assoc	NE Louisiana	PHD	74	Arkansas	1986
Chee, Kew-Chul	Asst	York Univ	PHD		NYU	1999
Chemmanur, Thomas J.	Asst	Columbia	PHD	90	NYU	1990
Chen, Andrew H.	Prof	So Methodist	PHD	69	Berkeley	1983
Distinguished Professor of Finance						
Chen, Carl R.	C-Pr	Dayton	PHD	77	Georgia	1977
Chen, Chang-Yi	Prof	CS-Chico	PHD	85	Oregon	1984
Chen, Chao	Assoc	CS-Northrdge	PHD	88	Maryland	1988
Chen, Chuan Yu		Montclair St	PHD		NYU	
Chen, Haiyang	Asst	Youngstown	MA	87	Kent St	
Chen, Kuang C.	Prof	CS-Fresno	PHD		Ohio St	1988
Chen, Nai-Fu	Prof	Calif-Irvine	PHD	75	Berkeley	1989
Chen, Ren-Raw	Asst	Rutgers-N Br	PHD	90	Illinois	1990
Chen, Son-Nan	Prof	Maryland	PHD	75	Georgia	
Chen, Su-Jane	Asst	Wis-Eau Clar	PHD	88	Missouri	1991
Chen, Yea Mow	Prof	San Fran St	PHD	84	Ohio St	1984
Chen, Zhiwu	Asst	Wisconsin	PHD	90	Yale	1990
Cheney, John B.	Assoc	Cen Florida	DBA		Tenn	1977
Cheng, Joseph M.	Assoc	Ithaca	PHD	86	SUNY-Bin	1983
Cheng, Louis T. W.	Asst	Murray State	DBA		LSU	1989
Cheng, William I.	Asst	Tuskegee	PHD	90	SUNY-Bin	1990
Cherin, Tony C.	Assoc	San Diego St	PHD			1982
Cherry, Richard	Prof	Lamar	PHD		Texas	1966
Cherukuri, U. Rao	Prof	CS-Stanislau	PHD	72	N Carol	1970
Cheshier, Patericia	Prof	CS-Sacrament	PHD	82	Nebraska	1984
Cheung, C. S. Sherman	Asst	McMaster	PHD		Illinois	
Chew, I. Keong	C-Ac$	Kentucky	PHD	77	S Carol	
Chhachhi, Indudeep S.	Asst	W Kentucky	DBA	90	So Illin	1990
Chiang, Raymond	C-Pr	U Miami	PHD	79	Penn	1985
Chiang, Thomas C.	Prof	Drexel	PHD		Penn St	1981
Chikaonda, Mathias	Asst	Memorial Un	PHD	90	Mass	1988
Chinloy, Peter	Assoc	American U	PHD	74	Harvard	1991
Realtor Chair and Homer Hoyt Faculty Fellow						
Chishty, Muhammod	Asst	W Illinois				
Chiu, Shean-Bi	Assoc	Nat Taiwan U	PHD	89	Washingt	1989
Cho, Dongsae	Assoc	Old Dominion				
Cho, Sung-il	Asst	Syracuse	PHD	89	Michigan	1987
Choate, George Marc	Prof	Willamette	PHD	70	Wash	1974
Choe, Hyuk	Asst	Penn State	PHD	90	Chicago	1990
Chohan, Ray V.	Prof	St Ambrose	PHD	75	Port St	1978
Choi, Chang K.	Prof	Chicago St	DBA		UCLA	
Choi, Dosoung	Assoc	SUNY-Buffalo	PHD	80	Penn St	1986
Choi, Ducksang	Asst	Metro State	DBA	91	Miss St	1990
Choi, J. Jay	Prof	Temple	PHD		New York	
Choi, Kwang S.	Assoc	Old Dominion	PHD	72	Cinn	1971
Choi, Seungmook	Asst	Nev-L Vegas	PHD	79	Texas	1991
Choi, Yoon K.	Asst	Texas-Dallas	PHD	90	Michigan	1990
Chollet, Deborah J.	Assoc	Georgia St	PHD		Syracuse	
Chong, Beng S.	Asst	Dayton	PHD	90	Wash U	1990
Chopin, Marc	VAsst	North Texas	PHD	91	Tx A&M	1991
Chopra, Navin	Asst	Temple	PHD		Michigan	
Chorun, Joseph	Assoc	Adelphi	PHD	65	Columbia	
Chou, Yu-Min	Prof	Mich-Dearbor	PHD	59	Illinois	1966
Choudhury, Santosh K.	Prof	Norfolk St	PHD		Northwes	1974
Chow, Edward	Asst	Santa Clara	PHD	90	Indiana	1990
Chow, Kewn Victor	Asst	W Virginia	PHD	89	Alabama	1989
Chowdhry, Bhagwan	Asst	UCLA	PHD	89	Chicago	1988
Chowdhury, Monayem	Prof	Cheyney				
Christensen, Bent	Asst	New York U	MS			
Christensen, Donald G.	Asst	Wichita St	PHD	88	S Carol	1988
Christiansen, William A.	Assoc	Florida St	PHD	83	Utah	1983
Christianson, Charles	Asst	Luther	MBA	75	S Dakota	1974
Christie, William G.	Asst	Vanderbilt	PHD	89	Chicago	19-8
Christner, Ronald	Assoc	Loyola-N Orl	PHD	71	Minn	1974
Christofi, Andreas C.	Assoc	Penn St-Harr	PHD	84	Penn St	1986
Chu, Chen-Chin	Assoc	Memphis St	PHD	84	Illinois	1984

Chua, Jess	Prof	Univ Calgary	PHD	76	Michigan	1979
Chua, Lena	Asst	Hawaii–Manoa	PHD	91	Ariz St	1991
Chugh, Lal C.	C-Ac	Mass–Boston	PHD	70	Harvard	1985
Chung, Kee-Ho	Assoc	Memphis St	PHD	86	Cinn	1988
Chung, M. C. (Marcus)	Assoc	CS–Sacrament	PHD	91	Mich St	1989
Chung, Ronald	Asst	Trenton St	ABD		Drexel	1991
Churchill, John	Asst	Arcadia Univ	PHD			1982
Ciancanelli, Penelope L.	Lect	Manches Inst	PHD		New York	1988
Claggett, E. Tylor	Asst	Wake Fr–Grad	PHD	79	Houston	1988
Clapp, Benjamin	Asst	Moorhead St	MBA	76	America	1990
Clapp, John M.	Prof	Connecticut	PHD	74	Columbia	1981
Clark, Donald W.	Assoc	Carson–Newm	MBA		Memph St	1981
Clark, Frank L.	C-Pr	E Illinois	PHD	75	Arkansas	1990
Clark, Jeffrey A.	Assoc	Florida St	PHD	80	Illinois	1983
Clark, Peter K.	Prof	Cal–Davis	PHD		Harvard	
Clark, Robert M.	Dean	Rockhurst	PHD	88	Syracuse	1991
Clark, Susan B.	Prof	Franklin	MBA	84	Ohio St	1987
Clarke, Alex	Lect	W Australia	MCOM	91	W Austra	1983
Clarke, Gerald L.	Inst	Boston Univ	BS		MIT	
Clarke, James J.	Assoc	Villanova	PHD	72	Notre Dm	1972
Clarke, Jere W.	Retir	So Conn St	PHD		Virginia	
Clauretie, Terrence	Prof	Nev–L Vegas	PHD		Wash St	1988
Claypool, Gregory A.	Assoc	Youngstown	PHD	88	Kent St	
Clayton, Gary E.	Prof	No Kentucky	PHD	73	Utah	1980
Clayton, Ronnie J.	C-Ac	Cen Florida	PHD		Georgia	1988
Cleveland, Paul	Asst	Birminghm So	PHD	85	Tx A&M	1990
Cliffe, Cheryl	SLect	U Auckland	MCOM			1987
Clinebell, John M.	C-Ac	No Colorado	DBA	88	S Illin	1987
Cloninger, Dale O.	Prof	Houston–Cl L	DBA	73	Fla St	1974
Clouse, Maclyn L.	C-Ac	Denver	PHD		U Wash	1977
Clyde, William	Assoc	Quinnipiac	PHD		Edinburg	
Coats, Pamela K.	Prof	Florida St	PHD	78	Nebraska	1978
Cobb, Kenneth	Asst	Tx Southern	MBA		N Ill	
Cochran, John S.	Prof	Georgia St	PHD	61	Harvard	1967
Cochran, R. Bruce	Assoc	San Jose St				
Cochran, Steven J.	Asst	Villanova	PHD	88	Cinn	1987
Cockerham, Mary	Inst	So Miss	MBA	83	So Miss	1983
Cockrum, William M.	Adj	UCLA	MBA	61	Harvard	1984
Cohen, J. Kalman	Prof	Duke	PHD		Car Mel	
Cohen, Neil	Assoc	George Wash	DBA	75	Virginia	
Cohn, Richard A.	Prof	Hartford	MBA		Stanford	
Colantuoni, Ido E.		Southeastern	PHD		NYU	
Cole, C. Steven	Asst	North Texas	PHD	89	Arkansas	1988
Cole, David W.	Prof	Ohio State	DBA	65	Indiana	
Cole, John A.	Asst	Florida A&M	PHD		Michigan	
Coles, Jeffrey L.	Assoc	Utah	BA	79	Pomona	1983
Collins, J. Markham	Prof	Tulsa	PHD	80	Oklahoma	1979
Collins, M. Cary	Asst	Tennessee	PHD		Georgia	
Colwell, Peter F.	Prof	Illinois	PHD	73	Wayne St	1973
Comeskey, Harry A.	Asst	N Car–Wilmin	DBA	83	Colorado	1984
Committe, Thomas Carrol	Prof	West Florida	PHD	66	Alabama	1967
Conine Jr., Thomas E.	C-Pr	Fairfield	PHD	79	New York	1980
Conn, Robert L.	C-Pr	Miami U–Ohio	PHD	73	Houston	1989
Connell Jr., Frederick L.	Asst	SE Louisiana	PHD	88	Fla St	1983
Connelly, Dennis E.	C-Ac	St Marys–Cdn				
Connolly, Robert A. on leave to Univ of North Carolina	Asst	Calif–Irvine	PHD	82	Maryland	1985
Connor, Gregory	Lect	London Econ	PHD	82	Yale	1991
Conover, James A.	Asst	North Texas	PHD	89	Tx A&M	1989
Conover, Roger	Asst	Azusa Pacif	MA		Sn Diego	1991
Conrad, James	Prof	Indianapolis	PHD		Purdue	1978
Conrad, Jennifer S.	Asst	No Carolina	PHD	86	Chicago	1985
Conroy, Robert M.	Assoc	Virg–Grad	DBA		Indiana	
Consler, John E.	Assoc	LeMoyne	DBA	78	Colorado	1984
Constand, R. L.	Asst	Hawaii–Manoa	PHD	89	Fla St	1988
Constantinides, George M. Leon Carroll Marshall Professor of Finance	Prof	Chicago	DBA	74	Indiana	1978
Conway, Gerald	Asst	Wayne St Col	MSE	73	Chadron	1975
Conway, Larry	Prof	Toledo	PHD		Illinois	1975
Conway, Paul F.	Assoc	Notre Dame	MSC	51	SUNY-Alb	1956
Conway, Steve	Asst	Wis–Stev Pt	MBA		Wiscon	1989
Conyers, Alex D.	Assoc	Morehead St	MBA		Kentucky	1958
Cook, Alan	Prof	Baylor	PHD		Arkansas	1969
Cook, Cline G.	Assoc	Columbus	PHD	87	Geo St	1985
Cook, David	Asst	Calvin	MBA		Grand V	
Cook, Douglas O.	Asst	Colorado	PHD	87	Texas	1987
Cook, Richard	Asst	Colo–Denver				
Cook, Tom	Assoc	Denver	PHD		U Wash	1983
Cooley, Clyde J.	Prof	Weber State	PHD	77	Utah	1978

156

Name	Rank	School	Degree	Yr	Univ	Yr
Cooley, Philip L.	Prof	Trinity	PHD	73	Ohio St	1985
Dick & Peggy Prassel Distinguished Professor of Business Administration						
Cooney, John W.	Inst	Wash State	ABD		Utah	1990
Cooney, Peter W.	Lect	U Manitoba	MBA	79	Manitoba	1978
Cooper, James R.	Prof	Georgia St	JD		Penn	
Cooper, Ken	Prof	Ohio Northrn	PHD	84	Minn	1986
Cooper, Rick	Asst	Wayne State	PHD	90	Vanderbi	1990
Cooper, S. Kerry	Prof	Texas A&M	PHD	71	Texas	1975
Lamar Professor						
Cooperman, Elizabeth S.	Asst	Baltimore	PHD		Georgia	
Copeland, Laurence	Prof	Un Stirling	PHD	85	Manchest	1991
Copeland, Thomas	Adj	New York U				
Copley, Ronald E.	Assoc	N Car-Wilmin	PHD	81	S Carol	1982
Corbett, Richard B.	Prof	Florida St	PHD	74	Geo St	1980
Independent Life & Accident Insurance Company Professor						
Corcione, Frank P.	Assoc	Scranton	PHD	75	Lehigh	1978
Corcoran, Charles	Assoc	Wis-Rvr Fall	PHD		Minn	1988
Corhay, Albert	Asst	Limburg	MBA	80	Liege	1989
Cornell, Bradford	H-Pr	UCLA	PHD	75	Stanford	1979
Cornett, Marcia M.	Assoc	So Illinois	PHD	83	Indiana	1990
Corrado, Charles J.	Asst	Missouri	PHD		Arizona	1990
Correll, Mark	Inst	Colorado	PHD	86	Wiscon	1988
Cortes, Bienviendo	Asst	Pittsburg St	PHD		Okla St	
Cosset, Jean-Claude	Prof	Univ Laval	PHD		Columbia	
Costello, Ann	Assoc	Hartford	PHD		Penn	
Cotner, John S.	Asst	Loyola-Maryl	PHD		St Louis	1989
Coutts, Andrew	Lect	Univ Leeds	MA			1989
Cowan, Arnold R.	Asst	Iowa State	PHD	88	Iowa	1988
Cox, Arthur T.	Asst	No Iowa	PHD	91	Iowa	1988
Cox, Charles M.	Assoc	Brigham Yg	PHD	78	U Wash	1965
Cox, Edwin B.	Prof	Boston Univ	PHD		Penn	
Cox, John Carrington	Prof	MIT	PHD			
Normura Professor of Finance						
Cox, Larry A.	Asst	Georgia	PHD		S Carol	
Cox, Raymond A. K.	Assoc	Cen Michigan	PHD	86	Mich St	1989
Cox, Samuel H.	Prof	Michigan St	PHD		LSU	
A.J. Pasant Chair in Life Insurance and Financeial Services						
Coyne, Christopher	Asst	St Joseph	PHD	86	Temple	1978
Coyne, Thomas J.	Prof	John Carroll	PHD		WstrnRes	1981
Crabb, Ronald R.	Asst	Wis-Whitewat	PHD		Madison	1986
Crane, Donald B.	Prof	CS-Fullerton	DBA		S Calif	1976
Crane, Dwight B.	Prof	Harvard	PHD	65	Car Mel	1969
Crary, David T.	Prof	Louisiana St	PHD	66	Ohio St	1972
Crawford, John E.	Asst	David Lipsc	PHD		Alabama	
Crawford, Peggy Joyce	Assoc	George Mason	PHD	79	Purdue	1982
Crego, Carl R.	Asst	Pace	DBA		Geo Wash	1985
Cretien, Paul D.	Prof	Baylor	PHD		Texas	1985
Creviston, D. Carlene	Inst	Ball State	MA	62	Ball St	1973
Crew, Michael A.	H-Pr	Rutgers-Newk	PHD		Bradford	
Crick, T.	Assoc	Detroit Merc	PHD	81	Iowa	1981
Crocker, Kevin	Asst	Athabasca Un	MBA	82	Windsor	1986
Crockett Jr., John H.	C-Ac	George Mason	PHD	75	N Carol	1985
Cromwell, Nancy	Asst	So Alabama	PHD		Georgia	1991
Crosby, Suzanne M.	Asst	Iona	PHD	89	No Ill	1988
Cross, Mark L.	Assoc	Louisiana Te	PHD		Missouri	1987
Croteau, Barbara A.	C-As	N Adams St	MBA		Providen	
Crowley, Frederick D.	Asst	Ind-Purdue	PHD	84	NYU	1982
Crum, Lawrence Lee	Prof	Texas	PHD	61	Texas	1969
Texas Commerce Bancshares, Inc., Centennial Professor in Commercial Banking						
Crum, Roy Lee	C-Pr	Florida	PHD	74	Texas	1974
Crunkleto, Jon R.	Assoc	Old Dominion	PHD		S Carol	1978
Crutchley, Claire E.	Asst	Auburn	PHD		Va Tech	1989
Cudd, Robert M.	Prof	SE Louisiana	PHD		Arkansas	1977
Cudjoe, Kwamena A.	Assoc	Ark-Pine Blf	PHD		Penn St	1987
Cummings, Michael	Asst	Barton	MBA		E Carol	1983
Cummins, J. David	Prof	Pennsylvania				
Harry J. Loman Professor of Property & Liability Insurance						
Cunningham, Dixon C.	Prof	Furman	DBA	70	Virginia	1983
Cunningham, Donald F.	Assoc	Baylor	PHD		Ohio St	1984
Cuny, Charles	Asst	Calif-Irvine	PHD	89	Stanford	1989
Curammeng, Mary	Inst	Hawaii Pacif	MACC		Hawaii	
Curcio, Richard J.	Prof	Kent State	PHD	73	Penn St	1971
Curley, Anthony J.	Prof	Penn State	PHD	69	Penn	1970
Curley, Michael D.	C-Pr	Kennesaw St	PHD	74	Kentucky	1984
Currie, David M.	Assoc	Rollins	PHD	76	S Carol	1978
Curtis, Wayne C.	Prof	Troy St	PHD	71	Miss St	1989
Curtis, William	H-As	Hardin-Simm	ABD	76	Texas	1976
Cutler, Mary M.	Asst	Central Conn	PHD			1987
Cyr, Don	Assoc	Saskatchewan	ABD		Alberta	1990
D'Antonio, Lou	Assoc	Denver	DBA		Colorado	1980

D'Arcy, Stephen P.	Assoc	Illinois	PHD	82	Illinois	1981
D'Souza, Rudolph E.	Assoc	Delaware	PHD		So Carol	
Dadgostar, B.	Assoc	Lakehead U	PHD			1983
Dagher, Samir P.	Prof	Marywood	PHD	74	Ohio St	1989
Daghestani, Eddie	Assoc	Barry	PHD		Colorado	1988
Dahl, Drew C.	Asst	Utah State	PHD	85	Tenn	1988
Dahlquist, Julie D.	Asst	St Marys-Txs	ABD		Tx A&M	
Daigler, Robert T.	Assoc	Fla Internat	PHD	76	Oklahoma	
Daines, Robert H.	Prof	Brigham Yg	DBA	66	Indiana	1959
Dale, Walter R.	Asst	Chicago St	LLM	83	J Marsha	1989
Dalrymple, Brent B.	Prof	Tx-Pan Amer	PHD	70	LSU	1989
Damanpour, Faramarz	Prof	Jms Madison	PHD	77	Texas	1980
Damodaran, Aswath	Assoc	New York U	PHD	85	UCLA	
Dandapani, Krishnan	Assoc	Fla Internat	PHD		Penn St	
Danford, Gregory	Assoc	Augustana SD	PHD	87	Wash St	1990
Daniel, Cornelia M.	Asst	Westfield St	PHD		Mass	1990
Daniel, Donnie L.	C-Pr	So Miss	PHD	73	Illinois	1977
Daniels, Kenneth N.	Asst	Virg Comm	PHD	91	Conn	1990
Dann, Larry	Prof	Oregon	PHD	80	UCLA	1977
Richard W. Lindholm Professor of Finance and Taxation						
Dare, William	Asst	Fla Atlantic	ABD		Tx Tech	1991
Dark, Frederick H.	Asst	Iowa State	PHD	87	Utah	1988
Darnell, Jerome C.	H-Pr	Colorado	DBA	65	Indiana	1965
Darr, Frank	Asst	Ohio State	JD		Ohio St	
Dash Jr., Gordon H.	C-Pr	Rhode Island	DBA	78	Colorado	1979
DaSilva Rosa, Raymond	STut	W Australia	BCOM	85	W Austra	1986
Daskin, Alan J.	Asst	Boston Univ	PHD		MIT	
Dasso, Jerome J.	Prof	Oregon	PHD	64	Wiscon	1966
H. T. Miner Professor of Real Estate						
Datta, Sudip	Asst	Bentley	PHD	89	SUNY	1989
Daves, Phillip R.	Asst	Tennessee	PHD		N Carol	
Davidge, William	Prof	Miss College	PHD	75		1988
Davidson III, Wallace N.	Prof	So Illinois	PHD	82	Ohio St	1989
Rehn Professor of Finance						
Davis, Alfred	Assoc	Queen's Univ	PHD		Penn St	1983
Davis, Eleanor	Inst	Clarkson	MBA	85	Plymouth	1989
Davis, Harry M.	C-Pr	Appalach St	PHD		Georgia	1977
Davis, Kevin T.	Prof	Melbourne U	MEC	72	ANU	1985
Davis, Maria F.	Asst	St Marys-Txs	MBA	77	Trinity	
Davison, Carl W.	Inst	Minot St	MBA		S Illin	1989
Dawson, Steven	C-Pr	Hawaii-Manoa	PHD	71	Michigan	1971
Day, Ted E.	Assoc	Texas-Dallas	PHD	81	Stanford	1990
De La Torre, Chris	Asst	Nebraska	PHD	90	Texas	1989
De Mong, Richard F.	Prof	Virginia	DBA		Colorado	
De, Soumendra N.	Asst	Evansville	DBA	88	So Illin	1988
Dean, Stephen F.	Inst	Georgia St	MI		Geor St	
DeAngelo, Harry	Prof	So Calif	PHD	77	UCLA	1991
Charles E. Cook/Community Bank Chair in Banking Finance & Business Economics						
Deans, Robert H.	Dean	CS-Long Bch	PHD	66	Pitt	
Deastlov, Frank	Assoc	Western Conn				
Deaves, Richard W.	Asst	McMaster	PHD		Toronto	
DeBondt, Werner	Asst	Wisconsin	PHD	85	Cornell	1984
Debrecht, Dennis M.	Asst	Carroll	PHD		Iowa St	1984
Deely, Thomas J.	Inst	Providence	MBA		St Johns	1976
DeFusco, Richard A.	Assoc	Nebraska	PHD	85	Tenn	1985
Degabriele, M. Rosalle	Asst	New So Wales	MCOM		NS Wales	1989
DeGennaro, R. P.	Asst	Tennessee	PHD		Ohio St	
Delgado, Francisco	Asst	Duke	PHD		Penn	
DelIva, Wilfred L.	Assoc	Villanova	PHD	80	Oklahoma	1987
DeLosSantos, Adora	Asst	Robt Morris	PHD		Penn St	
DeMarzo, Peter	Asst	Northwestern	PHD	89	Stanford	
Demaskey, Andrea	Asst	Nevada-Reno	PHD	87	Kent St	1986
Dempsey, Michael	Lect	Univ Leeds	PHD			1990
Denard, Deborah	Asst	Jackson St	TD		Tx So	1988
Denis, David J.	Asst	Virg Tech	PHD	88	Michigan	1989
Denis, Diane K.	Asst	Virg Tech	MBA	81	Cranfiel	1989
Denker, Claudia	Asst	Montana	DBA	90	La Tech	1990
Dennick-Ream, Zane A.	Asst	Robt Morris	MBA		Iowa	
Denning, Karen Craft	Asst	W Virginia	PHD	86	Pitt	1987
Dennis, Charles N.	Prof	So Miss	PHD	72	Arkansas	1972
Dermine, Jean	Assoc	INSEAD	PHD	82	Louvain	1982
Dermody, Jaime Cuevas	Asst	Ill-Chicago	PHD		Penn	1984
Desai, Anand S.	Asst	Florida	PHD		Michigan	1987
Deshpande, Shreesh D.	Asst	San Diego				
Desreumaux, James O.	Assoc	Corpus Chris	DBA		Miss St	
Detemple, Jerome	Assoc	Columbia	PHD	83	Penn	1984
DeThomas, Arthur R.	Prof	Valdosta St	DBA		Miss St	1977
Devaney, Michael T.	Assoc	SE Missouri	PHD	82	Arkansas	1988
DeVille, Susan	Asst	Baldwin-Wal	PHD		Case Wes	
Devine, John W.	Prof	Murray State	PHD	62	Indiana	1963

Dhatt, Yoshwonb	Assoc	So Colorado	PHD		
Dheeriya, Prakash L.	Prof	CS-Dominquez			
Dhillon, Upinder S.	Asst	SUNY-Bingham	PHD	86 LSU	1987
Dhir, Krishna S.	Dir	Penn St-Harr	DBA	75 Colorado	1991
Diallo, Alahassane	Assoc	E Michigan	PHD	85 Ohio St	1985
Diamond, Douglas W.	Prof	Chicago	PHD	80 Yale	1979
Dibee, Khalil	Prof	Seattle	PHD	62 Texas	1964
Dickens, Ross N.	Asst	Louisiana Te	DBA	Tenn	1991
Dickerson, Bodil	Inst	Oregon State	MBA	84 Oreg St	1981
Dickey, Ron	Prof	F Dick-Madis	PHD		
Dickinson, Amy	Asst	Fla Atlantic	PHD	89 Fla St	1989
Dierkens, Nathalie	Asst	INSEAD	PHD	86 MIT	1987
Dike, Stephen	Adj	Southeastern	PHD		
Dilbeck, Harold R.	Emer	CS-Long Bch			
Dill, Bernard	Prof	Bloomsburg	DBA	71 Geo Wash	1968
Diltz, J. David	Assoc	Tx-Arlington	PHD	80 Illinois	1987
Dimkoff, Gregg	C-Pr	Grand Valley	PHD	78 Mich St	1975
Dimovski, Bill	Lect	Deakin Univ	MBA	82 Geo St	1985
Diskin, Barry A.	Prof	Florida St	PHD	82 Geo St	1980
Diz, Fernando	Asst	Syracuse	PHD	89 Cornell	1989
Do, Andrew Q.	Asst	San Diego St	PHD	LSU	1990
Dobson, John	Assoc	Cal Poly-SLO	PHD	88 S Carol	1990
Dodds, Colin J.	Prof	St Marys-Cdn			
Doenges, R. Conrad	Prof	Texas	DBA	65 Colorado	1964
Arthur Andersen & Co. Alumni Centennial Professor in Finance					
Doerpinglaus, Helen I.	Asst	So Carolina	PHD	89 Penn	
Doherty, Neil A.	Prof	Pennsylvania			
Dokko, Yoon	Asst	Illinois	PHD	84 Penn	1984
Dolde, Walter	Assoc	Connecticut	PHD	73 Yale	1990
Domian, Dale Louis	Asst	Michigan St			
Dominick, John A.	Prof	Arkansas	PHD	Alabama	1970
Arkansas Bankers Assoc Chair in Banking & J.W. Bellamey Chair of Bank & Fin					
Domonkos, John A.	C-Ac$	Cleveland St	PHD	72 Case Wes	1969
Donahue, Thomas	Prof	Baldwin-Wal	DBA	S Calif	
Donaldson, Gordon	Prof	Harvard	DCS	56 Harvard	
Donaldson, John B.	Prof	Columbia	PHD	76 Car Mel	1977
Donleavy, G. D.	Asst	Un Hong Kong			
Doran, Paul	Lect	London Econ	PHD	85 Glasgow	1990
Dorfman, Mark S.	Prof	Ark-Ltl Rock	PHD	Illinois	
Dorigan, Michael	Asst	St Johns	PHD		
Dorp, Kieter	Asst	St Marys-Cdn			
Dothan, Michael	Prof	Minnesota	PHD		
Dougherty, Kevin	Asst	Wis-Parkside	PHD	91 Arizona	1990
Douglas, Patricia C.	Asst	Mary Baldwin	MS	90 Virginia	1990
Doukas, John	C-Pr	Old Dominion	PHD	NYU	1989
Dowen, Richard J.	Assoc	No Illinois	PHD	83 SUNY Bin	1983
Dowling, William A.	C	Augusta	DBA	84 Tenn	1990
Downe, Edward	C	New Haven	PHD	N Sch Re	
Downey, Gerald	Prof	Mass-Lowell	PHD	71 Boston C	
Downs, Thomas W.	Assoc	Alabama	PHD	Purdue	1989
Doyel, Tom	Prof	CS-Fresno	PHD	71 UCLA	1970
Doyle, Barry W.	Assoc	San Francisc	PHD	Oregon	
Dran Jr., John J.	Assoc	No Illinois	PHD	70 Kent St	1982
Dravid, Ajay R.	Asst	Pennsylvania	PHD	90 Stanford	1989
Drenk, Dean	Assoc	Montana St	PHD	74 Michigan	
Drescher, Sol	Assoc	NY Inst Tech	PHD		
Driemeier, Donald H.	Assoc	Mo-St Louis	DBA	69 Wash U	1965
Driscoll, Vincent	C	Quinnipiac	PHD	N Sch So	
Driver, Betty A.	VLect	Murray State	MBA	MurraySt	1983
Driver, Robert E.	C-Ac	Houston Bapt	PHD	73 Texas	1988
Prince-Chavanne Professor in Christian Business Ethics					
Droms, William G.	Prof	Georgetown	DBA	75 Geo Wash	1973
Drzycimski, Eugene	Prof	Wis-Oshkosh	PHD	66 Mich St	1970
Duan, Jin-Chuan	Asst	McGill Univ	PHD	Wiscon	1986
Dubofsky, David A.	Assoc	Texas A&M	PHD	82 U Wash	1981
Duchatelet, Martine	Assoc	Barry	PHD	Stanford	1989
Ducy, Mary E.	Asst	Tx Southern	MSA	Geo Wash	
Dudley, Dean A.	Prof	E Illinois	PHD	65 U Wash	1985
Duett Jr., Edwin H.	Asst	Miss State	PHD	87 Georgia	1987
Duffie, J. Darrell	Assoc	Stanford	PHD	84 Stanford	1984
Duggal, Rakesh	Asst	SE Louisiana	PHD	Arkansas	1989
Dugger, Patty I.	Prof	David Lipsc	EDS	Peabody	
Duhala, Karen	Assoc	Indiana-PA	PHD	87 Penn St	1990
Dukas, Stephen P.	Asst	Kansas State	PHD	90 Fla St	1990
Dukes, William P.	Prof	Texas Tech	PHD	68 Cornell	1968
Dumas, Bernard	Prof	Pennsylvania	PHD	73 Columbia	1990
Nippon Life Professor of Finance					
Duncan, Frederick H.	Assoc	Winthrop	PHD	S Carol	
Dunkeiberg, John	Assoc	Wake Forest	PHD	S Carol	1983
Dunlap, James W.	Dean$	Ind-Purdue	PHD	63 Arkansas	1991

Name	Rank	School	Degree	Yr	From	Yr
Dunlop, Ian	Lect	W Australia	PHD	90	Queensla	1988
Dunn, Bradford	Asst	Utica	MS			1984
Dunn, Michael	Prof	CS-Northrdge	PHD	71	UCLA	1968
Dunning, John	VProf	Rutgers-Newk	PHD		Upsala	
State of New Jersey Professor of International Business						
Dunsdon, David	Inst	Oregon State	MBA	80	Cen Mich	1981
Dunstan, James C.	Prof	Virg-Grad	DBA	73	Virginia	1973
Durst, David R.	Prof	Akron	DBA	72	Geo St	1968
Duvic, Robert C.	Lect	Texas	PHD	90	Texas	1989
Dwyer, Jr., Paul F.	Asst	Siena Coll	JD		New Eng	1987
Dybvig, Philip H.	Prof	Wash Univ	PHD	79	Yale	1988
Boatmen's Bancshares Professor of Banking and Finance						
Dyer, Michael A.	Asst	Bowling Gr	ABD		Illinois	1991
Dyl, Edward A.	H-Pr	Arizona	PHD	73	Stanford	1987
DyReyes, Felix	Prof	Metro State	PHD	74	Iowa St	1977
Eades, Kenneth M.	Assoc	Virg-Grad	PHD		Purdue	
Eagle, David M.	Asst	Eastern Wash	PHD	86	Minn	1989
Eaker, Mark R.	Prof	Virg-Grad	PHD		Stanford	
Business and Political Economy Chair						
Eakins, Stanley G.	Assoc	East Carol	PHD	90	Ariz St	1990
Earl Jr., John H.	Assoc	Richmond	PHD		Ariz St	1981
Easterwood, John C.	Asst	Houston	PHD	85	Texas	1984
Eastman, Kevin L.	Asst	Florida St	ABD		Penn	1989
Ebeid, Fred J.	Prof	W Illinois	PHD		Illinois	1970
Eberhart, Allan C.	Asst	Georgetown	PHD	89	S Carol	1989
Eberle, Jeanette	Asst	Hardin-Simm	PHD	91	Columbia	1990
Eberly, Janice C.	Asst	Pennsylvania	PHD	91	MIT	1991
James G. Campbell, Jr. Memorial Term Assistant Professor of Finance						
Echevarria, David	Asst	Mass-Lowell	PHD	88	Mass	
Eck, James Robert	Prof	Washburn	PHD	79	Illinois	1979
Eckbo, Espen	C	British Colu				
Eddy, Albert R.	Assoc	Loyola-Maryl	PHD		SUNY Buf	1984
Edelman, Richard B.	Prof	American U	DBA	75	Maryland	1983
Edelstein, Robert H.	Prof	Cal-Berkeley	PHD		Harvard	
Chair in Real Estate Development						
Ederington, Louis H.	Assoc	Oklahoma	PHD	72	Wash U	1989
Edgeworth, Hubert C.	Assoc	Florida St	PHD	57	Alabama	1957
Edleson, Michael	Asst	Harvard				
Edmond, Steve	Asst	Clark Atlant	MBA		Tx South	
Edmonds, Charles P.	Prof	Auburn	PHD	72	Arkansas	1973
Edmonds, Jim	Asst	Freed Hardem	JD	80	Tenn	1983
Edmondson, Rey	Inst	Athens	MBA		Alabama	1975
Edmondson, Robert	Asst	Barton	MBA		Wake For	1991
Edmunds, John C.	Assoc	Babson	DBA		Harvard	
Eduardo, Marcelo	Asst	Delta State	MBA	86	Delta St	1986
Edwards, Adrian	Prof	W Michigan	PHD	67	Ohio St	
Edwards, Charles	VProf	Belmont	PHD		N Carol	
Edwards, Franklin R.	C-Pr	Columbia	PHD	64	Harvard	1966
Edwards, Pamela	Lect	Manches Inst			Manchest	1990
Edwards, Robert G.	Prof	Henderson St	PHD	68	Arkansas	1969
Ehrhardt, Michael C.	Asst	Tennessee	PHD		Ga Tech	
Ehsani, Hassan B.	Asst	Mass-Boston	PHD	87	Houston	1991
Ehud, I. Ronn	Assoc	Texas	PHD	83	Stanford	1988
Eicher, Jeffrey	C-Ac	Clarion	JD		Pitt	1983
Eisemann, Peter C.	Prof	Georgia St	PHD	74	Michigan	1974
Eisenbeis, Robert A.	C-Pr	No Carolina	PHD	71	Wiscon	1982
Wachovia Professor of Banking; Associate Dean of Research						
Eisenhauer, Joseph G.	Asst	Canisius	PHD	91	SUNY-Buf	1989
Eiteman, David K.	Prof	UCLA	PHD	59	Northwes	1959
Ekern, Steinar	Prof	Norwegian	PHD		Stanford	
Ekman, Peter D.	Asst	Kansas State	PHD	89	Purdue	1989
Ekpoudom, Edidiong O.	Assoc	Hampton	PHD		Nebraska	
Elan, Don	Assoc	San Jose St				
Elayan, Fayez A.	Asst	SW Missouri	PHD	85	LSU	1990
Eldridge, Robert M.	Asst	Fairfield	DBA	87	Geo Wash	1988
Elebash, Clarence C.	C-Pr	West Florida	DBA	75	Fla St	1976
Elfakhani, Said	Assoc	Saskatchewan	PHD			1988
Elias, Carlos		Manhattan				
Elike, Uchenna I.	Asst	Alabama A&M	PHD		Alabama	
Ellert, James C.		Intl Mgt Dev	PHD		Chicago	
Elliott, Robert Stephen	Assoc	NW St of La	PHD		La Tech	
Ellis, Barry	Asst	SE Okla St	MBA	80	E Texas	1982
Ellis, David M.	Asst	Texas A&M	PHD	91	N Carol	1990
Ellis, John W.	Assoc	Colorado St	PHD		Mich St	
Ellis, M. E.	Assoc	St Johns	PHD		S Carol	
Elsaid, Hussein H.	Prof	So Illinois	PHD	68	Illinois	1967
Elston, Frank A.	Asst	E New Mexico	PHD	79	Virginia	1988
Elton, Edwin J.	Prof	New York U	PHD	70	Car Mel	
Nomura Professor of Finance						
Ely, David P.	Asst	San Diego St	PHD		Ohio St	1986

Name	Rank	School	Degree	Yr	Where	Yr
Emami, Aristotle	Asst	Adelphi	PHD	81	Wash St	
Emanuel, David C.	Assoc	Texas-Dallas	PHD	81	Stanford	1991
Emery, Douglas R.	Prof	SUNY-Bingham	PHD	77	Kansas	1989
Emery, Gary W.	D-Ac	Oklahoma	PHD	78	Kansas	1987
Emery, John T.	C-Pr	CS-Fullerton	PHD		Wash	1985
Emery, Richard F.	C-As	Linfield	MBA	71	ENMU	1986
Emerzian, A. D. Joseph	Prof	Connecticut	PHD	55	New York	1948
Eng, Maximo	Prof	St Johns	PHD	66	NYU	
Engberg, Holger L.	Assoc	New York U	PHD	63	Columbia	
Engler, George N.	Prof	CS-L Angeles	PHD	69	UCLA	1975
English, John	SLect	Tasmania	MBA			1989
Epplin, Maryellen P.	Inst	Central Okla	ABD		Okla St	1991
Erickson, John R.	Assoc	CS-Fullerton	PHD		CA-Davis	1979
Erickson, Mary K.	Lect	George Mason	MBA	85	G Mason	1985
Erickson, Suzanne M.	Asst	Seattle	PHD	87	U Wash	1986
Escarraz, Donald R.	Prof	North Dakota	PHD	64	Okla St	1984
Esensoy, Yilmaz	Prof	Alabama A&M	PHD	69	Ohio St	
Essayyad, Musa	Assoc	Alaska-Ancho	PHD	85	Alabama	1985
William H. Seward Professor of International Finance						
Essig, James	Asst	Ramapo	PHD		New York	
Etebari, Ahmad	Assoc	New Hampshir	PHD	79	N Texas	1980
Etter, Wayne E.	Prof	Texas A&M	PHD	68	Texas	1969
Ettinger, Marilyn	Asst	Jersey City	MBA		NYU	
Eubanks, Dorothy G.	Assoc	David Lipsc	MA		Peabody	
Eun, Cheol S.	Assoc	Maryland	PHD	81	New York	
on leave to Pennsylvania						
Evans, Dorla A.	Assoc	Alabama-Hunt	PHD	85	Arkansas	1991
Evans, Jocelyn	Asst	Iowa	PHD	91	So Carol	1991
Evans, Michael D.	Lect	Adelaide	MBA			1989
Evensen, Donald	Prof	Luther	MBA	48	Northwes	1950
Ewald, Peter K.	Prof	Lg-Isl-Post	PHD		NYU	
Ewedemi, Soga O.	Prof	Clarion	PHD		Penn	1988
Ewert, David C.	Prof	Georgia St	PHD	68	Stanford	1969
Ewing, Janet S.	H-Ac	Mary Baldwin	ABD		Va Comm	1977
Eyssell, Thomas H.	Asst	Mo-St Louis	PHD		Tx A&M	
Ezzamel, Mahmoud	Prof	Manches Inst	PHD		Sohampto	1990
Ezzell, John R.	Prof	Penn State	PHD	79	Penn St	1970
Fabozzi, Frank J.	VProf	MIT	PHD			
Fabritius, Michael M.	Prof	Mary Hrdn-By	PHD	87	Texas	1987
Fairbanks, John G.	Asst	Ferris State	MBA		Cen Mich	1980
Fairburn, Wayne A.	Prof	Central Wash	PHD	75	Mich St	1972
Fairchild, Keith WM	Assoc	Tx-S Antonio	PHD	86	Texas	1981
Fairchild, Lisa M.	Asst	Loyola-Maryl	BBA			1991
Falkowski, Daniel C.	Assoc	Canisius	PHD	72	New York	1975
Fama, Eugene F.	Prof	Chicago	PHD	64	Chicago	1963
Theodore O. Yntema Distinguished Service Professor of Finance						
Fanara, Philip	C-Pr	Howard	PHD	80	Indiana	1985
Fang, Hsing	Prof	CS-L Angeles	PHD	86	Ariz St	
Fang, Jimmy	Lect	City Poly HK	PHD	90	CUNY	1991
Farhi, Victor	Assoc	Lg-Isl-Post	PHD		NYU	
Faria, Hugo J.	Asst	Northeastern	PHD		S Carol	1988
Farr, William Kendrick	Asst	Georgia Col	PHD		Georgia	1985
Farragher, Edward J.	Assoc	Oakland	PHD	71	Illinois	1987
Farsio, Farzad	Asst	E Montana	PHD	89	Claremon	1987
Faseruk, Alexander J.	Assoc	Memorial Un	PHD	90	Mass	1988
Fatemi, Ali M.	H-Pr	Kansas State	PHD	79	Okla St	1980
Robert F. Hagans Professor						
Fauchald, Thomas	Assoc	Bemidji St	MS		N Color	1982
Faulhaber, Bert C.	Prof	Ball State	PHD	56	Insbruck	1978
Fedenia, Mark	Asst	Wisconsin	PHD	88	Wiscon	1986
Fehrs, Don	Asst	Notre Dame	PHD	87	Fla St	
Feiner, J.	Inst	SUNY Old Wes	ABD			1976
Feinstein, Steven P.	Asst	Boston Univ	PHD		Yale	
Feist, William R.	C-Ac	Monmouth	PHD	87	Temple	1966
Feldhaus, William R.	Assoc	Georgia St	PHD		Geo St	
Feldman, David	Asst	Ill-Chicago	PHD		Northwes	
Feldman, Stanley	Assoc	Bentley	PHD	76	New York	1988
Felgran, Steven D.	Asst	Northeastern	PHD		Yale	1989
Felheim, Robert	Assoc	Adelphi	PHD	74	NYU	
Feller, James F.	Asst	Mid Tenn St	PHD	79	Florida	1984
Fellows, Paul	Assoc	NE Missouri	PHD	85	Illinois	1991
Feltmate, Ian	Lect	Arcadia Univ	ABD	90	W Ontar	1919
Felton, James M.	Asst	Cen Michigan	PHD	90	Arkansas	1989
Fenster, Steven R.	VProf	Harvard				
Ferner, Jack D.	Lect	Wake Fr-Grad	MBA	55	Harvard	1971
Ferreira, Eurico J.	Assoc	Indiana St				
Ferri, Michael G.	Prof	George Mason	PHD	75	N Carol	1987
Ferris, Stephen P.	Assoc	Virg Tech	PHD	84	Pitt	1983
on leave to Memphis State						
Ferson, Wayne E.	Assoc	Chicago	PHD	82	Stanford	1983

Fetherston, Thomas A.	Asst	Alabama-Birm	PHD	85	Rutgers	1987
Fewings, David E.	Assoc	Western Wash	PHD	75	Toronto	1985
Field, Irv	Prof	Wash State	PHD	66	Oregon	1966
Fielding, William T.	Prof	Jacksonvl St	PHD		S Carol	1968
Fields, Joseph A.	Assoc	Connecticut	PHD	86	Penn St	1984
Fields, M. Andrew	Assoc	Delaware	PHD		Va Tech	
Figlewski, Stephen	Prof	New York U	PHD	76	MIT	
Filbeck, Greg	Asst	Miami U-Ohio	PHD	86	Kentucky	
Filer, John E.	Prof	So Alabama	PHD		Chicago	1987
Finch, J. Howard	Asst	Tenn-Chattan	ABD		Alabama	1991
Fineberg, George		Southeastern	MBA		American	
Finkelstein, John M.	C-Ac	New Mexico	PHD	76	Penn	1984
Finkler, Steven A.	Prof	New York-Gr	PHD	78	Stanford	1984
Finlay, Jim	C-Ac	W Illinois	MBA		La Tech	1984
Finn, Frank J.	Dean	Queensland	PHD	81	Queensld	1969
Finnerty, Joseph E.	Prof	Illinois	PHD	74	Michigan	1984
Finucane, Thomas J.	Assoc	Syracuse	PHD	86	Cornell	1985
Fischer, Donald E.	Prof	Texas-Tyler	DBA	65	Wash	1990
Fischer, Gerald C.	Prof	Temple	PHD	60	Columbia	1967
Fischer, Klaus P.	Asst	Univ Laval	PHD	85	Tx A&M	1990
Fish, Gerald	Lect	Loughborough	BA		Wales	
Fishcer, Klaus P.	Asst	Fordham				
Fisher, Charles C.	Prof	Pittsburg St	PHD		Wash St	
Fisher, Jeffrey D.	Assoc	Indiana				
Fisher, Lawrence	Prof	Rutgers-Newk	PHD		Chicago	
First Fidelity Bank Reseach Professor						
Fishman, Michael	Asst	Northwestern	PHD	86	Chicago	
Fitzgerald, John F.	C-Pr	Ball State	PHD	71	Wiscon	1984
Fitzgerald, Pat	Prof	Okla City	PHD		Texas	1981
Fitzpatrick, Brian	Asst	Rockhurst	PHD	90	St Louis	1990
Flanigan, George B.	Prof	N Car-Greens	PHD	73	Iowa	1973
Flannery, Mark J.	Prof	Florida	PHD		Yale	1989
Barnett Bank Eminent Scholar						
Fleming, Donald E.	Prof	Central Okla	DBA	74	Tx Tech	1976
Fleming, Garry A.	Assoc	Roanoke Col	PHD		Kentucky	1987
Flesaker, Bjorn	Asst	Illinois	PHD	90	Berkeley	1990
Fletcher, Donna	Asst	Bentley	PHD	91	LeHigh	1991
Fletcher, Harold D.	Prof	Loyola-Maryl	PHD		Illinois	1981
Fletcher, J. Stuart	Asst	Appalach St	PHD		Fla St	1988
Fletcher, John L.	Prof	Tenn-Martin	PHD		Miss	
Fletcher, Kenneth	Inst	Txs-Perm Bas	ABD		Tx Tech	
Fletcher, Peggy L.	Lect	Northeastern	ABD		Pitt	1985
Fletcher, Robert G.	Prof	CS-Bakersf	PHD	71	UCLA	1974
Flory-Truett, Lila	D-Pr	Tx-S Antonio	PHD	72	Iowa	1975
Flower, George M.	Asst	Houston Bapt	MBA	83	Wiscon	19
Flowers, Edward B.	Assoc	St Johns	PHD		Geo St	
Floyd, Charles F.	Prof	Georgia	PHD		N Carol	
Fluck, Roland F.	Prof	Fort Lewis	DBA	84	Colorado	1984
Fluker, John E.	Dean$	Ark-Pine Blf	PHD		Houston	1989
Foerster, Steve R.	Asst	W Ontario	PHD		Penn	1987
Folks, William R.	Prof	So Carolina	DBA	70	Harvard	1969
Followill, Richard A.	Asst	Appalach St	PHD		Alabama	1985
Foo, Jennifer	Asst	Stetson	PHD		Northeas	
Foost, James D.	Assoc	Indianapolis	PHD		S Carol	1982
Foote, William	Assoc	LeMoyne	PHD	84	Fordham	1988
Forbes, Ronald W.	Prof	SUNY-Albany	PHD	68	SUNY-Buf	1968
Forbes, Shawn M.	Prof	Alabama-Hunt	PHD	85	Georgia	1988
on leave to Georgia Southern, 1991-92						
Ford Jr., Robert M.	Asst	LaSierra	MBA	86	LomaLind	1986
Ford, Deborah A.	Assoc	Baltimore	PHD		Penn	
Ford, John	Prof	Maine	PHD	77	Harvard	1981
Ford, Joseph William	C-Ac	Iona	PHD	66	Fordham	1984
Ford, Kent	Asst	Dickinson St				
Ford, William F.	Prof	Mid Tenn St	PHD	66	Michigan	1991
Weatherford Chair of Finance						
Forsaith, David M.	Lect	Flinders Un	MSC	75	London	1990
Forster, Margaret M.	Asst	Ohio State	PHD		Cornell	
Forsyth, John D.	Prof	Duke	PHD		Illinois	
Fortin, Rich	Asst	New Mex St	PHD	88	Kansas	1988
Fortson, James C.	Prof	Georgia	PHD	69	Georgia	1969
Foster, Douglas F.	Assoc	Duke	PHD		Cornell	
Foster, F. Douglas	Asst	Duke	PHD		Cornell	
Foster, Paul L.	Prof	St Joseph	DBA	69	Virginia	1979
Foster, Phillip	Assoc	Metro State	PHD	68	Oregon	1976
Foster, Richard W.	Asst	Colo-Denver				
Foster, Robert D.	Prof	Am Grad Intl	PHD	68	Oregon	
Fountain, J. R.	Prof	CS-Sacrament	PHD	77	UCLA	1976
Fowler, David J.	C-Ac	York Univ	PHD		Toronto	1983
Frame, Robert J.	Prof	So Methodist	PHD	66	Colorado	1966
France, Virginia Grace	Asst	Illinois	PHD	86	Chicago	1988

Francfort, Alfred J.	Prof	Jms Madison	PHD	72	Pitt	1983
Francis, Jack Clark	Prof	CUNY-Baruch	PHD	69	U Wash	
Franke, Janice R.	Asst	Ohio State	JD		Ohio St	
Frankfurter, George M.	Prof	Louisiana St	PHD	71	SUNY-Buf	1987
Lloyd F. Collette Endowed Chair of Insurance and Financial Markets						
Frankle, Alan W.	Prof	Boise State	PHD		Arizona	1984
Franko, Lawrence	Prof	Mass-Boston	DBA	69	Harvard	1986
Fraser, Donald R.	Prof	Texas A&M	PHD	69	Arizona	1972
Fraser, Pat	Lect	Dundee	PHD	90	City	1987
Frasier, Charales E.	Assoc	David Lipsc	MA		Alabama	
Frazier, Jennifer	Asst	Jms Madison		90	Jms Madi	1991
Fredman, Albert J.	Prof	CS-Fullerton	PHD		UCLA	1975
Fredrikson, E. Bruce	Prof	Syracuse	PHD	63	Columbia	1966
Free, Veronica A.	Prof	No Alabama	PHD	70	Miss St	1984
Freeman, James		Columbia	MBA	69	Wharton	1990
Freitas, Lewis P.	Prof	Hawaii-Manoa	PHD	66	Columbia	1966
Fremault, Anne	Asst	Boston Univ	PHD		Penn	
French, Dan W.	C-Ac	Tx Christian	PHD	79	La Tech	1984
French, Kenneth R.	Prof	Chicago	PHD	83	Rochest	1983
Leo Melamed Professor of Finance						
Frenois, Jean-Pierre	Assoc	HEC-Montreal				
Freund, Steven	Asst	Penn State	PHD		NYU	1989
Fricke, Cedric	Prof	Mich-Dearbor	PHD	59	Michigan	1960
Frieder, Larry A.	Prof	Florida A&M	PHD		Arizona	
Friedland, Seymour	Prof	York Univ	PHD		Harvard	
Friedman, Harry M.	Adj	New York U	PHD	72	Cal-SanB	
Friedman, Hersey H.	Prof	CUNY-Brookly	PHD			1986
Friedman, Joseph	C-Pr	Temple	PHD		Berkeley	
Frino, Alessandro	Asst	U Wollongong	MPHI		Camb	1990
Frohlich, Cheryl J.	Asst	North Fla	PHD		Illinois	
Froot, Ken	VProf	Harvard				
Frost, Ceri E.	Lect	Univ Wales	BSC	84	Aberys	1986
Frost, Peter A.	Prof	U Washington	PHD	66	UCLA	1969
Fruhan, William E.	C-Pr	Harvard	DBA	70	Harvard	
Fry, Clifford	Asst	Houston	PHD	72	Tx A&M	1975
Fucaloro, Anthony	Dean$	Claremont	PHD	69	Arizona	1974
Fugar, Chris	Assoc	Dillard	PHD			
Fuhrmann, Thomas		St Joseph				
Fukasawa, Yoshikazu	Prof	Midwest St	PHD		Kans St	1978
Fulghieri, Paolo	Asst	Columbia	PHD	87	Penn	1987
Fuller, Beverly R.	Asst	Portland St	PHD	87	Va Tech	1987
Fuller, Floyd	C	Lees-McRae				
Fuller-Love, Nerys	Lect	Univ Wales	MBA	87	Aberys	1989
Fulmer Jr., John G.	H-Pr	Tenn-Chattan	PHD	70	Alabama	1977
Vieth Professor						
Fung, Hung-Gay	Asst	Baltimore	PHD		Geo St	
Furneis, Bill	Asst	Winthrop	PHD	90	Toronto	1988
Furst, Richard W.	Dean	Kentucky	DBA	68	Wash	1981
Gadd, Susan G.	Asst	Cumberland	MS	89	Kentucky	1990
Gaertner, Robert	Assoc	Lk Superior	MBA		Notre Dm	1965
Gagnon, Jean-Marie	Prof	Univ Laval	PHD	70	Chicago	1961
Gagnon, Louis	Asst	Queen's Univ	PHD		Toronto	1989
Gahir, Fikry S.	Prof	Utah	PHD	66	Wiscon	1970
Gahlon, James	Assoc	Minnesota				
Gallagher, Timothy J.	Prof	Colorado St	PHD		Illinois	
Gallinger, George W.	Asst	Arizona St	PHD		Purdue	1977
Galloway, James		Rochest Tech	PHD		Virginia	
Galvan, Mary	Asst	St Xavier	PHD		N Ill	1987
Gandal, Neil S.	Asst	Boston Univ	PHD		Berkeley	
Gandhi, Dev	Prof	Univ Ottawa	PHD	76	Wharton	1982
Gardner, Eldon J.	Assoc	U Lethbridge	PHD			1982
Gardner, Mona J.	Dean	Ill Wesleyan	PHD		Cinn	1988
Adlai H. Rust Professor of Finance/Insurance						
Gardner, William	Asst	San Francisc	PHD	59	Indiana	1975
Garg, Ramesh	Prof	E Michigan	DBA	74	Kent St	1978
Garino, James	Assoc	Athens	MA		Indiana	1968
Garman, Mark B.	Prof	Cal-Berkeley	PHD	69	Car Mel	1969
Garnett, Robert H.	Assoc	SW Texas St	PHD	81	Penn	1982
Garrison, Sharon H.	Assoc	East Tenn St	PHD	83	Tx-Arlin	1986
Gart, Alan	Prof	Mass-Dartmou	PHD	67	Penn	1989
Gash, Dennis N.	C-As	Aurora	MS	78	Northwes	1989
Gasper, Juli-Ann	Assoc	Creighton	PHD	84	Nebraska	1982
Gatti, James F.	Assoc	Vermont	PHD	72	Cornell	1972
Gatzlaff, Dean H.	Asst	Florida St	PHD	90	Florida	1990
Gaumnitz, Jack E.	Prof	Kansas	PHD	67	Stanford	1967
Gaunt, Deborah S.	Inst	Georgia St	MI		Geor St	
Gaunt, Larry D.	Prof	Georgia St	PHD		Geo St	
Gaus, Kenneth	Adj	Providence	MBA		Penn	1990
Gay, Gerald D.	Prof	Georgia St	PHD		Florida	
Gay, R. Keith	Asst	USAF Academy	MBA		UCLA	

Name	Rank	School	Degree	Year	From	Year
Gazmararian, George	C-Pr	Alma	MBA		Detroit	1966
Charels A. Dana Professor of Business Administration						
Geddert, John M.	Asst	Nebraska	PHD	89	Purdue	1989
Geiger, Joseph J.	Prof	Idaho	EDD	77	Colorado	1988
Geltner, David M.	Asst	Cincinnati	PHD	89	MIT	1989
Gendreau, Brian	Adj	New York U	MA	76	JohnsHop	
Gendreau, Richard J.	Prof	Bemidji St	MBS		St Cloud	1969
Gendron, Michel	Assoc	Univ Laval	PHD		Brit Col	1985
Gennotte, Gerard	Asst	Cal-Berkeley	PHD	85	MIT	1985
Gentry, James A.	Prof	Illinois	PHD	66	Indiana	1966
George, Thomas J.	Asst	Ohio State	PHD		Michigan	
Gerdsen, Julie B.	Asst	Xavier	PHD	81	Cinn	1988
Geske, Robert L.	Assoc	UCLA	PHD	77	Berkeley	1977
Ghandhi, Jamshed K. S.	Assoc	Pennsylvania	PHD	60	Cambridg	1965
Ghannadian, Frank	Asst	Mercer-Atlan	PHD		Geo St	1988
Ghanty, A. Sam	Asst	WI-Green Bay	PHD	82	Wiscon	1984
Ghazanfari, Farrokh		CS-Pomona	DBA	85	Miss St	1990
Ghee, William K.	Prof	Baylor	PHD		Penn	1981
Ghosh, Asim	Asst	Rider	PHD		Kentucky	
Ghosh, Chinmoy	Asst	Connecticut	PHD	86	Penn St	1986
Ghosh, Satyajit P.	Asst	Scranton	PHD	90	SUNY-Buf	1986
Giaccotto, Carmelo	Assoc	Connecticut	PHD	78	Kentucky	1981
Gibbons, Michael R.	Prof	Pennsylvania	PHD	80	Chicago	1989
Drexel Burnham Lambert Professor of Investment Banking						
Gibbs, Paul	SLect	Bournemouth	BA			1991
Gibson, Frank F.	C-Pr	Ohio State	JD	52	New York	
Gibson, Robert A.	Asst	Old Dominion	MS		Wiscon	1985
Gibson, Robert W.	Prof	Deakin Univ	PHD	76	Cinn	1977
Gilberg, Erika	Asst	Illinois St	PHD	86	S Ill	1989
Giles, Leon G.	Prof	Denver	PHD	71	Illinois	1970
Gill, Edward	VProf	CS-Chico	PHD	68	Oregon	1991
Giller, Marshall	Assoc	Ferris State	PHD			1978
Gillespie, William B.	Assoc	St Louis	PHD		Florida	
Gilmer, R. H.	Assoc	Miss State	PHD	82	Illinoia	1988
Gilmore, James E.	Dean	Sam Houston	EDD	69	Houston	1956
Gilroy, N.	Lect	U New Englan	MBA			1991
Gilson, Preston	Asst	Fort Hays St	MA	82	Sangamon	1988
Gilson, Stuart C.	Asst	Harvard				
Gilster, John E.	Assoc	Michigan St				
Gitman, Lawrence J.	Prof	San Diego St	PHD		Cinn	1989
Giunta, A. John	Prof	Scranton	PHD	56	Syracuse	1960
Gjerde, Oystein	Asst	Norwegian	DOEC			
Gjerum, Per Ivar	Asst	Norwegian				
Glascock, John L.	Assoc	Louisiana St	PHD	84	N Texas	1988
Glasgo, Philip W.	Assoc	Xavier	PHD	80	Ohio St	1984
Gleason, Anne E.	Asst	Oklahoma St	PHD	90	Fla St	1989
Glen, Jack	Asst	Pennsylvania	PHD	87	Northwes	1987
Alumni of Goldman Sachs Term Assistant Professor of Finance						
Glenn, David W.	Assoc	Utah	PHD	74	Stanford	1975
Glosten, Larry R.	Assoc	Columbia	PHD	80	Northwes	1989
Glubok, Allan	Prof	Ark-Ltl Rock	DBA		Wash U	
Gniewosz, Gerhardt	Asst	U Wollongong	MCOM			1990
Goddard, Jack B.	Inst	NE Okla St	MS	76	N Txs St	1976
Goebel, Paul	Assoc	Texas Tech	PHD	80	Georgia	1980
Goetzmann, William	Asst	Columbia	PHD	90	Yale	1990
Goff, Delbert C.	Asst	Appalach St	PHD	91	Fla St	1991
Goff, J. Larry	Prof	Fort Lewis	JD	72	Oklahoma	1985
Goho, Thomas S.	Assoc	Wake Forest	PHD		N Carol	1977
Golbe, Devra	Assoc	CUNY-Hunter	PHD		Brown	
Goldberg, Lawrence G	Prof	U Miami	PHD	72	Chicago	1981
Goldenberg, David H.	Assoc	Rensselaer	PHD		Florida	1986
Goldman, Sam	Assoc	New Mex St	JD	65	Northwes	1980
Goldsten, Joseph	Prof	Wash & Lee				
Golec, Joseph H.	Asst	Clark	PHD	86	Wash U	
Gombola, Michael J.	Assoc	Drexel	PHD		So Carol	1985
Gomersall, Nicholas	Asst	Luther	PHD	90	Cornell	1967
Gonzalez, Jose A.	Assoc	Youngstown	PHD	81	Kent St	
Goodacre, Alan	Asst	Un Stirling	PHD	82	Exeter	1981
Goode, Rudyard B.	Prof	Montana	PHD	53	Virginia	1974
Goodman, Seymour S.	Prof	Tulane	PHD	59	J Hopkin	1959
Goolsby, William C.	C-Pr	Wash State	PHD	74	Wiscon	1989
Goon, Robert		Bridgeport				
Gordon, Bruce L.	Inst	No Alabama	MA	86	Alabama	1986
Gordon, Myron J.	Prof	Univ Toronto	PHD		Harvard	1970
Gordon, Robert	Adj	New York U				
Gordon-McNeil, Elizabeth	Lect	Howard	MPA	88	Howard	1988
Goree, Janace Harvey	Assoc	Jackson St	JD		Illinois	1974
Gorman, Raymond F.	Assoc	Miami U-Ohio	DBA	82	Indiana	
Gorton, Gary Bernard	Assoc	Pennsylvania	PHD	83	Rochest	1990
Goslings, Jan Willem	Prof	Limburg	PHD	74	Amsterdam	1989

Name	Rank	School	Degree	Yr	Deg School	Yr
Gosnell, Thomas F.	Asst	U Miami	PHD	87	Va Tech	1987
Gould, Lawrence I.	H-Pr	U Manitoba	PHD	75	Toronto	1985
Goulet, Waldemar M.	Dean	Wright State	PHD	73	Mich St	1975
Gover, Timothy D.	Prof	E Illinois	MS	61	Illinois	1963
Grace, Steven H.	V-Ac	Tx Southern	PHD		Houston	
Graddy, Duane B.	Prof	Mid Tenn St	PHD	74	Lehigh	1972
Graham, Alexander Steven	Asst	Mississippi	PHD		Queen's	
Graham, Lise	Asst	Wis-La Cross	ABD		Miss St	1991
Graham, Sharon S.	Assoc	Cen Florida	PHD		Penn St	1984
Grambo Jr., Ralph W.	Assoc	Scranton	PHD	73	Penn	1973
Granger, George L.	Prof	East Tenn St	PHD	71	Penn	1961
Grant, Clare	Asst	Un Stirling	MS	86	Glasgow	1987
Grant, Donald	Dean$	Azusa Pacif	EDD		So Calif	1991
Grant, Dwight	Prof	New Mexico	PHD	74	Penn	1985
Gray, Otha L.	Prof	Lander	PHD	61	Alabama	1985
Greaney Jr., Walter T.	Prof	Boston Coll	PHD	60	Harvard	
Grebis, Thomas J.	Asst	Drexel	MBA		Drexel	1958
Green, Richard C.	Assoc	Carnegie Mel	PHD		Wiscon	1982
Greenbaum, Stuart I.	Prof	Northwestern	PHD	64	JHopkins	
Norman Strunk Distinguished Professor of Financial Institutions; Assoc Dean						
Greenhut, John G.	Assoc	Ariz St-West	PHD			1989
Greenleaf, James A.	Assoc	Lehigh	PHD	73	New York	1970
Greenlee, Robert	Assoc	Emporia St	EDS	64	Kan St	1967
Greenwald, Bruce	Prof	Columbia	PHD	78	MIT	1991
Greer, Gaylon E.	Prof	Memphis St	PHD	74	Colorado	1986
Fogelman Professor of Real Estate						
Greer, Jack	Asst	Oral Roberts	MBA	65	Oklahoma	1990
Gregory, Deborah W.	Asst	Georgia	PHD	87	Florida	1988
Gregory, Owen K.	Assoc	Ill-Chicago	PHD		Case Wes	
Gregory, W.	Lect	U New Englan	MEC			1990
Gregory-Allen, Russell B.	Asst	Rutgers-Camd	PHD		N Txs St	
Gressis, Nicolas	Prof	Wright State	PHD	75	Penn St	1979
Greubel, Robert T.	Prof	NE Okla St	PHD	72	Arkansas	1965
Griepentrog, Gary L.	Assoc	Wis-Oshkosh				
Grier, Paul C.	Assoc	SUNY-Bingham	PHD	71	New York	1976
Griffin, C. Ramon	Assoc	Metro State	PHD	79	Geo St	1986
Griffin, Paul A.	Prof	Cal-Davis	PHD		Ohio St	
Griffith, Reynolds	Assoc	S F Austin	PHD	66	Texas	1989
Griffiths, Mark	Asst	Wis-Milwauke	PHD	90	W Ontari	1988
Griggs, Frank	Assoc	Grand Valley	PHD	90	Ariz St	1990
Griggs, Jack	Dean	Abilene Chr	PHD	71	Texas	1991
Grim, John L.	Assoc	Youngstown	PHD	66	Kent St	
Grimshaw, Alan E.	Assoc	Towson State	DBA	79	Maryland	1987
Grinblatt, Mark S.	Assoc	UCLA	PHD	82	Yale	1981
Gritta, Richard D.	Prof	Portland	DBA	71	Maryland	1972
Gronwoller, Paul L.	Asst	Wyoming	PHD			1985
Groppelli, Angelico	Prof	Hofstra	PHD	70	NYU	1977
Gross, M. A. Ernestine	Asst	New So Wales	PHD		Sydney	1986
Gross, Thomas	Asst	Wis-Plattev	MBA		Madison	1991
Grossman, Sanford J.	Prof	Pennsylvania	PHD	75	Chicago	1989
Steinberg Trustee Professor of Finance						
Groth, John C.	Prof	Texas A&M	PHD	76	Purdue	1975
Grube, R. Corwin	Prof	Drake	PHD	74	Mich St	1988
Gruber, Martin J.	C-Pr	New York U	PHD	66	Columbia	
Nomura Professor of Finance						
Grundy, Bruce	Lect	Pennsylvania	PHD	78	Chicago	1990
Donald B. Stott Lecturer in Finance						
Grunewald, Alan E.	Prof	Michigan St	PHD	55	Wiscon	
Gudikunst, Arthur C.	Assoc	Bryant	PHD	74	Renssel	1990
Guedes, Jose	Prof	So Methodist	PHD	90	Ohio St	1990
Guenther, Harry P.	Prof	No Michigan	DBA	59	Indiana	1989
Guidry, K.	Asst	Nicholls St	PHD			1990
Guin, Larry D.	Assoc	Murray State	DBA		Miss St	1978
Guithues, Henry J.	Prof	St Louis	PHD	64	St Louis	
Gullett, Nell S.	Asst	Tenn-Martin	MBA		Tenn	
Gultekin, Mustafa N.	Assoc	No Carolina	PHD	84	New York	1985
Gultekin, N. Bulent	Assoc	Pennsylvania	PHD	76	Penn	1990
Gunay, Erdal	Asst	Univ Windsor				
Gunter, Rick	Inst	Abilene Chr	MBA	87	W Tx St	1990
Gunthorpe, D.	Asst	Tennessee	PHD		Florida	
Guo, Chen	Asst	Univ Ottawa	PHD			1990
Guo, Enyang	Asst	Millersville	PHD	91	Va Tech	1982
Gup, Benton E.	Prof	Alabama	PHD	66	Cinn	1983
Robert Hunt Cochrane/Alabama Bankers Chair						
Gupta, Atul	Asst	Bentley	PHD	85	Texas	
Gupta, Keshav	Asst	Bentley	PHD	84	Pitt	1987
Gupta, Manak C.	Prof	Temple	PHD	67	UCLA	
Gupta, Manoj	Asst	Wichita St	PHD	90	Illinois	1990
Gurley, Darryl E. J.	Lect	Northeastern	ABD		Colorado	
Gustavson, Sandra G.	H-Pr	Georgia	PHD		Illinois	

Guttentag, Jack M.	Prof	Pennsylvania	PHD	58 Columbia	1962
Jacob Safra Professor of International Banking					
Guttha, Raj	Assoc	Bloomsburg			1988
Gwaliam, D.	Lect	Univ Wales			
Gyourko, Joseph E.	Assoc	Pennsylvania	PHD	84 Chicago	1984
Hachey, George	C-Ac	Bentley	PHD	85 New Hamp	1983
Hackbart, Merl M.	Prof	Kentucky	PHD	68 Kans St	
Hackert, Ann M.	Asst	Idaho State	PHD	87 Iowa Sta	1984
Hackett Jr., Charles Wilson	Prof	Texas	DBA	55 U Wash	1966
The Capitol City Savings Regents Fellow					
Hadaway, Beverly L.	Assoc	Texas	PHD	80 Alabama	1980
Haddad, Kamal M.	Prof	San Diego St	PHD	Nebraska	1981
Haddad, Mahmoud M.	Asst	Wayne State	PHD	84 Alabama	1984
Hademenos, George	Asst	Southern	PHD	Houston	
Hadley, Garland R.	Prof	Midwest St	PHD	74 Missouri	1983
Hagerman, Robert L.	Prof	SUNY-Buffalo	PHD	72 Rochest	1982
Hagerty, Kathleen M.	Asst	Northwestern	PHD	85 Stanford	
Hagias, James	Assoc	Illinois St	PHD	75 Cinn	1986
Haight, G. Timothy	C-Pr	Towson State	DBA	80 Geo Wash	1989
Hajizadeh, Avaz	Prof	N Adams St	PHD	Renssel	
Hakala, Donald R.	H-Pr	East Txs St	PHD	Indiana	
Hakanson, Nils H.	Prof	Cal-Berkeley	PHD	66 UCLA	1969
Sylvan C. Coleman Professor of Finance and Accounting					
Hakim, Sam	Asst	Neb-Omaha	MA	Cal St	
Haley, Charles W.	Prof	U Washington	PHD	68 Stanford	1966
Hall, Anita J.	Inst	Clarion	MS	Penn St	1977
Hall, Jr., John R.	Asst	Missouri	ABD	Indiana	1991
Hall, Katherine H.	Lect	Flinders Un	LLB	Adelaide	1990
Hall, Pamela L.	Asst	Western Wash	PHD	91 La Tech	1990
Hall, Yvonne C.	Assoc	New Hamp Col	PHD	Col St	
Halloran, John A.	Assoc	Notre Dame			
Halpern, Paul	Prof	Univ Toronto	PHD	Chicago	1971
Halpin, Annette A.	Asst	Beaver	ABD	Drexel	1983
Halsey, Ken	Prof	Wayne St Col	PHD	73 N Colora	1987
Haltiner, James R.	Prof	Wm & Mary	DBA	Virginia	1976
Hamada, Robert S.	Prof	Chicago	PHD	69 MIT	1966
Edward Eagle Brown Professor of Finance					
Hamao, Yasushi	Asst	Columbia	PHD	87 Yale	1990
Hamid, Shahid	Asst	Fla Internat	PHD	88 Maryland	
Hamid, Shaikh A.	Inst	Boston Univ		Dhaka	
Hamilton, Janet G.	Asst	Portland St	PHD	86 Mich St	1986
Hamilton, Karen		Rhode Island			
Hamilton, Robert	Lect	Loughborough	MPHL	Glasgow	
Hamilton, Sally A.	Asst	Santa Clara	PHD	87 UCLA	1988
Hamilton, Thomas R.	Asst	St Marys-Txs	ABD	Tx Tech	
Hammerbacher, Irene M.	Prof	Iona	PHD	69 NYU	1969
Hammermeister, John F.	Inst	Augustana IL	MBA	Oregon	
Hammond, J. D.	Dean	Penn State	PHD	61 Penn	1961
Hampton, John J.	Prof	Insurance	DBA	Geo Wash	
Han, Ki C.	Asst	Suffolk	PHD	Mich St	
Han, Li-Ming	Asst	Wash State	PHD	87 Texas	1988
Hanawa, Toshiya	Prof	Hitotsubashi	DBA	80 Hitotsub	1969
Hancock, D'Anne Gorum	Asst	Mo-St Louis	PHD	N Orlean	
Hand, John H.	Prof	Auburn	PHD	65 MIT	1974
Handa, Puneet	Asst	New York U	PHD	86 Iowa	
Handley, Mark	Inst	Frostburg St	MBA	Ball St	1988
Handorf, William C.	Prof	George Wash	PHD		
Haney, Jack	Inst	NE Okla St	MBA		1991
Haney, Richard L.	Assoc	Texas A&M	PHD	74 Indiana	1978
Hankins, Kenneth P.	Prof	Youngstown	PHD	79 Arkansas	
Hannum, John E.	Asst	Alfred	PHD	N Carol	1987
Hanrahan, J. Robert	Prof	Brock Univ	MBA	60 Harvard	1975
Hansen, Robert	Assoc	Dartmouth	PHD	84 UCLA	1983
Hansen, Robert S.	Prof	Virg Tech	PHD	78 Florida	1979
Hansen, Terje	Prof	Norwegian	PHD	Yale	
Hanson, Robert C.	Asst	San Diego St	PHD	Utah	1987
Hanweck, Gerald A.	Prof	George Mason	PHD	Wash U	1986
Harawa, Rex	Asst	SUNY-Geneseo	PHD	SUNY-Bin	1989
Hardcastle, Rodney	Asst	Pacific Unio	MBA	89 Gold Gt	1989
Hardigree, Donald W.	Asst	Nev-L Vegas	PHD	Georgia	1990
Hardin, William F.	Prof	Arkansas	PHD	66 N Carol	1968
Hardouvelis, Gikas	Assoc	Rutgers-N Br	PHD	84 UC	1989
Hardt II, Henry W.	Assoc	Buena Vista	MBA	Arkansas	1983
Hardwick, Phil	Prof	Bournemouth	PHD		1974
Harjes, Richard H.	Inst	Arizona	ABD		
Harju, Melvin	Prof	La St-Shreve	PHD	72 Florida	1977
Harlow III, W. Van	Asst	Arizona	PHD	86 Texas	1986
Harlow, Charles	Prof	CS-Long Bch	DBA	68 S Calif	1968
Harlow, Forrest W.	Prof	Angelo State	PHD	76 N Texas	1983
Harmel Jr., Robert	Asst	Midwest St			

Name	Rank	School	Degree	Yr	PhD From	Yr
Harpaz, Giora	Assoc	CUNY-Baruch	PHD		Indiana	
Harper, Charles P.	Prof	San Jose St	PHD	79	Tx A&M	1984
Harrington, Diana R.	C-Pr	Virg-Grad	DBA		Virginia	
Harrington, John	Prof	Seton Hall	PHD	77	New York	
Harrington, Scott E.	Prof	So Carolina	PHD	77	Illinois	
Harris Jr., J. M.	Assoc	Clemson	PHD	80	S Carol	1986
Harris Snr., Malcolm C.	Asst	New So Wales	PHD		Conn	1991
Harris, Ellie	Asst	Minnesota	PHD			
Harris, Frederick	Assoc	Wake Fr-Grad	PHD		Virginia	1990
Harris, Kimberly H.	Asst	Wm Jewell	JD	78	Kansas	1986
Harris, Malcolm C.	Assoc	St Johns	PHD			
Harris, Milton	Prof	Chicago	PHD	74	Chicago	1987

Chicago Board of Trade Professor of Finance and Business Economics

Harris, Robert S.	Prof	Virg-Grad	PHD		Princeto	

C. Stewart Sheppard Professor of Business Administration

Name	Rank	School	Degree	Yr	PhD From	Yr
Harris, Thomas C.	Asst	New So Wales	PHD		UCLA	1991
Harriss, James D.	Asst	N Car-Wilmin	DBA	88	Miss St	1986
Hartl, Robert J.	Assoc	So Indiana	PHD	77	Arkansas	1989
Hartviksen, K. R.	D-Ac	Lakehead U	MBA		York	1979
Hartzell, David J.	Assoc	No Carolina	PHD	85	N Carol	1988
Harvey, Campbell R.	Assoc	Duke	PHD	86	Chicago	
Harvey, Mahlon O.	Lect	U Manitoba	MBA	70	Wash St	1973
Harvey, Roger K.	Emer	Ohio State	DBA	67	Indiana	1967
Hasbrouck, Joel	Assoc	New York U	PHD	81	Penn	
Haskins, James P.	Asst	No Colorado	PHD	91	Colo St	1987
Haslem, John A.	Prof	Maryland	PHD	67	N Carol	
Hass, Jerome E.	Prof	Cornell	PHD	69	Car Mel	1967
Hassan, M. Kabir	Asst	New Orleans	PHD	90	Nebraska	1990
Hassanein, Saad	Prof	Marymount	PHD		Catholic	1988
Hasseldine, D. John	Lect	Canterbury	MCOM	87	Canterbu	1988
Hasty, John M.	Prof	Tenn State	PHD	73	Geo St	1973
Hatch, James E.	Prof	W Ontario	PHD		Michigan	1972
Hatem, John J.	Asst	Geo Southern	PHD	90	LSU	1990
Hatfield, Gay B.	Asst	Mississippi	DBA		La Tech	
Hathaway, Neville	Assoc	Melbourne U	PHD			1984
Haugen, Robert	Prof	Calif-Irvine	PHD	68	Illinois	1989
Hawes, Elizabeth	Asst	Keene State	MBA	84	Mass	1986
Hawkins, Clark A.	Prof	New Mex St	PHD	64	Purdue	1985
Hawley, Delvin D.	Asst	Mississippi	MBA		Mich St	
Hay, Richard	Prof	Pittsburg St	PHD		Kent St	
Haye, Eric	Asst	St Johns	PHD			
Hayes, III, Samuel L.	Prof	Harvard				
Haynes, James F.	H	Athens	PHD		Vanderbi	1981
Hays, Fred H.	Prof	Mo-Kansas Ct	DBA		Kent St	1971
Hays, Patrick Allen	Assoc	W Carolina	PHD	77	N Carol	1985
Haywood, Charles F.	Prof	Kentucky	PHD	55	Calif	
Haywood, Dale	Prof	Northwood	PHD	80		1972
Hazen, Marinos	Assoc	Cedarville	ABD		Cleve St	1983
He, Hua	Asst	Cal-Berkeley	PHD	90	MIT	1989
He, Jia	Asst	Houston	PHD	89	Penn	1991
Heal, Inez G.	Assoc	Youngstown	MBA	76	Youngstn	
Healy, Gerald	Asst	Westfield St	CLU		Amer Col	1981
Hearth, Douglas P.	H-Ac	Arkansas	PHD		Iowa	1989
Heathcotte, Bryan	Prof	Am Grad Intl	DBA	70	Indiana	
Heaton, Hal B.	Prof	Brigham Yg	PHD	83	Stanford	1982
Hebner, Kevin	Asst	York Univ	PHD		Queen's	
Heck, Jean Louis	Assoc	Villanova	PHD	83	S Carol	1983
Heck, Tom	Assoc	Jamestown	MS	75	N Dakota	1977
Heflin, Thomas L.	Prof	CS-Sacrament	PHD	72	Oregon	1984
Hegde, Shantaram P.	Assoc	Connecticut	PHD	80	Mass	1990
Heggestad, Arnold A.	Prof	Florida	PHD	73	Mich St	1974

William H. Dial Professor; Director, Financial Institutions Center

Name	Rank	School	Degree	Yr	PhD From	Yr
Heier, Jan R.	Asst	Auburn-Montg	DBA	86	Miss St	1986
Hein, Scott E.	C-Pr	Texas Tech	PHD	79	Purdue	1983
Heinowitz, Harvey J.	Asst	Adelphi	MBA	75	Adelphi	
Helms, Billy P.	H-Pr	Alabama	PHD	73	Tenn	1973
Helmuth, John	Assoc	Rochest Tech	PHD		S Carol	1981
Heltne, Mari	Assoc	Luther	PHD	88	Arizona	1968
Hemler, Michael L.	Asst	Duke	PHD	88	Chicago	
Hempel, George H.	Prof	So Methodist	PHD	64	Michigan	1977

Corrigan Professor of Finance

Hendershott, Patric H.	Prof	Ohio State	PHD	65	Purdue	

Galbreath Professor of Real Estate

Name	Rank	School	Degree	Yr	PhD From	Yr
Henderson Jr., Glenn V.	Prof	Cincinnati	DBA	74	Fla St	1987
Henderson, Malcolm R.	Prof	Columbus	PHD	65	Alabama	1970
Hendrickson, Hildegard R.	Prof	Seattle	PHD	66	U Wash	1967
Henin, Claude G. J.	C-Pr	Univ Ottawa	PHD			1971
Hennigar, Elizabeth S.	Assoc	San Diego	DBA		Indiana	
Henrie, G.	Assoc	Univ Windsor				
Henry, James B.	Dean	Louisiana St	PHD	70	Syracuse	1984

Henry, John	Prof	Georgia SW	PHD		Alabama	
Henry, William L.	Asst	Clarion	JD		West Vir	1974
Henry, William Ray	Prof	Georgia St	PHD	57	N Carol	1970
Hensel, A. C.	Assoc	Lakehead U	MBA		Case Wes	1970
Hensler, Douglas A.	Asst	Tx-Arlington	PHD	89	U Wash	1991
Henssler, Gene W.	Prof	Kennesaw St	PHD	71	Michigan	1986
Herbst, Anthony F.	Prof	Txs-El Paso	PHD		Purdue	1987
Herring, Richard J.	Prof	Pennsylvania	PHD	73	Princeton	1972
Herst, Arthur	Prof	Limburg	PHD	81	Rotterd	1989
Hertzel, Michael G.	Asst	Arizona St	PHD		Oregon	1987
Herzog, John P.	Prof	Simon Fraser				
Heshmat, Shahram	Asst	Sangamon St				
Heskel, David G.	C-Ac	Bloomsburg				1976
Hess, Daniel	Assoc	Seattle Pac	PHD	82	Arizona	1987
Hess, Patrick	Assoc	Minnesota	PHD			
Hessel, Chris	Assoc	CUNY-Baruch	PHD		NYU	
Heston, Steven	Asst	Yale	PHD		Car Mel	1989
Hettenhouse, George W.	Prof	Indiana	PHD	70	Purdue	1969
Heuson, Andrea J.	Assoc	U Miami	PHD	82	Illinois	1982
Heuson, William G.	Prof	U Miami	PHD	54	St Louis	1948
Hevert, Kathleen T.	Asst	Boston Coll	PHD		N Carol	
Hexter, J. Lawrence	Prof	Kent State	PHD	66	Wiscon	1974
Hietala, Pekka	Assoc	INSEAD	PHD	87	Stanford	1987
Higgins, Charles J.	Assoc	Loyola Marym	PHD	85	Claremon	1982
Higgins, David	Assoc	Dallas	PHD	79	Texas	
Higgins, Robert C.	Prof	U Washington	PHD	69	Stanford	1967
Hill, Kendall Pat	C-Ac	Alabama-Birm	PHD	81	Okla St	1982
Hill, Ned C.	C-Pr	Brigham Yg	PHD	76	Cornell	1987
Hill, Roger P.	C-Pr	N Car-Wilmin	PHD	68	Mich St	1970
Hilliard, Jimmy E.	Prof	Georgia	PHD	72	Tenn	1972
C. Herman & Mary Virginia Terry Chair of Finance						
Hillion, Pierre	Assoc	INSEAD	PHD	88	UCLA	1987
Hindelang, T. J.	H-Pr	Drexel	DBA	73	Indiana	1973
Hindy, Ayman M.	Asst	Stanford	PHD	90	MIT	1990
Hines, D. Spencer	Assoc	Hawaii Pacif	MBA	82	Pepperdi	1989
Hines, Mary Alice	Prof	Washburn	PHD	67	Ohio St	1982
C. W. King Chair of Real Estate and Finance						
Hinton, Walter Val	Prof	Delta State	PHD	82	Arkansas	1989
Hiremath, B. N.	Prof	Fisk				
Hiris, Lorene	Asst	Lg-Isl-Post	MBA		Lg Isl	
Hirschey, Mark	Prof	Kansas	PHD	77	Wiscon	1988
Hirshleifer, David A.	Assoc	UCLA	PHD	85	Chicago	1984
Hirt, Geoffrey A.	C	DePaul	PHD		Illinois	
Hite, Gailen L.	Assoc	Columbia	PHD	75	U Wash	1987
Hitselberger, Thomas E.	V-As	Loyola-Maryl	MA		Geo Wash	1986
Hittle, Linda C.	Asst	San Diego St	PHD		Colorado	1987
Hlawitschka, Walter F.	Asst	Fairfield	PHD	89	Virginia	1988
Ho, Hsien-Chan	C $	Nat Taiwan U	PHD	85	Texas	1986
Ho, T. S.	Lect	U Lancaster	PHD		Lancaste	
Ho, Y. K.	Head	City Poly HK	PHD	79	Wiscon	1990
Ho, Y. W.	SLect	City Poly HK	MSC	82	Manchest	1989
Hoban Jr., James P.	Prof	Ball State	PHD	76	Utah	1976
Hobson, Hugh	Prof	Jms Madison	PHD	76	Georgia	1983
Hochman, Shalom J.	Assoc	Houston	PHD	80	Toronto	1980
Hocking, Ralph T.	Prof	Shippensburg	DBA	72	Kent St	1972
Hodges Jr., J. Frank	Prof	Geo Southern	PHD	73	Georgia	1980
Hodgin, Robert F.	Assoc	Houston-Cl L	DA		No Illin	
Hodrick, Robert J.	Prof	Northwestern	PHD	76	Chicago	
Tokai Bank Professor of International Finance						
Hoeven, James A.	Assoc	Colorado St	PHD		Colo St	
Hofflander, Alfred E.	Prof	UCLA	PHD	64	Penn	1966
Hoffmeister, J. Ronald	Assoc	Arizona St	PHD		Illinois	1983
Hogan, Arthur M. B.	Asst	George Mason	PHD	88	Texas	1988
Hogan, Stephen	Assoc	E Illinois	PHD	77	Oklahoma	1990
Hogenboom, Marion	Asst	Elmhurst	MM		Northwes	1984
Holbrook, S. Thomas	Prof	Tenn State	PHD	74	Georgia	1971
Holden, Craig	Asst	Indiana				
Holder, Mark E.	Asst	Valparaiso	ABD		Kent St	1990
Holderness, Clifford	Asst	Boston Coll	JD		Stanford	
Holdren, Don P.	Prof	Marshall	PHD	79	Nebraska	
Holland, John B.	SLect	Glasgow Univ	PHD	78	CNAA	1979
Holland, Kevin M. P.	Lect	Univ Wales	BSC	80	Bangor	1989
Holland, Michael M.	Asst	Villanova	DBA	75	S Calif	1982
Holliday, Richard	Assoc	Insurance	MA		Insuranc	
Hollinger, Robert D.	Prof	Kansas State	PHD	64	Ks St	1966
Holman Jr., Walter R.	Assoc	Loyola-Maryl	PHD		Syracuse	1982
Holt, Arthur L.	Prof	Towson State	PHD	67		1975
Holthausen, D.	H-Pr	N Carol St	PHD	74	Northwes	1976
Homafair, Ghassem	Prof	Mid Tenn St	PHD	82	Alabama	1982
Hong, Derek M.	Inst	USAF Academy	MBA		Stanford	

Name	Rank	School	Degree	Yr	From	Yr
Hood, Jerry M.	Prof	Loyola-N Orl	PHD	71	Tx Tech	1989
Hood, William	Asst	Mercer-Macon	MBA	84	N Carol	1984
Hooks, Jon A.	Asst	Albion	PHD	89	Mich St	1989
Hopewell, Michael H.	Assoc	Oregon	PHD	72	U Wash	1969
Hopusch, Edgar	Assoc	Grambling St	DBA	70	Colorado	1983
Hoque, Monzurul	Asst	Loyola-Chicg	PHD		Illinois	1988
Horton, Howard	Asst	Mary Hrdn-By	MBA	80	SW Tx St	1981
Horton, Joanne	Tutor	Univ Wales	BSC	90	Aberys	1991
Horvath, Philip A.	Prof	Bradley	DBA	75	Kent St	1977
Horvitz, Paul M.	Prof	Houston	PHD	58	MIT	1977

Judge James A. Elkins Professor of Banking and Finance

Horwitz, Ronald M.	Prof	Oakland	PHD	64	Mich St	1979
Hoskins, Colin	Prof	Univ Alberta	PHD	67	Manchest	1966
Hourigan, Frank E.	Assoc	Insurance	EDM		Columbia	
Houston, Arthur L.	Assoc	San Diego St	PHD		U Wash	1986
Houston, Joel F.	Asst	Florida	PHD		Penn	1987
How, Janice	STut	W Australia	BCOM	89	W Austra	1989
Howard, Barbara	Inst	SUNY-Geneseo	MBA		Renssela	1988
Howard, Charles Thomas	Assoc	Denver	PHD		U Wash	1978
Howard, Lorraine M.	Asst	Temple	ABD		Penn	
Howard, Robert	Assoc	N Carol A&T	PHD	78	Ohio St	
Howard, Sue Beck	Inst	North Fla	MBA	83	Fla St	
Howat, John D.	Assoc	Wis-Whitewat	PHD		Illinois	1976
Howcroft, J. Barry	SLect	Loughborough	MSC		Wales	
Howe, John S.	Assoc	Louisiana St	PHD	81	Purdue	1988
Howe, Keith M.	Prof	DePaul	PHD		Nebraska	

Dr. William M. Scholl Professor of Finance

Howe, Thomas S.	Asst	Illinois St	PHD	86	Tx Tech	1985
Hoyt, Dick	Assoc	Nev-L Vegas	PHD			
Hoyt, Robert	Asst	Georgia				
Hsia, Chi-Cheng	Prof	Portland St	PHD	74	UCLA	1988
Hsiao, James C.	Prof	So Conn St	PHD		Conn	
Hsiao, P.	Prof	San Fran St	PHD	89	S Calif	1989
Hsieh, Chen-Ho		La St-Shreve	PHD	90	LSU	1989
Hsieh, David A.	Assoc	Duke	PHD		MIT	
Hsin, Chin-Wen	Asst	CUNY-Baruch	PHD		Illinois	
Hsu, Der-Ann	Prof	Wis-Milwauke	PHD	73	Wiscon	1977
Hsu, H. Christine	Prof	CS-Chico	PHD		Penn St	
Huang, Chi-fu	Prof	MIT	PHD			
Huang, Gow-Cheng	Asst	Alabama St	PHD	91	Alabama	1989
Huang, Roger	Assoc	Vanderbilt	PHD	80	Penn	1988
Hubbard, Carl M.	Assoc	Trinity	PHD	75	Tx Tech	1975
Hubbard, Elbert W.	Assoc	Virg Comm	PHD	73	Cinn	1981
Huberman, Gur	Prof	Columbia	PHD	80	Yale	1989
Huckins, Larry	Asst	CUNY-Baruch	PHD		Chicago	
Huckins, Nancy	Asst	Hofstra	MPHI	91	CUNY	1991
Hudgins, Sylvia C.	Asst	Old Dominion	PHD		Va Tech	1989
Hudson, Carl D.	Asst	Auburn	PHD		Ariz St	1988
Huffman, Stephen P.	Asst	Wis-Oshkosh	PHD	90	Fla St	
Huggins, Kenneth M.	Assoc	Metro State	PHD	73	Tx Tech	1988
Hughes, William	Asst	Louisiana St	PHD	90	Georgia	1990
Hulbert, William	Assoc	W New Eng	MA		Syracuse	1972
Hull, John C.	Prof	Univ Toronto	PHD		Cranefld	1988
Hull, Robert M.	Asst	Washburn	PHD	90	Kansas	1990
Humphrey, David B.	Prof	Florida St	PHD	69	Berkeley	1991

The Fannie Wilson Smith Eminent Scholar Chair in Banking

Humphrey, John A.	Assoc	W Ontario	DBA		Harvard	1968
Hung, Mao-Wei	Asst	McGill Univ	PHD		Northwes	1990
Hunkins, Donald	Prof	Northwood	BA	71		1978
Hunt, Atha	Assoc	Chicago St	JD		DePaul	1975
Hunt, Jerry G.	Prof	East Carol	PHD	68	Colorado	1975
Hunter Jr., Richard	C $	Seton Hall	JD	76	Notre Dm	
Hunter, Hugh O.	Prof	Eastern Wash	DBA	76	S Carol	1980
Hunter, William C.	Assoc	Emory	PHD	79	Northwes	1980
Huntley, Kennes C.	Prof	Mankato St	PHD		Iowa	1967
Huntsman, Blaine	Prof	Utah	PHD	68	Penn	1969
Hussain, Riaz	Assoc	Scranton	PHD	73	J Hopkin	1967
Hussan, Mahboubal	Asst	New Hamp Col	MA		New Hamp	
Huston, Kevin	Asst	Marian	JD		Duke	1989
Hutchins, Robert C.	Prof	San Diego St	PHD	71	S Calif	1968
Hutchins, Ron	Assoc	E Michigan	PHD	77	Missouri	1977
Hutchinson, P.	H-Pr	U New Englan	PHD			1979
Hykes, Richard	Inst	Drexel	MBA		New York	1988
Hynes, Tim	Lect	St Fran Xav				
Hysom, John Leland	Assoc	George Mason	PHD	73	American	1977
Ibbotson, Roger	Prac	Yale	PHD		Chicago	1984
Ice, Randall D.	Asst	Central Okla	MBA	82	Michigan	1984
Ikein, Augustine	Assoc	Delaware St	PHD		Atlanta	
Ikenberry, David	Asst	Rice				
Iledare, Wumi	Asst	Fayetteville	PHD		W Virg	

Name	Rank	School	Degree	Yr	Degree School	Yr
Ilter, Selim S.	C	St John Fish	PHD		Geo St	
Impson, C. Michael	Asst	North Texas	DBA	87	La Tech	1987
Ingersoll, Jon	Prof	Yale	PHD		MIT	1982
Ingram, Franklin Jerry	Prof	NE Louisiana	PHD	79	S Carol	1986
Ingram, Marcus	Asst	Clark Atlant	PHD		Geo St	1991
Ingram, Virginia C.	Asst	Kennesaw St	MA	79	Cen Fla	1986
Ingram, William c.	Prof	David Lipsc	PHD		W Virgin	
Inman, James E.	Prof	Akron	JD	71	Akron	1966
Inman, Robert	Prof	Pennsylvania	PHD	71	Harvard	1971
Senior Fellow, Leonard Davis Institute of Health Economics						
Inselbag, Isik	Adj	Pennsylvania	PHD	73	Columbia	1979
Ip, Yiukeung	Prof	Chinese HK				
Irons, Edward D.	Dean	Clark Atlant	DBA	60	Harvard	1990
Isakson, Hans R.	Prof	No Iowa	PHD	78	Wiscon	1990
Isberg, Steven C.	Asst	Baltimore	PHD		SUNY-Bin	
Isimbabi, Michael		Morgan State	PHD			
Iskandar, Mai E.	Asst	No Illinois	PHD	86	Missouri	1991
Israel, Ronen	Asst	Michigan	PHD	89	Northwes	1987
Issa, Ahmad D.	Prof	W Michigan	PHD	67	Illinois	
Ivry, David A.	Prof	Hartford	MBA		Wharton	
Iwarere, Jide	Asst	Howard	PHD	87	Georgia	1986
Izan, Hy	Prof	W Australia	PHD	78	Chicago	1981
Jabbour, George	Asst	George Wash	PHD			
Jacklin, Charles J.	Asst	Stanford	PHD	85	Stanford	1987
Jackson III, William E.	Asst	Boston Univ	PHD		Chicago	
Jackson, James F.	Assoc	Oklahoma St	PHD	64	Texas	1963
Jackson, Raymond	C-Pr	Mass-Dartmou	PHD	67	Boston U	1973
Jackson, Robert L.	Inst	David Lipsc	MA		Cen Mich	
Jacobs, Donald P.	Dean	Northwestern	PHD	57	Columbia	
Gaylord Freeman Distinguished Professor of Banking						
Jacobs, Stanley	Assoc	Central Wash	DBA		Kent St	1983
Jacquier, Eric	Asst	Cornell	PHD	91	Chicago	1990
Jadlow, Janice W.	H-Ac	Oklahoma St	PHD		Okla St	1984
Jaffe, Jeffrey	Assoc	Pennsylvania	PHD	72	Chicago	1973
Jaffee, Dwight M.	Prof	Cal-Berkeley	PHD	68	MIT	1991
Jagannathan, Ravi	Assoc	Minnesota				
Jaggia, Priscilla	Asst	Mass-Boston	PHD	90	Indiana	1990
Jagtiani, Julapa	Asst	Syracuse	PHD	89	NYU	1990
Jahera, John S.	C-Ac	Auburn	PHD		Georgia	1980
Jakacky, Gary	Asst	Westfield St				
Jalan, Pradeep		Univ Regina				
Jalilvand, Abolhassan	C-Ac	Concordia U				
James, Charles J.	Prof	St Louis	PHD	70	St Louis	
James, Christopher	Prof	Florida	PHD	78	Michigan	1989
SunBank/William H. Dial Eminent Scholar						
James, Dennison M.		Southeastern	MA		Howard	
Jameson, Mel	Asst	Nev-L Vegas	PHD		Berkeley	1989
Janakiramanan, S.	Asst	SUNY-Albany	PHD	85	Minn	1985
Jang, Hasung	Asst	Korea Univ	PHD			1990
Janjigian, Vahan	Asst	Northeastern	PHD		Va Tech	1990
Jankowske, Wayne C.	Assoc	Xavier	PHD	75	Kentucky	1978
Jankowski, Joel R.	C-Ac	Tampa	ABD		Columbia	1986
Janowsky, Dale	Adj	Niagara				
Janus, Frank	Assoc	Pace	PHD		NYU	1965
Jarrell, Gregg A.	Prof	Rochester	PHD		Chicago	
Jarrell, Sherry L.	Asst	So Methodist	PHD	91	Chicago	1990
Jarrow, Robert A.	Prof	Cornell	PHD	79	MIT	1979
Ronald P. and Susan E. Lynch Professor of Investment Management						
Jassim, Amir A.	Prof	CS-Fresno	PHD		Georgia	1985
Jay, Nancy	Asst	Gannon				
Jayaraman, Narayanan	Asst	Georgia Tech	PHD	86	Pitt	1986
Jean, William H.	Prof	Alabama	PHD	64	Purdue	1973
Jefferis Jr., Richard H.	Asst	Colorado	PHD	85	Stanford	1990
Jegadeesh, Narasinhan	Asst	UCLA	PHD	87	Columbia	1987
Jen, Frank C.	Prof	SUNY-Buffalo	PHD	63	Wiscon	1964
Manufacturers & Traders Trust Co. Professor of Banking and Finance						
Jender, Jaime	VAsst	Wash Univ	PHD	88	Yale	1991
Jeng, Jau-lian	Asst	CS-Northrdge	PHD	91	CS-Domin	1991
Jenkins, Sarah B.	Asst	George Wash	PHD			
Jennings, Edward H.	Prof	Ohio State	PHD		Michigan	
Jennings, Robert H.	Prof	Indiana	PHD	59	Indiana	1967
Jennings, William	C $	CS-Northrdge	PHD	81	UCLA	1977
Jensen, Gerald R.	Asst	No Illinois	PHD	87	Nebraska	1987
Jensen, R. H. Marlin	Asst	Auburn	PHD		Tx A&M	1988
Jeong, Jinho	SLect	Univ Otago	PHD	91	Georgia	1991
Jernberg, Mary Jean	Inst	Mankato St	MBA		Mankato	1990
Jessell, Kenneth A.	Assoc	Fla Atlantic	PHD	85	Fla St	1983
Jin, Hyung Ki	Prof	CS-Pomona	DBA	71	S Calif	1977
Jo, Hoje	Asst	Santa Clara	PHD	86	Florida	1990
Joehnk, Michael D.	Prof	Arizona St	PHD		Arizona	1982

Jog, Vijay Mukund	Assoc	Carleton Un				
Johannes, James M.	C-Pr	Wisconsin	PHD	78	Wiscon	1984
First Wisconsin Professor of Banking						
Johansen, Thomas C.	Asst	Fort Hays St	PHD	90	Okla St	1989
John, Kose	Prof	New York U	PHD	78	Florida	
Johnsen, Thomajean	Asst	Denver	PHD		Colorado	1988
Johnsen, Thore	Prof	Norwegian	PHD		Carnegie	
Johnson, Arnell	Asst	Central Okla	ABD		Oklahoma	1980
Johnson, Clarke C.	Prof	Pace	PHD		Purdue	1979
Johnson, Craig	Prof	CS-Hayward	PHD	68	UCLA	1980
Johnson, Dale A.	Assoc	South Fla	DBA	73	Geo St	1970
Johnson, Dana J.	Prof	Virg Tech	PHD	76	Kent St	1976
Johnson, David	Asst	No Colorado	PHD	89	Tenn	1990
Johnson, David	Assoc	Pepper-Malib	PHD	89	Cinn	1991
Johnson, Eldon C.	Prof	Central Wash	MS		Colo St	1977
Johnson, Harry M.	Prof	Connecticut	PHD	62	Penn	1962
Johnson, Hazel J.	Assoc	Louisville	PHD	87	Florida	1990
Johnson, James M.	Prof	No Illinois	PHD	75	Ohio St	1987
Johnson, James R.	Assoc	Meredith	PHD		Duke	1979
Johnson, Jaqueline	Lect	W Australia	MCOM	90	W Austra	1985
Johnson, Joseph E.	Prof	N Car-Greens	DBA	69	Geo St	1969
Johnson, Keith B.	H-Pr	Connecticut	DBA	63	Wash U	1963
Johnson, Keith H.	Assoc	Kentucky	PHD	70	Illinois	
Johnson, Larry J.	Assoc	Tulsa	DBA	80	Indiana	1984
Johnson, Lewis D.	Assoc	Queen's Univ	PHD		Toronto	1981
Johnson, Linda L.	Assoc	Appalach St	PHD		Georgia	1981
Johnson, Mark S.	Asst	Idaho	PHD	87	Wash St	1987
Johnson, R. Larry	Prof	New Hamp Col	DBA		Geo Wash	
Johnson, R. Stafford	C-Pr	Xavier	PHD	76	Kentucky	1980
Johnson, Ramon E.	Prof	Utah	PHD	66	Wiscon	1965
Johnson, Raymond M.	Assoc	Auburn-Montg	PHD		Okla St	1970
Johnson, Richard D.	Assoc	Colorado St	PHD		Oregon	
Johnson, Robert R.	Asst	Creighton	PHD	88	Nebraska	1984
Johnson, Robert W.	Prof	Purdue	PHD	52	Northwes	1964
Johnson, Shane A.	Asst	Bowling Gr	PHD		LSU	1991
Johnson, Stephen A.	Asst	Txs-El Paso	PHD		Alabama	1987
Johnson, Timothy E.	Prof	Cincinnati	PHD	71	Illinois	1970
Johnston, Robert Dail	Assoc	George Mason	PHD	74	Alabama	1976
Jones Jr., Ray G.	Prof	Appalach St	DBA		Miss St	1973
Jones, C. A.	H	East Anglia	PHD		Hull	1985
Jones, Charles P.	Prof	N Carol St	PHD	69	N Carol	
Jones, Edward J.	Assoc	Utica	MBA			1976
Jones, Gail Graham	Prof	Jacksonvl St	JD		Alabama	1973
Jones, Jo Ann	Dean	Georgia Col	PHD	77	La Tech	1976
Jones, Lawrence D.	Prof	British Colu				
Jones, Robert	Prof	W Michigan	PHD	78	Notre Dm	
Jones, Steven L.	Asst	Georgia	PHD	88	Purdue	1988
Jones, Wesley W.	Inst	Geo Southern	MBA	89	Geo So	1990
Jordan, Bradford	Assoc	Missouri	PHD		Florida	
Jordan, James	Assoc	Virg Tech	PHD	80	N Carol	
Jordan, Susan D.	Asst	Missouri	PHD		Georgia	
Jordan-Wagner, James	Asst	E Illinois	PHD	89	N Texas	1990
Jorgensen, Jerry L.	Prof	Utah	PHD	65	Penn	1965
Jorion, Philippe	Assoc	Columbia	PHD	83	Chicago	1984
Jornsten, Kurt	Prof	Norwegian	DREK		Linkopin	
Jose, Manuel L.	Assoc	Akron	PHD	83	Va Tech	1990
Joshi, Yash Pal	Asst	Northeastern	PHD		Pitt	1989
Joy, O. Maurice	Prof	Kansas	PHD	69	N Carol	1969
Joyce C. Hall Distinguished Professor of Business						
Joyce, Theodore	Assoc	CUNY-Baruch	PHD		CUNY	
Jozsa Jr., Frank P.	Assoc	Pfeiffer	PHD	77	Geo St	1991
Jud, G. Donald	H-Pr	N Car-Greens	PHD	71	Iowa	1971
Jung, A.	Prof	San Fran St	PHD	90	Berkeley	1989
Jung, Minje	Asst	Mississippi	PHD	89	Fla St	
Junkus, Joan C.	Assoc	DePaul	PHD		Illinois	
Jurn, Iksu	Asst	Saginaw Vall	PHD	89	Nebraska	1990
Kadapakkam, Palani-Rasan	Asst	Houston	PHD	85	Michigan	1985
Kaen, Fred R.	Prof	New Hampshir	PHD	72	Michigan	1973
Kahl, Alfred L.	Assoc	Univ Ottawa	PHD			1974
Kahl, Douglas R.	Assoc	Akron	PHD	81	Iowa	1989
Kahn, Shulamit B.	Asst	Boston Univ	PHD		MIT	
Kairys Jr., Joseph Peter	Asst	W Ontario	PHD	90	Chicago	1990
Kaitz, Edward M.	Prof	Marymount	PHD		Harvard	
Kalay, Avner	Prof	Utah	PHD	79	Rochest	1987
Kale, Jayant R.	Asst	Georgia St	PHD		Texas	
Kallberg, Jarl G.	Assoc	New York U	PHD	79	Brit Col	
Kallianiotis, Ioannis	Assoc	Scranton	PHD	85	CUNY	1990
Kalra, Rajiv	Assoc	Moorhead St	PHD	89	Cinn	1989
Kalyman, Ansil	Prof	Univ Toronto	PHD		Yale	1975
Kam, Thomas	Asst	Hawaii Pacif	MBA		Hawaii	

Name	Rank	School	Degree	Yr	From	Yr
Kamae, Hiroshi	Prof	Hitotsubashi	DBA		Hitotsub	1984
Kamara, Avraham	Asst	U Washington	PHD	86	Columbia	1984
Kamath, Ravindra R.	Prof	Cleveland St	PHD	76	Cinn	1976
Kamma, Sreenivas	Asst	Indiana	PHD	87	SUNY-Buf	
Kanatas, George	C-Pr	South Fla	PHD	78	J Hopkin	1990
Kandel, Shmuel	Assoc	Tel Aviv Un				
on leave to Pennsylvania						
Kane, Edward J.	Prof	Ohio State	PHD	60	MIT	
Kang, Eun	Asst	CS-S Marcos	PHD	91	Penn	1991
Kang, Han Bin	Assoc	Illinois St	PHD	84	Illinois	1985
Kang, Jun-Koo		Rhode Island	MS	86	Iowa St	1991
Kannan, Srinivasan	Asst	Texas A&M	PHD	86	Illinoia	1986
Kao, Glenda Wenchi	Asst	Dayton	PHD	84	Illinois	1991
Kaplan, Steven Neil	Asst	Chicago	PHD	88	Harvard	1988
Kapoor, Ashok K.	Asst	Marist	ABD			1988
Kapplin, Steven D.	Prof	South Fla	PHD	79	Geo St	1974
Karafiath, Imre	Assoc	North Texas	PHD	83	Tx A&M	1984
Karbens, John	Assoc	Hawaii Pacif	EDD		Hawaii	
Karcic, Berislav	Prof	Iona	PHD	66	Columbia	1959
Kare, Dilip K.	Asst	North Fla	PHD		Tx Arlin	
Kareken, John	C-Pr	Minnesota	PHD			
Minnesota Chair in Banking and Finance						
Karels, Gordon V.	Assoc	Nebraska	PHD	79	Purdue	1986
Kares, Peter	Assoc	South Fla	PHD	68	Purdue	1969
Karna, Adi S.	Prof	Ind-Purdue	PHD	68	Ohio St	1984
Karolyi, G. Andrew	Asst	Ohio State	PHD	89	Chicago	
Karpoff, Jonathan M.	Assoc	U Washington	PHD	82	UCLA	1983
Karumanchi, V. R.	Asst	Alabama A&M	MS		Alab A&M	
Kashefinejad, Djavad	C-Pr	CS-Pomona	PHD	81	Claremon	1980
Katsimbris, George	Prof	Bridgeport	PHD		Conn	
Harvey Hubbell Professor of Economics & Finance						
Katz, Rachelle	C-Pr	Loyola Marym	PHD	80	Stanford	1976
Katz, Steven	Assoc	CUNY-Baruch	PHD		NYU	
Kau, James B.	Prof	Georgia	PHD		Wash	
C. Herman & Mary Virginia Terry Distinguished Chairholder in Business Adm						
Kauer, Robert T.	Asst	Case Western	PHD		Case Wes	
Kauffman, Daniel E.	C-Pr	Winona State	PHD		Nebraska	1983
Kaufman, Daniel J.	C-Ac	Wright State	PHD	86	Ohio St	1985
Kaufman, George G.	Prof	Loyola-Chicg	PHD		Iowa	1981
John Smith Professor						
Kaufman, Richard F.	Prof	CS-Sacrament	PHD	77	Tx-Arlin	1979
Kaufold, Howard S.	Adj	Pennsylvania	PHD	81	Princeto	1980
Kaul, Gautam	Asst	Michigan	PHD	85	Chicago	1985
Kavesh, Robert A.	Prof	New York U	PHD	54	Harvard	
Marcus Nadler Professor of Finance and Economics						
Kaywan, Sayeed	Asst	Towson State	PHD		American	1982
Kazarian, Dickran	Asst	Michigan	PHD	91	Chicago	1991
Kazemi, Hossein B.	Asst	Massachusett	PHD	85	Michigan	
Keane, Simon M.	Prof	Glasgow Univ	PHD	76	Glasgow	1969
Kearns, Daniel	Asst	Hawaii Pacif	MBA		Chaminad	
Keasey, Kevin	Prof	Univ Leeds	PHD	81		1990
Keasler, Terrill R.	Asst	Appalach St	PHD		Alabama	1987
Keat, Paul G.	Assoc	Am Grad Intl	PHD	59	Chicago	
Keating, William	Asst	Bentley	PHD	91	Arizona	1990
Keck, Peggy	Prof	W Kentucky	EDD		Oklahoma	1968
Keefe, M.	Inst	SUNY Old Wes	ABD			1985
Keenan, W. Michael	Assoc	New York U	PHD	67	Car Mel	
Kehr, James B.	Assoc	Miami U-Ohio	PHD	74	Ohio St	
Keim, Donald B.	Assoc	Pennsylvania	PHD	83	Chicago	1981
Keliiliki, Dale K.	Asst	Brighm Yg-HI	MS	71	Brig Yg	1972
Kellison, Stephen G.	C-Pr	Georgia St	MS		Nebraska	
Kelly, Al	Prof	NW Missouri	PHD		Kentucky	1975
Kelly, Gary Wayne	Asst	Miss State	PHD	88	Alabama	1984
Kelly, James M.	Assoc	LaSalle	PHD		Geo St	1978
Kelm, Kathryn	Asst	Emporia St	ABD		Missouri	1992
Kemp, Robert S.	Assoc	Virginia	DBA	81	Fla St	
Kendall, Coleman S.	Asst	Ill-Chicago	ABD			
Kendall, Leon	Prof	Northwestern	DBA	56	Indiana	
Kendree II, Jack M.	Assoc	SC-Coastal	PHD	89	S Carol	1985
Kennedy, Robert E.	Prof	Arkansas	PHD		Texas	1957
Kennedy, William F.	Assoc	N Car-Charl	PHD		Va Tech	1978
Kenney, Peppi	Asst	W Illinois				
Kensinger, John W.	Assoc	North Texas	PHD	83	Ohio St	1991
Keown, Arthur J.	Prof	Virg Tech	DBA	74	Indiana	1974
Kerr, Halbert	Prof	Wash State	PHD	76	U Wash	
Kerr, Helen J.	Lect	U Auckland	BCOM			1990
Kerry, Mike	STut	Deakin Univ	BCOM		Melbourn	1988
Kersey, Bruce L.	Prof	East Txs St	PHD	70	LSU	1970
Kesler, David W.	Assoc	Winona State	MBA		Kansas	1984
Kester, George W.	Assoc	Bucknell	DBA	83	Virginia	1983

Name	Rank	School	Degree	Yr	From	Yr
Kester, W. Carl	Prof	Harvard				
Ketcham, David C.	Asst	Bryant	PHD	88	Penn St	1991
Ketcher, David N.	Asst	Drake	PHD	91	Missouri	1990
Ketterer, Juan	Asst	Carnegie Mel	PHD	88	Minn	1988
Keys, James D.	Inst	Fla Internat	MBA	87	Fla Intl	
Khaki, Mohammed	Lect	CS-Chico	ABD		Oregon	1988
Khaksari, Shahriar	C-Ac	Suffolk	PHD		St Louis	
Khalil, Mohammed	Prof	US Intl				
Khan, A. Qayyum	Asst	N Car-Charl	PHD		Geo St	1989
Khan, Bahadur	SLect	Bournemouth	MA			1974
Khan, Bibi Zorina	Lect	Northeastern	PHD		UCLA	1990
Khan, Rauf A.	Prof	CS-San Bern	DBA	73	Colorado	1976
Khan, Walayet	Asst	Evansville	PHD	90	Arkansas	1989
Khanna, Naveen	Asst	Michigan	PHD	86	Northwes	1985
Khazeh, Khashayar	Assoc	Salisbury St	PHD	85	Tenn	1985
Kholdy-Sabety, Shady		CS-Pomona	PHD	84	Ca-SanBr	1990
Khoury, Nabil	C-Pr	Univ Laval	PHD	68	Indiana	
Khoury, Sarkis J.	Prof	Cal-Riversid	PHD		Penn	1984
Kidwell, David S.	Dean	Minnesota	PHD	75	Oregon	1991
Kierhan, Joseph	Asst	F Dick-Madis	PHD			
Kierulff, Herbert	Prof	Seattle Pac	DBA	66	S Calif	1980
Kihlstrom, Richard E.	C-Pr	Pennsylvania	PHD	68	Minn	1979

Ervin Miller-Arthur M. Freedman Professor of Finance

Kim, Chan-Wung	Asst	Mass-Boston	PHD	91	Iowa	1991
Kim, Chang-soo	Asst	St Johns	PHD			
Kim, Chongyoul	Asst	LeMoyne	PHD	82	Rutgers	1986
Kim, David J.	Prof	Indiana St	PHD		Wiscon	1975
Kim, Dongcheol	Asst	Rutgers-N Br	PHD	89	Michigan	1989
Kim, Dongman	Assoc	CS-San Bern	PHD	90	Ariz St	1990
Kim, E. Han	Prof	Michigan	PHD	75	SUNY-Buf	1980

Fred M. Taylor Professor of Business Administration

Kim, Hie-Jip	Prof	Korea Univ	PHD			1969
Kim, Hyung K.	Prof	Minn-Duluth	PHD	67	U Wash	
Kim, Kee S.	Assoc	SW Missouri	PHD	78	Texas	1988
Kim, Moon K.	Prof	Syracuse	PHD	74	Illinois	1975
Kim, Sang-Hoon	Assoc	Monmouth	PHD		Wiscon	1987
Kim, Sangphill	Asst	Bentley	PHD	84	Ohio	1988
Kim, Seung Hee	Prof	St Louis	PHD	69	New York	
Kim, Suk H.	D-Pr	Detroit Merc	PHD	75	St Louis	1977
Kim, Taewon	Prof	CS-L Angeles	PHD	86	Georgia	1987
Kim, Tong Suk	Asst	San Diego St	PHD		Ohio St	1989
Kim, Wheegook	Adj	Southeastern	PHD			
Kim, Y. C.	Asst	Clemson	PHD	87	Ohio St	1991
Kim, Yang H.	Prof	Alabama A&M	PHD		Utah	
Kim, Yong H.	Prof	Cincinnati	PHD	81	Penn St	1978

CBA Faculty Fellow

Kim, Yong O.	Asst	Rutgers-Newk	PHD		New York	
Kim, Yu K.	Asst	Hofstra	PHD	91	Rutgers	1990
Kimball, Ralph C.	C-Ac	Babson	PHD		Berkeley	
King, Jules		Florida A&M	PHD		Stanford	
King, Roger	Prof	So Miss	PHD	69	Tx Tech	1969
Kini, Omesh	Asst	Penn State	PHD		Purdue	1986
Kinsman, Michael	Prof	Pepper-L Ang	PHD	75	Stanford	1975
Kirby, Robert O.	Prof	Texas A&I	DBA	74	Tx Tech	1974
Kirk, Eugene	C-As	St Bonaventu	PHD	73	Boston C	1972
Kirklin, W. Wayne	Assoc	Heidelberg				
Kish, Richard J.	Asst	Lehigh	PHD	88	Florida	1988
Kishimoto, Naoki	Asst	Duke	PHD		NYU	
Kiss, Robert	Asst	E Michigan	PHD	90	Kent St	1990
Kittrell, Fred J.	Prof	Mid Tenn St	PHD	70	Miss	1971
Klaasen, Thomas A.	Prof	Txs Wesleyan	PHD	69	Mich St	1989
Klagstad, Harold L.	Asst	Wis-Milwauke	PHD	90	Purdue	1985
Klaudt, William J.	C-Ac	Jamestown	MED	64	Black Hl	1967
Klayman, Elliot I.	Assoc	Ohio State	LLM		Harvard	
Kleeven, Herman		Limburg				1991
Kleidon, Allan W.	Assoc	Stanford	PHD	83	Chicago	1982
Kleiman, Robert	Assoc	Oakland	PHD	86	Mich St	1985
Klein, Daniel P.	Asst	Bowling Gr	PHD		Kansas	1989
Klein, Linda S.	Asst	Connecticut	PHD	87	Fla St	1988
Klein, Richard H.	Assoc	Clemson	PHD	69	Texas	1978
Klemkosky, Robert	C-Pr	Indiana	PHD	71	Mich St	

Fred T. Greene Professor of Finance

Kling, John	Assoc	Wash State	PHD	83	Purdue	1988
Klock, David R.	Prof	Cen Florida	PHD		Illinois	1981
Klock, Mark S.	Assoc	George Wash	JD	88	Maryland	
Kluger, Brian D.	Asst	Cincinnati	PHD	83	Tulane	1987
Knez, Peter	Lect	Wisconsin	ABD		Penn	1991
Knight, John R.	Asst	Connecticut	PHD	90	LSU	1990
Knutson, Jerry L.	Dean	St Martin				
Kobos, Chester	Asst	Marist	PHD		Fordham	1982

Name	Rank	School	Degree	Yr	From	Yr
Koch, Paul D.	Assoc	Kansas	PHD		Mich St	1988
Koch, Timothy W. Chair of Banking	Prof	So Carolina	PHD	76	Purdue	
Kochman, Ladd M.	Assoc	Kennesaw St	DBA	80	Kentucky	1988
Kodres, Laura E.	Asst	Michigan	PHD	88	Northwes	1989
Koedijk, Kees	Assoc	Limburg	PHD	89	Rotterd	1991
Koehler, Cortus T.	Prof	CS-Sacrament	PHD	72	Claremon	1973
Kohers, Theodore	Prof	Miss State	PHD	71	Oregon	1971
Kohli, Raj K.	Asst	Ind-So Bend	DBA	90	Miss St	1990
Kokus, Jr., John	Assoc	American U	PHD	71	American	1969
Kolari, James W.	Assoc	Texas A&M	PHD	80	Ariz St	1980
Kolb, Robert W.	Prof	U Miami	PHD	74	N Carol	1983
Kolbe, Phillip T.	Asst	Memphis St	PHD	88	Arizona	1989
Kolodny, Richard	C-Pr	Maryland	PHD	72	New York	
Kon, Stanley J.	Prof	Michigan	PHD	76	SUNY-Buf	1982
Kooros, Syrous K.	Dean	Nicholls St	PHD			1991
Kooti, Ghanbar	Assoc	Albany State	PHD	80	Mich St	
Kopecky, Kenneth J.	Assoc	Temple	PHD		Brown	
Kopp, Thomas	H-Ac	Siena Coll	PHD	83	SUNY-Bin	1984
Koppenhaver, Gary D.	Assoc	Iowa State	PHD	80	Iowa	1988
Korajczyk, Robert A.	Assoc	Northwestern	PHD	83	Chicago	
Korkie, Robert	Prof	Univ Alberta	PHD	73	Wash	1973
Korth, C. M.	Prof	So Carolina				
Kothare, Meeta	Asst	Texas	PHD	91	Rocheste	1991
Kouatly, Youssef I.	Prof	Hartford	PHD		Penn	
Koundinya, Raina	Assoc	Mass-Lowell	PHD	77	NYU	
Koutmos, Gregory	Asst	Catholic				
Koveos, Peter	Assoc	Syracuse	PHD	77	Penn St	1982
Krabbenhoft, Alan	Asst	Roosevelt	ABD		Wayne St	1991
Kracaw, William A.	C	Penn State				
Krainer, Robert	Prof	Wisconsin	PHD	64	Michigan	1964
Kramer, Jeffrey A.	Lect	Connecticut	PHD	89	Conn	1981
Krausz, Joshua	Prof	Yeshiva	PHD	79	Renssela	1987
Kravel, George R.	Prof	St Cloud St	DBA	79	Colorado	1980
Krehbiel, Timothy L.	Asst	Oklahoma St	PHD		Purdue	1989
Kremer, Ann S.	Asst	Michigan St	MBA		U Wash	
Kremer, Joseph W.	Asst	Notre Dame	PHD		S Carol	
Kretlow, William J.	C-Ac	Houston	PHD	67	Purdue	1971
Kretovich, Duncan J.	Asst	Mich-Flint	PHD	85	Mich St	1988
Krienke, Albert B.	Prof	Midwest St	PHD		Txs A&M	1965
Krinsky, Itzhak	Assoc	McMaster	PHD		McMaster	
Krishnamurti, Chandrasekhar on leave of absence 1992-93 to India	Asst	Eastern Conn				
Krishnan, Ramesh	Asst	Memorial Un	PHD	88	Northwes	1991
KrishnaSwamy, C. R.	Prof	W Michigan	PHD	83	Tenn	1977
Kromis, Stephen G.	Assoc	NW St of La	PHD		La Tech	
Kroncke, Charles O.	Dean	Texas-Dallas	PHD	68	Minn	1988
Krouse, Clem	Prof	Cal-Santa Br				
Krueger, Mark K.	Asst	Colorado	PHD	89	Illinois	1988
Krueger, Thomas	Assoc	Wis-La Cross	PHD	88	Kentucky	1989
Krull, Steven	Asst	Hofstra	PHD	90	CUNY Bar	1986
Kuhle, James L.	Prof	CS-Sacrament	PHD	85	Texas	1984
Kuhlman, Bruce R.	Asst	Toledo	PHD		Florida	1988
Kuhlmann, Arkadi	Inst	Am Grad Intl				
Kuipers, Kenneth J.	Prof	Calvin	MA		Mich St	
Kulatilaka, Nalin	Assoc	Boston Univ	PHD		MIT	
Kulkarni, Mukund S.	Assoc	Penn St-Harr				
Kumar, Hari	Asst	Alaska-Fairb				
Kumar, Parmeswar C.	Assoc	American U	PHD	75	Penn St	1980
Kumar, Praveen	Asst	Carnegie Mel	PHD	81	Stanford	1985
Kumar, Raman	Asst	Virg Tech	PHD	85	Pitt	1984
Kummer, Donald R.	H-Ac	Mo-St Louis	PHD	75	Oregon	
Kundey, Gary E.	C $	Columbus	PHD	75	Florida	1974
Kuniansky, Harry R.	Prof	Augusta	DBA	70	Geo St	1980
Kunz, David	Assoc	SE Missouri	PHD	88	St Louis	1990
Kunz, Jeffrey T.	Asst	Carroll	MS		Wiscon	1981
Kuo, Cheng-Kun	Prof	Nat Taiwan U	PHD	86	Texas	1989
Kutasovic, Paul	Assoc	NY Inst Tech	PHD			
Kutner, George W.	Asst	Marquette	PHD		Northwes	1985
Kwan, Clarence C. Y.	Prof	McMaster	PHD		Ottawa	
Kwan, Edmond	Prof	CS-S Marcos	PHD	72	Cornell	1990
Kwan, Simon	Asst	Arizona	PHD	90	N Carol	1990
Kwok, Chuck C. Y.	Asst	So Carolina				
Kyle, Albert S.	Assoc	Cal-Berkeley	PHD	81	Chicago	1987
Kyle, Alfred	Assoc	Duke				
Laatsch, Francis E.	Asst	Bowling Gr	PHD		Oklahoma	1988
LaBarge, Karin	Asst	Rutgers-Camd	PHD		Berkeley	
LaBarge, Richard A.	Prof	Rutgers-Camd				
Lacey, Nelson J.	Assoc	Massachusett	PHD	85	Penn St	
Lahey, Karen E.	Assoc	Akron	PHD	85	Fla St	

174

Lai, Gene C.	Asst	Rhode Island	PHD	87	Texas	1988
Lai, Sung-Chung	Prof	CS-L Angeles	PHD	88	S Calif	1987
Lai, Tsong-Yue	Prof	CS-Fullerton	PHD		Yale	1991
Lai, Van Son	Asst	Univ Laval	PHD	85	Georgia	1989
Laird, Thomas	Assoc	Fla Atlantic	PHD	77	Miami	1974
Laiss, Barry		CS-Fresno				
Lajaunie, John	Asst	Nicholls St	ABD			1991
Lakehal-Ayat, Merouane	Asst	St John Fish	MIM		Denver	
Lakonishof, Josef	Prof	Illinois	PHD	76	Cornell	1987
Lam, Chun H.	Assoc	So Methodist	PHD	77	Duke	1981
Lamb, Reinhold P.	Asst	N Car-Charl	PHD	90	Fla St	1990
Lamb, Robert B.	Prof	New York U	PHD	70	London	
Lamberson, Morris A.	Prof	Cen Arkansas	PHD	72	Arkansas	
Lambert Jr., Eugene W.	Assoc	St Edwards	PHD	63	Alabama	1989
Lambert, William R.	Assoc	Brigham Yg	DBA	69	Indiana	1962
Lamm-Tennant, Joan	Assoc	Villanova	PHD	83	Texas	1989
LaMonica, Judith A.	Asst	Insurance	MS		Brooklyn	
Lamoureux, Christopher G.	Assoc	Wash Univ	PHD	85	Syracuse	1989
Lamy, Robert E.	Assoc	Wake Fr-Grad	PHD		LSU	1990
Lancaster, M. Carol	Asst	Richmond	PHD	84	Ariz St	1989
Landsea, William F.	Assoc	U Miami	PHD	66	Illinois	1965
Lane, Sarah J.	Asst	Boston Univ	PHD		Stanford	
Lane, William R.	Assoc	Louisiana St	PHD	76	N Carol	1977
LaNear, Richard E.	Assoc	Missouri So	PHD		Miss	1987
Lang, Darla F.	Asst	SW Texas St	ABD		Houston	1991
Lang, Larry	Asst	New York U				
Lang, Larry R.	Prof	Wis-Oshkosh	PHD	73	Mich St	1972
Lange, David	Asst	Auburn-Montg	DBA	89	Kentucky	1990
Lange, Helen P.	Asst	New So Wales	MCOM		NS Wales	1989
Lange, Paul M.	C-Pr	CS-Fresno	JD	65	Minn	1968
Langmead, John	SLect	Bournemouth	MSC			1974
Langohr, Herwig	Prof	INSEAD				
Langston, Rosemary	Dean$	Winona State	PHD		Minn	1978
Lanser, Howard P.	Assoc	Notre Dame	PHD	72	Purdue	1971
Lapoint, James J.	Asst	SW Louisiana	MS	64	So Miss	1964
Larrain, Maurice	Assoc	Pace	PHD		Columbia	1989
Larsen Jr., Glen	Asst	Tulsa	DBA	89	Indiana	1990
Larsen, James E.	Asst	Wright State	PHD	87	Nebraska	1987
Lash, Nicholas A.	Prof	Loyola-Chicg	PHD		Wayne St	1980
Lasher, William	Asst	Nichols Col	PHD	77	So Metho	1988
Lashgari, Malek	C-Ac	Hartford	PHD		NYU	
Lasik, John	Asst	Central Wash	MBA		Miss St	1985
Lasser, Dennis J.	Asst	SUNY-Bingham	PHD	84	Indiana	1988
Lathovich, Sharon		Ashland				
Latimer, Steve	Adj	New York U				
Laudor, Charles R.	Asst	Adelphi	PHD	70	Columbia	
Laughton, David	Asst	Univ Alberta	PHD	87	MIT	1987
Launie, Joseph	Prof	CS-Northrdge	PHD	68	UCLA	1965
Laux, Paul A.	Asst	Texas	PHD	88	Vanderbi	1989
Lavallee, Mario	Prof	HEC-Montreal				
Lavely, Joseph A.	Prof	Longwood	PHD	70	Iowa	1989
Lawrence, David B.	Prof	Drake	PHD	79	Iowa St	1979
Lawrence, Edward C.	Assoc	Mo-St Louis	PHD	82	Penn St	1982
Lawson, Larry L.	Assoc	Central Conn	PHD			1989
Lawson, William	Assoc	Carleton Un				
Le, S. V.	Assoc	CS-Long Bch	PHD			1986
Leabman, Jerry	Asst	Bentley	MST	84	Bentley	1987
Leach, J. Christopher	Asst	Pennsylvania	PHD	88	Cornell	1988
Donaldson, Lufkin & Jenrette Term Assistant Professor of Finance						
Leake, Richard	Assoc	Luther	ABD	75	Ohio	
Lease, Ronald C.	Prof	Utah	PHD	73	Purdue	1973
LeClair, Robert T.	C	Villanova	PHD	72	Northwes	1986
Lecompte, Richard L.B.	Asst	Wichita St	PHD	87	Texas	1989
Lecraw, Donald J.	Prof	W Ontario	DBA		Harvard	1975
Ledford, Manfred H.	Assoc	U Miami	PHD	73	Kentucky	1973
Lee, Bong-Soo	Asst	Minnesota	PHD			
Lee, Boyden	Assoc	New Mex St	PHD	71	Manchest	1980
Lee, Chan H.	Prof	Mankato St	PHD		No Illin	1982
Lee, Chung	Prof	Korea Univ	PHD			1968
Lee, Daniel	Assoc	CS-Fullerton	PHD		Berkeley	1990
Lee, David	Lect	Melbourne U	BEC	77	ANU	1990
Lee, Hei Wai	Asst	South Fla	PHD	89	Illinois	1990
Lee, Insup	Assoc	Delaware	PHD		Houston	
Lee, Jae Ha	Asst	Oklahoma	PHD	88	Indiana	1989
Lee, Jeong Wan	Asst	North Dakota	PHD	86	Texas	1986
Lee, John T.	C-Pr	Mid Tenn St	PHD	77	Georgia	1984
Lee, Moon H.	H $	Saskatchewan	PHD	74	Chicago	1970
Lee, Philip H.	Assoc	Merrimack	MBA	57	Syracuse	
Lee, Philip J.	Lect	Univ Sydney	MCOM		NS Wales	1990
Lee, Phill Sang	Prof	Korea Univ	PHD			1982

Lee, Sang	Asst	Nicholls St	PHD			1991
Lee, Scott	Asst	Texas A&M	PHD	90	Oregon	1990
Lee, Suk H.	Asst	Loyola-Chicg	PHD		So Calif	1988
Lee, Sung	Asst	St Johns	PHD			
Lee, Tsun-Siou	Prof	Nat Taiwan U	PHD	88	Berkeley	1988
Lee, Unro	Asst	Pacific	PHD	86	Purdue	
Lee, Wayne Y.	Prof	Kent State	PHD	73	UCLA	1991
Firestone Chair of Corporate Finance						
Lee, Yongho	Asst	McMaster	PHD		Northwes	
Lee, Youngho	Assoc	Howard	PHD	81	Geo Wash	1986
Lee, Yul	Asst	Missouri	PHD		Texas	
Leeds, Eva M.	Asst	Frank & Mars	PHD			1987
Lees, Francis A.	Prof	St Johns	PHD	61	NYU	1960
Leftwich, Richard W.	Prof	Chicago	PHD	80	Rochest	1979
Legg, Thomas D.	Assoc	St Cloud St	BA	75	Minn	1989
Legler, John B.	Prof	Georgia	PHD	67	Purdue	1971
Lehmann, Bruce N.	Prof	Columbia	PHD	83	Chicago	1981
Leinberger, Gary	Assoc	Millersville	PHD	83	Okla St	1986
Leinheiser, Frederick D.	Asst	York of PA	MBA		Shippens	1980
Leistikow, Dean A.	Asst	Fordham	PHD		Brown	1987
Leitch, Gordon	Adj	Portland	PHD	87	Tulane	1991
Leland, Hayne E.	Prof	Cal-Berkeley	PHD	68	Harvard	1974
Arno A. Rayner Professor of Finance and Management						
Lemaire, Jean	Prof	Pennsylvania				
Joseph Wharton Term Professor of Insurance & Actuarial Science						
Lemer, George	Dean	U Lethbridge	PHD		McGill	1981
Lemke, Graham	Inst	Penn State	ABD		Cornell	
Lensberg, Terje	Prof	Norwegian	DOEC			
Lentz, George H.	Asst	Indiana	MBA	82	Indiana	
Leon, G.	Assoc	SUNY Old Wes	PHD			1990
Leonard, David C.	Prof	Miami U-Ohio	PHD	76	Illinois	
Leonard, Paul A.	Prof	SUNY-Albany	PHD	80	Oregon	1987
Lepley, William H.	Asst	Wis-Milwaukee	PHD	87	Wiscon	1986
Lerner, Eugene M.	Prof	Northwestern	PHD	54	Chicago	
Lerner, Joshua	Asst	Harvard				
LeRoy, Stephen	Prof	Cal-Santa Br				
LeRoy, Stephen	Prof	Minnesota				
Carlson Professor of Finance						
Lerro, Anthony J.	C-Pr	Stetson	PHD		Alabama	1988
Lessard, Jeffrey P.		Rochest Tech	PHD	83	Arkansas	1989
Letterman, Denise	Asst	Robt Morris	MBA		Penn St	
Leung, Wai-Kin	Asst	Louisiana St	PHD	86	Texas	1986
Leverett Jr., E. J.	Prof	Georgia	DBA		Indiana	
Levi, Donald R.	C-Pr	Wichita St	PHD	74	Wash St	1980
Levich, Richard M.	Prof	New York U	PHD	77	Chicago	
Levine, Jules M.	Prof	Lg-Isl-Post	DBA		Indiana	
Levine, Philip	Assoc	Yeshiva	PHD	74	Columbia	1989
Levy, Haim	Prof	Florida	PHD		Jerusale	1981
Walter J. Matherly Professor; Graduate Research Professor						
Levy, Jerome	Adj	New York U				
Lewellen, Wilbur G.	Prof	Purdue	PHD	67	MIT	1964
Lewis, Barbara J.	Assoc	Miami U-Ohio	PHD	83	Cinn	
Lewis, Chantee	Prof	Bryant	DBA		Geo Wash	
Lewis, Craig M.	Asst	Vanderbilt	PHD	82	Wiscon	1986
Lewis, John H.	Prof	S F Austin	DBA	75	La Tech	1969
Lewis, John R.	Prof	Florida St	PHD	69	Wiscon	1969
Lewis, Karen K.	Assoc	Pennsylvania	PHD	85	Chicago	1991
Lewthwaite, Barbara Jayne	Asst	Centenary	MBA		St Johns	1987
LeYouvnenu, David	Asst	Winthrop	DBA	88	La Tech	1988
Li, H. C.	Prof	Bryant	PHD	71	Mass	
Liang, Youguo	Asst	Cleveland St	PHD	91	Kentucky	1991
Liano, Kartono	Prof	Miss State	PHD	89	Alabama	1989
Liaw, K. Thomas	Asst	St Johns	PHD			
Liberman, Joseph	Assoc	Roosevelt	PHD	82	Chicago	1988
Liesz, Thomas	Assoc	Western St	PHD	89	Idaho	1990
Light, Jay O.	Prof	Harvard				
Ligon, James	Asst	Alabama	PHD		Penn	1991
Lilly III, Claude C.	Prof	Florida St	PHD	73	Geo St	1978
Limmack, Robin J.	Assoc	Un Stirling	MBA	75	Liverpoo	1978
Lin, Cheyeh	Assoc	Cincinnati	DBA	69	Indiana	1967
Lin, James W. H.	Asst	Montana St	PHD	87	Arizona	
Lin, Jason	Assoc	NE Missouri	PHD	85	Wayne St	1986
Lin, Ji-Chai	Asst	Louisiana St	PHD	88	Iowa	1988
Lin, Joung-yol	C	Nat Chengchi	PHD	85	Iowa	1979
Lin, Yu-Isung	Prof	Nat Taiwan U	PHD	76	Minnesot	1978
Lin, Yun	Assoc	Nat Taiwan U	PHD	87	Illinois	1987
Lindahl, Mary R.	Assoc	Alaska-Fairb	PHD	75	Illinois	1986
Lindley, James T.	Prof	So Miss	PHD	77	Georgia	1990
Lindsay, Robert	Prof	New York U	PHD	55	Harvard	
Lindsey, Richard	Lect	Yale	PHD	91	Berkeley	1991

Name	Rank	School	Degree	Yr	Univ	Yr
Lindsley, David A.	Assoc	Toledo	PHD		Michigan	1972
Lindvall, John R.	Prof	Cal Poly-SLO	DBA	73	Illinois	1973
Ling, David C.	Assoc	Florida	PHD		Ohio St	1989
Linke, Charles M.	Prof	Illinois	PHD	66	Indiana	1966
Linn, Scott C.	Assoc	Oklahoma	PHD	82	Purdue	1989
Linneman, Peter D.	Prof	Pennsylvania	PHD	77	Chicago	1978
Albert Sussman Professor of Real Estate						
Lipscomb, Joseph B.	Assoc	Tx Christian	PHD	78	Houston	1977
Litka, Michael P.	Prof	Akron	JD	58	Iowa	1971
Little, James T.	Assoc	Wash Univ	PHD	77	Minn	1971
Litvan, John K.	Assoc	SW Missouri	PHD	81	Arkansas	1980
Litzenberger, Robert H.	Prof	Pennsylvania	PHD	69	N Carol	1986
Edward Hopkins, Jr. Professor of Investment Banking						
Liu, Crocker H.	Asst	New York U	PHD	88	Texas	
Liu, Pu	Assoc	Arkansas	PHD		Indiana	1984
Livingston, Miles B.	Prof	Florida	PHD		New York	1982
on leave to College of William & Mary, 1991-92						
Livingston, Thomas	Assoc	Charleston	PHD	77	S Carol	1977
Lloyd, William P.	Prof	Auburn	DBA	73	Indiana	1979
Lo, Andrew W.	Assoc	MIT	PHD			
Lo, Harry	Asst	Northern St	PHD	86	Geo St	1989
Lockett, Michael	Asst	Illinois St	PHD	87	Tx Tech	1985
Lockwood, Larry J.	C-As	Tx-Arlington	PHD	82	Purdue	1982
Loewenstein, Uri	Asst	Utah	MBA	81	NYU	1984
Logue, Dennis	Prof	Dartmouth	PHD	71	Cornell	1974
Loh, Charmen	Asst	Rider	PHD		Arkansas	
Lonergan, Janis	C-Ac	Augustana IL	PHD	78	So Ill	1976
Long Jr., John B.	Prof	Rochester	PHD	71	Car Mel	1969
Long, Michael	Assoc	Rutgers-Newk	PHD		Purdue	
Longmore, Dean R.	C-Pr$	Idaho State	PHD	80	Missouri	1979
Longstaff, Francis A.	Asst	Ohio State	PHD	87	Chicago	
Lonie, A. Alasdair	Lect	Dundee	MA	62	Glasgow	1982
Loo, Ching-Hsing	Prof	CS-L Angeles	PHD	84	Ohio St	1985
Lopilato, Carol	Prof	CS-Dominguez	PHD	80	S Calif	1975
Lord, Beverly R.	Asst	Canterbury	BCOM	91	Canterbu	1991
Lord, Richard A.	Asst	Georgia Col	PHD		Tx-Arlin	1988
Lorie, James H.	Prof	Chicago	PHD	47	Chicago	1947
Eli B. and Harriet B. Williams Professor of Business Administration						
Losey, Robert L.	Assoc	American U	PHD	77	Kentucky	1982
Loughlin, John	Inst	St Louis				
Louton, David	Asst	Bryant	PHD	91	Mich St	1991
Love, William	Assoc	Wis-Stev Pt	PHD		Arkansas	1982
Lucas, Deborah	Asst	Northwestern	PHD	88	Chicago	
Luckie Jr., William Vernon	Asst	Mercer-Macon	MBA	68	Miss	1976
Luckstone Jr., Harold C.	Asst	Insurance	MA		NYU	
Luehrman, Timothy	Assoc	Harvard				
Luft, Carl F.	Asst	DePaul	PHD		Geo St	
Lui, Y. H.	SLect	City Poly HK	MA	85	Lancast	1989
Lummer, Scott L.	Assoc	Texas A&M	PHD	83	Purdue	1983
Lund, Mark	Prof	Luther	PHD	75	Iowa St	1969
Lunden, John H.	Assoc	Ferris State	MBA		Michigan	1988
Lupo, Theresa	Inst	Lg-Isl-Post	MBA		Lg Isl	
Lusht, Kenneth M.	C-Pr	Penn State	PHD		Geo St	
Lutz, Robert A.	Asst	Weber State	BA	86	Utah	1991
Lymberopoulos, P. John	Prof	Colorado	PHD	65	Texas	1964
Lyn, Esmeralda	Assoc	Hofstra	PHD	82	CUNY Bar	1982
Lyn, Thomas L.	Prof	Rockhurst	PHD	70	Missouri	1975
Lynch, Gene C.	Prof	Arkansas	PHD		Texas	1973
Lynch, Larry A.	Assoc	Roanoke Col	PHD		Va Tech	1978
Lynge, Morgan J.	Assoc	Illinois	PHD	75	Michigan	1974
Ma, Christopher K.	Assoc	Texas Tech	PHD	83	Illinois	1988
Maberly, Edwin D.	Assoc	No Arizona	PHD		Tx A&M	1987
MacDonald, Don N.	Asst	North Texas	PHD	84	Tx A&M	1989
MacDonald, John A.	Asst	SUNY-Albany	PHD	87	Va Tech	1987
MacDonald, Ronald	Prof	Dundee	PHD		Manchest	1989
MacDonald, S. Scott	Assoc	Texas Tech	PHD	83	Tx A&M	1984
MacDougall, Shelley	Lect	Arcadia Univ	ABD		Bradford	1987
Mace, J. R.	SLect	U Lancaster	MS		London	
Mackay, Robert J.	Prof	Virg Tech	PHD	72	N Carol	1972
Mackenzie, David L.	Asst	New So Wales	MCOM		NS Wales	1988
Mackie, Wayne	Prof	Saginaw Vall	PHD	86	Mich St	1977
MacKinlay, A. Craig	Prof	Pennsylvania	PHD	85	Chicago	1985
MacMillan, L. W.	Assoc	Univ Calgary	PHD	86	Arizona	1987
MacMinn, Richard D.	Assoc	Texas	PHD	78	Illinois	1981
MacPhee, William A.	Adj	Illinois	MBA	72	Vanderb	1990
Macve, Richard H.	H-Lec	Univ Wales	MSC	76	London	1979
Madan, Dilip	Asst	Maryland	PHD	75	Maryland	
Madan, Rippy	Inst	Frostburg St	MBA		Marshall	1990
Madaris, Michael	Asst	So Miss	PHD	89	Alabama	1989
Madden, Gerald P.	Assoc	Fairfield	PHD	76	Penn St	1985

Madhavan, Ananth N.	Asst	Pennsylvania	PHD	88	Cornell	1988
W. P. Carey & Co. Term Assistant Professor of Finance						
Madrigal, Vincent	Asst	New York U	PHD	89	Princeto	
Madura, Jeff	Prof	Fla Atlantic	DBA	83	Fla St	1987
Maese, Judy	Assoc	New Mex St	PHD	82	Oregon	1980
Magiera, Frank T.	Asst	Wyoming	PHD			1987
Magner, Richard M.	Prof	Youngstown	MSED	57	Westmins	
Mahajan, Arvind	Assoc	Texas A&M	PHD	80	Geo St	1980
Mahajan, Y. Lal	Assoc	Monmouth	PHD		No Ill	1979
Maher, John E.	Retir	So Conn St	PHD		Harvard	
Maher, Matt	Asst	Boise State	PHD		Illinois	1989
Maheswaran, Srinivasan	Asst	Wash Univ	ABD	91	Minn	1991
Mahle, Stephen	VAsst	Virg Tech	PHD	84	Ohio St	1986
Mais, Eric L.	Asst	Hawaii-Manoa	PHD	88	S Carol	1988
Major, John B.	Assoc	CS-Hayward	PHD	73	Illinois	1988
Makhija, Anil K.	Assoc	Pittsburgh				
Malatesta, Paul H.	Assoc	U Washington	PHD	69	Rocheste	1980
Maldonado-Bear, Rita	Prof	New York U	PHD	69	New York	
Malitz, Ileen	Assoc	F Dick-Madis	PHD		Maryland	1990
Malko, J. Robert	Prof	Utah State	PHD	72	Purdue	1987
Mallett, James E.	Assoc	Stetson	PHD		Wayne St	1984
Malley, Susan L.	Assoc	Fordham	PHD	80	NYU	
Malone, Chris B.	Lect	Massey Univ	MBS			1986
Malone, Rodney Phil	Assoc	Mississippi	PHD	74	Florida	1973
Maloney, Kevin	Assoc	Dartmouth	PHD	83	U Wash	1983
Maloney, Paul J.	D-As	Providence	MBA		McGill U	1980
Mamoozadeh, G. Abbas	C	Silppery Roc	PHD		Kent	1981
Manakyan, Herman	Asst	W Kentucky	PHD	88	Alabama	1984
Manaster, Steven	Prof	Utha	PHD	77	Chicago	1983
Mandelker, Gershon N.	Prof	Pittsburgh	PHD		Chicago	
Mandell, Lewis	Prof	Connecticut	PHD	70	Texas	1980
Maness, Terry S.	C-Pr	Baylor	DBA		Indiana	1972
Carr P. Collins Professor of Finance						
Mangla, Inayat U.	Prof	W Michigan	PHD	78	Mich St	
Mangos, Nicholas C.	Lect	Flinders Un	MBA	85	Adelaide	1990
Manley, John	Prof	Seton Hall	MBA	81	Baruch	
Mann, Harvey	C-Pr	Brock Univ	PHD	72	New York	1987
Mann, Steven V.	Asst	So Carolina	PHD	87	Nebraska	
Manning, Christopher A.	Assoc	Loyola Marym	PHD	83	UCLA	1986
Mansinghka, S.	Prof	San Fran St	PHD	71	UCLA	1975
Mansur, Iqbal	Assoc	Widener	PHD	84	Cinn	1985
Mantripragada, Krishna G.	Prof	Ball State	PHD	71	Minn	1979
Manuel, Timothy A.	Asst	Montana	PHD	88	S Carol	1991
Marchesini, Roberto	Assoc	Houston-Cl L	PHD		Texas	
Marcus, Alan	Assoc	Boston Coll	PHD		MIT	
Marcus, Richard	Assoc	Wis-Milwauke	PHD	83	Chicago	1985
Margotta, Donald G.	Assoc	Northeastern	PHD		N Carol	1983
Markou, Peter J.	Dean	N Adams St	MSBA		Suffolk	
Markovich, Denise E.	Assoc	North Dakota	PHD	79	Manitoba	1986
Markovich, Michael	Prof	Lg Isl-Brook	PHD		Paris	
Markowitz, Harry	Prof	CUNY-Baruch	PHD		Chicago	
Speiser Distinguished Professor						
Marks, Barry R.	Prof	Houston-Cl L	PHD		Purdue	
Maroney, Patrick F.	Prof	Florida St	JD	75	Florida	1981
Marple, Wesley W.	Prof	Northeastern	DBA	67	Harvard	1966
Marr Jr., M. Wayne	Prof	Clemson	PHD	83	Tx Tech	1980
Marsh, Terry A.	Assoc	Cal-Berkeley	PHD	81	Chicago	1986
Marsh, William H.	Prof	S Car-Aiken	PHD		S Carol	
Marshall, David	Asst	Miami U-Ohio	PHD	88	Illinois	
Marshall, David	Asst	Northwestern	PHD	88	Car Mel	
Marshall, John F.	Assoc	St Johns	PHD		SUNY-SBr	
Marshall, Paul	Asst	Widener	PHD			
Marshall, Richard D.	Prof	Rutgers-Newk	LLB	56	Howard	1972
Marshall, Robert A.	C-Pr	Florida St	PHD	68	Penn	1976
Kathryn Magee Kip Professor of Life Insurance						
Marshall, S. Brooks	Assoc	Jms Madison	PHD	85	Virginia	1985
Marston, Felicia C.	Asst	Virginia	PHD		N Carol	
Marston, Richard	Prof	Pennsylvania	PHD	72	MIT	1972
James R. F. Guy Professor of Finance & Economics						
Martel, Robert	Asst	Bentley	MS	66	MIT	1989
Martell, Terry	Assoc	CUNY-Baruch	PHD		Penn St	
Martin, David	Asst	St Bonaventu	PHD	91	St Louis	1988
Martin, David	Prof	SUNY-Geneseo	PHD		Syracuse	1966
Martin, David A.	Assoc	Albright	DA	80	Lehigh	1983
Martin, Deryl W.	Asst	Tenn Tech	PHD	88	Tx A&M	1988
Martin, Gerald D.	Prof	CS-Fresno	PHD		Ariz St	1980
Martin, John D.	Prof	Texas	DBA	73	Tx Tech	1980
The Margaret & Eugene McDermott Centennial Professor in Banking & Finance						
Martin, Kenneth J.	Asst	Iowa	PHD	87	Purdue	1987
Martin, Linda J.	Assoc	Arizona St	DBA		La Tech	1980

178

Martin, Rinne	Prof	Oral Roberts	PHD	84	Cincinna	1977
Martin, Roger E.	Asst	Keene State	ABD		Vanderb	1985
Martinelli, Patrick A.	Prof	Loyola-Maryl	PHD		Ohio St	
Martini, Christine	Lect	Melbourne U	MSC		Melbourn	1991
Maskooki, Kooros	Assoc	Mass-Dartmou	PHD	77	Nebraska	1981
Mason, Scott P.	Prof	Harvard				
Mason, W. Joe	Assoc	East Tenn St	PHD	87	S Carol	1984
Masotti, Lou	Prof	Northwestern	PHD	64	Northwes	
Masson, Jean L.	Asst	Univ Ottawa	PHD	89	Rochest	1991
Masulis, Ronald	Prof	Vanderbilt	PHD	78	Chicago	1990
Mateer, Robert N.	Assoc	Liberty	MBA		Tulane	1984
Mathews, Clive M. H.	Lect	Flinders Un	MBS	89	Massey	1990
Mathis, F. John	C-Pr	Am Grad Intl	PHD	66	Iowa	
Mathur, Iqbal	C-Pr	So Illinois	PHD	74	Cinn	1977
Matsumoto, Keishiro	Assoc	So Conn St	PHD		Minn	
Matthews, Warren	C-Ac	Texas A&I	PHD		Tx A&M	1972
Mattson, Kyle Logan	Asst	Rochest Tech	DBA	88	Kentucky	1989
Mauer, David C.	Asst	Wisconsin	PHD	86	Purdue	1986
Maulden, Hoyt P.	Assoc	Embry-Riddle	MSBA	68	Geo Wash	1985
Maung, Mya	Prof	Boston Coll	PHD	61	Catholic	1966
Maxwell, Charles E.	Assoc	Murray State	PHD		Cinn	1988
Maxwell, Philip H.	Assoc	Jms Madison	PHD	74	Fla St	1974
May, Marvin M.	Adj	UCLA	PHD	69	UCLA	1972
May, Ralph	Asst	SW Okla St	PHD	75	Purdue	1989
Mayer, John M.	Lect	Assumption	MBA	80	Babson	1982
Mayers, David	Prof	Ohio State	PHD		Rochest	
Shepard Professorship in Insurance						
Mayne, Lucille S.	Prof	Case Western	PHD	66	Northwes	
Maynes, Elizabeth M.	Asst	York Univ	PHD		Queen's	1986
Mayo, Herbert	Prof	Trenton St	PHD	69	Rutgers	1982
Mazumdar, Sumon	Asst	McGill Univ	PHD		So Meth	1990
Mazzeo, Michael A.	Asst	Michigan St	PHD		Indiana	
McAloon, Joseph	Asst	Fitchburg St	MBA		S Dakota	1984
McArthur, John H.	Dean	Harvard	DBA		Harvard	1959
McBain, Michael L.	Asst	Marquette	PHD		Mass	1985
McCabe, George M.	Prof	Nebraska	PHD	75	Penn	1981
McCabe, James R.	C-Ac	Louisville	PHD	74	Missouri	1973
McCaffrey, Michael A.	Asst	Indiana-PA				
McCallum, John S.	Prof	U Manitoba	PHD	73	Toronto	1973
McCarthy, David	Asst	Skidmore	MBA		Stanford	1991
McCarthy, Joseph	Assoc	Bryant	DBA	83	Colorado	1989
McCarthy, Neil T.	Assoc	GMI	PHD	77	Renssela	1973
McCarty, Daniel E.	C-Pr	Fla Atlantic	PHD	73	Geo St	1981
McClaughlin, Robyn M.	Asst	Boston Coll	PHD		MIT	
McClean, Larry E.	Assoc	Fayetteville	PHD		Syracuse	
McClung, Jacquetta J.	Dean	Cameron	PHD	85	Oklahoma	1990
McClymont, Trevor L.	Assoc	LaSierra	DBA	88	Int Gr S	1991
McCollough, W. Andrew	Prof	Florida	PHD	71	Florida	1969
McConnell, Dennis	Asst	Maine	PHD	82	Maryland	
McConnell, John J.	Prof	Purdue	PHD	74	Purdue	1976
McCord, Sammy O.	Assoc	Auburn	PHD	71	Arkansas	1973
McCormack, Joseph Patrick	Asst	Houston-Cl L	PHD		Tx A&M	
McCue, Thomas E.	Assoc	Duquesne	PHD		N Carol	
McCulloch, Wendell	Prof	CS-Long Bch	J			1974
McDaniel, Wm R.	Prof	Fla Atlantic	PHD	75	Geo St	1975
McDonald, Bill D.	Prof	Notre Dame				
McDonald, James E.	Asst	No Colorado	DBA	88	La Tech	1989
McDonald, James L.	C-Ac	North Texas	PHD	79	Oklahoma	1976
McDonald, John G.	Prof	Stanford	PHD	67	Stanford	1968
The IBJ Professor of Finance and Business School Trust Faculty Fellow 90-91						
McDonald, Robert L.	C-Pr	Northwestern	PHD	82	MIT	
McElreath Jr., R. B.	Assoc	Clemson	PHD	76	Geo St	1987
McElroy, Jerome L.	C-Pr	St Marys-Ind	PHD	71	Colorado	1982
McEnally, Richard W.	Prof	No Carolina	PHD	69	N Carol	1973
Meade H. Willis, Sr. Professor of Investment Banking						
McEvoy, Chris P.	Lect	Loughborough	MSC		Bradford	
McFadyen, James	Prof	Fran Marion	PHD	73	Kentucky	1989
McGaughy, Cheryl A.	Inst	Angelo State	MBA	76	Miss	1984
McGee, Paul	Asst	Salem State	MS		Boston C	1990
McGoun, Elton G.	Asst	Bucknell	PHD	87	Indiana	1987
McGowan Jr., Carl B.	VAsoc	Mich-Flint	PHD	80	Mich St	1991
McGrath, Francis J.	Prof	Iona	PHD	69	Fordham	1979
McGregor, Michael	Inst	Ark-Monticel	MBA	87		
McInish, Thomas H.	Prof	Memphis St	PHD	78	Pitt	1982
Wunderlich Chair of Excellence in Finance						
McIntosh, Willard	Asst	Kentucky	PHD	87	N Tx St	
McIntyre Jr., James Edgar	Asst	Mississippi	PHD		Georgia	
McKee Jr., Gilbert James	Prof	CS-Pomona	PHD	72	Claremon	1969
McKenna, Frederick W.	Asst	So Alabama	PHD		S Carol	1985

Name	Rank	School	Degree	Yr	Univ	Yr
McKenzie, Richard Bunn	Prof	Mississippi	PHD	72	Va Tech	
Hearin-Hess Professor of Economics and Finance; on leave to Cal-Irvine						
McKenzie, Roger I.	Asst	Brighm Yg-HI	MBA	67	Harvard	1982
McKernan, John F.	Lect	Glasgow Univ	MBA			1990
McKinney, William	Inst	Angelo State	MA	77	Txs A&M	1984
McKinnon, John B.	Dean	Wake Fr-Grad	MBA	61	Harvard	1989
McKown, Ellen	Assoc	Central Okla	PHD	79	Oklahoma	1980
McLain, Louis	Asst	Txs Wesleyan	MBA	76	So Meth	1978
McLanahen, Craig	Dean$	Salem State	MBA			
McLeod, Robert W.	Assoc	Alabama	PHD		Texas	1978
McLintock, A. J.	Asst	East Anglia	BCOM		Edinburg	1980
McMahon, Richard G. P.	Assoc	Flinders Un	MBA	80	Adelaide	1978
McManis, Bruce	H-Pr	Nicholls St	PHD			1978
McManus, Ginette		St Joseph				
McMeen, Albert R.	Asst	Lg Isl-Brook	MBA	66	Columbia	
McNamara, Michael J.	Asst	Rhode Island	PHD	88	Nebraska	1988
McNeil, Melanie	Inst	No Illinois	MS	89	No Ill	1989
McNew, Ben B.	Prof	Cen Arkansas	PHD		Texas	
Carmichael Professor of Economics						
McNichol, Kathleen	Inst	LaSalle				
McNulty, James	Assoc	Fla Atlantic	PHD	75	N Carol	1989
McQueen, Grant R.	Asst	Brigham Yg	PHD	89	U Wash	1989
McRostie, Clair M.	Prof	Gustavus Ado	PHD	64	Wiscon	1957
McWee, Wayne	Assoc	Longwood	EDD		N Colo	1984
McWilliams, Victoria B.	Asst	Ariz St-West	PHD			1990
Mead, Ken	Asst	Insurance	MA		Rutgers	
Meador, Joseph Wayne	Prof	Northeastern	PHD		Penn	
Means Jr., Dwight B.	Asst	Memphis St	PHD	84	Pitt	1989
Mech, Timothy	Asst	Boston Coll	PHD		Rochest	
Medeweitz, Jeanette N.	Asst	Neb-Omaha	MS		St Louis	
Medley, William	Asst	Rio Grande	JD	80	Akron	1987
Megbolugbe, Isaac F.	Asst	American U	PHD	83	Penn	1991
Megginson, William L.	Asst	Georgia	PHD	86	Fla St	1986
Mehdian, Seyed M.	Asst	Temple	PHD		So Illin	
Mehra, Anita	Asst	Wis-Milwauke	PHD		Temple	1991
Mehra, Rajnish	Prof	Cal-Santa Br				
Mehran, Hamid	Asst	Boston Coll	PHD		N Carol	
Mehran, Jamshid	Assoc	Ind-So Bend	PHD	83	Arkansas	1986
Mehta, Dileep R.	Prof	Georgia St	DBA	65	Harvard	1973
Mei, Jiaping	Asst	New York U				
Meiburg, Charles O.	Prof	Virg-Grad	PHD	60	Virginia	
J. Harvie Wilkinson Jr., Professor of Business Administration						
Melicher, Ronald W.	Prof	Colorado	DBA	68	Wash U	1969
William H. Baughn Distinguished Scholar						
Mello, Antonio S.	VAsst	MIT	PHD			
Mellon, W. Giles	Prof	Rutgers-Newk	PHD		Princeto	
Melnyk, Z. Lew	Prof	Cincinnati	PHD	61	Mich St	1964
Memon, Iqbal A.	Asst	Fort Lewis	DBA	84	Miss St	1988
Mendelson, Morris	Prof	Pennsylvania	PHD	50	Cornell	1961
Mendenhall, Richard	Asst	Notre Dame				
Mensah, Samuel	Lect	Mich-Flint	ABD		Toronto	1991
Mercer, Jeffrey M.	Asst	No Illinois	PHD	91	Tx Tech	1991
Meric, Gulser	Assoc	Glassboro St	PHD		Lehigh	1987
Meric, Ilhan	Prof	Rider	PHD		Lehigh	
Merikas, Andreas G.	Asst	Miss State	PHD	88	Oklahoma	1987
Merrier, Patricia	C-Pr	Minn-Duluth				
Merriken III, Harry E.	Assoc	Loyola-Maryl	PHD		Maryland	1980
Merton, Robert C.	Prof	Harvard	PHD	70	MIT	
Merville, Larry J.	Prof	Texas-Dallas	PHD	71	Texas	1973
Messina, J.	Prof	San Fran St	PHD	79	Berkeley	1977
Messner, Stephen D.	Prof	Connecticut	DBA	66	Indiana	1966
Mettlen, Robert D.	Prof	Texas	DBA	69	Indiana	1966
Lamar Savings Centennial Professor in Finance						
Meulbroek, Lisa	Asst	Harvard				
Meurer Jr., Emil M.	Assoc	New Orleans	PHD		Nebraska	
Meyer, James E.	C	Okla City	PHD		N Carol	1987
Meyer, Richard L.	Prof	South Fla	PHD	71	Wiscon	1970
Meyer, Thomas O.	Asst	Toledo	ABD		Ohio St	1989
Mian, Shezad	Asst	Emory	PHD	87	Rochest	1989
Michaely, Roni	Asst	Cornell	PHD	90	NYU	1990
Michel, Allen J.	Assoc	Boston Univ	PHD		Cornell	
Michelson, Stuart	Asst	E Illinois	PHD	91	Kansas	1991
Mickens, Al	Assoc	SUNY Old Wes	PHD			1978
Middleton, Mary	Assoc	Ogelthorpe	PHD	88	Georgia	1988
Miestchovich Jr., Ivan J.	Assoc	New Orleans	PHD	86	So Miss	1978
Mikaya, Ivy Locke	Asst	Florida St	ABD		Florida	1990
Mikhail, Azmi D.	Prof	Ohio Univ	PHD	62	Ohio St	1967
Mikkelson, Wayne H.	Assoc	Oregon	PHD	80	Rochest	1984
Miles, James A.	Prof	Penn State	PHD		Penn St	1980
Milgrim, Herbert	Prof	CS-Dominguez	PHD	68	NYY	1972

Name	Rank	School	Degree	Age	PhD From	Year
Millar, James A.	Prof	Arkansas	PHD	71	Oklahoma	1970
Miller, Charles W.	Assoc	Marymount	MBA		Geo Wash	
Miller, Edward M.	Prof	New Orleans	PHD		MIT	
Miller, Jerry D.	Prof	West Txs St	PHD		LSU	1970
Gene Edwards Professor of Finance						
Miller, John R.	Asst	Mercer-Atlan	MBA		Geo St	1975
Miller, Merton H.	Prof	Chicago	PHD	52	JohnsHop	1961
Robert R. McCormick Distinguished Service Professor of Finance						
Miller, Norman G.	Prof	Cincinnati	PHD	77	Ohio St	1980
Miller, Otis	Prof	Wm Jewell	PHD		Missouri	1978
Miller, Richard K.	Asst	Robt Morris				
Miller, Robert E.	C-Ac	No Illinois	PHD	75	Kansas	1989
Miller, Roger L.	Assoc	No Illinois	PHD	65	Illinois	1976
Miller, Ronald K.	Assoc	Oklahoma St	PHD		Missouri	1981
Miller, Thomas	Prof	Kennesaw St	DBA	74	Indiana	1989
Miller, Walter	Assoc	Quinnipiac	PHD		NYU	
Millington, Kent	Asst	Idaho State	MBA		Brig Yg	
Mills, Dixie L.	Prof	Illinois St	PHD	80	Cinn	1980
Mills, Edwin S.	Prof	Northwestern	PHD	56	Birmingh	
Alan E. Peterson Distinguished Professor of Finance						
Mills, Geofrey T.	Assoc	No Iowa	PHD	79	Illinois	1983
Milonas, Nikos	Assoc	Massachusett	PHD	84	Baruch	
Milton, David	Asst	Bentley	MBA	85	Bentley	1983
Min, Sungky	Asst	SW Louisiana	PHD	90		1990
Minahan, John R.	VAsst	Babson	PHD		MIT	
Mintz, Seymour D.	Assoc	Insurance	JD		Toura Lw	
Mirus, Rolf	Prof	Univ Alberta	PHD	73	Minn	1971
Mishra, Banamber	Asst	McNeese St	PHD		Alabama	
Mishra, Banikanta	Asst	Emory	PHD	85	NYU	1988
Mishra, Chandra	Asst	Loyola-Chicg	PHD		Houston	1990
Misra, Lalatendu	Assoc	Tx-S Antonio	PHD	85	Texas	1982
Misumi, Takashi	Asst	Hitotsubashi	DBA		Hitotsub	1990
Mitchell, Jason	STut	W Australia	MACC	89	W Austra	1990
Mitchell, John B.	Asst	Cen Michigan	DBA	78	Kent St	1975
Mitchell, John M.	C-Ac$	Geneva	MBA	62	Pitt	1962
Mitchell, Karlyn	Prof	N Carol St	PHD	82	Michigan	
Mitchell, Kay	Asst	Barton	MBA		Campbell	1986
Mitchell, Mark L.	Asst	Chicago	PHD	87	Clemson	1990
Mitenko, Graham R.	Asst	Neb-Omaha	DBA		Memphis	
Mitra, Devashis	Prof	New Brunswic	PHD	91	Mass	1991
Mittler, Dale L.	Assoc	Capital	MBA		Capital	1978
Mittoo, Usha R.	Asst	U Manitoba	PHD	88	Brit Col	1988
Mittra, Sid	Prof	Oakland	PHD	62	Florida	1967
Miura, Ryozo	Prof	Hitotsubashi	PHD	76	UCB	1989
Mizrach, Bruce	VAsst	Pennyslvania				
visiting from Boston College						
Mlynaryk, Peter M.	Prof	CS-Fullerton	DBA	72	S Calif	1967
Mobilia, Pam	Asst	CUNY-Brookly	PHD			1991
Modani, Naval K.	Assoc	Cen Florida	PHD		So Carol	1983
Modest, David M.	C-Ac	Cal-Berkeley	PHD	81	MIT	1986
Modrow, William G.	Asst	South Fla	MS	63	Tx A&M	1963
Moeller, Susan	Asst	E Michigan	PHD	85	Mich St	1990
Moh'd, Mahmound	Asst	St Marys-Cdn				
Mohammad, Latiff	Lect	Clark Atlant	MBA		Atlanta	
Mohan, Daniel	Assoc	West Chester	PHD		Rutgers	1980
Mohan, Nancy K.	Asst	Dayton	PHD	86	Cinn	1987
Mohan, Santhosh	Asst	Ohio Northrn	PHD	90	Indiana	1991
Moini, Abdol H.	Assoc	Wis-Whitewat	PHD		Alabama	1985
Moizer, Peter	C-Pr	Univ Leeds	MA	83		1989
Mokkelbost, Per	Prof	Univ Calgary	PHD	73	Minn	1975
Mole, David	SLect	City Poly HK	PHD	87	Toronto	1989
Moloney, Damian	STut	Melbourne U	MCOM	91	Melbourn	1990
Monath, Donald R.	Assoc	Louisville	PHD	69	Florida	1969
Monroe, Margaret	Asst	Ill-Chicago				
Monroe, Margaret	Asst	Wayne State	PHD	81	Florida	1991
Monroe, Robert J.	Dean	Tulsa	DBA	70	Indiana	1981
Moody, George E.	Prof	Arkansas St	DBA		Indiana	
Mooney, Stephen P.	Assoc	St Cloud St	MS	82	So Meth	1986
Mooradian, Robert M.	Asst	Florida	PHD		Penn	1988
Moorcroft, Christian	Asst	Luther	MBA	85	Wi-LaCro	1966
Moore, B. C.	Assoc	Delta State	ABD		Miss	1986
Moore, Craig L.	C-Pr	Massachusett	PHD	72	Syrcuse	
Moore, Gary	Asst	Toledo				
Moore, Keith	Adj	New York U				
Moore, Larry	Asst	Memphis St	JD	76	Wash U	1967
Moore, Perry G.	Inst	David Lipsc	MA		Alabama	
Moore, Ronald W.	Adj	Harvard				
Moore, Scott	Asst	John Carroll	PHD	89	Kentucky	1986
Moore, William T.	Assoc	So Carolina	PHD	82	Va Tech	
Moosa, Suleman A.	Prof	CS-Chico	PHD	72	Penn	1980

Moosally, Joseph G.	Prof	Mankato St	PHD		Iowa	1969
Morck, Randall	Prof	Univ Alberta	PHD	86	Harvard	1986
Moreau, Art	Asst	McGill Univ	PHD		Iowa	1986
Morgan, Alfred D.	Prof	So Conn St	PHD		Harvard	
Morgan, Celia A.	C $	SW Texas St	PHD	71	Houston	1971
Morgan, Doug	Prof	Cal-Santa Br				
Morgan, George Emir	Prof	Virg Tech	PHD	77	N Carol	
Morgan, I. G.	Prof	Queen's Univ	PHD		Chicago	1978
Morin, Roger-Andre	Prof	Georgia St			Penn	
Morison, Ian C.	Prof	Loughborough	MA		Oxford	

Midland Group Professor of Banking and Finance

Morris, Barry K.	Prof	No Alabama	PHD	74	Arkansas	1974
Morris, Gene P.	Assoc	CS-Long Bch	MA			1967
Morris, Howard	Asst	Hillsdale	MBA	88	Penn	1991
Morris, James R.	Prof	Colo-Denver	PHD		Berkeley	
Morrison, Dianne	Inst	Wis-La Cross	MBA	87	Wis-LaCr	1990
Morrissey, Thomas F.	Prof	Case Western	PHD	70	Syracuse	
Morse, Joel N.	Assoc	Baltimore	PHD		Mass	
Mortazavi, Saeed	Prof	CS-Humboldt	PHD	83	Texas	1984
Morton, Allen D.	Asst	Western Conn			Penn	
Morton, Andrew	Asst	Ill-Chicago				
Moser, Ernest R.	H-Ac	NE Louisiana	PHD	73	Tx A&M	1976
Moses, Edward A.	Prof	Rollins	PHD	70	Georgia	1989
Moshirian, Farlborz	Asst	New So Wales	PHD		Monash	1990
Moss, Jimmy D.	Assoc	Lamar	PHD		Miss St	1986
Mossman, Charles	Asst	U Manitoba	ABD		W Ontari	1990
Mostaghimi, Mehdi	Assoc	So Conn St	MS		W Mich	
Mougoue, Mbodja	Asst	Cleveland St	PHD	89	N Orlean	1989
Mountain, Dean C.	Assoc	McMaster	PHD		W Ontari	
Movassaghi, Hormoz	Asst	Ithaca	ADB	91	Wiscon	1988
Moy, Ronald	Asst	St Johns	PHD			
Moyer, R. Charles	Prof	Wake Fr-Grad	PHD		Pitt	1988

Integon Chair in Finance

Mudaliar, Vishwa	Assoc	CS-Northrdge	PHD	85	So Carol	1982
Mueller, Paul A.	C-Ac	Bowling Gr	DBA	77	Kentucky	1976
Muhtaseb, Majed R.	Asst	CS-Pomona	PHD	87	Tenn	1988
Mukherjee, Tarun K.	Prof	New Orleans	DBA		Tx Tech	
Mulherin III, J. H.	Assoc	Clemson	PHD	84	Calif	1988
Mull, Rick	Asst	New Mex St	PHD	90	Georgia	1990
Mullineaux, Donald J.	C-Pr	Kentucky	PHD	71	Boston C	

Du Pont Chair in Banking and Finance

Mullins, Helena M.	Asst	Oregon	PHD	90	Berkeley	1990
Mullins, James E.	Prof	St Ambrose	MA	65	Marquett	1969
Mullis, David L.	Assoc	SC-Spartanbu	DBA	74	Miss St	1986
Mulugetta, Abraham	Assoc	Ithaca	PHD	86	Wiscon	1984
Mumey, Glen	C-Pr	Univ Alberta	PHD	65	Wash	1970
Mun, Kyung	Asst	NE Missouri	PHD	91	Va Tech	1991
Muoghalu, Michael	Asst	Pittsburg St	DBA		La Tech	
Murphy, J. Austin	Assoc	Oakland	PHD	84	Georgia	1984
Murphy, James T.	Prof	Tulane	PHD	62	Iowa	
Murphy, Neil B.	Prof	Virg Comm	PHD	86	Illinois	1988
Murray, Barbara	Assoc	Mich-Dearbor	PHD	67	Wayne St	1978
Murray, Michael J.	Prof	Winona State	PHD		Notre Dm	1986
Murray, Peter	Dean	Chaminade	MBA		Penn	1966
Murthy, Shashidhar N.	Asst	Rutgers-Newk	PHD		Columbia	
Muscarella, Chris J.	Assoc	Penn State	PHD	83	Purdue	
Musser, William M.	Inst	Penn St-Harr	MBA	75	Geo Wash	1978
Musson, H. S.	Assoc	Univ Windsor				
Mustafa, Chowdhury	Asst	Louisiana St	PHD	88	CS-Diego	1988
Musumeci, James J.	Asst	American U	PHD	87	Texas	1991
Muthuswamy, Jayram	Asst	Duke	PHD	90	Chicago	
Myer, Francis C. Neil	Asst	Cleveland St	PHD	89	St Louis	1989
Myers, Phyllis S.	Assoc	Virg Comm	PHD	84	S Carol	1982
Myers, Stewart Clay	Prof	MIT	PHD	67	Stanford	1966

Gordon Y. Billard Professor of Finance

Nabar, Prafulla	Asst	So Methodist	PHD	86	NYU	1987
Nachman, David C.	H-Pr	Georgia Tech	PHD	73	Northwes	1973
Nadig, Narayanaswamy	Asst	Benedict Col	MBA		Atlanta	
Nadler, Paul S.	Asst	Rutgers-Newk	PHD		New York	
Nagarajan, K. V.	Asst	Laurentian	PHD	87	Buffalo	
Nagy, Robert	Asst	WI-Green Bay	PHD	80	Miss	1988
Naidu, G. N.	Prof	Illinois St	PHD	76	Iowa	1976
Najand, Mohammed	Asst	Old Dominion	PHD		Syracuse	
Najarajan, S.	Asst	McGill Univ	PHD		Northwes	1988
Nam, Sang-Koo	Prof	Korea Univ	PHD			1983
Nance, Deana Renee	Asst	Louisiana Te	PHD		N Texas	1989
Nanisetty, Prasad	Asst	Indiana	PHD	86	Michigan	
Nanney, Jerry	C-Pr	Olivet	PHD	80	Ocean Pa	1989
Narayanan, M. P.	Asst	Michigan	PHD	83	Northwes	1986
Narayanaswamy, C. R.	Assoc	Idaho	PHD	84	Temple	1990

Narron, Charlie C.	Prof	Mars Hill	MA	58	E Carol	1958
Nash, Robert	Prof	Texas A&I	PHD		Tx A&M	1971
Nash, Timothy	Assoc	Northwood	MA	87		1981
Nashif, Mazin K.	Prof	CS-Dominguez	PHD	72	Nebraska	1973
Nasseh, Alireza	Assoc	St Louis	PHD		Mich St	
Nast, Donald A.	C-Ac	Florida St	PHD	75	Penn St	1974
Natell, Timothy	Prof	Minnesota				
Gelco Professor of Finance						
Nathan, Alli	Asst	Univ Calgary	PHD	90	Queens	1989
Navare, Jyoti	PLect	Bournemouth				1991
Nawalkha, Sanjay	Asst	Balitmore			Mass	
Nawrocki, David N.	Assoc	Villanova	PHD	76	Penn St	1981
Nayar, Nandkumar	Asst	Oklahoma	PHD	88	Iowa	1988
Nazar, Vivian	Asst	Ferris State	MBA		London	1988
Neal, Robert S.	Asst	U Washington	PHD	87	Chicago	1987
Neave, E. H.	Prof	Queen's Univ	PHD		Berkeley	1991
Neely, Walter P.	Prof	Millsaps	PHD	74	Georgia	1980
Neilsen, James F.	Prof	Oregon State	DBA	72	Colorado	1974
Nelson, Daniel B.	Asst	Chicago	PHD	88	MIT	1988
Nelson, David T.	Prof	Bentley	PHD	74	Wiscon	1983
Nelson, Edward A.	Assoc	CS-San Bern	PHD	68	UCLA	1987
Nelson, Jack M.	Assoc	Insurance	PHD		Penn	
Nelson, Jeryl	Inst	Wayne St Col	MBA	87	S Dakota	1986
Nelson, John	Prof	Luther	MBA	65	Iowa	1958
Nelson, Mark J.	Prof	Weber State	PHD	69	Oregon	1973
Nelson, Ramona	Asst	Luther	MBT	85	Minn	1975
Nelson, William B.	Assoc	Indiana NW	PHD	74	Rice	1979
Nemec, Richard	Asst	Texas A&I	ABD		Kentucky	1990
Netter, Jeffry M.	Asst	Georgia	PHD	88	Ohio St	1989
Neustel, Arthur D.	VAsst	Cen Florida	PHD		Va Tech	1984
Neveu, Raymond P.	Prof	So Maine	PHD	68	Pitt	1982
Newbould, Gerald D.	Prof	Nev-L Vegas	PHD		Liverpol	1988
Newman, Joseph A.	Asst	No Illinois	PHD	89	Tennesse	1989
Ng, Lilian K.	Asst	Texas	PHD	89	Penn	1989
Ng, Victor K.	Asst	Michigan	PHD	89	Calif	1989
Ngassam, Christopher	Asst	Delaware	PHD		Tx-Arlin	
Nguyen, Hong V.	Assoc	Scranton	PHD	81	SUNY-Bin	1979
Nichols, Michael	Inst	St Louis				
Nicol, Robert	Prof	Melbourne U	PHD	72	UCLA	1974
Niden, Cathy M.	Asst	Notre Dame	PHD	88	Chicago	
Niehaus, Gregory R.	Assoc	So Carolina	PHD	85	Wash U	
Nielsen, Carl C.	Assoc	Wichita St	PHD	66	Nebraska	1968
Nielsen, Lars T.	Assoc	INSEAD	PHD	85	Harvard	1989
Nielson, Norma L.	Prof	Oregon State	PHD	79	Penn	1985
Niendorf, Robert M.	Prof	Wis-Oshkosh	PHD	69	Wiscon	1969
Nikbakht, Ehsan	Assoc	Hofstra	PHD	82	Geo Wash	1982
Nikolaos, Adamou	Asst	Russell Sage	PHD			1989
Nimalendran, Mahendrarajah	VAsst	Florida	PHD		Michigan	1990
Noe, Thomas H.	Asst	Georgia St	PHD		Texas	
Noehl, James	Asst	Moorhead St	MBA	69	Minn	1972
Nohr, Timothy W.	Inst	Wichita St	MBA	86	Wichita	1986
Nolen Jr., James A.	Lect	Texas	MBA	76	Texas	1980
Noorbakhsh, Abbas	Assoc	Slippery Roc	PHD		Kansas	1990
Noreiko, Gary	Assoc	So Colorado	PHD			
Norgaard, Richard L.	Prof	Connecticut	PHD	62	Minn	1969
Noronha, Gregory	Asst	Old Dominion				
Norrie, Gweneth	STut	Deakin Univ	BCOM	83	Deakin	1983
Norton, Edgar A.	Asst	F Dick-Madis	PHD	84	Illinois	1988
Nosari, E. Joe	Prof	Florida St	PHD	72	Kentucky	1970
Noti, Gabriel	Asst	New So Wales	PHD		NS Wales	1972
Noulas, Athansios		Bridgeport				
Nourse, Hugh O.	Prof	Georgia	PHD		Chicago	
Nowak, Paul	Assoc	Drury	PHD	79	Fla St	
Nowicki, Lawrence W.	Asst	Adelphi	PHD	84	Paris	
Ntoko, Alfred Ngome	Asst	SUNY Oswego	PHD	85	SUNY-Bin	1985
Nunn Jr., Kenneth P.	Assoc	Connecticut	PHD	79	Mass	1979
Nunnally Jr., Bennie H.	C $	N Car-Charl	DBA		Virginia	1978
Nunthirapakorn, Thakol	Prof	Youngstown	PHD	84	Arkansas	
Nuven, Diep	Asst	Catholic				
Nwanna, Gladson	Assoc	Morgan State				
Nye, Blaine	Prof	San Francisc	PHD	84	Stanford	1988
Nye, David J.	Prof	Florida	PHD	73	Penn	1971
Nye, William A.	Prof	San Diego St	PHD	62	Penn	1962
Nyerges, Richard T.	Assoc	S Ill-Edward	PHD	72	Mich St	1980
O'Brien, Patrick	Dean	Jacksonvl St	PHD	77	Okla St	1991
O'Brien, Thomas J.	Assoc	Connecticut	PHD	80	Florida	1986
O'Connell, William E.	Prof	Wm & Mary	DBA	67	Indiana	
Chessie Professor of Business Administration						
O'Connor, Dennis J.	Prof	CS-Fullerton	PHD	67	SocResea	1971
O'Donnell, John L.	Prof	Michigan St	DBA	54	Indiana	

Name	Rank	School	Degree	Yr	Deg School	Yr
O'Hanlon, J.	SLect	U Lancaster	MA		Lancaste	
O'Hara, H. Thomas	Assoc	Suffolk	PHD			
O'Hara, Maureen	Prof	Cornell	PHD	79	Northwes	1979
O'Leary, Harold	Assoc	Fla Southern	DBA			1978
O'Neil, Barbara	Asst	Jersey City	MBA			
O'Neill, June	Prof	CUNY-Baruch	PHD		Columbia	
O'Sullivan, P.	Assoc	SUNY Old Wes	PHD			1975
Odom, Oris L.	C-Pr$	Texas-Tyler	DBA	79	Oklahoma	1983
Odutola, Adelaja	Inst	Virg Union	MS		Va State	1983
Ofek, Eli	Asst	New York U				
Ofer, Aharon R.	V	Northwestern	PHD	73	Penn	
Officer, Dennis T.	Assoc	Kentucky	PHD		Arkansas	1979
Officer, Robert	Prof	Melbourne U	PHD			1986
Ogawa, Eiji	Assoc	Hitotsubashi	DBA		Hitotsub	1988
Ogden, Joseph P.	Assoc	SUNY-Buffalo	PHD	82	Purdue	1988
Oglesby, Nicholas P.	Lect	N Car-Greens	BS		Virginia	1985
Ogum, George	Asst	Virginia St	DBA		Memphis	1990
Oh, Gyutaeg	Asst	Iowa	PHD	91	Yale	1991
Oh, John S.	Dean$	Portland St	PHD	78	Virginia	1979
Oh, Kap-Soo	Asst	Drexel	PHD		Penn	1988
Okere, Vivian O.	Asst	Providence	PHD		Rhde Isl	1987
Okleshen, Henry N.	C-Pr	Mankato St	PHD		Arkansas	1980
Okoruwa, Ason	Asst	No Iowa	PHD	85	Georgia	1991
Olienyic, John P.	Assoc	Colorado St	PHD		Colo St	
Olsen, Gary L.	C-Ac	Carroll	PHD		Marquett	1975
Olsen, Robert A.	Prof	CS-Chico	PHD	74	Oregon	1975
Olson, Alden C.	Retir	Mich State	PHD		Minn	
Olson, Bruce H.	Prof	Miami U-Ohio	DBA	61	Indiana	
Olson, Gerard	Asst	Villanova	PHD	88	Drexel	
Olson, Howard G.	Asst	Wis-Whitewat	PHD		Madison	1977
Omberg, Edward	Assoc	San Diego St	PHD		UCLA	1989
Opler, Tim	Asst	So Methodist	PHD	90	UCLA	1991
Oppedahl, Richard A.	Prof	South Dakota	PHD	67	Wash	
Oppenheim, Alan J.		Montclair St	PHD		NYU	
Oppenheimer, Henry R.	Assoc	Rhode Island	PHD	79	Purdue	1987
Osaghae, Vincent	Inst	Chicago St	MBA	86	Gov St	1989
Osborne, Dale K.	Prof	Texas-Dallas	PHD	63	Kentucky	1984
Osborne, John W.	C-As	Morehead St	MBA		E Kentuc	1977
Osteryoung, Jerome S.	Prof	Florida St	PHD	71	Geo St	1974
Ottaviani, Alberto	Asst	Iona	MBA	83	Iona	1982
Otuteye, Eben	Asst	New Brunswic	PHD	90	Queen's	1987
Oveisi, Hadi F.	Dean	St Edwards	PHD	79	Texas	1981
Overstreet, George A.	Assoc	Virginia	PHD		Alabama	
Owen, Mike		Montana St	MS	63	MIT	
Owens, Emiel W.	Assoc	Houston	PHD	56	Ohio St	1971
Owens, James K.	Prof	West Txs St	DBA		Harvard	1978
Owers, James	Assoc	Georgia St	PHD			1991
Owers, James E.	Prof	Massachusett	PHD	82	Ohio St	
Oxenford, Jerry	Asst	Wis-Plattev	MBA		Iowa	1982
Ozatalay, Savas	H	Widener	PHD			
Paccess, Tania	Tutor	Flinders Un	BEC	91	Flinders	1991
Pace, Dan	Asst	Valparaiso	PHD	91	Fla St	1991
Pace, Kelley R.	Assoc	Alaska-Fairb	PHD	85	Georgia	1986
Pachraraj, Raj A.	Assoc	Bowling Gr	PHD		Ohio St	1976
Packer, James	Assoc	Cen Arkansas	DBA		LSU	
Padgham, Gene L.	Inst	Jacksonvl St	MBA		Jack St	1981
Padmanabhan, Prasad	Asst	Penn State	PHD		McGill	1988
Page, Alfred N. T. C. Clarke Professor	Dean	Wm & Mary	PHD	64	Chicago	1990
Page, Daniel E.	Assoc	Auburn	PHD		Georgia	1984
Page, Frank H.	Asst	Alabama	PHD		Illinois	1991
Pak, Simon	Assoc	Fla Internat	PHD	80	Berkeley	
Palasvirta, Asmo P.	Assoc	Memorial Un	PHD	85	Utah	1991
Palmer, Bruce Allen	Prof	Georgia St	PHD		Penn	
Palmer, Michael	Assoc	Colorado	PHD	67	Wash	1967
Palmisciano, William		Rhode Island				
Palmon, Oded	Assoc	Rutgers-N Br	PHD	81	Chicago	1988
Palumbo, George M.	Prof	Canisius	PHD	77	Syracuse	1978
Pan, Fung-Shine L.	Assoc	CS-Hayward	PHD	86	Berkeley	1990
Pan, Ming-Shiun	Assoc	Shippensburg	PHD		Alabama	1989
Panici, Joseph	Asst	W Illinois				
Pantalone, Coleen C.	Assoc	Northeastern	PHD		Iowa St	1981
Panton, Don Bradley	Prof	Tx-Arlington	PHD	72	Arizona	1989
Papaioannou, George J.	C-Ac	Hofstra	PHD	79	Penn St	1982
Papasyriopoulos, Nicholas	SLect	Univ Otago	PHD	90	Wiscon	1990
Pappas, James L.	Dean	South Fla	PHD	68	UCLA	1986
Parameswakan, Sunil	Asst	Iowa	PHD	91	Duke	1991
Parham, Jack	Asst	Hillsdale	MBA		Virginia	1991
Parham, W. Jackson	Inst	David Lipsc	MBA		Virginia	
Parhizgari, Ali M.	Prof	Fla Internat	PHD	76	Maryland	

184

Name	Rank	School	Degree	Yr	From	Yr
Parikh, Rajeev	Assoc	St Bonaventu	PHD	82	Buffalo	1982
Park, Hoon	Asst	Cen Florida	PHD		Geo St	1988
Park, Hun Y.	Assoc	Illinois	PHD	82	Ohio St	1982
Park, Jinsop	Asst	Cal-Riversid	PHD		Berkeley	1987
Park, Jinwoo	Asst	Kansas State	PHD	90	Iowa	1990
Park, John C.	Prof	Frostburg St	PHD		Nebraska	1970
Park, Jong H.	Assoc	Kennesaw St	PHD	74	Okla St	1988
Park, Sangsoo	Asst	SUNY-Buffalo	PHD	90	Chicago	1990
Parker, George C.	Prof	Stanford	PHD	67	Stanford	
Parker, Joseph	Prof	New Haven	PHD		Oklahoma	
Parker, Michael E.	Asst	NE Louisiana	DBA	91	Miss St	1990
Parker, Robert S.	Dean	Georgetown	PHD	69	Wharton	1986
Parkinson, Ken	Adj	New York U				
Parry, David L.	Prof	CS-Pomona	PHD	76	S Calif	1980
Parry, Jennifer R.	Head$	Massey Univ	MBS			1988
Parsegian, Elsa	Assoc	Youngstown	PHD	85	Pitt	
Parson, Wayman	Asst	Hampton	JD		N Car Ce	1988
Parsons, John Emery	Asst	MIT	PHD			
Partain, Robert T.	Dean	Texas-Tyler	PHD	67	Texas	1986
Partch, M. Megan	Assoc	Oregon	PHD	81	Wiscon	1981
Pashley, Mary M.	Asst	Tenn Tech	PHD	86	Tennesse	1986
Pasmantier, Anita	Prof	Seton Hall	PHD	89	Fordham	
Patchias, James C.	Assoc	Adelphi	MPHL	84	NYU	
Patel, Ajay	Asst	Missouri	PHD		Georgia	
Patin Jr., Roy P.	Assoc	McNeese St	DBA	80	Miss St	1980
Patnaik, Promode K.	Prof	Alabama A&M	PHD		Alabama	
Patridge, Dan C.	Prof	Mt Allison U				
Fred C. Manning Professor						
Patterson, C. S.	Assoc	Concordia U				
Patterson, Douglas M.	Assoc	Virg Tech	PHD	78	Wiscon	1980
Patterson, Harlan R.	Prof	Ohio Univ	PHD	63	Mich St	
Patton, Charles H.	Adj	Memphis St	JD	75	Memph St	1986
Patton, Robert	Dean	So Maine				
Paulas, John	Assoc	Lg Isl-Brook	MBA		Columbia	
Paulson, Albert S.	Prof	Rensselaer	PHD	67	Va Tech	1972
Pawlukiewicz, James E.	Asst	Xavier	PHD	91	Kentucky	1989
Payne, Bruce C.	C-Pr$	SW Louisiana	PHD	77	La St	1975
Peacock, Ken	Dean$	Appalach St	PHD	79	LSU	1983
Pearson, Neil D.	Prof	Rochester	PHD		MIT	
Peavler, Rosemary C.	Asst	Morehead St	DBA		Kentucky	1983
Peavy III, John W.	Prof	So Methodist	PHD	78	Tx-Arlin	1979
Mary Jo Vaughn Rauscher Chair in Financial Investments						
Peck, Earl M.	Prof	Baldwin-Wal	PHD	74	Colorado	
Peck, Sarah	Asst	Iowa	PHD	91	Rochest	1990
Peevey, Robert M.	Asst	Houston	PHD	91	Tx A&M	1991
Pelaez, Rolando F.	Assoc	Houston-Down	PHD		Houston	1986
Pencek, Thomas A.	Asst	SUNY-Fredoni	DBA		Miss St	1988
Penkar, Samuel H.	Assoc	Houston-Down	PHD	84	Miss St	1984
Pennacchi, George G.	Assoc	Illinois	PHD	84	MIT	1990
Pennington, James W.	Asst	Kennesaw St	ABD		Harvard	1990
Perdue, Daniel Grady	Asst	Houston-Cl L	PHD		Alabama	
Pereira, Fabio T.	Asst	So Alabama	PHD		Alabama	1988
Perez, Robert	Assoc	Iona	PHD	66	NYU	1982
Perfect, Steven B.	Asst	Florida St	PHD	91	Texas	1990
Perkins, Charles A.	C-Ac	Missouri Wes	PHD		Geo Wash	1991
Perlick, Walter W.	Prof	Cal Poly-SLO	PHD	73	Penn St	1979
Perotti, Enrico C.	Asst	Boston Univ	PHD		MIT	
Perrakis, Stylianos	Prof	Univ Ottawa	PHD	70	Berkeley	1970
Perry, James E.	Assoc	Babson	PHD		Oklahoma	
Perry, Larry G.	Assoc	Arkansas	DBA		La Tech	1982
Perry, Philip	Assoc	SUNY-Buffalo	PHD	79	Berkeley	1985
Persons, John C.	Asst	Ohio State	PHD	91	Chicago	
Pertl, Mars	C-Ac	Memphis St	PHD	74	Iowa	1982
Perumpral, Shalini E.	Assoc	Radford	PHD		Va Tech	1975
Pescatrice, Donn	Assoc	Iona	PHD	75	Purdue	1983
Pescow, Michael		St Joseph				
Petersen, Mitchell A.	Asst	Chicago	PHD	90	MIT	1990
Peterson, David R.	Prof	Florida St	PHD	81	N Carol	1981
Peterson, James	Asst	Notre Dame				
Peterson, Jeffrey	Asst	St Bonaventu	PHD	91	Alabama	1984
Peterson, Manferd	C-Pr	Nebraska	PHD	71	Mich St	1976
Peterson, Pamela P.	Prof	Florida St	PHD	81	N Carol	1981
Peterson, Richard L.	Prof	Texas Tech	PHD	66	Michigan	1982
Briscoe Professor of Bank Management						
Petrovich, James	Asst	Jackson St	MBA		W Fla	1984
Petry, Glenn	Prof	Wash State	DBA	73	Colorado	1973
Petrych, William	Prof	Youngstown	MA	57	Ohio St	
Pettengill, Glenn	Assoc	Emporia St	PHD	76	Arkansas	1989
Pettijohn, James B.	Assoc	SW Missouri	PHD	80	Nebraska	1982
Pettit Jr., L. C.	Assoc	Virginia	DBA		Virginia	

Pettit, R. Richardson	Prof	Houston	PHD	69	UCLA	1977	
Duncan Professor of Finance							
Pettway, Richard H.	Prof	Missouri	PHD	65	Texas		
Missouri Bankers Chair							
Petway, C. Briggs	Asst	Barton	MA		N Car St	1989	
Peyser, Paul	Assoc	George Wash	PHD	79	Wiscon		
Pfaff, Philip	Assoc	Canisius	PHD	73	Mich St	1979	
Pfleiderer, Paul C.	Assoc	Stanford	PHD	82	Yale	1981	
Pham, Toan M.	Asst	New So Wales	MCOM		NS Wales	1974	
Phelps, Katherine L.	Asst	Ind-So Bend	PHD	88	S Carol	1987	
Philippatos, G. C.	Prof	Tennessee	PHD		New York		
Distinguished Chaired Professor of Banking and Finance							
Phillips, Aaron L.	Asst	American U	DBA	86	So Illin	1989	
Phillips, Gordon	Asst	Purdue	PHD	91	Harvard	1991	
Phillips, Herbert E.	Prof	Temple	PHD	68	U Wash	1973	
Phillips, Joseph M.	Assoc	Creighton	PHD	82	Notre Dm	1982	
Phillips, Michael	Assoc	Austin Peay	ABD			1991	
Phillips, Michael	Prof	CS-Northrdge	PHD	82	CS-Domin	1985	
Phillips, Philip	Prof	Seton Hall	PHD	62	New York		
Phillips, Robert Wesley	C-Pr	Richmond	DBA	69	Indiana	1974	
Phillips, Susan M.	Prof	Iowa	PHD	73	LSU	1974	
Phillips, William	Assoc	Memphis St	CLU	78	Memphis	1965	
Picconi, Mario J.	Prof	San Diego	PHD		Rutgers		
Pichler, Pegaret	Asst	Maryland	PHD	90	Stanford		
Pickett, H. R.	Assoc	N Carol Cen	DBA	73	Virginia	1982	
Pikas, Ann	Adj	Niagara					
Pilotte, Eugene A.	Asst	Wyoming	PHD			1988	
Pilotte, Sheree	Asst	Wyoming	PHD			1989	
Pilzer, Arthur		Southeastern	MBA		American		
Pilzer, Paul	Adj	New York U	MBA	76	Penn		
Pinches, George E.	Prof	Kansas	PHD	68	Mich St	1977	
Pindyck, Robert Stephen	Prof	MIT	PHD	71	MIT	1971	
Mitsubishi Bank Professor of Finance							
Pinegar, Michael J.	Assoc	Brigham Yg	PHD	82	Utah	1987	
Pinkerton, John M.	Prof	Virg Tech	PHD	79	Florida	1977	
Piper, Beverly	Assoc	Ashland	MS	78	Toledo	1979	
Piper, Thomas R.	Prof	Harvard					
Pittman, Debbie	Inst	Rhodes	ABD		Memphis		
Pitts, C. G. C.	Asst	East Anglia	PHD		Oxon	1964	
Pitts, Robert	Prof	Gettysburg	PHD		Harvard		
Planisek, Sandra	Assoc	Grand Valley	PHD	80	Kent St	1985	
Plath, D. Anthony	Asst	N Car-Charl	DBA		Kent St	1987	
Platt, Harlan D.	Assoc	Northeastern	PHD		Michigan	1981	
Platt, W. G.	Prof	San Fran St	PHD	73	Wayne	1976	
Plattueu, Robert	Prof	CS-Fullerton	PHD		Michigan	1991	
Pletcher, Dale D.	Prof	CS-Sacrament	DBA	74	Kent St	1975	
Pliska, Staney R.	Prof	Ill-Chicago	PHD				
Plosser, Charles I.	Dean$	Rochester	PHD	76	Chicago	1978	
Fred H. Gowen Professor of Business Administration							
Poe, Jerry B.	Prof	Arizona St	DBA	63	Harvard	1974	
Poindexter, Eugene O.	Prof	West Georgia	PHD	70	Syracuse	1977	
Poindexter, J. C.	Prof	N Carol St	PHD		Ohio St		
Polakoff, Michael	Asst	Syracuse	PHD	87	SUNY Bin	1988	
Policano, Andrew J.	Dean	Wisconsin	PHD	75	Brown	1991	
Polonchek, John A.	Assoc	Oklahoma St	PHD		Ga Tech	1983	
Polson, Houston H.	C-As	Bellevue	JD	89	Creighto	1985	
Ponarul, Richard R.	Prof	CS-Chico	PHD		Chicago		
Poole, R. Clifton	Dean	Richmond	PHD	74	S Carol	1975	
Poon,	Lect	U Lancaster	PHD		Lancaste		
Poon, Percy S.	Asst	Nev-L Vegas	PHD		LSU	1989	
Pope, Ralph A.	Assoc	CS-Sacrament	DBA	84	Miss St	1989	
Poplin, Toby L.	Assoc	Pfeiffer	MA	68	Appal St	1976	
Porte, David	Asst	Marquette	PHD		W Ontar	1988	
Porter, Robert J.	Assoc	So Carolina	PHD	65	N Carol		
Potter, Thomas A.	Asst	North Dakota	DBA	86	Colorado	1986	
Potts, J. Franklin	Assoc	Baylor	PHD		LSU	1968	
Potts, Tom L.	Assoc	Baylor	PHD		Illinois	1971	
Poulsen, Annette B.	Assoc	Georgia	PHD	83	Ohio St	1987	
Pourian, Heydar	Assoc	W Carolina	PHD	80	Wis-Milw	1984	
Power, David M.	Lect	Dundee	MSC	87		1987	
Power, Fred B.	Prof	South Fla	MED	64	Florida	1964	
Power, Mark L.	Assoc	Iowa State	PHD	81	Iowa	1983	
Pradhan, Surendra	Assoc	CS-Hayward	PHD	85	Tx-Dalla	1985	
Prag, Jules	Asst	Claremont	PHD	88	Rochest	1986	
Prakash, Arun J.	C-Pr	Fla Internat	PHD	81	Oregon		
Prasad, Devendra	Asst	Tx-S Antonio	PHD	90	Oklahoma	1988	
Prasad, Rose M.	Assoc	Cen Michigan	PHD	87	Cinn	1985	
Pratt, Brian	Asst	U Lethbridge	PHD			1990	
Pratt, Hugh	Asst	U Manitoba	PHD	91	Florida	1991	
Pratt, Richard T.	Prof	Utah	MBA	62	Utah	1966	

Preece, Dianna C.	Asst	Louisville	PHD	90	Kentucky	1989
Preston, John G.	Assoc	Boston Coll	DBA	65	Harvard	1969
Prestopino, Chris J.	Prof	CS-Chico	PHD	74	Penn	1972
Prezas, Alexandros P.	Assoc	Suffolk	PHD		Northwes	
Price, Kelly	Assoc	Wayne State	PHD	76	Michigan	1982
Prill, Ed	Asst	Colorado St	PHD		Illinois	
Pringle, John J.	Prof	No Carolina	PHD	72	Stanford	1973
C. Knox Massey Professor of Business Administration						
Prisman, Eliezer	Assoc	York Univ	DSC		ITIsrael	1989
Pritchard, Robert E.	Prof	Glassboro St	EDD		Penn	1971
Pritchett, S. Travis	Prof	So Carolina	DBA	69	Indiana	1973
Proctor, James E.	Assoc	Wofford	PHD	76	Clemson	1981
Puelz, Robert	Asst	Memphis St	PHD	90	Georgia	1990
Puffer, Marlene	Asst	Univ Toronto	ABD		Rochest	1990
Pugh, Dwight A.	Assoc	Ohio Univ	PHD	69	Ohio U	1969
Pugh, William N.	Asst	Auburn	PHD		Fla St	1986
Puglisi, Donald	Prof	Delaware	DBA	72	Indiana	1971
Pullara, Santo J.	Prof	Mass-Lowell	PHD	62	Syracuse	
Pulley, Lawrence B.	Assoc	Wm & Mary	PHD		Virginia	1985
Pullman, Howard W.	Prof	Youngstown	PHD	73	Columbia	
Purchas, Graeme	Lect	Canterbury	BCOM	65	Victoria	1989
Puri, Tribhuvan	Asst	Temple	PHD		Tennesse	
Puri, Yash	Prof	Mass-Lowell	DBA	77	Indiana	
Pyatt, Edward J.	Prof	Hampton	PHD	85	Temple	1984
Pyle, David H.	Prof	Cal-Berkeley	PHD	68	MIT	1968
Willis H. Booth Professor of Banking and Finance						
Pyun, C. S.	Prof	Memphis St	PHD	66	Georgia	1970
Query, Tim	Assoc	Indiana St				
Quigg, Laura J.	Asst	Illinois	PHD	91	Berkeley	1990
Quinn, Frances A.	Asst	Merrimack	MS		Bentley	
Quinn, Patrick	H-Pr	Wis-Superior	EDD		No Illin	1971
Quintero, Socorro M.	Asst	South Fla	PHD	89	Texas	1990
Raad, Elias A.	Asst	Ithaca	PHD	89	Alabama	1989
Rabinovitch, Ramon	Assoc	Houston	PHD	74	New York	1980
Racette, George A.	Assoc	Oregon	PHD	72	U Wash	1974
Racster, Ronald L.	Prof	Ohio State	PHD	67	Illinois	1968
Radcliffe, Robert C.	Assoc	Florida	PHD	71	Ohio St	1971
Radosevich, Barbara	Inst	Colo-Denver	EDS		West St	
Ragas, Wade R.	Prof	New Orleans	PHD	76	Ohio St	1976
Rahgozar, Reza	Assoc	Wis-Rvr Fall	PHD		Claremon	1987
Rahim, Naizur	Asst	Chris Newpor	MBA		Hampton	1988
Rahimian, Eric N.	Assoc	Alabama A&M	PHD		Indiana	
Rahman, Hamid	Asst	Old Dominion				
Rahman, Mahmud	Asst	E Michigan	PHD	91	Texas	1991
Rahman, Shafiqur	Asst	Portland St	PHD	86	Illinois	1986
Rahmlow, Harold F.	Asst	St Joseph	PHD	65	Wash St	1987
Rahnama, Masha	Asst	Winona State	PHD		Iowa St	1990
Rai, Anoop	Asst	Hofstra	PHD	87	Indiana	1988
Rainish, Robert	Prof	New Haven	PHD		CUNY	
Rajan, Murli	Asst	Scranton	MBA	85	Scranton	1989
Rajan, Raghuram	Asst	Chicago	PHD	91	MIT	1991
Rajanikanth, Nareseeyappa	Inst	Miss Vall St	MS		Miss St	1987
Rakes, Ganas K.	C-Pr	Ohio Univ	DBA		Wash U	
O'Bleness Professor of Banking and Finance						
Ralser, Tom	Asst	Mesa State				
Ralston, August	Prof	Iowa State	PHD	73	Penn	1982
Ramakomud, Sriprinya	C-Ac	Howard	PHD	63	Indiana	1977
Ramakrishnan, Kumoli	Asst	Hofstra	PHD	85	Texas	1985
Ramamurtie, Sailesh	Asst	Georgia St	PHD		Minn	1990
Ramanlal, Pradipkumer	Asst	So Carolina	PHD	91	Michigan	
Ramanujam, Srinivasa	Assoc	Insurance	PHD		Brown	
Ramaswamy, Krishna	Prof	Pennsylvania	PHD	78	Stanford	1985
Ramcharran, Harridutt	Asst	Akron	PHD	78	SUNY-Bin	1986
Ramirez, Gabriel	Lect	SUNY-Bingham	PHD	88	Geo St	1988
Ramjee, Anju	Assoc	No Kentucky	PHD	87	Cinn	1988
Ramjee, Balasubramani	Assoc	No Kentucky	PHD	87	Cinn	1988
Randall, Maury R.	C-Ac	Rider	PHD		New York	
Randle, Paul A.	Prof	Utah State	PHD	70	Illinois	1970
Randolph, William L.	Assoc	Norfolk St	PHD		Alabama	1989
Rangan, Nanda K.	Assoc	So Illinois	PHD	86	Tx A&M	1986
Rankin, David Foster	C-Pr	Southern Ark	PHD		Miss	1968
Rao, Narendar	Asst	NE Illinois	PHD	89	Cinn	1990
Rao, Ramesh	Assoc	Texas Tech	PHD	85	Tx Tech	1987
Rao, Ramesh K. S.	Prof	Texas	DBA	78	Indiana	1978
Rao, Spuma	Asst	SW Louisiana	PHD	88	Miss St	1988
Rao, Yedla K.	Prof	Alabama A&M	PHD	64	Maryland	
Rappaport, Allen	Prof	No Iowa	PHD	68	Texas	1982
Rashid, Muhammad	Prof	New Brunswic	PHD		Queen's	1985
Rathinasamy, Rathina S.	Asst	Ball State	PHD	87	Tennesse	1988
Ratner, Mitchell	Asst	Rider	PHD		Drexel	

Name	Rank	School	Degree	Yr	From	Yr
Ravenscraft, David J.	Assoc	No Carolina	PHD	80	Northwes	1987
Raver, Daniel H.	Asst	Geneva	MBA	85	Pitt	1980
Ravichandran, R.	Asst	Colorado	PHD	86	Iowa	1988
Ravid, S. Abraham	Assoc	Rutgers-Newk	PHD		Cornell	
Raviv, Artur	Prof	Northwestern	PHD	74	Northwes	
Ray, Marvin E.	Prof	Valdosta St	PHD	74	Arkansas	1974
Ray, Russ	Assoc	Louisville	PHD	78	Michigan	1983
Ray, Terry T.	C	Indiana-PA				
Rayborn, William	Asst	Mississippi	DBA		Memphis	
Rayhorn, Charles	Asst	No Michigan	ABD		Colorado	1989
Rayome, David	Asst	No Michigan	MBA	88	Akron	1990
Ready, Mark	Asst	Wisconsin	PHD	90	Cornell	1990
Rebello, Michael	Asst	Georgia St	PHD		Texas	1990
Rebelo, Sergio	Asst	Northwestern	PHD	88	Rochest	
Reddy, Venkat	Asst	Colorado Spr	ABD		Penn St	1991
Redle, David A.	Asst	Akron	JD	80	Akron	1981
Redman, Arnold L.	Assoc	W Kentucky	PHD	79	Illinois	1985
Redmer, Timothy A. O.	Prof	Regent	PHD	89	Va Comm	1991
Redmon, Alonzo L.	Assoc	N Carol A&T	PHD	87	N Carol	
Reed, Debra	Lect	Texas A&M	PHD	82	Purdue	1982
Reed, Morris	Asst	East Central	MBA	70	Hawaii	1975
Reeder, Danny B.	Asst	Okla Baptist	PHD	91	Okla St	1991
Rees, David J.	SLect	Murdoch Univ	PHD			1991
Regan, Edward	Adj	New York U	LLD	74	SUNY	
Rege, Udayan	Prof	Brock Univ	PHD	74	W Ontar	1984
Reiber, Ronald R.	Assoc	Canisius	PHD	74	Arizona	1971
Reichenstein, William	Assoc	Baylor	PHD		Ntr Dame	1990
Powers Chair of Investment Management						
Reichert, Alan K.	Prof	Cleveland St	PHD	75	Ohio St	1989
Reid, Donald W.	Assoc	So Alabama	PHD		Kentucky	1990
Reiff, Wallace W.	Prof	Cen Florida	DBA	62	Indiana	1970
Reiling, Henry B.	Prof	Harvard	JD	65	Columbia	
Reilly, Frank K.	Prof	Notre Dame	PHD		Chicago	
Reilly, Raymond R.	Assoc	Michigan	PHD	70	Penn St	1970
Reinganum, Marc R.	Prof	Iowa	PHD	79	Chicago	1987
Reinhart, Walter J.	C-Ac	Loyola-Maryl	PHD		N Carol	1984
Reints, William W.	Prof	San Diego St	PHD	66	U Wash	1966
Remaley, William	Prof	Susquehanna	PHD	71	New York	1973
Remmers, H. Lee	Prof	INSEAD	PHD	67	Manchest	1962
Rendleman, Richard J.	Prof	No Carolina	PHD	76	N Carol	1983
Rentz, William F.	Assoc	Univ Ottawa	PHD	71	Rochest	1975
Rentzler, Joel	Prof	CUNY-Baruch	PHD		NYU	
Renwick, Fred B.	Prof	New York U	PHD	66	New York	
Resnick, Bruce	Assoc	Indiana				
Reuben, Lucy J.	Asst	Florida A&M	PHD		Michigan	
Reyes, Mario G.	Asst	Idaho	PHD	87	Arkansas	1985
Rezranian, Rasoul	Asst	NE Illinois	PHD	89	So Ill	1990
Rhea, Joy L.	Inst	Jacksonvl St	MBA		Samford	1984
Rhee, Moon-Whoan	Inst	Towson State	PHD	91	Maryland	1987
Rhee, S. Ghon	Prof	Rhode Island	PHD	78	Ohio St	1989
Rhee, Thomas A.	Assoc	CS-Long Bch	PHD			1988
Rhee, Yinsong	Prof	St Cloud St	PHD	85	Minn	1988
Rhim, Jong C.	Asst	So Indiana	PHD	90	Missouri	1989
Rhoads, Thomas B.		Southeastern	MS		Geo Wash	
Rhoda, Kenneth L.	Assoc	LaSalle	PHD		SUNY-Buf	1981
Rhys, H.	Lect	Univ Wales				1992
Rice, Edward M.	Assoc	U Washington	PHD	78	UCLA	1979
Rice, Michael L.	Prof	Alaska-Fairb	PHD	75	N Carol	
Rice, Sherman T.	Adj	New York U	PHD	50	Illinois	
Rich, James D.	Lect	Wis-Whitewat	MBA		Wis-Whit	1988
Rich, Steven Paul	Asst	Baylor	PHD		Indiana	1982
Richards, Charles	Asst	Austin Peay				1991
Richards, K.	SLect	Univ Wales				
Richards, R. Malcolm	Dean	Wichita St	PHD	74	Michigan	1991
Richards, Verlyn D.	Prof	Kansas State	PHD	66	Illinois	1965
Richardson, Linda L.	Assoc	Siena Coll	PHD		Arkansas	1991
Richardson, Matthew P.	Asst	Pennsylvania	PHD	89	Stanford	1989
Elliott Baim Term Assistant Professor of Finance						
Richey, Clyde	Prof	Colorado	PHD	69	Indiana	1969
Richey, Thomas Craig	Assoc	West Florida	ABD	61	Northwes	1968
Riddick, Leigh A.	Asst	American U	PHD	88	Wiscon	1989
Riddiough, Timothy R.	Asst	Cincinnati	PHD	91	Wiscon	1991
Ridge, Jenny	SLect	Massey Univ	MBS			1980
Riding, Allan L.	Prof	Carleton Un				
Rieber, William J.	C	Butler	PHD	79	Pitt	
Riehl, Heinz	Adj	New York U	PMD	74	Harvard	
Riener, Kenneth	Prof	Cal Poly-SLO	PHD	76	Purdue	1983
Rietz, Thomas	Asst	Northwestern	PHD	88	Iowa	
Riley, Neil	Assoc	Fran Marion	PHD	86	Miss	1991
Riley, William B.	C-Pr	W Virginia	PHD	76	Arkansas	1978

Name	Rank	School	Degree	Yr	PhD School	Yr
Rim, Hong K.	Assoc	Shippensburg	PHD		Penn St	1986
Rimbey, James N.	Asst	Arkansas	DBA		Kentucky	1988
Rini, Charles T.	Assoc	Cleveland St	DBA	71	Kent St	1975
Ritchey, Robert	Assoc	Texas Tech	PHD	81	Arizona	1982
Ritchie Jr., John C.	Prof	Temple	PHD	63	Penn	
Ritchken, Peter	Prof	Case Western	PHD		Case Wes	
Ritter, Jay R.	Assoc	Illinois	PHD	81	Chicago	1989
Rivard, Richard J.	Assoc	South Fla	PHD	78	Tx A&M	1977
Rivetti, Daniel A.	Assoc	San Diego	DBA		Kent St	
Rivoli, Pietra	Assoc	Georgetown	PHD	84	Florida	1983
Rix, James A.	Prof	Okla Chr	PHD		Arkansas	1989
Rizzuto, Tonald J.	Prof	Denver	PHD		New York	1975
Roayaei, Jean	Assoc	Fayetteville	PHD		Fla St	
Robb, Alan J.	H $	Canterbury	MCOM	76	Canterbu	1979
Robbins, Ed	Asst	Hawaii-Manoa	PHD	87	Stanford	1988
Roberson, John	AdjPr	Northwestern	MBA	64	Harvard	
Robertson, J. Fiona	Asst	Seattle	MA	82	Queens	1987
Robin, Ashok J.		Rochest Tech	PHD	79	SUNY-Buf	1989
Robinson, Christopher M.	Assoc	York Univ	PHD		Toronto	1983
Robinson, Michael J.	Assoc	Univ Calgary	PHD	89	W Ontari	1990
Robinson, Michael L.	Asst	St Marys-Ind	MBA	78	Loyola	1984
Robinson, Richard M.	Asst	E Kentucky	PHD		Oregon	1985
Robson, Keith	Lect	Manches Inst	PHD		Manchest	1988
Rocourt, George F.	Adj	Barry	ABD	75	JHopkins	1991
Roden, Foster	Prof	North Texas	PHD	70	N Texas	1974
Rodriguez, Ricardo J.	Asst	U Miami	PHD	86	Texas	1985
Roenfeldt, Rodney L.	C-Pr	So Carolina	DBA	72	Indiana	1974
Rogers, Ronald C.	Assoc	So Carolina	PHD	83	Ohio St	
Rojalski, Richard	Prof	Dartmouth	PHD	74	Michigan	1976
Roley, V. Vance	Prof	U Washington	PHD	77	Harvard	1983
Rolfe, Cecil	Prof	S Col 7th Dy	PHD	66	Maryland	1964
Roll, Richard W.	Prof	UCLA	PHD	69	Chicago	1976
Allstate Professor of Insurance and Finance						
Romano, Roberta	Prof	Yale	JD		Yale	1984
Rose, Clarence C.	Prof	Radford	PHD		Va Tech	
Rose, John T.	Prof	Baylor	PHD		Wash U	1984
Lacy Chair in Banking						
Rose, Lawrence	Prof	San Jose St	PHD	85	Tx A&M	1985
Rose, Peter S.	Prof	Texas A&M	PHD	69	Arizona	1969
Rose, Terry L.	Assoc	W Virginia	PHD	78	Illinois	1984
Rosen, Kenneth T.	Prof	Cal-Berkeley	PHD		MIT	
California Real Estate Chair						
Rosenbaum, E.	Prof	Univ Windsor				
Rosenberg, Seymour L.	C-Ac	Central Conn	PHD			1981
Rosenbloom, Jerry S.	C-Pr	Pennsylvania				
Frederick H. Ecker Professor						
Rosenfeld, Gerald	Adj	New York U				
Rosenfeld, James D.	C-Ac	Emory	PHD	81	NYU	1983
Rosenstein, Stuart N.	Asst	So Illinois	PHD	87	Colorado	1987
Rosensweig, Jeffrey A.	Asst	Emory	PHD	85	MIT	1988
Rosenthal, Leonard	Assoc	Bentley	PHD	77	CUNY	1983
Rosko, Peter	Assoc	Minnesota				
Ross, Donald G.	Asst	St Fran Xav				
Ross, Ray L.	Prof	Youngstown	PHD	73	Illinois	1978
Ross, Stephen	Prof	Yale	PHD		Harvard	1977
Rossell, Fred	Asst	Calif U-Penn	MBA		Calif-PA	1990
Rosser, Bruce A.	Lect	Adelaide	MEC			1989
Rossman, Joseph	Assoc	Texas A&I	PHD		Iowa St	1970
Rotenberg, Wendy D.	Asst	McMaster	PHD		Toronto	
Roth, Herbert J.	C-Pr$	Shippensburg	PHD	68	Ohio St	1968
Rothwell, John	Prof	Xavier	MBA		Xavier	1963
Rouse, J. R.	VInst	Clemson	MPA		Clemson	
Rouse, Michael	Inst	Simmons	MBA	81	Boston U	
Roussakis, Emmanuel N.	Prof	Fla Internat	PHD	68	Louvain	
Rouwenhorst, G.	Asst	Yale	PHD		Rochest	1990
Rowell, Dexter	Assoc	Chris Newpor	PHD		Penn	1981
Rowland, M.	Asst	Detroit Merc	MA	84	Wayne St	1990
Rowley, Allan	Tutor	Univ Wales	BSC	89	Aberys	1990
Roy, Jean	Prof	Univ Laval				
Rozeff, Michael S.	Prof	SUNY-Buffalo	PHD	74	Rochest	1989
Louis M. Jacobs Professor of Corporate Financial Management						
Rozycki, John	Asst	Drake	PHD	91	Penn St	1990
Ruback, Richard	Prof	Harvard				
Rubash, Arlyn R.	Assoc	Bradley	PHD	75	Penn St	1974
Rubash, Marjorie A.	Inst	Bradley	MBA		Bradley	1988
Rubens, Jack H.	C-Ac	Bryant	DBA	84	Kent St	1991
Rubin, Bruce L.	Assoc	Old Dominion	PHD		Case Wes	1981
Rubinstein, Mark E.	Prof	Cal-Berkeley	PHD	71	UCLA	1972
Rudd, E. Ann	Inst	Miami U-Ohio	ABD			
Rudolf, Uwe	Assoc	Luther	MBA	78	S Calif	1968

Name	Rank	School	Degree	Yr	Institution	Yr
Rudolph, Patricia M.	Prof	Alabama	PHD		N Carol	1976
Ruggeri, Paul J.	Assoc	Siena Coll	ABD		Renssela	1984
Rumsey, John	Assoc	Univ Toronto	PHD		York	1991
Runyon, Richard	C-Pr	CS-Long Bch	DBA	70	S Calif	1968
Ruscher, Charles	Asst	Jms Madison		89	Jms Madi	1990
Rush, David F.	H-Pr	Colorado	DBA	71	Indiana	1968
Rush, Robert	Prof	Houston Bapt	PHD		Texas	
Rushing, Philip J.	Adj	Illinois	PHD	71	Illinois	1975
Russell, P. O.	Asst	East Anglia	MA		Manchest	1981
Russell, Paul W.	Prof	Buena Vista	EDD		N Carol	1967
Rust, A.	Prof	F Dick-Madis	PHD			
Ryan, Carolyn J.	Assoc	Salem State	PHD		Clark	1990
Ryan, Jr., Robert J.	Asst	Ithaca	PHD	89	Syracuse	1990
Ryan, Peter J.	Assoc	Univ Ottawa	PHD			1971
Ryksund, Conrod	Prof	Luther	PHD	70	Chicago	1954
Ryngaert, Michael D.	Asst	Florida	PHD	88	Chicago	1987
Rystrom, David S.	Assoc	Western Wash	PHD	82	Oregon	1983
Sa-Aadu, Jarjisu	Assoc	Iowa	PHD	80	Wiscon	1981
Sabrin, Murray	Asst	Ramapo	PHD		Rutgers	1985
Sachdeva, Darshan	Prof	CS-Long Bch	PHD			1977
Sachdeva, Kanwal S.	Assoc	San Diego St	PHD			1976
Sachlis, J. Minor	Assoc	George Wash	DBA	75	Maryland	
Sacley, William	Asst	So Miss	PHD	90	Nebraska	1990
Sahlman, William A.	Prof	Harvard				
Said, Hassan A.	Asst	Livingston	MBA		Cl Insur	1988
Saidi, Reza	Asst	Catholic				
Saint-Pierre, Jacques	Prof	Univ Laval	PHD	70	Louvain	
Sakariya, Sohanraj	Assoc	St John Fish	MBA		Cal St	
Sakata, Jenny	Inst	Hawaii Pacif	MACC		Hawaii	
Salam, Ahmad	Prof	Widener	PHD			
Salavitabar, Hadi	Assoc	SUNY-N Paltz	PHD	82	SUNY-Bin	1982
Sale III, Tom S.	H-Pr	Louisiana Te	PHD		LSU	1965
Salehizadeh, Mehdi	Prof	San Diego St	PHD			1980
Salib, Anis B.	Prof	Alabama A&M	PHD		Vanderb	
Salinger, Michael	Assoc	Boston Univ	PHD		MIT	
Salvatore, Valentino	Prof	Creighton	PHD	54	Nebraska	1954
Samprone Jr., Joseph C.	Assoc	Georgia Col	PHD		Cal-SanB	1983
Samuelson, William F.	Assoc	Boston Univ	PHD		Harvard	
Sanders, Anthony B. on leave to Univ of Chicago	Assoc	Ohio State	PHD	79	Georgia	
Sanders, Ralph	Asst	South Fla	PHD	88	SUNY	1991
Sanders, Thomas	Asst	So Maine	PHD	87	Colorado	1988
Sanger, Gary C.	Assoc	Louisiana St	PHD	80	Purdue	1985
Sankaran, Jayanthi	Asst	Hofstra	ABD	91	Syracuse	1991
Sant, Rajiv	Asst	Iowa	PHD	87	Pitt	1985
Santini, Donald	Asst	Babson			Boston U	
Santomero, Anthony M. Richard King Mellow Professor of Finance	Prof	Pennsylvania	PHD	71	Brown	1972
Santoro, Lawrence	Asst	Insurance	MA		CUNY	
Sardy, Hyman	C-Pr	CUNY-Brookly	PHD			1957
Sarig, Oded on leave to Pennsylvania	Assoc	Tel Aviv Un				
Sarkar, Asani	Asst	Illinois	PHD	89	Penn	1989
Sarmas, Paul	Asst	CS-Pomona	PHD		Claremont	1991
Sarmas, Paul	Asst	Chapman	PHD		Claremont	1985
Sartoris, William L.	Assoc	Indiana	PHD	70	Purdue	
Sarver, F. Lee	Asst	Mid Tenn St	PHD	87	Tenn	1991
Satyanarayan,		Rockhurst	MA	85	Toledo	1991
Sauer, David A.	Asst	Dayton	ABD		Michigan	1991
Saunders, Anthony	Prof	New York U	PHD	81	London	
Sauter, Frederick	Asst	Susquehanna	MBA	67	Columbia	1967
Sauve, Lucie	Asst	Univ Ottawa	PHD			1987
Savage, Helen	Asst	Youngstown	MS	83	Akron	
Sawyer, Granville	Prof	Seton Hall	PHD	85	Tenn	
Sawyer, James A.	Assoc	U Miami	PHD	64	Illinois	1964
Scahill, Edward M.	Asst	Scranton	PHD	83	SUNY-Bin	1989
Scanlon, Kevin P.	Asst	Notre Dame	PHD		Florida	
Schachter, Barry	Assoc	Tulane				
Schadler, Frederick P.	Asst	East Carol	PHD	87	S Carol	1988
Schaffer, Burton F.	Prof	CS-Sacrament	DBA	76	S Calif	1975
Schall, Lawrence D.	C-Pr	U Washington	PHD	69	Chicago	1968
Schallheim, James S.	Assoc	Utah	PHD	80	Purdue	1980
Schalow, David L.	Assoc	CS-San Bern	PHD	84	Arkansas	1991
Schar, Kurt		Intl Mgt Dev	DBA		Harvard	
Scharfstein, David	Asst	MIT	PHD			
Schary, Martha A.	Asst	Boston Univ	PHD		MIT	
Schatzberg, John D.	Assoc	New Mexico	PHD	84	Michigan	1990
Schauer, David	Assoc	Txs-El Paso	PHD		Notre Dm	
Schell, Richard	Asst	Northwood	MBA	70		1988
Schellenger, Michael H.	Asst	Wis-Oshkosh	DBA		Arkansas	

Name	Rank	School	Degree	Yr	Grad School	Yr
Schellhorn, Carolin D.	Lect	Northeastern	ABD		Texas	
Scherr, Frederick C.	Prof	W Virginia	PHD	79	Pitt	1977
Schickele, Sandra	Prof	Sonoma State	PHD	77	Chicago	1973
Schilbred, Cornelius M.	Prof	Norwegian	DOEC			
Schirm, David C.	Assoc	John Carroll	PHD	83	Penn St	1984
Schlapman, Richard	Prof	Minot St	EDD		N Dakota	1964
Schleef, Harold	C-Pr	Lewis & Clrk	PHD	77	Chicago	
Schlenker, Austin	D-Ac	Mercer-Atlan	PHD		Cal-Coas	1984
Schlesinger, Harris	Prof	Alabama	PHD		Illinois	1987
Frank Park Samford Chair of Insurance						
Schmidt, Ned	Inst	NE Okla St	MBA			1991
Schmitz, Paula	Asst	SW Texas St	PHD	91	Texas	1990
Schnabel, Jacques A.	Prof	Wilfrid Laur	PHD		NS Wales	1986
Schneeweis, Thomas	Prof	Massachusett	PHD	77	Iowa	
Schneid, Daniel L.	Assoc	Cen Michigan	PHD	74	Ohio St	1978
Schnitzel, Paul E.	Prof	CS-L Angeles	PHD	71	NYU	1974
Scholes, Myron S.	Prof	Stanford	PHD	69	Chicago	1983
Frank E. Buck Professor of Finance						
Schooley, Diane K.	Asst	Boise State	DBA		Colorado	1989
Schotman, Peter	Assoc	Limburg	PHD	89	Rotterd	1991
Schranz, Mary S.	Asst	Lehigh	PHD	88	Wash U	1990
Schroath, Frederick W.	Asst	Kent State	PHD	87	S Carol	1985
Schrock, Robert D.	Prof	Mo-Kansas Ct	PHD	70	Kansas	1965
Schubert, Walter	Assoc	LaSalle	PHD		Rutgers	1980
Schultz, Jeffrey A.	Prof	Christian Br	PHD		Case Ins	
Schultz, Paul H.	Asst	Ohio State	PHD	88	Chicago	
Schutte, David	Prof	North Texas	PHD	81	Minn	1989
Schwartz, Alan	Prof	Yale	LLB		Yale	1987
Schwartz, Arthur L.	Prof	South Fla	PHD	75	Oregon	1982
Schwartz, Eduardo S.	Prof	UCLA	PHD	75	Brit Col	1986
California Professor of Real Estate and Land Economics						
Schwartz, Leonard	Asst	Memphis St	JD	79	Wayne St	1986
Schwartz, Robert A.	Prof	New York U	PHD	66	Columbia	
Schwarz, Thomas V.	Asst	So Illinois	PHD	84	Fla St	1988
Schweig, Barry B.	Assoc	Creighton	PHD	77	Penn	1981
Schweitzer, Robert	C-Pr	Delaware	PHD		Duke	
Schweizer, Timothy	Asst	Luther	PHD	88	Arkansas	1980
Schwert, G. William	Prof	Rochester	PHD		Chicago	
Gleason Professor of Finance & Statistics						
Schweser, G. Carl	C-Ac	Iowa	PHD	76	Georgia	1976
Scott Jr., David F.	Prof	Cen Florida	PHD		Florida	1982
Chairholder/Della Philips-Martha D. Schenck Chair: American Private Enterpris						
Scott, David	Prof	Valdosta St	PHD	73	Arkansas	1975
Scott, Elton	Assoc	Florida St	DBA	74	Fla St	1975
Scott, James R.	Asst	SW Missouri	ABD		Georgia	1988
Scott, Jonathan A.	Assoc	Temple	PHD	80	Purdue	
Scott, Julia	Assoc	Bishop's Un				
Scott, Louis O.	Assoc	Georgia	PHD	82	Virginia	1989
Scott, Robert	Prof	CS-Chico	PHD	61	Harvard	1987
Scott, William	Prof	Illinois St	PHD	71	Houston	1984
Scribner, Curtis D.	Asst	Pittsburg St				
Scroggins Jr., William A.	Assoc	Jacksonvl St	DBA		Miss St	1979
Scull, Robert W.	Assoc	Mary Wash	PHD		Mass	1987
Seale, William E.	Prof	George Wash	PHD	75	Kentucky	
Sealey, Calvin W.	Asst	McGill Univ	PHD		Georgia	1980
Sears, John T.	Prof	St Fran Xav				
Sears, Paul	Assoc	Baldwin-Wal	PHD		Case Wes	
Sears, R. Stephen	Prof	Texas Tech	PHD	80	N Carol	1988
Seck, D.	Asst	Univ Windsor				
Seegers, Weldon	Lect	CS-Long Bch	MBA			
Seeley, Eric	Asst	CUNY-Hunter	PHD		New York	
Seifert, Bruce	Assoc	Old Dominion	PHD		Michigan	1984
Seifert, James A.	Assoc	Marquette	PHD		Wiscon	1976
Seitz, Neil E.	Prof	St Louis	PHD	73	Ohio St	1973
Selby, Michael	Read	London Econ	PHD	83	London	1987
Selden, Larry	Prof	Columbia	PHD	76	Penn	1976
Selender, Arthur	Asst	Limburg	MBA	85	Chicago	1989
Seligman, Barnard	Prof	Pace				
Sells Jr., Traylor D.	Lect	Corpus Chris	BBA		Southwes	
Seltzer, David F.	Asst	Wis-Parkside	PHD	89	Arizona	1989
Sen, Nilanjan	Asst	Radford	PHD		Va Tech	
Sen, Swapen	Asst	Mich Tech	ABD		Nebraska	1991
Senbet, Lemma W.	Prof	Maryland	PHD	75	SUNY Buf	
William Mayer Professor of Finance						
Senchack Jr., Andrew J.	Prof	Texas	PHD	73	UCLA	1973
First Republican Corp. Professorship in Business Administration						
Serraino, William J.	Prof	Miami U-Ohio	PHD	62	Ohio St	
Seth, Sarabjeet	Asst	Houston	PHD	57	Michigan	1985
Settle, John W.	Assoc	Portland St	PHD	78	U Wash	1984
Severiens, Jacobus T.	Prof	Kent State	PHD	72	Iowa	1983

Name	Rank	School	Degree	Yr	Grad School	Yr
Severn, A.	Assoc	Detroit Merc	PHD	69	Penn	1988
Severns, Roger	Prof	Mankato St	PHD		Nebraska	1987
Seward, J. Allen	Asst	Baylor	PHD		Penn	1976
Seward, James	Asst	Dartmouth	PHD	87	Wiscon	1987
Sewell, Susan P.	Asst	East Carol	PHD	90	Tx-Dalla	1990
Seyedian, Mojtaba	Assoc	SUNY-Fredoni	PHD		SUNY	1984
Seyhun, H. Nejat	Asst	Michigan	PHD	84	Rochest	1984
on leave to Univ of Chicago						
Sfiridis, James M.	Asst	Central Conn	PHD			1990
Shade, Phil	Assoc	Neb-Kearney	DBA		Indiana	1982
Shahrokhi, Manuchehr	Prof	CS-Fresno	PHD		Ohio St	1986
Shaked, Israel M.	Assoc	Boston Univ	DBA		Harvard	
Shakorri, Ken	Prof	CS-Bakersf	PHD			1986
Shalagan, Susan	Asst	Hartford	PHD		Pace	
Shang, Paul	Asst	Illinois Tch	PHD	90	Northwes	1989
Shank, Todd	Asst	Portland	ADB	91	Cen Fla	1991
Shankar, S. Gowri	Asst	SUNY Oswego	PHD	91	Syracuse	1990
Shanken, Jay A.	Prof	Rochester	PHD		Car Mel	
Shanker, Latha	Assoc	Concordia U				
Shanmugam, Bala	Asst	New So Wales	PHD		Wollong	1988
Shao, John	Asst	Okla City	PHD		Va Tech	1991
Shao, Lawrence P.	Asst	Fordham	PHD		Tenn	1989
Shapiro, Alan C.	Prof	So Calif	PHD			
Theodore and Ivadelle Johnson Professor Finance & Business Economics						
Shapiro, Arnold F.	C-Pr	Penn State	PHD		Penn	
Shapiro, Steven	Asst	New Haven	PHD		Geotown	
Sharathchandra, Gopalakrishn	Asst	So Methodist	PHD	89	Berkeley	1988
Sharef, G. A.	Prof	Bellarmine	PHD		Alabama	
Sharma, Jandhyala L.	Assoc	Cleveland St	PHD	75	Arkansas	1979
Sharma, Maneesh K.	Asst	NE Louisiana	PHD	91	Alabama	1991
Sharp, J. Franklin	Prof	Pace	PHD		Purdue	1985
Sharp, Peter A.	Prof	CS-Sacrament	PHD	84	Claremon	1982
Sharpe, Ian G.	Head	New So Wales	PHD		Stanford	1985
Shastri, Kuldeep	Assoc	Pittsburgh				
Shaw, David C.	Prof	W Ontario	PHD		Penn	1968
Shawcross, Roger K.	Asst	Suffolk	MS		Rhode Is	
Shawky, Hany A.	Assoc	SUNY-Albany	PHD	78	Ohio St	1978
Shedlarz, Robert J.	Prof	Akron	JD	72	Notre Dm	1972
Sheehan, Dennis P.	Assoc	Purdue	PHD	81	Berkeley	1986
Shefrin, Hersh	Prof	Santa Clara	PHD	74	London	1979
Shelan, Catherine	Asst	Ill-Chicago	PHD		Columbia	
Shelor, Roger M.	Asst	Louisiana Te	DBA		Kentucky	1989
Shen, Fred	Asst	Un Waterloo	PHD	89	Brit Col	1990
Shen, Qi	Asst	Michigan	PHD	91	Penn	1991
Shenkel, William M.	Prof	Georgia	PHD		Wash	
Sheridan, Patrick J.	Asst	Siena Coll	MBA		Siena C	1979
Sherman, Ann	Asst	Wisconsin	PHD	87	Minn	1987
Sherman, Hugh D.	Asst	York of PA	ABD		Temple	
Sherman, Jerome F.	Assoc	Creighton	PHD	73	Miss	1976
Sherman, Michael D.	Assoc	Toledo	PHD		Purdue	1980
Sherrouse, M. Teresa	Assoc	Augusta	ABD		Georgia	1975
Shetty, Anand	Asst	Iona	PHD	87	Pitt	1988
Shibakawa, Rinya	H-Pr	Hitotsubashi	DE	80	Hitotsub	1990
Shick, Richard A.	Dean	Canisius	PHD	73	SUNY-Buf	1978
Shiekh, Amir	Asst	Indiana	PHD	87	Calif	
Shih, Feng-Ying L.	Asst	Rider	MBA		Drexel	
Shimizu, Yoshinori	Prof	Hitotsubashi	DBA		Hitotsub	1977
Shin, Hung-Sik	Asst	Frostburg St	PHD		Pitt	1991
Shin, Kilman	Prof	Ferris State	PHD		Conn	1989
Shin, Tai S.	Prof	Virg Comm	PHD	69	Illinois	1978
Shin, Young-Seock	Asst	Virg Tech	PHD	89	Penn	1989
Shinkel, B.	Assoc	Detroit Merc	PHD	76	Purdue	1989
Shipman, William A.	C-Pr	Wartburg	PHD	77	Pitt	1972
Shirvani, Hassan M.	Assoc	St Thomas-Tx	PHD		Harvard	1986
Shivdasani, Anil	Asst	Univ Calgary	PHD	91	Ohio St	1991
Shome, Dilip K.	Assoc	Virg Tech	PHD	83	Florida	1982
Short, Helen	Lect	Univ Leeds	BA		Kent St	1990
Short, James L.	Prof	San Diego St	PHD	73	UCLA	1973
Shovlain, Ray	Prof	St Ambrose	MBA	80	St Ambro	1982
Showers, Vince E.	Asst	Bradley	PHD	88	Ohio St	1987
Shrader, Mark J.	Asst	Gonzaga	PHD	88	Tx Tech	1988
Shrieves, Ronald E.	Prof	Tennessee	PHD	72	UCLA	1972
Shrikhande, Milind	Asst	Georgia Tech	PHD	91	Penn	1991
Shtzel, Elwood W.	Asst	Siena Coll	MBA		New Hamp	1980
Shubik, Martin	Prof	Yale	PHD		Princet	1963
Shull, Bernard	Prof	CUNY-Hunter	PHD		Wiscon	
Shull, David M.	Asst	Miami U-Ohio	PHD	88	Indiana	
Shulman, Joel M.	Assoc	Wayne State	PHD	84	Mich St	1988
Shum, Connie	Asst	Corpus Chris	DBA		La Tech	
Shyam-Sunder, Lakshmi	Asst	Dartmouth	PHD	89	MIT	1987

192

Name	Rank	School	Degree	Yr	From	Yr
Sibbald, Peter G.	Prof	CS-Pomona	PHD	77	Claremon	1977
Sibley, Albin M.	Prof	Loyola-N Orl	PHD	72	S Carol	1979
Sicherman, Neil W.	Assoc	So Carolina	PHD	86	Florida	
Sick, Gordon A.	C-Ac	Univ Calgary	PHD	81	Brit Col	1988
Siddiqi, Mazhar	Asst	North Texas	ABD		U Wash	1991
Siegel, Andrew F.	Prof	U Washington	PHD	77	Stanford	1983
Siegel, Daniel R.	Prof	U Washington	PHD	83	Stanford	1990
Siegel, Fred W.	Assoc	Louisville	PHD	74	Illinois	1977
Siegel, Jeremy J.	Prof	Pennsylvania				
Siegel, Rachel	Asst	Lyndon State	MPPM		Yale	1990
Siergiej, Lalana	Assoc	Bloomsburg	ABD		Kent St	1989
Sigler, Kevin J.	Asst	N Car-Wilmin	PHD	86	Nebraska	1981
Sihler, William W.	Prof	Virg-Grad	DBA	65	Harvard	1967
Ronald Edward Trzcinski Professor of Business Administration						
Silber, William L.	Prof	New York U	PHD	66	Princeto	
Sillah, Marion	Assoc	Morehouse	PHD		S Carol	1987
Silvers, J. B.	Prof	Case Western	PHD		Stanford	
Elizabeth M. & William C. Treuhaft Professor of Management						
Silverstein, Ethel	Asst	NY Inst Tech	MBA			
Sim, Ah Boon	Asst	New So Wales	PHD		Concordi	1989
Simkowitz, Michael A.	Prof	Indiana	PHD	70	NYU	
Simmons, George B.	Prof	Fla Internat	PHD	61	Indiana	
Distinguished Service Professor						
Simmons, Joseph T.	Prof	South Dakota	PHD	74	Nebraska	1975
Simmons, Mark	Asst	S F Austin	PHD	87	Tx A&M	1987
Simms, John M.	Asst	N Car-Greens	PHD		N Carol	1985
Simonds, Richard R.	C-Pr	Michigan St	PHD		Michigan	1974
Simonson, Donald G.	Prof	New Mexico	PHD	72	Michigan	1971
Simpson, W. Gary	Prof	Oklahoma St	PHD		Txs A&M	1978
OBA Chair of Commercial Bank Management						
Sims Jr., Edwin C.	Prof	W Illinois	PHD		Columbia	1972
Singer, Robert	Inst	St Louis				
Singer, Ronald F.	Assoc	Houston	PHD	75	Mich St	1982
Singh, Ajai K.	Asst	Iowa State	PHD	88	Iowa	1987
Singh, Dayal	C-Pr	Marshall	DBA	65	Indiana	
Singh, Manoj	Asst	Boston Coll	PHD		Purdue	
Singh, Ranjit	Lect	Melbourne U	MEC	90	Monash	1991
Singleton, J. Clay	Dean	North Texas	PHD	79	Missouri	1991
Singleton, Kenneth J.	Prof	Stanford	PHD	77	Wiscon	1987
C.O.G. Miller Distinguished Professor of Finance						
Sinha, Sidharth	Asst	Massachusett	PHD	87	Berkeley	
Sinha, Tapen	Assoc	Bond Univ	PHD	86	Minn	1989
Sinkey Jr., Joseph F.	Prof	Georgia	PHD	71	Boston C	1976
Georgia Banking Association Professor of Finance						
Sinow, David M.	Adj	Illinois	PHD	82	Illinois	1986
Sirmans Jr., Clemon F.	Prof	Connecticut	PHD	76	Georgia	1991
Sirmans, G. Stacy	Assoc	Florida St	PHD	80	Georgia	1988
Sirmon, William A.		So Miss				
Sirri, Erik R.	Asst	Harvard				
Sisneros, Phillip M.	Asst	Houston	PHD	89	Tx Tech	1991
Skingle, J.		Univ Regina				
Skinner, David L.	Asst	S Ill-Edward	PHD	87	Mich St	1988
Skipper, Harold D.	Prof	Georgia St	PHD		Penn	
Skomp, Stephen E.	Prof	Bowling Gr	DBA		Oklahoma	1986
Skully, Michael T.	Assoc	New So Wales	MBA		Utah	1973
Slezak, Steve L.	Asst	Michigan	PHD	89	Calif	1989
Slovin, Myron B.	Prof	Louisiana St	PHD	72	Princeto	1987
Premier Bank/Chuck McCoy Distinguished Professorship in Financial Institution						
Smart, Scott	Asst	Indiana				
Smidt, Seymour	Prof	Cornell	PHD	54	Chicago	1956
Nicholas H. Noyes Proessor of Economics and Finance						
Smiley, Barry A.	D-Pr	NW St of La	DBA		La Tech	
Smith Jr., Clifford W.	Prof	Rochester	PHD		N Carol	
Clarey Professor of Finance and Economics						
Smith, Barry D.	H	New Mex St	PHD	83	Penn	1986
Smith, Brian F.	Asst	Wilfrid Laur	PHD		Western	1987
Smith, Charles	Asst	Txs-El Paso	ABD		Tx Tech	1991
Smith, Charles R.	Prof	CS-Fresno	PHD		Penn St	1980
Smith, Chris	Asst	Mo-Kansas Ct	PHD		Indiana	1989
Smith, David	Asst	SUNY-Albany	PHD	89	Va Tech	1989
Smith, Donald J.	Assoc	Boston Univ	PHD		Berkeley	
Smith, Halbert C.	Prof	Florida	DBA	62	Illinois	1971
Smith, James F.	Prof	No Carolina	PHD	71	So Meth	1988
Smith, Keith V.	Prof	Purdue	PHD	66	Purdue	1979
Smith, Marc T.	Asst	Florida	PHD		Ohio St	1986
Smith, Michael L.	Assoc	Ohio State	PHD		Minn	
Smith, Milton E.	Prof	Brigham Yg	PHD	81	Utah	1966
Smith, Patricia	Inst	Tarleton St	MBA	84	Tarleton	1984
Smith, Patricia B.	Asst	New Hampshir	PHD	87	New York	1989
Smith, Patrick	Assoc	Central Wash				

Name	Rank	School	Degree	Yr	From	Yr
Smith, Richard	Asst	Ark Tech	PHD	74	Texas	1991
Smith, Richard L.	C-Pr	Arizona St	PHD		UCLA	1981
Smith, Rodney F.	Prof	SUNY-Fredoni	PHD		Mass	
Smith, Ronald	Prof	CUNY-Hunter	DBA		LSU	
Smith, Roy C.	Prof	New York U	MBA	66	Harvard	
Smith, Solomon S.	Dean$	Fisk	PHD		So Illin	
Smith, Stanley D.	Dean	Arkansas	PHD	79	Ariz St	1985
Smith, Stephen D.	Prof	Georgia Tech	PHD	80	Florida	1986

Mills Bee Lane Professor of Banking and Finance; on leave to Geo St Spring 92

Smith, Thomas M.	Asst	Duke	PHD		Stanford	
Smith, Wallace F.	Prof	Cal-Berkeley	PHD		U Wash	
Smith, Weldon	Asst	East Central	MBA	72	Oklahoma	1980
Smith, Weldon L.	Prof	S F Austin	PHD	74	Tx A&M	1966
Smolen, Gerald E.	Prof	Toledo	PHD		Tenn	1986
Snow, Karl N.	Asst	No Carolina	PHD	91	Chicago	1990
Snyder, D.	Prof	St Marys-Cal	PHDJ	71	Penn St	1990
So, Jacky C.	C-Ac	S Ill-Edward	PHD	83	Ohio St	1983
Soenen, L. A.	Prof	Cal Poly-SLO	DBA	77	Harvard	1989
Sohn, Ira		Montclair St	PHD		NYU	
Sohrabian, Ahmad	Assoc	CS-Pomona	PHD	84	Ca-SanBr	1986
Solandro, Daniel	Asst	Virg Comm	PHD	90	Pitt	1989
Solberg, Donald	Asst	Wis-Milwauke	PHD	87	Nebraska	1987
Soldofsky, Robert M.	Emer	Iowa	PHD	54	Wash U	1954

Murray Professor

Soliman, Mostafa	Assoc	Prairie View	PHD		Iowa St	1971
Solomon, E. Ray	Prof	Florida St	PHD	62	Wiscon	1962

Midyette Eminent Scholar Chair in Insurance

Solomon, Lynnette K.	C	S F Austin	PHD	70	Arkansas	1979
Solt, Michael E.	Assoc	San Jose St				
Somanath, V. S.	Prof	San Fran St	PHD	81	New York	1988
Song, Kean P.		Prairie View				
Song, Moon	Asst	San Diego St	PHD		Ohio St	1988
Sonnenreich, William	Adj	New York U				
Sonstelie, Jon		Cal-Santa Br				
Sorensen, Donald E.	C-Ac$	Wis-Whitewat	PHD		Wiscon	1976
Sortino, F.	Prof	San Fran St	PHD	81	Oregor	1980
Soundararajan, L.	Asst	Georgia Col	ABD		Georgia	1988
Sounders, Edward M.	Asst	Northeastern	PHD		Geo St	1985
Spahr, Ronald W.	Prof	Wyoming	PHD			1974
Spangler, Gordon	Assoc	Salem State	PHD		Tufts	1984
Sparling, Beverly	Asst	Siena Coll	ABD		Renssela	1988
Sparrow, Gregory B.	Inst	No Illinois	MBA	80	No Ill	1980
Spatt, Chester S.	Prof	Carnegie Mel	PHD	79	Penn	1979
Speaker, Paul J.	Assoc	W Virginia	PHD	81	Purdue	1981
Spellman, Lewis J.	Prof	Texas	PHD	71	Stanford	1971
Speltz, John	Asst	Denver	PHD	90	Fla St	1990
Spencer, Austin Harvey	Prof	W Carolina	PHD	72	Indiana	1980
Spencer, Theresa	Asst	Meredith	PHD		N Car St	1985
Speros, Jonathan	Inst	Boston Univ	ABD		Boston C	
Spiegel, Matthew	Asst	Columbia	PHD	87	Princet	1986
Spiess, Katherine	Asst	Notre Dame				
Spilde, Roger		Concordia	ABD			
Spillane Jr., Edward Joseph	Assoc	Webster	PHD	73	St Louis	1986
Spindt, Paul	Prof	Tulane				
Spivey, Christopher B.	Prof	Citadel	PHD		N Texas	
Spivey, M. F.	Assoc	Clemson	PHD	87	Tenn	1987
Sprecher, C. Ronald	C-Pr	East Carol	PHD	69	Illinois	1989
Springer, T. M.	Asst	Clemson	PHD	86	Georgia	1988
Sprinkle, Richard	Assoc	Txs-El Paso	PHD			
Sprow, James	Asst	Grand Valley	ABD	87	Wash St	1991
Spruill, Charles R.	Prof	Pfeiffer	PHD	75	So Illin	
Spudeck, Raymond E.	Asst	Cen Florida	DBA		Tx Tech	1987
Squires, Jan R.	Assoc	SW Missouri	DBA	84	Virginia	1987
Sridharan, U. V.	Asst	Clemson	PHD	90	Iowa	1989
Srinivasan, Gopalan	Prof	New Brunswic	PHD		IMM-Indi	1987
Srinivasan, Venkatesan	Asst	Northeastern	PHD		Cinn	1985
Srivastava, Ashwani K.	Asst	Carleton Un				
Srivastava, Sanjay	Prof	Carnegie Mel	PHD	82	MIT	1982
Srivastava, Suresh	Asst	Alaska-Ancho	PHD	88	Maryland	1987
Sruggs Jr., Leslie S.	Assoc	Memphis St	PHD	74	Vanderbt	1969
Staats, William F.	Prof	Louisiana St	PHD	65	Texas	1971

Louisiana Bankers' Association Chair of Banking

Stack, Robert T.	H	Hawaii-Hilo	PHD	78	Mich St	1984
Stadtmueller, Katherine	Lect	Connecticut	JD	86	Boston C	1991
Stambaugh, Robert F.	Prof	Pennsylvania	PHD	81	Chicago	1979

Ronald O. Perelma Professor of Finance

Stancill, James	Prof	So Calif	PHD	65	Penn	1964
Stangeland, David	Asst	U Manitoba	ABD		Alberta	1991
Stanger, Anthony M. J.	Tutor	Flinders Un	BCOM	84	Tasmania	1989
Stanio, Raymond F.	Asst	American Int	MBA	64	Hartford	1983

194

Name	Rank	School	Degree	Yr	University	Yr
Stanley, Craig E.	Prof	CS-Sacramento	PHD	74	Claremon	1981
Stanley, Darrol	Prof	Pepper-L Ang	DBA	73	So Calif	1973
Stanley, Kenneth L.	Dean	Valdosta St	PHD	78	Purdue	1984
Stanley, Marjorie T.	Prof	Tx Christian	PHD	53	Indiana	1965
Stanley, Thomas O.	Assoc	Nicholls St				
Stanley, William	Assoc	NY Inst Tech	MBA			
Stansell, Stanley R.	Prof	East Carol	PHD	71	Georgia	1988
Stanton, Richard H.	Asst	Cal-Berkeley	PHD	91	Stanford	1991
Stanton, Thomas	Prof	Fran Marion	DBA	74	Geo Wash	1983
Stapleton, R. C.	Prof	U Lancaster	PHD		Sheffiel	
Starks, Laura T.	Assoc	Texas	PHD	81	Texas	1987
Statham, Pamela	Dean	W Australia	PHD	80	Monash	1991
Statman, Meir	C	Santa Clara	PHD	79	Columbia	1979
Stavenga, Mink	Dean$	US Intl				
Steeley, James M.	VAsst	Wash Univ	PHD	90	Warwick	1990
Steger, Randy A.	Asst	David Lipsc	DBA		Kentucky	
Stendardi, Edward J.	Assoc	St John Fish	MBA		SUNY-Alb	
Stensland, Gunnar	Asst	Norwegian				
Stephens, Alan A.	Assoc	Utah State	PHD	80	Utah	1984
Sterbenz, Frederic	Assoc	Wyoming	PHD			1981
Sterk, William E.	Prof	San Diego St	PHD		Wiscon	1978
Stern, M.	Asst	Tennessee	PHD		Virginia	
Stern, Stephen M.		Southeastern	MBA		Wharton	
Sternberg, Joel R.	Asst	Arizona	PHD	86	Stanford	1990
Sternberg, Theodore	Asst	Vanderbilt	PHD	89	Berkeley	1989
Stevens, Donald L.	Prof	Colo-Denver	PHD	71	Mich St	1982
Stevens, Jerry L.	Assoc	Richmond	PHD	81	Illinois	1986
Stevenson, Ben	Prof	Adrian	PHD		Ohio St	1980
Stevenson, Richard A.	Prof	Iowa	PHD	65	Mich St	1967
Stewart Jr., Samuel S.	Prof	Utah	PHD	70	Stanford	1973
Stewart, Brent A.		Citadel				
Stewart, Lewis M.	Asst	Geo Southern	MBA	60	Tx Tech	1970
Stewart, Robert E.	Asst	Troy St	MBA	65	Mississi	1967
Stick, Henry H.	Assoc	Dayton	PHD	57	Ohio St	1975
Stickels, Perry James	Assoc	CS-Fullerton	PHD		Claremon	1977
Stiefel, Leanna	Assoc	New York-Gr	PHD	72	Wiscon	1976
Stine, J. Bert	Assoc	S F Austin	DBA	84	La Tech	1986
Stitzel, Thomas E.	Prof	Boise State	PHD		Oregon	1975
Stock, Duane R.	Assoc	Oklahoma	PHD	79	Illinois	1979
Stockdale, John M.	Prof	CS-Sacramento	PHD	70	Iowa	1969
Stocker, John	Asst	Tampa	ABD		Kent St	1991
Stoffels, John D.	C $	Marquette	PHD	69	Mich St	1980
Stoll, Hans R.	Prof	Vanderbilt	PHD	66	Chicago	1980
Walker Professor of Finance						
Stoller, Linda	Lect	Babson	JD		Boston U	
Stolz, Richard W.	Prof	CS-Fullerton	PHD		Mich St	1987
Stone, Bernell K.	Prof	Brigham Yg	PHD	68	MIT	1986
Stoughton, Neal M.	Assoc	Calif-Irvine	PHD	83	Stanford	1986
Stout, R. Gene	Prof	Cen Michigan	PHD	72	Iowa St	1981
Stovall, Robert H.	Adj	New York U	MBA	57	New York	
Stover, Roger	Prof	Iowa State	DBA	75	Virginia	1979
Stowe, John D.	C-Pr	Missouri	PHD	74	Houston	1980
Straley, William	Assoc	Ogelthorpe	PHD	79	Auburn	1990
Strebel, Paul		Intl Mgt Dev	PHD		Princeto	
Strickland, Thomas H.	Assoc	Mid Tenn St	PHD	79	Oklahoma	1988
Strickland, William A.	Inst	Lg-Isl-Post	MBA		Lg Isl	
Strock, Elizabeth A.	Asst	Boston Coll	PHD		Mass	
Strong, John S.	Assoc	Wm & Mary	PHD		Harvard	1985
Strong, Robert	Assoc	Maine	PHD	83	Penn St	1983
Stroyny, Alvin	Lect	Wis-Milwauke	MBA	75	Wiscon	1990
Stuart, Charlie	Prof	Cal-Santa Br				
Stubblefield, Ronald		Southeastern	MSW		NYU	
Stuck, Charles	Asst	Ashland	MBA	85	Xavier	1985
Stuhldreher, Thomas J.	Prof	Clarion	DBA		Kent St	1985
Stulz, Rene M.	Prof	Ohio State	PHD		MIT	
Riklis Chair of Business and its Environment						
Stutzer, Michael	Assoc	Minnesota				
Stutzman, James F.	Asst	SW Texas St	PHD	82	Houston	1988
Subrahmanyam, A.	Asst	Columbia	PHD	90	UCLA	1990
Subrahmanyam, Marti G.	Prof	New York U	PHD	74	MIT	
Suchanek, Gerry	Assoc	Iowa	PHD	77	Northwes	1989
Sugrue, Timothy F.	Asst	George Mason	PHD	85	Mass	1997
Suk, David	Asst	Rider	PHD		Drexel	
Sukhwani, Manobarlal	Asst	Duquesne	ABD		Pitt	
Sullivan Jr., Frank L.	Adj	New York U	MBA	71	Penn	
Sullivan, A. Charlene	Assoc	Purdue	PHD	78	Purdue	1978
Sullivan, John	Lect	Wis-Whitewat	MBA		Wis-Whit	1984
Sullivan, Michael	Asst	Fla Internat	ABD	88	Yale	
Sullivan, Michael J.	Asst	Nev-L Vegas	PHD	89	Fla St	1991
Sullivan, Timothy	Prof	Bentley	PHD	71	Michigan	1980

195

Name	Rank	School	Degree	Yr	Univ	Yr
Sultan, Jahangir	Asst	Bentley	PHD	86	Arizona	1989
Sumi, Barbara	Assoc	Northwood	MS	80		1980
Sun, Tong-sheng	Asst	Columbia	PHD	87	Stanford	1990
Sun, Y. Elizabeth	Assoc	San Jose St				
Sundaram, Anant	Asst	Dartmouth	PHD	87	Yale	1986
Sundaram, Sridhar	Asst	Emporia St	DBA	90	Illinois	1989
Sundaran, Srinivasan	Asst	Ball State	PHD	90	Cinn	1991
Sundaresan, Suresh	Prof	Columbia	PHD	80	Car Mel	1980
Sunderman, Mark A.	Asst	Wyoming	PHD			1985
Sung, Hyun Mo	Asst	Loyola-Chicg	PHD		Illinois	1990
Sung, Jaeyoung	Asst	Ill-Chicago				
Sushka, Marie E.	Prof	Arizona St	PHD		Geotown	1984
Sussman, M. Richard	C-Pr	Cen Michigan	PHD	61	Michigan	1978
Sutton-Bell, Nancy S.	Assoc	Florida St	PHD	85	Georgia	1983
Svenden, Bjorn	Asst	Norwegian				
Swales, George S.	H-Ac$	SW Missouri	PHD	84	Arkansas	1982
Swang, Axel W.	C-Pr	David Lipsc	PHD		Alabama	
Swanson, Diane	Asst	Robt Morris	MA		Missouri	
Swanson, H. Gene	Asst	Loyola-Maryl	PHD			1991
Swanson, Jr. Paul J.	Assoc	Cincinnati	PHD	62	Illinois	1967
Swanson, Peggy E.	Prof	Tx-Arlington	PHD	78	So Meth	1978
Swanson, Richard N.	Prof	Mankato St	EDD		Florida	1968
Swanton, Donald W.	C-Ac	Roosevelt	PHD	74	Northwes	1978
Swartz, L. Mick	Asst	U Manitoba	ABD		Iowa	1991
Sweeney, Larry E.	Asst	Ball State	PHD	85	W Virg	1988
Sweeney, Richard J.	Prof	Georgetown	PHD	72	Princeto	1989
Sullivan/Dean Chair in International Business						
Sweeney, Robert	Assoc	Wright State	PHD	85	S Carol	1989
Sweeney, Timothy	C-Pr	Bucknell	PHD	72	Penn St	1980
Sweeting, Robert C.	SLect	Manches Inst	PHD		Keele	1979
Swensen, Philip R.	Prof	Utah State	DBA	72	Indiana	1975
Swensen, R. Bruce	Assoc	Adelphi	DSW	82	Columbia	
Swidler, Steven	Asst	Tx-Arlington	PHD	81	Brown	1988
Swift, Ernest W.	Assoc	Georgia St	PHD		Oklahoma	
Swindle, C. Sloan	Asst	Lehigh	PHD	91	Florida	1991
Swinnerton, G.	Asst	Detroit Merc	PHD	88	Kent St	1989
Synn, Wonhi J.	Asst	Elon	PHD	89	SUNY-Buf	1989
Szakmary, Andrew C.	Asst	So Illinois	PHD	91	N Orlean	1991
Szewczyk, Sam	Asst	Drexel	PHD		Penn St	1987
Tabwiztchi, S.	Assoc	SUNY Old Wes	PHD			1975
Taggart, Robert A.	Prof	Boston Coll	PHD		MIT	
Tai, Lawrence	Assoc	Loyola Marym	PHD	83	Geo St	1990
Tainer, Elevina	Asst	St Xavier	PHD			
Taitt, Arthur	Prof	CS-Northrdge	DBA	59	Indiana	1965
Tallman, Gary D.	Prof	No Arizona	DBA		Colorado	1976
Talmor, Eli	Assoc	Calif-Irvine	PHD	81	N Carol	1989
Tamarkin, Maurry J.	Assoc	Clark	PHD	79	Wash U	
Tamule, Harold B.	Asst	Providence	PHD		Mass	1990
Tandon, Kishore	Assoc	CUNY-Baruch	PHD	80	Pitt	
Tang, Alex	Asst	Morgan State	PHD		Houston	
Tang, Nai-Pan	Asst	McGill Univ	PHD		Northwes	1991
Tankersley, Irvin Lee	Prof	Memphis St	JD	73	Tulane	1973
Tannous, George F.	Assoc	Saskatchewan	PHD	88	Rhd Isl	1984
Tarhan, Vefa	C-Pr	Loyola-Chicg	PHD		CA-SanBr	1978
Tatsch, Paul A.	Assoc	Pacific	PHD	77	SUNY	
Taussig, Russell A.	Prof	Hawaii-Manoa	PHD	62	Berkeley	1970
Tavis, Lee A.	Prof	Notre Dame	DBA		Indiana	
C. R. Smith Professor						
Tavokkol, Amir	Asst	Kansas State	PHD	79	Ks St	1988
Tawarangkoon, W.	Asst	So Alabama	PHD		Mississi	1989
Taylor, Dean G.	Prof	Colo-Denver	PHD		Chicago	
Taylor, John N.	H-Pr	Alaska-Fairb				
Taylor, Keith L.	Prof	Sonoma State	PHD	81	Ariz St	1985
Taylor, Richard W.	Prof	Arkansas St	PHD	76	LSU	1984
Taylor, S.	Read	U Lancaster	PHD		Lancaste	
Taylor, Shannon	H $	Montana St	PHD	76	Colorado	
Taylor, Stephen L.	Assoc	Univ Sydney	PHD		NS Wales	1985
Taylor, Walt	Assoc	So Miss	PHD	73	Penn St	1991
Taylor, William M.	Assoc	Rice	PHD	79	Chicago	1988
Teall, John		Bridgeport				
Teall, John	Adj	New York U				
Tedefalk, Rolf	Prof	New Haven	PHD		Minn	
Tehranian, Hassan	C-Pr	Boston Coll	PHD		Alabama	
Templeton, William K.	Asst	Butler	PHD	90	Kent St	
Tennyson, Sharon	Asst	Pennsylvania				
Matthew R. Kornreich Term Assistant Professor						
Terry, Andy	Asst	Ark-Ltl Rock				
Terry, Rory	Asst	Oklahoma St	ABD		Utah	1991
Tessitore, Anthony	Asst	Rutgers-Newk	ABD		Baruch	
Tezel, Ahmet	Assoc	St Joseph	PHD	73	Berkeley	1985

Name	Rank	School	Degree	Yr	Univ	Yr
Thakor, Anjan	Prof	Indiana	PHD	79	Northwes	
Thapa, Samanta B.	Asst	W Kentucky	PHD	88	Geo St	1988
Tharthare, Suresh K.	Asst	St Joseph	PHD	87	Temple	1985
Thatcher, Janet S.	Prof	Wis-Whitewat	PHD		Wiscon	1986
Thatcher, John	Assoc	Wis-Whitewat	PHD		Madison	1991
Theerathorn, Pochara	Asst	Memphis St	PHD	83	Northwes	1989
Theodossiou, Panayiotis T.	Asst	Clarkson	PHD	87	CUNY	1989
Thiagarajan, Kuttalam R.	Asst	Prairie View	MA		Annamali	
Thibeault, Andre	Assoc	Univ Laval	PHD	84	West Ont	
Thies, Clifford F.	Asst	Baltimore	PHD		Boston C	
Thiewes, Harold	Prof	Mankato St	PHD		Iowa	1984
Thode, Stephen F.	Assoc	Lehigh	DBA	80	Indiana	1982
Thomas, Annie	Assoc	Babson	PHD		Yale	
Thomas, David J.	Assoc	St Cloud St	PHD	79	Nebraska	1980
Thomas, Martin	Asst	Drexel	PHD	90	Penn St	1989
Thomas, Patrick	Prof	Trenton St	PHD	74	Kentucky	1980
Thomas, Sam	Inst	Drexel				
Thompson II, Donald J.	Assoc	Georgia St	DBA		Harvard	
Thompson, A. Frank	H-Pr	No Iowa	PHD	77	Nebraska	1990
Thompson, Bradley	Tutor	Tasmania	BCOM			1989
Thompson, G. Rodney	H-Pr	Virg Tech				
Thompson, Howard E.	Prof	Wisconsin	PHD	64	Wiscon	1963
Thompson, J.	Prof	St Marys-Cal	MBA	63	Chicago	1979
Thompson, J. C.	Asst	E Kentucky	DBA	90	Kentucky	1991
Thompson, Raymond	Assoc	Pitts-Johnst	DBA	84	Nova	1980
Thompson, Rex	Prof	So Methodist	PHD	78	Rochest	1988
Caruth Professor of Financial Mangement						
Thoren, Raymond	C	SUNY-Plattsb	MBA		St Johns	1970
Thorley, Steven	Asst	Brigham Yg	PHD	91	U Wash	1991
Thornton, Billy	Asst	Emory	PHD	89	Harvard	1989
Thosar, Satish B.	Asst	Mass-Boston	PHD	89	Indiana	1989
Thrower, Ellen	Prof	Insurance	PHD		Geo St	
Thygerson, Kenneth	Prof	CS-San Bern	PHD	73	Northwes	1990
Tibbits, Garry E.	Assoc	U Wollongong	MCOM		Auckland	1977
Timme, Stephen G.	Assoc	Georgia St	PHD		Geo St	
Timmons, Douglas J.	Asst	Tx-S Antonio	PHD	86	Florida	1986
Tinic, Seha M.	C-Pr	Texas	PHD	70	Cornell	1985
James A. Elkins Centennial Chair in Finance						
Tippett, Mark J.	Lect	Univ Wales	MSC	69	Wales	1988
Tipton, James McCall	Assoc	Baylor	PHD		Florida	1980
Tirtiroglu, Dogan	Asst	Salisbury St	PHD	91		1991
Titman, Sheridan D.	Prof	UCLA	PHD	81	Car Mel	1980
To, Minh Chau	Assoc	HEC-Montreal				
Todd, Janet	Asst	Delaware	ABD		Mich St	1991
Tofteland, Elmer	Assoc	Northwood	MBA	78		1981
Tole, Thomas M.	Assoc	Auburn	DBA	74	Oklahoma	1974
Tollen, Robert D.	Assoc	Txs-El Paso	PHD		Texas	1972
Tompkins, C.	Prof	Univ Bath				
Tonietti, Marco E.	Prof	CS-Fullerton	PHD	72	St Louis	1970
Tonks, Ian	SLect	London Econ	PHD	83	Warwick	1991
Torabzadeh, Khalil M.	Assoc	Radford	PHD		Miss St	
Torous, Walter N.	Assoc	UCLA	PHD	81	Penn	1988
Torregrosa, Paul	Asst	Marquette	PHD		Va Tech	1988
Tourani Rad, Alireza	Asst	Limburg	MBA	84	Leuven	1988
Toyne, Michael	Asst	LaSalle				
Trahan, Emery A.	Asst	Northeastern	PHD		SUNY-Alb	1988
Tran, Trong	Adj	Southeastern	PHD			
Trapani, John M.	Prof	Tulane				
Travlos, Nickolaos G.	Assoc	Boston Coll	PHD		NYU	
Trennepohl, Gary L.	C-Pr	Texas A&M	PHD	76	Tx Tech	1986
Trent, Paul A.	Prof	Siena Coll	MBA		Long Is	1977
Trevino, Ruben C.	Asst	Seattle	PHD	80	Alabama	1987
Triantis, Alex	Asst	Wisconsin	PHD	88	Stanford	1989
Trieschmann, James S.	Prof	Georgia	DBA		Indiana	
Dudley L. Moore, Jr. Chairholder						
Trifts, Jack W.	Assoc	Rollins	PHD	84	Florida	1989
Trigeorgis, Lenos	Asst	Boston Univ	PHD		Harvard	
Trimble, Donald	Assoc	Skidmore	MBA		Harvard	1986
Trinidad, Jose	Asst	LaSalle	MBA		Rutgers	1988
Tripathy, Niranjan	Asst	North Texas	PHD	87	Tx Tech	1987
Tripp, James D.	Asst	W Illinois	MBA		Drury	1990
Trippi, Robert	Prof	CS-Long Bch	PHD			1989
Trivoli, George W.	Prof	Jacksonvl St	PHD	70	Virginia	1990
Trostle, Randolph L.	Assoc	Elizabethtwn	PHD	72	Lehigh	1970
Troughton, George H.	Prof	CS-Chico	PHD	61	Mass	1987
Truett, Dale	Prof	Tx-S Antonio	PHD	67	Texas	1973
Trussler, Susan	Asst	Scranton	PHD	89	Penn St	1985
Trzcinka, Charles	Prof	SUNY-Buffalo	PHD	80	Purdue	1980
Tseng, Kuo-Cheng	Prof	CS-Fresno	PHD		Penn St	1984
Tsetsekos, George	Asst	Drexel	PHD		Tenn	1988

Name	Rank	School	Degree	Yr	Univ	Yr
Tso, P. S.	Asst	Un Hong Kong	PHD			1979
Tucker, Alan L.	Assoc	Temple	PHD	86	Fla St	
Tucker, Michael T.	Asst	Fairfield	DBA	88	Boston	1988
Tuckman, Bruce	Asst	New York U	PHD	88	MIT	
Tufano, Peter	Asst	Harvard				
Turnbull, S. M.	Prof	Queen's Univ	PHD		Brit Col	1990
Turner, Betty	Asst	Guilford				
Turner, Robert G.	Prof	Florida St	PHD	69	Kentucky	1970
Turner, Terry L.	Prof	South Dakota	PHD	73	Car Mel	
Turtle, Harry J.	Asst	U Manitoba	PHD	91	Alberta	1990
Turtle, John P.	Dean	Univ Regina	PHD	74	Wash	1981
Tuttle, Donald L.	Prof	Indiana	PHD	65	N Carol	1970
Tuzzolino, Frank A.	Assoc	Am Grad Intl	PHD	87	Ariz St	
Twark, Allan J.	Prof	Kent State	PHD	59	Illinois	1966
Tyler, R. Stanley	Assoc	So Illinois	JD	52	Illinois	1970
Tyree, Donald A.	C-Pr	St Louis	PHD	59	Texas	
Tzang, Dah Nein	Prof	San Fran St	PHD	86	Illinois	1989
Uchida, Mark	Assoc	Butler	PHD	76	Illinois	
Udell, Gregory F.	Assoc	New York U	PHD	83	Indiana	
Ulivi, Ricardo M.	Prof	CS-Dominguez	PHD	81	Arkansas	1985
Unal, Haluk	Asst	Maryland	PHD	85	Ohio St	
Uppal, Jamshed	Asst	Catholic				
Upstrom, John P.	Assoc	Loras	MBA	82	Ill St	1984
Upton, David E.	Assoc	Virg Comm	PHD	76	N Carol	1987
Urrutia, Jorge L.	Assoc	Loyola-Chicg	PHD		Texas	1985
Ursel, Nancy D.	Asst	Univ Windsor				
Uselton, Gene C.	Prof	Texas A&M	PHD	70	Texas	1979
Uzoau, Ben	Assoc	SE Missouri	PHD	74	Columbia	1986
Vaidya, Ramesh	Asst	Minn-Duluth	PHD	81	Cornell	
Vaidyanathan, Ravi	Asst	NE Okla St	DBA	91		1991
Vaillet, Claude	Prof	INSEAD	PHD	76	Northwes	1978
Valenti, Dennis	Lect	E Michigan	MBA	84	Mich St	1989
Valentine, Jerome L.	Assoc	Southwestern	PHD		N Texas	1988
John Shearn Chair in Business Administration						
Valerio, Nicholas	Asst	Emory	PHD	91	Penn	1990
Van Auken, Howard E.	Assoc	Iowa State	PHD	80	Oklahoma	1980
Van Geem, Henry	Assoc	Midwest St	DBA		Tx Tech	1964
Van Horne, James C.	Prof	Stanford	PHD	64	Northwes	1965
A. P. Giannini Professor of Banking and Finance						
Van Inwegen, Greg	Asst	Syracuse	PHD	91	Penn	1991
Vandenberg, Pieter A.	Prof	San Diego St	DBA	72	S Calif	1969
VandenDool, Peter	Prof	CS-Stanislau	PHD	66	Oregon	1970
Vanderheiden, Paul A.	Assoc	Wis-Eau Clar	PHD	80	Florida	1983
Vang, David O.	Asst	St Thomas-MN	PHD		Iowa St	1988
Vanlandingham, Marguerite H.	Prof	Clarion	PHD		Florida	1981
Varaiya, Nikhil P.	C	San Diego St	PHD	83	U Wash	1988
Varamini, M. Hossein	Asst	St Norbert	PHD	85	Kans St	1987
Varela, Oscar A.	Assoc	New Orleans	PHD	81	Alabama	1982
Varian, Hal R.	Prof	Michigan	PHD	73	Berkeley	1977
Reuben Kempf Professor of Economics						
Varjavand, Reza	Assoc	St Xavier	PHD		Oklahoma	1986
Varma, Raj	Asst	Delaware	PHD		Penn St	
Vasconcellos, Geraldo M.	Asst	Lehigh	PHD	86	Illinois	1988
Vasigh, Bijan	Asst	Embry-Riddle	PHD	84	SUNY	1990
Vasseer, Potkin	Prof	CS-Dominquez				
Vaughan, Emmett J.	Prof	Iowa	PHD	63	Nebraska	1963
J. E. Partington Professor						
Vaughn Jr., Edward S.		Stonehill	JD		Suffolk	1981
Vaughn, Donald E.	Prof	So Illinois	PHD	61	Texas	1970
Vaziri, Mohammad T.	Prof	CS-San Bern	PHD	79	Oklahoma	1986
Veit, E. Theodore	Prof	Rollins	PHD	77	Arkansas	1988
Vellenga, Daniel R.	C-Pr	CS-Stanislau	PHD	74	Mich St	1986
Venkataraman, Subramanyan	VAsst	Florida	PHD		Wiscon	1988
Venkatesh, P. C.	Asst	Cincinnati	PHD	83	Florida	1991
Vennos, Spyros	Assoc	Towson State	DSC	68		
Verbrugge, James A.	H-Pr	Georgia	PHD	68	Kentucky	1968
Hiles Professor of Finance						
Verma, Avinash Kumar	Asst	Massachusett	PHD	88	Berkeley	
Verma, Savita	Asst	York Univ	PHD		Brit Col	1989
Vermaelen, Theo	C-Pr	INSEAD	PHD	80	Chicago	1987
Vermaelen, Theo	Prof	Limburg	MBA	76	Chicago	1989
Vernor, James D.	Assoc	Georgia St	PHD		Wiscon	
Vetsuypens, Michael R.	Asst	So Methodist	PHD	83	U Wash	1986
Vetter, Daniel E.	Assoc	Cen Michigan	PHD	83	Nebraska	1988
Vetzal, Ken	Asst	Un Waterloo	ABD		Toronto	1990
Vihtelic, Jill Lynn	Asst	St Marys-Ind	MBA	82	Mich St	1987
Vila, Jean-Luc	Asst	MIT	PHD	85	Paris	
Vilbert, Michael J.	Asst	USAF Academy	ABD		Wharton	
Vines, Tim		La St-Shreve	ABD		Tenn	1989
Vishny, Robert W.	Prof	Chicago	PHD	85	MIT	1985

Name	Rank	School	Degree	Yr	Inst	Yr
Visscher, Sue L.	Asst	Toledo	PHD		Indiana	1987
Viswanath, P. V.	Asst	Rutgers-Newk	PHD		Chicago	
Viswanathan, K. G.	Asst	Hofstra	PHD	91	Tenn	1989
Viswanathan, S.	Assoc	Duke	PHD		Northwes	
Volkan, Ara G.	C-Pr	West Georgia	PHD	79	Alabama	1989
Volkman, David A.	Inst	Neb-Omaha	BA		Nebraska	
Voorheis, Frank L.	Assoc	Wayne State	PHD	66	Mich St	1969
Vopel, Ronald P.	Prof	Youngstown	PHD	75	Pitt	
Vor der Landwehr, Dale	Assoc	Am Grad Intl	PHD	74	Wayne St	
Vora, Ashok	Prof	CUNY-Baruch	PHD		Northwes	
Vora, Gautam	Asst	New Mexico	PHD	82	Indiana	1989
Voris, Frank K.	Lect	Aurora	MBA	81	No Illin	1985
Voss, Richard	Asst	W Illinois				
Vu, Liem	Asst	Albany State				
Wachowicz Jr., John M.	Assoc	Tennessee	PHD		Illinois	
Wachter, Susan M.	Assoc	Pennsylvania	PHD	74	Boston C	1974
Wade, Charles	Assoc	Texas Tech	PHD	66	Oklahoma	1965
Wade, Charles M.	Assoc	West Florida	PHD	77	Miss	1980
Wade, J.	Prof	San Fran St	PHD	72	Stanford	1969
Wagner, Cecilia	Prof	Seton Hall	PHD	88	China	
Wahab, Mahmoud	Asst	Hartford				
Waheed, Amjad	Asst	East Tenn St	PHD	91	So Ill	1991
Wajstaub, Sandra	Lect	Wilfrid Laur	MBA		Manitoba	1990
Wakeman, Douglas J.	Assoc	Meredith	PHD		N Carol	1984
Walgren, Blaine	Assoc	CS-Fullerton	PHD		U Wash	1990
Walia, Tirlochan S.	Assoc	Indiana-PA				
Walker, Angela	Inst	Akron				
Walker, C. Lankford	Assoc	E Illinois	PHD	80	Georgia	1987
Walker, David A.	Prof	Georgetown	PHD	68	Iowa St	1973
Walker, Ella J.	Inst	West Txs St	MBA		W Txs St	1980
Walker, Ernest Winfield	Prof	Texas	DBA	53	Indiana	1954

Lawrence D. Gale Chair Emeritus in Small Business and Entrepreneurship

Name	Rank	School	Degree	Yr	Inst	Yr
Walker, Joe	Asst	Alabama-Birm	PHD	79	Tx A&M	1987
Walker, Lawrence C.	SLect	Texas A&M	PHD	72	Tx A&M	1984
Walker, Matthew	Inst	N Dakota St	ABD		Texas	1990
Walker, Michael C.	Prof	Cincinnati	PHD	71	Houston	1985
Walker, Milan Mark	Asst	Mississippi	PHD		Mich St	
Walker, Moses S.	Prof	Fayetteville	PHD		Iowa St	
Walker, Ronald J.	C-Pr	Cedarville	DBA	86	Kent St	1978
Walker, William H.	Assoc	SE Missouri	DBA	82	La Tech	1987
Walkling, Ralph A.	Assoc	Ohio State	PHD		Maryland	
Wall, Richard A.	Prof	Canisius	PHD	84	SUNY-Buf	1981
Wallace, Nancy E.	Asst	Cal-Berkeley	PHD		Michigan	
Wallace, Robert	Asst	Gannon	DBA		Kent St	
Wallace, William W.	Dean	Old Dominion	PHD	62		
Wallenbrock, Terry	Asst	Otterbein	MBA	82	Michigan	1983
Waller, Edward R.	Asst	Tulsa	PHD	88	Ariz St	1986
Waller, N. G.	Asst	Clemson	PHD	86	Texas	1988
Walls, Edward L.	Prof	N Car-Charl	DBA	70	Harvard	1971

R. S. Dickson Professor of Finance

Name	Rank	School	Degree	Yr	Inst	Yr
Walter, Ingo	Prof	New York U	PHD	66	New York	

Dean Abraham L. Gitlow Professor of Finance, Chairman of International Bus

Name	Rank	School	Degree	Yr	Inst	Yr
Walter, Terry S.	Prof	Univ Sydney	PHD		WA	1990
Walter, William J.	Assoc	Tri State	MBA	61	Northwes	1972
Walther, Carl H.	Prof	CS-Sacrament	PHD	83	Mich St	1984
Walz, Daniel T.	Dean	Trinity	PHD	81	Wash U	1982
Wang, Ko	Assoc	CS-Fullerton	PHD		Texas	1988
Wang, Louie K.	Asst	Tenn Tech	PHD	88	Northwes	1988
Wang, Tay-Chang	Assoc	Nat Taiwan U	PHD	88	Penn	1988
Wansley, James W.	Prof	Tennessee	PHD		S Carol	
Ward, Charles W.R.	H-Pr	Un Stirling	PHD	80	Reading	1985
Ward, David J.	Prof	Wis-Oshkosh				
Warfel, William		Indiana St				
Warga, Arthur	Prof	Wis-Milwauke	PHD	77	Michigan	1991
Warner, Jerold B.	Prof	Rochester	PHD		Chicago	
Warrack, Brian D.	Assoc	Wilfrid Laur	PHD		Alberta	1975
Warren, Stanton A.	Assoc	Niagara	PHD		SUNY-Buf	1981
Warschauer, Thomas	Prof	San Diego St	PHD			1977
Washam, James O.	Inst	Arkansas St	ABD		Miss	1989
Washington, Dorothy M.	Inst	NW St of La	MBA		Michigan	
Waterhouse, John	D-Pr	Un Waterloo	PHD	72	U Wash	1973
Waters, Alan Rufus	Prof	CS-Fresno	PHD		Rice	1986
Waters, Gola E.	Prof	So Illinois	PHD	70	Iowa	1965
Watson, Robert	Lect	Manches Inst	BA		Hull	1988
Watts, Ross L.	Prof	Rochester	PHD	71	Chicago	1971

Rochester Telephone Corporation Professor

Name	Rank	School	Degree	Yr	Inst	Yr
Watts, William A.	Prof	Txs-Perm Bas	PHD	66	Iowa	
Weatherford, Alan M.	Assoc	Cal Poly-SLO	PHD	86	Tx-Dalla	1986
Weaver, Carl G.K.	Prof	Jms Madison	PHD	75	Fla St	1980
Weaver, Daniel	Asst	Marquette	PHD		Rutgers	1990

Name	Rank	School	Degree	Yr	PhD From	Yr
Weaver, H. Bruce	C-Pr	Lycoming	JD			
Weaver, William C.	Assoc	Cen Florida	PHD		Geo St	1985
Webb, David	Prof	London Econ	PHD	75	London	1991
Webb, Gwendolyn P.	Asst	CUNY-Baruch	PHD		NYU	
Webb, James R.	Prof	Cleveland St	PHD	79	Illinois	1989
Webb, R. Brian	Asst	Indiana				
Webb, Robert I.	Assoc	Virginia	PHD		Chicago	
Weber, Carlene	Asst	CS-Bakersf	PHD			1989
Weber, David W.	Prof	Montana	DBA	73	Colorado	1974
Weber, Marsha	Asst	Moorhead St	MBA	88	Moorhead	1989
Weber, Richard E.	Prof	Monmouth	PHD		Rutgers	1979
Webster Jr., George H.	C-As	St Joseph	PHD	81	SUNY-Bin	1980
Webster, Allen L.	Assoc	Bradley	PHD	79	Fla St	1990
Webster, Patricia C.	Asst	Bradley	PHD	90	Kentucky	1990
Wee, Warren	Assoc	Hawaii Pacif	PHD	82	U Wash	1988
Weed, Norman L.	C-Pr	Houston-Cl L	PHD	68	Tulane	1974
Weeks, David E.	Asst	New Mexico	PHD	87	Texas	1986
Weeks, Wayne	Assoc	E Michigan	DBA	78	Kent St	1978
Wehmeyer, Willadee	Assoc	MidAmer Naz				
Wei, Peihwang P.	Asst	New Orleans	PHD		LSU	1989
Weight, G.Dale	Dean	Willamette	PHD	68	Oregon	1990
Weiher, Kenneth E.	Assoc	Tx-S Antonio	PHD	75	Indiana	1975
Weil, David	Lect	Boston Univ	PHD		Harvard	
Weil, Leonard	Adj	UCLA	BA	43	UCLA	1987
Weingartner, Martin	Prof	Vanderbilt	PHD	62	Carnegie	1977
Weinraub, Herbert J.	Assoc	Toledo	PHD	72	Mich St	1970
Weis, Charles	Prof	Tenn State	PHD		Ariz St	
Weiss, Donald E.	Assoc	No Illinois	PHD	76	Wiscon	1974
Weiss, Jeffrey	Assoc	CUNY-Baruch	PHD		Wiscon	
Weiss, Kathleen A.	Asst	Michigan	PHD	88	Florida	1988
Weiss, Nitzan	Prof	NY Inst Tech	PHD			
Welch, H. Oliver	Prof	Piedmont	DBA		Geo St	
Welch, Ivo I.	Asst	UCLA	PHD	91	Chicago	1990
Welch, Jonathan B.	C-Pr	Northeastern	PHD		Conn	
Welch, Oliver	Prof	Clark Atlant	PHD		Geo St	1991
Welch, Robert G.	Prof	Midwest St	PHD		OregonSt	1966
Welch, Robert L.	Assoc	Brock Univ	PHD	89	SUNY-Buf	1978
Welch, William	Assoc	Fla Internat	PHD	74	Michigan	
Welker, James E.	Asst	Indiana-PA				
Weller, Paul	Assoc	Iowa	PHD	81	Essex	1990
Wells, Bill		No Alabama				
Wells, Gary R.	Prof	Idaho State	PHD	71	Utah	1972
Wells, Grant J.	Prof	Ball State	PHD	73	Wiscon	1966
Wendelburg, George	Inst	Delaware St	MBA		Temple	
Wentz, Arthur G.	C-Ac	Akron	PHD	69	Ohio St	1982
Werner, Ingrid M.	Asst	Stanford	PHD	90	Rochest	1990
West, Bill W.	Prof	CS-Sacrament	JD	72	Berkeley	1970
West, David A.	Prof	Missouri	PHD	61	Arkansas	
West, Richard R.	Dean	New York U	PHD	64	Chicago	
Westerfield, Randolph W.	C-Pr	So Calif	PHD			
Charles B. Thornton Professorship in Finance						
Weston, J. Fred	Prof	UCLA	PHD	48	Chicago	1949
Warren C. Cordner Professor of Money and Financial Markets						
Wetmore, Jill L.	Assoc	Saginaw Vall	PHD	88	Mich St	1981
Whaley, Robert E.	C-Pr	Duke	PHD		Toronto	
Wheat, Charles M.	Assoc	S F Austin	PHD	68	Arkansas	1988
Wheatley, Simon	Asst	U Washington	PHD	86	Rocheste	1984
Whitaker, William M.	H-Pr	Geo Southern	PHD	68	Kentucky	1989
Whitbread, Joseph E.		Stonehill	PHD		Syracuse	1989
Whitcomb, David K.	Prof	Rutgers-Newk	PHD	68	Columbia	1975
White, Alan	Assoc	Univ Toronto	PHD		Toronto	1988
White, Charles	Assoc	New Hamp Col	PHD		Ohio St	
White, Daniel L.	Prof	Georgia St	PHD		Northwes	
White, Garland M.	Asst	Virginia St	MC		Richmond	1958
White, Harry L.	Asst	Boise State	PHD		Tx A&M	1988
White, John B.	Asst	Geo Southern	PHD	85	Virginia	1989
White, Larry R.	Assoc	Miss State	PHD	85	Georgia	1984
White, Mark A.	Asst	Virginia	PHD		Mich St	
White, Mark V.	Inst	Wyoming	ABD			1991
White, Richard E.	Assoc	North Fla	PHD	73	Missouri	1973
White, Robert W.	Assoc	W Ontario	PHD		MIT	1980
White, Susan	Lect	Texas	PHD	90	Texas	1989
Whitelaw, Robert F.	Asst	New York U				
Whitford, David T.	Assoc	Illinois	PHD	80	Georgia	1977
Whitman, Andrew	Prof	Minnesota				
Whitmire, Ray E.	Prof	Corpus Chris	PHD		Texas	
Whitney, Howard R.	D-Pr	Franklin	PHD	71	Oregon	1979
Whittaker, Maria C.	Asst	Ohio State	JD		Chicago	
Whyte, Ann Marie	Asst	Cleveland St	PHD	91	Fl Atlan	1991
Wiant, Kenneth	Asst	Fla Atlantic	PHD	91	S Carol	1990

Name	Rank	School	Degree	Yr	From	Yr
Widicus, Wilbur W.	C-Pr	Oregon State	PHD	64	Columbia	1964
Wieand, Kenneth F.	Prof	South Fla	PHD	70	Wash U	1980
Wier, Peggy	H-Ac	Oregon	PHD	81	Rochest	1982
Wiggins, C. Donald	Prof	North Fla	DBA		La Tech	
Wiggins, James B.	Asst	Cornell	PHD	86	MIT	1986
Wilbourn, Macon	Asst	Auburn-Montg	DBA		Miss St	1982
Wilbratte, Barry F.	C-Pr	St Thomas-Tx	PHD		Tulane	
Wilbur, Robert W.	Assoc	San Diego St	PHD		U Wash	1974
Wilcox, James A.	Assoc	Cal-Berkeley	PHD	80	Northwes	1978
Wilcox, Steve	Assoc	Mankato St	PHD		Nebraska	1991
Wiles, Kenneth W.	Asst	No Carolina	PHD	91	Texas	1990
Wiley, C. Jeffery	Asst	Fla Southern	MBA			1978
Wilford, Walton T.	Prof	New Orleans	PHD	64	So Meth	1986
Wilhelm, William J.	Asst	Boston Coll	PHD		LSU	
Willcocks, Geoff	PLect	Bournemouth	MBA			1987
Williams II, Ira	Dean	Alabama A&M				
Williams, Alex O.	C-Pr	Clark Atlant	PHD		Penn	
Robert Woodruff Professor						
Williams, Bismarck	Prof	Roosevelt	ABD		Chicago	1964
Williams, Edward E.	Prof	Rice	PHD	68	Texas	1978
Henry Gardiner Symonds Professor						
Williams, Griff	SLect	Bournemouth	MBA			1991
Williams, James	Assoc	CS-Northrdge	PHD	64		1982
Williams, John D.	Prof	Akron	DBA	71	Kent St	1969
Williams, John E.	Prof	Morehouse	PHD		Geo St	1976
Mills B. Lane Professor of Banking and Finance						
Williams, Melvin D.	Assoc	St Thomas-MN				
Williams, Michael E.	SLect	Texas	PHD	80		1988
Williams, Norman C.	C-Ac	Tenn Tech	PHD	72	Arkansas	1972
Williams, Numan A.	Prof	Ball State	PHD	73	Wiscon	1973
Williams, Richard E.	Assoc	Wright State	PHD	72	Mich St	1965
Williams, Sandra	Inst	Moorhead St	MBA	85	Moorhead	1988
Williams, Sarah	STut	Deakin Univ	BCOM	83	Deakin	1983
Williams, Stuart L.	Assoc	Wm & Mary	PHD		Syracuse	1972
Williams, William M.	Assoc	Arkansas St	PHD	78	Miss St	1978
Williamson, J. Peter	Prof	Dartmouth	DBA	61	Harvard	1961
Willner, Ram	Asst	Dartmouth	DBA	86	Harvard	1987
Wilson, Arthur J.	Asst	Case Western	PHD	90	Chicago	
Wilson, Berry K.	Asst	Georgetown	PHD	88	NYU	1988
Wilson, Brent	Assoc	Brigham Yg	DBA	79	Harvard	1982
Wilson, Bruce R.	Assoc	Massey Univ	MECO	74	New Eng	1970
Wilson, Dwayne	Dean	Freed Hardem	PHD	91	Miss	1975
Wilson, J.	Prof	N Carol St	PHD	66	Oklahoma	
Wilson, Joseph W.	Prof	CS-Fresno	PHD		Arkansas	1982
Wilson, Michael J.	Asst	NW Missouri	MSBA		S Illin	1986
Wilson, William E.	Asst	Hawaii-Hilo	PHD	90	Indiana	1989
Wilt Jr., Glenn A.	Assoc	Arizona St	PHD	63	Michigan	1963
Winder, Robert	Assoc	Chris Newpor	PHD		Rutgers	1991
Wingender, John R.	Assoc	Oklahoma St	PHD		Nebraska	1985
Winger, Bernard J.	Prof	Dayton	ABD		Cinn	1966
Wingler, Tony R.	Assoc	N Car-Greens	DBA		Kentucky	1976
Winick, Bernard S.	Assoc	Akron	JD	64	Akron	1979
Winkler, Daniel T.	Asst	N Car-Greens	PHD		S Carol	1986
Winn Jr., Edward L.	Prof	Belmont				
Winn, Daryl	Assoc	Colorado	PHD	73	Michigan	1971
Winter, Ralph	Prof	Univ Toronto	PHD		Berkeley	1979
Winters, Drew	Asst	Wis-Milwauke	PHD	87	Georgia	1991
Winton, Andrew	Asst	Northwestern	PHD	90	Penn	
Wirick, Ronald G.	Assoc	W Ontario	PHD		W Ontar	1979
Withrow, Linda	Prof	St Ambrose	MBA	84	St Ambro	1987
Wittschen Jr., J. Harvey	Prof	Citadel	PHD		Alabama	
Witzenburg, James	Inst	Hofstra	MBA	83	Hofstra	1987
Wobbekind, Richard	Asst	Colorado	PHD	84	Colorado	1985
Woerheide, Walter J.	C-Pr	Rochest Tech	PHD	77	Wash U	1990
Wolf, Avner	Assoc	CUNY-Baruch	PHD		Columbia	
Wolf, Harold Arthur	Prof	Texas	PHD	58	Michigan	1968
Wolfe, Edward R.	Assoc	W Kentucky	PHD	76	Kentucky	1984
Wolfe, Glenn A.	Asst	Toledo				
Wolfenbarger, J. Larry	C-Pr	Georgia Col	PHD		Tenn	1987
Wolff, Christian	C-Pr	Limburg	MBA	84	Chicago	1988
Womack, Douglas	Prof	SW Louisiana	PHD	71	Alabama	1971
Wong, Alan	Assoc	Indiana SE	PHD	85	N Texas	1985
Wong, D. W. S.	Asst	Un Hong Kong	MBA			1976
Wong, K. A.	Visit	City Poly HK	PHD	75	Liverpoo	1991
Wong, Matthew	Asst	St Johns	PHD			
Wong, S.	Prof	San Fran St	PHD	65	Berkeley	1967
Wong, Shee Q.	Assoc	Minn-Duluth	PHD	83	Wi-Milwa	
Woo, Li-Anne	Asst	New So Wales	BCOM		NS Wales	1986
Wood Jr., Oliver G.	Prof	So Carolina	PHD	65	Florida	1965
Wood, David D.	Assoc	Appalach St	DBA		La Tech	1985

Name	Rank	School	Degree	Yr	Inst	Yr
Wood, J. Stuart	Assoc	Loyola-N Orl	PHD	78	NYU	1984
Wood, Justin	VAsoc	Ohio State				
Wood, Larry	Inst	Univ Calgary	MBA	82	Calgary	1983
Wood, Robert A.	Prof	Memphis St	PHD	78	Pitt	1990
Distinguished Professor of Finance						
Wood, Sally	Tutor	W Australia	MBA	90	W Austra	1991
Woodard, Nelson	Asst	New Mexico	ABD		Virginia	1988
Woodbury, Denise	Asst	Florida St	ABD		Utah	1989
Woodliff, David	Lect	W Australia	BCOM	82	W Austra	1991
Woodruff, Catherine	Asst	Houston	PHD	84	Texas	1989
Woodruff, Criss G.	Asst	Radford	ABD		Miss st	
Woods, Donald H.	Prof	Georgia St	DBA	65	Harvard	1970
Woods, Ivan	Read	Melbourne U	PHD			1978
Woods, John C.	Asst	F Dick-Madis	PHD	89	New York	1990
Woodside III, B. Perry	Assoc	Charleston	PHD	74	S Carol	1987
Woodward, Richard S.	Prof	Univ Calgary	PHD	81	Exeter	1982
Woody, James R.	Prof	USAF Academy	DBA		Virginia	
Woolridge, J. Randall	Prof	Penn State	PHD		Iowa	1979
Wort, Donald H.	Prof	CS-Hayward	PHD	73	Mich St	1984
Worzala, Elaine	Asst	Colorado St				
Wright, David J.	Asst	Notre Dame	PHD		Illinois	
Wright, Fred E.	Emer	W Virginia	MA	50	W Virg	1951
Wright, Gene	Inst	David Lipsc	MBA		Vanderb	
Wright, Thomas V.	Assoc	St Louis	PHD		Wash U	
Wrightsman, Dwayne E.	Prof	New Hampshir	PHD	64	Mich St	1964
Wrolstad, Mark A.	Assoc	Winona State	DBA	83	Colorado	1989
Wu, Chunchi	Assoc	Syracuse	PHD	82	Illinois	1982
Wu, H. K.	Prof	Alabama	PHD	63	Penn	1972
Wyatt, James C.	Asst	Tenn-Chattan	MBA	90	Tenn-Cha	1991
Wyatt, Jeffrey G.	Asst	Miami U-Ohio	PHD	89	S Carol	
Wyatt, Robert W.	Assoc	No Iowa	PHD	78	Iowa	1980
Wyatt, Steve B.	Assoc	Cincinnati	PHD	80	Tx-Dalla	1987
Wynant, Larry	C	W Ontario	DBA		Harvard	1976
Yaari, Uzi	Assoc	Rutgers-Camd	PHD		Chicago	
Yang, Chau-Chen	Assoc	Nat Taiwan U	PHD	89	Illinois	1989
Yang, Tyler	Asst	CS-Long Bch				1991
Yanow, Richad	Prof	N Adams St	MBA		Harvard	
Yasar, Geyikdazi	Prof	SUNY Old Wes	PHD			1983
Yasuhara, Akio	Asst	Rhode Island	PHD	82	Ohio St	1988
Yau, Jot K.	Asst	George Mason	PHD	88	Mass	1988
Yavas, Burhan F.	C-As	CS-Dominguez	PHD	83	S Calif	1983
Yazdipour, Rassoul	Assoc	CS-Fresno	PHD		Ohio St	1987
Yeager, Frederick Conrad	Prof	St Louis	PHD	72	W Virgin	
Yener, Demir	Assoc	Babson	PHD		Gazi	
Yobaccio, Elizabeth J.	Asst	Bryant	DBA	91	Boston U	1991
Yoder, James A.	Asst	So Alabama	PHD		Florida	1988
Yohannes, Arefaine	Assoc	Mich-Dearbor	PHD	76	Northwes	1985
Yook, Ken C.	Assoc	St Cloud St	PHD	89	Nebraska	1989
Yoon, Yeomin	Prof	Seton Hall	PHD	75	Penn	
Yoshida, Kosaku	Prof	CS-Dominguez	PHD	75	NYU	1975
Young, Allan	Prof	Syracuse	PHD	67	Columbia	1971
Young, Colin M.	Asst	Bentley	PHD	82	London	1986
Young, E. Neil	Assoc	Florida St	JD	65	Miss	1972
Young, Leslie	Prof	Texas	PHD	71	Oxford	1983
V. F. Neuhaus Centennial Professor in Finance						
Young, Martin R.	SLect	Massey Univ	MA			1990
Young, Peter C.	Prof	St Cloud St	PHD	88	Minn	1987
Young, Philip J.	Asst	SW Missouri	PHD	90	Arkansas	1990
Young, Suzanne Lee	Lect	Texas	MA	76	Canterbu	1983
Yousif, Salah A.	Asst	Alabama A&M	MA		Howard	
Yu, Geungu	Asst	SW Louisiana	PHD	86	Miss St	1987
Yun, Yong-Sup	Prof	Korea Univ	PHD			1984
Yung, Kenneth K.	Asst	Old Dominion	PHD		Geo St	
Yuyuenyongwatana, Robert P.	Asst	St Johns	PHD			
Zacharias, John	Asst	Emory	PHD	91	Penn	1990
Zaher, Tarek		Indiana St				
Zaima, Janis K.	Prof	San Jose St	PHD	80	U Wash	1986
Zalewski, David A.	Asst	Providence	ABD		Clark	1990
Zaman, M. Raquib	C-Pr	Ithaca	PHD	70	Cornell	1974
Zantout, Zaher	Asst	Rider				
Zapatero, Fernando	Asst	Texas	PHD	91	Columbia	1991
Zaporowski, Mark P.	Assoc	Canisius	PHD	85	SUNY-Alb	1984
Zarruk, Emilio	Asst	Fla Atlantic	PHD	85	LSU	1990
Zdanowicz, John S.	Prof	Fla Internat	PHD	71	Mich St	
Zeldes, Stephen	Assoc	Pennsylvania	PHD	84	MIT	1982
Zemedkun, Wold	Assoc	Norfolk St	MA		Columbia	1977
Zender, Jaime E.	Asst	Utah	PHD	88	Yale	1988
Zenner, Marc	Asst	No Carolina	PHD	89	Purdue	1989
Zetts, Jerome E.	Prof	Youngstown	MBA	67	Wayne St	
Zhang, Chu	Asst	Univ Alberta	ABD		Chicago	1991

Name	Rank	School	Degree	Yr	Deg School	Yr
Zhang, G.	Asst	Un Waterloo	ABD		Brit Col	1991
Zhang, H.	Asst	Laurentian	PHD	87	Concordi	
Zhou, Guofu	Assoc	Wash Univ	PHD	90	Duke	1990
Zhu, Yu	Adj	New York U				
Zietlow, John	Assoc	Indiana St	PHD		Memphis	1989
Zin, Stanley E.	Asst	Carnegie Mel	PHD	87	Toronto	1988
Zinger, J. T.	Assoc	Laurentian	MBA	78	Western	
Zinkhan, Christian	C $	Campbell	DBA		Miss St	1987
Ziobrowski, Alan	Asst	Lander	PHD	90	Kent St	1991
Ziobrowski, Brigitte J.	Assoc	Augusta	ABD		Kent St	1991
Ziorklui, Sam	Asst	Howard	PHD	86	Howard	1984
Zissu, Anne-Marie	Asst	Temple	PHD		CUNY	
Zivney, Terry L. Harris Chair of Excellence	Prof	Tenn-Chattan	PHD	84	Geo St	1988
Zocco, Dennis	Assoc	San Diego	PHD		Lehigh	
Zock, Richard	Prof	CS-Hayward	DBA	71	Colorado	1984
Zorn, Thomas S.	Assoc	Nebraska	PHD	78	UCLA	1981
Zou, Liang	Asst	Limburg	MBA	86	Leuven	1990
Zumpano, Leonard V. Chair of Real Estate	Prof	Alabama	PHD	76	Penn St	1975
Zumwalt, J. Kenton	C-Pr	Colorado St	PHD		Missouri	
Zussman, David	Dean	Univ Ottawa	PHD			
Zwiebel, Jeffrey	Asst	Stanford	ABD	91	MIT	1991
Zwirlein, Thomas J.	Asst	Colorado Spr	PHD		Oregon	1984
Zychowicz, Edward	Asst	Hofstra	PHD	89	SUNY-Bin	1989